Research, Invention, and Innovation Congress (RI2C 2025)

E3S Web of Conferences Volume 679 (2025)

Bangkok, Thailand
19-20 August 2025

ISBN: 979-8-3313-3147-4

Printed from e-media with permission by:

Curran Associates, Inc.
57 Morehouse Lane
Red Hook, NY 12571

Some format issues inherent in the e-media version may also appear in this print version.

For additional information, please contact EDP Sciences – Web of Conferences at the address below.

EDP Sciences – Web of Conferences
17, Avenue du Hoggar
Parc d'Activité de Courtabœuf
BP 112
F-91944 Les Ulis Cedex A
France

Phone: +33 (0) 1 69 18 75 75
Fax: +33 (0) 1 69 28 84 91

contact-edps@webofconferences.org

Additional copies of this publication are available from:

Curran Associates, Inc.
57 Morehouse Lane
Red Hook, NY 12571 USA
Phone: 845-758-0400
Fax: 845-758-2633
Email: curran@proceedings.com
Web: www.proceedings.com

TABLE OF CONTENTS

List of Conference Chair

1. **Conference chair**
Prof.Dr. Somrerk Chandra-ambhorn (KMUTNB, Thailand)
Assoc.Prof.Dr. Kampanart Theinnoi (KMUTNB, Thailand)
Prof.Dr. Titipong Lertwiriyaprapa (KMUTNB, Thailand)

2. **Co-conference chair**
Asst.Prof.Dr. Wanlop Kitisatorn (KMUTNB, Thailand)
Assoc.Prof.Dr. Nonchanutt Chudpooti (KMUTNB, Thailand)
Assoc.Prof.Dr. Santi Chuetor (KMUTNB, Thailand)

3. **General secretary**
Dr. Chaniga Chuensangjun (KMUTNB, Thailand)

4. **International Advisory Board**
Prof.Dr.Ing. Edmund Haberstroh (RWTH Aachen University, Germany)
Prof.Dr. Yasushi Umeda (The University of Tokyo, Japan)
Prof.Dr. Yang Zhigang (Tsinghua University, China)
Assoc.Prof.Dr. Sanjay Mavinkere Rangappa (KMUTNB, Thailand)
Prof. Dr. Yu-Shen Cheng (National Yunlin University of Science and Technology, Taiwan)
Prof.Dr. Hassan El Bari (Ibn Tofail University, Morocco)
Prof.Dr. Jayapriya Jayaprakash (Anna University, India)
Assoc.Prof.Dr. Nagaraju Kottam (Ramaiah Institute of Technology, India)
Prof.Dr. Petar Yordanov Antov (University of Forestry, Bulgaria)
Prof.Dr. Ponnusami Venkatachalam (SASTRA Deemed University, India)
Prof.Dr. Show Pau-Loke (Khalifa University, United Arab Emirates)
Prof.Dr. R. Gnanamoorthy (Indian Institute of Technology Madras, India)

5. **Scientific Committee**

Kampanart Theinnoi, KMUTNB, Thailand
Wanlop Kitisatorn, KMUTNB, Thailand
Peerapong Pornwongthong, KMUTNB, Thailand
Danai Torrungrueng, KMUTNB, Thailand
Titipong Lertwiriyaprapa, KMUTNB, Thailand
Nonchanutt Chudpooti, KMUTNB, Thailand
Attaphon Kaewvilai, KMUTNB, Thailand
Chaiyut Sumpavakup, KMUTNB, Thailand
Thamrongsin Siripongsakul, KMUTNB, Thailand
Pornsak Srisungsitthisunti, KMUTNB, Thailand

Watchareewan Jitsakul, KMUTNB, Thailand
Sak Sittichompoo, KMUTNB, Thailand
Chaniga Chuensangjun, KMUTNB, Thailand
Sangwon Kittiwittayapong, KMUTNB, Thailand
Sophit Jamtaworn, KMUTNB, Thailand

6. **Publication Committee**

Assoc.Prof.Dr. Nonchanutt Chudpooti
Asst.Prof.Dr. Wanlop Kitisatorn
Assoc.Prof.Dr . Santi Chuetor
Asst.Prof.Dr. Peerapong Pornwongthong

7. **Organizing Committee (KMUTNB, Thailand)**

Prof.Dr. Somrerk Chandra-ambhorn
Assoc.Prof.Dr. Kampanart Theinnoi
Asst.Prof.Dr. Wanlop Kitisatorn
Asst.Prof.Dr. Peerapong Pornwongthong
Prof.Dr. Titipong Lertwiriyaprapa
Assoc.Prof.Dr. Rungsima Yeetsorn
Assoc.Prof.Dr. Amarin Ratanavis
Assoc.Prof.Dr. Nonchanutt Chudpooti
Assoc.Prof.Dr . Santi Chuetor
Asst.Prof.Dr. Chaiyut Sumpavakup
Dr. Chaniga Chuensangjun
Jittima Suwarat
Kraisuk Boonpardit
Kanjana Ngampojjanawong
Udomporn Duangngoen

8. **Innovative Sustainable Science (iSS) Editor**

Managing Editor: Santi Chuetor, KMUTNB, Thailand

Editorial Board Member:
Professor Shaily Mahendra, University of California Los Angeles, USA
Dr. Marttin Paulraj Gunduppali, University of Alberta, Canada
Professor Yu-Shen Cheng Yun, National Yunlin University of Science and Technology, Taiwan
Ts.Dr.Hoo Peng Yong, Universiti Malaysia Perlis, Malaysia

Secretary: Chaniga Chuensangjun, KMUTNB, Thailand

9. Innovative Sustainable Science (iSS) Academic Committee

Assoc. Prof. Dr.Kitirote Wantala	Khon Kaen University
Assoc. Prof. Dr.Petch Jearanaisilawong	KMUTNB
Assoc. Prof. Dr.Thirawudh Pongprayoon	KMUTNB
Dr.Arnon Setsungnern	KMUTT
Dr.Patikorn Sriphirom	Silpakorn University
Asst. Prof. Dr.Benjamaporn Wonganu	KMUTNB
Asst.Prof.Dr.Arnon Khamkeaw	KMUTNB
Dr.Jakkapop Phanthasri	NANOTEC
Asst. Prof. Dr.Suchata Kirdponpattara	KMUTNB
Dr.Diana Jose	KMUTNB
Dr.Nida Arshad	KMUTNB
Ms. Nichaphat Kitiborwornkul	KMUTNB
Dr.Vanarat Phakeenuya	KMUTNB
Assoc. Prof. Dr.Sathaporn Chuepeng	Kasetsart University
Assoc. Prof. Dr.Supak Tontisirin	KMUTNB
Assoc. Prof. Dr.Patcharin Worathanakul	KMUTNB
Asst. Prof. Dr.Sunanta Chuayprakong	KMUTNB
Assoc. Prof. Dr.Suttinun Phongtamrug	KMUTNB
Asst. Prof. Dr.Komthep Silpcharu	KMUTNB
Asst. Prof. Dr.Awat Wisetsai	KMUTNB
Asst. Prof. Dr.Kritamorn Jitrangsri	Walailak University
Dr.Khemmathin Lueangwattanapong	Kasetsart University
Dr.Kanjanawadee Singkronart	MTEC
Assoc. Prof. Dr.Panchika Prangkio	Chiang Mai University
Assoc. Prof. Dr.Atthasit Tawai	KMUTNB
Assoc. Prof.Dr.Nopphon Weeranoppanant	Chulalongkorn University
Dr.Chonlatep Usaku	Chulalongkorn University
Asst.Prof.Dr.Wanwitoo Wanmolee	KMUTNB
Dr.Wethaka Chaocharoen	Phetchaburi Rajabhat University
Asst. Prof. Anirut Kantasa-ard	Burapha University
Asst.Prof.Dr. Poomiwat Phadungbut	Mahidol University
Assoc.Prof.Dr. Sasithorn Kongruang	KMUTNB
Assoc.Prof.Dr. Sirikhwan Tinrat	KMUTNB
Asst.Prof.Dr. Theerawut Phusantisampan	KMUTNB
Dr.Nicharee wisuthiphaet	KMUTNB
Asst.Prof.Dr. Nichanan Tepsuparungsikul	Silpakorn University
Asst.Prof.Dr. Panwajee Payongsri	Mahidol University

Aim and Scope of Ri2C2025

The 6th Research, Invention, and Innovation Congress (RI2C 2025) is co-organized by IEEE Thailand Section (Antennas & Propagation (AP)/Electron Devices (ED)/Microwave Theory & Techniques (MTT) Joint Chapter), Electrical Engineering/Electronics, Computer, Telecommunications, and Information Technology Association (ECTI), Thai Institute of Chemical Engineering And Applied Chemistry (TIChE.), and King Mongkut's University of Technology North Bangkok (KMUTNB). The RI2C 2025 aims to bring together individuals from academic, research, and business to share practice solutions for Shaping the Sustainable Future with Research & Innovation.

The first RI2C took place in the year 2019 and has continued annually with support from academic association. This year RI2C 2025 will accept a research papers within three main categories, including: Innovative Electricals and Electronics (iEE), Innovative Mechanical and Materials (iMM), Innovative Sustainable Science (iSS), several of which have different tracks within them. We would like to invite KMUTNB's collaborators worldwide to attend the RI2C 2025 to exchange their experiences and re-vow our relationship in academic and research affairs. All those wishing to participate are welcomed to submit a research paper to present their work, which can be an oral or poster presentation through one of the official topics. The high-quality, original research papers will be submitted for publication following peer review to the proceedings indexed by Scopus. Moreover, the conference participants will have an opportunity to attend several keynote presentations on new indicators and directions in research and development in the multidisciplinary fields of the Innovation for Sustainability.

To this end, the Conference Committee is pleased to announce the Call for Papers for the 6th Research, Invention, and Innovation Congress (RI2C 2025), on August 19 - 20, 2025, take place in Bangkok, Thailand. With the experience of previously running five successful events, we are confident that the year 2025 will witness an even greater success of the RI2C 2025.

Session: Innovative Sustainable Science (iSS)
Venue: Asawin Grand Convention Hotel in Bangkok, Thailand
Conference date: 19-20 August 2025

Explore the highlight video and browse through photos from the RI2C 2024 event on the official website: https://www.ri2c-kmutnb.com

Some photos for iSS session

The 6th Research, Invention, and Innovation Congress (RI2C 2025)
Shaping the Sustainable Future with Research & Innovation
19 – 20 August 2025
CERTIFICATE

Research, Invention,
and Innovation Congress

Statement of Peer review

In submitting conference proceedings to BIO Web of Conferences, I certify to the Publisher that I adhere to the **Policy on Publishing Integrity** of the journal in order to safeguard good scientific practice in publishing.

1. All articles have been subjected to peer review administered by the proceedings editors.
2. Reviews have been conducted by expert referees, who have been requested to provide unbiased and constructive comments aimed, whenever possible, at improving the work.
3. Proceedings editors have taken all reasonable steps to ensure the quality of the materials they publish and their decision to accept or reject a paper for publication has been based only on the merits of the work and the relevance to the journal.

Title, date and place of the conference

RI2C 2025 - The 6th Research, Invention, and Innovation Congress
(Bangkok, Thailand, August 19 - 20, 2025)

Proceedings editor(s):

Dr. Marttin Paulraj Gunduppali

Professor Yu-Shen Cheng Yun

Professor Dr.Shaily Mahendra

Ts.Dr.Hoo Peng Yong

Date and editor's signature

17, avenue du Hoggar - PA de Courtabœuf – BP 112 - 91944 Les Ulis Cedex A (France)
Tél. : 33 (0)1 69 18 75 75 - Fax : 33(0)1 69 07 45 17 – www.edpsciences.org

 https://doi.org/10.1051/e3sconf/202567901001

Locational Analysis of Off-Site Hydrogen Production Facilities Considering Hydrogen Refueling Station Clusters

Kasin Ransikarbum [1*], *Bathrinath* Sankaranarayanan[2], *Hartmut* Zadek[3], and *Jettarat* Janmontree[3]

[1]Industrial Engineering, Ubonratchathani University, Thailand
[2]Mechanical Engineering, Kalasalingam Academy of Research and Education, India
[3]Institute for Engineering of Products and Systems, Otto-von-Guericke University Magdeburg, Germany

Abstract. The Hydrogen Supply Chain (HSC) encompasses the entire process of producing, storing, transporting, and distributing hydrogen for various applications from the upstream to the downstream operations. In the transportation sector, the downstream process involves delivering hydrogen to Hydrogen Refuelling Stations (HRSs) for the end use of diverse Fuel Cell Electric Vehicles (FCEVs) types. This study aims to analyze strategic locations for off-site hydrogen production facilities to distribute hydrogen to existing HRSs, using a case study of HRSs in Germany. Specifically, the K-means algorithm with the elbow method, a popular unsupervised machine learning approach, is initially used to determine the optimal number of HRS clusters and partition them based on latitude and longitude. Next, the rectilinear minisum optimization model is applied to evaluate the strategic location of an off-site hydrogen production facility, considering locational data and population density in specific postal codes. Our results could assist policymakers for infrastructure expansion and support the development of regional or national hydrogen roadmaps relevant to HSC.

1 Introduction and Motivation

The Hydrogen Supply Chain (HSC) encompasses various activities, including hydrogen production, storage, transportation, and distribution for use in diverse applications [1]. One of the key applications of hydrogen is in the transportation sector, where the downstream process involves delivering hydrogen for use in various types of Fuel Cell Electric Vehicles (FCEVs). According to the IEA's Sustainable Development Scenario [2], hydrogen demand is projected to reach 90 million metric tons by 2030 and exceed 500 million metric tons by 2070. While hydrogen consumption in the transportation sector is currently limited, it is expected to grow significantly, becoming the dominant sector by 2050 and beyond. Figure 1 illustrates the anticipated growth of hydrogen demand across various applications.

A well-developed HSC in transportation is essential for enabling the widespread adoption of FCEVs, providing a cleaner alternative to fossil fuels. Currently, the transportation sector remains a major contributor to greenhouse gas (GHG) emissions, primarily due to the dominance of internal combustion engine vehicles that rely on gasoline and diesel. Many countries and regions worldwide, including the European Union (EU), the United States, China, and others, have established policies to achieve a low-carbon economy, aiming to significantly reduce GHG emissions and transition toward cleaner

energy sources by 2050 [3, 4]. The Paris Agreement, in particular, plays a key role by requiring participating

countries to detail their plans for reducing GHG emissions and adapting to the impacts of climate change [5].

The growing concerns over climate change and air pollution have intensified efforts to transition toward green mobility solutions based on alternative energy, including battery electric vehicles (BEVs) and hydrogen FCEVs. These alternative energy vehicles, in particular, offer a range of benefits that are transforming the transportation sector, in which benefits and challenges have been extensively discussed in a number of studies, which support a shift toward a sustainable transportation ecosystem, an energy independence and an effort to combat climate change [6].

* Corresponding author: kasin.r@ubu.ac.th

This study focuses on the midstream and downstream processes of the HSC. Specifically, it aims to analyze strategic locations for off-site hydrogen production facilities to distribute hydrogen to existing Hydrogen Refueling Stations (HRSs) using a case study of Germany's network and infrastructure. Assessing the location of off-site hydrogen production facilities clearly affects the distribution performance in HSC. Initially, the K-means algorithm, a popular unsupervised machine learning approach, is used to assess HRS locations and cluster them based on latitude and longitude following the elbow method. Then, the rectilinear minisum optimization model is applied to determine the strategic location of an off-site hydrogen production facility, considering locational data and population density within specific postal codes of HRSs.

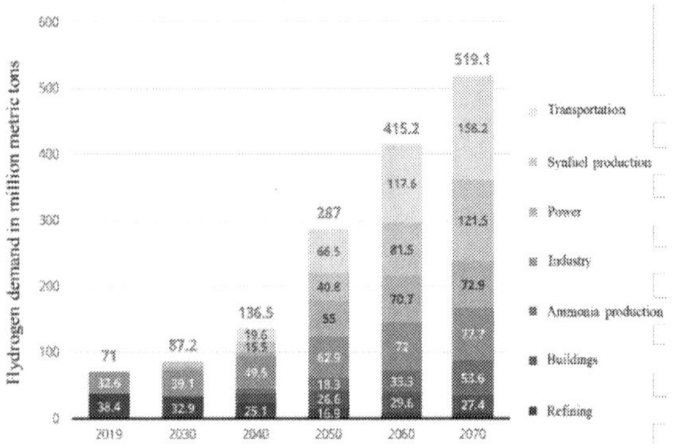

Fig. 1. Expected hydrogen demand growth for diverse applications [7]

We note that this assessment is part of an ongoing study aimed at further evaluating and modelling the HSC network by integrating upstream, midstream, and downstream operations. The manuscript is structured as follows: Section 2 presents the relevant literature and methodology, Section 3 discusses data collection and case study analysis, and Section 4 concludes with future research directions.

2 Literature and Methodology

2.1 Related Literature

The HSC consists of three key stages: upstream, midstream, and downstream. In the upstream stage, hydrogen is produced from various sources, categorized by different colors based on production methods. These include gray hydrogen (natural gas reforming), blue hydrogen (natural gas reforming with carbon capture), and green hydrogen (electrolysis powered by renewable energy). The midstream stage involves hydrogen storage, where it can be compressed (CH_2 in gaseous form) or liquefied (LH_2) and transported via tube trailers, cryogenic tankers, pipelines, or ships, depending on its physical state. Cryogenic technology is typically required to store and transport liquefied hydrogen at extremely low temperatures. The downstream stage focuses on end-use applications, one of which is transportation, such as Fuel Cell Electric Vehicles (FCEVs) [8]. Figure 2 illustrates a typical HSC, and Table 1 presents the key differences between compressed and liquefied hydrogen based on storage and transportation requirements [9-11].

The Hydrogen infrastructure in the transportation sector encompasses all essential components and facilities required to meet the hydrogen fuel demand of FCEVs. This network follows the "Well-to-Wheel" process, referring to the entire energy lifecycle—from hydrogen production to delivery via HRSs. Hydrogen infrastructure can be established using two primary approaches. The first, off-site hydrogen production, follows a centralized model in which hydrogen is produced in large quantities at a central facility and then transported to refueling stations. Alternatively, on-site hydrogen production involves generating hydrogen directly at refueling stations using small-scale production units, reducing the need for extensive transportation.

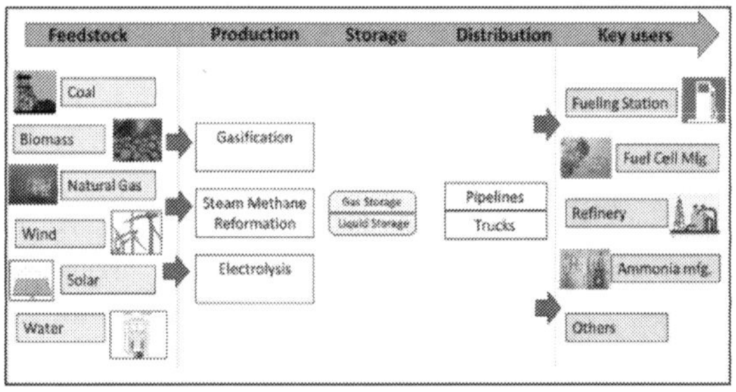

Fig. 2. Hydrogen supply chain structure

Table 1. Key logistical aspects of hydrogen form

Details	Compressed hydrogen (CH_2)	Liquefied hydrogen (LH_2)
Storage pressure	350–700 bar	~1 bar (Cryogenic tank)
Energy density	Low at 38 g/l	High at 71 g/l
Transport distance	Short to medium distance (e.g., tube trailers, pipeline)	Long-distance transport (e.g., cryogenic tankers)
Infrastructure cost	Low	High
Energy losses	Approx. 10–15% for compression	Approx. 30–40% for liquefaction

Modeling the HSC presents significant challenges, particularly in efficiency and infrastructure, as highlighted in several studies. For instance, challenges in the upstream process include evaluating hydrogen sources, integrating renewable energy for a green HSC, and assessing the feasibility of various hydrogen production methods [12]. The midstream stage involves challenges such as site selection for hydrogen plants, storage optimization, efficiency assessment, and distribution mode evaluation. Additionally, studies on the downstream stage address barriers to hydrogen demand, demand-supply balance, HRS assessment, and network design and optimization [13, 14].

Despite growing research on the HSC, significant gaps remain in midstream facility location and downstream integration of HRSs. The strategic placement of off-site hydrogen production facilities, considering existing HRSs, remains underexplored. Thus, this study's evaluation of locations for off-site hydrogen production facilities, based on clusters of HRSs, can provide valuable insights into the viability of hydrogen infrastructure.

2.2 Methodology

In this study, the HRS cluster is initially analyzed using the K-means algorithm, and the strategic off-site production facility is later assessed using the rectilinear-minisum optimization model. The K-means clustering method is an unsupervised machine learning algorithm that classifies data into K clusters by minimizing intra-cluster variance [15]. Specifically, the K-means algorithm seeks to achieve the minimum sum of squares. It iteratively adjusts observational data, partitioning them into K sets with the objective of minimizing the sum of squared differences within clusters. To ensure proper classification, the exact number of clusters must be specified as input. The schematic of the K-means analysis is shown in Figure 3

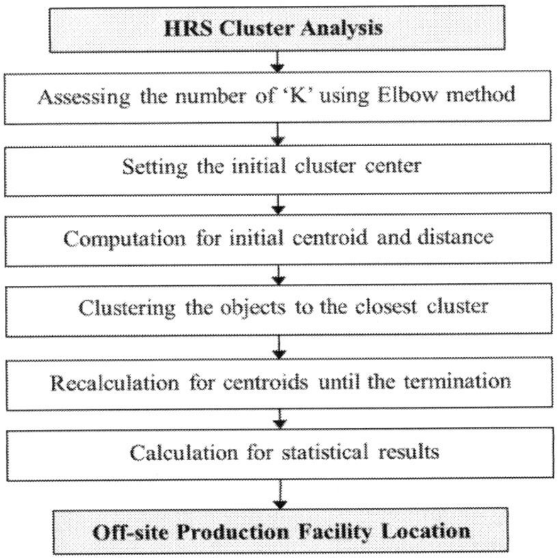

Fig. 3. Methodology flow of the study

Next, after cluster formation, the rectilinear-distance minimization model is applied to determine the optimal location of the centralized hydrogen production facility within each cluster. This model aims to minimize the sum of absolute differences in the respective coordinates, using rectilinear distance as the primary metric along with the density weight of each data point. Rectilinear distance is particularly suitable for evaluating travel distances in structured environments, such as city networks or facilities with grid-like layouts, making it an appropriate choice for this study. The mathematical notation for the rectilinear-distance minimization model is presented in Equations (1)–(2), where $d(X,P_i)$ is the function to compute rectilinear distance between each HRS and the optimal facility, (a_i, b_i) are latitude and longitude parameters of each HRS, (x, y) are decision variables, and D_i is the population density of each postal code, respectively. The model is particularly well-suited for planning infrastructure like hydrogen production facilities, where logistics and accessibility are key factors in minimizing costs and improving service efficiency. The K-means clustering and its variants have been applied for locational analysis in diverse studies (e.g., [15]).

$$\text{Minimize} \quad f(X) = \sum_i d(X,P_i)\cdot D_i \tag{1}$$

$$d(X,P_i) = \sum_i |x-a_i| + \sum_i |y-b_i| \tag{2}$$

3 Case Study and Analysis

https://doi.org/10.1051/e3sconf/202567901001

3.1 Case Study

In this subsection, we discuss the data collection and analysis for HRSs. Data were initially collected from the Hydrogen Analysis Resource Center [16], which provides information on existing and planned HRSs outside of the United States. As shown in Figure 4, the top five nations with the most HRSs are China, followed by South Korea, Japan, Germany, and France, respectively. Germany, in particular, has 138 HRSs, with 101 active stations and 37 planned (non-active) stations.

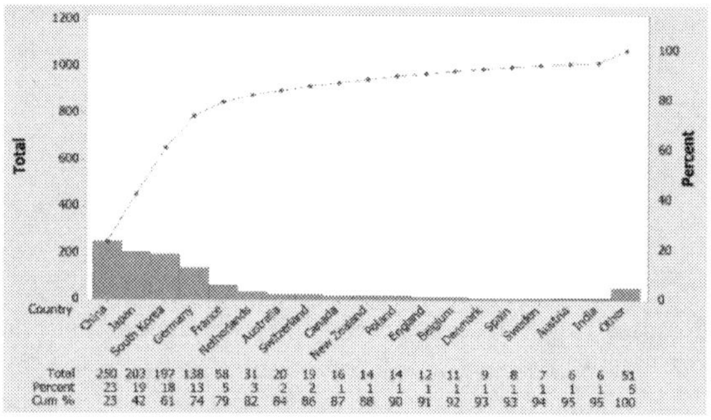

Fig. 4. Pareto chart of HRSs by country

In this study, data related to active HRSs in Germany are collected and refined for further analysis of HRS clusters and potential locations for off-site hydrogen production facilities. Table 2 presents selected data for active HRSs in Germany, including the index for HRS, city location, postal code, population in the respective postal area, and postal area details. Next, the HRS addresses based on Zip code are used to obtain the latitude and longitude coordinates of each location for further analysis. Figure 5 illustrates the existing locations of HRSs in the case study, mapped using the Geographic Information System (GIS) [17].

Table 2. Key logistical aspects of hydrogen form

HRSxx	City/Town	Zip code	Population	Area
HRS1	Aachen	52070	26,939	9.10
2	Bad Homburg	61352	23,778	17.20
3	Bad Rappenau	74906	22,356	73.55
4	Bayreuth	95448	27,672	33.50
5	Berg bei Hof	95180	1,981	38.90
HRS6	Berlin	10243	20,440	2.85
7	Berlin	12459	30,547	8.70
8	Berlin	13089	23,671	3.97
9	Berlin	12347	22,219	3.75
10	Berlin Charlottenburg	13593	20,185	4.55
HRS11	Berlin Mitte	10557	26,623	4.03
12	Berlin Schönefeld	12529	8,006	9.80
13	Biebelried	97318	1,216	22.70
14	Bonn	53121	22,593	5.60
15	Braunschweig	38112	33,240	21.80
HRS16	Bremen	28325	13,023	4.79
17	Brunsbüttel	25541	11,872	50.50
18	Derching	86316	30,886	80.10
19	Dortmund	44147	28,956	8.10
20	Dresden	01069	24,682	5.30
HRS21	Duisburg	47059	18,685	7.60
22	Düren	52353	28,841	31.40
23	Düsseldorf	40591	20,717	4.64
24	Flughafen Stuttgart	70771	41,042	29.89
25	Erfurt	99099	14,971	6.10
HRS26	Erlangen	91058	33,279	17.70
27	Essen	45327	21,551	6.20
28	Fellbach	70736	27,850	15.80
29	Flensburg	24983	6,306	61.30
30	Frankfurt	60528	32,173	17.90
HRS31	Frankfurt am Main	60314	22,772	3.91
32	Frankfurt am Main	65929	50,825	13.70
33	Frechen	50226	52,304	45.06
34	Freiburg	79108	39,554	21.20
35	Fürholzen	85376	2,810	16.10
HRS36	Fürth	90765	40,041	17.70
37	Geisingen	78187	6,215	73.75
38	Giengen an der Brenz	89537	19,806	44.05
39	Halle	6122	7,119	2.06
40	Hamburg	22335	22,693	7.80
HRS41	Hamburg	21079	69,243	30.90
42	Hamburg	20457	57,093	14.60
43	Hamburg	22525	31,517	8.20
44	Hamburg Bramfeld	22175	13,867	4.26
45	Hannover	30179	30,652	8.30
HRS46	Hasbergen	49205	11,119	21.37
47	Heidelberg	69124	24,490	15.50
48	Heidelberg	69123	34,659	17.70
49	Herten	45699	33,968	18.80
50	Hirschberg	69493	9,644	12.35
HRS51	Hofolding	85649	5,650	37.95
52	Husum	25813	23,960	25.80
53	Ingolstadt	85053	25,831	14.60
54	Irschenberg	83737	3,331	53.94
55	Kamen	59174	42,312	41.10
HRS56	Karlsruhe	76227	29,161	17.20
57	Kirchheim	36275	3,672	50.61
58	Koblenz	56072	16,694	23.60
59	Köln	51147	51,666	32.30
60	Laage	18299	6,555	114.90
HRS61	Laatzen	30880	41,960	34.16

https://doi.org/10.1051/e3sconf/202567901001

62	Landshut	84030	21,988	37.20
63	Leipzig	04157	10,681	3.35
64	Leverkusen	51373	45,041	14.00
65	Limburg an der Lahn	65552	2,749	4.88
HRS66	Lohfelden	34253	13,837	16.58
67	Magdeburg	39126	36,726	25.80
68	Metzingen	72555	23,118	34.55
69	Mönchengladbach	41236	16,316	4.02
70	Mülheim an der Ruhr	45472	21,596	8.00
HRS71	München	85356	23,698	33.60
72	München	81825	33,579	4.92
73	München	81737	30,930	5.40
74	München	80639	18,614	3.85
75	Münster	48163	36,896	63.50
HRS76	Neumünster	24539	30,533	24.90
77	Neuruppin	16816	19,616	48.30
78	Niebüll	25899	10,192	30.63
79	Nürnberg	90475	18,313	13.80
80	Oldenburg	26133	21,114	11.10
HRS81	Passau	94036	21,956	31.60
82	Passau	94036	21,956	31.60
83	Pentling	93080	6,398	32.47
84	Pforzheim	75177	18,926	13.30
85	Potsdam	14478	12,314	4.51
HRS86	Rastatt	76437	51,073	58.98
87	Ratingen	40882	18,624	34.40
88	Rheda-Wiedenbrück	33378	49,849	86.66
89	Rostock	18055	20,052	11.70
90	Saarbrücken	66117	16,003	9.40
HRS91	Schnelldorf	91625	3,670	51.43
92	Siegen	57074	22,009	26.10
93	Sindelfingen	71065	15,871	17.80
94	Stuhr-Großmackenstedt	28816	33,360	81.70
95	Ulm	89081	30,759	57.60
HRS96	Weiterstadt	64331	26,525	34.40
97	Wendlingen	73240	15,877	12.15
98	Wesseling	73240	15,877	12.15
99	Westre	25926	354	19.14
100	Wiesbaden	65205	42,721	30.60
HRS101	Wuppertal	42279	18,364	9.90

Fig. 5. GIS-based locations of HRSs in the case study

3.2 Results and Discussion

3.2.1 K-means-based HRS Cluster Analysis

We next discuss the HRS cluster analysis using the K-means algorithm. Initially, the appropriate parameter K, representing the number of clusters for all HRSs, is determined. Various methods exist for defining the number of clusters, with the elbow method applied in this study [18]. This method is a widely used graphical approach that visually identifies the optimal number of clusters. Specifically, the Within-Cluster Sum of Squares (WCSS) is computed and analyzed, representing the sum of squared distances between data points within a cluster and the cluster centroid for each varied K. The optimal number of clusters is identified at the "elbow point", where the rate of WCSS reduction significantly changes, as shown in Figure 6. Based on this approach, the number of clusters in this case study is determined to be four clusters.

Besides the elbow method, other techniques exist for determining the optimal number of clusters in clustering analysis including Silhouette method, Davies-Bouldin index, etc. Regardless, the elbow method is often considered superior in certain clustering situations due to its simplicity, ease of use, and interpretability. In this study, the K-means clustering algorithm based on the elbow method helps determine the regions with high concentrations of HRSs, which can guide the strategic placement of off-site hydrogen production facilities.

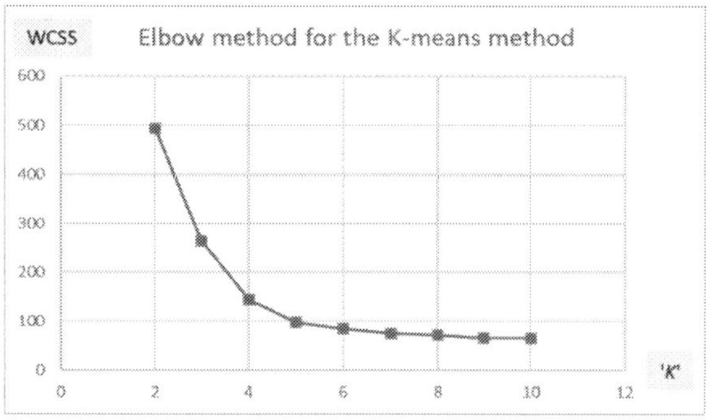

Fig. 6. The elbow method for the illustrated case study

Next, Table 3 presents a detailed analysis of the four HRS clusters based on the K-means algorithm. Specifically, there are 23, 19, 28, and 31 HRSs in each cluster, respectively. Additionally, Figure 7 illustrates the GIS-based map of the existing HRSs in the case study, classified by different clusters.

Table 3. Detailed data for HRS cluster

Cluster	# of HRS	HRS
1	23	HRS1, 14, 19, 21, 22, 23, 27, 33, 46, 49, 55, 58, 59, 64, 65, 69, 70, 75, 87, 88, 90, 92, 101
2	19	HRS15, 16, 17, 29, 40, 41, 42, 43, 44, 45, 52, 60, 61, 76, 78, 80, 89, 94, 99
3	28	HRS2, 3, 13, 18, 24, 30, 31, 32, 34, 37, 38, 47, 48, 50, 56, 57, 66, 68, 84, 86, 91, 93, 95, 96, 97, 98, 100
4	31	HRS4, 5, 6, 7, 8, 9, 10, 11, 12, 20, 25, 26, 35, 36, 39, 51, 53, 54, 62, 63, 67, 71, 72, 73, 74, 77, 79, 81, 82, 83, 85

Fig. 7. Classified HRSs based on four clusters

3.2.2 Off-Site Hydrogen Facility Location Analysis

Next, given the locational data based on latitude and longitude, as well as the population density for each postal code, the minisum rectilinear-distance model is applied to evaluate potential off-site hydrogen production facility locations. The rectilinear distance and postal density are chosen to ensure that street networks for distribution and the potential demand of FCEVs are accounted for when making strategic decisions about the hydrogen production facility. Initially, an overall analysis considering all 101 active HRSs in the case study is conducted as a baseline (i.e., HP0) as illustrated in Table 4. The analysis then presents decision variables related to the latitude and longitude for the proposed off-site hydrogen production facilities, which are (x, y) in the above equation. Specifically, HPG1, HPG2, HPG3, and HPG4 represent the proposed production facility locations for each HRS cluster group, as determined by the K-means algorithm analysis.

Table 4. Detailed data for HRS cluster

HP	# of HRS	Optimal latitude	Optimal longitude
HP0	101 (entire)	51.2724269073	9.9960513875
HPG1	23	51.1885798489	7.0011571164
HPG2	19	53.5460678291	9.9806254914
HPG3	28	49.4116533788	8.6691965074
HPG4	31	51.4901405987	13.0884493171

The results from the overall analysis for the strategic location of the off-site hydrogen production facility, considering all existing HRSs, are presented in Figure 8. The analysis takes into account both the rectilinear distance (km) and postal density (population per km²) to determine the optimal location. The overall minimum objective function value is found to be 680,475 people per kilometer. This indicates the lowest combined cost for the production facility placement when factoring in both travel distances and population density in the area.

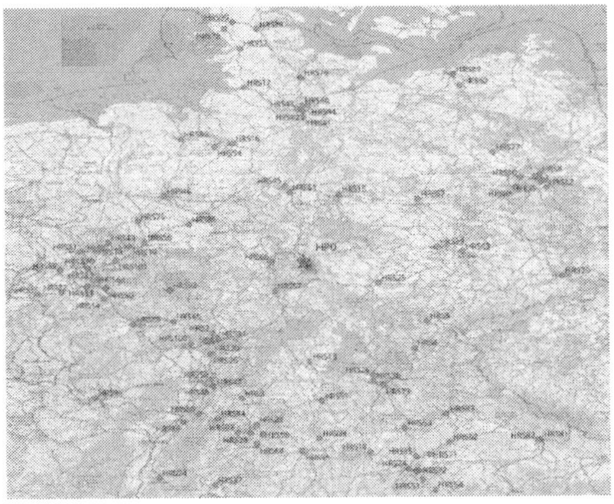

Fig. 8. Results of proposed hydrogen production facility (HP0) based on the entire 101 HRSs

In addition, Figures 9-12 provide a detailed breakdown of the analysis for each HRS cluster, showcasing how the objective function varies across different clusters. For Cluster 1, the objective function value is found to be 30,063. Cluster 2 shows a similar result with an objective function value of 28,586, reflecting slightly lower costs for strategic placement considering 23 and 19 HRSs in the clusters. In contrast, Cluster 3 presents a higher value of 34,706, highlighting a costlier location scenario with an increase in distribution cost for 28 HRSs. Finally, Cluster 4 stands out with the highest objective function value of 199,027, indicating a more significant logistical challenge in optimizing the placement of the hydrogen production facility within that cluster, given the largest number of HRSs and the greater dispersion of these locations. These results emphasize the varying degrees of complexity and cost-efficiency across different regions, guiding better-informed decisions for the development of the hydrogen infrastructure.

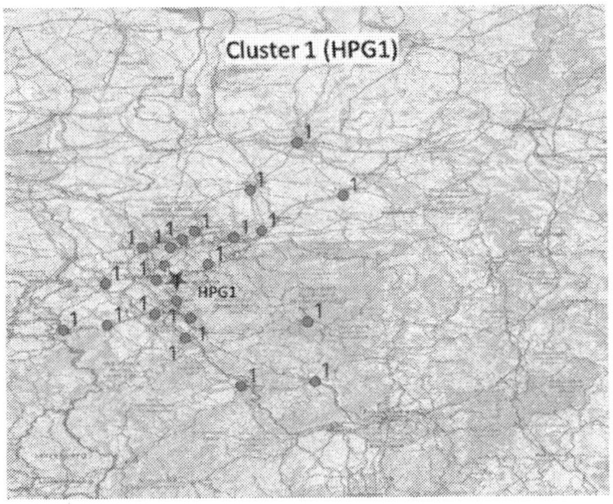

Fig. 9. Results of proposed hydrogen production facility (HPG1) based on the first cluster

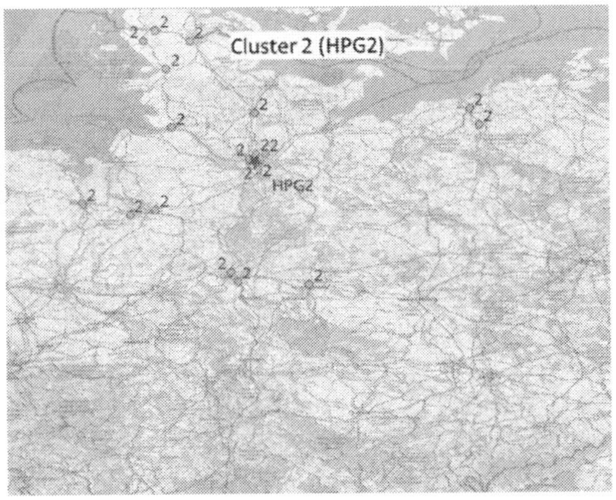

Fig. 10. Results of proposed hydrogen production facility (HPG2) based on the second cluster

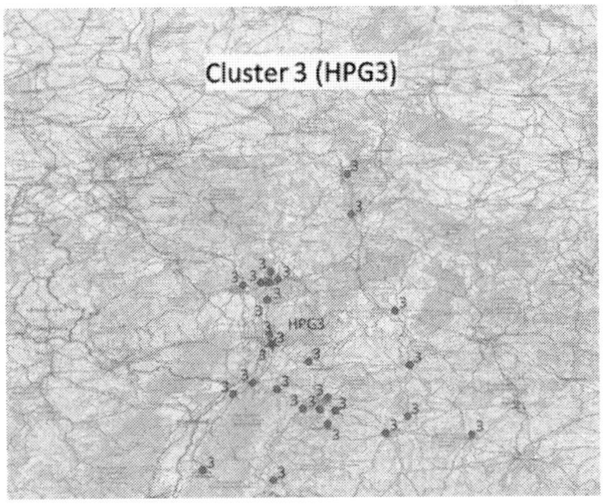

Fig. 11. Results of proposed hydrogen production facility (HPG3) based on the third cluster

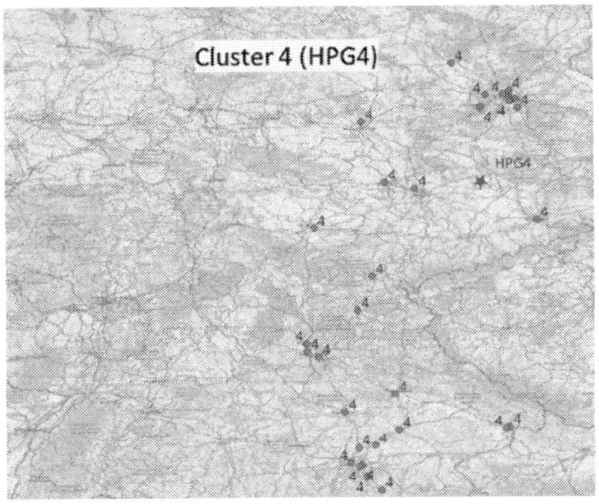

Fig. 12. Results of proposed hydrogen production facility (HPG4) based on the fourth cluster

3.2.3 Discussion and Policy Implication

In this study, the clustering analysis of HRSs using the K-means algorithm provides a structured approach to understanding regional distribution patterns, which is essential for assessing the logistics of the HSC. The identification of four distinct HRS clusters suggests varying geographical concentrations, which can significantly influence the placement of off-site hydrogen production facilities. Moreover, the sequential analysis using the rectilinear-minisum optimization model further refines these findings by identifying optimal locations for hydrogen production based on locational data and population density. Specifically, the optimal locations for off-site hydrogen production facilities for each cluster (i.e., HPG1–HPG4) offer tailored facility placements that align with localized demand.

The insights from this dual approach can contribute to enhancing strategic and tactical planning related to location and distribution, thereby informing future hydrogen infrastructure development. From a managerial perspective, these findings have significant implications for policymakers, investors, and energy infrastructure planners. First, by leveraging machine learning techniques and optimization models, decision-makers can adopt a data-driven approach to infrastructure expansion, minimizing inefficiencies and optimizing resource allocation [19]. Second, the spatial distribution of HRS clusters underscores the need for region-specific hydrogen production strategies, facilitating a balance between supply and demand. Additionally, incorporating population density into the decision-making process ensures that hydrogen production facilities are strategically placed to support future growth in FCEV adoption [20]. Furthermore, GIS-based analysis can assist policymakers in visualizing location and distribution plans [21]. By incorporating these insights into regional or national hydrogen roadmaps, stakeholders can foster a more resilient and cost-effective HSC, supporting the transition toward sustainable mobility.

4 Conclusion and Future research

This study provides a data-driven approach to optimizing the HSC by strategically locating off-site hydrogen production facilities based on existing HRSs in Germany. By employing the K-means clustering algorithm, four distinct HRS clusters were identified, revealing spatial distribution patterns that influence hydrogen logistics and infrastructure planning to balance hydrogen demand and supply within the HSC. Subsequently, the rectilinear-minisum optimization model was applied to determine the optimal locations for hydrogen production facilities, ensuring efficient distribution while considering population density and street network constraints.

This research provides practical implications to support policymakers in strategic and tactical planning for regional HSCs. Future research directions include exploring additional variables that may influence hydrogen production and distribution decisions, which could further refine facility placement and distribution strategies. Additionally, more complex methodologies can be integrated and extended to sequentially or simultaneously evaluate location and distribution planning within the HSC. One of our ongoing research projects also investigates FCEV-based routing analysis based on the extended Vehicle Routing Problem (VRP), given the analyzed locations. Furthermore, stochastic factors can be assessed, considering the uncertainties in both demand and supply. Expanding this research to other countries, including Thailand, for comparative studies or exploring other regions within Germany with emerging hydrogen economies could validate the model's applicability and provide comparative insights into different hydrogen infrastructure development approaches. Lastly, this study is part of our ongoing research aimed at further evaluating and modeling the HSC network by integrating upstream, midstream, and downstream core operations.

References

1. J. A. Riera, R. M. Lima, O. M. Knio, A review of hydrogen production and supply chain modeling and optimization. International Journal of Hydrogen Energy. **48**, 13731-13755 (2023). https://www.iea.org/
2. S. K. Dash, S. Chakraborty, M. Roccotelli, U. K. Sahu, Hydrogen fuel for future mobility: Challenges and future aspects. Sustainability. **14**, 8285 (2022)
3. X. Tian, C. An, Z. Chen, The role of clean energy in achieving decarbonization of electricity generation, transportation, and heating sectors by 2050: A meta-analysis review. Renewable and Sustainable Energy Reviews. **182**, 113404 (2023)
4. Q. Hassan, P. Viktor, T. J. Al-Musawi, B. M. Ali, S. Algburi, H. M. Alzoubi, M. Jaszczur, The renewable energy role in the global energy Transformations. Renewable Energy Focus. **48**, 100545 (2024)
5. M. Z. Chishti, X. Xia, E. Dogan, Understanding the effects of artificial intelligence on energy transition: The moderating role of Paris Agreement. Energy Economics. **131**, 107388 (2024)

6. F. Bai, F. Zhao, X. Liu, Z. Mu, H. Hao, Z. Liu, A comparative well-to-wheel analysis of renewable energy pathways for hydrogen and battery electric vehicles. Journal of Cleaner Production. **466**, 142832 (2024).
7. International Energy Agency (IEA), Global hydrogen demand by sector in the Sustainable Development Scenario, 2019-2070, IEA, Paris https://www.iea.org/
8. K. Ransikarbum, H. Zadek, J. Janmontree, Evaluating Renewable Energy Sites in the Green Hydrogen Supply Chain with Integrated Multi-Criteria Decision Analysis. Energies. **17**, 4073 (2024)
9. M. Aziz, Liquid hydrogen: A review on liquefaction, storage, transportation, and safety. Energies. **14**, 5917 (2021)
10. M. Reuß, P. Dimos, A. Léon, T. Grube, M. Robinius, D. Stolten, Hydrogen road transport analysis in the energy system: A case study for Germany through 2050. Energies. **14**, 3166 (2021)
11. U. S. Department of Energy (DOE) (2020). Hydrogen and Fuel Cell Technologies Office. URL: https://www.energy.gov/eere/fuelcells/
12. J. Janmontree, H. Zadek, K. Ransikarbum, Analyzing solar location for green hydrogen using multi-criteria decision analysis. Renewable and Sustainable Energy Reviews. **209**, 115102 (2025)
13. M. J. Kuby, A. S. Martinez, S. B. Kelley, G. Tal, Hydrogen station location analysis and optimization: Advanced models and behavioral evidence. Hydrogen Economy. 315-380 (2023)
14. G. Trencher, A. Edianto, Drivers and barriers to the adoption of fuel cell passenger vehicles and buses in Germany. Energies. **14**, 833 (2021).
15. K. Ransikarbum, D. Kritchanchai, W. Chanpuypetch, J. Niemsakul, Central Hospital Location and Distribution Planning Using Integrated K-Means and Vehicle Routing Algorithm in the Healthcare Chain. Oper. Supply Chain. Manag. Int. J. **17**, 299-315 (2024)
16. H2Tools. Hydrogen tools and resources. H2Tools. URL: https://h2tools.org/hyarc
17. QGIS geographic information system. QGIS Association. https://qgis.org
18. K. Shrikant, V. Gupta, A. Khandare, P. Furia, A comparative study of clustering algorithm. In Intelligent Computing and Networking: Proceedings of IC-ICN 2021. Singapore: Springer Nature Singapore, (2022), 219-235
19. M. A. Hossain, M. S. A. Mazumder, M. H. Bari, R. Mahi, Impact Assessment of Machine Learning Algorithms On Resource Efficiency And Management In Urban Developments. International Journal of Business and Economics. **1**, 1-9 (2024)
20. A. N. Sakib, F. Mehjabin, J. B. Schmidt, M. Haque, K. Saha, M. M. H. Bhuiyan, Harnessing hydrogen: A comprehensive literature review on strategic launching initiatives in the global energy market. International Journal of Energy Research. **2024**, 3265065 (2024)
21. S. Steidl, R. A. Peer, A. Alhamwi, W. Medjroubi, A. Z. Figueroa, J. Haas, GIS-Based modelling of hydrogen integration in urban energy systems–a systematic review. Current Sustainable/Renewable Energy Reports. 1-10 (2024)

Oxidation of NO to NO_2 with Ozone in Real Flue Gas Emitted from a Diesel Oil Combustor

Punya Promhuad[1,4], *Kampanart* Theinnoi[2,4], *Thawatchai* Wongchang[3,4], *Phurin* Chonpan[2], *Teerapong* Iamcheerangkoon[2], and *Sak* Sittichompoo[2,4*]

[1]Techno Park, King Mongkut's University of Technology North Bangkok, 10800 Bangkok, Thailand
[2]Department of Power Engineering Technology, College of Industrial Technology, King Mongkut's University of Technology North Bangkok, 10800 Bangkok, Thailand
[3]Department of Mechanical and Automotive Engineering Technology, Faculty of Engineering and Technology, King Mongkut's University of Technology North Bangkok, (Rayong Campus), 21120 Rayong, Thailand
[4]Research Centre for Combustion Technology and Alternative Energy (CTAE), King Mongkut's University of Technology North Bangkok, 10800 Bangkok, Thailand

Abstract. To reduce nitrogen oxides emissions (NOx) from flue gas, selective catalytic reduction (SCR) or adsorption using various solution are efficient methods. However, nitric oxide (NO) needs to be oxidised into nitrogen dioxide (NO_2) to enhance NOx removal performance. This paper presents the effects of operating parameter of a dielectric barrier discharge (DBD) reactor on ozone (O_3) generation which ozone was utilised to oxidise NO into NO_2 in the real flue gas from diesel oil burner. A cylindrical DBD configuration with 1.5 mm electrode gap and effective discharge volume ranged from 13.8 cm^3 were chosen to produce O_3-rich air for oxidising NO. Using concentrated O_2 instead of air as O_3 source could enhance O_3 formation (8.57 g/kWh vs. 44.08 g/kWh). NO conversion to NO_2 by O_3 was strongly dependent on O_3/NO ratio. Additionally, thermal O_3 decomposition by heat energy in flue gas also substantially reduced O_3 which must be compensated by using excess O_3/NO ratio. At flue gas temperature of 407°C, O_3/NO ratio of 6.37 was required to complete oxidise NO into NO_2. The optimal NO conversion efficiency of 2.93 g/kWh was realised at flue gas resident time of 313 ms and flue gas temperature of 483°C.

1 Introduction

Rapid Combustion of carbon-containing fuel (e.g. fossil fuels) has been the main source of carbon emissions such as carbon dioxide (CO_2) which associates with greenhouse effect that raises global surface temperature [1]. The rise of average global temperatures leads to extreme patterns of climate which adversely affect environment, ecosystem, and quality of life. Nitrogen oxides (NOx) is another air pollutant that emitted from complete combustion as the result of Thermal NOx [2]. High nitrogen-containing fuel could also produce high level of NOx emission [3] through fuel-NOx and prompt-NOx pathways [4]. High concentration of NOx emitted into the atmosphere results in acid rain which causes corrosion to buildings, and anything made from metals. It is of importance to manage the level of NOx to mitigate the negative consequences.

Selective catalytic reduction (SCR) [5] is a well-established aftertreatment technology for NOx reduction. SCR operates by injecting reagent (e.g. ammonia (NH_3) or urea ($(NH_2)_2CO$)) which reduces NOx into N_2 and H_2O through $4NH_3 + 4NO + O_2 \rightarrow 6H_2O + 4N_2$ and $4NH_3 + 2NO_2 + O_2 \rightarrow 6H_2O + 3N_2$ reactions [6]. However, these reactions proceed at slow pace and take relatively extended duration to complete compared to $4NH_3 + 2NO + 2NO_2 \rightarrow 6H_2O + 4N_2$ reaction which is known as 'fast-SCR' reaction [7]. Fast SCR reaction takes approximately 1 s or shorter to complete, hence; the process is more likely to complete within the catalyst. To achieve fast SCR reaction, the ratio between NO_2 to NO (NO_2/NO ratio) must equal to unity [8]. However, for flue gas from liquid and solid fuels combustion, NO is the only gas species emitted. Therefore, it is crucial to increase the NO_2/NO ratio which can be performed by oxidising NO into NO_2.

NO can be oxidised with O_2 in the presence of platinum (Pt) catalyst [9] via the general reaction: $NO + O_2 \rightarrow NO_2$. Even though, NO to NO_2 conversion could take place from 90 to 500°C, but conversion efficiency trends to reduce as gas temperature increase. Furthermore, conversion efficiency of catalytic process reaches approximately 60 % at 350 °C due to the nature of oxidation catalyst. On the other hand, NO can be effectively oxidised into NO_2 using O_3 [10] via $NO + O \rightarrow NO_2$ and $NO + O_3 \rightarrow NO_2 + O_2$ reactions [11]. In general, dielectric barrier discharge (DBD) [12, 13] is the most common O_3 generation method which utilises high voltage (HV) electricity to convert oxygen into ozone. Air is the most universal feedstock for ozone production due to the abundance availability. However, ozone yield and ozone efficiency are lower than using higher oxygen concentration mixture or pure oxygen as feedstock [14] due to ozone decomposition by catalytic reactions of NO

* Corresponding author: sak.s@cit.kmutnb.ac.th

and NO_2 [11]. Overall, ozone injection technique is a practical method to oxidise NO into NO_2 on-site where high conversion efficiency and low maintenance are important aspects of implementation.

The interaction between NO and O_3 is well documented [15-17]. However, most preliminary studies were conducted at laboratory-scale using simulated flue gas [15] or only NO, O_2, and N_2 mixtures [18]. Many studies conducted the experiment without the presence of water [19], small experiment scale [17], low gas temperature [18], and long residence time [20]. It is important to understand the effect of the abovementioned parameters which are encountered in real-world situations e.g. moisture content, sulphur, particles, short residence time, high temperature, and larger system's scale. Therefore, the experimental investigation with real flue gas at elevated flow rate will reduce the gap between theoretical studies and the actual application of ozone injection technique.

This paper presents an experimental investigation of a step-up scale of NO oxidation from small diesel oil burner using ozone injection to promote NO_2 formation. Our work investigates the effects of ozone production parameters (e.g. high voltage discharge voltage and frequency, inlet feed oxygen concentration) on the characteristics of ozone-rich air and the effects residence time and flue gas temperature on NO oxidation process.

2 Material and methods

2.1 Ozone production from DBD reactor

For DBD reactor employed in this study, most metal parts were fabricated from stainless steel 304 using multiple DBD cells connected in parallel in the same configuration experimented in [21] and [22]. Although, the main different was the material of the dielectric barrier which borosilicate glass tubes with outer diameter of 23 mm and glass tube wall thickness of 1.5 mm were used as dielectric barrier which mounted with inner electrodes. The gap between outside the dielectric barrier and outer electrodes was 1.5±0.5 mm. The total number of DBD cell was 12 cells which resulted in effective discharge volume of 13.8 cm^3. Dry air and bottled oxygen (99.99%) were used as oxygen source for ozone production. Feed air flow rate was regulated by a mass flow controller (MFC) (SMC model (PF2A750 – F02 - 27) at fixed flow rate of 20.0 LPM. A Trek 10/10B-HS high voltage power supply (HVPS) was used to produce high voltage (HV) electricity for the DBD reactor. The Trek HVPS's output signal was controlled by square wave generated by a Keysight DSOX1204 digital storage oscilloscope which also monitored the output HV voltage and current for calculating discharge electrical power. In this study, discharge voltage between 7 to 10 kV (peak) and discharge frequency between 100 to 500 Hz were used during the experiment. Figure 1 illustrates the discharge waveform monitored by Trek 10/10B-HS's outputs which depicts the phase shift of current profile compared to that of discharge voltage profile. The leading phase shift observed in the discharge current is indicative of a capacitive load, which arises from the inherent geometric configuration of the DBD reactor. This is the feature that is commonly observed in typical ozoniser [23]. Specific energy density (SED) between 425 - 996 J/L were used which could be written as the ratio of electric input power (P_{in} in W) to DBD reactor inlet air mixture flow rate ($\dot{V}_{air}$ in LPM) as shown in equation (1).

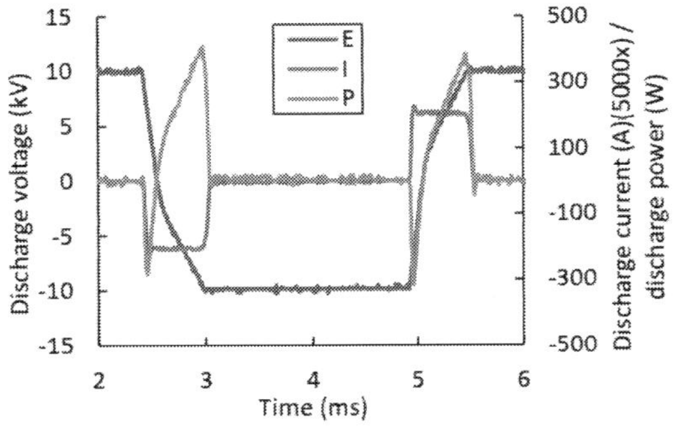

Fig. 1. DBD waveform at 10 kV$_{peak}$/ 600 Hz.

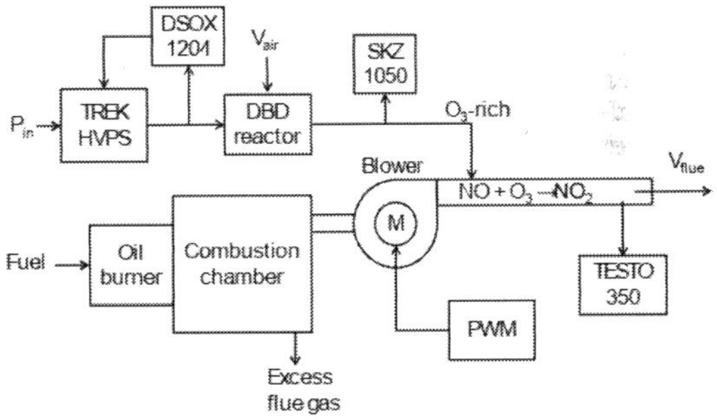

Fig. 2. Schematic diagram of experiment setup.

$$SED = 60 \times \frac{P_{in}}{\dot{V}_{air}} \quad (1)$$

A SKZ 1050-O_3 portable analyser was utilised to quantify the amount of O_3 generated from the DBD reactor. Hence, ozone production rate ($\dot{m}_{ozone}$, g/h) could be calculated by equation (2). Where ρ is ozone density (g/L) at a given temperature and pressure, and C is ozone concentration in (ppm-vol).

$$\dot{m}_{ozone} = 60 \times \rho \times \dot{V}_{air} \times \frac{C}{1000000} \quad (2)$$

To quantify the amount of ozone produced per one unit of electricity, specific ozone production (SOP) (in g/kWh) is depicted in equation (3). Where P_{in} represents the total electrical input power of the high voltage power supply system (HVPS and DSOX1204) measured by a power meter.

$$SOP = \dot{m}_{ozone} \times \frac{1000}{P_{in}} \quad (3)$$

2.2 Oxidation of NO in flue gas using ozone

Diesel oil burner, Olympia SL-3LP, was operated with 30% excess air with mean diesel fuel flow rate of 5.54 kg/h generated flue gas containing gas compositions as shown in Table 1. Gas species in the flue gas stream such as NO, NO_2, CO, CO_2, and O_2 were volumetrically quantified by a Testo 350 flue gas analyser.

Table 1. Baseline flue gas compositions (volumetric).

NO (ppm)	NO_2 (ppm)	CO (ppm)	CO_2 (%)	O_2 (%)
55.4	1.7	12.24	11.3	5.01

The turbine side of an automotive turbocharger was mechanically coupled to a DC motor to form an in-house built flue gas blower. Flue gas flow rate ($\dot{V}_{flue}$) was regulated by controlling the DC motor using pulse width modulation (PWM) technique. Tracer gas method [24] was used to measure the flue gas flow rate. Four different flue gas flow rates were experimented which resulted in 250 to 831 ms residence time for reaction between NO and O_3 to form NO_2. Residence time of NO and O_3 was the reciprocal of GHSV (Gas Hourly Space Velocity) as shown in equation (4) where volume of reactor is the volume of pipe section between O_3 injection port and Testo350 sampling port. Figure 2 illustrates the experimental setup utilised in this experimental investigation.

$$Residence\ time = GHSV^{-1} = \left(\frac{\dot{V}_{gas}}{V_{reactor}}\right)^{-1} \quad (4)$$

3 Results and discussions

3.1 Ozone production characteristics of DBD reactor

Figure 3 illustrates the concentration of O_3 and NO_2 at the outlet of the DBD reactor for operating duration of 900 seconds (15 minutes) with dry air as feedstock. The chart reveals that O_3 and NO_2 concentrations started to increase 60 seconds after the HVPS was turned on. Subsequently, the concentrations of O_3 and NO_2 rapidly increased until the 400th second, while the HVPS input power sharply declined. NO_2 is formed after O_3 formation based on high O_3/NO_2 ratio during early operation of HVPS which suggests that O_3 was generated first from oxygen in air via $O_2 + e \rightarrow 2O + e$ and $O + O_2 \leftrightarrow O_3$ reactions. Then, NO was produced through $N_2 + O \leftrightarrow NO + N$ reaction. Simultaneously, HV discharge also generated N via $N_2 + e^- \rightarrow 2N$ reaction which acted as a precursor for NO formation through $N + O_2 \leftrightarrow NO + O$ reaction. In this case, the absence of H_2O in dry air inhibited the formation of NO via OH + N pathway. The high O_3 concentration ($O_3/NO >= 1$ [25]) favoured NO oxidation into NO_2 through $NO + O_3 \rightarrow NO_2 + O_2$ and $NO + O \rightarrow NO_2$ reactions [22]. Due to substantial concentrations of O_3, no trace of NO was detected as the entire NO was converted into NO_2. It is reasonable to infer that $O + O_2 \leftrightarrow O_3$ and $NO + O_3 \rightarrow NO_2 + O_2$ reactions are ozone-consuming process that limits ozone yield in addition to the gas temperature increased by joules-heating phenomenon [26]. It can be observed that O_3/NO_2 ratio reached near steady-state around the value 1.9 after HVPS operated approximately 300 seconds. No significant change of O_3/NO_2 ratio was observed indicating the limit of O_3 production.

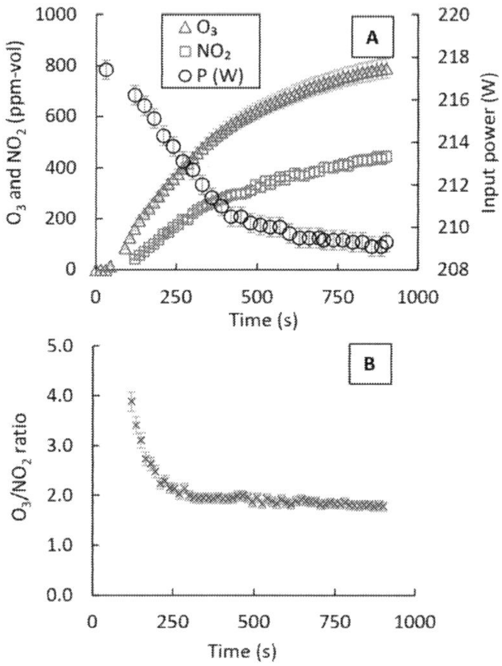

Fig. 3. Time evolution of O_3 and NO_2 production, and O_3/NO_2 ratio from DBD reactor at 10kV and 200 Hz.

As ozone generation progressed, HVPS input power started to decline which was due to the convergence toward equilibrium of gas compositions within discharge zone of the DBD reactor. The compositions of gases within the DBD reactor were believed to substantially influences the capacitance and the equivalence series resistance of the DBD reactor. Assuming the inductance of the circuit remains constant, a reduction in capacitance led to an increase in the capacitive reactance (X_c) of the DBD reactor, as defined by $X_C=(2\pi fC)^{-1}$. The elevated reactance imposed greater impedance to current flow, thereby attenuating the discharge current and consequently resulted in a decrease in the input power of the HVPS.

Figure 4 depicts the effect of HVPS operating frequency on O_3 and NO_2 production characteristics which higher discharge frequency increases number of discharge repetition in given period. As the result, more oxygen (O) and nitrogen (N) radicals could be generated which linearly enhanced ozone production rate as illustrated in Fig.4A. Similarly, the radical N and O facilitated the formation of NO which subsequently oxidised into NO_2 in an overall linear trend similar to that of O_3. Although, O_3 and NO_2 concentrations appeared to increase concurrently, a slight declined of O_3/NO_2 ratio (Figure 4B) at higher discharge frequency indicates that O_3 production rate increased less rapidly than the rate of NO_2 formation. The formation of NO_2 in the context of O_3 production is considered undesirable because it diverts energy away from dissociation of O_2 molecules and decreases the efficiency of O_3 production. Figure 4C illustrates that ozone yield increases with higher discharge frequency as the results of greater number of times of energy injection to feed gas per given duration [13]. It should be noted that the ozone yield reported in this study may appear lower compared to values presented in literature reviews (in the "introduction" section). This discrepancy arises from the differing methodologies used to measure electrical power. In this work, ozone yield was calculated based on the total input power of the system, which accounts for all energy losses. Consequently, the results presented here offer a realistic assessment of system performance and are directly applicable for scaling purposes in future implementations utilising this dataset.

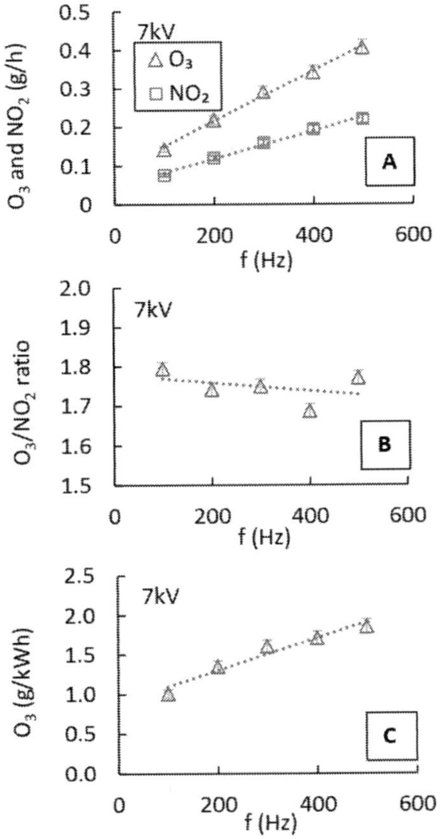

Fig. 4. Effect of discharge frequency and voltage on O_3 and NO_2 productions, O_3/NO_2 ratio, and O_3 yield.

On the other hand, Figure 5A demonstrates the effect of HVPS supply voltage on O_3 and NO_2 production characteristics. Overall, increasing discharge voltage seemed to exhibit similar effect on O_3 production rate as increasing the discharge frequency by effectively increase energy into the O_2 dissociation process. Increasing discharge voltage enhanced specific energy density applied to air feedstock which raised input energy for O_2 and N_2 excitation to produce O and N radicals and resulted in higher O_3 and NO_2 concentrations in product mixture. The O_3/NO_2 ratio in Figure 5B demonstrates different trend to that of Fig.4B which O_3/NO_2 increases from 1.8 toward 1.9 with higher discharge voltage. The results reveal that increasing discharge voltage had significant impact on O_3 generation at given discharge frequency. In this scenario, the increase discharge voltage led to the rate of O_3 formation exceeded that of NO_2, which is considered advantageous for optimising the ozone generation process. Figure 5C displays that O_3 yield rose from approximately 2 g/kWh to 7 g/kWh when increased discharge voltage from 7 to 10 kV. This indicates that discharge voltage played a significant role in ozone production efficiency. Nevertheless, the discharge voltage is fundamentally constrained by the dielectric strength of the insulation materials used within the high-voltage circuitry, including the ceramic insulator employed in the DBD reactor. Increasing the discharge voltage necessitates a larger reactor geometry and results in greater overall system weight. Thus, while higher discharge voltages may enhance ozone yield, they do so at the expense of increased reactor size, weight, and component costs required to withstand elevated electrical stresses. Ozone yield obtained by using air as oxygen feedstock reached a maximum value of 7 g/kWh at 10 kV and 500 Hz in this study.

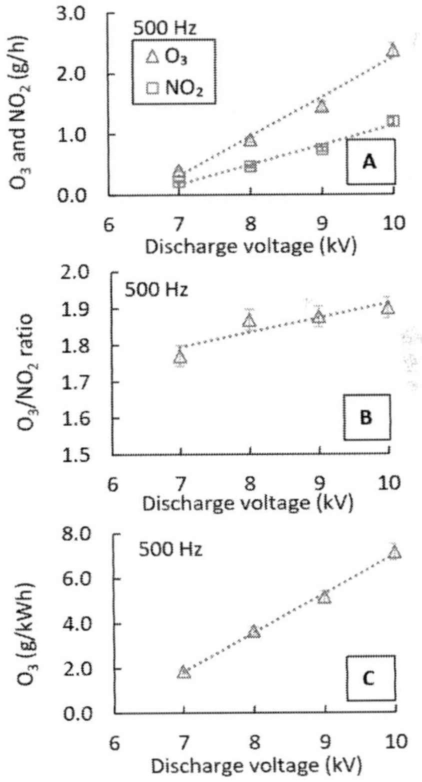

Fig. 5. Effect of discharge frequency and voltage on O_3 and NO_2 productions, O_3/NO_2 ratio, and O_3 yield

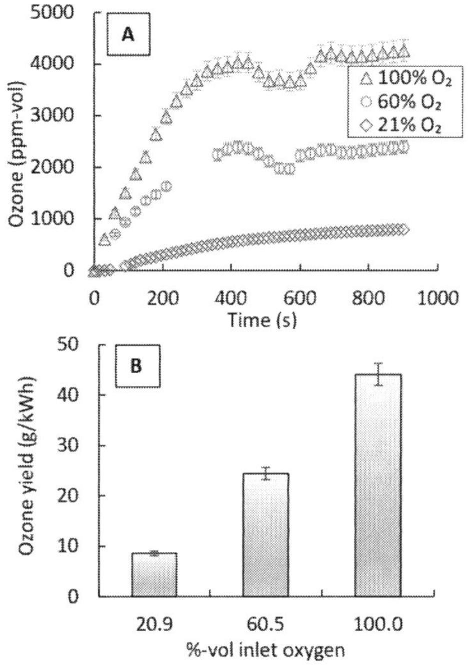

Fig. 6. Time evolution of different air feed oxygen concentrations on ozone production (A), and ozone yield (B) from DBD reactor at 10kV and 200 Hz.

Figure 6A illustrates the concentration of O_3 and NO_2 at the outlet of DBD reactor when different inlet O_2 concentrations applied over 900 seconds with discharge voltage and frequency of 10 kV and 200 Hz, respectively. The higher O_2 concentrations in feed air resulted higher O_3 concentrations due to greater chance of collision between free electrons and oxygen molecules. O_3 concentrations climbed up sharply during the first 300 seconds after HVPS was operated and reached the first peak around 400th second for both 60.5% and 100% O_2 feeds. However, a noticeable O_3 concentration fluctuation can be observed which followed by a steady increase and the concentration started to plateau soon after. The fluctuation was thought to occur as the result of unstable flow rate of oxygen flow controller which such a pattern persisted for both 60.5% and 100% O_2 feed conditions. At 900th second, ozone concentration of 784, 2392, and 4241 ppm-vol were observed with inlet O_2 feed of 21%, 60.5%, and 100%, respectively. The data indicate a positively correlated, slightly superlinear relationship between inlet oxygen concentration and outlet ozone concentration. Specifically, a 2.88-fold increase in oxygen concentration (from 21% to 60.5%) resulted in a 3.05-fold increase in ozone output concentration (784ppm→2392ppm), while a 4.76-fold increase in oxygen inlet concentration (from 21% to 100%) led to a 5.41-fold increase in ozone outlet concentration (784ppm→4241ppm). These findings suggest that the efficiency of ozone formation improves with higher oxygen availability, potentially due to enhanced reaction kinetics or reduced energy losses in the HV discharge process. The exclusion of N_2 from the input feed contributed to the enhanced O_3 yield, as it allowed the HV discharge energy to be fully directed toward the dissociation of oxygen molecules for ozone formation. In the absence of N_2, energy is not diverted toward the formation of NO_2, an undesired byproduct, thereby improving the overall efficiency of the ozone generation process. As shown in Figure 6B, an increase in oxygen concentration from 21% to 60.5% resulted in a sublinear enhancement of ozone yield, with a 2.85-fold increase from 8.57 g/kWh to 24.46 g/kWh. In contrast, elevating the oxygen concentration from 21% to 100% produced a mildly superlinear response, yielding a 5.14-fold increase in ozone output, reaching 44.08 g/kWh. These observations underscore the critical role of oxygen purity in maximizing ozone production efficiency of a DBD reactor. However, the energy requirements associated with generating high-purity oxygen must be carefully considered to assess the practical viability of employing enriched oxygen feeds in real-world applications.

3.2 Oxidation of NO in real flue gas using ozone

After the ozone generation characteristics have been established, a diesel oil burner was operated and allowed to heat up and reached a steady state which flue gas temperature and compositions were approximately constant. Ozone flow rate between 0.88 to 4.74 g/h was injected into flue gas stream 80 cm upstream the sampling port which was corresponding to approximately 13 times of the flue gas pipe inside diameter. This was done to ensure that ozone could react well with NO molecules. Increasing ozone injection rate resulted in reduced NO concentration which NO was oxidised and formed NO_2 as shown in Figure 7A. Based on the linear equation obtained from the results, to completely oxidise NO into NO_2, 4.572 g/h of O_3 is required which corresponds to O_3/NO ratio of 6.145 (Figure 7B). According to the stoichiometry of $NO + O_3 \rightarrow NO_2 + O_2$ reaction, only O_3/NO ratio of 1.0 is needed [25]. However, in practice, approximately 5 times more of O_3/NO ratio was needed to realise complete NO oxidation which was due to high flue gas temperature that caused O_3 decomposition via $O + O_2 \leftrightarrow O_3$ and $O_3 + O \rightarrow O_2$ pathways. The short residence time (831 ms) for the O_3 to react with NO in the flue gas stream was the main reason for the need to use an excessive amount of O_3. If high rate of O_3 injection is performed and O_3/NO ratio is further enhanced, NO_2 can be oxidised into higher NOx such as NO_3 which ultimately form N_2O_5 as end-product through $NO_2 + NO_3 \rightarrow N_2O_5$ reaction. This is an important step for improving NOx removal applications using alkaline solution [27]. For application to enhance fast-SCR reaction, only 50% of NO in flue gas would be needed to oxidise into NO_2 to obtain NO_2/NO ratio equals 1. Based on Figure 7C, it results in 1.748 g/h of ozone needed which corresponds to O_3/NO of 2.35 and NO conversion efficiency of approximately 1.0 g/kWh as depicted in Figure 7D. The lowered O_3/NO ratio means the smaller excess ozone required and higher system's efficiency can be realised.

 https://doi.org/10.1051/e3sconf/202567901002

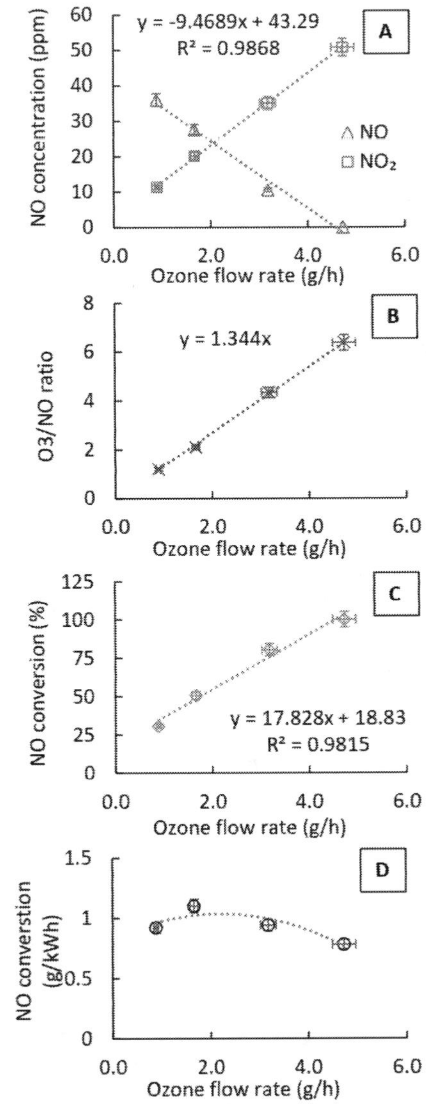

Fig. 7. Effect of input ozone flow rate on NOx emission characteristics at flue gas flow rate of 270 LPM.

Figure 8 demonstrates the effect of flue gas flow rate on NOx emission characteristics when constant ozone injection of 3.3 g/h was supplied to the flue gas stream. The greater flue gas flow rate means higher number of NO molecules introduced at given duration as depicted in Figure 8A which effectively reduced O_3/NO ratio as depicted in Figure 8B. As a result, higher amounts of unconverted NO could be observed because of significant lower O_3 flow rate compared to NO molar flow rate. This was reflected in the NO_2 flow rate shown in Figure 8A. The higher flue gas flow rate resulted in a higher flue gas temperature due to the shorter time for the hot gas within the flue gas pipe limits heat transfer to the pipe wall, thereby effectively minimising heat loss.

Figure 8C illustrates the invert correlation between flue gas temperature and its time of residence in the reaction zone section. The combination of high temperature flue gas and increased flue gas flow rate that decreased O_3/NO ratio resulted in larger amount of NO introduced, more O_3 destruction [23] and reduced NO_2 formation. At given O_3 injection rate, flue gas flow rate of 750 LPM demonstrated NO conversion of 50% with the peak NO conversion efficiency of 2.93 g/kWh. Further increase the flue gas flow rate will lead to NO conversion (both % and g/kWh) reduction as illustrated in Figure 8D.

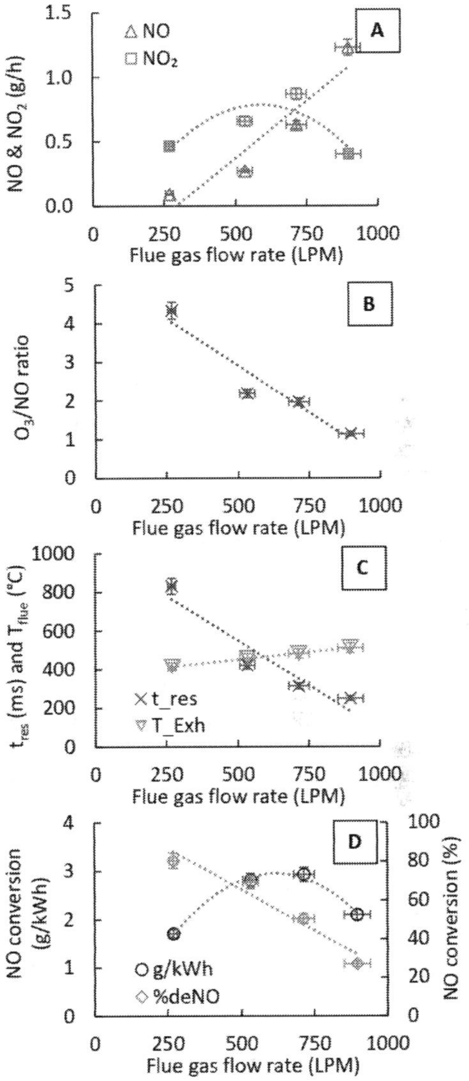

Fig. 8. Effect of flue gas flow rate on NOx emission characteristics at constant ozone injection rate.

4 Conclusions

This work experimentally investigated the effect of real flue gas at elevated temperature and volumetric flow rate on NO oxidation into NO_2 by means of injecting O_3. Ozone production characteristic of the in-house built DBD reactor fed with various concentration of oxygen and high voltage discharge conditions were evaluated. The proposed DBD reactor could reach the maximum ozone yield of 44.08 g/kWh with 100% oxygen feed. The generated O_3 was injected into the flue gas stream generated by a diesel oil burner to evaluate NO conversion to NO_2. The findings reveal that flue gas temperature played a significant role on O_3 destruction which reduced O_3 to react with NO. The higher flue gas flow rate reduces the gas residence time, which minimised heat loss through the flue gas duct. The optimised flue gas flow rate could enhance NO conversion by balancing between minimising O_3 destruction and maximising resident time for the reaction. Consequently, an excess O_3/NO ratio was required to achieve complete oxidation of NO into NO_2, in this case; O_3/NO ratio > 6 was required to entirely oxidise NO. The findings in this study can help NOx aftertreatment engineers to improve the operating condition of NO oxidation system using ozone to enhance SCR performance in real world conditions. Further investigation on NO oxidation using in-situ analytic tools will shed light on the underlying NO to NO_2 mechanisms.

This research budget was allocated by National Science, Research and Innovation Fund (NSRF), and King Mongkut's University of Technology North Bangkok (Project No. KMUTNB-FF-68-B-26).

References

1. T. Skytt, S. N. Nielsen, B.-G. Jonsson, Global warming potential and absolute global temperature change potential from carbon dioxide and methane fluxes as indicators of regional sustainability – A case study of Jämtland, Sweden. *Ecol. Indic.* **110**, 105831 (2020). https://doi.org/10.1016/j.ecolind.2019.105831
2. Y. B. Zeldovich, ZELDOVICH 1959. *Zh. Eksp. Teor. Fiz.* **36**, 964 (1959)
3. D. Erdemir, I. Dincer, A perspective on the use of ammonia as a clean fuel: Challenges and solutions., *John Wiley & Sons. Inc. Chichester, UK.*, 2021
4. H. Xiao, A. Valera-Medina, P. J. Bowen, Study on premixed combustion characteristics of co-firing ammonia/methane fuels. *Energy*. (2017). https://doi.org/10.1016/j.energy.2017.08.077
5. I. Nova, E. Tronconi, Urea-SCR Technology for deNOx After Treatment of Diesel Exhausts. *Johnson Matthey Technol. Rev.* **59**, 221–232 (2014). https://doi.org/10.1007/978-1-4899-8071-7
6. R. Villamaina, I. Nova, E. Tronconi, T. Maunula, M. Keenan, Effect of the NH4NO3 Addition on the Low-T NH3-SCR Performances of Individual and Combined Fe- and Cu-Zeolite Catalysts. *Emiss. Control Sci. Technol.*. **5**, 290–296 (2019). https://doi.org/10.1007/s40825-019-00140-3
7. C.-N. Kuo, C.-S. Li, Y.-L. Lai, S.-I. Yen, Metal-Doped Mesoporous MnO2-CeO2 Catalysts for Low-Temperature Pre-Oxidation of NO to NO2 in Fast SCR Process. (2023). https://doi.org/10.3390/catal13040694
8. W.-J. Li, T.-Y. Li, M.-Y. Wey, Preferred enhancement of fast-SCR by Mn/CeSiOx catalyst: Study on Ce/Si promotion and shape dependence. *Chem. Eng. J.* **403**, 126317 (2021). https://doi.org/10.1016/j.cej.2020.126317
9. M. Okubo, T. Kuwahara, Chapter 3 - Principle and design of emission control systems. M. Okubo and T. B. T.-N. T. for E. C. in M. D. E. Kuwahara, Eds. Butterworth-Heinemann. 53–143. (2020). https://doi.org/10.1016/B978-0-12-812307-2.00003-1
10. M. Okubo, T. Kuwahara, Chapter 4 - Operation examples of emission control systems. M. Okubo and T. B. T.-N. T. for E. C. in M. D. E. Kuwahara. Eds. Butterworth-Heinemann. 145–210. (2020). https://doi.org/10.1016/B978-0-12-812307-2.00004-3
11. N. Osawa, T. Tsuji, R. Ogiso, Y. Yoshioka, Effect of nitrogen addition to ozone generation characteristics by diffuse and filamentary dielectric barrier discharges at atmospheric pressure*. *Eur. Phys. J. Appl. Phys.* **78**, (2017). [Online]. Available: https://doi.org/10.1051/epjap/2017160471
12. K.-M. Lin, T.-Y. Liao, J.-Y. Lin, M. Abrar, Y.-X. Chen, Analysis of ozone generation in a planar atmospheric pressure air dielectric barrier discharge reactor. *Plasma Sources Sci. Technol.* **32**, 25007 (2023). https://doi.org/10.1088/1361-6595/acb812
13. M. Tański, A. Reza, D. Przytuła, K. Garasz, Ozone Generation by Surface Dielectric Barrier Discharge. *Appl. Sci.* **13**, (2023). https://doi.org/10.3390/app13127001
14. L. Wei, H. Deng, G. Neretti, Y. Zhang, Ozone yield limit in low temperature plasmas based on thermodynamics. *Eur. Phys. J. D.* **73**, 136 (2019). https://doi.org/10.1140/epjd/e2019-90560-y
15. M. Zhang *et al.*, Intensification of NOx Conversion over Activated Coke by Ozone Oxidation for Sintering Flue Gas at Low Temperatures. *ACS Omega.* **6**, 13484–13495 (2021). https://doi.org/10.1021/acsomega.1c01722
16. Y. Nie, L. Xu, Y. Yang, D. He, Y. Mei, Mechanism investigation on yellow phosphorus inducing O, O3 and OH• radicals in phosphate rock slurry for high-efficiency NO oxidation. *Sep. Purif. Technol.* **312**, 123435 (2023). https://doi.org/10.1016/j.seppur.2023.123435
17. L. Liu, B. Shen, M. Si, F. Lu, Performance and mechanism of MnOx/γ-Al2O3 for low-temperature NO catalytic oxidation with O3/NO ratio of 0.5. *Fuel Process. Technol.* **222**, 106979 (2021). https://doi.org/10.1016/j.fuproc.2021.106979
18. Z. Zhang, H. Xi, S. Zhou, W. Zhou, M. Shreka, Efficient removal of NOx from simulated marine exhaust by using O3-Na2SO3: Experimental factors and optimization analysis. *Fuel.* **313**, 122659 (2022). https://doi.org/10.1016/j.fuel.2021.122659

19. F. Meng *et al.*, Promotional effect of surface fluorine on TiO2: Catalytic conversion of O3 and H2O2 into ·OH and ·O2− radicals for high-efficiency NO oxidation. *Chem. Eng. J.* **424**, 130358 (2021). https://doi.org/10.1016/j.cej.2021.130358
20. S. Bhowmick, A. Badiwal, K. T. Shenoy, Removal of NOx using ozone injection and subsequent absorption in water. *Chem. Eng. J. Adv.* **15**, 100511 (2023). https://doi.org/10.1016/j.ceja.2023.100511
21. M. Holub, S. Kalisiak, T. Borkowski, J. Myskow, R. Brandenburg, The Influence of Direct Non-Thermal Plasma Treatment on Particulate Matter (PM) and NOx in the Exhaust of Marine Diesel Engines. *Polish J. Environ. Stud.* **19**, 1199–1211 (2010). [Online]. Available: http://apps.webofknowledge.com/full_record.do?product=UA&search_mode=GeneralSearch&qid=1&SID=R2NLPhmYMEEtpS9Gxa8&page=1&doc=9
22. H. Yamasaki *et al.*, Pilot-Scale NOx and SOx Aftertreatment by Semi-Dry Plasma-Chemical Hybrid Process in Glass-Melting-Furnace Exhaust Gas. *Plasma Chem. Plasma Process.* **42**, 51–71 (2022). https://doi.org/10.1007/s11090-021-10193-4
23. S. Jodzis, M. Zięba, Energy efficiency of an ozone generation process in oxygen. Analysis of a pulsed DBD system. *Vacuum.* **155**, 29–37 (2018). https://doi.org/10.1016/j.vacuum.2018.05.035
24. R. A. Bryant, Uncertainty estimates of tracer gas dilution flow measurements in large-scale exhaust ducts. *Flow Meas. Instrum.* **61**, 1–8 (2018). https://doi.org/10.1016/j.flowmeasinst.2018.03.004
25. M. Si *et al.*, Review on the NO removal from flue gas by oxidation methods. *J. Environ. Sci.*, **101**, 49–71 (2021). https://doi.org/10.1016/j.jes.2020.08.004
26. K.-M. Lin, K.-C. Wang, Y.-S. Chang, S.-Y. Chuang, Gas Heating Mechanisms in Atmospheric Pressure Helium Dielectric-Barrier Discharges Driven by a kHz Power Source. (2020). https://doi.org/10.3390/app10217583
27. Z. Zhu, B. Xu, Purification Technologies for NOx Removal from Flue Gas: A Review. (2022). https://doi.org/10.3390/separations9100307

Design and Development of an Energy-Efficient Suki Sauce Stirrer: a Novel Concept Study

Khridsadakhon Booddachan[1], *Nipon* Bhuwakietkumjohn[1], *Jittimon* Wongsa[1,2], *Surachet* Sichamnan[3], *Yongliang* Li[4], and *Thanya* Parametthanuwat [1,2*]

[1] Faculty of Industrial Technology and Management, King Mongkut's University of Technology North Bangkok (Prachinburi Campus), 25230 Prachinburi, Thailand
[2] KMUTNB Techno Park Prachinburi, King Mongkut's University of Technology North Bangkok (Prachinburi Campus), 25230 Prachinburi, Thailand
[3]Thermal Energy and Distillation Engineering Research Unit (in the process and equipment designed) Faculty of Industry and Technology, Rajamangala University of Technology Isan, Sakonnakhon Campus
[4]Birmingham Centre for Energy Storage and School of Chemical Engineering, University of Birmingham, Birmingham, B15 2TT, United Kingdom

Abstract. This study presents the design and evaluation of an energy-efficient sukiyaki sauce stirrer incorporating thermosyphon technology to reduce both heating time and fuel consumption. The conventional method requires continuous stirring for 180 minutes to reach the target temperature of 85°C, consuming approximately 3.5 kg of LPG. To address this inefficiency, a novel thermosyphon system was developed and integrated into the stirrer pot. The apparatus comprises twelve AISI 304 stainless steel thermosyphon tubes (25.4 mm OD, 54.5 cm length) mounted on a custom-built structure. Water was used as the working fluid, filled to 50% of the evaporator volume to facilitate effective heat transfer via phase change. Experimental testing, using a mixture of water and granulated sugar to simulate sukiyaki sauce, demonstrated that the target temperature was achieved in 80 minutes, reducing heating time by over 50% and saving 0.84 kg of LPG. The findings confirm that thermosyphon-assisted heat transfer, combined with active stirring, significantly enhances thermal efficiency and shortens the processing time. Notably, microbial testing conducted in accordance with the Ministry of Public Health's standards revealed no contamination during production. This approach offers a promising, energy-conserving solution for food preparation processes, particularly in small scale or individually operated cooking applications.

1 Introduction

FOOD DE MAGICAL CO., LTD operates The Rock Shabu restaurant chain, specialising in grilling and shabu set meals. Its product range includes fresh ingredients such as meats, vegetables, and fruits, as well as processed items like black shabu soup and sukiyaki dipping sauce. As part of its commitment to continuos innovation and quality enhancement, the company participated in the Pre-Talent Mobility Project at King Mongkut's University of Technology North Bangkok (KMUTNB). The project aimed to improve production processes, extend the shelf life of sukiyaki dipping sauce, and elevate overall product standards. The company has been certified with Primary GMP (Good Manufacturing Practice) by the Ministry of Public Health, authorising the production of sukiyaki dipping sauce, soup bases, and a variety of sauces. Its prototype sukiyaki dipping sauce has also received FDA approval for commercial distribution.

In response to the expansion of its restaurant branches and ongoing business negotiations both domestically and internationally, the company is preparing to increase its production capacity. However, the existing sukiyaki sauce production method remains highly labour-intensive, relying on manual stirring in a single-layer stainless steel pot heated by an LPG gas stove. This method lacks precise control over stirring speed, exposes workers to excessive heat and physical strain, and often results in inconsistent stirring, leading to sauce burning, production losses, and quality fluctuations. To overcome these limitations, the company has proposed the development of an advanced sukiyaki sauce stirring system. The improved design will feature a double-layered pot to prevent the thick and viscous sauce from burning; a thermosyphon unit to enhance energy efficiency; and specially designed stirring blades powered by a regulated drive system.

The upgraded system will also incorporate controls for adjusting stirring speed and duration, a real-time display of sterilisation temperatures, and integrated process monitoring; however, these features are not discussed in detail within this paper. These enhancements aim to boost production capacity, ensure product uniformity, reduce waste and processing time, and lower both labour and energy costs.

*Corresponding author : thanya.p@itm.kmutnb.ac.th

Figure 1 illustrates a two-phase closed thermosyphon (TPCT), which is a type of wickless heat pipe that facilitates heat transfer through evaporation and condensation processes. Unlike conventional heat pipes, which depend on capillary action to return condensate, the TPCT employs gravitational force for liquid return. In this system, the evaporator is strategically placed at the lowest point, allowing gravity to effectively assist in circulating the working fluid. TPCTs are known for their straightforward design, low thermal resistance, high thermal performance, and economical manufacturing. These attributes have led to their widespread adoption in multiple applications, such as waste heat recovery, electronic cooling, turbine blade temperature control, and solar thermal systems [1-3].

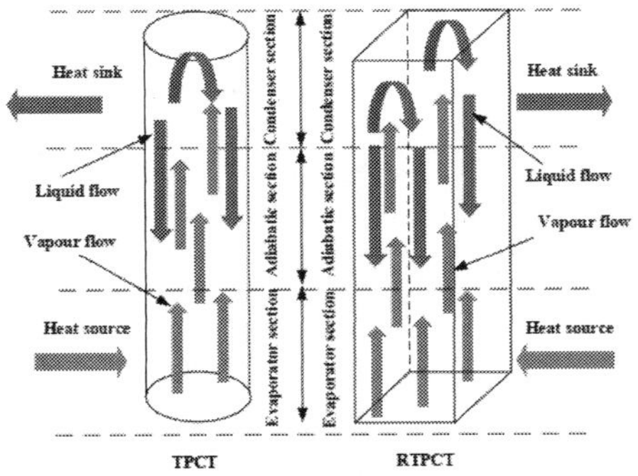

Fig. 1. Structure and functional concept of a TPCT system [1].

Nevertheless, additional investigation is necessary to thoroughly evaluate the feasibility and applicability of these approaches within real-world engineering contexts. This study focuses on the development of an energy-efficient sukiyaki sauce stirrer, introducing a novel TPCT-based design [4]. This system incorporates a uniquely engineered TPCT that relies solely on water as the working fluid to transport heat from the evaporator to the condenser, eliminating the need for any external power input. The primary objective is to evaluate the system's effectiveness and its ability to maintain optimal temperature regulation during the sauce preparation process.

2 Development Concept and Experimental Configuration

2.1 Design of Thermosyphon System and Stirring Device

The thermosyphon kit used in this study, developed in accordance with ESDU 80013 [5] , has a total length of 545 mm, comprising both the evaporator and condenser sections. An adiabatic section was omitted, as the design is tailored to align with the optimised tank length for this specific application. The thermosyphon is constructed from AISI 304 stainless steel tubing with an internal diameter of 25.4 mm. A total of twelve tubes are employed, with deionised (DI) water serving as the working fluid. The thermosyphons are evenly distributed along the inner circumference of the pot, with a center-to-center distance of 10 cm. The pot is constructed from AISI 304 stainless steel, with an internal diameter of 650 mm, an external diameter of 680 mm, and a height of 800 mm, resulting in a total volume of 100 liters.

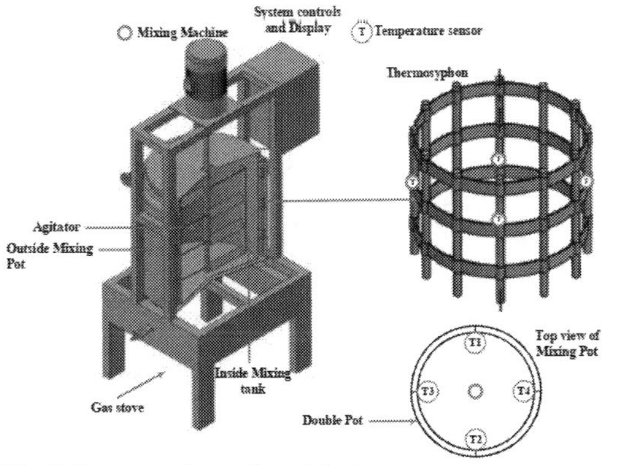

Fig. 2. Process and experimental setup.

Figure 2 shows the positioning of the experimental setup adjacent to the suki sauce stirrer machine. For each trial, 100 litres of Suki Sauce were used in the mixing process. The system schematic shown in Figure 2 includes a gas stove (LPG) heater as the primary heat source. To monitor thermal performance, seven type-K thermocouples (± 0.1°C accuracy) were installed and connected to a Yokogawa DX200 data acquisition system, which supports up to 20 input channels and measures temperatures ranging from −200°C to 1100°C. The thermocouples were strategically positioned throughout the system to capture the temperature distribution and facilitate effective process control and display.

The heat transfer rate Q_{Pot} and heat flux q_{Pot} at the evaporator section of the TPCT can be determined using Equations (1) and (2), respectively [3, 4], [6]:

$$Q_{POT} = m_{LPG} LHV_{LPG} \left(T_{Company} - T_{start}\right) \quad (1)$$

$$q_{Pot} = \frac{Q_{Pot}}{A_{eap,TPCT}} \quad (2)$$

The heat transfer rate of the sukiyaki sauce (SS) within the storage tank was determined at the condenser section, based on Equations (3) and (4) [3, 4], [6]:

$$Q_{SS} = mc_{p,SS} \left(T_{SS,final} - T_{SS,first}\right) / t \quad (3)$$

$$q_{CB} = \frac{Q_{CB}}{A_{CB\ \mathrm{tank}}} \quad (4)$$

The effectiveness (ε) of HE-TPCT was determined by comparing the actual heat flux to the maximum heat flux obtained through TPCT, which can be calculated using equation (5) [3, 4], [6].

$$\varepsilon_{HETPCT} = \frac{Q_{actual}}{Q_{max}} = \frac{Q_{SS}}{C_{\min}(T_e - T_{Pot})} \qquad (5)$$

2.2 Design Concept and Thermosyphon Selection

The primary production process employed by the company involves stirring and boiling sukiyaki sauce until it reaches a temperature of 85°C. Once this target temperature is achieved, the sauce is held at boiling for an additional 30 minutes to effectively eliminate pathogens such as Staphylococcus aureus and Salmonella spp. To optimise this process, a thermosyphon system was integrated into the boiling pot, and combined with mechanical stirring., This integration enhances heat transfer efficiency from the bottom to the top of the vessel and improves overall temperature distribution. Upon reaching 85 °C, the thermosyphon assists in maintaining a stable temperature and retaining heat throughout the process. The underlying design concept is shown in Figure 3.

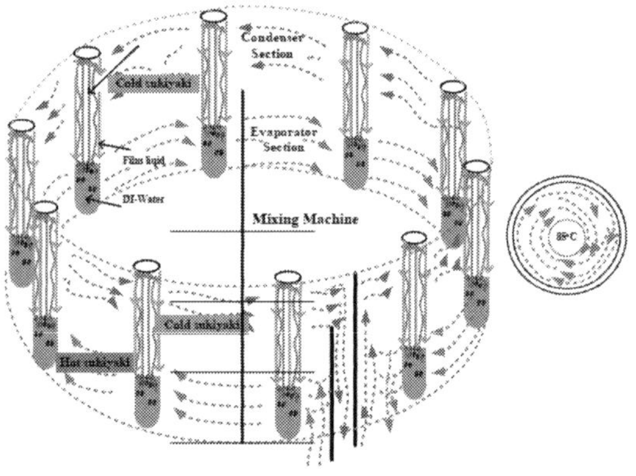

Fig 3. Design Concept and Thermosyphon Selection.

2.3 Microbiological Quality Analysis of the Sukiyaki Sauce Products

Sukiyaki sauce samples were sterilised by heating at 85°C for 30 minutes using a kettle equipped with a thermosyphon to ensure even temperature distribution. Achieving the specified temperature and time parameters during sterilisation is critical for eliminating spoilage microorganisms as well as pathogenic microbes that pose health risks to consumers.

The microbiological quality of the sukiyaki sauce was assessed according to standard analytical methods. This included the determination of total plate count, and the detection of yeasts and moulds using the BAM method (2001) [7], Bacillus cereus (BAM, 2020) [8], Clostridium perfringens (BAM, 2001) [9], Staphylococcus aureus (BAM, 2016) [10], Escherichia coli via the Most Probable Number (MPN) method (BAM, 2020) [11], and Salmonella spp. (BAM, 2022) [12]. These analyses were conducted in accordance with the Community Product Standard TISI 466/2547 for sukiyaki sauce, as well as the Ministry of Public Health Notification No. 201 B.E. 2543 (Under Thailand government) governing specific types of sauces.

3 Results and Discussion

3.1 Investigation into the Reduction of Stirring Time in a Sukiyaki Sauce Pot with and without Thermosyphon Integration

Figure 4 presents the experimental results obtained from trials involving the heating of 100 litres of sukiyaki sauce initially at ambient room temperature. The findings revealed a significant reduction in the time required to reach the target temperature when a thermosyphon was integrated into the system. Without the thermosyphon, the sukiyaki sauce required 100 minutes to reach 88°C. However, when the thermosyphon was employed, the same temperature was achieved in just 80 minutes. This represents a 30-minute reduction in heating time, equivalent to a 20% improvement in thermal response. These results clearly demonstrate that incorporating a thermosyphon into the heating system substantially enhances heat transfer efficiency and significantly reduces overall processing time [13, 14].

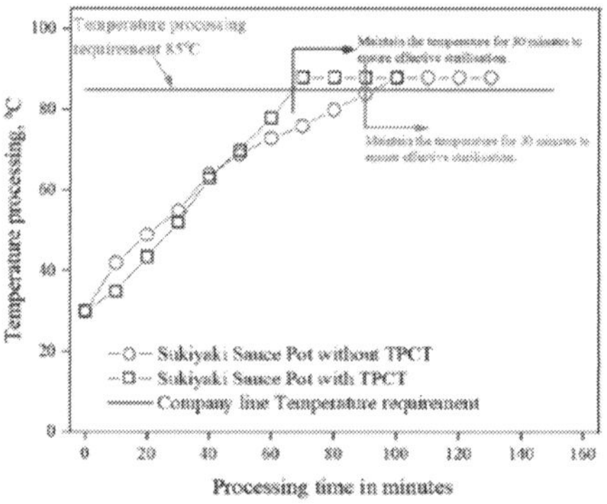

Fig 4. Temperature profiles of sukiyaki sauce with and without TPCT during thermal processing.

3.2 Distribution temperature

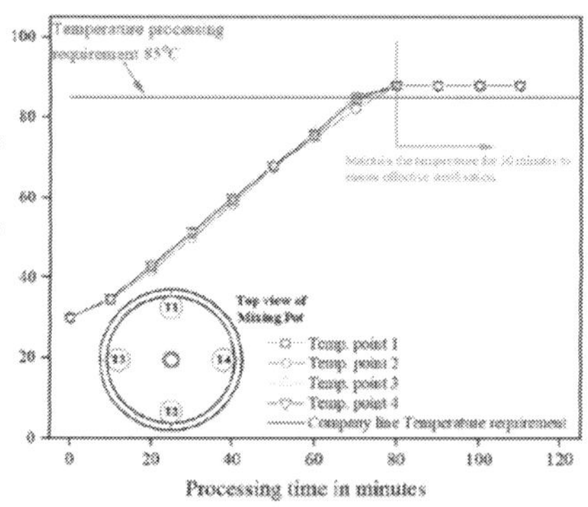

Fig 5. Temperature distribution at four measurement points during the heating of sukiyaki sauce using a TPCT-integrated system.

Figure 5 presents the temperature distribution of a plain water and sukiyaki sauce mixture processed using a system integrated with a thermosyphon. The results demonstrate a high degree of thermal uniformity across all four measurement points. Compared to the vendor's conventional sauce-stirring method, this configuration achieved the target temperature of 85°C more rapidly. During the heating process, the temperature variation at any given time remained within ±5°C. Notably, after 80 minutes, all measurement points consistently exceeded 85°C. These findings support the results shown in Figure 4, confirming that the integration of a thermosyphon, combined with mechanical stirring, substantially enhances heat distribution [13, 15]. This improvement is attributed to the thermosyphon's ability to efficiently transfer heat from the bottom to the top of the vessel, thereby ensuring consistent temperature control and meeting the thermal requirements specified by the company.

3.3 Fuel Consumption and Economic Viability

Table 1. Comparison of fuel consumption during sukiyaki sauce heating with and without thermosyphon integration.

Description of Test	Fuel Consumption (kg)	Fuel Saved (%)
Fuel consumption by vendor during traditional sukiyaki sauce heating	3.5 kg	
Fuel consumption during heating of water mixed with Sukiyaki Sauce and thermosyphon	2.66 kg	24.00%

The data presented in the table 1 indicate that the integration of a thermosyphon into the sukiyaki sauce stirring system led to a notable reduction in fuel consumption. Specifically, fuel usage decreased by 0.84 kilograms per session, representing a 24% reduction. This outcome demonstrates that the thermosyphon, when employed as a heat transfer enhancement device within the sauce pot, effectively contributes to lowering production costs by reducing both heating time and energy consumption [13]. The overall efficiency of the system with the thermosyphon installed was calculated to be 27%.

3.4 Microbiological Quality Analysis of Sukiyaki Sauce Products

Table 2. shows that the sukiyaki sauce sample exhibited a pH value below 4.6, thereby classifying it as a low-acid food in accordance with the Ministry of Public Health Announcement No. 144, B.E. 2535 (Under Thailand government). Microbiological analysis of the product, which was processed using a sukiyaki sauce pot equipped with a thermosyphon system, demonstrated that the total viable microbial count was below 10,000 CFU/g. Yeast and mould counts were less than 10 CFU/g, *Bacillus cereus* and *Clostridium perfringens* were each detected at levels below 10 CFU/g, and *Staphylococcus aureus* did not exceed 100 CFU/g.

Table 2. Microorganism counts detected in sukiyaki sauce samples.

Properties	Quality criteria	Microbial count of the sample
Total plate count (CFU/g)	$<1.0 \times 10^4$	$<1.0 \times 10$
Yeast and Mold (CFU/g)	$<1.0 \times 10^2$	$<1.0 \times 10$
Bacillus cereus (CFU/g)	$<1.0 \times 10^2$	$<1.0 \times 10$
Clostridium perfringens (CFU/g)	$<1.0 \times 10^3$	$<1.0 \times 10$
Staphylococcus aureus (CFU/g)	$<1.0 \times 10^2$	$<1.0 \times 10$
Escherichia coli (MPN/mL)	<3.0	<3.0
Salmonella spp. (in 25 g)	Not Detected	Not Detected

Escherichia coli, determined using the Most Probable Number (MPN) method, was found to be less than 3 MPN/mL, while *Salmonella spp.* were not detected. These findings confirm that the sukiyaki sauce product complies with the microbial quality standards stipulated in the Community Product Standard (TISI 466/2547) for sukiyaki sauce, as well as the Ministry of Public Health Announcement No. 201, B.E. 2543 (Under Thailand government), which governs specific types of sauces.

4 .Conclusion

This project successfully transitioned sukiyaki sauce production from a labour-intensive manual process to a machine-assisted system. This shift has effectively addressed key challenges previously encountered in the manual stirring process, such as the inability to maintain consistent quality, operator fatigue due to high ambient temperatures, and the increasing viscosity of the sauce, which often led to burning and production losses. A double-layered stirring pot was designed and developed to prevent the thick sauce from burning, complemented by the integration of a thermosyphon system to ensure uniform, rapid, and energy-efficient heat distribution. These enhancements have led to notable improvements in product quality, increased production capacity, reduced material waste, minimised production time, operational costs, and labour as well as energy consumption. As a result, the prototype suki sauce stirring machine was produced, yielding standardised products that have achieved FDA registration. The project has also fostered the development of additional products for future expansion and facilitated knowledge transfer through collaborative activities with business and industrial sectors.

The installation of a thermosyphon within a standard packaging stirrer pot often introduces internal obstructions that may compromise the efficiency of cooking, stirring, and mixing operations. Moreover, the materials employed in the construction of the thermosyphon may pose a potential risk of food contamination. To mitigate these issues, it is critical to carefully evaluate the thermosyphon's design, fabrication methods, and installation procedures to ensure efficient heat dissipation while maintaining hygienic conditions. The results of this study confirm the feasibility of such an implementation and demonstrate its effectiveness in preserving product cleanliness and minimizing the risk of contamination. Nevertheless, minor limitations persist, particularly concerning the interference observed during product loading and unloading processes, which may necessitate further optimization of the system's spatial configuration.

This research was funded King Mongkut's University of Technology North Bangkok with Contract no. KMUTNB-RTM-66-3, Pre-Talent Mobility Project. The authors would like to thank Miss Keawalin Chumchuen and Mr. Suparach Pattamon for their valuable assistance in the development and testing phases of this project in collaboration with FOOD DE MAGICAL CO., LTD.

References

1. T. Chompookham, S. Sichamnan, N. Bhuwakietkumjohn, T. Parametthanuwat, The rectangular two-phase closed thermosyphon: A case study of two-phase internal flow patterns behaviour for heat performance. *Archives of Thermodynamics*. **41**, (2020)
2. S. Khandekar, Y. M. Joshi, B. Mehta, Thermal performance of closed two-phase thermosyphon using nanofluids, *Thermal Science*. **47**, 667–695 (2008)
3. D. Reay, P. Kew, *Heat pipe, Theory, Design And Application*. Fifth edit. Butterworth-Heinemann, 2006
4. T. Parametthanuwat, N. Bhuwakietkumjohn, S. Sichamnan, K. Booddacha, J. Wongsa, Design of a chocolate tempering machine with thermosyphon installation–a new concept study. in *E3S Web of Conferences*, (EDP Sciences, 2025)
5. Anon., *Heat pipes-general information on their use, operation and design, Data Item No. 80013*. . London: Engineering : Sciences Data Unit, (1980).
6. F. P. Incropera, D. P. DeWitt, T. L. Bergman, A. S. Lavine, *Fundamentals of heat and mass transfer*. **6**. (Wiley New York, 1996)
7. Larry Maturin (ret.) and James T. Peeler (ret.), "BAM Chapter 3: Aerobic Plate Count | FDA." Accessed: (2025). [Online]. Available: https://www.fda.gov/food/laboratory-methods-food/bam-chapter-3-aerobic-plate-count
8. A. K. E. J. R. (ret.), S. M. H. (ret.), R. W. B. (ret.) Sandra M. Tallent, BAM Chapter 14: Bacillus cereus | FDA. Accessed: (2025). [Online]. Available: https://www.fda.gov/food/laboratory-methods-food/bam-chapter-14-bacillus-cereus
9. E. Jeffery Rhodehamel (ret.) and Stanley M. Harmon (ret.), "BAM Chapter 16: Clostridium perfringens | FDA." Accessed: May 14 (2025). [Online]. Available: https://www.fda.gov/food/laboratory-methods-food/bam-chapter-16-clostridium-perfringens
10. J. H. R. W. B. (ret.), and G. A. L. (ret.) Sandra Tallent, "BAM Chapter 12: Staphylococcus aureus | FDA." Accessed: May **14**, (2025). [Online]. Available: https://www.fda.gov/food/laboratory-methods-food/bam-chapter-12-staphylococcus-aureus
11. S. D. W. (ret.), M. A. G. (dec.), W. B. Peter Feng (ret.), "BAM Chapter 4: Enumeration of Escherichia coli and the Coliform Bacteria | FDA." Accessed: May 14, (2025). [Online]. Available: https://www.fda.gov/food/laboratory-methods-food/bam-chapter-4-enumeration-escherichia-coli-and-coliform-bacteria
12. H. W. A. J. (ret.), B. G. G. Z., T. H. (ret.) Wallace H. Andrews (ret.), BAM Chapter 5: Salmonella | FDA. Accessed: 14 (2025). [Online]. Available: https://www.fda.gov/food/laboratory-methods-food/bam-chapter-5-salmonella
13. T. Parametthanuwat, S. Rittidech, K. Booddachan, Thermosyphon installation for energy thrift in a smoked fish sausage oven (TISO). *Energy*. (2010). https://doi: 10.1016/j.energy.2010.03.010
14. M. F. Robitoh *et al.*, Effect of mixing particles on the thermal performance of three-phase closed thermosyphon. *International Communications in Heat and Mass Transfer*. **163**, 108758 (2025). https://doi.org/10.1016/j.icheatmasstransfer.2025.108758
15. S. Thongdang, S. Sichamnan, S. Chokphoemphun, A. Donmuang, N. Pipatpaiboon, Case study of design and construction of dehydration for paddy by heat exchanger rectangular two-phase closed thermosyphon (DP-HE/RTPCT). *Case Studies in Thermal Engineering*. **57**, 103951 (2024). https://doi: 10.1016/J.CSITE.2023.103951

Is urban development around Laem Chabang Port, Thailand, sustainable?

Nitin Agarwala [1], *Worawut* Poma [2*], *Effi Helmy* Ariffin [3], *Abdullah* Açık [4], *Ikha* Magdalena [5,6], *Punarut* Sirichokpokin [2], *Narthsirinth* Netirith [2], *Naruphun* Chotechuang [2], *Htet Khaing* Kyi Lin [2], *R.* Nagalakshmi [7], *Lanlila* Chitsom [8], and *Chalida* Pohma [9]

[1] Naval War College, Verem, Goa, India
[2] Faculty of International Maritime Studies, Kasetsart University, Sri Racha Campus, Thailand
[3] Institute of Oceanography and Environment, Universiti Malaysia Terengganu, Malaysia
[4] Maritime Faculty, Dokuz Eylül University, Turkey
[5] Faculty of Mathematics and Natural Sciences, Bandung Institute of Technology, Indonesia
[6] Center for Coastal and Marine Development, Institut Teknologi Bandung, Indonesia
[7] Department of Civil Engineering, SRM Institute of Science and Technology, KTR, TN, India
[8] CNNC Joint Venture, 88 Bangna-Trad 30 Rd., Debaratna Bangna-Tai, Bangna, Bangkok, Thailand
[9] Faculty of Engineering and Technology, Siam Technology College, Thailand

Abstract. Mega ports are believed to urbanize their surrounding areas quickly. However, literature confirming that they actually accelerate long-term land-use development is limited. There is, hence, a need to investigate land-use changes before and after the development of a port to evaluate the interconnection and influence between such ports and their neighboring areas. This study aims to evaluate historical land-use changes between 1975 and 2021 around Laem Chabang port, the biggest container port in Thailand, using satellite images obtained from Google Earth and the U.S. Geological Survey. Standard procedures of spatiotemporal analysis were implemented for analysis. Key findings show that urbanization was rapid during the port development planning and construction phase but slowed down soon after. Accordingly, one can infer that mega ports may be considered only as a temporary catalyst for surrounding urbanization and do not bring about urbanization on a permanent basis. This study is considered important as it provides a good understanding of the relationship between urbanizing and ports and can help develop a strategy to establish a balance between coastal urban development and environmental protection.

1 Introduction

Seaports are essentially anthropogenic marine structures that extend land functions into the ocean and act as key linkages in international logistics and supply chains [1-2]. They have evolved over time not only to serve ships but also to offer value-added services such as packaging and labeling, as well as to create jobs in port zones. Port locations are selected to optimize land access in navigable waters by providing commercial trade with sheltered places where ships can be safely loaded, unloaded, refueled, or repaired. Seaports play a vital role in maritime transportation and trade facilitation, significantly influencing local, regional, and national economic, social, and environmental developments. Nowadays, ports help expand the world economy and act as engines of economic growth for a nation by providing a connection to the growing world trade. In the past, the topic of ports and their impact on the economy has been discussed in several studies. Chang et al. [3] concluded that ports stimulate economic growth at both the country and regional levels. Port development significantly raises the land value of the neighboring port area as businesses and industries take advantage of the benefits offered and mushroom in the region [4].

Ports, shipping activities, environment, and urbanization are intertwined [6-8]. The ports affect the sustainability (e.g., human well-being, green cover areas, ecosystem, biodiversity protection, and pollution management, etc.). Coastal communities and their well-being are one of the vital components of sustainable development [9]. Hence, many researchers have focused on the impacts of port development on urban expansion and land-use evolution. An extensive review regarding the sustainable development of ports and urban complexity is presented by Nebot et al. [10], who mention the vital role of ports in integrated coastal zone management. Ports and coastal areas have undergone physical transformations due to intensive port-driving competitive processes relating to land-use and port relationships. Specifically to Port Sudan,

* Corresponding author : worawut.po@ku.th

Hawash et al. [11] highlighted that the urban development rate outstripped the population growth rate, resulting in land being used for urbanization faster. Similarly, in China, Shu et al. [12] found vast urban expansion adjacent to Taicang Port in Fuqiao, China, and suggested that differentiated policies should be formulated to guide the proper expansion of urban land.

With significant developments occurring in these port areas, numerous undesirable consequences have been studied in greater detail by various researchers, including water quality degradation, coastal resource degradation, and air quality issues [13]. Port-driven urbanization can negatively affect the allocation of coastal resources. Economically, Deng et al. [14] found that these ports do not significantly contribute to economic growth. In return, since industries are concentrated in the vicinity of major ports, they significantly affect the lives of employees and their family members, sometimes even leading to conflicting land-use at unprecedented rates with the main competition being between residential and recreational services for access to limited coastal space. Our traditional belief that port-induced urbanization is always good for coastal inhabitants may not be the case if we consider aspects from these publications.

Since urban expansion always requires adequate infrastructure preparations (including coastal structures, transportation networks, water, and electricity), and those infrastructures come with costs and environmental impacts [15], it is essential that the urban growth pattern around mega ports be correctly comprehended. An incorrect idea of whether a mega port temporarily or permanently stimulates city expansion patterns can result in wasteful investments. Thus, this raises our research question of whether a port can continuously accelerate surrounding urbanization or it just creates only a short-term impact on coastal urban development. This study thus aims to answer this question by investigating land-use changes around Laem Chabang Port, the biggest container port in

Thailand. The study is considered important as it can help the government, city planners, and coastal managers to create a strategic urban development plan for areas surrounding the ports.

2 Study site and methodology

Thailand has a coastline of 3,148 km with over 4,000 km of waterways for both domestic and coastal transportation. For this study, we aim to focus on Laem Chabang (LCB) port.

2.1 Laem Chabang Port description

Laem Chabang (LCB) port is one of the major deep-sea ports of South Asia, located in Chonburi province. It is characterized as the most efficient container port by leading international deep seaports, with 80% of the international trade of Thailand being handled by this port alone. The development of the LCB port was undertaken in three phases. In the first phase, construction continued from 1987 to 1991. The second phase of construction began in 1997 and was completed in 2000. In 2025, the third phase is being constructed (Figure 1). The LCB port has been one of the main economic drivers for Thailand, hosting numerous small and large industries and, systematically decentralizing economic prosperity, and speeding up rural development. On the other hand, rapid urban area expansion, accelerated by the presence of the LCB port, has created conflicts among other coastal users. In addition, coastal problems such as maritime traffic and accidents, decreased marine life presence, marine debris, and wastewater discharge into the ocean emerged due to this urban development.

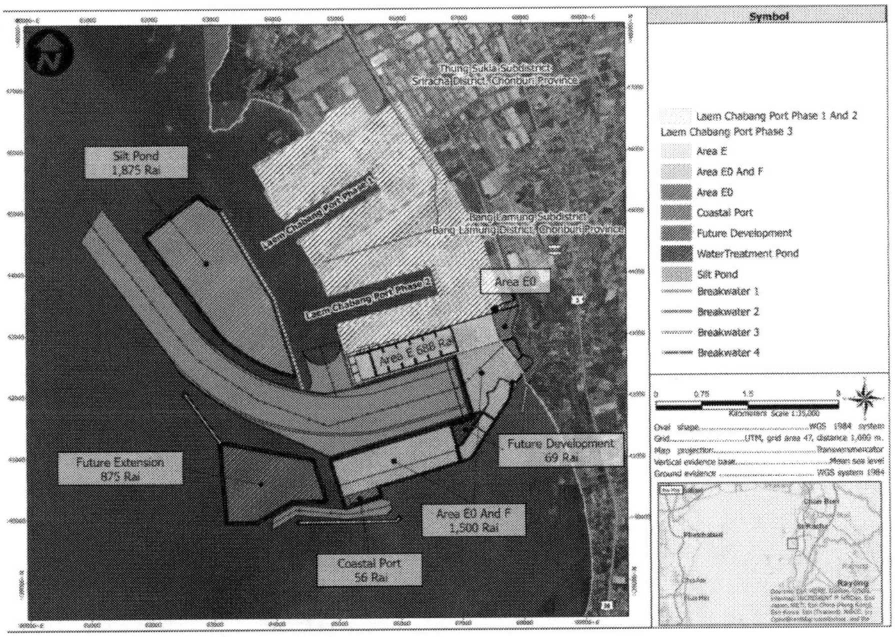

Fig. 1. Laem Chabang Port (sources: [30, 31])

2.2 Methodology

The applications of remote sensing (RS) and geographical information systems (GIS) have been widely applied in data acquisition to obtain timely and accurate spatial data on land cover, assessing the spatiotemporal changes of marine and coastal resources [16]. The remotely sensed images can effectively monitor land-use conditions, serving as an excellent data source for coastal landforms and land-use change analysis [17]. GIS provides a flexible platform to collect, store, display, and analyze digital data necessary for change detection. It has been widely applied in the context of port-related matters, as seen in the study of Gao et al. [18], where they applied GIS to measure China's port accessibility from the perspective of land-sea coordination. Ayotamuno et al. [19] examined changes in land use and economic activities between 1986 and 2005 in a residential complex in Port Harcourt, Nigeria that was originally developed for senior civil servants and military personnel, showing the rapid expansion of commercial activities within what was exclusively a residential area. Sonde et al. [20] applied RS satellite data to investigate fast unrestricted growth due to domestic use and industrialization around Jawaharlal Nehru Port Trust in India. Hence, applying RS and GIS to analyze historical urbanizing characteristics at the LCB port in Thailand was considered feasible and appropriate.

High-resolution satellite images for the LCB port were freely available from two sources: the U.S. Geological Survey (USGS) and Google Earth. These satellite images were available for the period commencing 1975. Images chosen for this study were those that did not have any cloud covering the study area or that allowed the authors to see land use characteristics clearly. Information on the year of construction of the port was gathered. Although LANDSAT imagery, provided by USGS, had a rather coarse resolution, it had been popularly applied in many coastal urban land cover transformations. More recent satellite images were extracted from Google Earth because of their higher image resolution. In order to find noticeable changes, the USGS or Google Earth satellite images were collected in a 5-year interval (4-6 years) from 1975 to 2021, as detailed in Table 1., depending on image availability and cloud cover. They were later processed to obtain land-use cover percentages of pre- and post-port development. The methodology framework adopted in the study is illustrated in Figure 2. The authors carefully rectified and geo-referenced the images. Then, we conducted field surveys and ground truthing. At a later step, the authors applied visual interpretation to discriminate residential areas, sea areas, and agricultural/forest areas. Afterward, land-use maps from 1975 to 2021 were created. Finally, the authors were able to analyze the change in the land use around the LCB port.

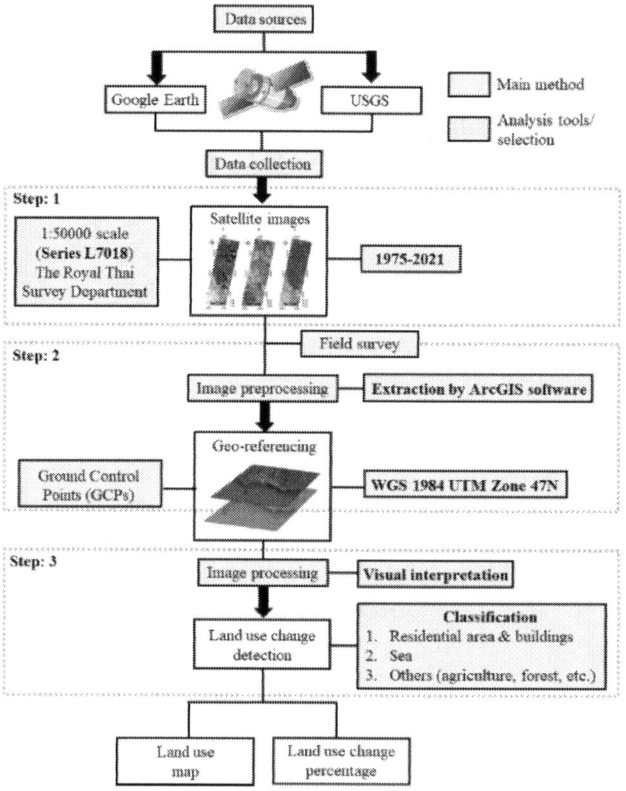

Fig. 2. Flowchart illustrating steps to monitor land-use changes at the LCB port

Table 1. Data used in this study

Focus Area	Image sources	Satellite	Image Date
Laem Chabang Port	Google Earth		10/8/2021
			6/11/2016
			9/1/2011
			29/12/2006
			31/12/2001
	USGS	Landsat 5	15/11/1996
		Landsat 5	2/11/1996
		Landsat 5	31/12/1986
		Landsat 2	8/10/1976
		Landsat 2	31/12/1975

3 Results

Land-use transformation around the LCB port from 1975 to 2021 is presented in Table 2 and Figure 3. One observes that agricultural, forest, and undeveloped lands decreased from 50 sq. km in 1975 to 12.3 sq. km in 2021. It can be observed that the urbanization rate around the LCB port surged sharply during the port planning stage. The urbanization rate was approximately 0.72% per year (from 1975 to 1986) but jumped to 1.4% per year (from 1986 to 1991). If the LCB port had not been constructed in 1991, the urbanization rate would have increased steadily instead of aggressively, as observed. Another sharp rise in urbanization rate around the LCB port was observed during 2011 – 2016 when the port publicized its third phase expansion by reclaiming 1,600,000 sq.m. The 3rd phase feasibility study happened during 2011-2016, followed by the conduct of environmental and health impact assessment (EHIA), which was approved by the cabinet in October 2018. That is why one can notice the surge in urbanization rate during 2011-2016. The non-linear urbanizing transformation rate, as analyzed, is seen in Figure 3 and Figure 4. One notices that the LCB port saw growth in residential areas and buildings within a 5-km radius. This growth was from 0.7 sq. km in 1975 to 36.6 sq. km in 2021.

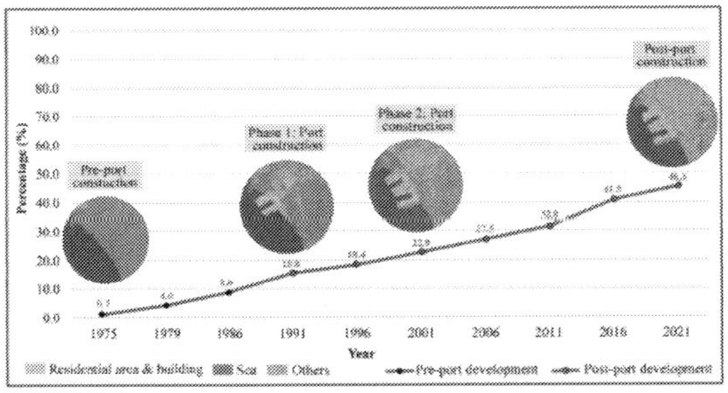

Fig. 3. Percentage of urbanization from 1975 to 2021 in the radius of 5 km around the LCB port

Table 2. Urbanization rate from 1975 to 2021 in a radius of 5 km around the LCB port

Type of land use									
Year	Port		Residential area and buildings		Sea		Others		Total area (km²)
	Area (km²)	Percentage	Area (km²)	Percentage	Area (km²)	Percentage	Area (km²)	Percentage	
2021	7.7	9.7	36.6	46.3	22.5	28.5	12.3	15.5	
2016	7.7	9.7	32.8	41.5	22.5	28.5	16.0	20.3	
2011	7.7	9.7	25.3	32.0	22.5	28.5	23.6	29.8	
2006	7.7	9.7	21.8	27.5	22.5	28.5	27.2	34.3	
2001	7.7	9.7	18.1	22.9	22.5	28.5	30.8	38.9	79.1
1996	7.7	9.7	14.5	18.4	25.9	32.8	33.2	41.9	
1991	5.5	6.9	11.9	15.1	25.9	32.8	35.8	45.2	
1986	5.5	6.9	6.8	8.6	28.7	36.2	43.7	55.2	
1979	-	-	3.2	4.0	28.7	36.2	47.3	59.8	
1975	-	-	0.5	0.7	28.7	36.2	50.0	63.1	

4 Discussion

Land-use change is a process associated with both natural and anthropogenic activities that have profound impacts on human settlements and the coastal environment. Ports are an essential link within a complex system of societal and environmental interactions, especially in coastal zones. In this study, urbanization change analysis was based on establishing the LCB port as a time node. It was observed that prior to port planning and construction, the urban expansion rate was limited. When the project of developing a port was announced, the growth rate of residential areas sharply increased and continued for a few years. This trend is similar for nearly all infrastructure projects across the world and is based on an expected demand wherein speculators tend to invest in undeveloped areas at low rates to make quick profits when the project eventually develops. However, such urbanization cannot continue for long and hence sees a drop, as observed in this study. The study area shows similar trends and results to show that while there is a concerted view that mega ports lead to extensive urbanization in surrounding areas, this is not entirely true, and such projects can best provide such growth and development for a short period, which depends entirely on demand. Once the demand is met, further urbanization slows before the fresh expansion of the port is declared. This trend is considered similar to any other infrastructure project. Similarly, it is undeniable that mega ports, regardless of their magnitude of influence, transform undeveloped land into residential and industrial buildings, which, too, is akin to other infrastructure projects. Since vast land tracks in the countryside and forest areas have been converted to urban territory to deal with rapid population growth and to sustain economic growth in the port area, there is a need for proper management schemes to manage coastal areas and control unplanned urbanization in the port region. Only such a managed effort will ensure that the ill effects of urbanization, such as pollution through plastics, chemicals, sewage, oil, nutrients, litter, shipping-related pollution such as wastewater discharge and ballast water [7, 21] and many more, can be avoided.

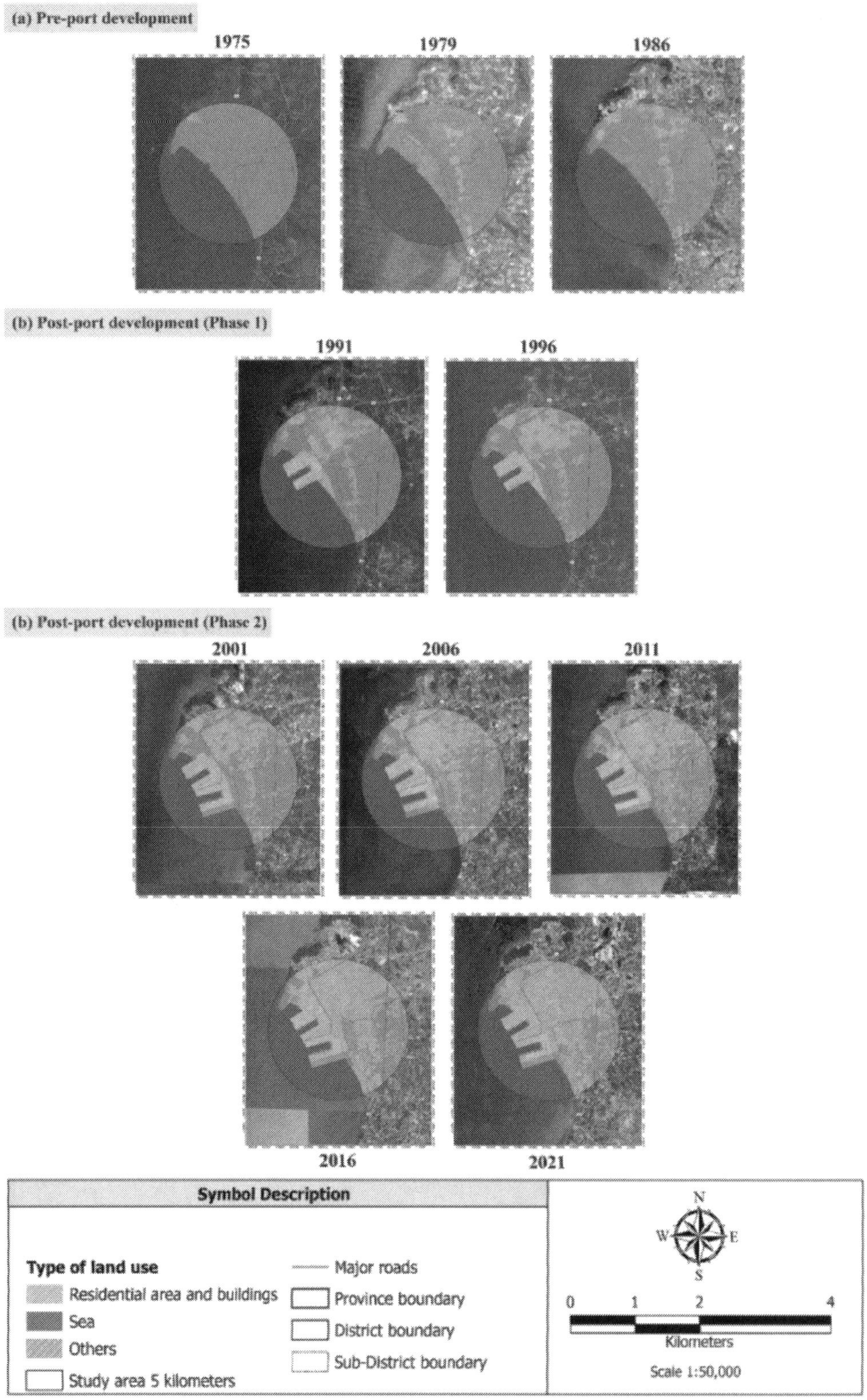

Fig. 4. Land cover map around the LCB port in a 5-km radius

It is important to mention that different ports have different development bases and hence may result in a disparity in their surrounding land-use patterns. The Semarang port of Indonesia is a live example of this disparity. When it was developed, the area surrounding the port had been profoundly impacted. Although the port successfully promoted economic growth in coastal areas that benefited neighboring communities, it induced environmental pollution and urban traffic congestion because of the high population density around the port region. Yet another example is the Port Harcourt in Nigeria, which is the largest harbor and center of petroleum activities in Nigeria. The port city saw an urbanization increase of over 300% during 1986-2003, expanding from 135 sq. km to 550 sq. km, displaying remarkable changes in land use [22]. This was possible due to limited opportunities available for the local population, which encouraged the movement of the population to the port city and, hence, enhanced urbanization. One notices that the geographical location of the port and the goods it handles (such as processing of goods, logistics operations, shipbuilding, or ship repairing) can also alter the direction of development followed by the port city. Accordingly, these cities may become 'maritime hubs', 'secondary service centers', 'specialized waterfront cities', or just distressed urban areas, thereby dictating the resulting urbanization and pollution patterns in these areas. In recent times, with a focus on sustainability, improved transportation and digitalization in ports have altered the relationship between a port and its hinterland, thereby ensuring that the ills of pollution emanating from ports can be reduced. This has also encouraged urbanization to move to the hinterland, encouraging the decongestion of the port and its surrounding areas.

As countries look for economic growth and find the maritime sector as a growth engine to propel such economic growth, the development of ports and maritime sectors is natural to happen. However, one needs to be careful of the downsides of the resulting unabated and unplanned urbanization, which demands continuous involvement of policymakers in fine-tuning the governing policies to provide the requisite economic growth while ensuring that the ills of such growth are kept to a minimum. It should also be remembered that by merely developing a port infrastructure cannot guarantee its success with an existing demand. While demand for own shipping can be a starting point, it cannot sustain mega ports, which require these ports to attract large-scale transshipment traffic.

The study shows that nearly every mega port in the world would have experienced the same pattern of urbanization around them, first with a sharp increase before the port construction, followed by a decline in growth rate soon after the construction was finished. A similar analysis, when undertaken for other port projects, such as Sihanoukville port in Cambodia and Penang port in Malaysia by the authors (not presented in this article) has brought similar results as obtained for the LCB port. Hence, the study can safely conclude that while the traditional belief that a port encourages urbanization of the surrounding area is true, it is limited to spikes that are driven by policy decisions related to further development and use of these ports. However, there is a need that such development and growth of ports be done in a planned manner with proper advanced technology [23] to ensure that sustainable growth and urbanization are achieved and the ills of environmental degradation, enlarged poverty gap, decay of a sense of community, and cultural conflicts can be avoided and kept to a minimum.

5 Conclusions

The evolution of land use at the LCB port in Thailand was investigated to develop a correlation between port development and urbanization in the surrounding areas of the port. It was observed that the urbanization rate due to development of port was accelerated only for a short duration before the port construction, which faded soon after the port began to operate before spiking again for a short duration. This trend is considered to be in line with other infrastructure projects, which display that such a surge in urbanization is linked to opportunists creating facilities when the project is announced for encashment, and then such urbanization is visible when the project facility is created to meet the demand of the working community and their families. Once the demand it met, the next surge is possible only if there is growth in the project. While this is true for most cases, there are variables such as commodities handled by the port, policy support, and social conditions that may govern the urbanization of surrounding areas of ports. Whatever the reason, it is essential that careful planning and effort are put in to ensure that the proposed development is sustainable, eco-friendly, and does not cause a negative impact on the coastal ecosystem, air quality, and biota of the region, which is otherwise a common downside of ports. If such urbanization effects are misunderstood or incorrectly estimated, they can lead to bad investments, as seen in Hambantota and Eemshaven, and undesirable social and environmental consequences.

The authors would like to thank all faculty members of the Faculty of International Maritime Studies, Kasetsart University for assisting and facilitating this research.

References

1. M. S .Abubakar, C. N. Nwoloziri, E. Newman, A. Hlali, A correlation of port users' patronage and tariff structure of Nigerian seaports: A study of Lagos Apapa port. Maritime Technology and Research. **7**, 272515 (2025). https://doi.org/10.33175/mtr.2025.271519
2. D. A. Syahrianda, Suadi, Djumanto, Service excellence at sea: User satisfaction with Belawan Samudera Fishing Port, Indonesia. Maritime Technology and Research. **7**, 270067 (2025). https://doi.org/10.33175/mtr.2025.270067
3. Y. T. Chang, S. H. Shin, P. T. W. Lee, Economic impact of port sectors on South African economy: An input–output analysis. Transport Policy. **35**, 333-340 (2014). https://doi.org/10.1016/j.tranpol.2014.04.006
4. C. Mlambo, The impact of port performance on trade: The case of selected African states. Economies. **9**, 135 (2021). https://doi.org/10.3390/economies9040135
5. M. N. Rooney, There's nothing better than land. : A migrant group's strategies for accessing informal settlement land in Port Moresby. In Kastom, Property and Ideology; McDonnell, S., Allen, M.G., Filer, C., Eds.; ANU Press: Australia. 111-144 (2017)
6. P. Premsamarn, T. K. Win, D. Watanabe, Assessing the impact of emission control areas policy on ship emissions in the Gulf of Thailand using AIS data. Maritime Technology and Research **7**, 275311 (2025). https://doi.org/10.33175/mtr.2025.275311
7. A. P. Onyena, O. R. Nwaogbe, Assessment of water quality and heavy metal contamination in ballast water: Implications for marine ecosystems and human health. Maritime Technology and Research. **6**, 270227 (2024). https://doi.org/10.33175/mtr.2024.270227
8. C. Saengsupavanich, Which eroding site is more urgent for the government?: a reflection from coastal communities. Journal of Coastal Conservation. **24**, 9 (2020). https://doi.org/10.1007/s11852-020-00729-9
9. G. Bulengela, I am a Fisher : Identity and livelihood diversification in Lake Tanganyika Fisheries, Tanzania. Maritime Technology and Research. **6**, 268718 (2024). https://doi.org/10.33175/mtr.2024.268718
10. N. Nebot, C. Rosa-Jiménez, R.P. Ninot, B. Perea-Medina, Challenges for the future of ports. What can be learnt from the Spanish Mediterranean ports?. Ocean and Coastal Management. **137**, 165-174 (2017). https://doi.org/10.1016/j.ocecoaman.2016.12.016
11. E. Hawash, A. El-Hassanin, W. Amer, A. El-Nahry, H. Effat, Change detection and urban expansion of Port Sudan, Red Sea, using remote sensing and GIS. Environmental Monitoring and Assessment. **193**, 1-22 (2021). https://doi.org/10.1007/s10661-021-09486-0
12. B. Shu, H. Zhang, Y. Li, Y. Qu, L. Chen, Spatiotemporal variation analysis of driving forces of urban land spatial expansion using logistic regression: A case study of port towns in Taicang City, China. Habitat International. **43**, 181-190 (2014). https://doi.org/10.1016/j.habitatint.2014.02.004
13. N. Agarwala, Project Green Ports: Are Indian ports on the right track?. Maritime Affairs: Journal of the National Maritime Foundation of India. **18**, 15-36 (2022). https://doi.org/10.1080/09733159.2022.2143134
14. P. Deng, S. Lu, H. Xiao, Evaluation of the relevance measure between ports and regional economy using structural equation modeling. Transport Policy. **27**, 123-133 (2013). https://doi.org/10.1016/j.tranpol.2013.01.008
15. C. Saengsupavanich, Coastal revetment design process in Thailand. WIT Transactions on the Built Environment. **170**, 33–44 (2017). https://doi.org/10.2495/CC170041
16. K. Abualhin, S. Abushaban, Predictive models of non-optically active coastal water quality parameters by remote sensing imagery. Maritime Technology and Research. **7**, 274944 (2025). https://doi.org/10.33175/mtr.2025.274944
17. C. Saengsupavanich, Morphological evolution of sand spits in Thailand. Marine Geodesy. **44**, 432-453 (2021). https://doi.org/10.1080/01490419.2021.1893873
18. J. Gao, Z. Wang, X. Yu, Accessibility measurement of China's coastal ports from a land-sea coordination perspective - An empirical study. Journal of Transport Geography. **105**, 103479 (2022). https://doi.org/10.1016/j.jtrangeo.2022.103479
19. A. Ayotamuno, A. E. Gobo, O. B. Owei, The impact of land use conversion on a residential district in Port Harcourt, Nigeria. Environment and Urbanization. **22**, 259-265 (2010). https://doi.org/10.1177%2F0956247810363529
20. P. Sonde, S. Balamwar, R. S. Ochawar, Urban sprawl detection and analysis using unsupervised classification of high resolution image data of Jawaharlal Nehru Port Trust area in India. Remote Sensing Applications: Society and Environment. **17**, 100282 (2020). https://doi.org/10.1016/j.rsase.2019.100282
21. D. M. S. Abessa, A. R. N. Gonçalves, M. U. de Carvalho, N. Spanghero, N.S.S. Do Nasicmento, M. Fornari, F.C. Perina, A.C.F. Cruz, Not all that glitters is gold: Glitter causes acute toxicity to nauplii of Artemia sp. Maritime Technology and Research. **6**, 270722 (2024). https://doi.org/10.33175/mtr.2024.270722
22. N. G. Dan-Jumbo, M. J. Metzger, A. P. Clark, Urban land-use dynamics in the Niger delta: the case of Greater Port Harcourt watershed. Urban Science. **2**, 108 (2018). https://doi.org/10.3390/urbansci2040108

23. A. S. Alamoush, A. I. Ölçer, Harnessing cutting-edge technologies for sustainable future shipping: An overview of innovations, drivers, barriers, and opportunities. Maritime Technology and Research. **7,** 277313 (2025). https://doi.org/10.33175/025.277313

Development of a simple colorimetric sensor for bacteria detection

Saowapa Thumsing Niyomthai[1,*], *Nattharika* Ratchatathammanit[1], *Sunisa* Phaosung[1], *Narumol* Kreua-ongarjnukool[1], and *Pitt* Supaphol[2,3]

[1]Department of Industrial Chemistry, Faculty of Applied Science, King Mongkut's University of Technology North Bangkok, 10800 Bangkok, Thailand

[2]The Petroleum and Petrochemical College, Chulalongkorn University, 10330 Pathumwan, Bangkok, Thailand

[3]The Center of Excellence on Petrochemical and Materials Technology, Chulalongkorn University, 10330 Pathumwan, Bangkok, Thailand

Abstract. Wound care is vital to prevent infections and inflammation that can lead to chronic wounds. This study developed a novel chitosan-based wound dressing incorporated with purple corn (Zea mays L.) extract as a colorimetric sensor for detecting bacterial infections. The dressings were prepared using 1.5% w/v chitosan, 2 mL glycerol, and varying amounts of purple corn extract (5–20 g). The formulation containing 20 g extract showed the highest anthocyanin content (177.10 ± 1.77 mg/L) and desirable mechanical properties, including a tensile strength of 0.26 ± 0.04 MPa, elongation at break of 23.75 ± 1.77%, and Young's modulus of 25.33 ± 1.96 MPa. SEM analysis revealed a smooth surface with uniform extract distribution. The water vapor transmission rate (734 ± 18 g/m²/day) indicated suitable moisture permeability for wound healing. The dressing exhibited clear pH-dependent color changes orange (pH 5.0), purple-brown (pH 7.4), and dark brown (pH 9.0) enabling visual detection of infection-related pH shifts. Additionally, it showed strong antibacterial activity. These results demonstrate that purple corn extract-infused chitosan dressing is a promising smart wound care material with dual functions: pH-responsive sensing and antibacterial protection.

1 Introduction

The skin is one of the most important organs in the human body, playing a critical role in maintaining homeostasis and protecting internal organs [1]. When skin is wounded, it can cause pain, inflammation, and physiological disturbances [2]. A wound refers to damage to the skin or underlying tissues in various forms, such as abrasions, surgical incisions, or punctures [3]. While small wounds may not require intensive care and can often be managed with basic treatment, if such wounds become infected and are not properly treated, they may develop into chronic wounds. Therefore, wound dressing is an important factor in promoting faster healing and preventing infection, which is one of the main causes of delayed wound healing [4].

Wound healing involves various cell types, including keratinocytes and fibroblasts [5]. Normally, the skin's pH ranges from 4.0 to 6.0, but after injury, the pH can rise to approximately 7.4. If the wound becomes infected, the pH may further increase to around 9.0. Thus, changes in pH are closely related to wound status and bacterial infection [6].

Wound dressings help absorb exudates and prevent external contamination. Materials commonly used in commercial wound dressings include polyurethane, polyethylene oxide, and silicone. However, for patients with burn wounds or deep wounds, frequent dressing changes are necessary, which leads to higher costs [7]. To address this, biodegradable wound dressings made from biopolymers have been developed. These materials are environmentally friendly, naturally degradable, and biocompatible, such as cellulose, collagen, chitosan, casein, and starch [8].

Chitosan is a biopolymer derived from chitin through deacetylation, which con-verts N-acetyl-D-glucosamine to glucosamine [9]. Chitosan possesses key functional groups, including amino ($-NH_2$) and hydroxyl (-OH) groups, which allow it to bind with proteins and dissolve in organic acids such as acetic, lactic, and citric acid [9]. These properties make chitosan suitable for wound dressing applications due to its biocompatibility, non-irritant nature, and biodegradability [10]. Additionally, chitosan exhibits antibacterial properties and accelerates the wound healing process [11]. It can also retain moisture at the wound site, promote faster healing, reduce scar formation [12], and effectively prevent bacterial infection [13].

Recently, there has been growing interest in using natural extracts for antibacterial purposes. Purple corn extract, which is rich in anthocyanins a type of natural pigment exhibits both antioxidant and antibacterial properties [14, 15]. Notably, the structure of anthocyanins is pH-dependent, enabling their use as pH indicators to detect infection in wounds [16].

*Corresponding author : saowapa.t@sci.kmutnb.ac.th

Purple corn (Zea mays L. var. purple corn) is native to South America, particularly Peru, and is known for its deep purple kernels rich in anthocyanins such as pelargonidin, cyanidin, and peonidin. These compounds exhibit strong antioxidant and antimicrobial properties [17]. Anthocyanins from purple corn are also more stable than those from many other sources, making them suitable for use in medical and cosmetic applications [18]. One of their key features is pH sensitivity—anthocyanins appear red in acidic conditions and turn purple or green as the pH becomes neutral or alkaline. This property allows them to serve as natural pH indicators, useful for detecting bacterial infections in wounds, which often cause an increase in wound pH [19].

This study, therefore, proposes the development of a wound dressing incorporating purple corn extract, aimed at both antibacterial activity and functioning as a pH-sensitive sensor for detecting bacterial infections in wounds.

2 Materials and Methods

2.1 Materials

Purple corn extract obtained from T. S. T. twin product. Chitosan, from crab shell was purchased from Sigma-Aldrich Germany. Acetic acid and Ethanol was purchased from Sigma Aldrich USA. All other chemical agents were of analytical grade.

2.2 Preparation of purple corn extract

Purple corn extract 5 g was dissolved in 200 mL of distilled water, then stirred and heated at 60°C for 90 minutes. The mixture was subsequently filtered, and the filtrate was centrifuged at 5,000 rpm for 10 minutes. The same procedure was repeated using 10, 15, and 20 g of purple corn extract, respectively.

2.3 Preparation of wound dressing containing purple corn extract

Chitosan (1.5 g) was dissolved in 2% v/v acetic acid solution and mixed with 2 mL of glycerol. The mixture was stirred at room temperature for 6 hours. Subsequently, 2 mL of 1% v/v glutaraldehyde was added and stirred for an additional 30 minutes. Then, 35 mL of purple corn extract solution was added to the hydrogel and stirred at room temperature for another 30 minutes. The resulting solution was centrifuged at 4000 rpm for 10 minutes. Finally, the mixture was dried at 60°C for 6 hours to obtain chitosan-based hydrogel wound dressing incorporated with purple corn extract.

2.4 Characterization

2.4.1 FTIR analysis

The wound dressing containing purple corn extract was analyzed using FTIR (PERKIN ELMER Spectrum One). The wound dressing containing purple corn extract was placed in the sample holder and scanned in the middle infrared region (400–4000 cm^{-1}), in order to investigate the infrared spectral characteristics of the wound dressing containing purple corn extract.

2.4.2 Morphological observation by SEM

Wound dressing containing purple corn extract were cut into 1 × 1 cm pieces. The cut samples were mounted onto aluminum stubs using carbon tape, ensuring that the surface of each sample was properly oriented for observation. The samples were then coated with a thin layer of gold for 1 minute prior to examination using scanning electron microscopy (SEM) to investigate their surface morphology.

2.4.3 Mechanical properties of the wound dressing containing purple corn extract

Wound dressing containing purple corn extract were cut into 1 × 4 cm pieces and tested following ASTM D882 standards using a Texture Analyzer (TA. XT Plus). The sample gauge length was set to 100.0 mm, and the load cell was set to 5 N. The crosshead speed for tensile testing was 60 mm/min. Each sample was tested three times.

2.4.4 Swelling Ratio

Wound dressing containing purple corn extract, were cut into 2 × 1 cm, were prepared and tested by weighing and recording the initial weight. The samples were then immersed in distilled water for 7 days, with the weight recorded at the following time points: 0.25, 0.50, 0.75, 1, 2, 3, 4, 5, 6, 12, 24, 48, 72, 96, 120, 144, and 168 hours. The swelling ratio was calculated using eq. 1.

$$\text{Swelling Ratio (\%)} = \frac{W_s - W_d}{W_d} \times 100 \quad (1)$$

where Ws is weight of the hydrogel after swelling at various time intervals (g) and Wd is weight of the dry hydrogel (g)

2.4.5 Water Vapor Transmission Rate (WVTR)

Wound dressing containing purple corn extract were sealed in containers with distilled water and weighed before and after sealing. The samples were then placed in a Desiccator for 1, 2, 3, 4, 5, 6, and 7 days. Each sample was tested in triplicate. The Water Vapor Transmission Rate (WVTR) was calculated using eq. 2.

$$\text{WVTR } (g \cdot m^{-2} \cdot day^{-1}) = \frac{W_0 - W_t}{A \cdot t} \quad (2)$$

where W_0 is Weight of the container with distilled water sealed with the hydrogel at the initial time (g), W_t is Weight of the container with distilled water sealed with the hydrogel at any given time (g), A is Cross-sectional area of the hydrogel in contact with water (m^2) and t is time (day)

2.4.6 Release efficiency of purple corn extract from wound dressing

Wound dressing containing purple corn extract were immersed in phosphate-buffered saline (PBS) and shaken at 37°C for 7 days. The samples were collected and replenished at the following time intervals: 0.25, 0.50, 0.75, 1, 2, 3, 4, 5, 6, 12, 24, 48, 72, 96, 120, 144, and 168 hours. The release of the extract was measured using a UV-Vis Spectrophotometer at a wavelength of 520 nm. The release efficiency was then calculated using eq. 3.

$$\text{Release Percentage} = \frac{M_t}{M_\infty} \text{ x } 100 \qquad (3)$$

Where M_t is Actual amount of the extract in hydrogel released at time (mg) and M_∞ is Total amount of compound initially loaded or total releasable amount (mg)

2.4.7 Antibacterial Efficacy of wound dressing containing purple corn extract using the Disk Diffusion Method

The bacterial suspensions of gram-positive bacterium S. aureus and gram-negative bacterium E. coli were spread evenly on TSA. Wound dressing containing purple corn extract, which were prepared for testing, were cut into circular pieces with a diameter of 1.0 cm. The plates were incubated at 37°C until bacterial growth covered the entire plate. The inhibition zone (clear zone) was then observed, and the diameter of the inhibition zone was measured. The obtained values were used to calculate the average and standard deviation to compare the antibacterial effectiveness following ASTM E1054-08

2.5 Evaluation of pH-responsive visible color change of the wound dressing containing purple corn extract

Wound dressing containing purple corn extract were cut into 3 × 3 cm pieces and immersed in phosphate-buffered saline (PBS) solutions at pH 5.0, 7.4, and 9.0 for approximately 30 minutes. The color change of the wound dressings was visually observed before and after immersion in PBS at each pH value.

3 Result and Discussion

3.1 Characterization

3.1.1 FTIR

The difference between the purple corn extract, hydrogel, and hydrogel containing purple corn extract was observed. The basic structure of the purple corn extract contains anthocyanins, which lack nitrogen groups, and thus no N-H stretching and C-N stretching are observed. In contrast, both hydrogel with and without purple corn ex-tract show N-H stretching and C-N stretching, along with other functional groups pre-sent, which are part of the fundamental structure of chitosan. This allows for the preliminary structural identification of the compounds in the purple corn extract, hydro-gel, and hydrogel containing the purple corn extract.

3.1.2 Morphological observation by SEM

From the morphological characteristics of the wound dressing films containing purple corn extract, the naked-eye observation showed that the films had a smooth, homogeneous, and continuous surface. Additionally, the morphological characteristics of the wound dressing films with purple corn extract revealed that the extract was evenly distributed on the film. This ensures that when applied, the purple corn extract will come into direct contact with the skin and exert antibacterial effects consistently across the entire dressing.

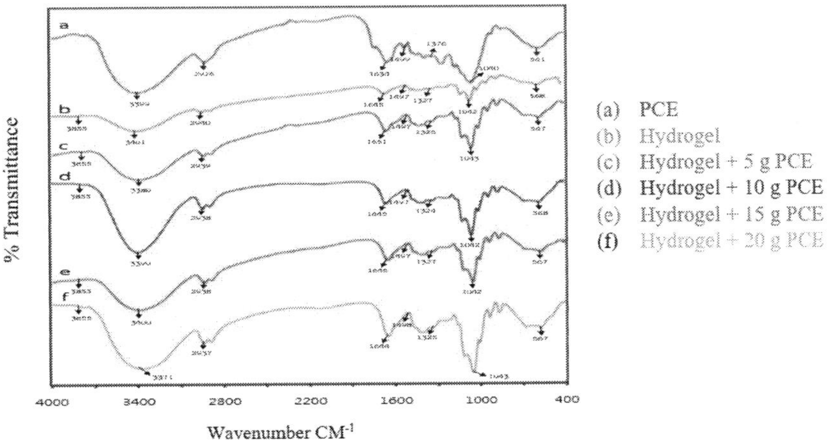

Fig. 1. FTIR spectrum of purple corn extract, hydrogel, and hydrogel containing purple corn extract

Table 1. Functional group of PCE, hydrogel, hydrogel+5 g PCE, hydrogel+10 g PCE, hydrogel+15 g PCE and hydrogel+20 g PCE

Wavenumber	PCE	Hydrogel	Hydrogel + 5 g PCE	Hydrogel + 10 g PCE	Hydrogel + 15 g PCE	Hydrogel + 20 g PCE
3865 (N-H stretching)	✗	✓	✓	✓	✓	✓
3399 (O-H stretching)	✓	✓	✓	✓	✓	✓
2926 (C-H stretching)	✓	✓	✓	✓	✓	✓
1634 (C=O stretching)	✓	✓	✓	✓	✓	✓
1499 (C=C stretching)	✓	✓	✓	✓	✓	✓
1327 (C-N stretching)	✗	✓	✓	✓	✓	✓
1040 (Aromatic ring C-H deformation)	✓	✓	✓	✓	✓	✓
561 (C-O stretching)	✓	✓	✓	✓	✓	✓

where ✓ is functional groups were observed
✗ is no functional groups were observed

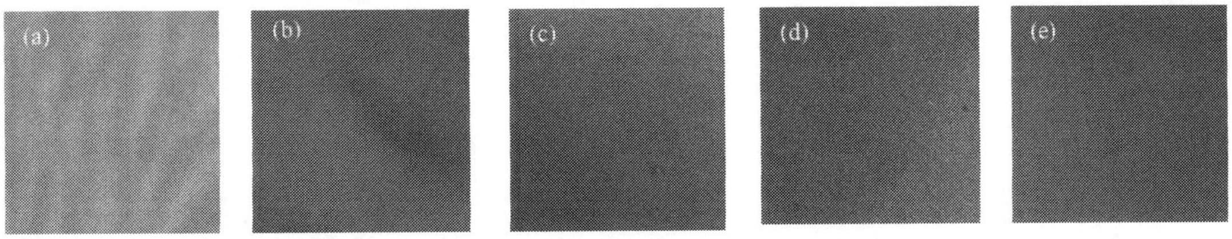

Fig. 2. Visual observation with the naked eye (a) Hydrogel, (b) Hydrogel+5 g PCE, (c) Hydrogel+10 g PCE, (d) Hydrogel+15 g PCE and (e) Hydrogel+20 g PCE

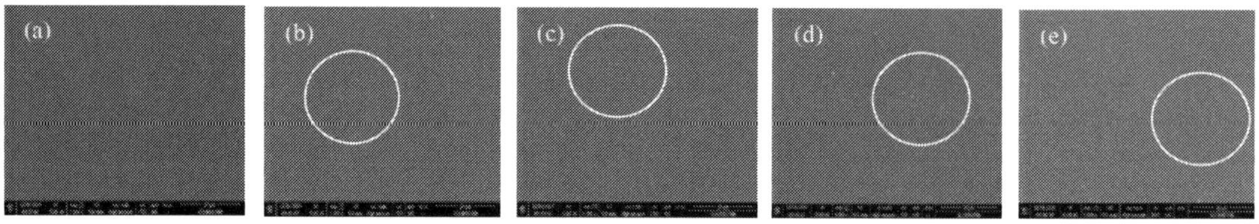

Fig. 3. SEM of surface (a) Hydrogel, (b) Hydrogel+5 g PCE, (c) Hydrogel+10 g PCE, (d) Hydrogel+15 g PCE and (e) Hydrogel+20 g PCE

3.1.3 Mechanical properties

As the concentration of purple corn extract (PCE) increases, the tensile strength, elongation at break, and Young's modulus decrease, indicating a change in the polymer structure and a reduction in mechanical strength with higher concentrations of PCE. The dressing containing 20 grams of purple corn extract exhibited a tensile strength of 0.26 ± 0.04 MPa, elongation at break of 23.75 ± 1.77%, and Young's modulus of 25.33 ± 1.96 MPa, which were lower than those of the commercially available hydro-colloid dressing, which had a tensile strength of 0.74 ± 0.02 MPa, elongation at break of 49.35 ± 3.53%, and Young's modulus of 41.59 ± 0.30 MPa. The results suggest that the dressing with a higher concentration of purple corn extract has reduced flexibility and strength. In contrast, dressings with lower concentrations of purple corn extract, such as 5 and 10 grams, exhibited better mechanical properties and retained good flexibility.

Table 2. Mechanical properties of commercial wound dressing, wound dressing and wound dressing containing purple corn extract (n=3)

Type of hydrogel	Tensile Stress (MPa)	Elongation at break (%)	Young's modulus (MPa)
Hydrogel	0.58±0.01	36.25±1.77	35.85±2.12
Hydrogel+5 g PCE	0.43±0.02	26.25±1.77	27.59±0.14
Hydrogel+10 g PCE	0.36±0.03	23.75±1.77	25.98±0.03
Hydrogel+15 g PCE	0.30±0.01	24.00±1.53	25.84±0.17
Hydrogel+20 g PCE	0.26±0.04	23.75±1.77	25.33±1.96
Commercial wound dressing[1]	0.74±0.02	49.35±3.53	41.59±0.30

[1] Commercial wound dressing (in the market)

3.1.4 Swelling Ratio

As time increases, the weight of both the wound dressing and the wound dressing containing purple corn extract swells most significantly at the 1-hour mark. The weight then slightly decreases at 4 hours, followed by an increase in weight as time progress-es. The initial decrease in swelling is due to the equilibrium of water in the dressing. Initially, the dressing absorbs water due to the driving force, and once excessive water absorption occurs, water is released to balance the chemical potential. Furthermore, it can be observed that as the concentration of purple corn extract increases, the swelling rate also increases. This is because the anthocyanins in the purple corn extract enhance the formation of hydrogen bonds with water, resulting in greater water absorption by the dressing. This affects the polymer structure, creating more pores and improving the swelling capacity of the dressing, leading to an increased swelling rate [20].

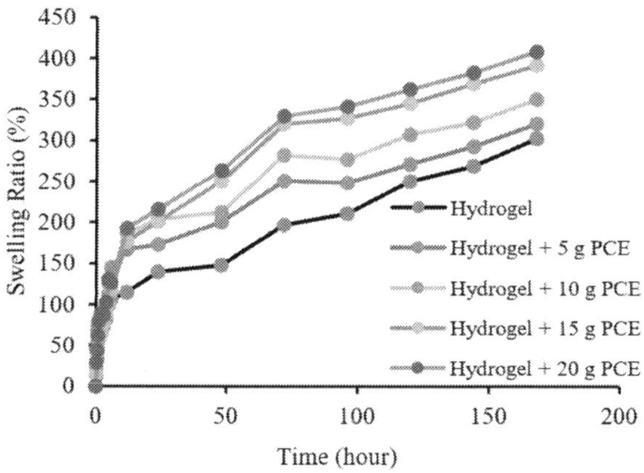

Fig. 4. Swelling Ratio at different times of the wound dressing and wound dressing containing purple corn extract (n=3)

3.1.5 Water Vapor Transmission Rate (WVTR)

The water vapor transmission rate (WVTR) of the wound dressing and the wound dressing containing purple corn extract also showed a decreasing trend over time. The WVTR was initially high but decreased within 7 days. The thickness of the film is one of the factors that affects the variation in water vapor transmission. As the thickness of the film increases, the WVTR decreases because the increased thickness lengthens the distance that water molecules must travel from one side of the film to the other. As a result, some water molecules are unable to pass through the film, thus lowering the WVTR [21]. The dressing containing 20 grams per milliliter of purple corn extract exhibited the lowest WVTR, 734 ± 18 g/m²/day, which is close to the WVTR of Te-gadermTM, a commercially available wound dressing, with a value of 862 g/m²/day, as reported by Nuutila, K. and Eriksson, E. [22]. This value is higher than the WVTR of the dressing without purple corn extract, which was 73 ± 3 g/m²/day.

https://doi.org/10.1051/e3sconf/202567901005

These findings indicate that, within 7 days, the dressing containing purple corn extract can effectively prevent external water from penetrating the wound during the healing process.

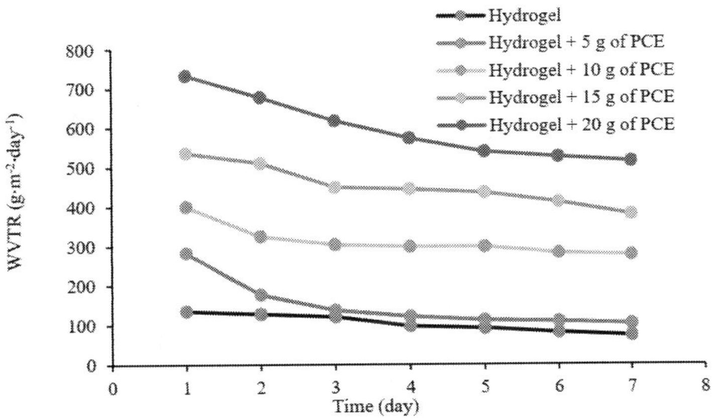

Fig. 5. WVTR of the wound dressing and wound dressing containing purple corn extract (n=3)

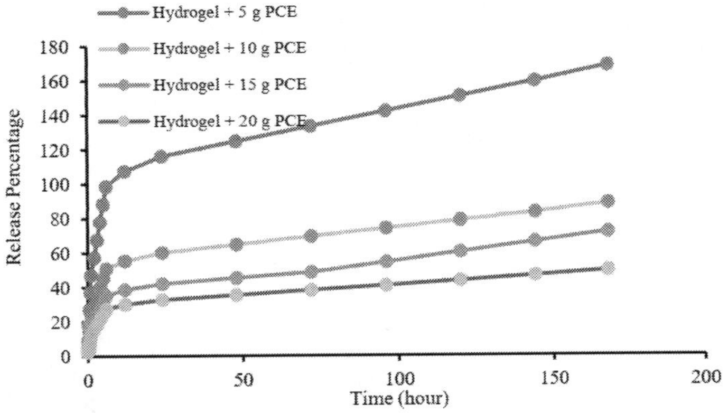

Fig. 6. Release efficiency of wound dressing containing purple corn extract (n=3)

3.1.6 Release efficiency of purple corn extract from wound dressing

The wound dressings containing 5 and 10 grams of purple corn extract released the extract rapidly from 15 minutes to 12 hours. After 12 hours, the release rate slowed and became more stable. When considering the maximum cumulative release percentage of the wound dressings containing 5 and 10 grams of purple corn extract, the values were 168.25 ± 0.29 and 88.33 ± 0.22, respectively. In contrast, the cumulative re-lease percentages of the wound dressings containing 15 and 20 grams of purple corn extract were lower, at 71.73 ± 13.33 and 49.39 ± 0.58, respectively. This is attributed to the larger molecular structure of the purple corn extract in the higher concentrations, which made it more difficult for the extract to diffuse out, resulting in a lower release amount compared to the 5 and 10-gram extract dressings.

3.1.7 pH-responsive visible color change

The wound dressings containing 5 and 10 grams of purple corn extract were not able to inhibit the growth of Gram-negative *E.* coli and Gram-positive *S.* aureus bacteria. However, the wound dressings containing 15 and 20 grams of purple corn extract were able to inhibit both Gram-negative *E.* coli and Gram-positive *S.* aureus. The inhibition zone diameters for *E.* coli were 11.25 ± 0.86 and 11.97 ± 1.13 millimeters, re-spectively. It was observed that the inhibition zone for *E.* coli was smaller than that for *S.* aureus due to the more complex and asymmetric cell wall structure of Gram-negative bacteria compared to Gram-positive bacteria, which allows for greater growth of Gram-negative bacteria. This shows that the purple corn extract in wound dressings weighing 15 and 20 grams can enhance the antibacterial efficacy of the dressing against both *E.* coli and *S.* aureus.

https://doi.org/10.1051/e3sconf/202567901005

Table 3. Visible color change of wound dressing containing purple corn extract at pH 5.0, 7.4, and 9.0

Type of hydrogel	Before the experiment	pH 5.0	pH 7.4	pH 9.0
Hydrogel + 5 g PCE				
Hydrogel + 10 g PCE				
Hydrogel + 15 g PCE				
Hydrogel + 20 g PCE				

3.1.8 pH-responsive visible color change

The wound dressing containing purple corn extract exhibits color changes. When exposed to a PBS solution at pH 5.0 or normal skin, the dressing appears orange. Upon injury, where the PBS solution has a pH of 7.4, the dressing changes to a purple-brown color. If bacterial infection occurs, with a PBS solution at pH 9.0, the dressing changes to a dark brown color.

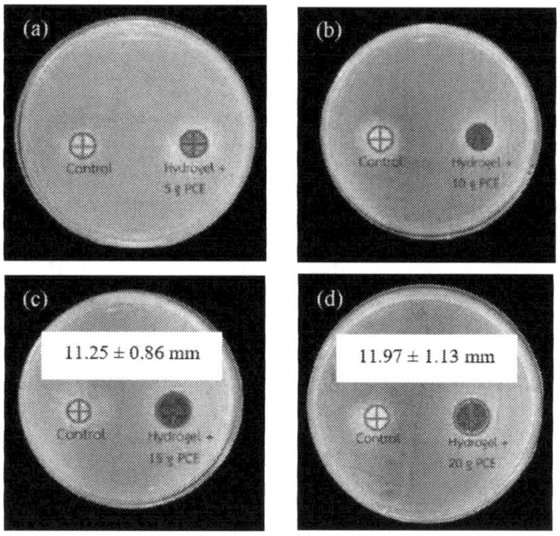

Fig. 7. Clear inhibition zone for Gram-negative *E. coli* of the wound dressing containing purple corn extract (a) 5 g PCE, (b) 10 g PCE, (c) 15 g PCE and (d) 20 g PCE

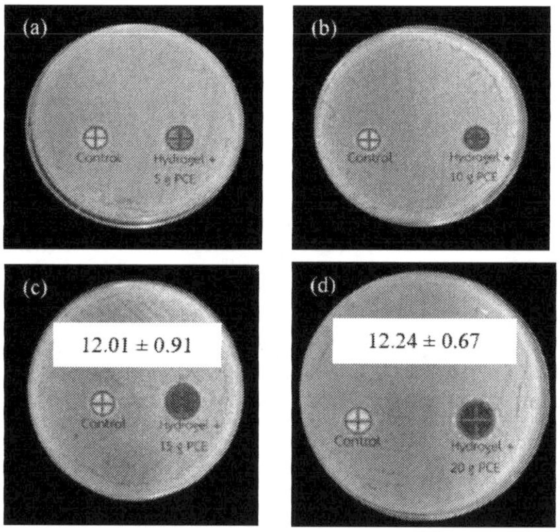

Fig. 8. Clear inhibition zone for Gram-positive *S. aureus* of the wound dressing contain-ing purple corn extract (a) 5 g PCE, (b) 10 g PCE, (c) 15 g PCE and (d) 20 g PCE

4 Conclusion

The wound dressing incorporated with purple corn extract demonstrated a uniform distribution throughout the film, ensuring direct skin contact and consistent antibacterial activity across the entire surface. The dressing exhibited a low water vapor transmission rate (WVTR) of 734 ± 18 g·m⁻²·day⁻¹, indicating its ability to effectively prevent external moisture penetration. Over time, the weight of both the control and the extract-loaded dressings gradually increased and reached equilibrium after 72 hours. Notably, the wound dressing containing 20 g of purple corn extract was soft and flexible, showing superior handling properties compared to commercial products. In addition, the dressing exhibited visible color changes in response to different pH values appearing orange at pH 5.0 (normal skin condition), purple-brown at pH 7.4 (injured condition), and dark brown at pH 9.0 (bacterial infection) indicating its potential as a colorimetric pH sensor for wound monitoring. Furthermore, the extract-loaded dressing effectively inhibited the growth of both Gram-negative *E. coli* and Gram-positive *S. aureus*, confirming its antibacterial efficacy. Overall, these findings suggest that the purple corn extract-based wound dressing is a promising candidate for smart wound care applications combining pH-sensing and antimicrobial functions.

The authors acknowledge the support received form the Department of Industrial Chemistry, Faculty of Applied Science, KMUTNB (KMUTNB-68-BASIC-33), (a), PPC, Chulalongkorn University, Thailand (b)

References

1. F. Feng, Z. Zhao, J. Li, Y. Huang, W. Chen, Multifunctional dressings for wound exudate management. *Progress in Materials Science.* **146**, 101328 (2024)
2. O. Eskilson, E. Zattarin, L. Berglund, K. Oksman, K. Hanna, J. Rakar, D. Aili, Nanocellulose composite wound dressings for real-time pH wound monitoring. *Materials Today Bio.* **19**, 100574 (2023).
3. National Pressure Injury Advisory Panel. Prevention and treatment of pressure ulcers: Clinical practice guideline. *International Journal of Nursing Practice.* **22**, 24–31 (2016).
4. X. Mu, H. Yu, C. Zhang, X. Chen, Z. Cheng, R. Bai, X. Wu, Q. Yu, C. Wu, Y. Diao, Nanoporous nitrocellulose liquid bandage modulates cell and cytokine response and accelerates cutaneous wound healing in a mouse model. *Carbohydrate Polymers.* **136**, 618–629 (2016)
5. S. Barrientos, O. Stojadinovic, M. S. Golinko, H. Brem, M. Tomic-Canic, Growth factors and cytokines in wound healing. *Wound Repair and Regeneration.* **16**, 585–601 (2008).
6. K. Kiti, C. Thanomsilp, O. Suwantong, The potential use of colorimetric pH sensor from Clitoria ternatea flower for indicating bacterial infection in wound dressing application. *Microchemical Journal.* **177**, 107277 (2022)
7. M. Burkatovskaya, G. P. Tegos, E. Swietlik, T. N. Demidova, A. P. Castano, M. R. Hamblin, Use of chitosan bandage to prevent fatal infections developing from highly contaminated wounds in mice. *Biomaterials*, **27**, 4157–4164 (2006)
8. M. Rinaudo, Chitin and chitosan: Properties and applications. *Progress in Polymer Science.* **31**, 603–632 (2006)
9. A. Moeini, P. Pedram, P. Makvandi, M. Malinconico, G. G. Ayala, Wound healing and antimicrobial effect of active secondary metabolites in chitosan-based wound dressings: A review. *Carbohydrate Polymers.* 233, 115839 (2020)
10. S. N. Hosseini, M. Jalaly, M. Heydari, A. Mirzapoor, Evaluation of a chitosan-based hydrogel containing graphene oxide and Scrophularia striata extract as an antimicrobial wound dressing. *South African Journal of Botany.* **171**, 199–208 (2024)
11. X. Qing, G. He, Z. Liu, Y. Yin, W. Cai, L. Fan, P. Fardim, Preparation and properties of polyvinyl alcohol/N–succinyl chitosan/lincomycin composite antibacterial hydrogels for wound dressing. *Carbohydrate Polymers.* **261**, 117875 (2021)
12. H. Li, M. Li, Anthocyanins from purple corn as antioxidants and their applications. *Journal of Food Science.* **81**, 2676–2685 (2016)
13. S. Charmongkolpradit, T. Somboon, R. Phatchana, W. Sang-aroon, B. Tanwanichkul, Influence of drying temperature on anthocyanin and moisture contents in purple waxy corn kernel using a tunnel dryer. *Case Studies in Thermal Engineering.* **25**, 100886 (2021)
14. Q. Wang, Y. Jiang, W. Chen, D. J. McClements, C. Ma, X. Liu, F. Liu, Development of pH-responsive active film materials based on purple corncob and its application in meat freshness monitoring. *Food Research International.* **161**, 111832 (2022)
15. M. G. S. Ursu, S. A. Milea, B. Păcularu-Burada, L. Dumitrașcu, G. Râpeanu, S. Stanciu, N. Stănciuc, Optimizing of the extraction conditions for anthocyanin's from purple corn flour (Zea mays L): Evidences on selected properties of optimized extract. *Food Chemistry*: X. **17**, 100521 (2023)
16. V. Sharma, P. Jha, Smart wound dressings using hydrogel matrices for pH sensing. Biomaterials. **245**, 119984 (2020)
17. J. Yang, B. Ou, L. Cheng, Antioxidant and antiproliferative activities of common edible purple corn (Zea mays L.) varieties from Peru. Journal of Agricultural and Food Chemistry. **57**, 7543–7548 (2009)
18. T. Tsuda, Dietary anthocyanin-rich plants: Biochemical basis and recent progress in health

benefits studies. Molecular Nutrition & Food Research. **56**, 159–170 (2012)
19. A. Castañeda-Ovando, M. de L. Pacheco-Hernández, M. E. Páez-Hernández, J. A. Rodríguez, C. A. Galán-Vidal, Chemical studies of anthocyanins: A review. Food Chemistry. **113**, 859–871 (2009).
20. D. Chelminiak-Dudkiewicz, A. Smolarkiewicz-Wyczachowski, K. Mylkie, M. Wujak, D. T. Mlynarczyk, P. Nowak, S. Bocian, T. Goslinski, M. Ziegler- Borowska, Chitosan-based films with cannabis oil as a base material for wound dressing application. *Scientific Reports*. **12**, 18658 (2022)
21. S.Y. Zhang, W. Xue, Z. Yu, Moisture barrier evaluation of SiOx/SiNx stacks on polyimide substrates using electrical calcium test. Thin Solid Films. **580**, 101-105 (2015)
22. K. Nuutila, E. Eriksson, Moist Wound Healing with Commonly Available Dressings. ADVANCES IN WOUND CARE. **10**, 685-698 (2021)

Evaluation of Anthocyanin Content, Color Stability, and Antibacterial Activity of Purple Corn Extract for Application in Colorimetric Sensors

Sunisa *Phaosung*[1], Nattharika *Ratchatathammanit*[1], Narumol *Kreua-ongarjnukool*[1], Pitt *Supaphol*[2,3], and Saowapa *Thumsing Niyomthai*[1,*]

[1]Department of Industrial Chemistry, Faculty of Applied Science, King Mongkut's University of Technology North Bangkok, Wongsawang, Bangsue, 10800 Bangkok, Thailand

[2]The Petroleum and Petrochemical College, Chulalongkorn University, Phyathai Road, Pathumwan, 10330 Bangkok, Thailand

[3]The Center of Excellence on Petrochemical and Materials Technology, Chulalongkorn University, Pathumwan, 10330 Bangkok, Thailand

Abstract. In recent years, increasing attention has been paid to plant-derived compounds as natural alternatives to synthetic chemicals in food, cosmetic, and healthcare applications. Purple corn (*Zea mays L.*) has attracted considerable interest due to its high anthocyanin content, which not only imparts a vibrant color but also exhibits antioxidant and antibacterial properties. This study aimed to evaluate the multifunctional potential of purple corn extract as both a natural pH indicator and an antibacterial agent. Anthocyanins were extracted from purple corn and analyzed using UV-Visible spectrophotometry. The extracts were tested in buffer solutions across a pH range of 2.0–12.0. The extracts color exhibited distinct transitions: reddish-purple under acidic conditions (pH 2.0–6.0), grayish-purple under neutral to slightly basic conditions (pH 7.0–9.0), and bluish-green under alkaline conditions (pH 10.0–12.0). Despite these variations, the maximum absorbance was observed at 520 nm, particularly at pH 1.0 and 4.5, where measurements were conducted for anthocyanin. FTIR spectroscopy confirmed the presence of functional groups including hydroxyl, alkyl, alkene, and aromatic ring, which are characteristic of phenolic and anthocyanin compounds. Quantitative analysis showed that total anthocyanin content peaked at 177.10 ± 24.68 mg/L, corresponding to increased extract concentrations. Antibacterial activity was assessed against *Escherichia coli* (Gram-negative) and *Staphylococcus aureus* (Gram-positive) using serial dilution method. The extract demonstrated bactericidal properties at concentrations ranging from 7.0–14.0 %w/v. Overall, the study highlights the potential of purple corn extract as a natural, eco-friendly pH-sensitive dye with significant antibacterial activity, suitable for application in food packaging, cosmetics, and biomedical fields.

1 Introduction

Thailand possesses rich biodiversity, particularly in vegetables and fruits that are widely consumed and utilized. Each plant species offers unique beneficial properties. Many Thai fruits and vegetables can be consumed fresh and are also used in traditional medicine. For example, tomatoes, papayas, and guavas are rich in antioxidants that help reduce the risk of chronic diseases such as cancer and heart disease [1]. In addition, fruits like pomelo, mangosteen, and mango are highly nutritious and can be incorporated into health products due to their abundance of vitamins and flavonoids [2].

Studies on red- and purple-colored fruits and vegetables have shown that they contain anthocyanins flavonoid their purple or red coloration. Anthocyanins antioxidant properties help protect cells from oxidative stress and reduce the risk of various diseases, particularly those related to vascular and neurological degeneration [3]. Plants such as purple corn, eggplant, red cabbage, and blueberries are rich sources of anthocyanins and hold great promise for diverse applications [4].

Anthocyanins are also notable for their pH-sensitive color changes, shifting from red in acidic conditions to purple or blue under alkaline conditions [5]. Beyond their color-changing ability, anthocyanins exhibit additional bioactivities including anti-inflammatory, anti-cancer, and anti-aging effects, making them promising agents in the prevention of chronic diseases such as cardiovascular disorders [6]. Research interest in anthocyanins continues to grow due to their safety and potential for incorporation into health-related products such as pharmaceuticals and dietary supplements [7].

In addition to these health benefits, anthocyanins have been increasingly recognized for their antimicrobial activity. Several studies have demonstrated that anthocyanins can inhibit the growth of various bacterial species by disrupting cell membranes, altering intracellular functions, and interfering with nucleic acid synthesis [8]. Specifically, anthocyanins extracted from purple corn have shown strong inhibitory effects against

*Corresponding author : saowapa.t@sci.kmutnb.ac.th

https://doi.org/10.1051/e3sconf/202567901006

both Gram-positive and Gram-negative bacteria, making them attractive candidates for natural antibacterial agents in food preservation and biomedical applications [8].

Purple corn (*Zea mays L.*) has gained attention as a rich source of anthocyanins, especially in its cob, which contains high levels of these compounds. In addition to antioxidant activity, purple corn also contains phenolic compounds that contribute to disease prevention, such as cancer and cardiovascular diseases [9]. Research has shown that anthocyanins extracted from purple corn cobs using ultrasonic-assisted extraction and acidified solvents can yield up to 7,869.26 µg CGE/g dry weight, highlighting its potential as a potent antioxidant source [10]. Furthermore, purple corn extract has demonstrated strong antibacterial activity against common foodborne and clinical pathogens [8].

Due to its pH-sensitive color-changing properties and high antioxidant content, purple corn is highly suitable for development as a natural pH indicator. The extract can serve as a colorimetric sensor capable of accurate pH detection in an environmentally friendly manner [11]. Applications include food packaging, cosmetic formulations, medical diagnostics, and chemical sensing [12].

This study aims to evaluate the multifunctional properties of purple corn extract, focusing on its potential as a colorimetric pH sensor and antibacterial agent. The sensor is expected to be safe, eco-friendly, and adaptable for future applications in industrial, medical, and nutritional fields [13].

2 Materials and Methods

2.1 Materials

Purple corn extract was obtained from T.S.T. Twin Product (Thailand). The bacterial strains used in this study were *Escherichia coli* (*E. coli*) ATCC 25922, a Gram-negative bacterium, and *Staphylococcus aureus* (*S. aureus*) ATCC 25923, a Gram-positive bacterium. All reagents and chemicals used were of analytical grade.

2.2 Preparation of purple corn extract

Different quantities (5, 10, 15, and 20 g) of dried purple corn extract powder were each dissolved in 200 mL of distilled water. The mixtures were stirred and heated at 60 °C for 90 minutes. After extraction, each sample was filtered and centrifuged at 5,000 rpm for 10 minutes to remove particulates. The resulting supernatant was used for subsequent analyses.

2.2.1 Determination of total anthocyanin content in purple corn extract

Purple corn extracts were prepared by dissolving 5, 10, 15, and 20 g of purple corn extract in distilled water. For total anthocyanin determination, the extracts were diluted with buffer solutions at pH 1.0 (potassium chloride-hydrochloric acid) and pH 4.5 (sodium acetate-acetic acid) in accordance with the pH differential method. The absorbance of each extract was measured using a UV-Visible spectrophotometer (Analytik Jena, Specord 210 Plus). These buffers provided controlled acidic environments that ensured accurate anthocyanin quantification while minimizing any interference from strong acids. The total anthocyanin content was then calculated using Equation 1. All extract concentrations (5, 10, 15, and 20 g of dried purple corn powder) were used in subsequent experiments, including pH stability and antibacterial activity tests, in order to determine the optimal concentration based on performance outcomes. The extract obtained from 20 g, which yielded the highest anthocyanin content, was included to evaluate its effectiveness compared to lower concentrations.

$$\text{References Anthocyanin (mg/L)} = \frac{\text{AŸMWŸDFŸ1000}}{\varepsilon \times l} \qquad (1)$$

where A is (A520 nm - A700 nm) pH 1.0 - (A520 nm - A700 nm) pH 4.5, MW is molecular weight of cyanidin-3-glucoside (g/mol), DF is dilute factor, "ε" is molar absorptivity (L•mol-1•cm-1) and l is optical path length of the cell (cm)

2.2.2 Color Stability of Anthocyanins in Purple Corn Extract at Different pH

The color stability of anthocyanins in purple corn extract was assessed using buffer solutions with pH values from 2.0 to 12.0. Color changes were visually observed, and absorbance spectra were recorded using a UV-Visible spectrophotometer (Analytik Jena, Specord 210 Plus).

This pH range was chosen because anthocyanins ars unstable below pH 2.0 and above pH 12.0 Staying within this range allowed clear color changes to be observed without degrading the pigment.

2.3 Characterization

2.3.1 FTIR analysis

The purple corn extract was analyzed using Fourier Transform Infrared Spectroscopy (FTIR) with a Perkin Elmer Spectrum One spectrometer. A drop of the extract was placed onto a potassium bromide (KBr) plate, which was then covered with another KBr plate to form a thin film. The sample was mounted on the sample holder and scanned in the mid-infrared region from 400 to 4000 cm^{-1} to obtain the FTIR spectrum

The spectrum was interpreted to identify characteristic absorption bands associated with anthocyanin compounds. These included a broad O-H stretching band near 3399 cm^{-1} (hydroxyl groups), C-H stretching around 2926 cm^{-1} (alkyl groups), aromatic C=C stretching at 1499 cm^{-1} and C-O bending vibrations near 1040 cm^{-1}, consistent with phenolic and glycosidic structures such as cyanidin-3-glucoside. The band assignments were based on published literature [14]

2.3.2 Determination of the Minimum Inhibitory Concentration (MIC) of Purple Corn Extract

The purple corn extract was used in liquid form, not as a powder; thus, the use of %w/v refers to the mass of dried purple corn powder originally dissolved in a given volume of solution. This unit was retained to reflect the concentration of the initial solid material in the extract preparation.

A 96-well microtiter plate was used to determine the minimum inhibitory concentration (MIC) of purple corn extract against Gram-negative *E. coli* and Gram-positive *S. aureus*. Positive control wells contained only tryptic Soy Broth (TSB), while negative control wells contained only purple corn extract without any bacterial onoculum. 14.0% w/v purple corn extract solution was pipetted 100 µL in column 1. TSB was added to columns 2–10 and 12, 50 µL per well. A serial two-fold dilution was performed to prepare extract concentrations of 14.0, 7.0, 4.0, 2.0, 1.0, 0.5, 0.2, 0.1, 0.06, and 0.03% w/v, each well was inoculated with 10^6 CFU/mL of bacterial suspension. After incubation at 37°C for 24 hours, turbidity was visually inspected and compared with the controls. Wells showing no visible turbidity were considered as exhibiting bacterial growth inhibition.

2.3.3 Determination of the Minimum Bactericidal Concentration (MBC) of Purple Corn Extract

A 10 µL aliquot of purple corn extract concentrations ranging from 0.03 % to 14.0% w/v, prepared as described in section 2.3.2, was pipetted onto solid agar medium. After MIC determination, 10 µL from wells that showed no turbidity were plated onto TSB agar and incubated at 37°C for 24 hours. The lowest concentration with no visible bacterial colony was recorded as the MBC.

3. Results and Discussion

3.1 Total anthocyanin content in purple corn extract

The UV-Vis absorbance spectra of purple corn extract at pH 1.0 and pH 4.5 are presented in Figure1 Across all extract concentrations, the maximum absorbance was consistently observed at 520 nm, which corresponds to the characteristics absorption of anthocyanins.

At pH 1.0, the spectra of the 15 g and 20 g samples showed little difference, which may be due to anthocyanin aggregation or optical saturation under highly acidic conditions. Anthocyanins tend to self-associate in flavylium cation form at low pH, limiting further increase in absorbance even with higher concentration [15]. In contrast, at pH 4.5, absorbance increased linearly with extract amount, indicating fewer molecular interactions and greater pigment stability in mildly acidic conditions [16].

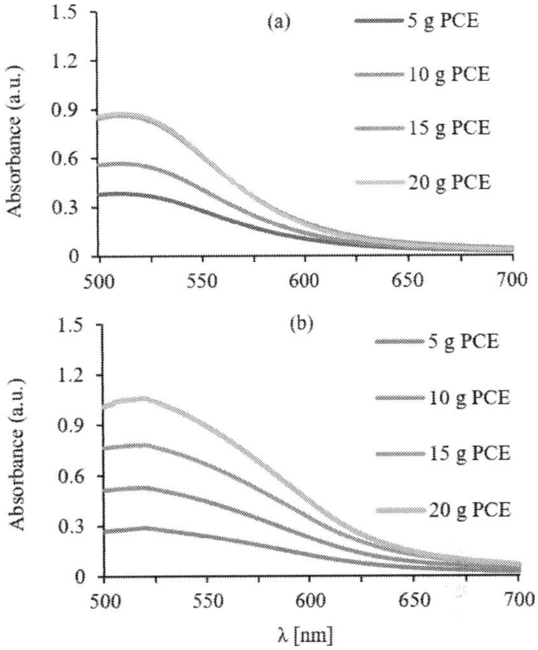

Fig. 1. UV-Vis absorbance spectra of purple corn extract solution at (a) pH 1.0 and (b) pH 4.5

As shown on Figure 2, the total anthocyanin content increased with extract weight, reaching 177.10 ± 24.68 mg/L in the 20 g sample. These results confirm that anthocyanin yield depends on extract concentration.

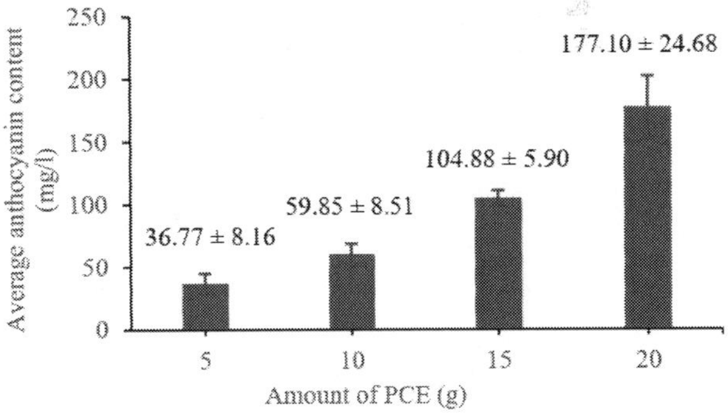

Fig. 2. The anthocyanin content in purple corn extracts weighing 5, 10, 15 and 20 g

3.2 Color Stability of Anthocyanins in Purple Corn Extract at Different pH

The results of the color change study of anthocyanins in purple corn extract in buffer solutions at pH 2.0–12.0 showed that at pH 2.0, 3.0, 4.0, 5.0, and 6.0, the extract appeared reddish-purple. At pH 7.0, 8.0, and 9.0, the color shifted to grayish-purple, while at pH 10.0, 11.0, and 12.0, the extract exhibited a darker bluish-green hue.

https://doi.org/10.1051/e3sconf/202567901006

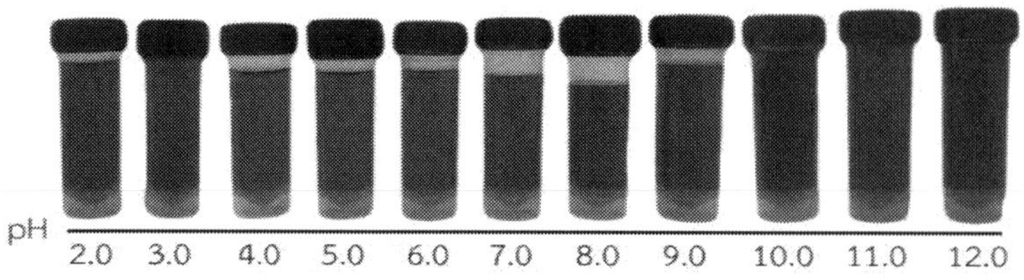

Fig. 3. Change color of Purple corn extract solution in buffer solution pH 2.0-12.0

The color transitions from red (pH 2-4) to reddish-purple (pH 5-8), deep purple (pH 9-10), and bluish-green (pH 11-12) is attributed to structural transformations of anthocyanins into flaylium cations, quinoidal bases, and chalcone forms. These pH dependent changes align with previous findings by Zhao et.al., who demonstrated how anthocyanins shift both in structure and color across varying pH conditions [17].

Similar behavior has been reported in anthocyanins from red cabbage, butterfly pea, and black rice, which also exhibit vivid and reversible pH-responsive color changes [18, 19]. These findings support their potential use in natural pH indicators.

3.3 Characterization

3.3.1 FTIR

The FTIR spectrum of purple corn extract revealed distinct absorption peaks at 3399 cm-ʃ (OóH stretching), 2926 cm-ʃ (CóH stretching), 1499 cm-ʃ (C=C stretching), and 1040 cm-ʃ (aromatic ring CóH deformation). These peaks correspond to functional groups commonly found in anthocyanin. The broad peak at 3399 cm-ʃ is associated with hydroxyl groups present in phenolic compounds, while the peak at 2926 cm-ʃ indicates C-H stretching from aliphatic chains. The absorption at 1499 cm-ʃ represents aromatic C=C bonds, and the 1040 cm-ʃ band is attributed to C-O stretching or bending vibrations in glycosidic linkages.

These spectral features confirm the presence of hydroxyl, alkyl, and aromatic ring structures, consistent with anthocyanins such as cyanidin-3-glucoside. No absorption bands related to nitrogen-containing groups were observed. The observed FTIR peaks are consistent with those reported in recent studies of anthocyanin-rich plant extracts, including the identification of hydroxyl, aromatic, and glycosidic groups [14].

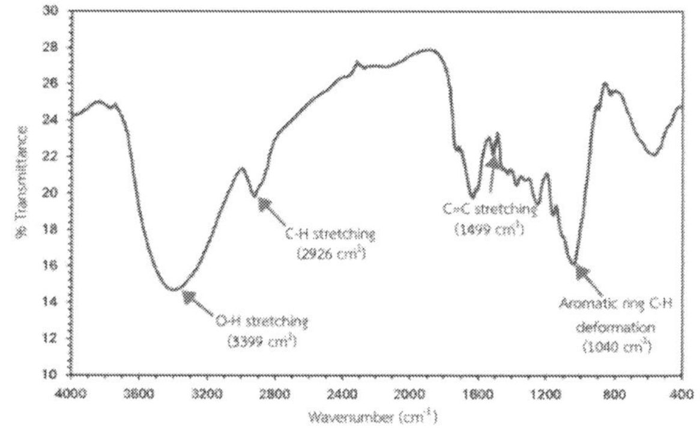

Fig. 4. FTIR spectrum of Purple corn extract solution

3.3.2 Minimum Inhibitory Concentration (MIC) of Purple Corn Extract

The experimental results showed that purple corn extract at concentrations of 7.0–14.0 % w/v effectively inhibited the growth of both Gram-negative *E. coli* and Gram-positive *S. aureus*. In the MIC assay, the bacterial inoculum was standardized to 10^6 CFU/mL, and the cultures were incubated at 37°C for 24 hours. Samples containing 7.0–14.0% w/v extract remained visibly clear, indicating no bacterial growth, similar to the negative control (TSB only). In contrast, lower concentrations and positive control (TSB with bacteria but without extract) showed visible turbidity due to bacterial proliferation.

https://doi.org/10.1051/e3sconf/202567901006

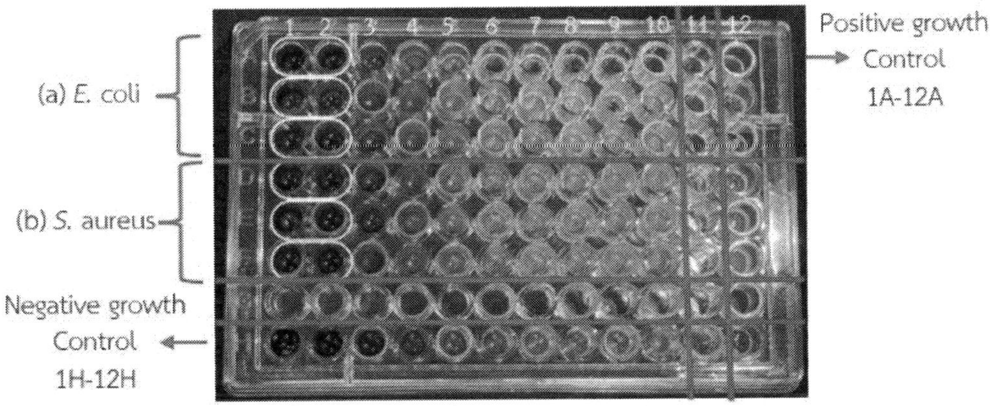

Fig. 5. MIC of Purple corn extract

3.3.3 Minimum Bactericidal Concentration (MBC) of Purple Corn Extract

The MBC of purple corn extract was determined by subculturing 10 µL from MIC wells that showed no turbidity onto TSB agar plates. After incubation at 37°C for 24 hours, the plates were examined for bacterial growth. The results demonstrated that purple corn extract at concentrations of 7.0–14.0% w/v showed no visible bacterial colonies for both Gram-negative *E. coli* and Gram-positive *S. aureus*, confirming that the extract at these concentrations exhibited bactericidal activity. In contrast, lower concentrations produced visible colonies, indicating killing of the bacteria.

The findings indicate that the MBC of purple corn extract is 7.0% w/v for both Gram-negative *E. coli* and Gram-positive *S. aureus* test organisms.

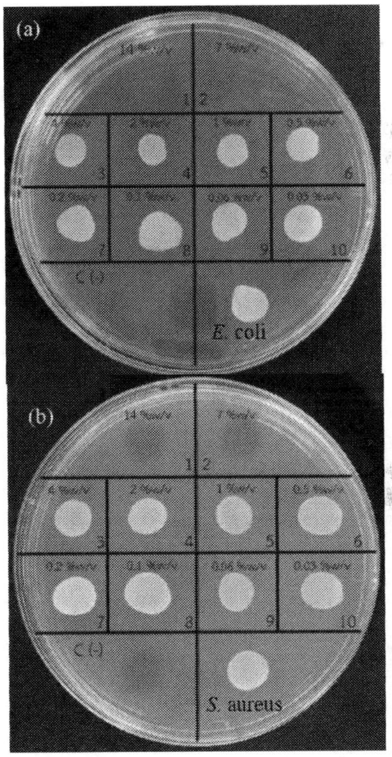

Fig. 6. MBC of Purple corn extract

4 Conclusions

This study demonstrated the multifunctional potential of purple corn extract as both a natural pH indicator and an antibacterial agent. The extract exhibited distinct and visually perceptible color transitions across a wide pH range (pH 2.0–12.0), which is consistent with the known pH sensitivity of anthocyanins reported in prior studies on red cabbage and hibiscus [18, 19]. Spectrophotometric analysis revealed a maximum absorbance at 520 nm and confirmed a high anthocyanin content up to 177.10 ± 24.68 mg/L. These findings are in agreement with previous reports on anthocyanin-rich plant sources [6, 7] and further highlight the concentration-dependent nature of the extract's colorimetric response. FTIR spectroscopy additionally verified the presence of phenolic and aromatic functional groups, reinforcing the conclusion that the extract contains key structural features typical of anthocyanins.

Moreover, the extract exhibited significant antibacterial activity against both *Escherichia coli* (Gram-negative) and *Staphylococcus aureus* (Gram-positive), with minimum inhibitory and bactericidal concentrations observed at 7.0% w/v. These results support its potential as a dual-function bioactive component, particularly for applications in food safety, smart packaging, and antimicrobial materials.

Future research should focus on incorporating the extract into biopolymer films or sensor matrices, evaluating its functional stability under practical storage and usage conditions, and investigating its antimicrobial efficacy against a broader spectrum of microorganisms. Overall, purple corn extract offers a promising, sustainable, and multifunctional natural alternative for use in food, cosmetic, and healthcare industries.

The authors acknowledge the support received form the Department of Industrial Chemistry, Faculty of Applied Science, KMUTNB-68-BASIC-33 (a), PPC, Chulalongkorn University, Thailand (b). This research is currently in the process of patent application.

References

1. R. Sompong, N. Tansakul, Thai traditional vegetables and fruits:Diversity and nutritional value. *Journal of Agricultural Science and Technology*. **21**, 215–222 (2019)
2. S. Chuenchom, A. Kongsuwan, Nutritional and health-promoting properties of Thai fruits. *Asian Journal of Food and Agro-Industry*. **13**, 45–53 (2020)
3. T. Noppakun, A. Watcharapasorn, Anthocyanins in colored fruits and vegetables: Health benefits and applications. *Thai Journal of Nutrition*. **26**, 133–141 (2021)
4. P. Khampan, P. Ratanatraiwong, Sources and extraction methods of anthocyanins in Thai plants. *Journal of Natural Products*. **17**, 77–85 (2020)
5. K. Saengkaew, A. Worachartcheewan, Anthocyanins as natural pH indicators and smart sensors. *Journal of Applied Science and Innovation*. **14**, 102–110 (2021)
6. S. Boonsong, W. Chaiyasit, Anti-inflammatory and anticancer potential of anthocyanins. *Journal of Medicinal Plants Research*. **16**, 128–136 (2022)
7. S. Wongsagul, T. Lekprichakul, Anthocyanin-based supplements and functional foods: Safety and efficacy. *International Journal of Food Science and Nutrition*. **28**, 91–98 (2023)
8. T. Chanthasena, T. Jaidee, Antibacterial properties of purple corn extracts. *Asian Journal of Microbiology and Biotechnology*. **19**, 110–116 (2023)
9. M. Phumthum, U. Srisawat, Bioactive compounds in purple corn (Zea mays L. var. ceratina). *Thai Journal of Agricultural Science*. **55**, 123–130 (2022)
10. W. Rungseevijitprapa, S. Chanthai, Ultrasonic-assisted extraction of anthocyanins from purple corn husk. *Food Chemistry and Biochemistry*. **48**, 72–80 (2021)
11. W. Kittikorn, T. Limboonreung, Eco-friendly pH sensors using natural pigments from purple corn. *Green Chemistry Letters and Reviews*. **13**, 289–297 (2020)
12. N. Nualkaew, U. Jittasopa, Application of purple corn extract as a natural colorimetric pH sensor. *Journal of Food and Cosmetic Science*. **18**, 55–62 (2023)
13. C. Yimyam, S. Tinnarat, Development of natural pH sensors from purple corn extract for industrial use. *Journal of Innovation in Applied Sciences*. **22**, 101–108 (2024)
14. A. Amanah, A. Aminullah, R. Martien, *Isolation and characterization of anthocyanin from black rice and their application in smart packaging*. Heliyon. **6**, e04543 (2020)
15. Z. Zhang et al, *Self-association and color stability of anthocyanins under acidic conditions*. Food chemistry. **344**, 128660 (2021)
16. T. Wu et al., *Structural transformations and stability of nthocyanin under various pH conditions: A review*. Trends in Food Science & Technology. **83**, 86-98 (2019)
17. L. Zhao et al., *Color and Structural changes of anthocyanins under different pH conditions: Experimental and computational approaches*. Food Chemistry. **314**. 126170 (2020)
18. N. T. Thuy et al., *Natural anthocyanins as pH-sensitive indicators: Recent advances and applications in food packaging*. Journal of Food Engineering. **356**, 111299 (2023)
19. Y. Li et al., *pH-responsive behavior of anthocyanins from butterfly pea flower and their application in smart packaging*. Food Hydrocolloids. **128**, 107609 (2022)

Modification and Characterization of Waxy and Native Tapioca Starches for Stabilizing Resveratrol Pickering Emulsion

Rapeeporn Wannarat[1], *Anchana* Pleanklay[1], *Suthida* Boonsith[2, 3], and *Sukanya* Thepwatee[1*]

[1]Department of Industrial Chemistry, Faculty of Applied Science, King Mongkut's University of Technology North Bangkok, 10800 Bangkok, Thailand
[2]Department of Chemical Engineering, Faculty of Engineering, Mahidol University, 73170 Nakhon Pathom, Thailand
[3]Expert Centre of Innovative Herbal Products, Thailand Institute of Scientific and Technological Research, 12120 Pathum Thani, Thailand

Abstract. Tapioca starch is a promising biopolymer for use as a solid particle stabilizer in Pickering emulsions. This study aimed to enhance the emulsifying performance of native (NS) and waxy (WS) tapioca starches through antisolvent precipitation followed by esterification with 3% (w/v) octenyl succinic anhydride (OSA). Structural and functional changes were characterized by SEM, XRD, DSC, FTIR, contact angle measurements, and degree of substitution analysis. The modifications transformed the starch morphology from smooth granules into rough, aggregated particles and reduced crystallinity, gelatinization enthalpy, and the intensity of characteristic functional groups. Both starch types exhibited similar structural changes; however, the modified native starch (NSp-OSA) showed higher hydrophobicity (contact angle: 103.73 ± 0.50°) than the modified waxy starch (WSp-OSA, 84.83 ± 0.60°), resulting in improved emulsion stability. Emulsion screening using jojoba oil identified optimal starch-to-oil ratios of 2.0:1.2 g/g for NSp-OSA and 1.0:1.2 g/g for WSp-OSA. These conditions were then applied for encapsulating resveratrol (RES). Due to the poor solubility of RES in oil, a ternary solvent system comprising of PEG 400, jojoba oil, and olive oil (0.1:0.5:0.5:0.5 g/g) was formulated to enhance solubility and emulsion uniformity. The NSp-OSA formulation produced more stable RES-loaded emulsions than WSp-OSA. This study demonstrates the potential of modified tapioca starches as bio-based stabilizers for emulsion-based delivery systems.

1 Introduction

Pickering emulsions, stabilized by solid particles instead of conventional surfactants, have gained increasing attention for applications in the food, pharmaceutical, and cosmetic industries due to their enhanced stability and biocompatibility [1]. Starch, a biodegradable and renewable biopolymer, is particularly attractive as an eco-friendly stabilizer [2]. Tapioca starch is abundant, inexpensive, and easily modified; however, native starch granules usually lack the amphiphilic properties required for effective stabilization of oil-in-water (O/W) emulsions [3]. To improve their emulsifying ability, several strategies such as particle size reduction and surface hydrophobization have been explored. Among these, esterification with octenyl succinic anhydride (OSA) is a widely used method to increase starch surface activity and promote interfacial adsorption in emulsion systems [4, 5].

Resveratrol (RES), a naturally occurring polyphenolic compound, has attracted considerable attention due to its antioxidant, anti-inflammatory, and anticancer properties. Despite its therapeutic potential, the practical use of RES in functional food, cosmetic, and pharmaceutical formulations is limited by its poor water solubility, low chemical stability, and limited bioavailability.

Emulsion-based delivery systems offer an approach to enhance the solubility and stability of RES in aqueous formulations [6]. Successful encapsulation requires a formulation that can dissolve RES efficiently in the oil phase while maintains emulsion stability during storage. Pickering emulsions stabilized by modified starch particles represent a promising and sustainable strategy to achieving these goals using food-grade, bio-based materials [7, 8].

This study focuses on improving the emulsifying properties of native (NS) and waxy (WS) tapioca starches for stabilizing RES-loaded Pickering emulsions. Antisolvent precipitation using ethanol was employed to reduce particle size, followed by esterification with 3% (w/v) OSA to enhance hydrophobicity. The modified starches (NSp-OSA and WSp-OSA) were characterized in terms of morphology, crystallinity, thermal behavior, chemical properties, and wettability using SEM, XRD, DSC, FTIR, degree of substitution, and contact angle analyses. Their performance as stabilizers was evaluated through emulsion screening with jojoba oil and subsequent RES encapsulation using a ternary oil mixture designed to enhance RES solubility. This work provides comparative insights into how structural and surface property differences between modified native and waxy tapioca starches influence their ability to stabilize RES-loaded Pickering emulsions.

*Corresponding author : sukanya.t@sci.kmutnb.ac.th

2 Materials and Methods

2.1 Materials

Waxy and native tapioca starches were supplied by Thai Wah Public Co., Ltd. (Thailand). Ethanol was obtained from the Liquor Distillery Organization (Thailand), while octenyl succinic anhydride (OSA) was sourced from Tokyo Chemical Industry Co., Ltd. (Japan). Hydrochloric acid was purchased from RCI Labscan Co., Ltd. (Thailand), and sodium hydroxide from Supelco Inc. Cosmetic-grade *trans*-resveratrol, jojoba oil, and olive oil were acquired from Chanjao Longevity Co., Ltd. (Thailand). Polyethylene glycol 400 (PEG 400, cosmetic grade) was provided by S. Tong Chemicals (1985) Co., Ltd. Unless otherwise specified, all chemicals used were of analytical grade.

2.2 Preparation of nanoprecipitated starch

Two types of tapioca starch—native starch (NS) and waxy starch (WS)—were subjected to particle size reduction via antisolvent precipitation using ethanol, also known as ethanol nanoprecipitation, following a method adapted from [9]. A 1% (w/v) starch suspension was prepared by dispersing 8.00 g of starch in 800 mL of deionized (DI) water and stirring continuously at 200 rpm and 100°C for 30 min to achieve complete gelatinization. Once a homogeneous starch solution was obtained, the mixture was allowed to cool to room temperature (~30°C) while stirring continued. Ethanol (160 mL) was then added dropwise at a constant rate under continuous stirring. The mixture was stirred for an additional 8 h at ambient temperature. Subsequently, it was refrigerated at approximately 4°C for 15 h to promote starch precipitation. The resulting precipitate was collected and freeze-dried for 48 h, or until completely dry, yielding native starch precipitate (NSp) and waxy starch precipitate (WSp).

2.3 OSA modification of nanoprecipitated starch

NSp and WSp were each weighed at 5.00 g and dispersed in 95.00 mL of DI water. The suspension was stirred at 200 rpm at 35°C, and the pH was adjusted to 8.0–8.5 using a 3% (w/v) sodium hydroxide solution. Octenyl succinic anhydride (OSA) was then added at a concentration of 3% (w/v), based on the dry weight of starch. The reaction was carried out for 3 h under continuous stirring. After the reaction, the pH of the mixture was adjusted to 6.5 using 0.5 M hydrochloric acid solution. The modified starch was recovered by centrifugation at 5,000 rpm for 3 min. The supernatant was discarded, and the precipitate was washed with DI water and centrifuged again under the same conditions. This washing step was repeated twice. The resulting precipitate was then washed twice with 97% (v/v) ethanol and dried in an oven at 40°C for 24 h. The final products obtained were designated as NSp-OSA and WSp-OSA.

2.4 Characterization of starch

2.4.1 SEM analysis

The morphology of tapioca starch granules before and after OSA modification was examined using a scanning electron microscope or SEM (JEOL JSM-7610FPlus) at 3000× magnification to evaluate granule shape and surface characteristics. Samples were mounted on SEM stubs using carbon adhesive tape and directly introduced into the chamber for imaging [10].

2.4.2 X-ray diffraction

The crystalline structure of native and modified starches was analyzed via X-ray diffraction (XRD) using a D2 PHASER diffractometer (Bruker, Germany) equipped with Cu-Kα radiation ($\lambda = 1.5406$ Å), operating at 30 kV and 10 mA. Scans were recorded over a 2θ range of 5° to 60°, with a step size of 0.02° and a dwell time of 0.6 s per step. The relative crystallinity was calculated using Equation (1) [11]:

$$\text{Crystallinity} = (\text{Area under the peaks}) \times 100 / (\text{Total curve area}) \quad (1)$$

2.4.3 Thermal properties

Thermal transitions, particularly gelatinization behavior, were assessed by differential scanning calorimetry (DSC). Prior to analysis, starch samples were dried to a moisture content of approximately 7.7%. Around 10.623 mg of starch was suspended in deionized water at 30% (w/w) and loaded into a 60 µL stainless steel pan (CODE03190029) sealed with a volatile-resistant lid and tygon O-rings. Samples were equilibrated overnight at room temperature. DSC analysis was conducted from 0°C to 120°C at a heating rate of 10°C/min under a nitrogen atmosphere (flow rate: 20 mL/min) [11, 12]. The onset (To), peak (Tp), and conclusion (Tc) temperatures, along with gelatinization enthalpy (ΔH), were analyzed.

2.4.4 FTIR

Functional groups of the starches were characterized using a FT-IR spectrometer (PerkinElmer Spectrum 100, USA). The samples were mixed with potassium bromide (KBr) and pressed into translucent pellets using a manual hydraulic press at 5 N/m^2 for 3 min. FT-IR spectra were collected in the 450–4000 cm^{-1} range with a resolution of 4 cm^{-1}, averaging eight scans per sample [13].

2.4.5 Contact angle

Surface wettability of the starches before and after OSA modification was evaluated using water contact angle measurements. Samples were compressed into flat pellets using a manual hydraulic press at 5 N/m^2 for 3 min. A 5 µL droplet of deionized water was dispensed onto the sample surface at a controlled rate of 0.5 µL/s using a microsyringe. Measurements were conducted using an optical contact angle system (OCA15 Plus, DataPhysics Instruments GmbH, Filderstadt, Germany) with a 6×

parfocal zoom lens [14]. Each sample was analyzed in triplicate for reproducibility.

2.4.6 Degree of substitution

The degree of substitution (DS) of OSA-modified starches was determined using a titration method adapted from [15]. In brief, 1.00 g of modified starch was dispersed in 25.0 mL of 2.5 M HCl in isopropanol and stirred at 300 rpm for 10 min at room temperature. Subsequently, 20.0 mL of 90% (v/v) aqueous isopropanol was added, and the slurry was stirred continuously for 30 min. The mixture was then centrifuged at 300 rpm for 30 min. The supernatant was titrated with 0.1 M NaOH using phenolphthalein as the indicator. The DS was calculated using Equation (2):

$$DS = [0.162 \times (A \times M) / W]/[1 - (0.210 \times (A \times M) / W)] \qquad (2)$$

where A is the volume of NaOH (mL), M is the molarity of NaOH (mol/L), and W is the weight of starch sample (g).

2.5 Pickering emulsion formulation and evaluation

The preparation of Pickering emulsions was adapted from the method described in [16]. NSp-OSA and WSp-OSA were dispersed in DI water according to the compositions listed in Table 1. The starch suspensions were stirred at 200 rpm and 35°C for 10 min to ensure homogeneity of the aqueous phase. Jojoba oil was then gradually added dropwise to the suspension while homogenizing with a high-speed homogenizer at 15,000 rpm. After the complete addition of oil, homogenization was continued for an additional 3 min. The resulting emulsions were transferred into glass vials for stability testing at room temperature (~30°C). The physical appearance of the emulsions was monitored at time intervals of 5 min, 30 min, 1 h, and 24 h. Once the optimal Pickering emulsion formulation for jojoba oil was identified, it was used for resveratrol (RES) encapsulation. The final formulation consisted of 0.5% (w/w) jojoba oil, 0.1% (w/w) RES, 0.5% (w/w) polyethylene glycol 400 (PEG 400), and 0.5% (w/w) olive oil, with DI water added to adjust the total formulation to 100% (w/w).

Table 1. Formatting sections, subsections and subsubsections.

NSp-OSA or WSp-OSA (g)	Jojoba oil (g)	DI water (g)
0.05	1.20	98.75
0.10		98.70
0.20		98.60
1.00		97.80
2.00		96.00

3 Results and discussion

3.1 SEM analysis

The morphological characteristics of NS, WS, NSp, WSp, NSp-OSA, and WSp-OSA were examined using SEM, as illustrated in Figure 1. Native starches (NS, WS) exhibited smooth, spherical granules (~15–16 µm). Ethanol precipitation (NSp, WSp) caused partial granule disruption and increased surface roughness. After OSA modification (NSp-OSA, WSp-OSA), granules lost their spherical shape, appearing as rough, stone-like aggregates. Both starch types showed similar morphological changes throughout the process.

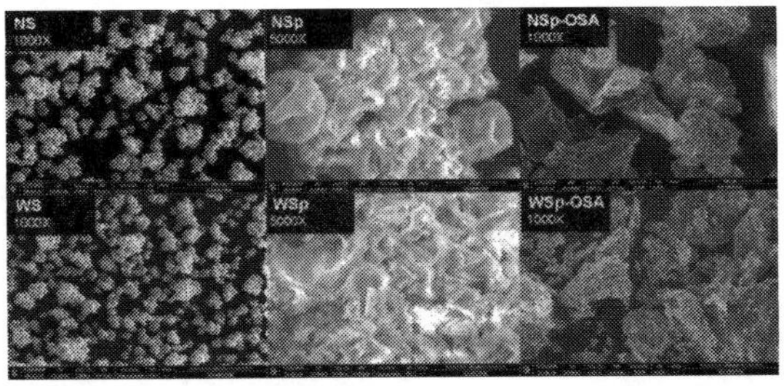

Fig. 1. SEM images of NSp, WSp, NSp-OSA, and WSp-OSA.

3.2 X-ray diffraction

Tapioca starch possesses a semicrystalline structure composed primarily of amylose and amylopectin. Native starches (NS and WS) exhibited distinct XRD peaks at 15°, 17°, and 23°, reflecting their high crystallinity (Figure 2). In contrast, ethanol-precipitated samples (NSp and WSp) showed broader peaks, indicating partial disruption of the crystalline regions. Following OSA modification, NSp-OSA and WSp-OSA displayed a single broad peak around 20°, suggesting significant structural rearrangement and a transition toward a more amorphous state due to esterification. Correspondingly, crystallinity decreased from 22.4% (NS) to 7.2% (NSp-OSA) and from 22.8% (WS) to 7.9% (WSp-OSA).

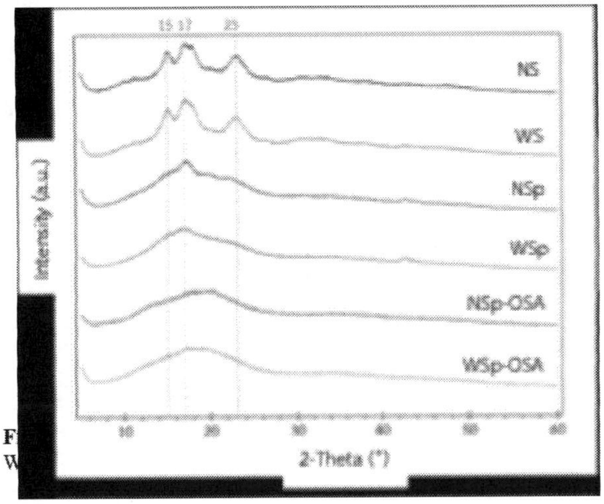

F
W

3.3 Thermal properties

Figure 3 and Table 2 show the DSC thermograms and thermal properties of NS, WS, NSp-OSA, and WSp-OSA, highlighting the impact of modification on starch gelatinization. Native starches (NS and WS) exhibited onset temperatures (To) of 62.16 ± 0.33°C and 66.38 ± 0.12°C, with peak temperatures (Tp) at 69.09 ± 0.12°C and 72.34 ± 0.23°C, respectively. In contrast, OSA-modified starches (NSp-OSA and WSp-OSA) showed significantly lower To values of 23.14 ± 1.14°C and 34.85 ± 0.09°C, along with a marked reduction in gelatinization enthalpy (ΔH)—from 16.16 ± 0.36 J/g to 0.18 ± 0.07 J/g for NSp-OSA, and from 17.43 ± 0.03 J/g to 0.96 ± 0.00 J/g for WSp-OSA.

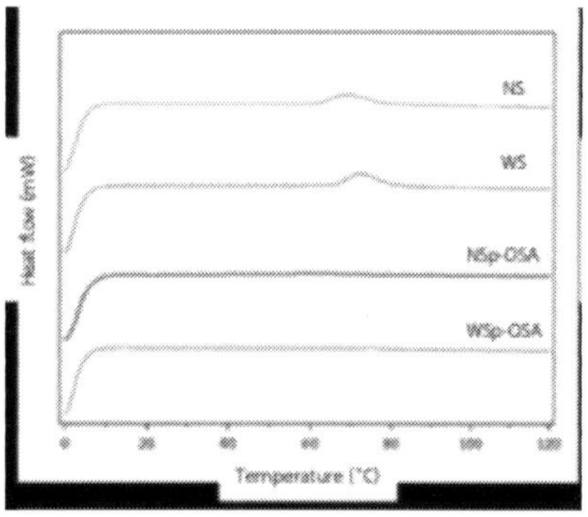

Fig. 3. DSC thermograms of NS, WS, NSp-OSA, and WSp-OSA.

These thermal changes indicate disruption of crystalline regions due to ethanol precipitation and OSA esterification, leading to reduced particle size, weakened hydrogen bonding, and delayed retrogradation. The lower gelatinization temperature enables the formation of gel-like surface layers under mild heating, enhancing particle surface activity and promoting more effective adsorption at the oil–water interface, thereby improving Pickering emulsion stability.

Table 2. Thermal properties of NS, WS, NSp-OSA, and WSp-OSA.

Sample	To (°C)	Tp (°C)	Tc (°C)	Enthalpy (ΔH, J/g)
NS	62.16 ± 0.33	69.09 ± 0.12	78.62 ± 0.33	16.16 ± 0.36
WS	66.38 ± 0.12	72.34 ± 0.23	80.43 ± 0.16	17.43 ± 0.03
NSp-OSA	23.14 ± 1.14	30.37 ± 0.51	34.93 ± 1.28	0.18 ± 0.07
WSp-OSA	34.85 ± 0.09	62.06 ± 0.08	68.60 ± 0.41	0.96 ± 0.00

3.4 FTIR

FT-IR analysis (Figure 4) confirmed the successful functionalization of tapioca starch with OSA. Native starches (NS and WS) exhibited characteristic absorption bands at ~3400 cm^{-1} (O–H stretching), 2920 cm^{-1} (C–H stretching), 1645 cm^{-1} (O–H bending of absorbed water), and 1018 cm^{-1} (C–O–C stretching of the glycosidic lickage). The ethanol-precipitated starches (NSp and WSp) showed broader O–H stretching bands, indicating increased hydrophilicity due to partial disruption of hydrogen bonding. In contrast, the OSA-modified starches (NSp-OSA and WSp-OSA) displayed new absorption peaks at 1720 cm^{-1} (C=O stretching of ester groups) and 1570 cm^{-1} (asymmetric stretching of $RCOO^-$), confirming successful esterification. However, these peaks were relatively weak, suggesting a low degree of substitution and indicating that complementary analytical methods may be required for further varification.

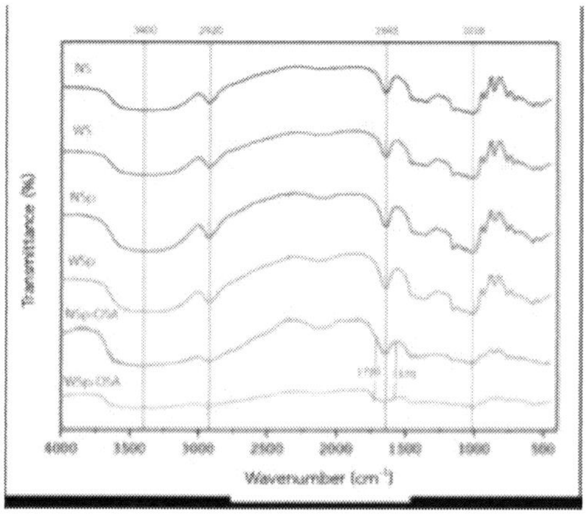

Fig. 4. FT-IR spectra of NS, WS, NSp, WSp, NSp-OSA, and WSp-OSA.

3.5 Degree of substitution and contact angle

The degree of substitution (DS) was evaluated to confirm the successful grafting of OSA onto starch molecules. The DS values for NSp-OSA and WSp-OSA were 0.032 ± 0.005 and 0.039 ± 0.009, respectively. As shown in Figure 5, native starches (NS and WS) exhibited water contact angles of 48.03 ± 1.28° and 52.63 ± 0.32°, respectively. These values increased slightly after ethanol precipitation to 65.00 ± 0.76° for NSp and 59.50 ± 0.36° for WSp. Following OSA modification, the contact angles increased significantly to 103.73 ± 0.50° for NSp-OSA and 84.83 ± 0.60° for WSp-OSA. This marked increase in hydrophobicity confirms the successful substitution of hydrophilic hydroxyl groups with lipophilic octenyl groups via esterification, in agreement with both FTIR and DS results.

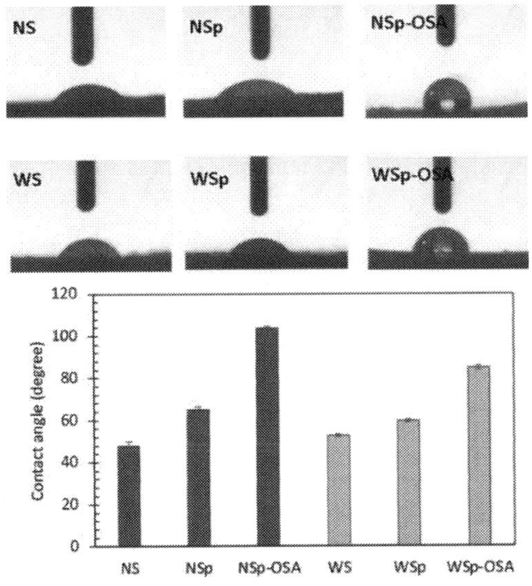

Fig. 5. Contact angle of NS, WS, NSp, WSp, NSp-OSA, and WSp-OSA.

3.6 Screening formulation of Pickering emulsion using NSp-OSA and WSp-OSA

To evaluate the emulsifying performance of modified tapioca starches, Pickering emulsions were prepared using 3% w/v NSp-OSA or WSp-OSA with varying starch-to-oil ratios, keeping the oil phase (jojoba oil) constant. Emulsion stability was assessed over 24 h at room temperature, as shown in Figure 6.

At lower starch-to-oil ratios (e.g., 0.05:1.2 g/g), emulsions appeared milky and homogeneous with minimal phase separation initially. Over time, both NSp-OSA-0.05 and WSp-OSA-0.05 showed slight creaming and increased clarity. Similar behavior was observed at 0.1:1.2 and 0.2:1.2 g/g, with gradual cream layer formation and minor starch sedimentation after 24 h.

At higher ratios (1.0:1.2 and 2.0:1.2 g/g), NSp-OSA-1.0 and NSp-OSA-2.0 emulsions remained stable with minimal separation, while WSp-OSA-1.0 showed slight sedimentation and WSp-OSA-2.0 displayed evident creaming and reduced stability.

In summary, NSp-OSA-2.0 and WSp-OSA-1.0 yielded the most stable emulsions. The greater contact angle of NSp-OSA (>90°) compared to WSp-OSA (~90°) enhanced its stabilizing ability. Excessive starch (e.g., WSp-OSA-2.0) resulted in foaming and instability.

Based on the results, the optimal Pickering emulsion formulations for resveratrol encapsulation were NSp-OSA-2.0 and WSp-OSA-1.0, which exhibited the most stable physical properties. These emulsions were selected for further use in encapsulating resveratrol.

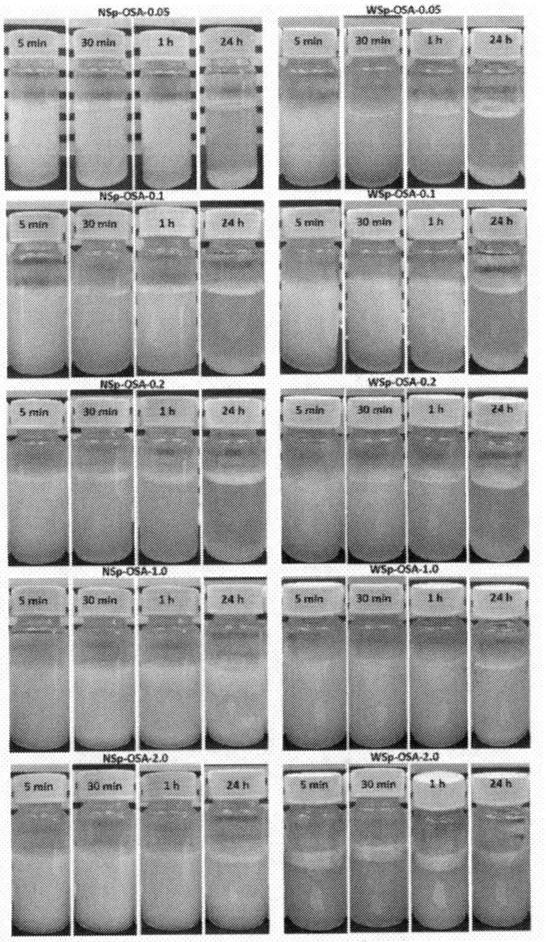

Fig. 6. Pickering emulsions prepared with NSp-OSA and WSp-OSA at various ratios and leave at room temperature for 24 h.

3.7 Solubility test and Pickering emulsion of RES

Prior to encapsulation in the Pickering emulsion, the solubility of RES was evaluated, as shown in Figure 7. In the first trial, using a 0.1:0.5 g/g ratio of RES to DI water, RES did not dissolve. Similarly, in the second trial, with a 0.1:0.5 g/g ratio of RES to jojoba oil (JO), RES remained undissolved. However, in the third trial, where a 0.1:0.5 g/g ratio of RES to PEG 400 (PEG) was tested, the RES dissolved completely, forming a clear solution.

To improve the solubility of 0.1 g of RES in jojoba oil (JO), a mixture of JO and PEG at a weight ratio of 0.5:0.5 was initially tested; however, slight phase separation was observed. Subsequently, the addition of olive oil (OO), forming a JO:PEG:OO mixture at a weight ratio of 0.5:0.5:0.5, resulted in enhanced solubility and a more homogeneous solution. Therefore, the formulation with a RES:PEG:JO:OO ratio of 0.1:0.5:0.5:0.5 g was selected for resveratrol encapsulation in the Pickering emulsion.

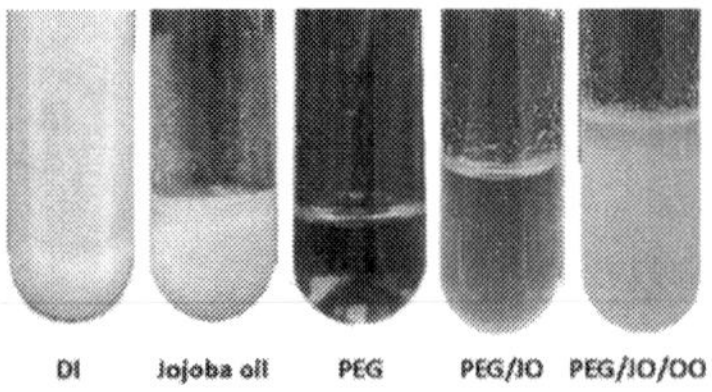

Fig. 7. Solubility of RES in DI water, JO, PEG400, and mixed solvents.

Pickering emulsion of RES using NSp-OSA and WSp-OSA were prepared using 1.2 g of oil phase comprising RES, PEG, JO, and OO at a weight ratio of 0.1:0.5:0.5:0.5. The emulsions were stored at room temperature (~30°C) for 24 h, as shown in Figure 8. The results indicate that the stability of the RES Pickering emulsions was significantly enhanced compared to those formulated with NSp-OSA-1.0 and WSp-OSA-2.0 in the presence of JO as the single oil component.

Fig. 8. Pickering emulsions of RES prepared using NSp-OSA-0.1 and WSp-OSA-2.0 with and oil phase comprising RES, PEG, JO, and OO at a weight ratio of 0.1:0.5:0.5:0.5, observed over a 24 h period at room temperature (~30 °C).

4 Conclusion

This study investigated the modification of native (NS) and waxy tapioca (WS) starches through antisolvent precipitation to reduce particle size and esterification with 3% (w/v) octenyl succinic anhydride (OSA) to enhance particle hydrophobicity for use in Pickering emulsion formulations. The modifications altered the starch morphology from smooth, spherical granules to rough, stone-like aggregates. Crystallinity decreased after modification, resulting in lower gelatinization enthalpy. Both starch types exhibited similar trends in morphology, crystallinity, thermal behavior, and functional group changes; however, they differed markedly in hydrophobicity, as reflected by water contact angles of 103.73 ± 0.50° for NSp-OSA and 84.83 ± 0.60° for WSp-OSA. This difference in surface hydrophobicity significantly affected their ability to stabilize Pickering emulsions.

Screening with jojoba oil identified optimal formulations at starch-to-oil ratios of 2.0:1.2 g/g for NSp-OSA and 1.0:1.2 g/g for WSp-OSA. These conditions were applied for resveratrol (RES) encapsulation. Solubility testing indicated that RES had poor solubility in jojoba but dissolved well in PEG 400, while the addition of olive oil improved the homogeneity of the oil phase. Consequently, a mixed oil system (RES: PEG : JO : OO at 0.1:0.5:0.5:0.5 g/g) was employed for preparing RES-loaded Pickering emulsions. This formulation significantly improved emulsion stability, with NSp-OSA demonstrating superior performance compared to WSp-OSA.

Overall, this study provides valuable insights into the functional enhancement of tapioca starches and their potential as bio-based stabilizers for emulsion-based delivery systems and other value-added applications.

We gratefully acknowledge the financial support from King Mongkut's University of Technology North Bangkok (Grant No. KMUTNB-67-BASIC-18). We also wish to express our appreciation to the Department of Industrial Chemistry, Faculty of Applied Science, King Mongkut's University of Technology North Bangkok, and the Department of Chemical Engineering, Faculty of Engineering, Mahidol University, for their generous assistance and access to critical analytical instruments.

Author contributions

Rapeeporn Wannarat.: Investigation and Methodology. **Anchana Pleanklay.**: Investigation and Methodology. **Suthida Boonsith.**: Conceptualization, Resources, and Validation. **Sukanya Thepwatee.**: Conceptualization, Data Curation, Formal Analysis, Graphic Preparation, Writing – Original Draft, Reviewing, and Editing, Funding Acquisition, Supervision, Project Administration, and Validation.

References

1. L. E. Low, S. P. Siva, Y. K. Ho, E. S. Chan, B. T. Tey, Recent advances of characterization techniques for the formation, physical properties and stability of Pickering emulsion. Adv. Colloid Interface Sci. **277**, 102117 (2020)
2. R. L. J. Almeida, S. S. Monteiro, N. C. Santos, N. S. Rios, E.S. dos Santos, Starch modification and its application in Pickering emulsion stabilization: a review. J. Food Meas. Charact.**18**, 4984-5003 (2024)
3. S. Ge, L. Xiong, M. Li, J. Liu, J. Yang, R. Chang, et al., Characterizations of Pickering emulsions stabilized by starch nanoparticles: Influence of starch variety and particle size. Food Chem. **234**, 339-47 (2017)
4. S. Simsek, M. Ovando-Martinez, A. Marefati, M. Sjöö, M. Rayner, Chemical composition, digestibility and emulsification properties of octenyl succinic esters of various starches. Food Res. Int. **75**, 41-9 (2015)
5. E. Agama-Acevedo, L. A. Bello-Perez, Starch as an emulsions stability: the case of octenyl succinic anhydride (OSA) starch. Curr. Opin. Food Sci. **13**, 78-83 (2017)

6. D.N. Dikmetas, H. Yenipazar, A. Can Karaca, Recent advances in encapsulation of resveratrol for enhanced delivery. Food Chem. **460**, 140475 (2024)
7. M. Matos, A. Marefati, P. Barrero, M. Rayner, G. Gutiérrez, Resveratrol loaded Pickering emulsions stabilized by OSA modified rice starch granules. Food Res. Int. **139**, 109837 (2021)
8. W. Bi, G. Liyuan, W. Wenjuan, X. Qiang, Skin targeting of resveratrol-loaded starch-based Pickering emulsions: preparation, characterization, and evaluation. Colloid Polym. Sci. **299**, 1383-95 (2021)
9. Y. Qin, C. Liu, S. Jiang, L. Xiong, Q. Sun, Characterization of starch nanoparticles prepared by nanoprecipitation: Influence of amylose content and starch type. Ind. Crops Prod. **87**, 182-90 (2016)
10. H. Dong, Q. Zhang, J. Gao, L. Chen, T. Vasanthan, Comparison of morphology and rheology of starch nanoparticles prepared from pulse and cereal starches by rapid antisolvent nanoprecipitation. Food Hydrocoll. **119**, 106828 (2021)
11. M. J. dos Santos Alves, P. M. Calvo Torres de Freitas, A.R. Monteiro, G. Ayala Valencia, Impact of the Acidified Hydroethanolic Solution on the Physicochemical Properties of Starch Nanoparticles Produced by Anti-Solvent Precipitation. Starch – Stärke, **73**, 2100034 (2021)
12. J. M. Fang, P. A. Fowler, C. Sayers, P. A. Williams, The chemical modification of a range of starches under aqueous reaction conditions. Carbohydr. Polym. **55**, 283-9 (2004)
13. H. Li, Y. Ma, L. Yu, H. Xue, Y. Wang, J. Chen et al., Construction of octenyl succinic anhydride modified porous starch for improving bioaccessibility of β-carotene in emulsions. RSC Adv. **10**, 8480-9 (2020)
14. L. Dai, C. Sun, Y. Wei, L. Mao, Y. Gao, Characterization of Pickering emulsion gels stabilized by zein/gum arabic complex colloidal nanoparticles. Food Hydrocoll. **74**, 239-48 (2018)
15. J. Zhang, C. Ran, X. Jiang, J. Dou, Impact of octenyl succinic anhydride (OSA) esterification on microstructure and physicochemical properties of sorghum starch. LWT. **152**, 112320 (2021)
16. B. Guo, C. Liu, L. Grossmann, J. Weiss, Pickering emulsion stabilized by hydrolyzed starch: Effect of the molecular weight. J. Colloid Interface Sci. **612**, 525-35 (2022)

Sequential Production of Levan and Xanthan Gum via Integrated Fermentation for Enhanced Carbon Utilization

Srividhya Krishnan[1], *Sivappriya* Nadimuthu[1], *Ratheeshkumar* Shanmugam[1], *Malinee* Sriariyanun[2], and *Ponnusami* Venkatachalam[1*]

[1]Bioprocess Intensification Laboratory, Center for Bioenergy, School of Chemical & Biotechnology, SASTRA Deemed University, Thirumalaisamudram, Thanjavur, India
[2]Biorefinery and Process Automation Engineering Center, Department of Chemical and Process Engineering, The Sirindhorn International Thai-German Graduate School of Engineering, King Mongkut's University of Technology North Bangkok, 10800 Bangkok, Thailand

Abstract. Microbial exopolysaccharides (EPS) have gained significant attention in recent years due to their diverse applications in food and healthcare sectors. These polymers can exist as either homo- or heteropolysaccharides depending on their monomeric sugar composition. Among these, levan, a fructose-based homopolymer, holds considerable potential in pharmaceutical and food applications. Its biosynthesis by *Bacillus* species using sucrose as the sole carbon source has been extensively studied. Similarly, xanthan gum, a heteropolysaccharide produced by *Xanthomonas campestris*, consists of a β-(1→4)-D-glucose backbone with trisaccharide side chains comprising mannose and glucuronic acid. Xanthan is widely utilized in the food industry as a stabilizer and rheology modifier. *Bacillus* spp. produces levan using a two-step enzymatic process. In the initial step, sucrose is hydrolysed into glucose and fructose. In the second step levan is formed by the polymerization of fructose units. This process leaves a glucose-rich spent medium, which is typically underutilized. The present study proposes a sequential fermentation strategy to valorize the residual glucose and improve overall carbon efficiency. In the first stage, fermentation of 100 g/L of pure sucrose was conducted using *B. subtilis* MTCC 441. Levan was precipitated from the culture broth using isopropyl alcohol (IPA), resulting in a yield of 0.39 g levan/g sucrose. Post-precipitation, the IPA was recovered and the clarified supernatant was concentrated and subjected to sugar profiling via HPLC. The analysis revealed 92.16 g/L of glucose and 10.43 g/L of residual sucrose, indicating significant glucose availability for further processing. To utilize, this residual glucose, the recovered broth was diluted and supplemented with essential micronutrients to formulate a medium containing 20 g/L of glucose for xanthan production. The second-stage fermentation was carried out using *X. campestris* NCIM 2956, which yielded 2.17 g/L of xanthan gum. The structural integrity and identity of the produced EPSs—levan and xanthan—were confirmed using NMR and FT-IR spectroscopy. This study presents a cost-effective and sustainable bioprocessing strategy that integrates levan and xanthan production via sequential fermentation, thereby enhancing carbon conversion efficiency and reducing downstream waste.

1 Introduction

Biopolymers are natural polymers produced by living organisms like plants or microbes that consist of repeating monomeric units covalently bonded to form larger molecules. They have versatile applications, especially in industries like food and medical, owing to their biocompatible, biodegradable and non-toxic nature [1]. Most of the microbial polysaccharides are carbohydrate-based, as these microorganisms transform the carbon and nitrogen into intracellular or extracellular polysaccharides through their unique metabolic pathways [2]. These microbial polysaccharides are usually water-soluble and have a distinct role in the food industries as they are used as stabilisers, emulsifiers, gelling agents, coagulants, etc, to improve the quality and texture of food [1].

Levan is one such fructose-based homopolysaccharide that has unique properties produced mainly using *Bacillus* spp. with sucrose as a primary carbon source. Studies have optimised the production conditions for levan [3]. Another commercially important biopolymer is the xanthan gum, which is produced *by Xanthomonas* sp. with glucose as the carbon source. It is a heteropolysaccharide consisting of repeating units of glucose, mannose, and glucuronic acid [4]. Both levan and xanthan are water-soluble exopolysaccharides with potential applications in the food industry.

During levan fermentation, the sucrose breaks into fructose and glucose, where the fructose molecules polymerise to yield levan by the action of the enzyme levansucrase. A major portion of the glucose produced is not consumed in levan production and hence remains as a byproduct in the fermentation broth. Post-fermentation the

*Corresponding author : vponnu@chem.sastra.edu

levan is obtained by precipitation using a suitable anti-solvent like isopropyl alcohol or ethanol. After product recovery, the spent solvent is recovered by distillation, and the spent media is discarded. Since this spent media contains residual fermentable sugars (mainly glucose and traces of sucrose and fructose), it can be converted to a bioproduct to improve the overall economy of the process. The novelty of this study lies in the development of an integrated bioprocess that utilizes residual fermentable sugars, primarily glucose, from levan fermentation spent media for the sequential fermentation of xanthan gum. The approach addresses a critical limitation in conventional levan production, unutilized by product glucose, by enabling its conversion into xanthan gum to improve overall economy of the process. Thus, this study could provide a potential way of producing two commercially important biopolymers (levan and xanthan) and enhancing carbon flux utilisation.

2 Materials and Methods

2.1 Microbial culture conditions

Two bacterial strains, *Bacillus subtilis* MTCC441 (Microbial Type Culture Collection, Chandigarh, India) and *Xanthomonas campestris* (NCIM 2954) (National Collection of Industrial Microorganisms, Pune, India) are used in the study. B. *subtilis* MTCC441 was cultured in Luria Bertani broth for 20 hours at 37°C, and MGYP (malt extract 3g/L, glucose 10g/L, yeast extract 3 g/L) was used for culturing *X. campestris* cells at 30°C for 24 hours.

2.2 Production media formulation and stage-I fermentation

The levan production was formulated according to the optimised protocol as per [3]. Briefly, the medium consists of pure sucrose (100 g/L), yeast extract (2 g/L), ammonium sulphate (3 g/L), potassium dihydrogen phosphate (1 g/L), magnesium sulphate (0.6 g/L), and manganese sulphate (0.2 g/L), with initial pH adjusted to 7 before autoclaving. About 10% (v/v) inoculum was added to 100 mL production media taken in 250 mL conical flask, and the fermentation was carried out at 37°C for 16 hours.

2.3 Levan recovery and residual sugar estimation

After the stage-I fermentation, the cells were centrifuged at 8000 rpm for 10 minutes and kept for drying at 60°C. The supernatant was adjusted to pH 11, and ice-cold isopropyl alcohol (IPA) at a 1:3 (supernatant: IPA) ratio was added. Followed by levan recovery by centrifugation at 8000 rpm for 10 minutes. The precipitated levan was kept for drying at 60°C.

The IPA is recovered from the spent medium using a rotary evaporator and concentrated spent media is obtained. The sugar fraction was analysed using High Performance Liquid Chromatography (HPLC) with a Carbo-sep CHO 782 Pb column equipped with a Refractive index (RI) detector. The sucrose, glucose and fructose remaining after the fermentation were estimated.

2.4 Stage - II fermentation

The xanthan gum fermentation media was formulated by diluting the sample to a glucose concentration of 20 g/L. The media was autoclaved, and 10 % (v/v) of seed culture was inoculated and kept for fermentation at 30°C for 5 days at 200 rpm.

2.5 Xanthan recovery and final sugar estimation

Followed by the fermentation period, the media was autoclaved at 121°C for 10 min. Then the cells were centrifuged at 8000 rpm for 10 minutes. The remaining supernatant was added with 1:3 ice-cold acetone to precipitate the xanthan gum. Finally, the acetone was recovered by distillation, and the residual media were analysed using HPLC.

2.6 Characterisation using NMR and FT-IR

The exopolysaccharides levan and xanthan produced were confirmed using ^{13}C NMR, ^{1}H NMR (JEOL 600 MHz NMR, JNM-ECZ600R/S1), and FT-IR (Perkin Elmer Spectrum 100) analysis. The samples were dissolved in D_2O for NMR analysis.

3 Results

3.1 Levan yield and remaining sugar estimation

In stage-I fermentation, the cell yield was about 3.23 ± 0.18 g/L, and the levan yield of 38.36 ± 0.41 g/L was achieved. The fermentation was started with 10 g of sucrose, following the fermentation levan was precipitated, and the supernatant was rotary evaporated. The amount of residual sugars in the concentrated media was found to be 1.46 g, 3.66 g, and 1.82 g of sucrose, glucose and fructose, respectively. Here, the remaining sucrose corresponds to the unconverted sucrose. The fructose amount is lower due to its dual usage in cell growth and levan production, while the glucose is only used for cell growth and maintenance.

For the stage - II fermentation, the xanthan media was formulated by diluting the supernatant to 20 g/L glucose concentration. Other xanthan production media compounds were supplemented.

3.2 Xanthan yield and final sugar estimation

The stage - II fermentation using *X. campestris* resulted in a biomass yield of 5.135 ± 0.1484 g/L, and xanthan yield of 2.170 ± 0.1838 g/L. The final sugar in the broth was estimated after stage - II fermentation, and the broth contained about 0.319 g of fructose. The residual sucrose was completely consumed by the *X. campestris* for its growth, and hence, sucrose was not present in the

https://doi.org/10.1051/e3sconf/202567901008

fermented broth. Similarly, glucose concentration was very less (0.033 g) in the broth as the *X. campestris* consumes glucose for its metabolism. The sugar level at each fermentation stage is shown in Figure 1.

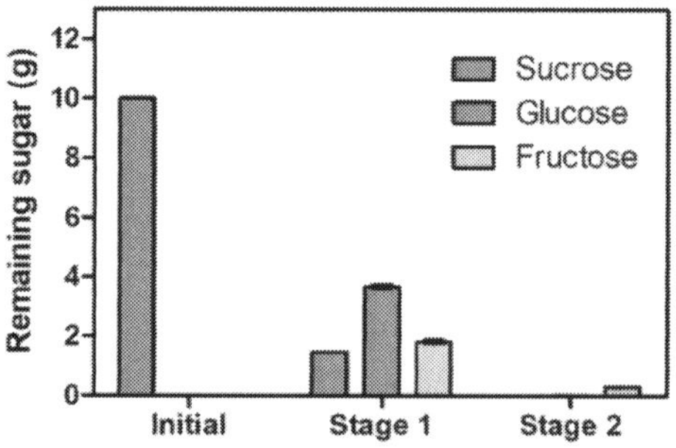

Fig. 1. Sugar remaining in the fermentation broth after each stage of fermentation

3.3 Levan and xanthan confirmation using NMR

Levan is a fructan polysaccharide composed of β (2-6)-linked fructosyl units with an initial α -D-glucopyranose residue, and it displays distinctive NMR characteristics that differentiate it from related fructans such as inulin. In the 1H NMR spectrum, the C6 methylene protons of the fructosyl backbone, indicative of β (2-6) linkages, resonate at 3.66 ppm and 3.49 ppm. Protons at C1 (3.85 ppm), C3 (4.13 ppm), and C4 (4.27 ppm) are attributed to hydrogen-bonding interactions that stabilize the polymer's helical conformation, while the C5 proton of the fructofuranose ring is observed downfield at 4.73 ppm due to deshielding by adjacent glycosidic bonds (Figure 2). The presence of an anomeric proton signal near 5.18 ppm confirms the α-D-glucose unit at the reducing end. In the 13C NMR spectrum, the signals for C2 (104 ppm) and C6 (60.66 ppm) are characteristic of the β (2-6) linkages, while peaks at 80.27 ppm (C5), 76.09 ppm (C3), 75.53 ppm (C4), and 62.09 ppm (C1) correspond to the respective carbons in the fructosyl units [5].

a)

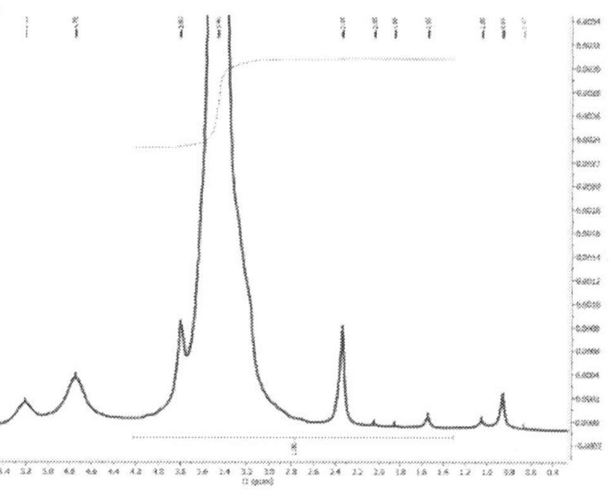

b)

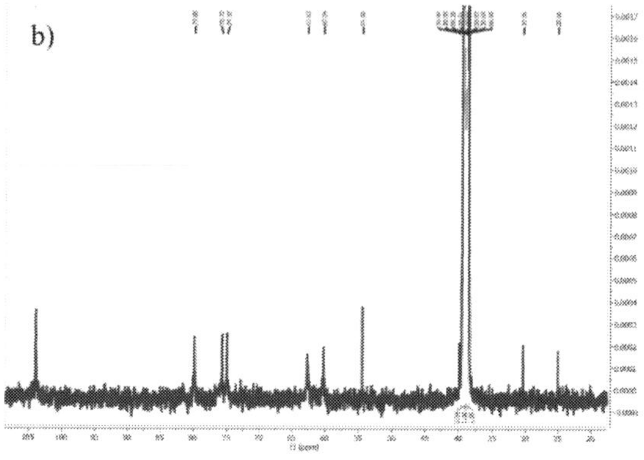

Fig. 2. NMR of levan polymer a). ^{1}H proton, b). ^{13}C carbon.

Xanthan, a cellulose-based polymer, has a side chain consisting of a mannose residue acetylated at C6, linked to galacturonic acid, followed by a terminal mannose bearing a pyruvate group. Proton NMR analysis reveals distinct structural features: the pyruvate methyl group is identified by a resonance at 1.16 ppm, while the acetyl methyl group appears at 1.90 ppm. The anomeric proton of the β -D-glucopyranosyl unit in the cellulose backbone is observed at 4.62 ppm, whereas the α -D-mannopyranosyl anomeric proton resonates at 4.74 ppm. The C5 proton of galacturonic acid, influenced by the carboxylate group, is detected at 4.49 ppm. Broad signals between 3.10–3.58 ppm correspond to hydroxyl protons, consistent with hydrogen bonding in the polysaccharide matrix [6-9]. A separate anomeric proton signal at 5.08 ppm further confirms the mannose residue in the side chain (Figure 3). These assignments align with xanthan's established structure, where acetyl and pyruvate substituents enhance solubility and rheological properties, while anomeric configurations stabilize the helical conformation critical for its functionality.

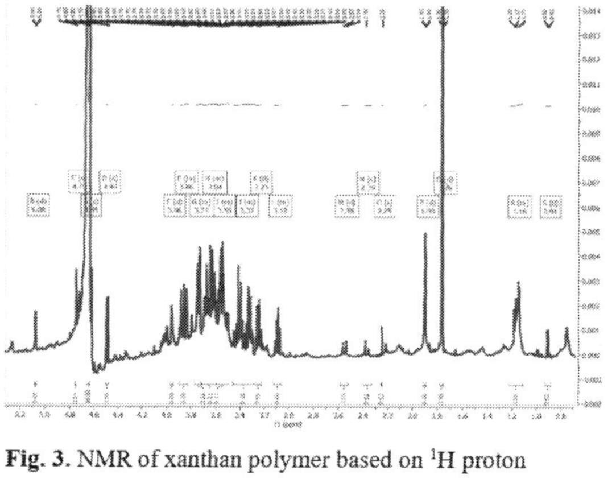

Fig. 3. NMR of xanthan polymer based on ^{1}H proton

3.4 Confirmation using FT-IR analysis

FTIR analysis of levan and xanthan reveals distinct spectral features corresponding to their chemical structures. For levan, characteristic peaks include a strong O H stretching vibration at 3392 cm^{-1} (hydroxyl group), a C–C stretch at 2929 cm^{-1} indicative of the furanose ring, a C–O stretch at 1346 cm^{-1} within hydroxyl groups, and a prominent ether linkage (C–O–C) at 1114 cm^{-1}. In contrast, xanthan shows a broad O–H stretch at 3450 cm^{-1} (hydroxyl groups), C–C and C–H stretching bands at 2883 cm^{-1} and 2817 cm^{-1} (both related to the furanose ring), and notable carbonyl absorptions at 1765 cm^{-1} (carboxylic acid) and 1633 cm^{-1} (acetyl group). Additional peaks include a C–O stretch at 1415 cm^{-1} (hydroxyl group) and an ether linkage (C–O–C) at 1117 cm^{-1}, further confirming the polysaccharide backbone and functional diversity of xanthan (Figure 4).

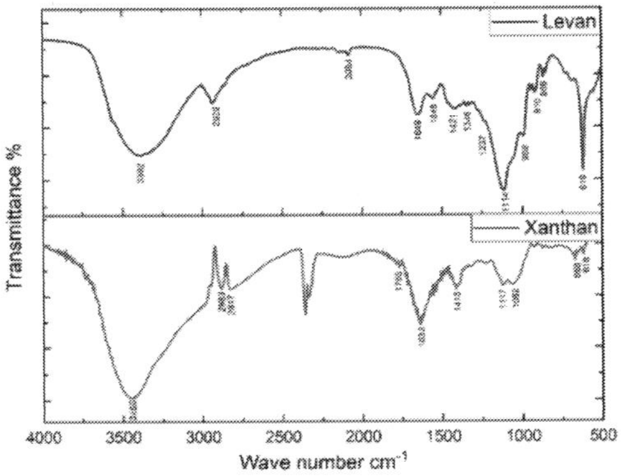

Fig. 4. FT-IR analysis of levan and xanthan

4 Discussion

Studies have demonstrated the co-production of polyhydroxyalkanoates (PHA) along with biohydrogen [10]. In a similar attempt by [11], co-production of PHB and violacein was achieved using *Iodobacter* sp PCH194 isolated from the Himalaya. Even the co-production of PHA and an exopolysaccharide was achieved [12] from pine hydrolysate as an alternative carbon source. In an attempt by [13], they have achieved co-production of P3HB (53 %) and gluconic acid (133 g/L) using *Halomonas elongate*. In a similar study by [14], they have co-produced PHA along with ethanol, where they have investigated on the impact of ethanol on carbon flux of the PHA production. All these studies have produced PHA or PHB polymer, which are usually obtained along with the cell biomass, and the supernatant contains the exopolysaccharides [14]. In an attempt by [16], they have achieved sequential production of PHA along with levan [17]. has previously reported sequential production of levan with poly-ε-lysine through microbial fermentation using sucrose as substrate. Therefore, we have tried to produce levan along with xanthan gum through microbial fermentation.

Here, in our presented study, we aimed to produce two biopolymers (levan and xanthan), both of which are exopolysaccharides secreted in the fermentation broth. Initially, the fermentation was started with sucrose (10 g) as a carbon source for the levan production. We were able to get around 38.36 ± 0.41 g/L of levan after the first fermentation. Following this, the media is left with 1.46 g of sucrose, 3.66 g of glucose and 1.82 g of fructose. For xanthan production, the left-out media was diluted five times to attain a 20 g/L (1.98 g) of glucose concentration, while the fructose of 0.98 g and sucrose of 0.79 g remained in the media. Upon the second fermentation, xanthan was produced at 2.17 ± 0.184 g/L. The final media remaining was left with 0.0328 g of glucose, 0.319 g of fructose and zero sucrose. From the results, we can infer that the *X. campestris* was able to consume sucrose and glucose to the maximum extent, along with fructose in moderation. Therefore, for further application of this study may include the strategy to utilize hydrolysate sugars obtained from biorefining process of lignocellulose biomass [18] for productions of levan and xanthan. This target will help to support the sustainable development goals, especially SDG12 and circular economy to reduce consumption of natural resources [19].

5 Conclusion

The production of levan and xanthan gum was achieved using a sequential fermentation method. From the results, we can observe that the spent media stream after the fermentation of levan can be efficiently used for the production of xanthan gum, in sequential fermentation. It can also be observed that the remaining sucrose and some amounts of fructose are also being utilised by the *X. campestris*, as it has the ability to consume both mono and disaccharides. From the study, it can be seen that one of its strengths lies in the efficient utilization of resources. This is a notable advantage, as research on the application of fructose is less common compared to other types of sugars. Therefore, this study has the potential to be further developed to add value in industrial applications. This integrated strategy helps in maximising the resource by improving the overall economic feasibility.

The Authors thank SASTRA DEEMED UNIVERSITY for the research facility and support. Srividhya Krishnan sincerely thanks CSIR for her Senior Research Fellowship (SRF), award no: 35110781, File no: 09/1095(18700)/2024-EMR-I.

References

1. J. Baranwal, B. Brajesh, F. Antonella, L. D. Giovanna, K. Amit, Biopolymer: A Sustainable Material for Food and Medical Applications, Polymers. **14**, 983 (2022). https://doi.org/10.3390/polym14050983
2. M. Sharma, T. Nihed, K. Imen, R. Tarek, Microbial Biopolymers: From Production to Environmental Applications—a Review, Applied Sciences. **14**, 5081 (2024). https://doi.org/10.3390/app14125081
3. Chidambaram, J. C. A. Sailaja, V. Bhuvaneshwari, K. S. Kartik, M. P. Krishna, R. S. Saravanan, V. Ponnusami, Studies on Solvent Precipitation of Levan Synthesized Using Bacillus Subtilis MTCC

441, Heliyon **5**, e02414 (2019). https://doi.org/10.1016/j.heliyon.2019.e02414

4. H. Li, X. Ronge, W. Zongji, L. Guantian, Advancements in Xanthan Gum-Based Film and Coating for Food Packaging, Carbohydrate Polymers. **356**, 123409 (2025). https://doi.org/10.1016/j.carbpol.2025.123409
5. B. Veerapandian, S. R. Shanmugam, S. Varadhan, K. K. Sarwareddy, K. P. Mani, V. Ponnusami, Levan Production from Sucrose Using Chicken Feather Peptone as a Low Cost Supplemental Nutrient Source, Carbohydrate Polymers. **227**, (2020). https://doi.org/10.1016/j.carbpol.2019.115361
6. S. Faria, L. O. P. Carmen, A. L. M. Sérgio, G. H. T. Manuel, M. R. Miriam, P.F. Francisca, L. C. Vicelma, Characterization of Xanthan Gum Produced from Sugar Cane Broth, Carbohydrate Polymers. **86**, 469–76 (2011). https://doi.org/10.1016/j.carbpol.2011.04.063
7. J. Kang, Y. Hongxia, L. Xinxue, H. Chao, L. Qin, C. Liting, Z. Jixiang, L. Yan, W. Shujun, G. Qingbin, Structural, Rheological and Functional Properties of Ultrasonic Treated Xanthan Gums, International Journal of Biological Macromolecules. **246**, 125650 (2023). https://doi.org/10.1016/j.ijbiomac.2023.125650
8. M. Rinaudo, M. Milas, F. Lambert, M. Vincendon, Proton and Carbon-13 NMR Investigation of Xanthan Gu. ACS Publications. (2002) https://doi.org/10.1021/ma00239a018
9. M. Takemasa, N. Katsuyoshi, Solution Structure of Molecular Associations Investigated Using NMR for Polysaccharides: Xanthan/Galactomannan Mixtures. *Journal of Physical Chemistry B.* **120**, 3027–37 (2016). https://doi.org/10.1021/acs.jpcb.5b11665
10. D. Thulasidharan, A. Arumugam, B. U. Kiran, Research and Economic Perspectives on an Integrated Biorefinery Approach for the Simultaneous Production of Polyhydroxyalkanoates and Biohydrogen. *International Journal of Biological Macromolecules.* **193**, 1937–51 (2021). https://doi.org/10.1016/j.ijbiomac.2021.11.025
11. V. Kumar, D. Sanyukta, K. Subhash, K. Sanjay, S. Dharam, Bioprocess for Co-Production of Polyhydroxybutyrate and Violacein Using Himalayan Bacterium *Iodobacter* sp. PCH194. Bioresource Technology. **319**, 124235 (2021). https://doi.org/10.1016/j.biortech.2020.124235
12. S. K. Bhatia, G. Ranjit, K. Byungchan, K. Suhyun, C. Do-Hyun, J. Heeju, K. Yun-Gon, K. Jae-Seok, Y. Yung-Hun, Coproduction of Exopolysaccharide and Polyhydroxyalkanoates from *Sphingobium Yanoikuyae* BBL01 Using Biochar Pretreated Plant Biomass Hydrolysate, Bioresource Technology. **361**, 127753 (2022). https://doi.org/10.1016/j.biortech.2022.127753
13. T. Leandro, M. Conceição Oliveira, M. Manuela R. da Fonseca, M. Teresa Cesário, Co-Production of Poly(3-Hydroxybutyrate) and Gluconic Acid from Glucose by Halomonas Elongata, Bioengineering. **10**, 643 (2023). https://doi.org/10.3390/bioengineering10060643
14. C. Rangel, D. L. Nídia, A. M. R. Maria, C. Gilda, Dynamics in the Profile of Biopolymers Produced by Mixed Microbial Cultures from Ethanol-Rich Feedstocks, Journal of Environmental Chemical Engineering. **12**, 112609 (2024). https://doi.org/10.1016/j.jece.2024.112609
15. de Siqueira, C. Edmilson, A. A. Aline, E. C. S. Páblo, P. S. B. Maria, M. H. Laureen, Polyhydroxyalkanoates and Exopolysaccharides: An Alternative for Valuation of the Co-Production of Microbial Biopolymers, Biotechnology Progress. **40**, e3412 (2024). https://doi.org/10.1002/btpr.3412
16. E. C. Siqueira, M. H. Laureen, Sequential Production of Two Biopolymers-Polyhydroxyalkanoate and Levan by Microbial Fermentation, Research, Society and Development. **12**, e25212340745–e25212340745 (2023). https://doi.org/10.33448/rsd-v12i3.40745
17. I. L. Shih, W. Tsaur-Chin, C. Shou-Zoo, L. Gen-Der, Sequential Production of Two Biopolymers-Levan and Poly-ε-Lysine by Microbial Fermentation, Bioresource Technology. **102**, 3966–69 (2011). https://doi.org/10.1016/j.biortech.2010.11.066
18. S. Areeya, E. J. Panakkal, P. Kunmanee, A. Tawai, S. Amornraksa, M. Sriariyanun, A. Kaoloun, N. Hartini, Y. S. Chen, M. Kchoau, S. Dasari, M. P. Gundupalli, A review of sugarcane biorefinery: From waste to value-added products, Applied Science and Engineering Progress. **17**, 7402 (2024). https://doi.org/10.14416/j.asep.2024.06.004
19. R. J. P. Latiza, R. V Rubi, Circular economy integration in 1G+2G sugarcane bioethanol production: application of carbon capture, utilization, closed-loop systems and waste valorization for sustainability, Applied Science and Engineering Progress. **18**, 7448 (2025). https://doi.org/10.14416/j.asep.2024.07.005

Characterisation and Optimisation of Succinoglycan from Garden Grass using *Agrobacterium radiobacter* NCIM 2443

Sharad J S[1], *Amrutha Shree* R[2], *Bhuvaneshwari* Veerapandian[2], *Saravanan Ramiah* Shanmugam[2,3], *Srividhya* Krishnan[2], *Nanthini Devi* Senthilventhan[2], *Malinee* Sriariyanun[4], and *Ponnusami* Venkatachalam[2,*]

[1]Department of Biotechnology, IIT Madras, Chennai, India
[2]Bioprocess Intensification Laboratory, Center for Bioenergy, School of Chemical & Biotechnology, SASTRA Deemed University, Thirumalaisamudram, Thanjavur, India
[3]Current Affiliation: Department of Biosystems Engineering, Auburn University, Auburn, Alabama, 36849 USA
[4]Biorefinery and Process Automation Engineering Center, Department of Chemical and Process Engineering, The Sirindhorn International Thai-German Graduate School of Engineering, King Mongkut's University of Technology North Bangkok, 10800 Bangkok, Thailand

Abstract. Succinoglycan is an exopolysaccharide that is produced mainly by soil-dwelling microorganisms. It has certain unique structural properties, making it a super viscosifying agent and a thermally stable gel. These properties are contributed by its acidic and water-soluble nature. This heteropolymer is made up of one galactose residue for every seven glucose residues and also includes certain non-carbohydrate residues, namely succinate, acetate and pyruvate. The polymer finds various applications as a thickener and emulsifier for the food industry, fluid loss agent for the cement industry, as a cosmetic additive, etc. Currently, commercial production of succinoglycan is mainly through conventional media. This has a direct effect on the production costs and thus limits the market potential of the biopolymer. This calls for researching low-cost carbon sources. One such carbon source is garden grass, which is being produced and wasted in tons every year. The present study aims to hydrolyze the waste garden grass using chemical methods to recover fermentable sugars and to use these sugars along with nutrient supplementation for succinoglycan production. Initially, we have characterized the garden grass, which had 19.13% extractives. Further, the cellulose content was estimated to be 31.11±2.70 %, and lignin content was estimated to be 16.05 %. The maximum reducing sugar of 0.54 g per g of grass was obtained using 2% H_2SO_4, which was further used for the production of succinoglycan using microbial fermentation with the *Agrobacterium radiobacter* NCIM 2443 strain. The carbon source, glucose concentration, and C:N ratio were optimized for maximum succinoglycan production. The produced polymer was then characterized using NMR and FT-IR analysis.

1 Introduction

Biopolymers are basically polymers that are produced by living things like microorganism. It can also be phrased as polymeric biomolecules. The carbohydrate-based polysaccharides are polymeric carbohydrate structures that have linear or branched polymers of sugars within them [1, 2]. Since these polymers are produced by living organisms, they are also biodegradable and their long chain lengths leave a very low carbon footprint [3]. Compared to synthetically produced polymers that have relatively simpler structure, biopolymers tend to have complex structural features and thus adopt unique 3D spatial geometries. It is these unique structures that give rise to biological activity for most of these biopolymers. Microorganisms are known to naturally produce many industrially important polysaccharides, polyesters, and polyamides. These biopolymers have a varying range of applications, from being used as viscosity modifiers to plastics based on their properties. These properties include viscosity-modifying effect, inertness, composition and molecular weights. Some microorganisms are of increasing interest based on their production of multifunctional polysaccharides including intracellular, structural, or exopolysaccharides [4].

Exopolysaccharides are secreted out into the surrounding environment by the microorganisms. There is a multitude of applications of biopolymers that extend to exopolysaccharides in the fields of pharmaceuticals and food industries [5]. Most microbial exopolysaccharides are identical to gums that are in current use [6]. Succinoglycan is one such commercially important polymer, which is acidic, water insoluble made up of β-1,2-glucan monomeric units. Succinoglycan with excellent thermal stability and remarkable viscosity enhancing properties was first isolated from *Alcaligenes faecalis* var. *myxogenes* in 1965 [7]. The polymer is primarily produced by soil dwelling bacteria. The applications of this biopolymer mainly extend to food industry and construction industry owing to its unique rheological and stability characteristics.

*Corresponding author : vponnu@chem.sastra.edu

Agrobacterium radiobacter is a facultatively aerobic, heterotrophic bacterium that metabolizes organic compounds for energy and growth. During oxidative respiration, the bacterium stores energy in the form of polyglucose molecules while oxygen acts as the terminal electron acceptor. This is not seen in the case of anaerobic respiration. It can produce succinoglycan-like EPS when grown on carbon sources like ethanol or glucose under diverse growth conditions. Furthermore, its metabolic flexibility and resilience suggest that *A. radiobacter* possesses the physiological robustness advantageous for biotechnological applications [8].

Green waste has increased due to rapid expansion and urbanisation, generating about tons of waste every year [9]. This biomass is rich in lignin, cellulose and hemicellulose, which can be potentially used for bioconversions based on the concept of biorefinery [10]. The major green waste includes the garden grass, whose composition ranges from cellulose, hemicellulose and lignin in the range of 25-40%, 25-50% and 10-30%, respectively. Thus, this is a potential resource for fermentable sugars, which in turn could be used for succinoglycan production.

Hence, this work focuses on the production of succinoglycan fermentation using *A. radiobacter* strain. Parameters like carbon source, carbon concentration, C/N ratio, and precipitation ratio for the maximum production of succinoglycan were optimised. The acid hydrolysate of waste garden grass was used as a carbon source for the succinoglycan fermentation.

2 Materials and methods

2.1 Procurement of chemicals

Sucrose, peptone, $MgSO_4$, Agar Type 1, $NH_4H_2PO_4$, sodium hydroxide and hydrochloric acid were purchased from Himedia Laboratories Pvt. Ltd. Yeast extract, galactose, $ZnCl_2$, acetone and isopropanol were purchased from Sisco Research Laboratories Pvt. Ltd. Glucose, KH_2PO_4, $FeSO_4.7H_2O$, $MnSO_4.H_2O$ and $CoCl_2.6H_2O$ were purchased from Merck Specialities Private Limited. Sulphuric acid was procured from Thermo Fischer Scientific India Pvt. Ltd. Nitric acid was purchased from Paxmy Speciality Chemicals.

2.2 Biomass collection and characterisation

2.2.1 Estimation of moisture and extractives

The biomass garden grass was collected from the premises of SASTRA Deemed to be University, Thanjavur. The sample was sieved with sieves of particle size (0.405 mm), and the experiments for each category were carried out. All characterisation protocols were followed as per NREL protocols.

For the moisture content, in a crucible, 1 g of grass was taken and kept at 105°C for 4 h on a hot plate. The moisture content was calculated as follows:

$$\text{Moisture (\%)} = ((a - b)/a) \times 100 \ldots\ldots\ldots\ldots\ldots (1)$$

Where, *a = initial weight of biomass before drying and b = weight of biomass after drying.*

For the extractives, about 20 g of grass was taken, and Soxhlet extraction was carried out with acetone as solvent. The sample was dried until a constant weight was reached. The weight loss was considered to be the extractives that include oils and terpenoids. The extractives (%) were given by:

$$\text{Extractives (\%)} = ((a-b)/a) \times 100 \ldots\ldots\ldots\ldots\ldots (2)$$

Where, *a = initial weight of the sample as received and b = weight of the dried sample after extraction.*

2.2.2 Estimation of cellulose and lignin

For the cellulose estimation, about 0.5 g of extractive-free grass was taken and added with 3 mL of reagent containing 80% acetic acid and nitric acid in the ratio 10:1. The mixture was heated to 100°C for 30 minutes. The sample was filtered using vacuum filtration. The residue containing the cellulose was washed until the colour changed to white and weighed to estimate the percentage of cellulose in the sample.

For the lignin estimation, about 0.5 g of the extract-free sample was taken and added with 3 mL of 72% H_2SO_4. The mixture was then incubated at 30°C with constant stirring of every 15 minutes for a period of 1 hour. The sample was filtered and diluted with distilled water to reach a final concentration of 4% H_2SO_4. The sample was autoclaved at 121°C and filtered with filter paper after adjusting the pH. For the estimation, about 2 mL of the filtrate was taken, along with 2 mL of 3% H_2SO_4. The optical density of the sample was measured at 208 nm using a UV-Visible spectrophotometer. The percentage of acid-soluble lignin (ASL) was estimated using the eqn. 3.

$$\%ASL = \frac{A}{\varepsilon}\frac{V}{W_{od}} \times DF \times 100 \ldots\ldots\ldots\ldots (3)$$

Where, A= optical density of the sample at 208 nm, ε = extinction coefficient of lignin at 208 nm (110 $L \cdot g^{-1} \cdot cm^{-1}$, NREL standard), DF = dilution factor, V = total volume of filtrate (L), and W_{od} = oven-dried weight of extractives free sample (g).

The solid residue obtained after filtering the sample was taken and dried at 108°C until constant weight was reached. The amount of acid-insoluble lignin (AIL) present was estimated using the following formula:

$$\% AIL = \frac{W_{ad}}{W_{od}} \text{x} 100 \ldots\ldots\ldots\ldots (4)$$

Where, w_{ad} = weight of the sample after drying, and w_{od} = oven-dried weight of extractives-free sample.

2.2.3 Estimation of total reducing sugar

10 mL of the filtered sample was taken, added with 10 mL of H_2SO_4 and kept for 1 h. After which, 1 mL of the

solution was taken and diluted in the ratio 1:100 with distilled water for further analysis. The sugar content in the sample was estimated using the DNS reagent. A DNS standard was also run simultaneously with known aliquots of glucose as a standard.

2.3 Microbial culture conditions and growth curve analysis

Strain of *Agrobacterium radiobacter* NCIM 2443 was obtained from National Centre for Cell Sciences, Pune. The culture was maintained in glycerol stocks at -20°C. *A. radiobacter* NCIM 2443 was grown on YEB medium containing 0.5 g/L of meat extract, 0.1 g/L of yeast extract, 0.5 g/L of peptone, 0.5 g/L of sucrose and 30 mg/L of $MgSO_4$ in 100 mL of distilled water. The cells were grown at 28°C for 48 h, at 150 rpm, and were used as seed culture for further experimentation.

For the growth curve, 1 % of the *A. radiobacter* cells were inoculated in YEB medium and kept at 150 rpm. The cell growth was measured at regular intervals of 2 h by measuring the optical density of the sample at 600 nm for a period of 5 days.

2.4 Sudan black screening test for succinoglycan

The grown cells of *A. radiobacter* were quadrant streaked on YEB agar plates and incubated at 28°C for 48 hours. Colonies were observed and added with 5 mL of 0.2 % Sudan Black reagent, and rinsed with 10 mL of absolute ethanol after 10 minutes.

2.5 Production media for succinoglycan

The production media contained 25 g/L sucrose, 1 g/L KH_2PO_4, 0.25 g/L $MgSO_4$, 1 g/L $NH_4H_2PO_4$ and 1 mL of trace elements solution (0.5 g $FeSO_4.7H_2O$, 0.2 g $MnSO_4.H_2O$, 0.1 g $CaCl_2$ and 0.1 g of $ZnCl_2$ in 100 mL of 0.1N HCl) in 100 mL distilled water [11]. The pH of the media was adjusted to 7. Seed culture of 10 mL was inoculated in the media, and a temperature of 28°C with 150 rpm was maintained.

2.6 Effect of carbon source

Three different sugars are taken as carbon sources, namely, glucose, sucrose and galactose, were formulated with other media components. The media contains 25 g/L carbon source (Glucose/ Sucrose/ Galactose), 1 g/L KH_2PO_4, 0.25 g/L $MgSO_4$, 1 g/L $NH_4H_2PO_4$ and 1 mL of trace elements solution (0.5 g $FeSO_4.7H_2O$, 0.2 g $MnSO_4.H_2O$, 0.1 g $CaCl_2$ and 0.1 g of $ZnCl_2$ in 100 mL of 0.1 N HCl) in 100 mL distilled water. The pH of the media was adjusted to 7. 10 mL of the seed culture was inoculated in the media, and a temperature of 28°C and an agitation of 150 rpm were maintained. After choosing the best carbon source, the concentration of the carbon source was varied (25 g/L, 50 g/L, 75 g/L and 100 g/L) to study the influence of the concentration of the carbon source.

2.7 Effect of carbon-nitrogen (C:N) ratio

The basic media contained 25 g/L glucose, 1 g/L KH_2PO_4, 0.25 g/L $MgSO_4$, $NH_4H_2PO_4$ (1.4 g/L, 0.547 g/L and 2 g/L) and 1 mL of solution containing trace elements (0.5 g $FeSO_4.7H_2O$, 0.2 g $MnSO_4.H_2O$, 0.1 g $CaCl_2$ and 0.1 g of $ZnCl_2$ in 100 mL of 0.1 N HCl) in 100 mL distilled water. Fermentation was carried out at pH 7, a temperature of 28°C, with an agitation speed of 150 rpm.

2.8 Recovery of succinoglycan

In the optimised media, the cells were inoculated, and the samples were withdrawn every 24 hours from day 0 to day 5. 10 mL of the sample was taken and centrifuged at 4°C at 8000 rpm for 15 minutes. The supernatant and the pellet were recovered and preserved separately. The pellet was dried in the hot air oven at 40°C, and the dry cell weight was calculated. 10 mL of the supernatant was taken and added to 10 mL of antisolvent. Acetone and isopropanol were chosen as antisolvents and added in ratios of 1:1, 2:1, 3:1, 4:1, and 5:1 to the supernatant. The precipitated polymer was dried at 40°C until it reached constant weight.

2.9 Production media using garden grass hydrolysate

The grass sample after acid hydrolysis was taken and filtered. The sample pH was adjusted to 7 and filtered again. 50 mL of the sample was taken and made up to 100 mL using distilled water and other production media components. Fermentation was carried out at pH 7, at temperature 28°C, with an agitation speed of 150 rpm.

2.10 Characterisation of succinoglycan

The produced succinoglycan sample was analysed using NMR and FT-IR to confirm its structural and functional groups.

3 Results and discussion

3.1 Biomass collection and characterisation

The moisture content of the garden grass was found to be 0.225 ± 0.014%. The extractives were found to be 19.14 ± 0.34%, and the total lignin content of the extractive-free sample was 19.85 ± 1.21%. In the present study, effectiveness of H_2SO_4 pretreatments for hydrolyzing grass biomass was assessed based on the yield of reducing sugars using the DNS assay. Acid pretreatment using 2% H_2SO_4 resulted in the highest sugar yield, 54.2 ± 0.82 g/100 g of grass biomass (Figure 1). This yield is consistent with established literature, wherein dilute acid hydrolysis effectively breaks down hemicellulose and partially hydrolyzes cellulose, liberating monomeric sugars [12, 13]. The mechanism involves hydrothermal degradation, where the concentrated acid facilitates cleavage of glycosidic linkages in hemicellulose and opens the lignocellulosic matrix, thereby improving cellulose accessibility.

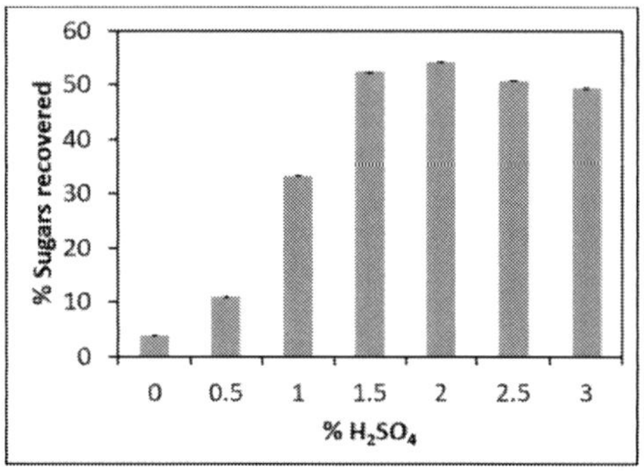

Fig. 1. Sugar recovered using different concentrations of sulphuric acid.

3.2 Sudan black test

The exopolysaccharide succinoglycan produced by certain rhizobial and soil bacteria, plays a significant role in biofilm formation, symbiotic interactions, and osmotic stress tolerance. In the current experiment, the Sudan Black B staining method was employed to assess the production of succinoglycan by *A. radiobacter.* Sudan Black B is a lipophilic azo dye commonly used to stain lipid-rich substances, including polyhydroxybutyrate (PHB) and other neutral lipids. However, in polysaccharide detection assays, it has a secondary application: it can bind non-specifically to hydrophobic components but does not interact with highly hydrated, gel-forming exopolysaccharides like succinoglycan. As reported by Liu et al. (1998), colonies that do not produce succinoglycan or other similar EPS typically absorb Sudan Black dye and exhibit black or dark blue coloration [12]. In contrast, succinoglycan-producing colonies retain a white or creamy appearance due to the exclusion of the dye by the gelatinous EPS layer, which forms a hydrated barrier around the cells and prevents dye penetration.

As shown in Figure 2, the bacterial streaks remain white and unstained following treatment with Sudan Black B. This indicates that the bacteria are actively producing a thick, hydrated layer of succinoglycan, which prevents the lipophilic dye from binding to the underlying cell wall or membrane structures. The uniformity and intensity of the unstained zone across multiple streaks further suggest robust and consistent EPS production across the bacterial population. This visual outcome serves as a qualitative confirmation of succinoglycan production. The gelatinous nature of the EPS is typical of succinoglycan, which is composed predominantly of glucose and galactose residues with pyruvyl, succinyl, and acetyl modifications that confer its anionic and viscous properties [14].

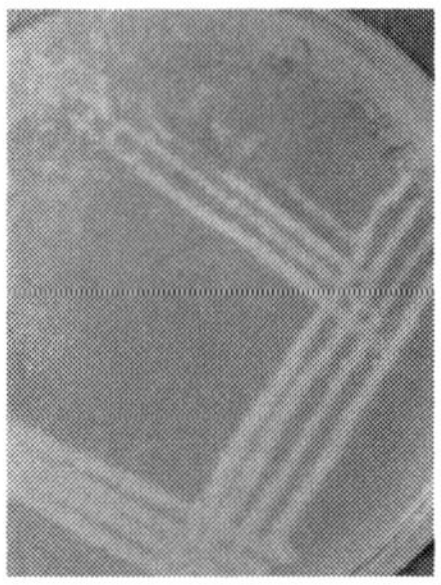

Fig. 2. Sudan black test for the production of succinoglycan by the *A. radiobacter*.

3.3 Growth curve analysis and succinoglycan production

The growth profile of the bacterial isolate was evaluated by measuring optical density at 600 nm over a 48-hour incubation period, as shown in Figure 3. The organism exhibited a distinct three-phase growth pattern typical of bacterial cultures. The initial lag phase, spanning 0–6 hours, likely reflected a period of physiological adaptation where the bacteria adjusted to the new growth environment and initiated metabolic reprogramming. This was followed by a pronounced exponential (log) phase from approximately 6 to 36 hours, which rapid cellular proliferation was observed, indicating active nutrient uptake and biomass accumulation. After 36 hours, the growth curve plateaued, signifying entry into the stationary phase, where nutrient depletion and accumulation of waste products began to limit further population expansion. This phase is often associated with the biosynthesis of secondary metabolites and extracellular biopolymers, including exopolysaccharides (EPS) such as succinoglycan.

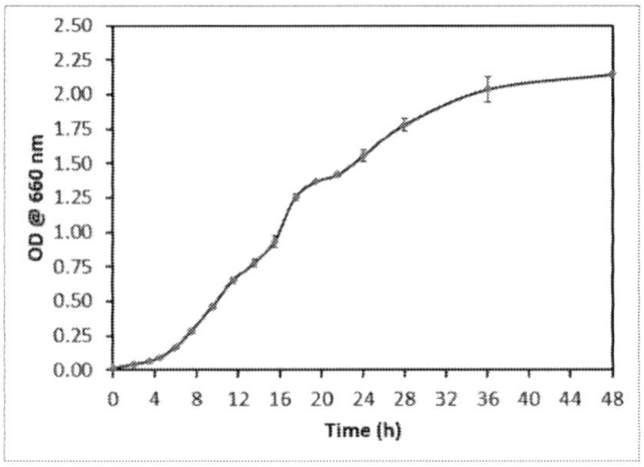

Fig. 3. Microbial growth curve representing the growth of the organism *A. radiobacter*.

Succinoglycan production was targeted specifically during the stationary phase, given that stress conditions such as nutrient limitation often upregulate EPS biosynthetic pathways. After fermentation, the culture broth was centrifuged to separate bacterial cells from the extracellular matrix. The supernatant was treated with an anti-solvent isopropanol to precipitate succinoglycan. A white, floating precipitate was clearly visible, as illustrated in Figure 4. The precipitate was recovered from the solution, consistent with characteristics described for succinoglycan-like EPS in previous studies. Isopropanol was chosen due to its polarity difference from water and its ability to precipitate high-molecular-weight polysaccharides without degradation. The extraction process was repeated from day 2 to day 5, confirming consistent and reproducible production. The white precipitate's appearance and timing strongly suggest successful recovery of succinoglycan, a high-viscosity biopolymer primarily composed of glucose and galactose, with succinyl, acetyl, and pyruvyl side groups contributing to its physical and chemical properties.

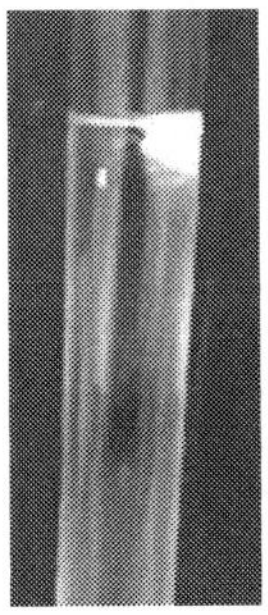

Fig. 4. Shows the white precipitate as a result of acetone precipitation

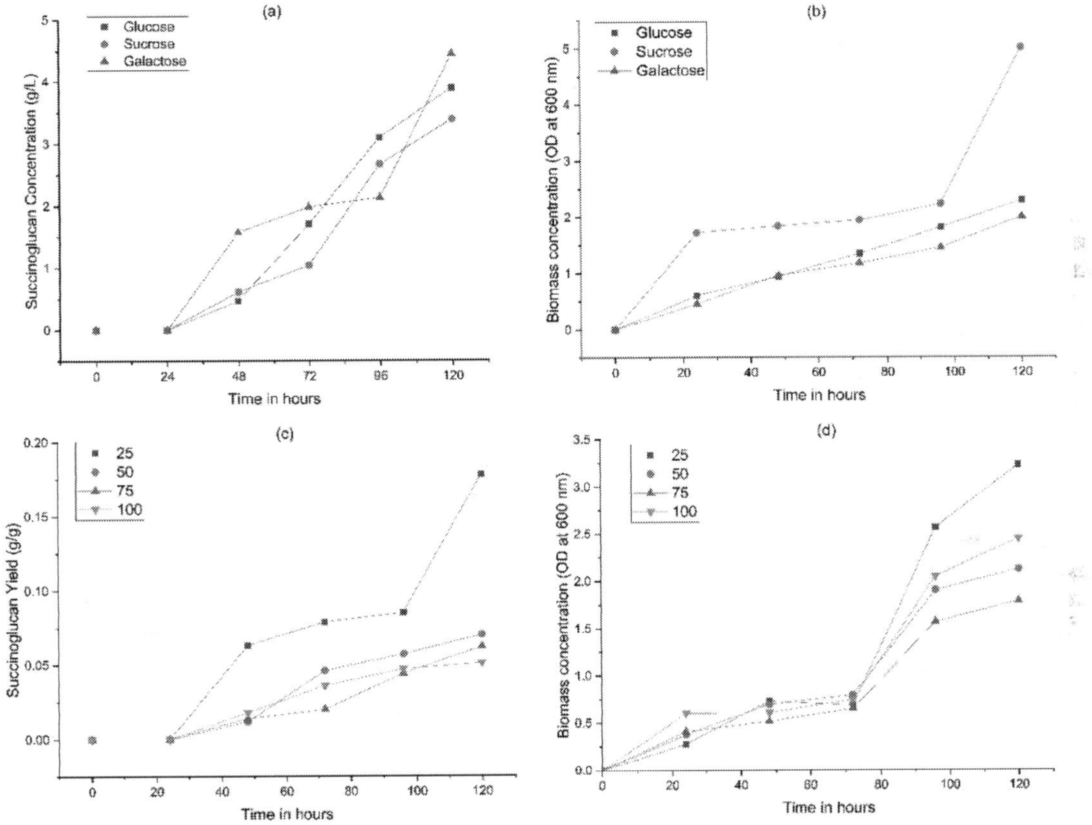

Fig. 5. Optimisation of Succinoglycan production: (a) succinoglycan concentration with different carbon sources, (b) biomass yield with different carbon sources, (c) succinoglycan yield at various glucose concentrations, and (d) biomass yield at various glucose concentrations.

Similar behavior has been reported in *A. radiobacter*, as described by [15], where succinoglycan production peaked during late-log and early stationary phases. This temporal association between growth kinetics and EPS production provides a basis for optimizing inoculum timing, culture duration, and recovery protocols in future bioprocess development.

3.4 Effect of carbon source

To investigate the influence of various carbon sources on succinoglycan production, three conventional sugars—glucose, galactose, and sucrose—were evaluated. Glucose and galactose were selected due to their known role as the principal monomeric constituents of succinoglycan [8]. Sucrose was included based on recent studies demonstrating its effectiveness in enhancing EPS production [11]. As shown in Figure 5 (a), succinoglycan production increased progressively with time for all three carbon sources. Among them, sucrose supported the highest final yield, reaching approximately 4.5 g/L by 120 hours. Glucose and galactose also promoted significant production, with final yields of approximately 3.8 g/L and 3.5 g/L, respectively. These trends are consistent with existing literature and support the hypothesis that sucrose acts as a more readily utilizable substrate for EPS biosynthesis. Furthermore, a conversion yield of 0.208 g of succinoglycan per gram of sucrose was recorded, indicating efficient biopolymer synthesis. Despite sucrose yielding the highest biomass and EPS production, glucose was chosen as the primary carbon source for subsequent optimization experiments. This choice was based on the relevance to practical applications involving lignocellulosic feedstocks, particularly grass biomass, which primarily contains cellulose composed of glucose units rather than disaccharides like sucrose.

To study the effect of concentration of glucose for succinoglycan production, fermentation trials were conducted at 25 g/L, 50 g/L, 75 g/L, and 100 g/L of glucose. The highest conversion yield was observed at 25 g/L, with a value of 0.177 ± 0.0018 g of succinoglycan per gram of glucose, aligning well with reports on optimal sucrose levels from previous studies. In contrast, increasing glucose concentration resulted in progressively lower yields: 0.07 g/g at 50 g/L, 0.062 g/g at 75 g/L, and 0.051 g/g at 100 g/L (Figure 5 (c)). This inverse relationship between glucose concentration and succinoglycan yield suggests possible catabolite repression or osmotic inhibition at higher sugar levels, which could impair metabolic flux toward EPS biosynthesis. Similar patterns have been observed in other polysaccharide-producing microbes, where moderate substrate concentrations favor polymer synthesis, while excessive sugar levels suppress secondary metabolite pathways.

3.5 Effect of Carbon/Nitrogen ratio

In this study, glucose was selected as the fixed carbon source based on its relevance to lignocellulosic hydrolysates, while ammonium dihydrogen phosphate was used as the nitrogen source. The carbon concentration was maintained constant, and the C:N ratio was varied by changing nitrogen levels to obtain molar ratios of 25:1, 50:1, and 75:1, respectively. These ratios were chosen based on previous studies suggesting that nitrogen-limiting conditions may favor exopolysaccharide production, particularly succinoglycan, in several microbial systems. As illustrated in Figure 6(a), the highest biomass yield was achieved at a C:N ratio of 25, followed closely by C:N 50. In contrast, the C:N 75 condition resulted in significantly reduced biomass accumulation. These findings indicate that higher nitrogen availability supports more cell growth, likely due to enhanced protein and nucleic acid biosynthesis necessary during exponential and stationary growth phases. Surprisingly, as shown in Figure 6(b), the highest succinoglycan yield was also observed at C:N 25, reaching 0.54 g of succinoglycan per gram of glucose consumed. Yields declined progressively with increasing C:N ratio, with the lowest production observed at C:N 75. This result is not fully consistent with previous literature, which often reports enhanced exopolysaccharide production under nitrogen-limited conditions, presumably as a microbial stress response mechanism that redirects carbon flux toward secondary metabolite pathways. The divergence observed in the present study may be attributed to the enhanced biomass productivity under higher nitrogen conditions, which may in turn support greater overall EPS biosynthesis through increased enzyme expression and metabolic activity. A similar observation was made by Pinedo et al. (2008), where moderate nitrogen availability promoted EPS production in certain rhizobial strains [16]. It is also plausible that the threshold for nitrogen limitation in this strain is higher than expected, and further experimentation with broader C:N ratios or different nitrogen sources may help clarify the optimal window for succinoglycan overproduction.

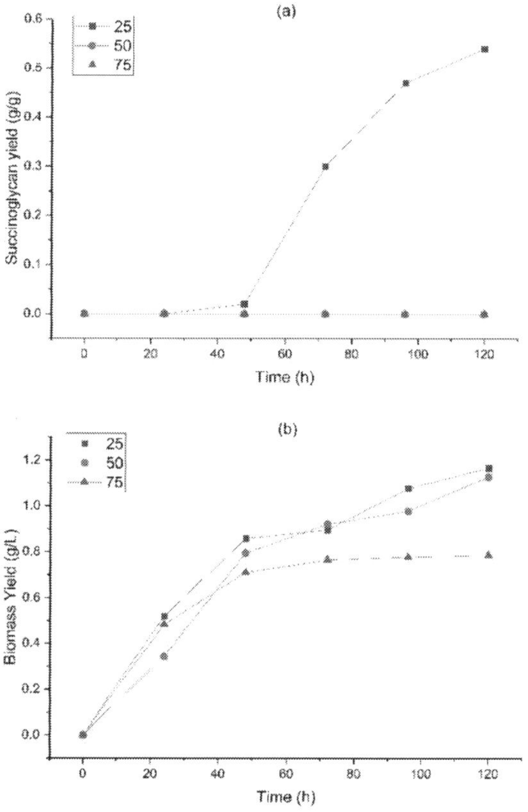

Fig. 6. Effect of carbon to nitrogen ratio (a) product yield and (b) biomass yield.

3.6 Succinoglycan recovery Total reducing sugar content

Downstream processing plays a major role in the efficient recovery and quantification of biopolymers such as succinoglycan and is equally important as upstream optimization. In this study, solvent precipitation was employed as the primary recovery technique, leveraging the poor solubility of succinoglycan in organic solvents such as acetone and isopropanol (IPA), as previously described by [17] To optimize recovery efficiency, different sample-to-solvent volume ratios (1:1 to 1:5) were evaluated for both acetone and IPA. The concentration of succinoglycan recovered under each condition is presented in Figure 7. Among the tested conditions, isopropanol at a 1:2 (supernatant: solvent) ratio was found to be the most effective, yielding a maximum succinoglycan concentration of 7.12 g/L, while at 1:1 ratio yield was only 4.7 g/L . Upon increasing the IPA ratio beyond 2, succinoglycan yield . In case of acetone, from 1:1 to 1:3 ratio, there was an increase in succinoglycan production from 3.42 g/L to 4.62 g/L, and at 1:4 ratio, the succinoglycan of about 6.2 g/L was obtained. Further increase in acetone ratio reduced polymer yield. This condition clearly outperformed all others, including corresponding acetone ratios, which consistently yielded lower concentrations. Isopropanol proved superior to acetone across all solvent ratios tested.

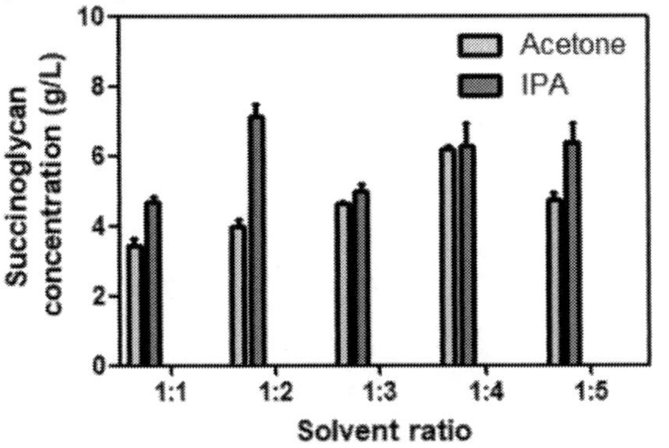

Fig. 7. Succinoglycan precipitation upon two different solvents

3.7 Characterization of succinoglycan

The structural features of the extracted biopolymer were characterized using ¹H Nuclear Magnetic Resonance (¹H-NMR) and Fourier Transform Infrared (FT-IR) Spectroscopy. The ¹H-NMR spectrum, presented in Figure 8, provides key insights into the monomeric composition and substitution pattern of the polymer. The chemical shifts observed at δ = 0.965 and 1.165 ppm represent methyl protons of pyruvyl groups. The acetyl protons are identified at δ = 1.808 ppm. The cluster ranging from δ = 3.052 to 4.022 ppm indicates the presence of β-glycosidic linkages between glucose and galactose units, confirming the polysaccharide backbone structure (Figure 8). The peak chemical shift at 4.075 gives out the solvent peak [8]. The lack of succinate addition to the polymer is evident from the result. It is postulated that the bacterium might be an exoH mutant, i.e. it lacks the gene to add the succinate moiety.

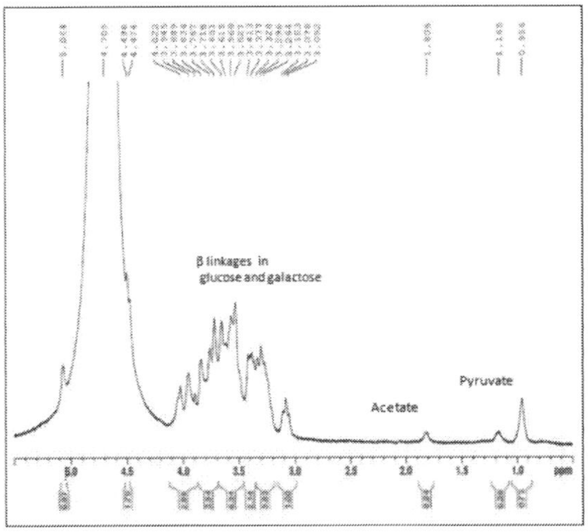

Fig. 8. H-NMR analysis of the biopolymer.

Further confirmation was obtained via FT-IR analysis, shown in Figure 9. A broad absorption band around 3300 cm⁻¹ corresponds to -OH stretching vibrations, typical of polysaccharides. The band near 1700 cm⁻¹ is assigned to -CH bending, while the signal at 1313 cm⁻¹ is attributed to carboxylic acid (COOH) functional groups. A strong band at 1070 cm⁻¹ confirms the presence of C–O–C and C–O stretching vibrations, reinforcing the polysaccharide structure [18]. However, subtle deviations in the FT-IR profile, particularly the diminished absorbance in regions typically associated with succinate groups, support the hypothesis that the biopolymer lacks succinylation. This observation aligns with prior reports on exoH-deficient strains, which produce succinoglycan without succinate moieties, leading to minor but consistent spectral shifts [19].

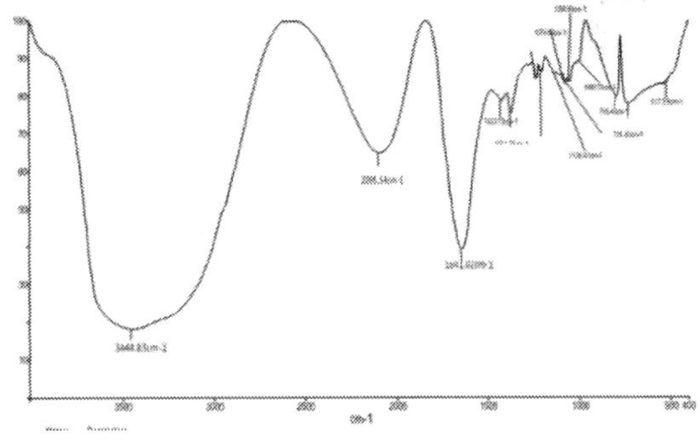

Fig. 9. FT-IR analysis of the biopolymer.

4 Conclusion

The compositional analysis of garden grass revealed its suitability as a lignocellulosic feedstock for biopolymer production. The biomass contained 19.13% extractives, comprising waxes, fatty acids, resin oils, and terpenoids. The cellulose content was determined to be 31.11 ± 2.70 %, while lignin accounted for 16.05 % of the dry weight. The moisture content was relatively low, at 0.18 %, indicating good storage stability and minimal pre-processing requirements. Acid hydrolysis using 2 % sulfuric acid yielded a maximum of 0.5909 g of reducing sugars per gram of grass, demonstrating the efficiency of the pretreatment method in converting polysaccharides into fermentable sugars. These hydrolysates were subsequently utilized as a substrate for the production of succinoglycan, an industrially significant extracellular biopolymer. Through systematic optimization of the conventional production media, it was found that a glucose concentration of 25 g/L combined with a carbon-to-nitrogen (C:N) ratio of 25 supported maximum succinoglycan synthesis. Given its abundance, low cost, and sustainable nature, garden grass serves as a viable alternative to conventional carbon sources for succinoglycan production, thus enhancing the economic feasibility of biopolymer manufacturing processes.

The Authors thank SASTRA Deemed University for the research facility and support. Srividhya Krishnan sincerely thanks CSIR for her Senior Research Fellowship (SRF), award no: 35110781, File no: 09/1095(18700)/2024-EMR-I. Nanthini Devi sincerely thank DST-Inspire (IF230140) for her Junior Research Fellowship.

References

1. P. Harmsen, W. Huijgen, L. Bermudez, R. Bakker (n.d.). Literature review of physical and chemical pretreatment processes for lignocellulosic biomass. Energy Research Centre of The Netherlands, Petten, The Netherlands. ECN-E—10-013. (2010)
2. A. K. Mohanty, M. Misra, L. T. Drzal (Eds.). Natural fibers, biopolymers, and biocomposites (0 ed.). CRC Press. (2005). https://doi.org/10.1201/9780203508206
3. M. R. Yates, C. Y. Barlow, Life cycle assessments of biodegradable, commercial biopolymers A critical review. Resources, Conservation and Recycling. **78**, 54–66 (2013).https://doi.org/10.1016/j.resconrec.2013.06.010
4. Ms. V. Gupta, Microbial production of biopolymers and polymer precursors. International Journal for Research in Applied Science and Engineering Technology. **10**, 47–54. (2022). https://doi.org/10.22214/ijraset.2022.45052
5. F. Freitas, V. Alves, I. Coelhoso, M. Reis, Production and food applications of microbial biopolymers. In J. Teixeira & A. Vicente, Engineering Aspects of Food Biotechnology. **20130952**, 61–88. CRC Press. (2013). https://doi.org/10.1201/b15426-5
6. A. Fatimi, Patentability of biopolymer-based hydrogels. The 25th International Electronic Conference on Synthetic Organic Chemistry. **39**, (2021). https://doi.org/10.3390/ecsoc-25-11653
7. T. Harada, Succinoglucan 10C3: A new acidic polysaccharide of alcaligenes faecalis var. myxogenes. Archives of Biochemistry and Biophysics. **112**, 65–69 (1965). https://doi.org/10.1016/0003-9861(65)90010-X
8. U. Halder, A. Banerjee, R. Bandopadhyay, Structural and Functional Properties, Biosynthesis, and Patenting Trends of Bacterial Succinoglycan: A Review. Indian Journal of Microbiology. **57,** 278-284 (2017). http://doi.org/10.1007/s12088-017-0655-3
9. X. Liu, Y. Xie, H. Sheng, Green waste characteristics and sustainable recycling options. Resources, Environment and Sustainability. **11**, 100098. (2023). https://doi.org/10.1016/j.resenv.2022.100098
10. S. Areeya, E. J. Panakkal, P. Kunmanee, A. Tawai, S. Amornraksa, M. Sriariyanun, A. Kaoloun, N. Hartini, Y. S. Cheng, M. Kchaou, S. Dasari, M. P. Gundupalli, A review of sugarcane biorefinery: from waste to value-added products. Applied Science and Engineering Progress. **17**, 7402-7402
11. J. Jeong, Y. Kim, Y. Hu, S. Jung, Bacterial succinoglycans: Structure, physical properties, and applications. Polymers. **14**, 276 (2022). https://doi.org/10.3390/polym14020276
12. T. A. Lloyd, C. E. Wyman, Combined sugar yields for dilute sulfuric acid pretreatment of corn stover followed by enzymatic hydrolysis of the remaining solids. Bioresource Technology. **96**, 1967–1977 (2005)
13. M. A. Khan, E. J. Panakkal, M. Sriariyanun, M. P. Gundupalli, S. Roddecha, K. Katam, J. Jayaprakash, K. Cheenkachorn, Dewaxing and Post-Pretreatment Washing: Impact on Sugar and Ethanol Yields from Tobacco Residue. Applied Science and Engineering Progress. **17**, 7495-7495 (2024)
14. M. Liu, J. E. González, L. B. Willis, G. C. Walker, A novel screening method for isolating exopolysaccharide-deficient mutants. Applied and Environmental Microbiology **64**, 4600–4602 (1998). https://doi.org/10.1128/AEM.64.11.4600-4602.1998
15. M. Stredansky, E. Conti, C. Bertocchi, M. Matulova, & F. Zanetti, Succinoglycan production by Agrobacterium tumefaciens. Journal of Fermentation and Bioengineering. **85**, 398–403 (1998). https://doi.org/10.1016/S0922-338X(98)80083-4
16. C. A. Pinedo, R. M. Bringhurst, D. J. Gage, Sinorhizobium meliloti mutants lacking phosphotransferase system enzyme HPr or EIIA are altered in diverse processes, including carbon metabolism, cobalt requirements, and succinoglycan production. Journal of Bacteriology, **190**, 2947–2956 (2008). https://doi.org/10.1128/JB.01917-07
17. G. T. Kalyanasundaram, M. Doble, M., S. N. Gummadi, Production and downstream processing of (1→3)- β-D-glucan from mutant strain of agrobacterium sp. ATCC 31750. AMB Express. **2**, 31. (2012). https://doi.org/10.1186/2191-0855-2-31
18. H. Gao, L. Yang, J. Tian, L. Huang, D. Huang, W. Zhang, F. Xie, Y. Niu, M. Jin, C. Jia, C. Zou, J. Huang, Z. Chang, X. Yang, D. Jiang, Characterization and rheological properties analysis of the succinoglycan produced by a high-yield mutant of rhizobium radiobacter ATCC 19358. International Journal of Biological Macromolecules. **166**, 61–70 (2021). https://doi.org/10.1016/j.ijbiomac.2020.10.087
19. M. Bakhtiyari, M. Moosavi-Nasab, H. Askari, Optimization of succinoglycan hydrocolloid production by agrobacterium radiobacter grown in sugar beet molasses and investigation of its physicochemical characteristics. Food Hydrocolloids. **45**, 18–29 (2015)

The influence of prebiotic encapsulated materials on the stability of probiotic

Pitsinee Karunborirak[1], *Sunee* Eadmusik[1], *Ratchanee* Charoen[2], *Kriangkrai* Phattayakorn[3], and *Wanticha* Savedboworn[1*]

[1]Department of Agro-Industry Technology and Management, Faculty of Digital Agro-Industry, King Mongkut's University of Technology North Bangkok, 25230 Prachinburi, Thailand
[2]Department of Innovation and Product Development Technology, Faculty of Digital Agro-Industry, King Mongkut's University of Technology North Bangkok, 25230 Prachinburi, Thailand
[3]Department of Food Technology and Nutrition, Faculty of Natural Resources and Agro-Industry, Kasetsart University, Chalermphrakiat Sakon Nakhon Province Campus, 47000 Sakon Nakhon, Thailand

Abstract. The impact on probiotics from insufficient protection of microcapsules necessitates the development of more effective probiotic encapsulation. This is achieved by using encapsulating agents and adding a double coating layer to the microcapsules to enhance structural strength. This study aimed to investigate the survivability of the bacteria probiotic *Lactobacillus plantarum* TISTR 2075 encapsulated with alginate, gellan gum, creatine monohydrate and different prebiotics by using extrusion technique and coated with chitosan and hyaluronic acid by layer-by-layer technique. The encapsulation efficiency (%EE) was tested and the physical characteristics, morphology and mechanical strength of the gel encapsulations were also evaluated. Findings indicated that the encapsulation of probiotics with prebiotic added increased the encapsulation efficiency (70-94 %). Moreover, the addition of pullulan provided the microcapsules with high mechanical strength. These results confirmed that the enhancement of prebiotic pullulan to the encapsulating agents had significant effects on the survivability of probiotic cells.

1 Introduction

Probiotics are microorganisms promoting gastrointestinal health and enhancing immune responses when dispensed in adequate amounts. They offer several health benefits to the host, and their potent viability is worthy of protection [1]. Beneficial microorganisms must be assigned as bacteria cells live that can tolerate the gastrointestinal tract and locate the colon [2]. Moreover, probiotics have great potential for immunomodulatory activity, and even neurological health [3]. During processing and storage, probiotics are sensitive under the technological and gastrointestinal tract that could lead to the instability of the survivability and activity of probiotic bacteria cells [4]. A significant concern of probiotics is the viability during the process, the storage, and the delivery.

Prebiotics are fibers and carbohydrates that the human body cannot be digested but nurture as nourishment for gut bacteria such as fructooligosaccharides (FOS), galactooligosaccharides (GOS), inulin, and resistant starch [5]. Their capability to preserve a healthy balance of intestine microorganism, raise the immune system, and enhance overall health [6, 7]. Encapsulation processes on the survival of *Lactobacillus plantarum* F1 and *Lactobacillus reuteri* 182 using the extrusion technique with 2% sodium alginate as encapsulation agent, combined with prebiotics, namely 4% trehalose and 2% inulin, and coated with 0.4% chitosan and subjected to freeze drier. The addition of trehalose and sodium alginate protected lactic acid bacteria (LAB) with the increasing of survival rate to more than 92.5%. The chitosan coating enhanced the spherical shape and improved mechanical strength. The prebiotic encapsulation resulted in better cell stability during one year storage, with values of 4.82 log CFU/g in alginate-trehalose beads and 5.64 log CFU/g in alginate-trehalose-inulin beads [8]. Kistaubayeva et al. [9] reported that the survival of *Lactobacillus rhamnosus* GG encapsulated with alginate and alginate plus pullulan were 74 and 94%, respectively. However, the viability of the probiotic was rapidly decreased in unencapsulated cells with low cell viability (43% survival rate). Apiwattanasiri et al. [10] suggested that the encapsulation of *Lactobacillus casei* using silk sericin-alginate-prebiotics and coated with silk sericin improved the survival rate of probiotic.

Microencapsulation is an encapsulation technique in which biocomponents are coated inside polymer microcapsules with nanometer to millimeter particles [11]. Microencapsulation technology is a well-confined method developed to conserve stability and protect active substances for long-term or within targeted delivery systems that help shield probiotics from adverse

* Corresponding author: Wanticha.s@agro.kmutnb.ac.th

conditions in the stomach [4]. Traditionally, encapsulation with prebiotics ensures that the probiotic cells have a persistent supply of a food source, offers additional protection, improve their stability, and ensure that prebiotics assist the growth of the probiotics once they reach the gut [12].

The stability of microencapsulation is reduced during processing, storage, and during gastric and intestinal simulation juice. The microcapsules are coated with multiple layers of coating or layer-by-layer to effectively deliver probiotics [13]. Polysaccharide-protein conjugates offer a new dimension in encapsulation system design. This technique enhances the stability of colloids by using electrostatic technique to neutralize charges [14].

Amino acid (Creatin monohydrate) is used to supplement the structure of the microcapsules. Amino acids have smaller molecules than proteins, so they can be better attached with hydrogels to the structure of the microcapsules. Therefore, the objective of this investigation aimed to study the survival of the encapsulation probiotic bacteria *L. plantarum* TISTR 2075 with different encapsulated hydrogels and prebiotics. After that, chitosan and hyaluronic acid were applied to the samples as layer-by-layer coating materials. Utilization of the charge difference of positively charged chitosan followed by negatively charged hyaluronic acid was applied. The physical and morphological characteristics of microcapsules were analysed.

2 Materials and methods

2.1 Cell culture condition

The cell strain *Lactobacillus plantarum* TISTR 2075 acquired from Bangkok MIRCEN, Thailand. The cells were subcultured in MRS broth (Merck, Germany) medium. The cell cultures were incubated at 37°C for 24 h. Cell pellets were obtained by centrifugation at 4000 rpm for 15 min.

2.2 Probiotic encapsulation

Microencapsulated probiotics used the extrusion method. As discussed in section 2.1, 100 mL culture of the cell was prepared, and 3 mL of cell pellets were harvested by centrifugation. Cell suspension of 10^{10} CFU/mL was added with 20 mL of sterile encapsulants as in comprising 2% sodium alginate (ALDRICH, Norway), 0.2% gellan gum (MySkinRecipes, Thailand), 0.5% creatine monohydrate (Shixing, China) and a variety of 1% prebiotic such as fucoidan (MySkinRecipes, Thailand), pullulan (MySkinRecipes, Thailand) and yeast beta glucan (Angel Humam Health,China). The treatments of the experiment are indicated in Table 1. Then, encapsulant was mixed and extruded by using a sterile syringe connected to a sterile needle (diameter 0.6 mm) into 100 mL sterile of 0.2 M $CaCl_2$ (KemAus, Australia) for 30 min. Subsequently, the microcapsules were washed in 0.1% sterile peptone solution and removed to 100 mL of 0.4% (w/v) chitosan solution for 30 min. Next layer coatings were carried into 100 mL of 1% (w/v) hyaluronic acid for 30 min.

Table 1. Treatments of probiotic encapsulation.

Treatments	Materials	Coating layers: 1% Chitosan + 1% Hyaluronic acid
AG-C (Control)	2% Sodium Alginate +1% Gellan gum	•
AGC-C	2% Sodium Alginate +1% Gellan gum +0.5% Creatine monohydrate	•
AGC-F-C	2% Sodium Alginate +1% Gellan gum +0.5% Creatine monohydrate +1% Fucoidan	•
AGC-Pu-C	2% Sodium Alginate +1% Gellan gum +0.5% Creatine monohydrate +1% Pullulan	•
AGC-Y-C	2% Sodium Alginate +1% Gellan gum +0.5% Creatine monohydrate +1% Yeast beta glucan	•

2.3 Efficiency of encapsulation

The efficiency of encapsulation assessed the viability of probiotics according to the encapsulation procedure using the following formula according to Apiwattanasiri et al. [10].

$$Encapsulation\ efficiency\ (EE, \%) = \frac{N}{N_0} \times 100 \quad (1)$$

Here, N_0 and N indicate the number of viable cells remaining before and after encapsulation (log CFU/g).

2.4 Morphological and size

The morphology and the size of the particles were examined by using a stereo microscope (Motic, DM-143-FBGG, China).

2.5 Color

The samples were determined using a lab scan XE colorimeter (HunterLab, ColorFlex, USA). Then it was apprized as L*, a*, b*, C*, h* values.

2.6 Water activity (a_w)

The water activity was analyzed by a water activity meter (Aqualab, 3TE, USA). The microcapsules were set in the plastic cup to be analyzed at 25 ± 2°C. The microcapsules were measured and replicated 3 times.

2.7 Mechanical strength

The microcapsules were determined using a texture analyzer (TA.XT plus). A P/36R probe was applied with a pre-test speed of 1.00 mm/s, test speed of 2.00 mm/s and post-test speed of 10.00 mm/s. Briefly, a rupture force utilized to a microcapsule was determined as a measure of mechanical stability.

2.8 Statistical assessment

All treatments were represented in triplicate. The results are presented as mean ± standard deviation. The ANOVA was used to identify, using SPSS 28 Software (IBM SPSS, Armonk, USA). Significance was determined as $p<0.05$.

3 Results and discussion

3.1 The encapsulation efficiency of microcapsules

As shown in Figure 1, the viability after encapsulation of all treatments tended to decrease after encapsulation. The encapsulation efficiency of probiotic *L. plantarum* TISTR 2075 by extrusion encapsulation technique in this study was found to be in the range of 71-94%. AGC-Y-C had the lowest encapsulation efficiency (71.83%). However, AG-C, AGC-C, AGC-F-C and AGC-Pu-C showed high encapsulation efficiency of higher than 90%. Pullulan is a polysaccharide that, when combined with proteins, increases the viscosity and structural strength of the microcapsules. The pullulan structure is a complex interlacing of fibers that increases the area available for probiotics to bind to the microcapsule structure [15]. Fucoidan is a polysaccharide with encapsulation properties. When used in combination with proteins and hydrogels, the encapsulation efficiency of fucoidan encapsulated probiotics is greatly improved. This is due to the difference in charge between the negative charge of the sulfate fucoidan and the positive charge of the protein [16]. Surprisingly, the AG-C sample without prebiotics and creatine monohydrate had an encapsulation efficiency comparable to that of the microcapsules with prebiotics and creatine monohydrate added. According to many researches, microcapsules without prebiotics may have a high encapsulation efficiency, but their survival rate following storage will be low. Jeznienė et al. [8] showed that encapsulation with prebiotic addition (inulin) provided a higher survival rate during storage than encapsulation without prebiotic addition. Thinkohkaew et al. [17] reported that the *Lactobacillus casei* microcapsules with added prebiotics (inulin) had a high probiotic survival rate of approximately 7.6 log CFU/g, but the microcapsules without added inulin had a survival rate of approximately 6.8 log CFU/g after 28 days at 4°C storage. The AGC-Y-C microcapsules decreased up to 2.99 log CFU/g, while the microcapsules encapsulated with other encapsulant reduced 0.10-0.66 log CFU/g. Consistent with the findings of Thinkohkaew et al. [18], the encapsulation efficiency of the encapsulated probiotic using alginate combined with gellan gum and coated with chitosan improved the survival rate from 80.35% to 97.82%. Gellan gum would improve the encapsulation efficiency
further through the ionic interactions with alginate. The use of beta-glucan-alginate encapsulation of *L. acidophilus* LA-5 via spray drying has an encapsulation efficiency between 78.20%. Yeast beta-glucan is an outstanding polysaccharide with a honeycomb-like structure. This structure, crosslinked with alginate, effectively locks in the probiotics and protects them [19]. Ahmadi et al. [19] showed that the encapsulation of probiotics supplemented with higher ratio of yeast beta glucan strengthened the structure of microcapsules and improved the efficiency of probiotic encapsulation. The microcapsules encapsulated by prebiotic supplementation and adding a layer to coat the microcapsules in two layers. The microcapsules had higher encapsulation efficiency and stability from adding a coating layer to the microcapsules. The single-layer coating of the microcapsules helped protect the probiotics from the unsuitable or adverse external conditions affecting probiotics. However, increasing the number of coating layers would diminish the effect on the probiotics encapsulated within the microcapsule structure [10].

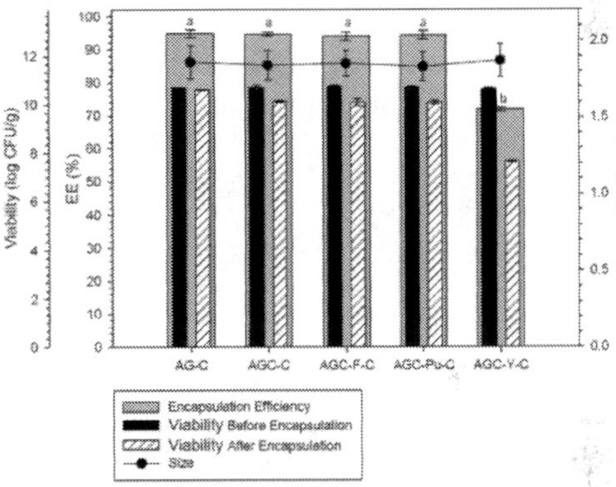

Fig. 1. The efficiency of encapsulation, viability before and after encapsulation, and particle size of microcapsules. Different letters on the top of the bar indicated a significant difference ($p<0.05$) between groups.

3.2 Morphological and particle size

Probiotics encapsulated with different types of encapsulants were examined under a stereo microscope. It can be seen that the microcapsules have a spherical shape, and the surface was smooth (Figure 2). The size and shape of microcapsules composed of different encapsulation agents appeared quite uniform with no significant difference ($p\geq0.05$) in sizes. The microcapsule sizes were in the range of 1.830-1.870 mm. Singh et al. [20] suggested that the microcapsules are 50 nm to 2 mm in size, have a spherical shape, consist of a core and shell structure, including particles that are dispersed within a sphere. The important thing for delivery and protection of the probiotics is a relatively quiet uniform in size and shape [17].

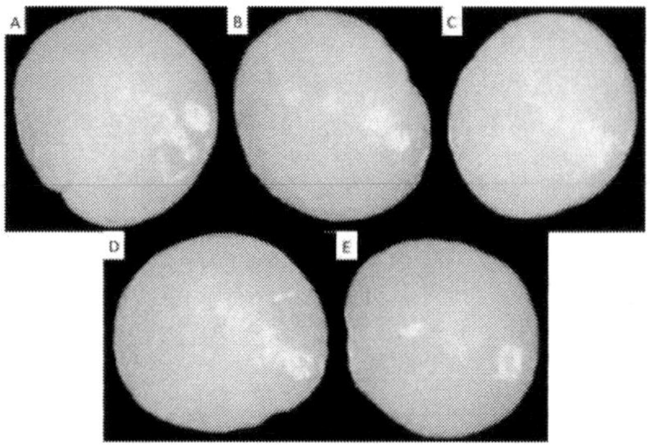

Fig. 2. Stereo microscopy images of microcapsules.
A: AG-C, B: AGC-C, C: AGC-F-C, D: AGC-Pu-C, E: AGC-Y-C.

3.3 Color

In this study, the L* a* and b* values of microcapsules have significant differences ($p<0.05$) in color properties, those were illustrated in Table 2. AGC-Pu-C had the highest L* value (58.217) and AGC-C exhibited the highest negative a* value (-2.653) indicates the degree of greenish. Also, AGC-F-C exhibited the highest positive b* value (6.537), showing a yellow hue. C* represents chroma or color saturation, and h* is the hue angle. The higher the chroma value, the higher the vibrant and pure colors starting from zero. The microcapsules had a low level of color vibrancy, but there were significant differences ($p<0.05$) in color vibrancy according to the composition of the encapsulant used. The hue value was significant difference ($p<0.05$) observed in the microcapsules that had the difference color range. The color analysis results indicated one of the important quality characteristics of microcapsules. The color value is influenced by many factors, for instance the concentration of the encapsulating material and the ratio of encapsulating material, which affect the color of microcapsules.

3.4 Water activity (a_w) and mechanical strength

From the study of water activity of fresh microcapsules, the water activity contents were in the range of 0.976-0.978, which was no significant ($p\geq0.05$) difference. The mechanical strength of microcapsules was evaluated by using a texture analyzer with rupture force (fracturability), which was assigned as a standard of mechanical stability or endurance of the sample against fracture. The microcapsules encapsulated probiotics with different types of encapsulant were shown in Figure 3. It was found that microcapsules from different encapsulants showed significant differences ($p<0.05$) in mechanical strength values. Especially, microcapsules encapsulated with AGC-Pu-C and AGC-C had the greatest mechanical strength with a value of 5.837 and 5.474 N, respectively. However, the microcapsules containing only alginate plus gellan gum and coated with chitosan and a second layer of hyaluronic acid showed the lowest mechanical strength (2.320 N). These results showed that the density of gel structure increased from the addition of composition in encapsulant and different prebiotics.

Table 3. Water activity of microcapsules.

Treatments	Water activity $(a_w)^{ns}$ ± SD
AG-C	0.977 ± 0.001
AGC-C	0.976 ± 0.002
AGC-F-C	0.976 ± 0.002
AGC-Pu-C	0.978 ± 0.001
AGC-Y-C	0.978 ± 0.001

ns: the value was no significant difference ($p\geq0.05$).

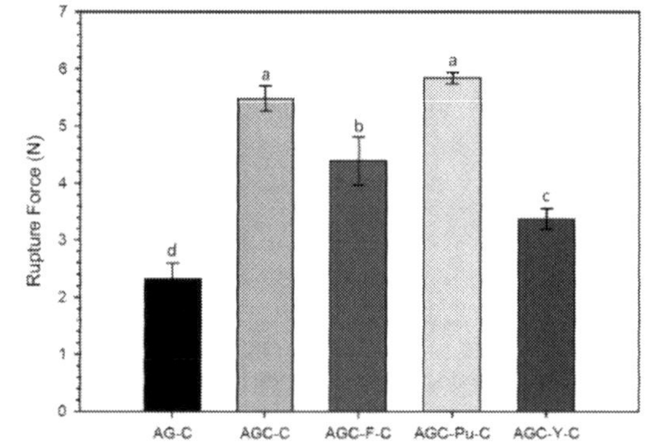

Fig. 3. The mechanical strength of gel microcapsules. Different letters (a-d) on the top of the bar denoted a significant difference ($p<0.05$) between groups.

Table 2. Color of microcapsules.

Treatments	Color ± SD				
	L*	a*	b*	C*	h*
AG-C	54.813 ± 0.031^{d}	-1.870 ± 0.035^{d}	4.383 ± 0.154^{d}	4.770 ± 0.156^{d}	113.123 ± 0.333^{a}
AGC-C	56.967 ± 0.012^{b}	-2.653 ± 0.147^{a}	5.990 ± 0.106^{b}	6.553 ± 0.153^{b}	113.893 ± 0.837^{a}
AGC-F-C	56.557 ± 0.006^{c}	-2.073 ± 0.038^{c}	6.537 ± 0.015^{a}	6.857 ± 0.012^{a}	107.643 ± 0.314^{c}
AGC-Pu-C	58.217 ± 0.040^{a}	-2.447 ± 0.038^{b}	6.460 ± 0.137^{a}	6.910 ± 0.147^{a}	110.707 ± 0.090^{b}
AGC-Y-C	53.393 ± 0.015^{e}	-0.883 ± 0.147^{e}	5.687 ± 0.134^{c}	5.757 ± 0.150^{c}	98.807 ± 1.207^{d}

Superscript letters (a-e) in the same column indicated a significant difference ($p<0.05$) between values.

4 Conclusion

This research showed that the encapsulation of probiotics with use hydrogel and prebiotic pullulan (AGC-Pu-C) enchanted the encapsulation efficiency, resulting in the probiotics surviving up to 10 log CFU/g after the extrusion encapsulation process. The addition of hyaluronic acid to the chitosan coating promotes the spherical shape of the microcapsules. This affects the structure of the microcapsules, resulting in increased strength and efficiency of the encapsulation to protect the probiotics. Furthermore, the mechanical strength was exhibited high. The composition of the encapsulation material that was chosen to use is crucial for developing probiotic encapsulation. Further research should be conducted on the selection of prebiotics that can be effectively utilized by probiotics and promote hydrogel in the microcapsule structure.

The authors would like to be thankful for the Faculty of Digital Agro-Industry and Graduate College, King Mongkut's University of Technology North Bangkok.

References

1. J. Plaza-Diaz, F. J. Ruiz-Ojeda, M. Gil-Campos, A. Gil, Mechanisms of Action of Probiotics. Adv Nutr. **10**, S49–S66 (2019). https://doi.org/10.1093/advances/nmy063
2. G.V. de Melo Pereira, B. de Oliveira Coelho, A.I.M. Júnior, V. Thomaz-Soccol, C.R. Soccol, How to select a probiotic? A review and update of methods and criteria. Biotechnology Advances. **36**, 2060–2076 (2018). https://doi.org/10.1016/j.biotechadv.2018.09.003
3. D. R. Silvaa, J. de Cássia Orlandi Sardib, N. de Souza Pitanguic, S. M. Roquee, A. C. B. da Silvaf, P. L. Rosalena, Probiotics as an alternative antimicrobial therapy: Current reality and future directions. Journal of Functional Foods. **73**, 104080 (2020). https://doi.org/10.1016/j.jff.2020.104080
4. S. Razavi, S. Janfaza, N. Tasnim, D.L. Gibson, M. Hoorfar, Microencapsulating polymers for probiotics delivery systems: Preparation, characterization, and applications. Food Hydrocolloids. **120**, 106882 (2021). https://doi.org/10.1016/j.foodhyd.2021.106882
5. I. A. Neri-Numa, G. M. Pastore, Novel insights into prebiotic properties on human health: A review. Food Research International. **131**, 108973 (2020). https://doi.org/10.1016/j.foodres.2019.108973
6. G. T. C. Delgadoa, W. M. S. C. Tamashirob, Role of prebiotics in regulation of microbiota and prevention of obesity. Food Research International. **113**, 183-188 (2018). https://doi.org/10.1016/j.foodres.2018.07.013
7. M. Cunningham, G. Vinderola, D. Charalampopoulos, S. Lebeer, M. E. Sanders, R. Grimaldi, Applying probiotics and prebiotics in new delivery formats - is the clinical evidence transferable? Trends in Food Science & Technology. **112**, 495-506 (2021). https://doi.org/10.1016/j.tifs.2021.04.009
8. S. Jeznienė, I. Bružaitė, A. Šipailienė, Application of biomacromolecules encapsulation systems for the long-term storage of *Lactobacillus plantarum* F1 and *Lactobacillus reuteri* 182. Heliyon. **10**, e26566 (2024). https://doi.org/10.1016/j.heliyon.2024.e26566
9. A. Kistaubayeva, M. Abdulzhanova, S. Zhantlessova, I. Savitskaya, T. Karpenyuk, A. Goncharova, Y. Sinyavskiy, The Effect of Encapsulating a Prebiotic-Based Biopolymer Delivery System for Enhanced Probiotic Survival. Polymers. **15**, 1752 (2023). https://doi.org/10.3390/polym15071752
10. P. Apiwattanasiri, R. Charoen, S. Rittisak, K. Phattayakorn, S. Jantrasee, W. Savedboworn, Co-encapsulation efficiency of silk sericin-alginate-prebiotics and the effectiveness of silk sericin coating layer on the survival of probiotic *Lactobacillus casei*. Food Bioscience. **46**, 101576 (2022). https://doi.org/10.1016/j.fbio.2022.101576
11. S. Chew, C. Tan, L. Pui, P. Chong, B. Gunasekaran, N.K. Lin, Encapsulation Technologies: A Tool for Functional Foods Development. IJITEE. **8** (5S) (2019)
12. W. Y. Koh, X. X. Lim, T. Tan, R. Kobun, B. Rasti, Encapsulated Probiotics: Potential Techniques and Coating Materials for Non-Dairy Food Applications. Appl. Sci. **12**, 10005 (2022). https://doi.org/10.3390/app121910005
13. S. Agriopoulou, S. Smaoui, M. Chaari, T. Varzakas, A. C. Karaca, S. M. Jafari, Encapsulation of Probiotics within Double/Multiple Layer Beads/Carriers : A Concise Review. Molecules. **29**, 2431 (2024). https://doi.org/10.3390/molecules29112431
14. A. N. Kovács, N. Varga, Á. Juhász, E. Csapó, Serum protein-hyaluronic acid complex nanocarriers: Structural characterisation and encapsulation possibilities. Carbohydrate Polymers. **251**, 117047 (2021). https://doi.org/10.1016/j.carbpol.2020.117047
15. J. Ma, C. Xu, H. Yu, Z. Feng, W. Yu, L. Gu, Z. Liu, L. Chen, Z. Jiang, J. Hou, Electro-encapsulation of probiotics in gum Arabic-pullulan blend nanofibres using electrospinning technology. Food Hydrocolloids. **111**, 106381 (2021). https://doi.org/10.1016/j.foodhyd.2020.106381
16. S. Kraithong, A. Theppawong, Y. Liu, P. Sangsawad, R. Huang, Fucoidan as an Encapsulant material: Applications and advantages in active agents and probiotic encapsulations. Food Chemistry. **477**, 143570 (2025). https://doi.org/10.1016/j.foodchem.2025.143570
17. K. Thinkohkaew, N. Aumphaiphensiri, T. Tangamornsiri, N. Niamsiri, P. Potiyaraj, I. Suppavorasatit, Inulin extracted from burdock root

(Arctium lappa L.) incorporated alginate/chitosan hydrogel beads for probiotics encapsulation. Journal of Agriculture and Food Research. **18**, 101405 (2024). https://doi.org/10.1016/j.jafr.2024.101405

18. K. Thinkohkaew, V. Jonjaroen, N. Niamsiri, A. Panya, I. Suppavorasatit, P. Potiyaraj, Microencapsulation of probiotics in chitosan-coated alginate/gellan gum : Optimization for viability and stability enhancement. Food Hydrocolloids. **151**, 109788 (2024). https://doi.org/10.1016/j.foodhyd.2024.109788
19. M. Ahmadi, F. Hashempour-Baltork, S. Shojaee-Aliabadi, M. J. Marand, F. Shahraz, A. M. Mortazavian, S. M. Hosseini, Effect of yeast cell wall and β-glucan on survival of *Lactobacillus acidophilus* LA-5 encapsulated in spray-dried cross-linked alginate microcapsules. LWT. **222**, 117662 (2025). https://doi.org/10.1016/j.lwt.2025.117662
20. M. N. Singh, K. S. Y. Hemant, M. Ram, H. G. Shivakumar, Microencapsulation: a promising technique for controlled drug delivery. RPS. **5**, 65-77 (2010)

Advancing the Regeneration of Diesel Particulate Filters through the Utilization of Ozone Generated by Non-Thermal Plasma: An Experimental Investigation

Tanapat Prodkornburee [1], *Pokpong* Arsa[1], *Teerapong* Iamcheerangkoon[1], *Sak* Sittichompoo [1,2], and *Kampanart* Theinnoi [1,2]*

[1] College of Industrial Technology, King Mongkut's University of Technology North Bangkok, Wongsawang, Bangsue, 10800 Bangkok, Thailand
[2] Research Centre for Combustion Technology and Alternative Energy (CTAE), Science and Technology Research Institute, King Mongkut's University of Technology North Bangkok, 10800 Bangkok, Thailand

Abstract. Particulate matter (PM2.5) from diesel engines poses significant environmental and health risks. Diesel Particulate Filters (DPF) mitigate emissions but suffer from soot accumulation, which increases back pressure and requires regeneration, often impractical at low urban driving temperatures. This study investigated Non-Thermal Plasma (NTP)-generated ozone and hydrogen for DPF regeneration, assessing their impact on particulate matter, pressure drop, and DPF lifespan. Experiments utilized a 4-stroke diesel engine, with ozone produced from pure oxygen or air through NTP at 20 VPP, 50-1000 Hz, and 5-10 L/min, and introduced into a soot-filled DPF at 200°C. Regeneration was monitored by differential pressure. Findings showed ozone effectively reduced DPF pressure drop, with pure oxygen at 1,000 Hz and 5 L/m yielding the best regeneration above 5,000 ppm ozone. Lower flow rates increased ozone concentration. Hydrogen addition of 3-6% did not significantly improve efficiency and caused system anomalies, possibly due to the formation of water. In conclusion, ozone is a promising, low-energy DPF regeneration solution, effective at temperatures ranging from 200-300°C to 600°C, which is ideal for urban conditions. Optimizing ozone generation is crucial, while hydrogen addition may not be beneficial.

1 Introduction

The escalating global concern over particulate matter (PM2.5) concentrations in the atmosphere presents a continuous and severe environmental and public health crisis, particularly in densely populated urban and industrial areas. Diesel engines are a primary contributor to PM2.5 pollution [1,2], disproportionately responsible for a larger share of emissions compared to gasoline vehicles, even when conforming to the Euro 6 emission standards [3]. This exceedance of emission limits highlights the urgent need for innovative and more effective exhaust after-treatment solutions [4]. A Diesel Particulate Filter (DPF) is a critical after-treatment device designed to capture particulate matter from the exhaust of diesel engines. However, DPF has a finite capacity for soot accumulation, leading to clogging, increased exhaust back pressure, and reduced engine efficiency. To restore filter performance, periodic regeneration is essential, involving the oxidation of accumulated soot [5]. Conventional regeneration methods, such as active and passive regeneration, often require high temperatures or substantial energy input, which are frequently impractical during typical urban driving cycles characterized by lower exhaust temperatures [6]. The challenge of PM2.5 emissions from diesel engines, coupled with the limitations of conventional DPF regeneration methods that struggle to operate efficiently at lower temperatures or with reduced energy consumption, necessitates the exploration of alternative, more versatile, and energy-efficient regeneration approaches. This investigates the efficacy of ozone (O_3) as a potent oxidizing agent for the low-temperature breakdown of particulate matter, thereby facilitating DPF regeneration in urban driving conditions [7]. To meticulously study the pressure drop across the DPF under various regeneration conditions [8]. To experimentally determine methods that can effectively increase the operational lifespan of the diesel particulate filter [9]. The generation of particulate matter from diesel engines is intrinsically linked to the chemical properties of diesel fuel and the dynamics of its combustion, often resulting from incomplete combustion and leading to the formation of soot through a multi-stage process involving inception, nucleation, growth, agglomeration, and aggregation [10–12]. Non-Thermal Plasma (NTP) technology offers an innovative method for ozone generation, which is crucial for DPF regeneration [13,14], as it can produce ozone at relatively low temperatures, enhancing energy efficiency. Oxidation is a fundamental chemical reaction in which soot, composed of solid carbon particles, reacts with oxidizing agents, such as ozone, to convert into gaseous products, including carbon dioxide or carbon monoxide.

*Corresponding author : kampanart.t@cit.kmutnb.ac.th

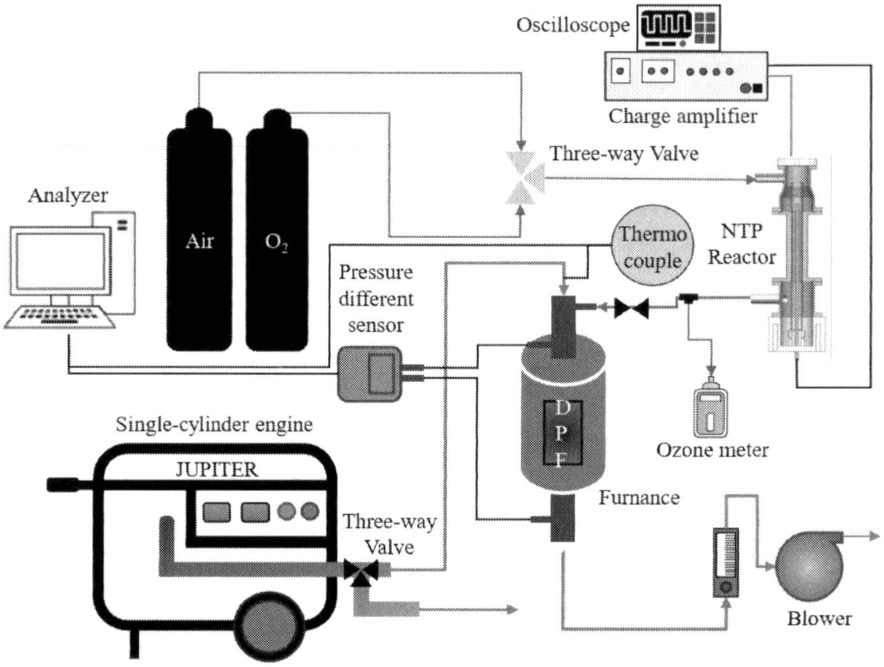

Fig. 1. Schematic diagram of the experimental setup for DPF regeneration using NTP.

The ability of ozone to facilitate this process at lower temperatures is essential [15,16]. DPF functions by trapping particulate matter; however, their finite capacity necessitates regeneration, which can be either active or passive. Both conventional methods have limitations in urban driving conditions [14]. Ozone's inherent instability and strong oxidizing capability can break down soot at significantly lower temperatures, around 200-300°C, compared to conventional methods, which operate at around 600°C, making it suitable for urban cycles. It also investigates hydrogen's potential to enhance this process by providing a localized heat source [17,18].

This study aims to address the critical challenge of PM 2.5 emissions from diesel engines. Conventional DPF regeneration methods are impractical in urban driving due to their high temperature and energy requirements. To propose a more effective solution using O_3 generated by NTP. This work aims to investigate the efficacy of this method in facilitating low-temperature DPF regeneration. The experiment examines the impact of factors such as gas feedstock and NTP frequency on regeneration performance, laying the groundwork for the development of cleaner and more efficient exhaust after-treatment technologies.

2 Experimental setup

The setup for DPF regeneration is depicted in the experimental system in Figure 1. The core components of the system included a Jupiter single-cylinder diesel engine, which served as the controlled source of particulate matter, and a DPF where soot accumulation and regeneration experiments were performed. To maintain the temperature of the DPF during regeneration, a furnace was integrated into the system. Gas generation for regeneration was achieved through the NTP reactor, and a blower was used to induce and control the gas flow throughout the system. The data were collected by the sensors placed within the system. Pressure differential sensors were installed at both the inlet and outlet of the DPF to measure the pressure drop across the filter accurately. Thermocouples were positioned to monitor temperatures at various points, including the DPF, ensuring that the desired thermal conditions were maintained. An ozone meter was incorporated to provide real-time measurements of ozone concentration, allowing for direct monitoring of the generated gas. The experimental setup comprised a specific array of tools and equipment, each selected for its role in ensuring precise control and accurate measurement during the investigation.

2.1 Experimental setup

A Jupiter model JP-D5GF diesel engine was employed as the consistent source of particulate matter. This is a 4-stroke, 1-cylinder engine. The engine detail was as shown in Table 1.

Table 1. The engine specifications.

	Value	Unit
Engine speed	3,000	Revolution per minute (rpm)
Displacement	406	Cubic centimeter (cc)
Power output	10	Horsepower (HP)
Voltage	220	Volt (V)
Output	5	Kilowatt (kW)

Table 2. The conditions and parameters of the experiment, using different gas inlets, consist of O_2 and air for ozone production.

Flow rate to NTP (L/m)	Gas inlet	Voltage (kV)	Frequency (Hz)
5	O_2	20	50
			500
			1,000
	Air		50
			500
			1,000
			500
			1,000
10	O_2		50
			500
			1,000
	Air		50
			500
			1,000
			500
			1,000

2.2 Tools and equipment

A Carbolite Eva vertical tube furnace was used to control the temperature of the DPF during regeneration experiments precisely. This furnace can maintain temperatures within a wide range, from 30°C to 3,000°C, ensuring that the DPF can be held at the desired exhaust gas temperature of 200°C during the regeneration. The blower features a 200 mm impeller diameter and is used to create and regulate the airflow throughout the experimental system. This ensured consistent gas flow rates for both ozone generation and DPF regeneration processes.

Table 3. The conditions for regeneration of DPF.

Engine speed (rpm)	Engine load (%)	Flow rate to NTP (L/m)	Gas inlet	Voltage (kV)	Frequency (Hz)
1,500	12	5	O_2	20	50
					500
					1,000
			Air		50
					500
					1,000

The NTP reactor was central to the ozone generation process. The principle of NTP involves electrical discharge to oxidize particles at low temperatures, a method chosen for its potential to extend DPF lifespan by avoiding high thermal stress. Specifically, the Indirect NTP (INTP) method was implemented to generate reactive chemical species for PM oxidation, thereby minimizing the production of secondary pollutants.

The commercial DPF used in this study was a silicon carbide (SiC) filter with modified a diameter to 23 mm and a length of 127 mm. Its specifications included a cell density of 200 cells per square inch (CPSI) and a wall thickness of 0.43 mm. Key properties for filtration performance were an average pore size of 11±5 μm and a porosity of 46±5%. The chemical composition of the SiC was measured to be 71±7%.

A Keysight model DSOX1204A oscilloscope was used for precise measurement and control of electrical signals, including voltage, frequency, and phase, within the NTP system.

An instrument capable of measuring pressure variations in the range of 0-25 kPa was installed at both the inlet and outlet of the DPF

Thermocouples type K were strategically placed to provide accurate temperature measurements throughout the system, within the DPF and the exhaust gas stream.

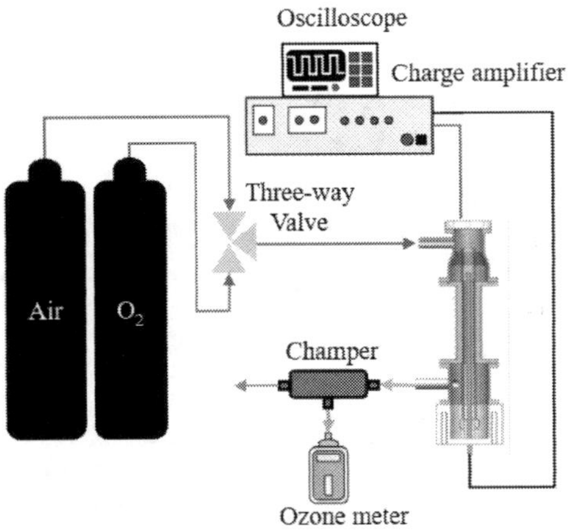

Fig. 2. Schematic diagram of the non-thermal plasma NTP system for ozone generation and measurement, with pure O_2 and air as feedstocks.

An ozone meter with a measurement range of 0-5,000 ppm was connected to the gas flow path to quantify the concentration of ozone produced by the NTP reactor in real-time. Ozone production was validated before initiating the engine experiments. The parameters and conditions governing ozone production are summarized in Table 2. In Figure 2, the diagram illustrates the system used to measure ozone concentration, featuring a three-way valve that allows for the selection of either pure O_2 or air. The selected gas was fed into the NTP reactor, where it generated ozone. The ozone meter then provided real-time measurements of the ozone concentration, enabling us to test various gas flow rates and frequencies to determine the optimal settings for ozone production.

2.3 The calculation of space velocity

The space velocity (SV, 1/h) is crucial for normalizing the gas flow rate relative to the volume of the catalyst or reactor, as follows:

$$SV = \dot{Q}/V \qquad (1)$$

Where Q represents the volumetric flow rate of the exhaust gas, and V denotes the volume of the reactor or catalyst.

$$V = \pi D^2 h/4 \qquad (2)$$

DPF Volume Calculation: The volume of the DPF was calculated using the standard formula for the volume of a cylinder by following:

The volumetric flow rate of exhaust gas ($\dot{Q}$) produced by the engine was determined using the engine's cylinder volume (V_e) and the number of exhaust emissions per operating cycle, as follows:

$$\dot{Q} = V_e \times n \qquad (3)$$

To ensure that the experimental conditions were scalable and comparable across different engine sizes, the space velocity was maintained consistently across various setups. This principle is expressed as:

$$SV_1 = SV_2 \qquad (4)$$

$$\frac{\dot{Q}_1}{V_1} = \frac{\dot{Q}_2}{V_2} \qquad (5)$$

The engine was running to its normal operating temperature, then exhaust gas was routed through the DPF for approximately 1 hour and 30 minutes to collect particulate matter. The collected particulate matter is deposited in the DPF, as illustrated in Figure 3. The DPF, now loaded with particulate matter, was then placed in the Cabolite oven and heated to the temperature of the exhaust gas. Ozone was generated using the NTP Reactor. The parameters and conditions of the experiment are shown in Table 3. To simulate real-world driving. The parameters of 1,500 rpm and 12% engine load are representative of a low-load, low-speed urban driving cycle [19]. A gas flow rate of 5 L/min was selected for testing. Experiments have shown that a lower flow rate results in a longer residence time for the gas within the NTP reactor. The extended residence time allows for more complete ozone formation, resulting in a higher overall ozone concentration and, consequently, a more effective regeneration performance.

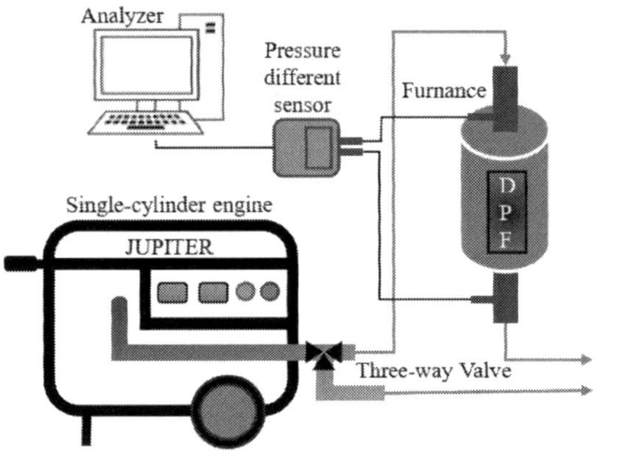

Fig. 3. Schematic diagram of the experimental setup of the engine for particulate matter collection.

3 Result and discussion

3.1 The comparative influence of air and oxygen on ozone production

When air is fed into the NTP reactor, the ozone production is significantly influenced by the frequency and flow rate. At a flow rate of 5 L/m, increasing the frequency substantially enhanced the ozone concentration, as indicated in Figure 4. Specifically, at 50 Hz, the ozone concentration was relatively low, ranging from 90 to 100 ppm. However, increasing the frequency to 500 Hz resulted in a notable increase to approximately 600 ppm, and further increasing it to 1,000 Hz yielded concentrations around 1,100 ppm.

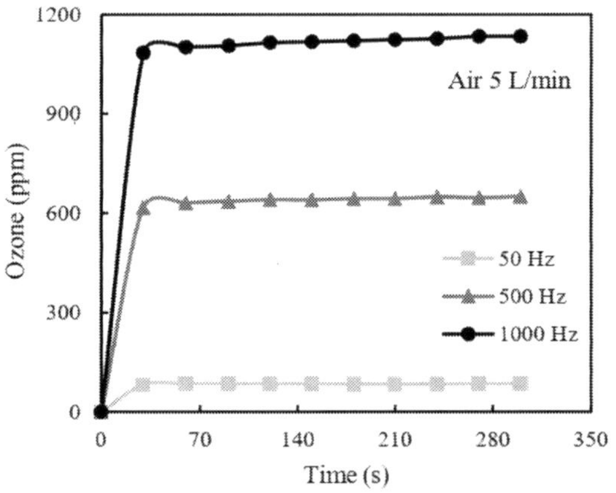

Fig. 4. Ozone production characteristics of the NTP reactor using an air inlet flow rate of 5 L/min at various frequencies.

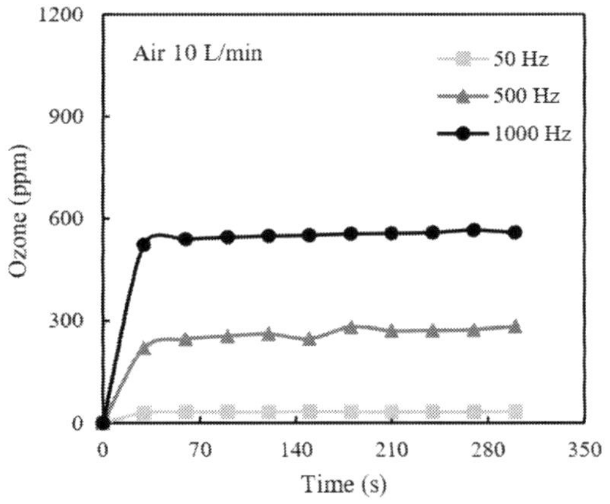

Fig. 5. Ozone production characteristics of the NTP reactor using an air inlet flow rate of 10 L/min at various frequencies.

This demonstrates a direct correlation between higher frequency and increased ozone output when using air. Conversely, when the flow rate of atmospheric air was increased to 10 L/m, as demonstrated in Figure 5, a substantial reduction in ozone concentration was observed across all frequencies compared to the 5 L/min condition. At 50 Hz, concentrations dropped to 30-40 ppm, at 500 Hz to 200 ppm, and at 1,000 Hz to 500 ppm. This reduction in ozone production at higher flow rates is attributed to a shorter residence time of the gas within the NTP reactor. With less time for plasma-induced reactions to occur, the efficiency of ozone formation decreases, resulting in lower ozone concentrations. This highlights that for optimal ozone generation, a balance between gas flow rate and reaction time within the plasma field is crucial. Utilizing pure oxygen as the feedstock improved the efficiency of ozone production. The Figure 6 illustrates that at a flow rate of 5 L/m, the ozone concentrations were significantly higher than those achieved with air. At 50 Hz, approximately 250 ppm of ozone was produced. At 500 Hz, the concentration surged to approximately 2,500 ppm, with production stabilizing after about 60 seconds. Notably, at 1,000 Hz, the ozone concentration exceeded the measurement range of the equipment, which has a maximum capacity of 5,000 ppm. This indicates that pure oxygen, being a more concentrated source of the reactant (O_2), allows for much higher ozone yields.

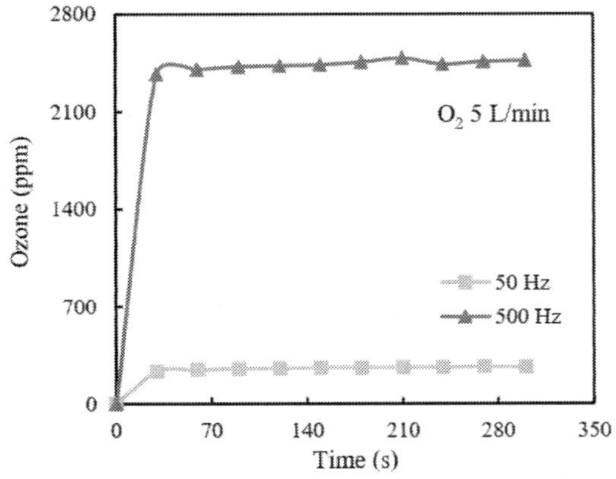

Fig. 6. Ozone production characteristics of the NTP reactor using an O_2 inlet flow rate of 5 L/min at various frequencies.

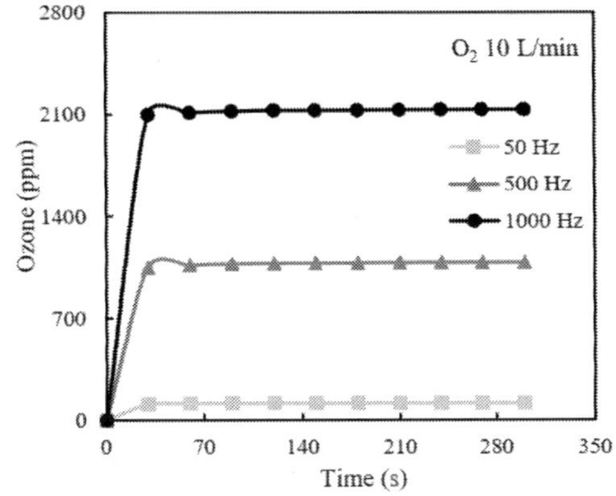

Fig. 7. Ozone production characteristics of the NTP reactor using an O_2 inlet flow rate of 10 L/min at various frequencies.

When the flow rate of pure oxygen was increased to 10 L/m, as shown in Figure 7, a similar trend of reduced efficiency due to shorter reaction time was observed. However, the absolute concentration remained higher than those from the air. At 50 Hz, approximately 115 ppm of ozone was produced. At 500 Hz, the concentration reached about 1,000 ppm, and at 1,000 Hz, it was around 2,000 ppm, also stabilizing after approximately 60 seconds. The results show the average ozone concentration achieved under various conditions of gas type, flow rate, and frequency.

The ozone production tests indicate that the gas flow rate has a direct impact on the efficiency of ozone generation. A flow rate of 5 L/m consistently produced higher ozone concentrations than 10 L/m, primarily because the lower flow rate allowed for a longer reaction time within the NTP reactor. This extended residence time facilitated the formation of more complete ozone. Furthermore, ozone production generally stabilized after approximately 60 seconds of operation, indicating a steady-state condition for the NTP system. The superior performance with pure oxygen highlights the importance of feedstock purity in maximizing ozone yield, particularly at higher frequencies.

3.2 The regeneration of DPF utilizing ozone under varying gas inlet compositions

The effectiveness of DPF regeneration was primarily assessed by monitoring the differential pressure across the filter, which directly correlates with the accumulation of particulate matter. A reduction in differential pressure indicates successful soot removal.

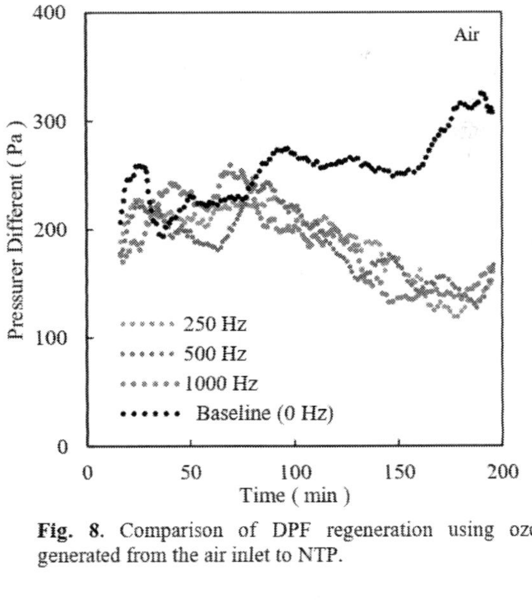

Fig. 8. Comparison of DPF regeneration using ozone generated from the air inlet to NTP.

The experiments involving ozone generated from atmospheric air demonstrated clear regeneration capabilities. The baseline shows the initial increase in differential pressure as soot was collected in the DPF during the first 60 minutes. After this soot loading phase, ozone injection commenced at a DPF temperature of 200°C for 2 hours. The results indicated that the differential pressure began to decrease noticeably around the 80-minute mark and eventually returned to a near-normal state by 180 minutes, as illustrated in Figure 8. This trend confirms the efficacy of ozone produced from atmospheric air in regenerating the DPF, with higher frequencies and thus higher ozone concentrations, generally leading to more effective regeneration. The ability to achieve regeneration at 200°C, significantly lower than the 600°C required for conventional thermal regeneration, highlights a key advantage for applications in low-temperature exhaust environments, such as urban driving.

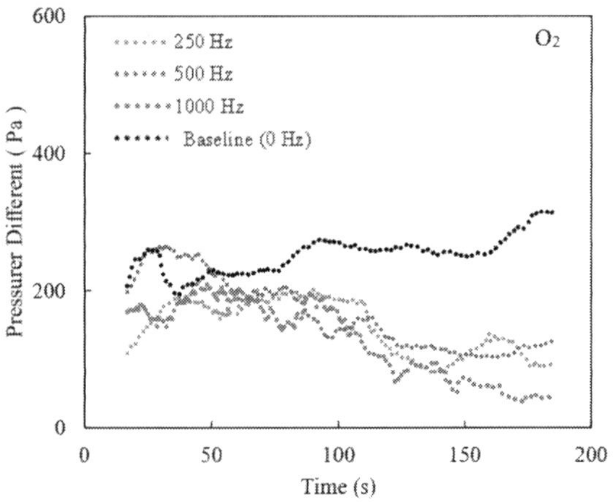

Fig. 9. Comparison of DPF regeneration using ozone generated from the air inlet to NTP.

Regeneration experiments using ozone generated from pure oxygen were expected to show superior performance due to higher ozone concentrations. Figure 9. illustrates these results. While the overall trend for regeneration was positive, some inconsistencies were observed in the differential pressure readings at 250 Hz and 1,000 Hz. These anomalies are hypothesized to stem from variations in the modified DPF devices used for each test or potentially from the presence of water within the exhaust system. The latter could be a consequence of experimental conditions, particularly if hydrogen were introduced in preliminary or subsequent tests that might have influenced the system. Despite these irregularities, the general pattern indicated that the DPF's pressure differential returned to normal levels within the 180-minute regeneration period, suggesting effective soot oxidation by ozone from pure oxygen.

The experimental investigation into the use of ozone and hydrogen for DPF regeneration has yielded several important conclusions regarding their efficacy and potential applications. The primary measurement, based on the differential pressure across the DPF, unequivocally indicates that ozone is highly effective in regenerating the DPF by reducing the accumulation of soot. This is particularly evident when ozone is generated from pure oxygen at higher frequencies, such as 1,000 Hz, which yields higher concentrations of ozone. The mechanism underlying this effectiveness lies in ozone's inherent instability, which leads to its decomposition into highly reactive free oxygen atoms. These atoms possess a strong oxidizing capability, enabling them to react directly with the carbonaceous particulate matter and soot in the DPF, converting it into gaseous products, such as carbon monoxide or carbon dioxide. Crucially, this ozone-driven oxidation occurs at significantly lower temperatures, typically around 200-300°C, compared to the approximately 600°C required for conventional DPF self-regeneration. This low-temperature capability represents a substantial advantage, making ozone a promising low-energy solution for DPF regeneration, especially suitable for operating conditions where exhaust temperatures are typically insufficient for passive regeneration, such as in urban driving cycles.

4 Conclusion

The experimental investigation into the use of ozone for DPF regeneration has yielded several important conclusions regarding its efficacy and potential applications. The experiment, which measures the differential pressure across the DPF, indicates that ozone is highly effective in regenerating the DPF by reducing the accumulation of soot. This is particularly evident when ozone is generated from pure oxygen at higher frequencies, such as 1,000 Hz, which yields higher concentrations of ozone. This study confirmed that higher frequencies of the power supply to the NTP system at 250, 500, and 1,000 Hz directly result in increased ozone production, which in turn leads to improved DPF regeneration performance. This oxidation occurs at significantly lower temperatures, typically around 200-300°C, compared to the approximately 600°C required for conventional DPF self-regeneration. This low-temperature capability represents a substantial advantage, making ozone a promising low-energy solution for DPF regeneration, especially suitable for operating conditions where exhaust temperatures are typically insufficient for passive regeneration, such as in urban driving cycles.

The future work, including further optimization of the NTP reactor parameters, particularly focusing on energy efficiency for ozone generation from pure oxygen, could be explored. Investigations into the long-term effects of ozone regeneration on DPF material degradation and catalyst durability would also be beneficial. Additionally, exploring alternative methods for low-temperature soot oxidation that do not introduce additional system complexities or by-products could be considered. The findings from this research provide a strong foundation for developing more energy-efficient and environmentally sound diesel exhaust after-treatment technologies.

References

1. G. F. Chen, Y. C. Lin, Y. C. Lin, C. C. Wang, W. H. Chen, Human and Ecological Risk Assessment: An International Journal. **28**, 802 (2022)
2. C. Y. Chao, W. Li, P. K. Hopke, F. Guo, Y. Wang, and R. J. Griffin, Environmental Pollution. **366**, 125381 (2025)
3. M. Clairotte, R. Suarez-Bertoa, A. A. Zardini, B. Giechaskiel, J. Pavlovic, V. Valverde, B. Ciuffo, C. Astorga, Environ Sci Eur. **32**, 1 (2020)

4. V. Rossi, L. Brocchi, M. Medda, S. Paltrinieri, F. Rulli, R. Tonelli, SAE Technical Papers. (2023)
5. Z. Meng, C. Chen, J. Li, J. Fang, J. Tan, Y. Qin, Y. Jiang, Z. Qin, W. Bai, K. Liang, Fuel. **262**, 116589 (2020)
6. P. qiang Tan, L. shuang Duan, E. feng Li, Z. yuan Hu, D. ming Lou, Appl Therm Eng. **178**, 115628 (2020)
7. W. Wang, Y. Cai, Y. Shi, J. Wang, N. Zhao, L. Ji, International Journal of Automotive Technology. **22**, 871 (2021)
8. Z. Meng, B. Zeng, J. Tan, Z. Chen, J. Ou, Fuel. **317**, 123353 (2022)
9. T. Yu, K. Li, Q. Wu, P. Yao, J. Ke, B. Wang, Y. Wang, Atmosphere. **14**, 314 (2023)
10. K. Mohiuddin, S. Park, Energy, Environment, and Sustainability. **55** (2019)
11. A. K. Agarwal and M. Krishnamoorthi, International Journal of Engine Research. **24**, 2807 (2023)
12. S. Rana, M. R. Saxena, R. K. Maurya, Environmental Science and Pollution Research. **29**, 15432 (2022)
13. Y. Yang, J. Fang, Z. Qin, P. Pu, C. Yi, Y. Yan, Z. Han, J Therm Anal Calorim. **148**, 5709 (2023)
14. Z. Zhang, R. Dong, G. Lan, T. Yuan, D. Tan, Environmental Science and Pollution Research. **30**, 39338 (2023)
15. Y. Shi, Y. Zhou, Z. Li, Y. Cai, X. Li, Y. He, J. Fang, Chemosphere. **302**, 134787 (2022)
16. J. Ding, M. Xie, Z. Li, Y. Wang, J Alloys Compd. **1010**, 178228 (2025)
17. Y. Shi, Y. He, Y. Cai, Z. Li, W. Wang, Y. Zhou, Y. Lu, Y. Yang, Journal of the Energy Institute. **102**, 268 (2022)
18. B. R. Stanmore, J. F. Brilhac, P. Gilot, Carbon N Y. **39**, 2247 (2001)
19. A. G. M. B. Mustayen, X. Wang, M. G. Rasul, J. M. Hamilton, and M. Negnevitsky, IOP Conf Ser Earth Environ Sci. **838**, 012013 (2021)

Investigation of NO and NO_2 Transformation in a Non-Thermal Plasma-Assisted SCR System with Cu/Al_2O_3

Pichitpon Neamyo[1,4], *Punya* Promhuad[2,4,*], *Warirat* Temwutthikun[2,4], *Sak* Sittichompoo[3,4], *Nuttapon* buntek[2], *Boonlue* Sawatmongkhon[3,4], *Thawatchai* Wongchang[1,4], and *Kampanart* Theinnoi[3,4]

[1]Department of Mechanical and Automotive Engineering Technology, Faculty of Engineering and Technology, King Mongkut's University of Technology North Bangkok (Rayong Campus), 21120 Rayong, Thailand
[2]KMUTNB Techno Park, King Mongkut's University of Technology North Bangkok, 10800 Bangkok, Thailand
[3]College of Industrial Technology, King Mongkut's University of Technology North Bangkok, 10800 Bangkok, Thailand
[4]Research Centre for Combustion Technology and Alternative Energy (CTAE), Science and Technology Research Institute, King Mongkut's University of Technology North Bangkok, 10800 Bangkok, Thailand

Abstract. This research investigates a hybrid methodology for the abatement of low-temperature NO_x by amalgamating non-thermal plasma (NTP) with a Cu/Al_2O_3 catalyst under conditions that simulate diesel exhaust. A catalyst consisting of 2 wt% Cu-loaded γ-Al_2O_3 was synthesized through the technique of incipient wetness impregnation and subsequently characterized using X-ray diffraction (XRD) and scanning electron microscopy with energy-dispersive X-ray spectroscopy (SEM–EDS), thereby confirming the presence of metallic Cu^0 and its uniform distribution. Plasma experiments were executed at input power levels of 20, 30, and 40 W. The results indicated that NTP in isolation effectively facilitated the oxidation of NO to NO_2, attributable to the generation of reactive species including O_3 and O*. Nevertheless, when this plasma treatment was employed in conjunction with the catalyst, both NO and NO_2 were concurrently eliminated via the rapid selective catalytic reduction (SCR) mechanism, resulting in substantially enhanced NO_x conversion rates. Further examination revealed that a reduction in the electrode gap resulted in an increase in electric field strength (E = V/d), which in turn amplified plasma reactivity. At a gap of 3 cm, the most significant NO_x reduction efficiency was attained due to improved NO oxidation and an optimal NO/NO_2 ratio entering the catalyst. In summary, this study elucidates that the efficacy of plasma-catalytic systems is influenced not solely by plasma power but also by the geometrical configuration of the reactor. These findings offer essential insights for the design of energy-efficient systems aimed at low-temperature NO_x control.

1 Introduction

Nitrogen oxides (NO_x), which predominantly include nitric oxide (NO) and nitrogen dioxide (NO_2), represent significant atmospheric contaminants primarily produced through combustion mechanisms in internal combustion engines [1]. Considerable emissions are also linked to external combustion sources, including coal- and gas-fired power generation facilities, industrial furnaces, and marine propulsion systems [2, 3]. These pollutants contribute to various environmental and public health concerns, encompassing acid precipitation, photochemical smog, the formation of ground-level ozone, and respiratory ailments [4, 5].

Selective Catalytic Reduction (SCR) has been extensively adopted as a proficient post-combustion technology for NO_x abatement, attaining substantial removal efficiencies under optimal thermal conditions (typically ranging from 250 to 400°C) [6, 7]. Nevertheless, SCR systems frequently experience diminished catalytic efficiency at lower temperatures, particularly during engine cold-start scenarios or during transient load conditions, wherein the reaction kinetics are adversely affected [8]. Furthermore, the necessity for ammonia or urea injection introduces the potential for ammonia slip, especially under conditions of suboptimal dosing or fluctuating thermal environments, which can result in secondary emissions and create the need for complex control strategies or supplementary catalysts (e.g., ammonia oxidation catalysts) [9].

To mitigate these constraints, Non-Thermal Plasma (NTP) technology has emerged as a promising solution for NO_x reduction at lower temperatures [10]. NTP systems harness energetic electrons generated during dielectric barrier discharges (DBDs) to initiate chemical transformations such as excitation, dissociation, and ionization without significantly elevating the overall gas temperature . A notably advantageous characteristic of NTP is its capacity to oxidize NO into NO_2, a more reactive species that plays a pivotal role in facilitating the rapid SCR pathway [11]:

* Corresponding author: punya.p@technopark.kmutnb.ac.th

$$NO+NO_2+2NH_3 \rightarrow N_2+3H_2O \qquad (1)$$

The production of reactive oxygen and nitrogen species (RONS), encompassing O, O_3, OH•, and NO_3, further amplifies the oxidation mechanism and concurrently aids in the elimination of additional pollutants, including unburned hydrocarbons and soot [12, 13]. Nonetheless, systems utilizing only plasma commonly encounter obstacles, such as insufficient conversion of NO_x, the generation of unwanted byproducts (e.g., N_2O, O_3), and a comparatively elevated energy expenditure per unit of pollutant eliminated [14].

To mitigate these limitations, hybrid plasma–catalyst systems have been suggested, wherein plasma serves as an initial gas-phase activation phase preceding a catalytic reactor [15, 16]. Among the diverse array of catalytic supports, copper-loaded γ-alumina (Cu/Al_2O_3) has emerged as a subject of interest due to its considerable surface area, thermal resilience, and capacity to interact synergistically with species generated by plasma [17]. The integration of copper enhances redox activity, promotes the adsorption and activation of NO_x, and facilitates the breakdown of intermediates such as N_2O_5, thereby contributing to a more thorough reduction of NO_x [18].

Despite the promising prospects presented by plasma–catalyst systems, significant knowledge deficits persist concerning the influence of plasma operating parameters (e.g., power level) and reactor architecture (e.g., electrode gap distance) on the generation of reactive species and the subsequent selective catalytic reduction (SCR) process [19]. Specifically, the function of electric field strength ($E = V/d$) in modulating plasma density, energy transfer, and NO/NO_2 speciation remains inadequately elucidated, particularly under dynamically optimized catalytic conditions [20].

The objective of this investigation is to explore the synergistic effects of non-thermal plasma (NTP) and a Cu/Al_2O_3 catalyst on the reduction of NO_x under conditions simulating diesel exhaust. This research concentrates on (i) analyzing the impact of plasma power input on the conversion of NO to NO_2, (ii) evaluating the efficacy of the plasma–catalyst hybrid system in facilitating the rapid SCR mechanism, and (iii) investigating the influence of reactor geometry, specifically the electrode gap, on plasma reactivity and the overall efficiency of NO_x abatement. The findings are intended to furnish a mechanistic comprehension and practical insights for the optimization of plasma-assisted SCR technologies applicable to low-temperature emission control scenarios.

2 Experimental

2.1 Material preparation

A supported catalyst, comprising 2 wt% copper on γ-alumina, was synthesized utilizing the incipient wetness impregnation technique. The support material, γ-alumina (Ajax Finechem, Australia), exhibited a specific surface area of 142 m^2/g, as evaluated by the Brunauer-Emmett-Teller (BET) methodology. The copper precursor, copper nitrate (Thomas Baker Chemicals, India), was solubilized in a minimal quantity of distilled water (0.5 cm^3). This aqueous precursor solution was subsequently introduced meticulously to 1 g of the support material. The resultant sample was then subjected to drying in an oven at 110 °C overnight to eliminate the solvent. The final catalyst was achieved following calcination in static air at a temperature of 600°C for a duration of 2 hours, facilitating the decomposition of the nitrate precursor and the formation of the copper oxide phase.

2.2 Materials characterization

The crystalline phases of the synthesized catalytic materials were determined through the application of X-Ray Diffraction (XRD) methodologies. Data acquisition was performed utilizing a Rigaku Miniflex 600 diffractometer, which operates utilizing Cu-Kα radiation ($\lambda = 1.5418$ Å). The XRD patterns were recorded within the 2θ range of 10° to 90° at a scanning rate of 2°/min. The surface morphology and elemental composition of the catalytic materials were investigated through the utilization of a ZEISS AURIGA Field Emission Scanning Electron Microscope (FE-SEM), which was integrated with an Oxford Instruments Energy-Dispersive X-ray (EDX) spectrometer to facilitate comprehensive elemental analysis.

2.3 Experimental setup

A laboratory-scale apparatus was developed to replicate the composition of diesel engine exhaust gas and to examine the reduction of NO_x utilizing a non-thermal plasma (NTP) reactor, succeeded by a catalytic converter. The schematic representation of the experimental setup is depicted in Figure 1. The system encompassed five principal components: gas mixing and delivery, preheating furnace, NTP reactor, catalytic converter, and exhaust gas analysis.

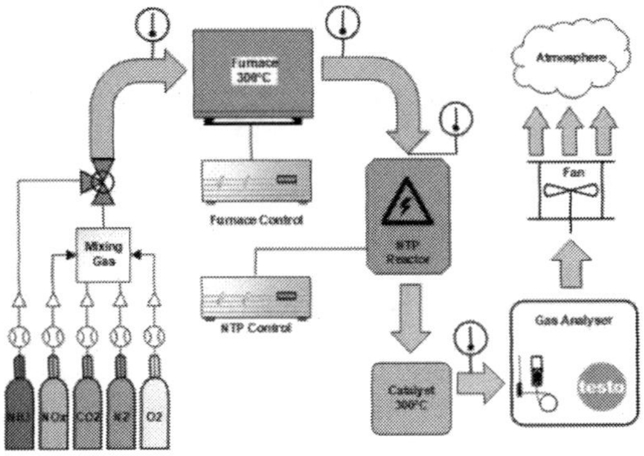

Fig. 1. Experimental configuration for plasma-assisted NO_x abatement utilizing non-thermal plasma (NTP) and a catalyst under conditions mimicking diesel exhaust.

The catalyst was packed in a quartz tube with an inner diameter of 0.5 inch (1.27 cm) and a bed height of 2 inches (5.08 cm), giving a geometric catalyst volume of approximately 6.4 cm^3. At a total gas flow rate of 10

L/min (600 L/h, normalised at 25°C and 1 atm), the gas hourly space velocity (GHSV) was calculated as ~9.4×10^4 h^{-1}. This GHSV value was constant for all plasma power conditions.

High-purity gas cylinders containing ammonia (NH_3), nitrogen (N_2), carbon dioxide (CO_2), nitrogen oxides (NO_x), and oxygen (O_2) were utilized to replicate the composition of exhaust gases. The specifications for each gas were delineated as follows: O_2 (99.95%), N_2 (99.95%), CO_2 (99.95%), NH_3 (1,000 ppm in N_2), and NO_x (1,000 ppm in N_2). Each gas line was fitted with a flow meter and a unidirectional valve to ensure accurate flow regulation and to avert backflow. The gases were subsequently introduced into a stainless-steel mixing chamber, wherein a homogeneous mixing process transpired. The aggregate gas flow rate was meticulously maintained at 10 L/min, with the volumetric concentrations of each constituent adjusted to correspond with the simulated exhaust composition, as elaborated in Table 1.

Table 1. Simulated exhaust gas composition used for plasma–catalytic NO_x reduction experiments.

Gas species	Concentration	Unit
O_2	13.5	%
NOx	120.3	ppm
NO	114.8	ppm
NO_2	5.4	ppm
CO_2	6.0	%
NH_3	117.0	ppm

The mixed gas stream was subjected to preheating via an electric furnace to simulate the thermal conditions characteristic of engine exhaust. The temperature of the furnace was systematically monitored utilizing thermocouples and regulated through a digital furnace controller. The temperature metrics were exhibited on a digital temperature monitor to ascertain uniform inlet conditions for the NTP reactor. The exhaust temperature was sustained at approximately 300°C throughout the duration of the experiment, as this temperature is deemed optimal for SCR applications. The preheated gas was subsequently routed into the NTP reactor, which was designed in a Dielectric Barrier Discharge (DBD) configuration. The reactor was energized by an alternating current (AC) high-voltage source (220 V), with the input electrical energy meticulously monitored using a calibrated watt meter. An independent control unit was employed to modulate the operating voltage and frequency of the plasma discharge. Power discharges of 30, 40, and 60 W were administered to the NTP section to assess the impact of plasma energy on the efficiency of NO_x removal. After the plasma treatment, the gas stream traversed through a catalytic converter filled with the catalyst under investigation. The catalyst zone was additionally equipped with a thermocouple to monitor temperature during operation, thereby ensuring optimal conditions for catalytic NO_x reduction. The outlet gas stream was conditioned by a gas regulator and subsequently directed through a fan system prior to being released into the atmosphere. A TESTO 350 gas analyser was utilized to quantify the concentrations of NO_x and other gaseous species in real-time. The Testo 350 provides sufficient resolution and accuracy for exhaust gas analysis, with specifications as follows: O_2 (resolution 0.01 vol.%, accuracy ±0.2 vol.%), NO (resolution 1 ppm, accuracy ±5 ppm for 0–99 ppm and ±5% of reading for 100–1999 ppm), and NO_2 (resolution 0.1 ppm, accuracy ±5 ppm for 0–99.9 ppm and ±5% of reading above 100 ppm). All gas concentrations reported in Table 1 (O_2 13.5 vol.%, NO 114.8 ppm, NO_2 5.4 ppm, NH_3 117 ppm, CO_2 6.0 vol.%) are therefore above the instrument's resolution limits and within the stated accuracy range. The collected data were transmitted to a computer for logging and subsequent analysis. Outlet NH_3 concentration was monitored using a handheld NH_3 gas detector (0–1000 ppm range, 1 ppm resolution, accuracy ±3% F.S.). No NH_3 slip was detected under any experimental condition. All electrical devices, inclusive of the furnace and plasma control units, were powered by a 220–250 VAC electrical source. Power consumption for the NTP reactor was recorded using a watt meter for the purpose of evaluating energy efficiency.

The NOx mass flow rate was calculated from the measured concentration difference (ΔC, ppm) using the following equation:

$$\dot{m}_{NO_x} = \frac{P \cdot \dot{V}_{gas} \cdot \Delta C \cdot MW}{R \cdot T \cdot 10^6}$$

where P is the system pressure (1 bar), $\dot{V}_{gas}$ is the total volumetric flow rate of the feed gas ($m^3\ s^{-1}$), ΔC is the NOx reduction in ppm (as NO_2 equivalent), MW is the molecular weight of NO_2 (46 g mol^{-1}), R is the universal gas constant (8.314 J mol^{-1} K^{-1}), and T is the absolute temperature (573 K). The calculated mass flow rate is expressed in g h^{-1}.

The specific NOx reduction, normalized to the plasma input power, was then obtained as:

$$\eta_{NO_x} = \frac{\dot{m}_{NO_x} \times 1000}{P_{in}}$$

where P_{in} is the plasma input power (W). The unit of η_{NOx} is g kWh^{-1}.

3 Result and Discussion

3.1 XRD Result

Figure 2 illustrates the X-ray diffraction (XRD) patterns corresponding to the Cu/Al_2O_3 catalyst. Distinct diffraction peaks attributable to both Cu and Al_2O_3 were detected. The existence of Cu was substantiated by its characteristic diffraction peaks observed at 2θ values of approximately 42° and 50°, which align with the standard diffraction pattern for metallic copper (Cu^0) as per JCPDS No. 04-0836 [21]. Moreover, distinctive peaks of Al_2O_3 were recognized at around 20°, 30°, 37°, 39°, 45°, 60°,

65°, 66°, and 79°, signifying the presence of the γ-Al_2O_3 phase as the support material [22].

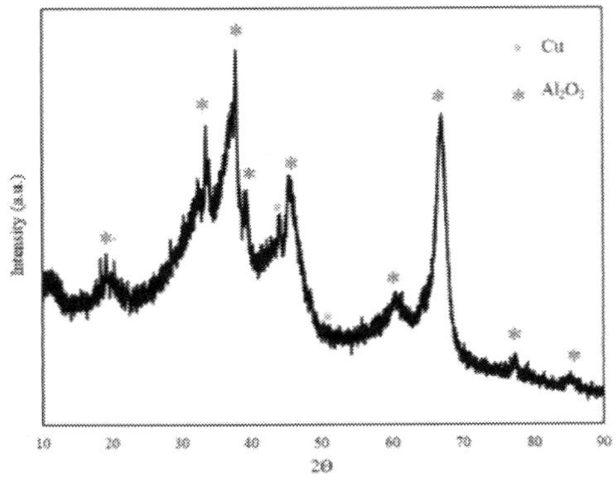

Fig. 2. XRD patterns of the Cu/Al_2O_3 catalyst indicating the presence of metallic Cu and γ-Al_2O_3 phases

The identification of metallic copper, in preference to copper oxide (CuO or Cu_2O), implies that the Cu species remain in a reduced state after the preparation of the catalyst, which is of considerable importance for redox reactions. Copper-based catalysts supported on γ-Al_2O_3 have been documented to play a pivotal role in facilitating the selective catalytic reduction (SCR) of NO_x with NH_3, particularly at low to moderate temperatures [23]. The well-dispersed Cu^0 species on the surface of Al_2O_3 significantly enhance electron transfer mechanisms and promote the interaction between NH_3 and NO_x, culminating in enhanced efficiency of NO_x conversion [24].

These observations corroborate the successful integration of Cu onto the Al_2O_3 support, which is essential for optimizing catalytic performance. The presence of crystalline Cu^0 further suggests robust thermal and structural stability under the prevailing reaction conditions, which will be elaborated upon in the subsequent section regarding NO_x reduction performance.

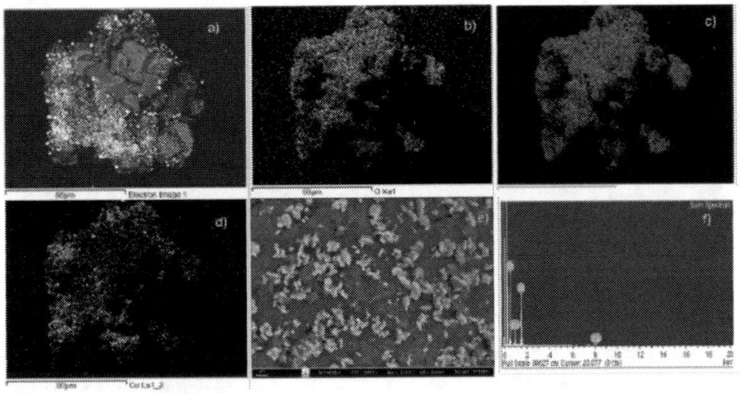

Fig. 3. SEM and EDS analyses reveal a uniform copper distribution on the γ-Al_2O_3 substrate. This finding confirms effective synthesis and supports enhanced NO_x reduction performance.

3.2 SEM-EDS Result

Figure 3 shows SEM micrographs and EDS mapping of the synthesized Cu/Al_2O_3 catalyst. Panel (a) presents the overall SEM image, while panels (b), (c), and (d) correspond to the EDS elemental mappings of oxygen (O), aluminum (Al), and copper (Cu), respectively. Panel (e) shows a higher magnification SEM image revealing surface morphology with well-dispersed particles, and panel (f) displays the EDS spectrum confirming the elemental composition.

The presence of oxygen and aluminum throughout the sample confirms the Al_2O_3 support, as also validated by the XRD peaks of γ-Al_2O_3 in Figure 2. Importantly, the EDS mapping in panel (d) shows that copper is evenly dispersed across the catalyst surface, without observable agglomeration. This observation is consistent with the XRD results in which metallic Cu^0 peaks were detected, suggesting successful incorporation of copper in its reduced form.

The high dispersion of copper is a critical factor for catalytic activity [25]. A uniform distribution of Cu species enhances the availability of active sites, promotes interaction with NO_x and NH_3, and improves the overall efficiency of the SCR process [26]. Moreover, the absence of copper oxide peaks in the XRD pattern and the fine dispersion in the EDS mapping both indicate that the synthesis method yields a high-quality catalyst with metallic Cu^0 well anchored on the Al_2O_3 surface.

This combination of XRD and EDS analyses strongly supports that the catalyst preparation was effective and that the resulting material possesses the structural and compositional features necessary for enhanced NO_x reduction performance under NTP-assisted conditions.

3.3 Analysis of NO and NO_2 Concentration under Different Power Conditions

As illustrated in Figure 4, the initial gaseous effluent exhibited concentrations of 114.82 ppm of nitrogen monoxide (NO) and 5.45 ppm of nitrogen dioxide (NO_2).

The introduction of a 20 W non-thermal plasma (NTP) resulted in a pronounced alteration in the concentrations of nitrogen oxides. The concentration of NO experienced a substantial decline, reducing to 46.00 ppm, which was concomitant with a marked elevation in the NO_2 concentration to 67.61 ppm. This finding underscores the significant oxidative potential inherent in the NTP environment. The conversion of NO to NO_2 can be attributed to reactions involving plasma-generated reactive oxygen species (ROS), predominantly atomic oxygen (O•) and ozone (O_3) [27]. These findings align with the following plasma-mediated reaction mechanisms [28]:

$$NO+O^* \rightarrow NO_2 \quad (2)$$
$$NO+O_3 \rightarrow NO_2 \quad (3)$$

In the case of Cu/Al_2O_3-only treatment (absent plasma influence), NO was reduced to 55.94 ppm while NO_2 remained undetectable at 0 ppm, signifying typical selective catalytic reduction (SCR) activity devoid of oxidative processes. When both NTP and Cu/Al_2O_3 were employed concurrently, NO further diminished to 39.00 ppm, and NO_2 was eliminated, indicating that plasma-generated NO_2 was rapidly consumed via the accelerated SCR reaction.

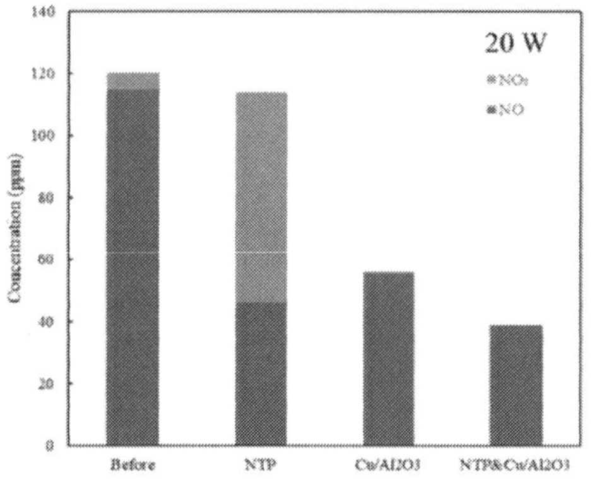

Fig. 4. Impact of solitary and synergistic applications of NTP and Cu/Al_2O_3 interventions on the concentrations of NO and NO_2 at a plasma power of 20 W.

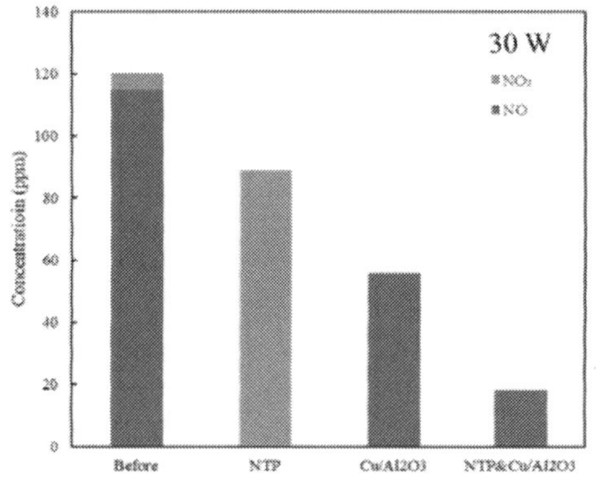

Fig. 5. Efficiency of NO oxidation and NO_x removal under 30 W plasma input with and without Cu/Al_2O_3 catalyst.

As illustrated in Figure 5, an escalation of the plasma power to 30 W significantly modified the reaction pathways. Under conditions exclusive to NTP, NO was completely oxidized to 0 ppm, resulting in a considerable increase in NO_2 concentration to 88.70 ppm. This observation signifies a heightened production rate of oxidizing species such as O• and O_3, which may subsequently lead to the formation of dinitrogen pentoxide (N_2O_5) through the ensuing reactions. Conversely, the catalyst-only system achieved a reduction of NO to 55.94 ppm without yielding any measurable NO_2. The synergistic effect of the combined NTP and Cu/Al_2O_3 system was markedly evident, as it drastically diminished NO concentration to 18.50 ppm while concurrently achieving complete removal of NO_2 (0 ppm). This reflects an exceptionally efficient conversion of NOx, which is ascribed to the facilitation of the rapid SCR mechanism, augmented by the presence of plasma-generated NO_2.

$$NO_2+O_3 \rightarrow NO_3+O_2 \quad (4)$$
$$NO_2+NO_3 \leftrightharpoons N_2O_5 \quad (5)$$

This transformation indicates that a fraction of NO_2 undergoes further oxidation to form N_2O_5 under conditions characterized by elevated ozone and high-energy plasma. Although N_2O_5 is not directly quantifiable via standard NO/NO_2 analysers, its generation signifies a transformation in NO_x speciation and may elucidate the observed minor discrepancy in NO_2 accumulation. Notably, N_2O_5 can also engage in NO reduction through reactions with ammonia (NH_3), thereby contributing to enhanced NO_x removal [29]:

$$N_2O_5+2NH_3 \leftrightharpoons N_2+3H_2O \quad (6)$$

This supplementary pathway offers an alternative route for plasma-assisted reduction, particularly in atmospheres abundant in ozone and ammonia. These reactions further augment the efficiency of NO_x abatement and exemplify the intricate interplay between plasma chemistry and catalytic activity. Consequently, the generation and subsequent degradation of N_2O_5 under non-thermal plasma conditions may contribute to the reduction of residual NO concentrations beyond conventional selective catalytic reduction pathways.

The influence of an elevated plasma power input of 40 W is illustrated in Figure 6. In the absence of a catalytic agent, the application of plasma treatment alone resulted in the total conversion of NO, thereby diminishing its concentration to 0 ppm. This phenomenon was accompanied by a pronounced increase in NO_2 concentration to 201.48 ppm, the peak level recorded, signifying that an excessive input of plasma energy facilitates extensive oxidation processes. Conversely, the Cu/Al_2O_3 catalyst demonstrated consistent performance under conditions of lower power, leading to a reduction of NO to 55.94 ppm.

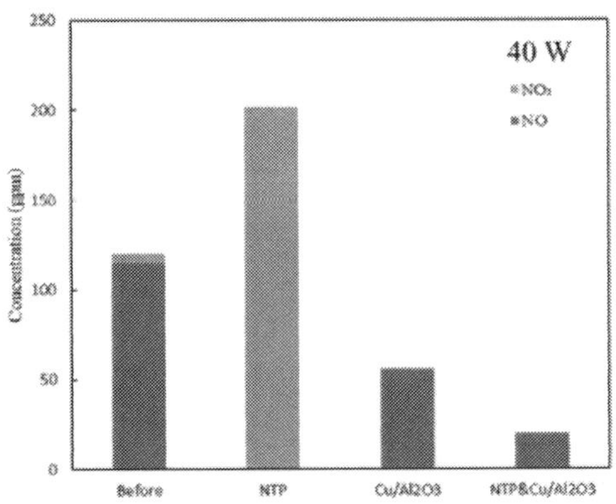

Fig. 6. Enhanced NO_2 formation and NO_x reduction by combined NTP and catalyst system at 40 W.

The synergistic capabilities of the hybrid system were most prominently observed under these experimental conditions. The integrated NTP + Cu/Al_2O_3 configuration achieved the minimal NO concentration at 25.38 ppm while simultaneously attaining complete elimination of NO (0 ppm). This observation suggests that the reactive oxidants, particularly NO_2, produced by the high-power plasma were effectively harnessed and consumed by the catalyst in the rapid selective catalytic reduction pathway, thereby reinforcing the collaborative interaction between the plasma- and catalyst-mediated reaction mechanisms. The pronounced increase in NO_2 concentration at 40 W can also be explained by the influence of the background gas composition. In the simulated exhaust, species such as O_2, N_2, CO_2, and NH_3 coexist with NO and NO_2. At sufficiently high plasma power, the energetic electrons promote additional dissociation of O_2 and partial excitation of N_2 These reactive species can subsequently participate in plasma-driven reactions, leading to further formation of NO and its oxidation to NO_2. For example, reactions between N_2 and O_2 under plasma excitation ($N_2 + O\bullet \rightarrow NO + N\bullet$, followed by $NO + O\bullet/O_3 \rightarrow NO_2$) can contribute significantly to the observed accumulation of NO_2. This synergistic effect explains why the highest NO_2 concentration was detected under NTP-only conditions at 40 W.

This trend became more pronounced at higher plasma wattages (30–40 W), where the increased discharge energy density intensified electron impact dissociation of O_2 molecules. As a result, larger amounts of reactive oxygen species (ROS), particularly atomic oxygen (O•) and ozone (O_3), were produced. These ROS accelerated the oxidation of NO into NO_2 through reactions (2) and (3), leading to a clear increase in NO_2 concentration under NTP-only conditions. In addition, at elevated wattages, a fraction of the formed NO_2 may undergo further oxidation to yield N_2O_5 in the presence of excess O_3. Although N_2O_5 was not directly detected by the analyser, its formation reflects a shift in NO_x speciation under high-energy plasma environments and further supports the explanation for the enhanced NO_2 accumulation observed.

When the Cu/Al_2O_3 catalyst was introduced, the change in NO with increasing NTP wattage can be explained by plasma–catalyst synergy. Higher discharge power intensifies electron-impact processes ($e^- + O_2 \rightarrow O\bullet + O\bullet + e^-$; $O\bullet + O_2 + M \rightarrow O_3 + M$), thus raising the flux of $O\bullet/O_3$ that oxidize NO to NO_2 ($NO + O\bullet/O_3 \rightarrow NO_2$). On the catalyst, Cu redox sites (Cu^{2+}/Cu^+) and the Al_2O_3 surface promote (i) NO oxidation via adsorbed O and nitrate/nitrite intermediates and (ii) SCR pathways once NH_3 is present in the feed. With increasing wattage, plasma-activated NH_3 (e.g., $NH_3 \rightarrow NH_2\bullet$) accelerates the surface steps of standard and fast SCR ($4NH_3 + 4NO + O_2 \rightarrow 4N_2 + 6H_2O$; $2NH_3 + NO + NO_2 \rightarrow 2N_2 + 3H_2O$), resulting in a net decrease of NO. At the highest wattage, competing side reactions (partial NH_3 oxidation to NO/NO_2, NO_2 decomposition, and site blocking by nitrate species) may moderate the net NO removal, yielding a plateau or slight rebound. Overall, the observed NO trend arises from the balance among plasma-phase NO oxidation, catalyst-mediated $NO \rightarrow NO_2$ and $NO \rightarrow N_2$ routes, and power-dependent side reactions.

To evaluate the energy performance of the system, the NOx mass flow rate (g/h) and the specific NOx reduction (g/kWh) were calculated based on inlet–outlet concentrations, flow rate, plasma input power, and the molecular weight of NOx (expressed as NO_2 equivalent). The results are presented in Table 2. As can be seen, the NTP-only case shows limited efficiency and even negative values at 40 W, confirming that plasma alone can promote NOx formation under high-energy conditions. In contrast, the NTP+Cu/Al_2O_3 configuration demonstrates much higher specific NOx reduction, with up to 2.36 g/kWh at 20 W, highlighting the synergistic effect between plasma activation and catalytic SCR pathways.

Table 2. Mass flow rate and specific NOx reduction under different plasma powers and operating conditions

Condition	Power (W)	Mass flow rate (g/h)	Specific NOx reduction (g/kWh)
NTP	20	0.0039	0.20
	30	0.0183	0.61
	40	-0.0470	-1.18
NTP+Cu/Al_2O_3	20	0.0471	2.36
	30	0.0590	1.97
	40	0.0550	1.38

3.4 Influence of Reactor Geometry on Plasma-Catalytic NO_x Reduction

The synergistic interaction between non-thermal plasma (NTP) and selective catalytic reduction (SCR) was rigorously examined by manipulating the electrode gap of the reactor while maintaining a constant plasma power output of 40 W. As elucidated in Figure 7 and Table 2, the spatial configuration of the plasma discharge region exerted a significant effect on the overall efficiency of NO_x reduction within the integrated system.

Table 3. Electrical Characteristics and Reactor Parameters at 40 W Plasm Power

Reaction Gap (cm)	Discharge Voltage (kV)	E (kV/cm)
6	43.3	7.2
4	32.0	8.0
3	27.4	9.1

The findings illustrate a distinct inverse correlation between the electrode gap and the conversion rate of NO. Optimal performance was observed at the minimum gap of 3 cm, where the resultant outlet NO concentration was diminished to its lowest level of approximately 20 ppm. Conversely, as the gap was expanded to 4 cm and subsequently to 6 cm, the outlet NO concentration exhibited an increase to approximately 30 ppm and 45 ppm, respectively.

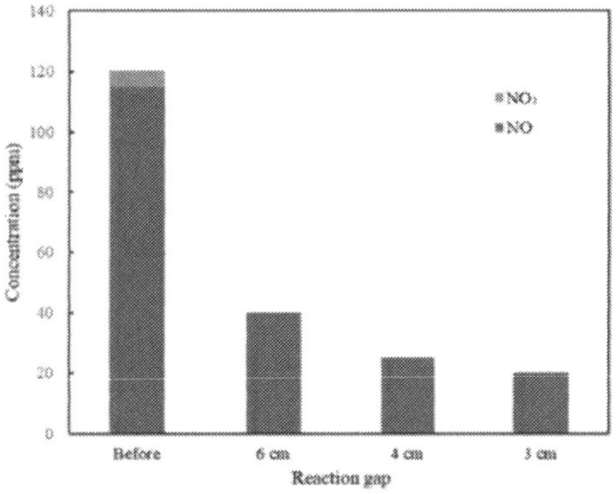

Fig. 7. The influence of reaction gap distance on the concentrations of NO and NO_2 during NTP operation at 40 W.

This observed pattern correlates directly with the strength of the electric field (E), which is determined by the equation $E=V/d$. Although the discharge voltage (V) experienced a reduction as the gap (d) was minimized, the resultant electric field exhibited a marked intensification, escalating from 7.2 kV/cm at a 6 cm gap to 9.1 kV/cm at a 3 cm gap. The augmented electric field facilitates the acceleration and energy of electrons, thereby enhancing the production rate of reactive oxygen and nitrogen species (RONS), including O•, O_3, and NO_3. The primary function of the plasma within this hybrid system is to effectively oxidize a fraction of the initial NO into NO_2. This plasma-generated NO_2 is essential for facilitating the highly efficient rapid SCR reaction on the subsequent Cu/Al_2O_3 catalyst. Consequently, the heightened plasma reactivity at the 3 cm gap establishes an optimal NO/NO_2 ratio that enters the catalyst bed, thereby maximizing the overall NO_x conversion. This observation underscores the critical importance of optimizing reactor geometry, not only for enhancing plasma performance but also for improving the synergistic efficacy of plasma-catalytic systems in the realm of pollution control.

4 Conclusion

This study demonstrates the effectiveness of a hybrid non-thermal plasma (NTP) and Cu/Al_2O_3 catalytic system for nitrogen oxides (NO_x) reduction at low temperatures resembling diesel exhaust conditions. A catalyst with 2 wt% Cu-loaded γ-Al_2O_3 was developed, showing highly dispersed metallic Cu^0 essential for enhancing selective catalytic reduction (SCR) activity. The combination of NTP and the catalyst created a synergistic mechanism utilizing plasma-generated oxidants with catalytic reduction processes. Adjusting the plasma input power revealed that NTP alone could efficiently oxidize nitric oxide (NO) to nitrogen dioxide (NO_2), with higher power levels (30–40 W) significantly increasing NO_2 production. However, when integrated with the Cu/Al_2O_3 catalyst, the generated NO_2 was rapidly consumed through SCR reactions, leading to superior NO_x conversion compared to individual treatments. The presence of intermediary species like N_2O_5 under high-energy plasma conditions further complicated and enhanced the plasma-assisted reaction network. Additionally, reactor geometry, specifically the electrode gap, was carefully analyzed. A smaller reaction gap (3 cm) produced the highest electric field intensity (9.12 kV/cm), increasing plasma reactivity and promoting NO oxidation, thus optimizing the NO/NO_2 ratio entering the catalytic zone. This condition achieved the lowest residual NO concentration (~20 ppm), underscoring the importance of geometric optimization for maximizing plasma–catalyst synergy. In conclusion, the results confirm that reactor design, plasma power adjustment, and catalyst integration are interconnected factors affecting NO_x reduction efficacy. These findings provide a scientific basis for advancing energy-efficient, low-temperature deNO_x technologies based on plasma-catalytic systems.

This research budget was allocated by National Science, Research and Innovation Fund (NSRF), and King Mongkut's University of Technology North Bangkok (Project No. KMUTNB-FF-68-B-26).

References

1. S. Meier, E.F.M. Koene, M. Krol, D. Brunner, A. Damm, G. Kuhlmann,A lightweight NO2-to-NOx conversion model for quantifying NOx emissions of point sources from NO_2 satellite observations, Atmos. Chem. Phys. 24, 7667–7686 (2024). https://doi.org/10.5194/acp-24-7667-2024
2. M.A. Gonzalez-Salazar, T. Kirsten, L. Prchlik, Review of the operational flexibility and emissions of gas- and coal-fired power plants in a future with growing renewables, Renewable and Sustainable Energy Reviews, 82 (2018) 1497–1513. https://doi.org/10.1016/j.rser.2017.05.278
3. Z. Ma, Y. Yang, P. Sun, H. Xing, S. Duan, H. Qu, Y. Zou, Analysis of marine diesel engine emission characteristics of different power ranges in China, Atmosphere, 12(9) (2021) 1108. https://doi.org/10.3390/atmos12091108

4. I. Manisalidis, E. Stavropoulou, A. Stavropoulos, E. Bezirtzoglou, Environmental and Health Impacts of Air Pollution: A Review, Frontiers in Public Health, 8 (2020) 14. https://doi.org/10.3389/fpubh.2020.00014
5. J. Sun, A.J. Barnes, D. He, M. Wang, J. Wang, Systematic Review and Meta-Analysis of the Association between Ambient Nitrogen Dioxide and Respiratory Disease in China, International Journal of Environmental Research and Public Health, 14(6) (2017) 646. https://doi.org/10.3390/ijerph14060646
6. G. Busca, L. Lietti, G. Ramis, F. Berti, Chemical and mechanistic aspects of the selective catalytic reduction of NOx by ammonia over oxide catalysts: A review, Applied Catalysis B: Environmental, 18(1–2) (1998) 1–36. https://doi.org/10.1016/S0926-3373(98)00040-X
7. S. Roy, M.S. Hegde, G. Madras, Catalysis for NOx abatement, Applied Energy, 86(11) (2009) 2283–2297. https://doi.org/10.1016/j.apenergy.2009.03.022
8. B. Guan, R. Zhan, H. Lin, Z. Huang, Review of state of the art technologies of selective catalytic reduction of NOx from diesel engine exhaust, Applied Thermal Engineering, 66(1–2) (2014) 395–414. https://doi.org/10.1016/j.applthermaleng.2014.02.021
9. M. Jabłońska, "Progress on noble metal-based catalysts dedicated to the selective catalytic ammonia oxidation into nitrogen and water vapor (NH3-SCO)," Molecules, vol. 26, no. 21, 6461, 2021, https://doi.org/10.3390/molecules26216461.
10. W. Temwutthikun, P. Promhuad, T. Iamcheerangkoon, B. Sawatmongkon, K. Theinnoi, S. Sittichompoo, An Experimental Investigation on Enhancing Nitrogen Oxides Reduction of Non-Thermal Plasma (NTP) Aftertreatment System with Silver-Base Catalyst with NTP Downstream SCR Catalyst Configuration. Materials Science Forum. (2024). https://doi.org/10.4028/p-CcFD5C
11. R. Gholami, C.E. Stere, A. Goguet, C. Hardacre, Non-thermal-plasma-activated de-NO_x catalysis, Philosophical Transactions of the Royal Society A: Mathematical, Physical and Engineering Sciences, 376(2110) (2018) 20170054. https://doi.org/10.1098/rsta.2017.0054
12. H. H. Kim, "Nonthermal plasma processing for air-pollution control: a historical review, current issues, and future prospects," Plasma Processes and Polymers, vol. 1, no. 2, pp. 91–110, 2004, https://doi.org/10.1002/ppap.200400028
13. M. Babaie, P. Davari, P. Talebizadeh, F. Zare, H. Rahimzadeh, Z. Ristovski, and R. Brown, "Performance evaluation of non-thermal plasma on particulate matter, ozone and CO_2 correlation for diesel exhaust emission reduction," Chemical Engineering Journal, vol. 276, pp. 240–248, 2015, https://doi.org/10.1016/j.cej.2015.04.086
14. S. Teodoru, Y. Kusano, and A. Bogaerts, "The effect of O_2 in a humid $O_2/N_2/NO_x$ gas mixture on NO_x and N_2O remediation by an atmospheric pressure dielectric barrier discharge," Plasma Processes and Polymers, vol. 9, pp. 652–689, 2012, https://doi.org/10.1002/ppap.201100187.
15. J. Van Durme, J. Dewulf, C. Leys, H. Van Langenhove, Combining non-thermal plasma with heterogeneous catalysis in waste gas treatment: A review, Applied Catalysis B: Environmental, 78(3–4) (2008) 324–333. https://doi.org/10.1016/j.apcatb.2007.09.035
16. H.-L. Chen, H.-M. Lee, S.-H. Chen, M.-B. Chang, S.-J. Yu, S.-N. Li, Removal of volatile organic compounds by single-stage and two-stage plasma catalysis systems: A review of the performance enhancement mechanisms, current status, and suitable applications, Environmental Science & Technology, 43(7) (2009) 2216–2227. https://doi.org/10.1021/es802679b
17. Y. Li, J. Su, J. Ma, F. Yu, J. Chen, and R. Li, "Novel straight synthesis of super-microporous Cu/Al2O3 catalyst with high CH4-SCR-NO activity," Catalysis Communications, vol. 65, pp. 6–9,2015, https://doi.org/10.1016/j.catcom.2015.02.020
18. K. Shimizu, H. Kawabata, H. Maeshima, A. Satsuma, and T. Hattori, "Intermediates in the selective reduction of NO by propene over Cu–Al2O3 catalysts: Transient in situ FTIR study," Journal of Physical Chemistry B, vol. 104, no. 13, pp. 2885–2893, 2000, https://doi.org/10.1021/jp9930705
19. V. Palma, M. Cortese, S. Renda, C. Ruocco, M. Martino, E. Meloni, A Review about the Recent Advances in Selected Nonthermal Plasma Assisted Solid–Gas Phase Chemical Processes, Nanomaterials, 10(8) (2020) 1596. https://doi.org/10.3390/nano10081596
20. J.T. Herron, Modeling studies of the formation and destruction of NO in pulsed barrier discharges in nitrogen and air, Plasma Chemistry and Plasma Processing, 21 (2001) 581. https://doi.org/10.1023/A:1012003218939
21. JCPDS-ICDD, Powder Diffraction File, Card No. 04-0836 (Cu), International Centre for Diffraction Data, Newtown Square, PA, USA.
22. S. Selpiana, D. N. Sari, E. Purwaningsih, Synthesis and characterization catalyst γ-Al_2O_3 and Al/γ-Al_2O_3, Indonesian Journal of Fundamental and Applied Chemistry, 7(1) (2022) 26–31. https://doi.org/10.24845/ijfac.v7.i1.26
23. J. Li, H. Chang, L. Ma, J. Hao, R.T. Yang, Low-temperature selective catalytic reduction of NOx with NH3 over metal oxide and zeolite catalysts—A review, Catalysis Today, 175 (2011) 147–156. https://doi.org/10.1016/j.cattod.2011.03.034
24. N. Jraba, T. Makhlouf, G. Delahay, H. Tounsi, Catalytic activity of Cu/η-Al_2O_3 catalysts prepared from aluminum scraps in the NH_3-SCO and in the

NH_3-SCR of NO, Environmental Science and Pollution Research, 29(6) (2022) 9053–9064. https://doi.org/10.1007/s11356-021-16206-1

25. M. Hattori, T. Hattori, M. Ozawa, The chemical state and Cu+ stability for three-way catalytic performance of Cu-added Al2O3 catalysts. (2023). https://doi.org/10.1016/j.apcata.2023.119515
26. B. Zhu et al., Insights into the active sites of copper species in CuO/SiO2 catalysts for NH3-SCR: Quantitative analysis and mechanism study. Fuel. (2024). https://doi.org/10.1016/j.fuel.2024.131341
27. P. Chonpan, K. Theinnoi, T. Iamcheerangkoon, P. Promhuad, S. Sittichompoo, Effects of operating parameters on dielectric barrier discharge non-thermal plasma ozone generator performance and NO Conversion. E3S web of conferences. **610**, 4001 (2025). https://doi.org/10.1051/e3sconf/202561004001
28. J. H. Bae, H. Lee, S.-C. Huh, S. Park, Nitric and Nitrous Acid Formation in Plasma-Treated Water: Decisive Role of Nitrogen Oxides (NO=1–3). Chemosphere. 143105 (2024). https://doi.org/10.1016/j.chemosphere.2024.143105
29. L. S. Ko, K. L. Pan, M. B. Chang, Deep oxidation of NO via catalytic ozonation. J Air Waste Manage Assoc.(2024). https://doi.org/10.1080/10962247.2024.2416047

The Study of Fragrance Encapsulation Using Zeolite

Natnicha Kongyang, *Sukanya* Sudmee, *Rapeeporn* Wannarat, and *Sukanya* Thepwatee

Department of Industrial Chemistry, Faculty of Applied Science, King Mongkut's University of Technology North Bangkok, Wong Sawang, Bang Sue, 10800 Bangkok, Thailand

Abstract. Aroma is a key component in food, cosmetics, and consumer products, significantly influencing human perception and satisfaction. However, most fragrances are volatile and susceptible to degradation upon exposure to air, heat, and light, reducing product quality and shelf life. Therefore, the development of efficient encapsulation systems for fragrance retention and controlled release is essential. This study investigates the use of zeolites—nanoporous materials with high specific surface areas and excellent adsorption capabilities—as encapsulation carriers for three commonly used cosmetic fragrances: D-limonene (DL), benzyl acetate (BA), and geraniol (GE), which vary in molecular size. The encapsulation efficiency (%EE) and loading efficiency (%LE) of each fragrance were evaluated and compared. The effect of incorporating Tween 80 (T80), a nonionic surfactant, into the system was also examined. Fragrance content and stability were analyzed using thermogravimetric analysis (TGA) one day after preparation and after 30 days of storage at ambient temperature. Results indicated that the presence of T80 helped stabilize %EE and %LE across different fragrance types, whereas in the absence of T80, encapsulation performance appeared more dependent on fragrance molecular characteristics. Additionally, retention studies revealed that systems containing T80 exhibited improved fragrance retention, particularly for low molecular weight, highly volatile compounds. These findings suggest that T80 may modulate the interaction between fragrance molecules and zeolite surfaces, improving both initial loading and long-term retention. This knowledge supports the development of more effective fragrance delivery systems for applications requiring sustained aroma release.

1 Introduction

Fragrance plays a vital role in consumer perception and product appeal in food, cosmetics, and household items [1-3]. However, due to the high volatility of most fragrance compounds, their aroma is rapidly lost when exposed to the atmosphere, leading to diminished product quality and a reduced lifespan of the fragrance. Encapsulation technology offers an effective strategy to protect fragrances, control their release, and prolong their sensory impact [4]. Zeolites have attracted interest as encapsulation materials because of their nanoporous architecture, large surface area, strong adsorption capabilities, and compatibility with biological systems, making them ideal carriers for volatile organic compounds [5-7]. Their pore size and surface characteristics are critical for the physical entrapment and selective adsorption of fragrance compounds.

In addition, formulation additives such as surfactants can significantly influence encapsulation performance. Tween 80 (T80), a non-ionic surfactant, is commonly used to stabilize emulsions and improve the dispersion of active compounds [8, 9]. In the context of fragrance encapsulation, T80 may affect the interaction between zeolites and fragrance molecules by modulating surface affinity or altering molecular mobility [10]. However, to the best of our knowledge, no previous studies have specifically investigated this effect.

Therefore, this study aims to develop an effective fragrance encapsulation system using natural zeolite in combination with T80 as the carrier and retention-enhancing agent for three model fragrance compounds: D-limonene (DL), benzyl acetate (BA), and geraniol (GE). These fragrances were selected based on their structural diversity, molecular weight, and common use in cosmetic applications [11-13]. Encapsulation was performed with and without the addition of 1% (w/v) T80 to assess its role in modifying fragrance–zeolite interactions. Encapsulation performance was evaluated through loading efficiency (%LE) and encapsulation efficiency (%EE), followed by stability assessment using thermogravimetric analysis (TGA) after 30 days of storage at ambient temperature. The effects of molecular characteristics and T80 on fragrance retention were compared. This work explores how molecular size, volatility, and surfactant-assisted modifications influence the encapsulation and long-term stability of fragrances in zeolite-based systems, contributing to the development of more efficient delivery platforms for products requiring prolonged aroma release.

2 Materials and Methods

2.1 Materials

Natural cosmetic-grade zeolite was purchased from Tropicalife Co., Ltd. (Thailand). Ethanol was obtained from the Liquor Distillery Organization (Thailand). Cosmetic-grade D-limonene (DL, 95.0%), geraniol (GE, 95.0%), and benzyl acetate (BA, 99.0%) were supplied by Chanjao Longevity Co., Ltd. (Thailand). Cosmetic-grade Tween 80 (T80, 90.0%) was provided by S. Tong Chemicals Co., Ltd. (Thailand). All chemicals were used as received without further purification.

2.2 Encapsulation of fragrance

The fragrance encapsulation procedure was based on methods described in earlier studies [4, 10]. Zeolite was pre-treated by drying in a vacuum oven (BINDER GmbH, Germany) at 80°C for 2 h. After pretreatment, 1.0 g of zeolite was dispersed into a solution of 15 mL ethanol and 0.200 g T80, with gentle stirring to ensure homogeneity. Then, 5 mmol of a selected fragrance compound was added to the mixture, which was continuously stirred at 60 °C using a magnetic stirrer set to 700 rpm until a dry, powder-like product was formed. The resulting fragrance-loaded zeolite powder was subsequently dried in a hot air oven (Model T6120, Heraeus Instruments, Germany) at 60°C for 2 h.

2.3 Characterization

2.3.1 UV-vis analysis of fragrance compounds

UV–vis absorption spectra of the fragrance molecules were recorded using a SPECORD 210 PLUS UV–vis spectrophotometer (Analytik Jena, Germany). Ethanol was used as both the solvent and blank in the spectral range of 190–1000 nm, using a quartz cuvette.

2.3.2 SEM

The surface morphology of the zeolite was examined using a scanning electron microscope (SEM, FEI QUANTA 450) at 5000× magnification. Prior to imaging, samples were dried in a vacuum oven at 80°C for 3 h, mounted on SEM stubs using carbon adhesive tape, coated with platinum (Pt) at 10 kV and 30 mA, and then directly introduced into the chamber for imaging.

2.3.3 X-ray diffraction

The crystalline structure of zeolite samples were analyzed using X-ray diffraction (XRD) using a D2 PHASER diffractometer (Bruker, Germany) equipped with Cu-Kβ radiation (λ = 1.3923 Å), operating at 40 kV and 30 mA. Scans were recorded over a 2θ range of 1° to 80°, with a step size of 0.02° and a scan speed of 1.20 °/min.

2.3.4 N_2 adsorption-desorption

Prior to nitrogen adsorption–desorption analysis, the zeolite sample was first heated in a vacuum oven at 80 °C for 3 h, followed by pretreatment under a nitrogen gas flow (50 mL/min) at 250°C for 4 h. The adsorption–desorption isotherm, specific surface area, pore size, and pore volume of the zeolite were determined via N_2 adsorption–desorption analysis conducted at -196°C using a BELSORP-mini instrument (BEL, Japan). The specific surface area was evaluated using the Brunauer–Emmett–Teller (BET) equation, while the pore size and pore volume were calculated using the Barrett–Joyner–Halenda (BJH) method [14].

2.3.5 Color measurement

Color analysis of the zeolite samples before and after fragrance loading was performed using the CIELAB color model and reported in the Lab color space using an eXact™ XP spectrophotometer (X-Rite, USA). In this model, the L value represents lightness, ranging from 0 (black) to 100 (white). The a* coordinate reflects the green-to-red spectrum, where negative values indicate green and positive values indicate red. The b* coordinate corresponds to the blue-to-yellow range, with negative values representing blue and positive values indicating yellow. The overall color change (ΔE) between the fragrance-loaded and natural zeolite samples was calculated using Equation (1) [15]:

$$\Delta E = \sqrt{\Delta L^2 + \Delta a^2 + \Delta b^2} \quad (1)$$

2.3.6 FTIR

Functional groups present in the starch samples were characterized using a FT-IR spectrometer (PerkinElmer Spectrum 100, USA). Each sample was blended with potassium bromide (KBr) and compressed into translucent pellets using a manual hydraulic press at a pressure of 5 N/m² for 3 min. Spectra were recorded in the range of 450–4000 cm^{-1} at a resolution of 4 cm^{-1}, with eight scans per sample.

2.3.7 TGA

Thermogravimetric analysis (TGA) was performed to determine the fragrance loading efficiency (%LE) and encapsulation efficiency (%EE). The analyzed samples included: zeolite, zeolite loaded with a fragrance molecule, and zeolite loaded with a fragrance molecule and Tween 80 (T80). Each sample (10 mg) was analyzed using a TGA/DSC 3+ thermogravimetric analyzer (Mettler-Toledo Ltd., Thailand) under an air atmosphere at a flow rate of 50 cm³/min. The temperature was ramped from 50 to 700°C at a heating rate of 10 °C/min. The %LE and %EE were calculated using Equations (2) and (3), respectively:

$$\%LE = \frac{W_F}{W_{ZL}} \times 100 \quad (2)$$

$$\%EE = \frac{W_F}{W_{F0}} \times 100 \quad (3)$$

where W_F is the weight of encapsulated fragrance, W_Z is the weight of zeolite, and W_{F0} is the initial weight of the fragrance loaded.

2.4 Fragrance retention

Fragrance retention was evaluated by storing the encapsulated fragrance samples in a desiccator at ambient temperature, following a method adapted from the literature [6]. After 30 days of storage, the samples were analyzed using TGA as previously described. The percentage of fragrance retention (%RT) was calculated using Equation (4):

$$\%RT = \frac{\%LE_{30}}{\%LE_0} \times 100 \quad (4)$$

where $\%LE_{30}$ is the loading efficiency after 30 days of storage and $\%LE_0$ is the initial loading efficiency.

3 Results and discussion

3.1 UV-vis spectra of fragrance compounds

Three fragrance molecules were investigated in this study: D-limonene (DL), benzyl acetate (BA), and geraniol (GE), as shown in Fig. 1. Geraniol is a terpene alcohol known for its characteristic rose-like scent. The UV–vis absorption spectra of the fragrance compounds are presented in figure 2. Both DL and GE exhibited maximum absorbance (λ_{max}) around 203 nm, while BA showed a λ_{max} at 207 nm, which aligns closely with previously reported values [16-18].

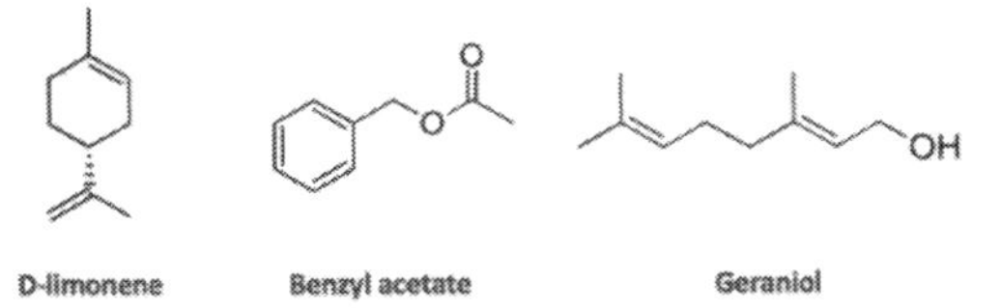

Fig. 1. Molecular structure of fragrance molecules used in this works.

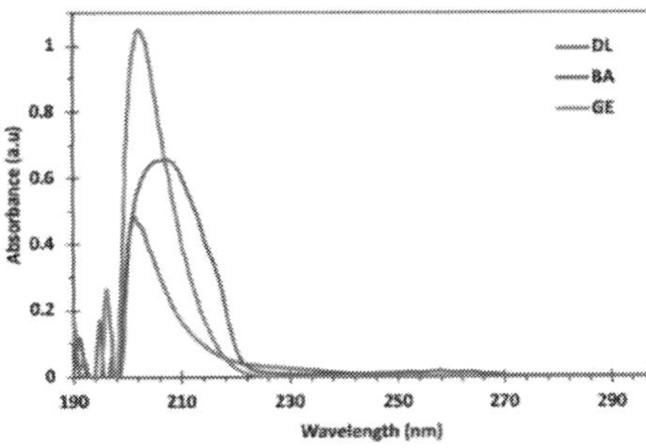

Fig. 2. UV-vis spectra of fragrance compounds.

3.2 SEM and N_2 adsorption-desorption analyses of zeolite

Zeolites are typically porous materials with a microporous structure, resulting in a high surface area that is suitable for adsorption applications. Their narrow pore distribution also enables controlled fragrance release. In this study, the morphology of the natural zeolite was examined using SEM, as shown in Figure 3(a). The SEM image reveals that the zeolite particles form aggregates with a highly rough surface, suggesting the presence of significant porosity.

To further confirm the porosity, N_2 adsorption–desorption analysis was performed to determine the specific surface area, pore size, and pore volume. As shown in Figure 3(b), the isotherm corresponds to type IV according to the IUPAC classification, indicating a mesoporous structure with pore sizes in the range of 2–50 nm [19]. The zeolite exhibited a specific surface area of 98.209 m^2/g, an average pore size of 10.9 nm, and a pore volume of 0.4852 cm^3/g. The relatively low surface area and large pore size are consistent with previous reports on natural zeolites [20-22].

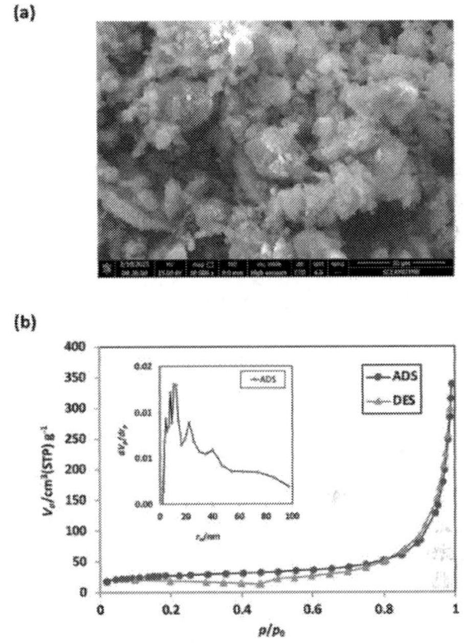

Fig. 3. (a) SEM image of zeolite at 10,000× magnification and (b) N_2 adsorption–desorption isotherm and pore size distribution curve.

3.3 X-ray diffraction

X-ray diffraction (XRD) analysis was conducted to investigate the crystalline structure of the natural zeolite. As illustrated in Fig. 4, the diffraction pattern was recorded over a 2θ range of 1° to 80°. The presence of sharp and well-defined peaks in the XRD pattern confirms the crystalline nature of the zeolite. The observed diffraction peaks correspond to the crystalline phase of clinoptilolite ($(K_2,Na_2,Ca)_3[Al_6Si_{30}O_{72}]\cdot 20H_2O$, IUPAC code: HEU), with characteristic peaks at 2θ values of 9.78°, 11.16°, 22.40°, and 29.92° [22, 23], as well as the crystalline phase of quartz, identified by a prominent peak at 2θ of 26.62° [21].

After fragrance loading (DL/Ze, BA/Ze, and GE/Ze), the XRD patterns and peak intensities remained largely unchanged compared to those of the natural zeolite, indicating that the loading process did not affect the

https://doi.org/10.1051/e3sconf/202567901013

crystalline structure of the zeolite. However, co-loading with Tween 80 (GE-Tw/Ze) showed a noticeable reduction in peak intensity, suggesting partial disruption of the crystal structure during the encapsulation process. Nonetheless, the overall structural stability of the zeolite was largely preserved following fragrance incorporation.

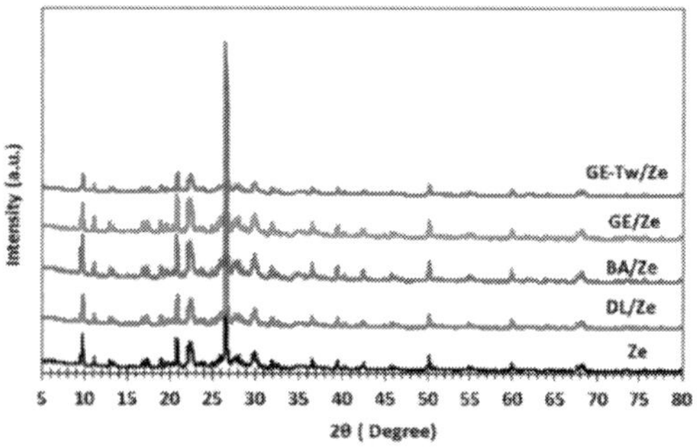

Fig. 4. XRD diffractograms of zeolite, fragrance-loaded zeolites, and geraniol-loaded zeolite with Tween 80.

3.4 Color analysis

The total color difference (ΔE) between the fragrance-loaded zeolite and natural zeolite was evaluated to assess the visual changes resulting from fragrance encapsulation, which is important for the quality control of commercial products, as such changes may affect the final appearance of the end products. The CIELAB color parameters of the zeolite samples are summarized in Table 1.

Table 1. Color of zeolite and fragrance-loaded zeolites with and without T80.

Sample	L*	a*	b*	ΔE
Ze	78.07 ± 0.02	5.23 ± 0.00	13.36 ± 0.01	-
DL/Ze	76.95 ± 0.01	5.10 ± 0.01	13.03 ± 0.01	1.16
BA/Ze	70.31 ± 0.01	5.79 ± 0.01	13.16 ± 0.01	7.79
GE/Ze	64.60 ± 0.00	7.78 ± 0.01	17.63 ± 0.01	14.36
DL-Tw/Ze	65.71 ± 0.01	7.92 ± 0.01	18.19 ± 0.10	14.23
BA-Tw/Ze	64.64 ± 0.01	8.62 ± 0.00	19.08 ± 0.00	15.05
GE-Tw/Ze	66.70 ± 0.00	7.92 ± 0.01	18.19 ± 0.10	12.72

In general, untrained human eyes can perceive color differences when ΔE exceeds 2. The greater the ΔE value, the more noticeable the difference to the human eye [24, 25].

Natural zeolite exhibited a high L* value along with positive a* and b* values, indicating a bright color with reddish and yellowish tones. After fragrance loading, noticeable changes in the color parameters were observed. The L* value tended to decrease, indicating a darker shade, while the a* and b* values increased, suggesting enhanced red and yellow components.

Among the tested fragrances, GE induced the most pronounced color change. The presence of T80 appeared to enhance this effect, which may be attributed to their larger molecular size and their interaction with the zeolite surface, potentially influencing surface properties and light reflection behavior.

3.5 FTIR

Figure 5. FT-IR spectra comparing (a) pure zeolite and individual fragrance molecules, (b) fragrance-loaded zeolite without T80, and (c) fragrance-loaded zeolite with T80.

FTIR spectrum of zeolite (Figure 5(a)) exhibits characteristic bands corresponding to Si–O(Si) and Si–O(Al) vibrations in the range of 1200–400 cm^{-1}. Additionally, absorption bands around 1600 cm^{-1} and 3700 cm^{-1} are attributed to H–O bending and stretching vibrations, respectively, indicating the presence of adsorbed water molecules within the zeolite structure [26].

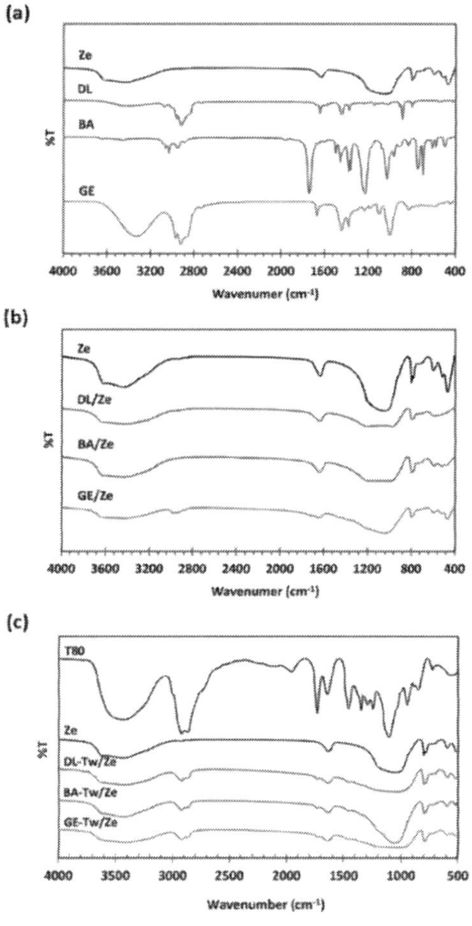

Fig. 5. FTIR spectra of (a) zeolite and fragrance compounds, (b) fragrance-loaded zeolites, and (c) fragrance-loaded zeolite with T80.

For D-limonene, the spectrum displays distinct peaks at 2975 cm^{-1} and 2920 cm^{-1}, assigned to C–H stretching

 https://doi.org/10.1051/e3sconf/202567901013

vibrations of methyl groups (–CH_3). The C=C stretching vibrations of both cycloalkene and disubstituted alkene structures are observed at 1645 cm^{-1}. CH_2 scissoring vibrations appear at 1452 cm^{-1} and 1376 cm^{-1}, while the =C–H out-of-plane bending of a terminal methylene group is noted at 887 cm^{-1} [27].

The FTIR spectrum of BA shows characteristic aromatic C–H stretching at 3035 cm^{-1}, a strong ester C=O stretching band at 1742 cm^{-1}, and C–O stretching of the ester group at 1229 cm^{-1}. Additionally, C–H out-of-plane bending vibrations of the aromatic ring are observed at 750 cm^{-1} and 698 cm^{-1}.

GE exhibits a broad O–H stretching band of the alcohol group at 3334 cm^{-1}. The C–H stretching vibrations of methyl groups (–CH_3) are observed at 2968 cm^{-1} and 2918 cm^{-1}. A prominent C=C stretching vibration of the alkene group appears at 1669 cm^{-1}, while the C–O stretching vibration of the alcohol functional group is detected at 1001 cm^{-1} [28].

Fragrance-loaded zeolite samples (DL/Ze, BA/Ze, and GE/Ze) (Figure 5 (b)) showed the major characteristic bands of the zeolite. However, distinct peaks corresponding to the fragrance molecules were generally not clearly observed, except in the GE/Ze sample, which showed peaks around 2976 cm^{-1} and 2939 cm^{-1}, corresponding to the C–H stretching of methyl groups (–CH_3), confirming the presence of geraniol. The absence of distinct fragrance peaks in the other sample maybe attributed to the low fragrance-to-zeolite ratio. Moreover, during the encapsulation process, fragrances with higher boiling points—such as geraniol—are more likely to remain entrapped within the zeolite matrix, resulting in higher residual content post-encapsulation.

In addition, the sample containing T80 (Figure 5(c)) exhibits weak signals of characteristic vibration bands corresponding to C–H stretching of hydrocarbon chains at 2925 cm^{-1} and C=O stretching of the ester group at 1737 cm^{-1}, confirming the presence of T80 after encapsulation [10].

3.6 Fragrance loading and encapsulation efficiencies

The fragrance loading efficiency (%LE) and encapsulation efficiency (%EE) were estimated and are presented in Fig. 6. As observed, the encapsulation systems containing T80 exhibited more consistent %LE and %EE values compared to systems without T80. In the presence of T80, the %LE of DL-Tw/Ze, BA-Tw/Ze, and GE-Tw/Ze ranged narrowly between 15–17%, while the %EE values were between 23–28%. In contrast, systems without T80 (DL/Ze, BA/Ze, and GE/Ze) showed substantial variation in both %LE (8-30%) and %EE (11-42%). These findings suggest that the presence of T80 contributes to improved consistency in the encapsulation of different fragrance molecules. However, additional analytical techniques such as TGA–MS or gas chromatography are recommended to confirm these results.

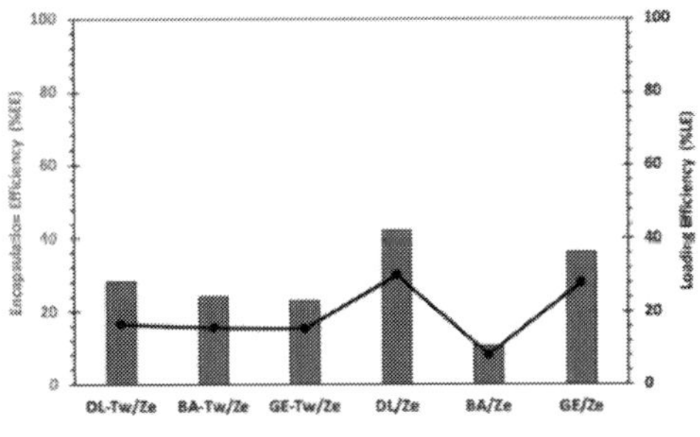

Fig. 6. Encapsulation efficiency (%EE, bar graph) and loading efficiency (%LE, line graph) of fragrance-loaded zeolite with and without the addition of T80.

3.7 Fragrance retention

To evaluate fragrance retention, the encapsulated samples were stored in a desiccator at ambient temperature for 30 days, after which the remaining fragrance content in the carriers was measured. As shown in figure 7, D-limonene—having the lowest molecular weight (136.23 g/mol) and boiling point (176°C)—exhibited the lowest retention. In contrast, geraniol, with the highest molecular weight (154.25 g/mol) and boiling point (230°C) among the tested compounds, showed the highest retention. Notably, the presence of T80 enhanced fragrance retention, particularly for low molecular weight and more volatile compounds such as D-limonene and benzyl acetate (150.18 g/mol, 134°C). The hydrophilic head of T80 can interact with the zeolite surface via hydrogen bonding, while its hydrophobic tail interacts with fragrance molecules through London dispersion forces. This dual interaction mechanism helps prolong the release of fragrance compounds. These findings highlight the significant role of T80 as a fragrance retention enhancer, suggesting its potential application in industrial formulations requiring prolonged aroma release.

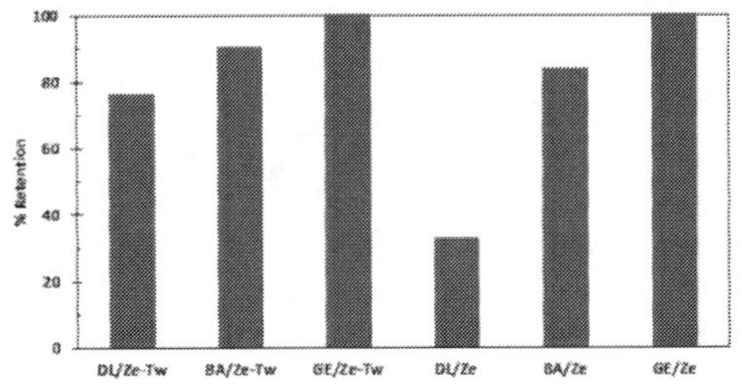

Fig. 7. Fragrance retention after storage at ambient temperature for 30 days.

4 Conclusion

This study highlights the effectiveness of natural zeolite as a carrier for fragrance encapsulation, particularly when modified with Tween 80 (T80). The incorporation of T80, a non-ionic surfactant, improved the uniformity of loading and encapsulation efficiency across structurally diverse fragrance molecules. Zeolite facilitated the entrapment and stabilization of fragrance molecules, while T80 improved molecular dispersion and retention, particularly for low molecular weight (small molecules) and volatile compounds such as D-limonene and benzyl acetate. The results underscore the synergistic role of zeolite and T80 in modulating encapsulation behavior and long-term fragrance retention, offering a promising approach for the development of advanced delivery systems with sustained aroma release for industrial applications.

This research was funded by Faculty of Applied Science, King Mongkut's University of Technology North Bangkok, Contract No. 680036. We gratefully acknowledge the Department of Industrial Chemistry, Faculty of Applied Science, King Mongkut's University of Technology North Bangkok, and the Department of Chemical Engineering, Faculty of Engineering, Mahidol University, for their valuable support and provision of essential analytical instruments.

Author contributions

Natnicha Kongyang.: Investigation and Methodology. **Sukanya Sudmee.**: Investigation and Methodology. **Rapeeporn Wannarat.**: Investigation and Methodology. **Sukanya Thepwatee.**: Conceptualization, Data Curation, Formal Analysis, Graphic Preparation, Writing – Original Draft, Reviewing, and Editing, Funding Acquisition, Supervision, Project Administration, and Validation.

References

1. R. S. Herz, M. Larsson, R. Trujillo, M. C. Casola, F. K. Ahmed, S. Lipe, M. E. Brashear, A three-factor benefits framework for understanding consumer preference for scented household products: psychological interactions and implications for future development. Cogn. Res.: Princ. Implic. **7**, 28 (2022). https://doi.org/10.1186/s41235-022-00378-6
2. R. K R, S. Gopi, P. Balakrishnan, Introduction to Flavor and Fragrance in Food Processing. Flavors and Fragrances in Food Processing: Preparation and Characterization Methods (American Chemical Society, 2022). http://doi.org/10.1021/bk-2022-1433.ch001
3. E. Guzmán, A. Lucia, Essential Oils and Their Individual Components in Cosmetic Products. Cosmetics. **8**, 114 (2021). https://doi.org/10.3390/cosmetics8040114
4. S. P. Costa, O. S. Soares, C. A. Aguiar, I. C. Neves, Fragrance carriers obtained by encapsulation of volatile aromas into zeolite structures. Ind. Crops Prod. **187**, 115397 (2022). https://doi.org/10.1016/j.indcrop.2022. 115397
5. K. Ayuningtyas, E. Kusrini, W.W. Prihandini, Development of fragrance carrier from Luffa acutangula using zeolite A. IOP Conf. Ser.: Mater. Sci. Eng. **1098**, 022005 (2021). https://doi.org/ 10.1088/1757899X/1098/ 2/ 022005
6. Z. Li, J. Huang, L. Ye, Y. Lv, Z. Zhou, Y. Shen, Y. He, L. Jiang, Encapsulation of highly volatile fragrances in Y zeolites for sustained release: Experimental and theoretical studies. ACS omega. **5**, 31925-31935 (2020). https:// doi.org/ 10.1021/acsomega.0c04822
7. S. Wang, D. Jiang, Z. Zhou, Y. Shen, L. Jiang, A novel photothermo-responsive nanocarrier for the controlled release of low-volatile fragrances. RSC Advances. **10**, 14867-14876 (2020) https://doi.org/10.1039/C9RA106 62F
8. Y. Tian, C. Lianghong, W. Zhang, Influence of Ionic Surfactants on the Properties of Nanoemulsions Emulsified by Nonionic Surfactants Span 80/Tween 80. J. Disper. Sci. Technol. **37**, 1511-1517 (2016). https:// doi.org/10.1080/01932691.2015.1048806
9. R. Wang, C. Ma, H. Yan, H. Zhao, P. Wang, S. Zhang, J. Ju, S. Yu, Z. Yin, Lecithin/Cholesterol/Tween 80 Liposomes for Co-Encapsulation of Vitamin C and Xanthoxylin. ACS Appl. Nano Mater. **7**, 5982-5995 (2024). https://doi.org/ 10.1021/acsanm.3c05884
10. F. Kerdmuanglek, T. Chomtong, S. Boonsith, T. Chutimasakul, J. Iemsam-arng, S. Thepwatee, Non-ionic surfactant-assisted controlled release of oxyresveratrol on dendritic fibrous silica for topical applications. J. Colloid Interface Sci. **646**, 342-353 (2023). https://doi.org/ 10.1016/j.jcis.2023.05.050
11. A. Kliszcz, A. Danel, J. Puła, B. Barabasz-Krasny, K. Możdżeń, Fleeting Beauty—The World of Plant Fragrances and Their Application. Molecules **26,** 2473 (2021). https://doi.org/10.3390/molecules26092473
12. P. Anandakumar, S. Kamaraj, M.K. Vanitha, D-limonene: A multifunctional compound with potent therapeutic effects. J. Food Biochem. **45,** e13566 (2021). https://doi.org/10.1111/jfbc.13566
13. W. Chen, A.M. Viljoen, Geraniol – A review update. S. Afr. J. Bot. **150**, 1205-1219 (2022). https://doi.org/ 10.1016/j.sajb.2022.09.012
14. G. Ye, Y. Sun, Z. Guo, K. Zhu, H. Liu, X. Zhou, M.O. Coppens, Effects of zeolite particle size and internal grain boundaries on Pt/Beta catalyzed isomerization of n-pentane. J. Catal. **360**, 152-159 (2018) https://doi.org/ 10.1016/j.jcat.2018.01.033
15. D. Tsivas, A. Vlyssides, A. Vlysidis, Monitoring of a III-Phase Olive Pomace Composting Process Using the CIELAB Colorimetric Method. Waste Biomass Valori. **12**, 5029-5039 (2021). https://doi.org/10.1007/s12649-021-01363-8
16. X. Feng, K. Feng, Q. Zheng, W. Tan, W. Zhong, C. Liao, Y. Liu, S. Li, W. Hu, Preparation and characterization of geraniol nanoemulsions and its antibacterial activity. Front. microbiol. **13**, (2022). https://doi.org/10.3389/fmicb.2022.1080300
17. B.R. Belem, G.V. Carapeto, M.G. Issa, H.G. Ferraz, Microemulsions: An Encapsulation Strategy to Increase the Thermal Stability of D-limonene. Pharmaceutics. **15**, 2564 (2023). https://doi.org/10.3390/ pharmaceutics15112564
18. D. McGinty, D. Vitale, C. S. Letizia, A. M. Api, Fragrance material review on benzyl acetate. Food Chem. Toxicol. **50**, S363-S84 (2012). https://doi.org/10.1016/ j.fct.2012.02.057
19. M. Thommes, K. Kaneko, A.V. Neimark, J. P. Olivier, F. Rodriguez-Reinoso, J. Rouquerol, S. S.W. Kenneth, Physisorption of gases, with special reference to the evaluation of surface area and pore

size distribution (IUPAC Technical Report). Pure Appl. Chem. **87**, 1051-1069 (2015). https://doi.org/10.1515/pac-2014-1117

20. A. Mockovčiaková, M. Matik, Z. Orolínová, P. Hudec, E. Kmecová, Structural characteristics of modified natural zeolite. J. Porous Mater. **15**, 559-564 (2008). https://doi.org/10.1007/s10934-007-9133-3
21. M. Silva, A. Lecus, Y. Lin, J. Corrao, Tailoring natural zeolites by acid treatments. J. Mater. Sci. Chem. Eng. **7**, 26-37 (2019). https://doi.org/10.4236/msce.2019.72003
22. M. Dosa, N. Grifasi, C. Galletti, D. Fino, M. Piumetti, Natural Zeolite Clinoptilolite Application in Wastewater Treatment: Methylene Blue, Zinc and Cadmium Abatement Tests and Kinetic Studies. Materials **15**, 8191 (2022). https://doi.org/10.3390/ma15228191
23. R. Malekian, J. Abedi-Koupai, S. S. Eslamian, Influences of clinoptilolite and surfactant-modified clinoptilolite zeolite on nitrate leaching and plant growth. J. Hazard. Mater. **185**, 970-976 (2011). https://doi.org/ 10.1016/ j.jhazmat.2010.09.114
24. O. E. Pecho, R. Ghinea, R. Alessandretti, M. M. Pérez, A. Della Bona, Visual and instrumental shade matching using CIELAB and CIEDE2000 color difference formulas. Dent. Mater. **32**, 82-92 (2016). https://doi.org/10.1016/j.dental.2015.10.015
25. T. U. Klinke, W. B. Hannak, K. Böning, H. A. Jakstat, E. Prause, Visual Tooth Color Determination with Different Reference Scales as an Exercise in Dental Students' Education. Dent. J. **11**, 275 (2023). https://doi.org/ 10.3390/dj11120275
26. O. Korkuna, R. Leboda, J. Skubiszewska-Zie̜ba, T. Vrublevs'ka, V. M. Gun'ko, J. Ryczkowski, Structural and physicochemical properties of natural zeolites: clinoptilolite and mordenite. Microporous Mesoporous Mater. **87**, 243-254 (2006). https://doi.org/10.1016/ j.micromeso.2005.08.002
27. I. H. Arachchilage, M. K. Patel, J. Basi, J. P. Harmon, Environmentally Friendly Radiation Hard d-Limonene and Laccol Copolymers Synthesized via Cationic Copolymerization. Polym. Eng. Sci. **60**, 607-618 (2020). https://doi.org/10.1002/pen.25319
28. K. N. Rosalina, T. Wukirsari, S. Handayani, S. Hudiyono, Utilization of Silica Gel for the Synthesis of Geranyl Laurate and Citronellyl Laurate. Bull. Chem. React. Eng. Catal. **19**, 350-360 (2024). https://doi.org/ 10.9767/bcrec.20159

Synergism of blended extract of *Ageratum houstonianum* and *Chromolaena odorata* leaves on the corrosion inhibitor of reinforcing steel in concrete composite

Madhab Gautam[1,2], *Laxman* Gupta[1], *Nabin* Pandey[1], *Nootan Prasad* Bhattarai[1*], and *Jagadeesh* Bhattarai [1†]

[1]Central Department of Chemistry, Tribhuvan University, Kirtipur 44618, Kathmandu, Nepal
[2]Department of Chemistry, Tribhuvan M. Campus, Tribhuvan University, Tansen 32500, Palpa, Nepal

Abstract. Corrosive degradation of reinforcing steel (RS) in concrete composite (ConC) is a significant factor contributing to the early collapse of reinforced concrete infrastructures. The degradation of the RS in ConC impacts if appropriate corrosion control efforts are not applied promptly. Plant-based green extracts have been recently used as anticorrosive materials to prevent RS corrosion. This study investigated the effectiveness of various concentrations of blended extracts from the leaves of *Ageratum houstonianum* and *Chromolaena odorata* (referred to as AHL-COL) in controlling the corrosion of reinforcing mild steel (RMS) in the ConC using a half-cell potential measurement with the help of the ASTM C876-22b standard. Performed the surface analysis using scanning electron microscopy with energy dispersive X-ray spectroscopy (SEM-EDS) to examine the anticorrosive actions of the AHL-COL concentrations. The corrosion probability (P_{corr}) of the RMS in concrete beams with 500-2000 ppm AHL-COL is synergistically lowered compared with the control concrete beam or even the presence of individual plant extracts, as evidenced by shifting the corrosion potential (E_{corr}) to a zone where the P_{corr} of the RMS should be < 10%, and also supported by electron microscopic, and SEM-EDS analysis.

1 Introduction

Reinforced concrete (RC) is one of the most widely used nano-composite structural materials over the last two centuries [1]. One of the reasons for the early damage of RC structures is the corrosion of reinforcing steel (RS). The RS corrodes in concrete composite (ConC) when it is in contact with ingressed water/moisture, salt ions (chloride, sulfate, sulfide), oxides of nitrogen, H_2S, CO_2, among other substances, through the concrete mix [2]. The RS is passivated in ConC through the formation of Fe_2O_3, which functions as protective layer on the mild steel in the highly alkaline concrete solution with a pH 13±0.5. Even so, when chlorides, sulfates, CO_2, moisture, and so on ingress through the pores of the ConC to the RS surface, such protective passive film undergoes breakdown by a decrease in pH <10 [3]. As a result, the corrosion phenomena of the RS in ConC become noticeable.

The corrosive damage of the RS occurs due to the reduction of strength, durability, and elasticity, i.e., most mechanical properties [4]. Corrosion scientists also emphasized the need for a meticulous corrosion control mechanism of the RS in ConC [5], which not only provides a guarantee for the structure's durability and strength but also causes damage to the environmental and economic aspects. The corrosive damage of the RS is a source of the early destruction (i.e., less than 50 years) of concrete structures (ConS). The restoration cost of the corroded ConS is around 3% of the gross domestic product of the developed countries [6]. The cost of RS corrosion in ConC depends on the severity of such a critically polluted environment [7].

To overcome such RS corrosion-based concrete impairment, researchers have widely practiced adding low concentrations of various synthetic chemicals as corrosion inhibitors for the significant improvement of the quality control of the RC properties like corrosiveness, durability, stability, and so on. An effective plant-based corrosion inhibitor enhanced adsorption capacity on metal surfaces in aqueous electrolytes, biofuels and their blends. However, few works have reported on plant-based extracts as corrosion inhibitors in concrete electrolytes. In recent years, some research groups like Ahmed & Ganesh [8], Ghoreishiamiri *et al.* [9], Bhattarai *et al.* [10], and Valdez-Salas *et al.* [11] have focused on the use of plant-based phytochemicals as green additives in ConC to control the early corrosive damages of mild steel in the RC infrastructures.

* Corresponding author : neutan08@ygmail.com
† Corresponding author : bhattarai_05@yahoo.com

The plant-based green additives contain a wide range of phytoconstituents, which are highly basic with high electron density and heteroatoms such as N, O, P, and S, serving as active centers for the adsorption onto the RS surface [12]. The increasing order of inhibition potency of the heteroatoms follows the sequence O<N<S<P [13]. In general, the plant-based corrosion inhibitors passivate the RS in ConS in two ways- either by enhancing the formation of a protective oxide film through a de-electronation effector by selectively adsorbing on the metal surface and by generating a barrier film that prevents ingress of corrosive agents through the ConC to the RS surface [14].

The plant-based extract also contains π-electrons in heterocyclic ring compounds, which adsorb onto the RS surface [15], following these four steps: (i) electrostatic interactions between charge-carrying phyto-molecules and metal ions, (ii) interaction between vacant d-orbital of the metal atom and lone pair electrons of N, S, or O hetero-atom, (iii) interaction between unoccupied d-orbital of the metal atom and π-electrons of the aromatic ring compounds, and (iv) combination of the above-mentioned three processes [16]. Thus, imparting a passive film formation through physical, chemical, or both adsorption processes.

In the last seven years, abundant numbers of phyto-constituents, extracted from different plant parts [17] exhibited as a potent green inhibitor in aqueous electrolytes to prevent metals corrosion. A few Nepali plants' leaves have been utilized to prepare plant-based corrosion inhibitors, which act as anti-corrosive agents for controlling the mild steel corrosion in aqueous environments, fossil fuels, and their blends. However, most of them are limitedly employed as green-based corrosion inhibitors in ConC to control the early corrosion damage of the reinforcing mild steel.

Researchers have thoroughly focused their work on inhibiting the corrosion of steel in chloride-contaminated concrete pore solution using leaf-based extracts from *Fatsia japonica* [18], *Urtica dioica* [19], *and Platanus acerifolia* [20] plants. They possess desirable properties as green corrosion inhibitors, which include heteroatoms such as nitrogen, oxygen, and sulfur, as well as aromatic ring phyto-compounds like alkaloids, flavonoids, phenols, polyphenols, amino acids, tannins, and terpenes. These phyto-compounds act as effective anti-corrosive agents. The adsorption process of physical, chemical, or both between phyto-molecules and metal surface is believed to be the most responsible factor in showing the efficacious corrosion-resistant properties of mild steel in corrosive environments [21].

In this context, a blended extract of *Ageratum houstonianum* and *Chromolaena odorata* leaves (AHL-COL) is exploited as a blended phyto-inhibitor in the present work for controlling the RS corrosion in ConC. Two alien plant species, among 40 species of the genus *Ageratum* in Nepal, are *Ageratum houstonianum* and *Ageratum conyzoides* [22]. Much work has been reported on the *Ageratum conyzoides* extract compared with the *Ageratum houstonianum* species. The aqueous extract of *Ageratum conyzoides* functioned as an anti-corrosive agent for preventing metallic degradation in aggressive electrolytes [23]. Previous work screened out the presence of some phyto-compounds (i.e., phenols, alkaloids, tannins, saponins, steroids, terpenes, and flavonoids) in the leaf extract of *Ageratum conyzoides* [24]. These findings highlighted the plant's rich profile of phyto-compounds and its potential for use in corrosion control applications [25].

The *Ageratum houstonianum* is a flowering shrub belonging to the Asteraceae family, and is an undesirable plants [26]. If people do not manage such unwanted plant, it creates adverse effects in agricultural production sectors. Thus, this study hypothesizes that the leaves of the unwanted *Ageratum houstonianum* can serve as practical and effective green corrosion inhibitors for mitigating the significant corrosion of various metals and alloys in aggressive electrolytes. It might be good for nature, farmers, and the public. In recent years, very few researchers have investigated the anti-corrosive properties of *Ageratum houstonianum* extract on SS-410 steel sheet in 0.5 M H_2SO_4. A corrosion inhibition efficiency of 93% was confirmed for SS-410 stainless steel in 0.5 M H_2SO_4 with 500 ppm *Ageratum houstonianum* extract from electrochemical and weight loss analysis [27].

Comparably, *Chromolaena odorata* (Siam weed and *Banmaraa* in Nepali) is a rapidly growing perennial flowering shrub species of the Asteraceae family, and it is also one of the alien plant species that harm the biodiversity of Nepal [28]. In literature, the ethanol extracts of *Chromolaena odorata* leaf extracts have been noted as an efficacious inhibitor for controlling steel corrosion in aqueous electrolytes [29]. In recent years, studies have reported that individual leaf extracts from both *Ageratum houstonianum* (AHL) and *Chromolaena odorata* (COL) have shown effective anticorrosive properties for mild steel in reinforced concrete, as per the ASTM C876-22b standard [30]. In particular, the addition of 2000-4000 ppm of each AHL or COL extract demonstrated superior corrosion-inhibiting properties than the RC slab without the plant extract [31].

In this context, the present study investigated the synergistic effects of blended extracts of both plant leaves (AHL-COL) for inhibiting the reinforcing mild steel corrosion in concrete using the half-cell potential method. The novelty of this work is that no other research has used the blended extract of both the *Ageratum houstonianum* and *Chromolaena odorata* leaves (AHL-COL) for the first time as green inhibitor against RMS in alkaline concrete composite. This research work recommends the possibility of the consequences of a practical blended plant-based corrosion inhibitor for the prolongation of the RC infrastructures.

2 Materials and Methods

Fresh, uninfected, and healthy leaves of *Ageratum houstonianum* and *Chromolaena odorata* plants were separately collected from the Sunawal area (27.6008° N, 83.6989° E) of Nawalparasi district, Nepal, as described elsewhere [31]. Both the collected plant species were identified as *Chromolaena odorata* L. (Siam weed or *Banmaraa* in Nepali) and *Ageratum houstonianum* Mill (Blue billygoat in English or *Bukejhar* in Nepali). Both plant species identified by the National Herbarium and Plant Laboratory, Plant Department, Godabari, Lalitpur, have their voucher numbers deposited at the office. The fresh leaves of these two plants were dried by placing them in a shaded area for a few weeks.

The air-dried leaves of both plants were separately pulverized for making plant powder, and stored in airtight plastic containers for extract preparation, as noticed in Figure 1(a). Two hundred grams of each plant powder were dipped in 400 mL of methanol for three weeks with regular stirring and filtered the phyto-bioactive solution using a Whatman filter [Figure 1(b)]. The filtrate solution was concentrated with a rotary evaporator [Figure 1(c)] to obtain a solid plant extract [Figure 1(d)].

Fig. 1. Freash leaves of *A. houtonianum* and *C. Odorata* plants and their dried powder (a), the powder soaked with methanol (b), a rotary evaporator machine (c) for the preparation of solid leaf extract (d).

The extract was kept inside a freezer at 4°C until used as an anti-corrosive additive in a concrete composite. The characteristic functional groups of both the plant extracts were ascertained from the FTIR and UV-Visible (SPECORD®200 PLUS, Germany) spectroscopic analysis. The phytochemical screening tests of the extract were conducted to confirm the presence of various phyto-molecules in the extract.

A rust-free thermo-mechanically treated (TMT) and corrugated 500 XD mild steel (MS) rod having a 12 mm diameter with a 300 mm long mild steel rod was reinforced in a concrete beam, as displayed in Figure 2(a). The chemical compositions of the mild steel rod are (wt. %), Fe (>98%) with impurities of C (0.17 to 0.25%), Si (0.4%), Mn (0.9%), S (0.05%), and P (0.05%) [32].

The reinforced concrete (RC) beam with 320 mm × 80 mm × 80 mm dimensions was fabricated using a concrete composite paste (Figure 2a). The concrete paste was prepared by mixing coarse gravel, fine river sand, and ordinary Portland cement (53 grades) powder in a 3:2:1 mass ratio, adding required amount of distilled water with 500 ppm-2000 ppm AHL-COL, as approved by the ASTM C1582/C1582M-11 standard [33]. The cement-water ratio was adjusted to about 0.45.

A total of four rectangular concrete beams were made with the control condition, 500 ppm, 1000 ppm, and 2000 ppm blended AHL-COL, using a rectangular casting box [Figure 2(c)]. The blended AHL-COL extract is a mixture of equi-amounts of the AHL and COL extracts. Additionally, the other eight beams were constructed using a concrete composite paste with AHL and COL at concentrations of 500 ppm, 1000 ppm, 2000 ppm, and 4000 ppm, respectively. About 20 mm of the RMS rod was exposed to one side of the concrete beam, and the equidistant four points (marked as 1, 2, 3, 4) were selected on the beam surface for the recording of the Ecorr, as illustrated in Figure 2(d).

After the preparation of the concrete beams, the E_{corr} of each of the four points was recorded at regular time intervals up to six months or more with the help of a digital multimeter (UNI-T Business, Hong Kong). The exposed end of the RS acted as the working electrode, which was attached to the +ve terminal of the multimeter. A reference electrode was connected to the −ve terminal of the multimeter, as demonstrated in Figure 2(d).

Fig. 2. Pictures of (a) materials of concrete nano-composite mixture and mild steel rod (a), concrete paste (b), fixed steel rod in a casting box (c), and corrosion potential measurement by a digital multi-meter (d).

The average E_{corr} of the four points of each concrete beam was taken for grading three corrosion probability conditions (PC_{corr}) of the RC beam, as approved by the ASTM C876-22b standard [32], which is summarized in Table 1. In this grading system, the average E_{corr} value is regarded as the indicator of the PC_{corr} of the RC beam. For example, if the noted E_{corr} value of the RMS in concrete locates more in a positive than −0.125 V (SCE), the reinforced concrete infrastructure is supposed to be beneath 10% corrosion risk (BCR<10) condition. In contrast, the RC could be rated as an above 90% corrosion risk (ACR>90) when the recorded E_{corr} value of the RMS is negative than, i.e., less than −0.276 V against SCE. It is believed that the RMS is an intermediate corrosion risk (ICR10-90) when the E_{corr} value is in between the BCR<10 and ACR>90 regions (i.e., −0.276 V to −0.176 V), as summarized in Table 1.

Optical images of the RMS surfaces before and after exposure to the extract-treated concrete composite paste were captured for surface analysis using a digital optical microscope. Additionally, the surface sensitive SEM/EDS technique was used to observe the changes in morphology and chemical composition of the RMS surface after exposure to ConC with varying plant concentrations.

Table 1. Average E_{corr} dependent corrosion probability condition (PC_{corr}) of the RMS in concrete beam, as approved by the ASTM C876-22b Standard [32].

Average E_{corr} (V vs SCE)	PC_{corr} of RMS in concrete beam
More negative than −0.126	Beneath 10% corrosion risk (BCR<10)
Between −0.276 to −0.126	Intermediate corrosion risk (ICR10-90)
More negative than −0.276	Above 90% corrosion risk (ACR>90)

3 Results and Discussion

For the approximate analysis of the methanol extract from both plants, an UV-visible spectrophotometer (SPECORD® 200 PLUS, Germany) was used to examine the extract under both UV and visible light, covering a wavelength range of 200-800 nm. This method effectively indicates the presence of π-bonding, σ-bonding, lone pairs of electrons, aromatic rings, and chromophores that are characteristic of the phyto-molecules in the analyzed plant extracts, as illustrated in Figure 3.

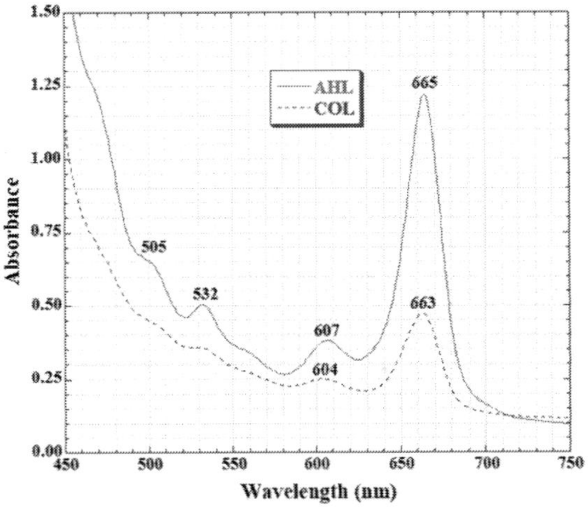

Fig. 3. Recorded UV-Visible spectra of AHL and COL.

The presence of these electronic states, lone pairs of electrons, and aromatic rings is assumed to be effective in controlling the corrosion of reinforcing metals in concrete mix. Results proclaimed the presence of four or more absorption peaks between 450 and 700 nm wavelengths in both plant extracts. The maxima at 505, 532, 607, and 665 nm for the AHL specimen and at 532, 604, and 663 nm for the COL specimen are the characteristics of some phytomolecules as reported in the literature [34]. The UV-Vis spectrophotometry study indicates the presence of secondary metabolites. Nevertheless, analysis of the complex nature of the methanol extracts of both plants using UV-Vis spectroscopy has some disadvantages [35]. Thus, the UV-Vis findings are supplemented by more reliable and pertinent analytical techniques of FTIR and GC-MS for the identification of secondary metabolites in plant-based extracts.

As illustrated in Figure 4, the FTIR absorption peak around 3345-3334 cm^{-1} is owing to O-H stretching vibration of hydrogen bonding [36], and around 2941-2927 cm^{-1} and 2856-2833 cm^{-1} are asymmetrical and symmetrical C-H stretch, respectively [37]. A broad and weak peak around 1720 cm^{-1} appears only in the AHL extract, which indicates the presence of either the N-containing or C=O group or both [36] in the methanol leaf extract of *Ageratum houstonianum*. The appearance of a strong peak around 1638-1616 cm^{-1} for both the plant extracts, and a very intense peak at 1505 cm^{-1} for AHL only indicates the presence of the C=O group in an aromatic ring compound [37].

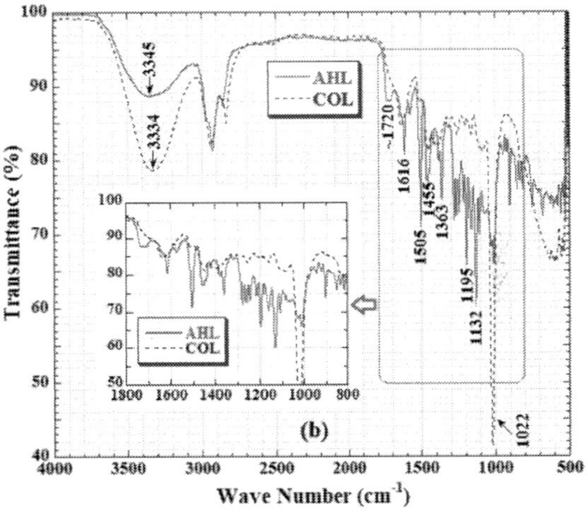

Fig. 4. FTIR spectra of AHL and COL.

Table 2. Assignment of the functional groups present in the AHL and COL extracts.

Wavenumber (cm^{-1})		Functional group	Ref.
AHL	COL		
3345 (b)	3334 (b)	O–H stretching due to H bonding	[36]
2927 (s)	2941 (s)	C–H (CH_2) asymmetric stretching	[37]
2856 (w)	2833 (w)	C–H (CH_3) symmetrical stretching	[37]
1720 (bw)	–	C–N stretching, C=O group	[36]
1616 (s)	1638 (s)	Aromatic C=C / C=O stretching	[42]
1577 (bw)	–	C–O vibration / aromatic C=C stretching	
1505 (vs)	1515 (vw)	Aromatic C=O stretching	[38]
1455 (s)	1449 (w)	C–H stretching/ aromatic C=C stretching	[39]
1421 (vw)	1400 (bw)	C–H bending	[40]
1363 (s)	–	Aromatic C=C stretching	[42]
1260 (w)	1257 (w)	C–O stretching of organic acids	[43]
1195 (vs)	1205 (vw)	Presence of –COOH group	[44]
1162 (s)	1162 (w)	C–H stretching	[39]
1132 (vs)	1102 (vw)		
1076 (vw)	1087 (w)	C–O ether stretching vibration	[45]
1016 (w)	1022 (vs)	O–H, C–H in plane bending of aromatics	[10]

Besides these diagnostic regions of the FTIR spectra, both AHL and COL extracts have absorption peaks in fingerprint regions of the spectra between 600-1400 cm^{-1} wave numbers, as summarized in Table 2. Peculiarly, the peak value at 1363 cm^{-1} for the AHL extract is probably due to the C=C stretches in the aromatic compounds [42]. These results confirm that both the leaf extracts of AHL and COL are enriched with anti-corrosive aromatic phyto-molecules, constituting hetero-elements such as O, N, and S. Consequently, a consolidated adsorption layer could be easily formed on the RMS surface, resulting from the delocalization of electrons between the more electronegative hetero-elements and the corroded metal surfaces [42].

The phytochemical screening test confirms the presence (+) or absence (−) of various secondary metabolites in the methanol leaf extracts of both AHL and COL, as summarized in Table 3. Alkaloids, flavonoids, phenols, steroids, saponins, and tannins are major secondary metabolites that can favor the development of a corrosion-resistant adsorbed layer between the mild steel and concrete composite. Meanwhile, the AHL showed negative tests for glycosides and carbohydrates in contrast with a positive test for the COL (Table 3).

The COL shows a negative test for terpenoids in contrast to the positive test for the AHL. Despite such experimental observations, previous tests reported that the terpenoid was also present in the leaf extract of the *Chromolaena odorata* plant [46]. The results of the secondary metabolite tests are almost congruous with the prior screening test reports on AHL [47] and COL [48] extracts. The configuration of these phyto-compounds in both the AHL and COL extracts, which are composed of heterogeneous organic molecules containing N, O, S, and aromatic ring compounds in their molecular structures, is the most responsible factor for the adsorption of the molecules onto the surface of corroded metal [49]. Hence, a mixture of AHL and COL (i.e., AHL-COL) extracts could be an effective inhibitor to control the corrosion of reinforcing metal in concrete structures.

Table 3. Results of screening tests for phyto-compounds present in AHL), and COL.

Tests	Phyto-compounds	AHL	COL
Dragendroff's	Alkaloids	+	+
Alkaline reagent	Flavonoids	+	+
Lead acetate	Phenols	+	+
Legal test	Glycosides	−	+
Salkowski	Terpenoids	+	−
Liebermann-Burchard	Steroids	+	+
Foam	Saponins	+	+
Ferric chloride	Tannins	+	+
Molisch's	Carbohydrates	−	+

Researching plant-based phyto-compounds as anti-corrosive additives in ConC would benefit concrete technologists, structural engineers, and corrosion scientists [50]. The plant-based extracts have an impact on extending the stability, reliability, and longevity of the reinforced concrete frameworks. Large amounts of concrete frameworks have faced the problems of unavoidable and unwanted corrosion phenomena of steel/metal embedded in concrete infrastructures.

To avoid such unexpectedly corrosive degradation of the steel/metal in concrete frameworks, an *in situ* electrochemical corrosion potential (E_{corr}) recording would be a conclusive, reliable, and cost- effective method to monitor different corrosion conditions (i.e., BCR<10, ICR10-90, and ACR>90) of the concrete infrastructures at regular intervals of time, as summarized above in Table 1.

Therefore, this study focused on observing the inhibitory effects of various concentrations of blended AHL-COL extract added in ConC to control CoS corrosion. We measured the corrosion potential (E_{corr}) at four points on each concrete beam over a period of up to six months, using the half-cell potential measurement method, and the results are illustrated in Figure 5. The figure demonstrates the changes in the E_{corr} of four surface-points (i.e., Pt-1, Pt-2, Pt-3, Pt-4) of the RMS in all four concrete beams with exposure time up to six months or more, which were made ready the concrete beam using the control ConC without the addition of the blended plant extract [Figure 5(a)], and by the inclusions of 500 ppm [Figure 5(b)], 1000 ppm [Figure 5(c)], and 2000 ppm [Figure 5(d)] AHL-COL extract in the ConC.

The E_{corr} value of the RC beams with different concentrations of the AHL-COL extract has been shifted towards a region of less than 10% corrosion probability (P_{corr}) after exposure to the RC beams between 15 and 180 days or more at ambient conditions, except the control RC beam. The E_{corr} value of all four points of the control RC beam without the addition of plant extract is shifted to a noble potential region by increasing the exposure time to about one month [Figure 5(a)]. However, with increasing the exposure times about one to three months, the E_{corr} of the control concrete beam has moved remarkably towards an intermediate corrosion risk (i.e., ICR10-90) region, and ultimately attained a steady state E_{corr} less noble than −0.275 V (SCE) during the exposure between 3 to 6 months or more, inferring a high corrosion risk of the RMS in the concrete beam without the plant extract.

The results revealed that the 500, 1000, and 2000 ppm AHL-COL improved the anti-corrosive properties of the ConC. Probably, a stable film formed on the RMS surface by the process of physical or chemical adsorption of phyto-compounds extracted from the plant-based extract [4]. The film prevents corrosive ions or molecules from entering the steel surface through the concrete nano-pores, as previously stated [51].

Besides, the variation of the E_{corr} with exposure time of the concrete beams with different concentrations of the blended AHL-COL extract is found to be time-dependent, as reported in previous studies [52]. The structure of the concrete beams with the AHL-COL extract should be denser through a high degree of hydration and low porosity at long exposure times, and hence decrease the diffusion coefficient of pollutant ions/molecules across the interfacial region of the concrete nano-matrix and reinforced metal surface. However, such phenomena should not be moved ahead in the case of the beam without the blended extract. Thence, the E_{corr} of the concrete beam without plant extract shifted to a less noble direction with time, as demonstrated in Figure 5(a).

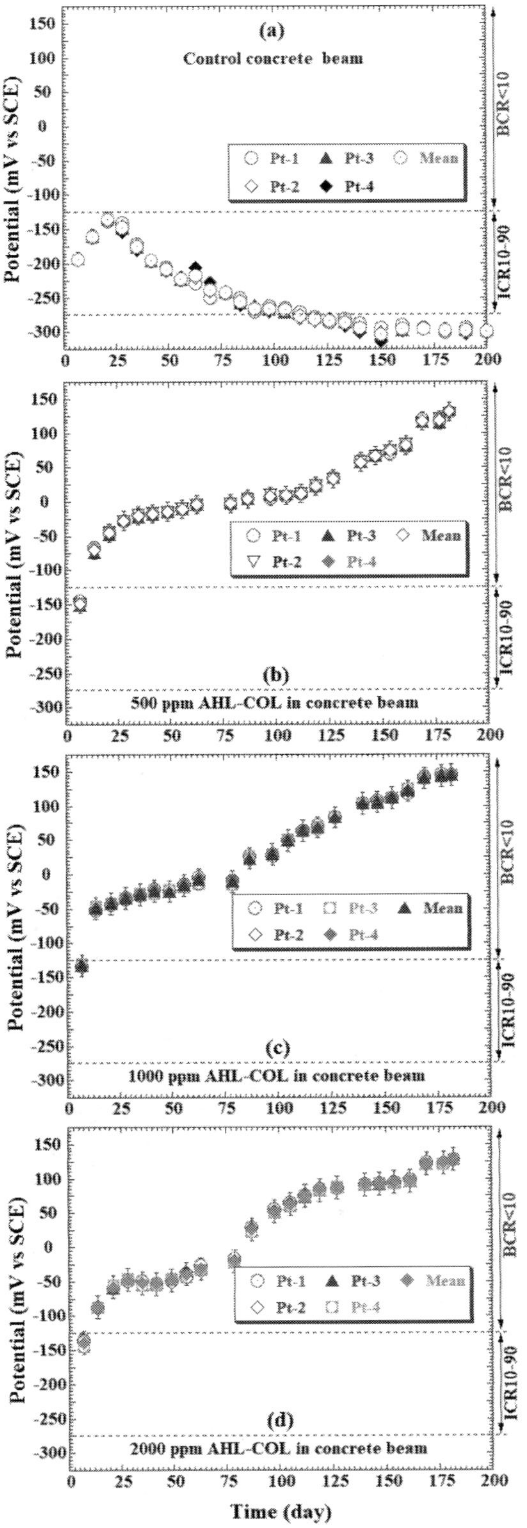

Fig. 5. The changes of electrochemical corrosion potential of the RMS in concrete beam at (a) control condition and with the additions of (b) 500 ppm (c) 1000 ppm and (d) 2000 ppm AHL-COL in concrete composite, as a function of exposure time at ambient atmosphere.

Additionally, Figure 6(a) summarizes the variation of the average E_{corr} values for all four points on each concrete beam, including standard error bars. As the exposure time increases, the average E_{corr} shifts to a more corrosion-resistant region (i.e., where BCR < 10), moving away from intermediate corrosion risk areas. A more stable protective layer is expected to form on the surface of the RMS in the presence of heterogeneous organic molecules containing N, O, S, and aromatic ring compounds. Also, it gives a meaningful indication that the standard deviation from the average E_{corr} is < 10 mV except in very few cases (<2%).

The outcomes revealed that localized corrosion of the RMS in ConC beam could not be expected with the additions of both plant extracts and their blended extracts. The phyto-compounds of the plant extract enhanced to form an anti-corrosive passive film across the interface between the mild steel and concrete matrix, which shifts the corrosion condition from the region of the intermediate corrosion to a region with less than < 10% chance of corrosion occurrence [30].

Furthermore, Figures 6(b), 6(c), and 6(d) illustrate the variation with the average E_{corr} of the RMS in concrete beams without (control) and with different concentrations of the plant-based three types of extracts (i.e., AHL, COL, blended AHL-COL). The motive of the study is to compare the inhibitory effects of the blended AHL-COL concentrations over the individual AHL or COL extract in preventing the corrosion of the RMS in the ConC. The same trend in the change of the average E_{corr} of the concrete beams with 500 to 2000 ppm AHL-COL, AHL, or COL is observed. However, the additions of 500-2000 ppm AHL-COL in the concrete beam showed significantly higher corrosion-inhibiting ability and expected high passivity strength compared with the concrete beams with the same concentrations of the individual AHL or COL extract. Consequently, it can be stated that the blended AHL-COL demonstrated a synergistic effect in inhibiting the corrosion of mild steel in the ConC.

The surface features of the embedded mild steel before and after reinforced in concrete composite (ConC) at control condition and with different concentrations of the blended HL-COL extract was also investigated from the recorded optical images of the sample specimens (Figure 7). The corrugated mild steel surface before reinforcement in concrete composite exhibits comparatively a smooth surface without notable defects, as shown in Figure 7(a).

In contrast, an optical image of the RMS surface, which was exposed in the control ConC, disclosed that the corrosion product has remarkably appeared on the metal surface compared to the optical images of the exposed sample specimens in a concrete with different concentrations of AHL-COL extract for about six months, as displayed in Figure 7(b). The images of the RMS surface in the concrete beam with 1000 ppm and 2000 ppm AHL-COL extracts are smooth without significant rust defects, as noticed in Figures 7(c), and 7(d). The E_{corr} results, as described above in Figs. 6 and 7, established the fact that the plant-based protective layers are successfully developed over the RMS surface after exposure to the ConC for long periods in the ambient atmosphere by adsorbing/interacting with the conjugated polar groups of the phyto-compounds on the RMS surface, which have sufficient electrophilic centers [53].

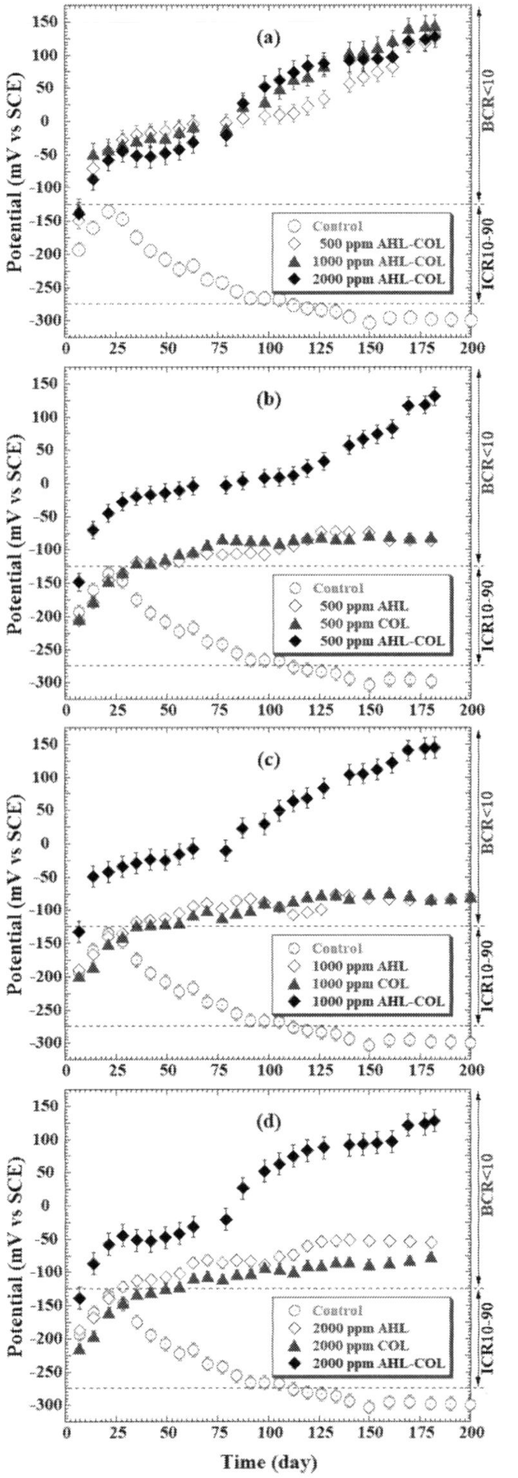

Fig. 6. Variation of the average corrosion potential of RMS in concrete beam with various concentrations of AHL-COL in concrete composite.

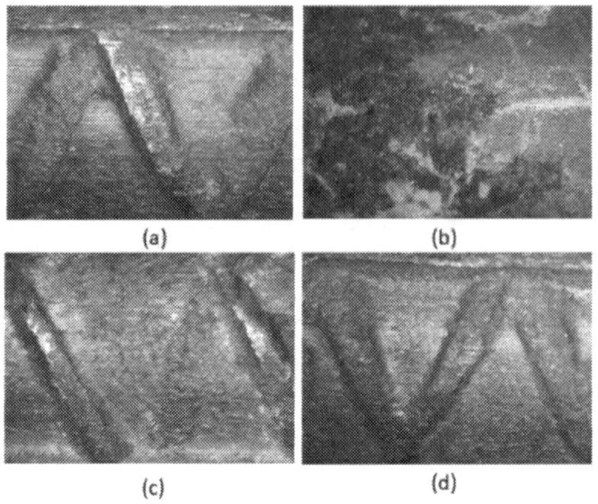

Fig. 7. Optical images of the mild steel (a) before, and after embedding in concrete composite (b) without plant extract, (c) with 1000 ppm AHL-COL, and (d) with 2000 ppm AHL-COL.

Accordingly, the RMS corrosion rate would progressively decline upon the addition of different amounts of the blended AHL-COL extract in ConC. It indicates the formation of a passive layer over the RMS surface in the concrete composite with blended extracts. Moreover, the morphological features and chemical compositions of the corroded RMS surface were investigated after exposing the sample specimens for six months or more in ConC using a scanning electron microscope (SEM) with an energy-dispersive X-ray (EDX) spectrometer. The results of the SEM/EDX analysis provide solid evidence supporting the relationship between E_{corr} variation and the corrosion-inhibiting efficiency of the RMS in ConS. This relationship highlights the impact on electrochemical potential values and identifies the areas at risk of corrosion. SEM images reveal that irregular rusting occurs on the surface of the RMS, which has crumbled into small fragments on the corroded surfaces of the reinforcing materials, as illustrated in Figure 8(a).

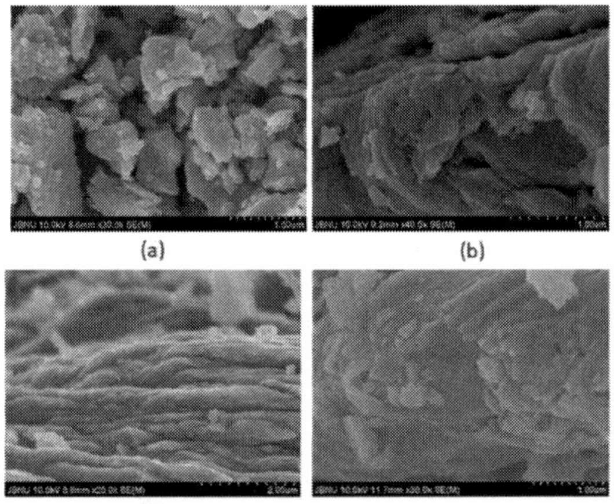

Fig. 8. SEM images of the RMS after reinforcing it for about six months in concrete composite (a) without extract (control), and with extracts of (b) 2000 ppm AHL, (c) 1000 ppm AHL-COL, and (d) 2000 ppm AHL-COL.

However, additions of 1000 ppm and 2000 ppm AHL-COL, including 2000 ppm AHL to the concrete composite, lower the possibility percentage of the RMS corrosion risk. The SEM image clearly shows that the corrosion-related surface imperfections are eliminated on the inhibited mild steel surface, demonstrating the increased inhibition efficacy of three different extracts, as in Figuers 8(b), 8(c) and 8(d). The RMS corrosion is controlled through the adsorption mechanism. Hence, the additions of 1000-2000 ppm AHL-COL lower the possibility of corrosion risk of the reinforcing concrete infrastructures, which is also supported by the results of the EDX analysis, as demonstrated in Figure 9.

EDS analysis reveals significant amounts of carbon and oxygen on the RMS surface after being embedded in the concrete mix under control conditions, as shown in Figure 9(a). Nevertheless, the amount of Fe on the corroded RMS surface is remarkably lower compared with the composition of the fresh mild steel rod (i.e., >98%). Such changes in the chemical components of the RMS surface in the control ConC reveal the formation of corrosion products of the iron oxide layer on the corroded steel surface [54].

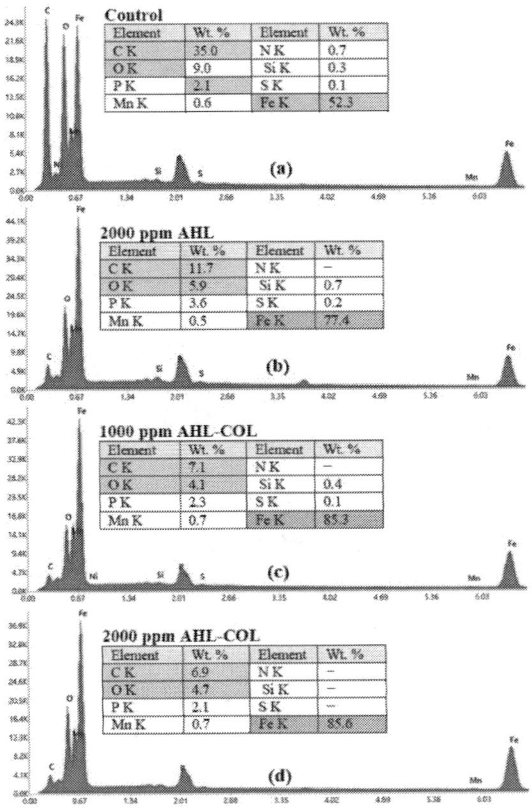

Fig. 9. EDX analysis of the RMS surfaces after exposed for six months in concrete composite (a) at control condition, and with blended (b) 1000 ppm AHL, (c) 1000 ppm AHL-COL and (d) 2000 ppm AHL-COL extracts.

When the RMS is exposed in concret beam with only 2000 ppm AHL and blended 1000-2000 ppm AHL-COL extracts, as shown in Figures 9(b), 9(c), and 9(d), respectively, the EDX spectrum shows comparatively lower oxygen and higher percentages of Fe, showing low corrosion risk on the RMS with the addition of the AHL or the blended AHL-COL extracts in the ConC. As a result, the formation of a protective thin oxide layer by the addition of AHL and AHL-COL extracts in the CNC enhances the anti-corrosive properties [55]. Among these three extracts, the blended two extracts (i.e., 1000 ppm & 2000 ppm AHL-COL) have shown better anti-corrosive behavior of the RMS in the concrete beam.

4 Conclusion

Based on the screening test, FTIR, UV-Vis spectroscopy, half-cell potential, and surface analysis, the experimental findings support the development of a novel plant-based concrete additive for the corrosion control of the RMS in the reinforced concrete beams. The blended extracts of *Ageratum houstonianu*m and *Chromolaena odorata* at concentrations of 500 ppm, 1000 ppm, and 2000 ppm exhibit a synergistic effect in inhibiting the corrosion of RMS in the reinforced concrete beam. It is primarily due to the formation of a compacte adsorption layer on the surfaces of the RMS.

The consequences of this work would be a breakthrough in understanding the knowledge on AHL-COL extract as noble green corrosion inhibitor for extending the lifespan of the RMS in concrete structures. The results of the present work permit the production of plant-based novel anti-corrosive concrete additives on a commercial scale to control SRC corrosion. A detailed study on the film formation mechanism using electrochemical impedance spectroscopy (EIS), linear polarization, and other relevant surface analysis techniques.

This research work was supported by the University Grants Commission (UGC) of Nepal under the Ph. D. Fellowship and Research Support No.: PhD-78/79-S&T-03 to author MG. The authors acknowledge Dr. Ishwor Pathak of Jeonbuk National University, South Korea, for providing SEM-EDS facilities.

References

[1] I. Marcos, J.-T. San-José, L. Garmendia, A. Santamaría, J.M. Manso, Central lessons from the historical analysis of 24 reinforced-concrete structures in northern Spain. *J. Cult. Heritage.* **20**, 649–659 (2016). https://doi.org/10.1016/j.culher.2016.03.003

[2] Y.P. Asmara, T. Kurniawan, A.G.E. Sutjipto, J. Jafar, Application of plants extracts as green corrosion inhibitors for steel in concrete- a review. *Indonesian J. Sci. Technol.* **3**(2), 158–170 (2018).

[3] A. Biparva, *Reinforced Concrete Corrosion: A Silent Killer*, (2016). https://www.constructioncanada.net/reinforced-concrete-corrosion-a-silent-killer

[4] G. Venkatesh, C. Kamal, P. Vennila, S. Kaya, M.G.L. Annaamalai, B.E. Ibrahimi, Sustainable corrosion inhibitor for steel embedded in concrete by Guar Gum: Electrochemical and theoretical analyses. *Appl. Surf. Sci. Adv.* **12**, 100328 (2022).

[5] S. Robuschi, A. Tengattini, J. Dijkstra, I. Fernandez, K. Lundgren, A closer look at corrosion of steel reinforcement bars in concrete using 3D neutron and X-ray computed tomography. *Cem. Conc. Res.* **144**, 106439 (2021).

[6] U.M. Angst, Challenges and opportunities in corrosion of steel in concrete. *Mater. Struct.* **51**(1), 4 (2018).

[7] M. Oki, S.A. Akintola, A.A. Adediran, P.P. Ikubanni, B.T. Ogunsemi, Reinforcement bar corrosion - causes and management. *J. Phys.: Conf. Ser.* **1378**(2), 022095 (2019).

[8] E.S.J. Ahmed, G.M. Ganesh, A comprehensive overview on corrosion in RCC and its prevention using various green corrosion inhibitors. *Buildings.* **12**(10), 1682 (2022).

[9] S. Ghoreishiamiri, P.B. Raja, M. Ismail, S.F.H. Karouei, P. Forouzani. *Areca catechu*: an eco-friendly corrosion inhibitor for reinforced concrete structures in corrosive medium. *J. Bio-Tribo-Corros.* 7, 22 (2021).

[10] J. Bhattarai, M. Somai, N. Acharya, A. Giri, A. Roka, N.P. Phulara, Study on the effects of green-based plant extracts and water-proofers as anti-corrosion agents for steel-reinforced concrete slabs. *E3S Web Conf.* **302**, 02018 (2021).

[11] B. Valdez-Salas, R. Vazquez-Delgado, J. Salvador-Carlos, E. Beltran-Partida, R. Salinas-Martinez, N. Cheng, M. Curiel-Alvarez, *Azadirachta indica* leaf extract as green corrosion inhibitor for reinforced concrete structures: corrosion effectiveness against commercial corrosion inhibitors and concrete integrity. *Materials.* **14**(12), 3326 (2021).

[12] R. Anitha, S. Chitra, V. Hemapriya, I. Chung, S. Kim, M. Prabakaran, Implications of eco-addition inhibitor to mitigate corrosion in reinforced steel embedded in concrete. *Constr. Build. Mater.* **213**, 246–256 (2019).

[13] B.E.R. Amitha, B.B.J. Basu, Green corrosion inhibitors for corrosion protection of metals and alloys: an overview. *Int. J. Corros.* **2012**, 1–15 (2012).

[14] N. Patni, S. Agrawal, P. Shah, Greener approach towards corrosion inhibition. *Chin. J. Eng.* **2013**, 784186 (2013).

[15] S.Z. Salleh, A.H. Yusoff, S.K. Zakaria, M.A.A. Taib, A. Abu Seman, M.N. Masri, M. Mohamad, S. Mamat, S. Ahmad Sobri, A. Ali, P.T. Teo, Plant extracts as green corrosion inhibitor for ferrous metal alloys: a review. *J. Cleaner Prod.* **304**,127030 (2021).

[16] I.B. Onyeachu, D.I. Njoku, S.C. Nwanonenyi, C.C. Ahanotu, K.M. Etiowo, Investigation into the adsorption and inhibition properties of sodium octanoate against CO_2 corrosion of C1018 carbon steel under static and hydrodynamic conditions. *Sci. Afr.* **20**, e01603 (2023).

[17] R. Naderi, A. Bautista, F. Velasco, M. Soleimani, M. Pourfath, Use of licorice plant extract for controlling corrosion of steel rebar in chloride-polluted concrete pore solution. *J. Mol. Liq.* **346**, 117856 (2022).

[18] Q. Wang, X. Wu, H. Zheng, L. Liu, Q. Zhang, A. Zhang, Z. Yan, Y. Sun, Z. Li, X. Li, Evaluation for *Fatsia japonica* leaves extract as green corrosion inhibitor for carbon steel in simulated concrete pore solutions. *J. Buil. Eng.* **63**, 105568 (2023).

[19] R. Naderi, A. Bautista, F. Velasco, M. Soleimani, M. Pourfath, Green corrosion inhibition for carbon steel reinforcement in chloride-polluted simulated concrete pore solution using *Urtica dioica* extract. *J. Buil. Eng.* **58**, 105055 (2022).

[20] Q. Liu, Z. Song, H. Han, S. Donkor, L. Jiang, W. Wang, H. Chu, A novel green reinforcement corrosion inhibitor extracted from waste *Platanus acerifolia* leaves. *Constr. Buil. Mater.* **260**, 119695 (2020).

[21] C. Verma, E.E. Ebenso, M. Quraishi, Ionic liquids as green and sustainable corrosion inhibitors for metals and alloys: An overview, *J. Mol. Liq.* **233**, 403–414 (2017).

[22] P. Satyal, A. Poudel, W.N. Setzer, Variation in the volatile phytochemistry of *Ageratum conyzoides*, *Am. J. Essent. Oils Nat. Prod.* **6**, 7–10 (2018).

[23] O.O. Adeyemi, O.O. Olubomehin, R.O. Bello, Investigation of *Ageratum conyzoides* aqueous extract as inhibitor for hydrochloric acid corrosion of SX 316 steel. *Acad. J. Sci. Eng.* **8**(1), 20–32 (2022).

[24] R. Chahal, A. Nanda, E.K. Akkol, E. Sobarzo-Sánchez, A. Arya, D. Kaushik, R. Dutt, R. Bhardwaj, M.H. Rahman, V. Mittal, *Ageratum conyzoides* L. and its secondary metabolites in the management of different fungal pathogens. *Molecules (Basel, Switzerland).* **26**(10), 2933 (2021).

[25] C.A. Coy-Barrera, L.D. Becerra, S.A. Torres-Cortés, V.C. Gonzalez, Eco-friendly corrosion inhibition study of croton extracts (Euphorbiaceae) for mild steel in HCl 1.0 M: experimental and theoretical studies. *Results Chem.* **16**, 102498 (2025).

[26] A. Lamsal, M.P. Devkota, D.S. Shrestha, S. Joshi, A. Shrestha, Seed germination ecology of *Ageratum houstonianum*: a major invasive weed in Nepal. *Plos One.* **14**(11), e0225430 (2019).

[27] R. Singh, D. Prasad, Z. Safi, N. Wazzan, L. Guo, De-scaling, experimental, DFT, and MD-simulation studies of unwanted growing plant as natural corrosion inhibitor for SS-410 in acid medium. *Colloids Surf. A.* **649**, 129333 (2022).

[28] K.K. Shah, I. Tiwari, S. Tripathi, S. Subash Subedi, J. Shrestha, Invasive alien plant species: A threat to biodiversity and agriculture in Nepal. *Agriways.* **8**(2), 62–73 (2020).

[29] M. M. Muzakir, F.O. Nwosu, S.O. Amusat, Mild steel corrosion inhibition in a NaCl solution by lignin extract of *Chromolaena odorata*. *Port. Electrochim. Acta.* **37**(6) 359–372 (2019).

[30] ASTM C876-22b, *Standard Test Method for Corrosion Potentials of Uncoated Reinforcing Steel in Concrete,* in Annual book of ASTM

standards, ASTM International, West Conshohocken, USA, (2022).

[31] N.K. Pandey, L. Gupta, J. Bhattarai, N.P. Bhattarai, An inhibitory prospect of leaf extracts of flossflower and yam for rebar steel corrosion in concrete aggregates. *E3S Web Conf.* **559**, 02008 (2024).

[32] M. Gautam, D. B. Subedi, J.R. Dhungana, M. Dhakal, K.P. Bohara, N.P. Bhattarai, J. Bhattarai, A sustainable approach for mitigating rebar corrosion in adverse conditions using *Phyllanthus emblica* (L.) leaf extract as concrete scale inhibitor. *Int. J. Corros. Scale Inhib.* **14**(3), 1522-1554 (2025).

[33] ASTM C1582/C1582M-11, *Standard Specification for Admixtures to Inhibit Chloride Induced Corrosion of Reinforcing Steel in Concrete,* in Annual book of ASTM standards, ASTM International, West Conshohocken, USA, (2017), pp. 10.

[34] T.K. Patle, K. Shrivas, R. Kurrey, S. Upadhyay, R. Jangde, R. Chauhan, Phytochemical screening and determination of phenolics and flavonoids in *Dillenia pentagyna* using UV–Vis and FTIR spectroscopy. *Spectrochim. Acta Part A.* **242**, 118717 (2020).

[35] B. Renuka, B. Sanjeev, D. Ranganathan, Evaluation of phyto-constituents of *Caralluma nilagiriana* by FTIR and UV-Vis spectroscopic analysis. *J. Pharmacogn. Phytochem.* **5**(2), 105–108 (2016).

[36] E. Safitri, H. Humaira, N. Nazaruddin, S. Susilawati, M. Murniana, N.D. Md Sani, *Dioscorea alata* L anthocyanin extract methanol as a sensitive pH active compound. *J. Phys.: Conf. Ser.* **1869**, 012058 (2021).

[37] A. Sulistiawan, W. Setyaningsih, A. Rohman, A new FTIR method combined with multivariate data analysis for determining aflatoxins in peanuts (*Arachis hypogaea*). *J. Appl. Pharm. Sci.* **12**(7), 199–206 (2022).

[38] P.P. Yue, Y.J. Hu, G.Q. Fu. C.X. Sun. M.F. Li, F. Peng, R.C. Sun, Structural differences between the lignin-carbohydrate complexes (LCCs) from 2-24 months old bamboo (*Neosinocalamus affinis*). *Int. J. Mol. Sci.* **19**(1), (2018).

[39] A. Inan Genc, S. Gok, S. Banerjee, F. Severcan, Valdecoxib recovers the lipid composition, order and dynamics in colon cancer cell lines independent of COX-2 expression: An ATR-FTIR spectroscopy study. *Appl. Spectrosc.* **71**(1), 105–117 (2017).

[40] J.M. Barcelo, A.M. Gatchallan, I.J.B. Aquino, D.R.E. Ollero, F.L.D. Cortez, T.M. Costales, L.A.Q. Marzo, FTIR spectrum and antimutagenicity of *coffea arabica* pulp and *Arachis hypogaea* test in relation to their *In vitro* antioxidant properties. *Asia Pac. J. Multidiscip. Res.* **3**(4), 99–108 (2015).

[41] U.J. Chukwu, T.O. Uchechukwu, O. Akaranta, Synthesis of new cation exchanger resins from chemically modified peanut (*Arachis hypogaea* L.) testa extract. *Int. J. Sci. Eng. Res.* 8(3), 523–529 (2017).

[42] J.E. Eziuka, I.B. Onyeachu, D.I. Njoku, S.C. Nwanonenyi, M.A. Chidiebere, E.F. Oguzie, *Elucidating the inhibition behaviour of Pterocarpus santalinoides* leaves extract on mild steel corrosion in H_2SO_4 solution–GC-MS, FTIR, SEM, Experimental and computational approach. *Moroccan J. Chem.* **11**(3), 579–593 (20223).

[43] C. Zhang, J. Deng, L. Lin, M. Li, X. Sheng, H. Xia, M. Lin, Use of ATR-FTIR spectroscopy and chemometrics for the variation of active components in different harvesting periods of *Lonicera japonica*. *Int. J. Anal. Chem.* **2022**, 8850914 (2022).

[44] M. Maczka, A. Ciupa, A. Gągor, A. Sieradzki, A. Pikul, B. Macalik, M. Drozd, Perovskite metal formate framework of [NH_2-CH^+-NH_2]Mn$(HCOO)_3$]: phase transition, magnetic, dielectric, and phonon properties. Inorg. Chem. **53**(10), 5260–5268 (2014).

[45] E. Fachriyah, M.A. Ghifari, K. Anam, Isolation, identification, and xanthine oxidase inhibition activity of alkaloid compound from *Peperomia pellucida*. *IOP Conf. Ser.: Mater. Sci. Eng.* **349**, 12017 (2018).

[46] K. Vijayaraghavan, J. Rajkumar, M.A. Seyad, Efficacy of *Chromolaena odorata* leaf extracts for the healing of rat excision wounds. *Vet. Med.* **62**(10), 565–578 (2017).

[47] S.K. Chandraker, M. Lal, M.K. Ghosh, V. Tiwari, T.K. Ghorai, R. Shukla, Green synthesis of copper nanoparticles using leaf extract of *Ageratum houstonianum* Mill. and study of their photocatalytic and antibacterial activities. *Nano Express* **1**(1), 010033 (2020).

[48] F. Odutayo, C. Ezeamagu, T. Kabiawu, D. Aina, G. Mensah-Agyei, Phytochemical screening and antimicrobial activity of *Chromolaena odorata* leaf extract against selected microorganisms. *J. Adv. Med. Pharm. Sci.* **13**(4), 1–9 (2017).

[49] S. Aribo, S.J. Olusegun, L.J. Ibhadiyi, A. Oyetunji, D.O. Folorunso, Green inhibitors for corrosion protection in acidizing oilfield environment. *J. Assoc. Arab Univ. Basic Appl. Sci.* **24**(1), 34–38 (2017).

[50] M. Sheydaei, The use of plant extracts as green corrosion inhibitors: a review. *Surfaces*. **7**(2), 380-403 (2024).

[51] A. Chaouiki, M. Chafiq, Y.G. Ko, A.H. Al-Moubaraki, F.Z. Thari, R. Salghi, K. Karrouchi, K. Bougrin, I.H. Ali, H. Lgaz, Adsorption mechanism of eco-friendly corrosion inhibitors for exceptional corrosion protection of carbon steel: Electrochemical and first-principles DFT evaluations *Metals*. **12**(10), 1598 (2022).

[52] D.V.P. Tran, Time-dependent model for evaluating corrosion potential and electrical resistivity of reinforced concrete. *Eng. J.* **25**(1), 125–135 (2021).

[53] K. Hjouji, E. Ech-chihbi, I. Atemni, M. Ouakki, T. Ainane, M. Taleb, Z. Rais, *Datura stramonium*

plant seed extracts as a new green corrosion inhibitor for mild steel in 1M HCl solution: Experimental and surface characterization studies. *Sustainable Chem. Pharm.* **34**, 101170 (2023).

[54] R. Jalab, A.B. Ali, M. Khaled, M. Abouseada, S. Al-Khalil, A. Al-Suwaidi, S. Hamze, I.H. Hussein, Novel polyepoxysuccinic acid-grafted polyacrylamide as a green corrosion inhibitor for carbon steel in acidic solution. *ACS Omega* **8**(19), 16673–16686 (2023).

[55] D.K. Verma, F. Khan, Green approach to corrosion inhibition of mild steel in hydrochloric acid medium using extract of spirogyra algae. *Green Chem. Lett. Rev.* **9**(1), 52–60 (2016).

Effect of Oxyhydrogen Injection on Particulate Matter Characteristics in Ethanol-Fuelled Gasoline Direct Injection Engines

Ketsiree Ketpirune [1, 2], *Pokpong* Arsa [1, 2], *Sak* Sittichompoo[1,2], *Nathinee* Theinnoi[3], *Boonlue* Sawatmongkhon[1,2] *Pichitpon* Neamyou[2,4], and *Kampanart* Theinnoi [1,2*]

[1]College of Industrial Technology, King Mongkut's University of Technology North Bangkok, Bangsue, 10800 Bangkok, Thailand
[2]Research Centre for Combustion Technology and Alternative Energy (CTAE), Science and Technology Institute, King Mongkut's University of Technology North Bangkok, Bangsue, 10800 Bangkok, Thailand
[3]Department of Ordnance Engineering, Chulachomklao Royal Military Academy, 26001 Nakhon Nayok, Thailand
[4]Department of Mechanical and Automotive Engineering Technology, Faculty of Engineering and Technology, King Mongkut's University of Technology North Bangkok (Rayong Campus), 21120 Rayong, Thailand

Abstract. This research examines the influence of HHO gas, produced through electrolysis, on particulate matter emissions and combustion efficiency within a GDI engine under steady-state operational conditions. HHO, which consists of a composite of hydrogen and oxygen, was injected at varied concentrations (0.5%, 1%, and 2%) into the engine's intake system to optimize combustion attributes. The findings indicated that the incorporation of HHO resulted in a reduction of total particulate mass and a shift in the geometric mean diameter towards diminished values, thereby signifying enhanced combustion and decreased soot production. The categorisation of particles into nucleation and accumulation modes demonstrated a concentration-dependent behaviour, wherein lower concentrations of HHO facilitated the formation of ultrafine particles, while higher concentrations of HHO favoured oxidation processes and particle aggregation. The combustion efficiency, as determined from the concentrations of carbon monoxide and carbon dioxide, exhibited a significant increase with the addition of HHO, reaching a maximum of 96.24% at a concentration of 1% HHO. These results substantiate the hypothesis that HHO enrichment fosters cleaner combustion and presents a viable strategy for mitigating particulate matter emissions in GDI engines without necessitating substantial modifications.

1 Introduction

Particulate matter (PM) emissions originating from road transportation have emerged as a critical concern for both environmental integrity and public health, particularly in urban locales characterised by high population density and elevated vehicular activity. Fine ($PM_{2.5}$) and ultrafine particulate emissions are derived from both exhaust and non-exhaust mechanisms, with internal combustion engines (ICEs) being a predominant source due to the inefficiencies associated with fuel combustion and the generation of particulates related to lubricants. [1, 3] Ultrafine particles pose particularly severe health risks, as their diminutive size facilitates deep infiltration into the human respiratory tract, thereby increasing the likelihood of serious health complications such as cardiovascular and pulmonary disorders. [4] In light of accumulating scientific data that correlates PM exposure with detrimental health effects, regulatory bodies across the globe have instituted progressively stringent emission regulations. This trend has catalysed extensive research into methodologies for PM mitigation, encompassing advancements in fuel formulation, combustion chamber architecture, exhaust after-treatment technologies, and optimization of in-cylinder combustion processes, all intended to curtail emissions without compromising engine performance or operational efficiency.

Among the myriads of strategies aimed at emission reduction, hydrogen (H_2) supplementation has garnered significant scholarly interest due to its advantageous combustion properties. H_2 is characterised by a high laminar flame speed, extensive flammability limits, and the absence of carbon content, all of which facilitate more complete and efficient combustion processes. In Gasoline Direct Injection (GDI) engines, where stratified charge operation and fuel-rich zones frequently lead to localized incomplete combustion and soot generation, the incorporation of H_2 into the intake air has been demonstrated to diminish both PM mass and number concentrations. [5, 6] This phenomenon is attributed to the enhanced propagation of the flame and the improved oxidation of intermediate species, which collectively inhibit the genesis of soot precursors. A range of experimental investigations has substantiated that even

* Corresponding author: kampanart.t@cit.kmutnb.ac.th

minimal quantities of H_2, when accurately introduced, can result in substantial reductions in PM emissions without negatively impacting combustion stability or thermal efficiency.

H_2 produced through electrolysis presents additional benefits for automotive applications. Electrolysers facilitate the generation of H_2 and oxygen from water utilizing electrical energy, ideally sourced from renewable systems, thereby enabling the production of H_2 with zero carbon emissions at the point of generation.[7] The capacity to produce H_2 on-demand obviates the necessity for high-pressure storage or external refuelling infrastructure, rendering this methodology particularly appealing for decentralized, small-scale applications. Compact electrolyser units can be seamlessly integrated into vehicle architectures, allowing for real-time, continuous delivery of H_2 into the intake system. This capability enables dynamic regulation of the combustion process and offers a practical, sustainable avenue for the in-situ reduction of PM emissions.

Although gasoline direct injection (GDI) engines are progressively adopted in contemporary automotive design due to their enhanced thermal efficiency, meticulous fuel metering capabilities, and elevated power output, they are intrinsically susceptible to increased particulate matter (PM) emissions in comparison to port fuel injection (PFI) systems. This phenomenon can be attributed mainly to the direct injection of fuel into the combustion chamber, which may result in suboptimal fuel–air mixing, particularly during transient operational conditions and cold start scenarios. To address these challenges, scholars have investigated the utilization of hydrogen (H_2) to improve combustion quality and diminish particulate matter formation. The incorporation of H_2, especially in the form of HHO gas (a synthesis of H_2 and oxygen) produced through electrolysis and introduced into the intake air, has exhibited promise in fostering a more uniform mixture formation and accelerating flame propagation, consequently mitigating soot production at its inception. Notably, this approach does not require extensive alterations to existing hardware, which resonates with broader initiatives aimed at promoting clean combustion through minimally invasive technological advancements.

The principal objective of this research endeavour is to examine the impact of electrolyser-generated HHO gas on the particulate matter emission characteristics emanating from a GDI engine. The investigation specifically concentrates on the way HHO supplementation influences particle size distribution, numerical concentration, and mass emissions under steady-state operational circumstances. Considering H_2's capability to enhance oxidation processes and decrease soot precursor formation, this study seeks to ascertain whether the introduction of HHO gas derived from electrolytic processes can effectively mitigate the particulate matter formation mechanisms that are intrinsic to GDI combustion.

2 Experimental Setup

2.1 Engine Test

The experimental configuration encompassed a four-cylinder, 1.3-litre Gasoline Direct Injection (GDI) engine, with detailed specifications delineated in Table 1, integrated with an eddy-current dynamometer (Hofmann Prüftechnik D3210 Elze) to facilitate accurate manipulation of engine load under steady-state operational conditions. All experimental trials were conducted at stoichiometric air–fuel ratios ($\lambda = 1$). Prior to the commencement of data collection, the engine was equilibrated at a coolant temperature of 310 K (±4 K), while the ambient relative humidity was sustained within a range of 60% to 80%. Emissions alongside fuel consumption metrics were meticulously recorded across a spectrum of steady-state speed and load conditions.

Table 1. Specification of GDI engine

Item	Value	Unit
Model	Mazda SKYACTIV G1.3	
Number of cylinders	4	Cylinders
Bore	71	mm
Stroke	82	mm
Displacement Volume	1298	cm^3
Compression Ratio	14:1	
Maximum Power	$62_{@5,400\ rpm}$	kW
Maximum Torque	$112_{@4,000\ rpm}$	Nm
Fuel System	Direct Injection	
Engine Aspirate	Naturally Aspirated	

In this investigation, HHO gas was synthesized utilizing an OH-series electrolyser system, as delineated in Table 2, which facilitates the generation of a composite of H_2 and oxygen through the electrolysis of water.[11] To enhance the conductivity and overall efficacy of the electrolysis process, the electrolyte solution consisted of water amalgamated with 37.5% Sodium Hydroxide (NaOH) by volume. This specific concentration was chosen to optimize H_2 output under consistent operational parameters. The resultant gas mixture is presented in Table 3.

Table 2. Specification of Electrolyser

Item	Value	Unit
Electrolyser Model	H180	
Electrolyte Composition	NaOH solution in Water	
Power	600	Watt
Capacity	1	Litre

In the present investigation, the experimental parameters entailed the modulation of the intake of the Gasoline Direct Injection (GDI) engine with diverse concentrations of Hydrogen-Hydrogen-Oxygen (HHO) gas generated through the process of electrolysis. The HHO gas, which is composed of a blend of diatomic hydrogen (H_2) and diatomic oxygen, was introduced at three distinct volumetric levels: 0.5%, 1%, and 2% of the intake air, as delineated in Table 3. The gas mixture was characterised by a composition of 63.36% H_2 and 18.55% oxygen by volume, with the residual fraction consisting of water vapor and minor trace gases. These gas mixtures were uniformly applied across all varying conditions of HHO blending. The principal aim of modifying the HHO concentration was to assess its impact on combustion behaviour, the formation of particulate matter, and combustion efficiency during steady-state engine operation, while ensuring a stoichiometric air-fuel ratio was preserved throughout all experimental trials.

Table 3. Concentration of H_2 and O_2 mixture in HHO gas is contingent upon the specific conditions applied.

%HHO	%H_2	%O_2
0.5	63.36%	18.55
1		
2		

2.2 Apparatus

In the present investigation, the generation of H_2 from an oxy-H_2 generator was scrutinized through the application of the Hsense H_2 detection system, aimed at replicating the delivery of HHO gas to the intake manifold of a gasoline direct injection (GDI) engine. Considering that the flow rate of the electrolyser was inadequate to satisfy the engine's requirements under loaded operational conditions, the Hsense system was utilized to accurately quantify the volume of H_2 generated during the electrolysis process. Situated downstream of the electrolyser, the Hsense sensor facilitated real-time monitoring of H_2 concentration and flow rate, thereby enabling precise estimation of the HHO gas produced. These empirical measurements were subsequently employed to construct and simulate the regulated introduction of HHO upstream of the throttle valve, with the objective of enhancing mixture homogeneity while preserving stoichiometric combustion conditions.

Gaseous emissions emanating from the engine's tailpipe were quantified employing a HORIBA MEXA-584L automotive emissions analyser, distinguished for its exceptional precision in monitoring a comprehensive spectrum of exhaust gas constituents. The analyser provides measurement accuracies of ±0.3 %vol for carbon monoxide (CO) within the 0–10%vol range, ±0.4%vol for carbon dioxide (CO_2) within the 0–20 %vol range, ±10 ppm for hydrocarbons (HC) within the 0–10,000 ppm range, and ±25 ppm for nitric oxide (NO) within the 0–5000 ppm range. The system guarantees remarkable linearity and repeatability, thereby furnishing reliable and consistent data for the assessment of engine gaseous emissions across diverse testing conditions. Moreover, the concentrations of CO and CO_2 acquired from the MEXA-584L were employed to compute combustion efficiency as delineated in Equation 1, offering significant insights into the completeness of the combustion process and aiding the interpretation of particulate formation patterns observed during the experimental [13].

$$CE = \frac{[CO_2] + ([CO] \times 0.5)}{[CO_2] + [CO] + (n \times [HC])} \quad (1)$$

Within the combustion efficiency equation, each variable signifies a distinct exhaust gas component pertinent to carbon oxidation. [CO_2] signifies the concentration of CO_2 present in the exhaust gas, articulated as a percentage by volume (vol%), which serves as an indicator of complete combustion. [CO] denotes the concentration of CO (also expressed in vol%), which arises from incomplete combustion and signifies partially oxidised carbon. The coefficient 0.5 corresponds to the oxidation level of CO, indicating that each CO molecule possesses only half the oxygen requisite for full conversion to CO_2. [HC] refers to the concentration of unburned hydrocarbons, initially quantified in parts per million (ppm) and subsequently converted to vol% by dividing by 10,000. This variable is contingent upon the number of carbon atoms within the hydrocarbon molecule based on the fuel type, typically 12 for gasoline (hexane), 3 for propane (LPG), and 1 for methane (CNG), thus quantifying the total unburned carbon content from hydrocarbons. Collectively, these variables facilitate the precise calculation of combustion efficiency through the evaluation of the extent of carbon oxidation within the exhaust stream.

In a concurrent manner, the characterization of particulate emissions was conducted utilizing a TSI Scanning Mobility Particle Sizer (SMPS), which quantified particle size distributions spanning from 7.50 to 294.3 nm, with a peak measurable concentration of 10^7 particles/cm³ attained through suitable dilution techniques.[14] Exhaust samples were channelled in a streamlined flow towards the SMPS for the purpose of real-time analysis, with the subsequent data processed employing Aerosol Instrument Manager software (version 10.3.1.0, TSI). Particle mass concentrations (μg/m³) along with size distributions were extracted for each experimental condition. The computation of particle mass was executed in accordance with the relationship articulated in Equation 2.

$$Particle\ Mass = \frac{\pi}{6} \times D_p \times N_p \times \rho_p \quad (2)$$

where denotes the particle diameter (nm), represents the number concentration (#/cm³), and indicates the particle density, which was presupposed to be 1.2×10^{-9} g/cm³. This methodology furnishes a robust assessment of particulate matter emitted from the exhaust system.

3 Result

3.1 Particle Size Distribution

The distribution of particle numbers (dN/dlogDp) ascertained under various HHO blending scenarios while maintaining a constant engine load and speed shown in fig. 1a. The baseline scenario (absence of HHO) displayed a preeminent particle mode in the range of 140–160 nm, with the particle number concentration consistently remaining beneath 1.0×10^6 #/cm³. The introduction of HHO resulted in notable alterations in particle number concentration. Specifically, at 0.5% and 1% HHO, the number concentration exhibited a modest increase yet migrated toward diminished particle sizes (~80–100 nm), signifying an enhancement in nucleation processes. Remarkably, the condition with 2% HHO manifested a pronounced peak at approximately 60 nm, with the number concentration surging to exceed 3.5×10^6 #/cm³. This significant escalation in the concentration of nucleation-mode particles implies that elevated HHO concentrations facilitate accelerated combustion and elevated flame temperatures, thereby promoting the generation of smaller particles, notwithstanding an overall improvement in combustion cleanliness. Figure 1b illustrates the distribution of particle mass, which exhibited an inverse relationship to the findings pertaining to particle number. The baseline condition displayed a prominent mass peak exceeding 700 µg/cm³ at approximately 160 nm, which is indicative of the accumulation mode. The incorporation of HHO gas at all concentrations resulted in a significant reduction in the overall particle mass, with the 2% HHO scenario demonstrating the most pronounced decrease. This finding suggests that while elevated concentrations of HHO may augment the quantity of nucleation-mode particles, they contribute minimally to the overall particulate mass owing to their reduced dimensions.

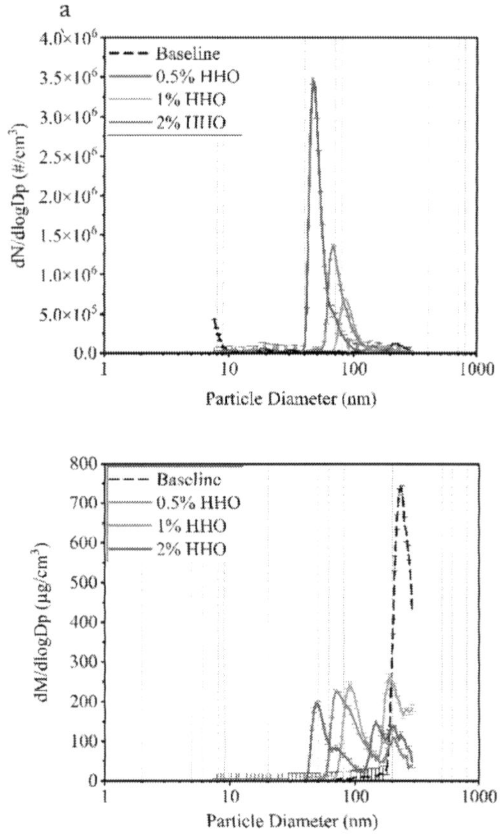

Fig. 1. An analysis of the distribution of a) particle Number and b) particle mass across each experimental condition.

In support of this observation, Figure 2 delineates the geometric mean diameter of the particles, which experienced a significant decline with HHO augmentation from 150.6 nm (baseline) to 81.5 nm (0.5% HHO), 103.5 nm (1% HHO), and 59.7 nm (2% HHO). This gradual transition towards smaller particle sizes underscores the impact of HHO on modifying combustion characteristics, culminating in enhanced fuel oxidation and diminished soot formation.

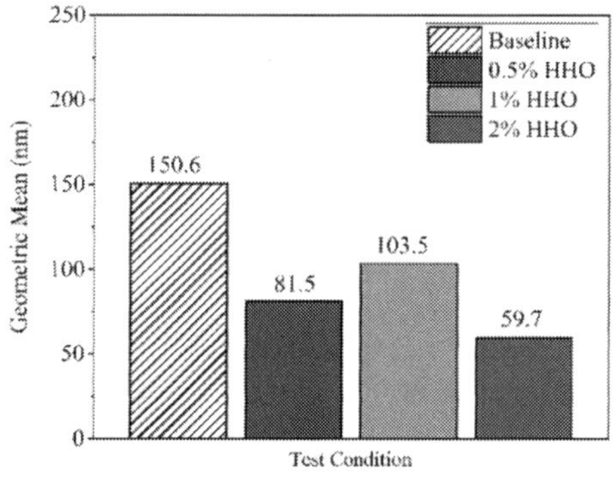

Fig. 2. Geometric Mean of Particle Diameter.

The categorisation of particles into nucleation mode (Dp ≤ 50 nm) and accumulation mode (Dp > 50 nm) elucidates the influence of HHO gas on particulate generation. As illustrated in Figure 3a, the concentration of particles within the accumulation mode exhibited a pronounced increase after the incorporation of HHO. The baseline condition recorded a total concentration of 1.56×10^6 #/cm³. Following the introduction of 1% HHO and 0.5% HHO, the accumulation mode particles escalated significantly to 1.38×10^7 and 1.37×10^7 #/cm³, respectively. Notably, the condition with 2% HHO produced a moderate accumulation concentration of 7.53×10^6 #/cm³, which, although inferior to the concentrations observed with 1% and 0.5% HHO, still indicates a considerable enhancement relative to the baseline. This alteration may suggest particle enlargement through agglomeration or a modification in combustion dynamics that favours the formation of larger soot particles under these specific conditions.

Conversely, the particle behaviour in nucleation mode, depicted in Figure 3b, exhibited a distinct pattern. The baseline particle count within the nucleation mode was determined to be 2.58×10^6 #/cm³. The supplementation with HHO revealed a pronounced dependence on the blending ratio. The condition with 0.5% HHO resulted in a substantial increase in nucleation particles, reaching 1.63×10^7 #/cm³, indicative of vigorous ultrafine particle formation. In contrast, both the 1% and 2% HHO conditions led to a decrease in nucleation particle concentrations to 5.76×10^5 and 1.03×10^6 #/cm³, respectively. These findings imply that lower concentrations of HHO may facilitate nucleation through heightened combustion temperatures and the formation of reactive radicals, whereas higher concentrations may promote soot oxidation and particle coagulation, thereby diminishing the numbers of ultrafine particles. This classification accentuates the dual role of HHO in influencing both particle size modes contingent upon its dosage.

a

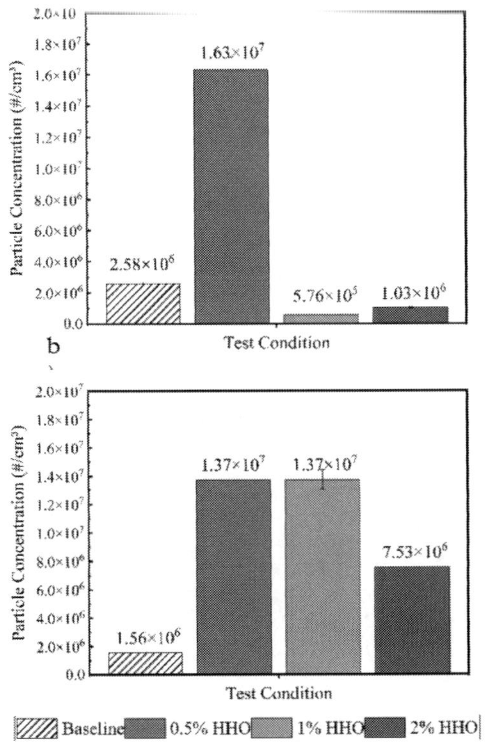

Fig. 3. Total particle number concentration for a) Nucleation Mode and b) Accumulation mode

3.2 Combustion Efficiency

The combustion efficiency outcomes, derived from the analysis of CO and CO_2 concentrations, furnish compelling corroborative evidence for the alterations observed in particle characteristics as measured by the SMPS. As illustrated in Figure 6, the baseline condition manifested a combustion efficiency of 88.35%, which reflects significant incomplete combustion, correlating with an increased particle mass and geometric mean diameter noted in the accumulation mode. The incorporation of HHO resulted in a notable enhancement in combustion efficiency, achieving a pinnacle of 96.24% at a concentration of 1% HHO, indicative of more thorough oxidation of carbonaceous materials and a concomitant reduction in CO emissions. This augmented efficiency is consistent with the pronounced decrease in particle mass and the transition towards smaller particle dimensions (as substantiated by the observed reduction in geometric mean diameter), thereby validating the hypothesis that HHO facilitates cleaner combustion processes. Even at a concentration of 2% HHO, notwithstanding a slight decline to 95.81% efficiency, the prevailing trend of diminished particle mass and diameter persisted, implying that the enhancement of combustion quality is instrumental in mitigating soot formation and reorganizing particle size distribution.

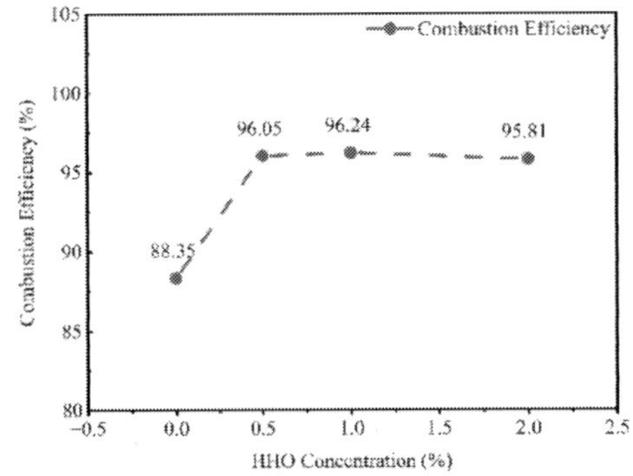

Fig. 4. The combustion efficiency associated with varying concentrations of HHO (hydrogen and oxygen)

4 Conclusion

This comprehensive investigation elucidated that the incorporation of HHO gas, which is generated through an on-demand electrolysis process, into a GDI engine system can profoundly affect both the emissions of particulate matter and the overall efficiency of combustion processes. The introduction of HHO into the combustion chamber was associated with a significant reduction in the mass of particulate emissions, alongside an observable transition towards smaller geometric mean diameters of these particles, which serves as a compelling indicator of more complete combustion processes and a concomitant suppression of soot formation in the exhaust. A meticulous classification of the emitted particles into distinct nucleation and accumulation modes has revealed that lower concentrations of HHO tend to promote the formation of ultrafine particulate matter, whereas elevated concentrations tend to enhance the oxidation of soot and facilitate the agglomeration of particles, leading to a more efficient combustion environment. Simultaneously, the combustion efficiency, which was quantitatively assessed through the analysis of CO and CO_2 concentrations in the exhaust, exhibited a remarkable improvement, achieving a peak efficiency of 96.24% when 1% HHO was supplemented, thereby providing substantial corroboration for the findings derived from the SMPS measurements. These insightful findings serve to affirm the considerable potential that HHO supplementation holds as a practical and minimally invasive methodology aimed at reducing particulate emissions while concurrently enhancing the quality of combustion in contemporary GDI engine technologies.

This research budget was allocated by National Science, Research and Innovation Fund (NSRF), and King Mongkut's University of Technology North Bangkok (Project No. KMUTNB-FF-68-B-26).

References

1. S. Etikyala, Particulate Formation in GDI Engines Towards Sustainable Transportation with Zero Emissions, Ph.D. dissertation, Dept. Thermo and Fluid Dynamics. (2022)
2. Z. Hu, Z. Lu, H. Zhang, B. Song and Y. Quan, Effect of oxidation temperature on oxidation reactivity and nanostructure of particulate matter from a China VI GDI vehicle. *Atmospheric Environment.* **256**, (2021). https://doi.org/10.1016/j.atmosenv.2021.118461
3. F. Bonatesta, E. Chiappetta and A. La Rocca, Part-load particulate matter from a GDI engine and the connection with combustion characteristics. *Applied Energy.* **124**, 366–376 (2014). https://doi.org/10.1016/j.apenergy.2014.03.030
4. N. Englert, Fine particles and human health – A review of epidemiological studies. Toxicology Letters. 235–242 (2004). https://doi.org/10.1016/j.toxlet.2003.12.035
5. J. Symonds, P. Price, P. Williams and R. Stone, Density of particles emitted from a gasoline direct injection engine. *Proc. 12th ETH Conf. Combustion Generated Nanoparticles*, Zurich, Switzerland, (2008)
6. H. Seong, K. Lee and S. Choi, Effects of engine operating parameters on morphology of particulates from a gasoline direct injection (GDI) engine. SAE Technical Paper. (2013). https://doi.org/10.4271/2013-01-2574
7. S. Wang, A. Lu and C. J. Zhong, Hydrogen production from water electrolysis: role of catalysts. *Nano Convergence.* **8**, (2021). https://doi.org/10.1186/s40580-021-00254-x
8. Singh, Akhilendra and Sharma, Nikhil and Agarwal, Ramesh and Agarwal, Avinash. Advanced Combustion Techniques and Engine Technologies for the Automotive Sector. (2020). https://doi.org/10.1007/978-981-15-0368-9
9. S. Madhu, Effects and Advantages of Gasoline Direct Injection System.
10. S. Liu, Z. Wang, H. K. Jia and L. Chen, Research on the influence of hydrogen and oxygen fuel obtained from water electrolysis on combustion stability of shale gas engines. *International Journal of Automotive Technology.* **20**, 119–125 (2019). https://doi.org/10.1007/s12239-019-0011-1
11. PARK, *Operation Manual for Oxy-Hydrogen Generator*.
12. HORIBA, *HORIBA Automotive Emission Analyzer MEXA-584L Instruction Manual*.
13. J. B. Heywood, *Internal Combustion Engine Fundamentals*. New York: McGraw-Hill. (1988)
14. M. A. Rahman, Q. Ou and D. Pui, Electrospray-Scanning Mobility Particle Sizer (ES-SMPS) technique: Superior sizing and multimodal characterization of colloidal nanoparticles compared to NTA and DLS. *Analytical Chemistry.* **96**, 18946–18956 (2024). https://doi.org/10.1021/acs.analchem.4c02891

Investigation of Bakuchiol-Loaded Beads Synthesis Using Coaxial Electrospray and their Stability

Apisittipong Srinusud[1], *Tanawan* Boonmee[1], *Chayanee* Suwimon[1], and *Nisalak* Trongsiriwat[1*]
[1]Department of Industrial Chemistry, Faculty of Applied Science, King Mongkut's University of Technology North Bangkok, Wongsawang, Bangsue, 10800 Bangkok, Thailand

Abstract. Bakuchiol, a meroterpene derived from *Psoralea corylifolia,* offers diverse skin benefits but is prone to degradation under environmental stress. This study aimed to encapsulate bakuchiol in alginate-based beads using coaxial electrospray to enhance its stability. Bead formation was optimized by varying sodium alginate concentrations, core-to-shell flow rates, and applied voltage. Optimal conditions (1.0% w/v alginate; 20:40 mL/min; 1000 V) yielded spherical, well-defined beads. Fourier-transform infrared (FT-IR) spectroscopy confirmed successful encapsulation. Stability tests demonstrated that the beads maintained structural integrity and bakuchiol retention under various storage conditions over 60 days. High retention (greater than 80%) was achieved in neutral and moderately acidic pH (3, 5 and 7) solutions and under both light and dark storage, underscoring the protective role of the alginate matrix. Conversely, exposure to alkaline pH induced degradation and diffusion-related loss. These findings indicate that coaxial electrospray-based alginate beads represent a promising delivery system for stabilizing bakuchiol, supporting its future application in cosmetic formulations.

1 Introduction

Bakuchiol (BK) is a meroterpene extracted from the seeds of *Psoralea corylifolia* [1, 4-6]. It has garnered increasing attention in the cosmetics and cosmeceuticals industries due to its broad range of skin benefits. These include reducing hyperpigmentation, minimizing wrinkles [5, 7-9], enhancing skin elasticity [5], stimulating collagen production [9], antioxidant, anti-inflammatory [10, 11], anti-acne and anti-bacterial [10, 13, 14]. Importantly, bakuchiol exerts these bioactivities with low skin irritation relative to retinol, making it suitable for sensitive skin types [5, 15]. As a result, bakuchiol has emerged as a promising natural alternative to retinol in anti-aging formulations [8-10, 16].

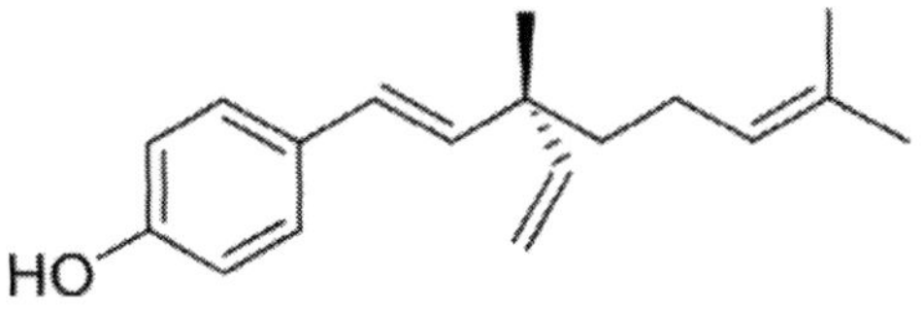

Fig. 1. Chemical structure of bakuchiol.

Chemically, bakuchiol (4-(3-ethenyl-3,7-dimethyl-1, 6-octadienyl)-phenol; $C_{18}H_{24}O$) [1] belongs to the meroterpenoid class, consisting of a phenolic group and an unsaturated hydrocarbon chain [1-4]. Due to its hydrophobic nature, bakuchiol dissolves readily in oils such as moringa and olive oil [16], as well as in organic solvents like ethanol and dimethyl sulfoxide (DMSO) [3, 11]. However, bakuchiol exhibits poor stability when exposed to light, oxygen, and heat, which can compromise its chemical integrity and biological efficacy [17-19].

Encapsulation technologies have been explored as a means of protecting active compounds from environmental degradation [20, 21]. Among various encapsulation approaches, polysaccharide-based systems are particularly attractive due to their biocompatibility and biodegradability [22]. Alginate, a natural polysaccharide derived from brown seaweed, is widely employed for encapsulation owing to its mild gelation process and excellent barrier properties [23, 24]. In the presence of calcium ions (Ca^{2+}), alginate chains undergo ionic crosslinking via interaction with guluronic acid residues, resulting in a dense and stable three-dimensional network commonly referred to as the "egg-box" structure [24, 25]. The alginate gel matrix offers mechanical stability and a protective barrier against external stressors [23, 26], making alginate an ideal candidate for encapsulating sensitive active ingredients like bakuchiol.

The coaxial electrospray technique offers an effective method for producing core–shell micro- and nanoparticles [27]. In this process, two immiscible liquids are co-delivered through a coaxial nozzle at controlled flow rates. When a high voltage is applied, the electric field overcomes the surface tension of the solution, generating a Taylor cone at the nozzle tip. This results in the emission of fine droplets toward the collector, typically containing a crosslinking solution [28]. The advantages of this

* Corresponding author : Nisalak.t@sci.kmutnb.ac.th

technique include high encapsulation efficiency, mild processing without heat, and the production of uniform particles [29-31].

This study provides a systematic investigation into the synthesis and stability of BK-loaded beads using coaxial electrospray. The primary objectives are to optimize the bead formation process, characterize the chemical and structural properties of the resulting beads, and evaluate the stability of encapsulated bakuchiol under various storage conditions including storage in calcium chloride solution and ultrapure water at room temperature under light and dark conditions, as well as in buffer solutions with pH values of 1, 3, 5, 7, and 9. Finally, the retained bakuchiol content in the beads was quantified. The insights gained from this work aim to support future applications in cosmetic formulations.

2 Materials and Methods

2.1 Materials

Bakuchiol was supplied from Chanjao Longevity Co. (Bangkok, Thailand). Sodium alginate, coconut oil and calcium chloride (food grade) were supplied from Krungthepchemi Co. (Bangkok, Thailand). Hydrochloric acid, sodium hydroxide, and methanol (AR grade) were supplied from Qrec Co. (New Zealand). Ultrapure water was obtained from the Department of Industrial Chemistry, Faculty of Applied Science, King Mongkut's University of Technology North Bangkok (KMUTNB).

2.2 Preparation of beads

Beads were prepared using a coaxial electrospray technique with a core-shell structure comprising an inner needle nested inside an outer needle. The core solution was prepared by dissolving bakuchiol in coconut oil at a concentration of 1% (v/v). The shell solution was prepared by dissolving sodium alginate in ultrapure water at concentrations of 1.0%, 1.5%, and 2.0% (w/w). A calcium chloride ($CaCl_2$) solution at 2.0% (w/v) was prepared in ultrapure water and used as the crosslinking bath to induce gelation during bead formation. The core and shell solutions were fed through a coaxial nozzle under controlled conditions. Details of the formulation and processing parameters are summarized in Table 1.

2.3 Fourier transform infrared spectroscopy

Fourier transform infrared (FT-IR) spectra were obtained using the PerkinElmer Spectrum 100 FT-IR Spectrometer to analyze the chemical composition of the prepared beads. The samples were prepared using the KBr pellet method. As the prepared beads were prone to moisture absorption, a drying process was required by placing them in a desiccator before grinding and compressing into transparent pellets. The pellets were scanned at a frequency of 4000-400 cm^{-1} for a total of 64 scans.

2.4 Optical microscope

The morphology of beads was characterized by optical microscope (Olympus). The beads were placed on a slide, then examined at 10X magnification.

Table 1. Process parameters for coaxial electrospray bead formation.

Parameters	Set	Unit
Bakuchiol; Core concentration	1	%w/v
Sodium alginate; Shell concentration	1, 1.5, 2	%w/v
$CaCl_2$; Collector concentration	1, 2, 3	%w/v
Flow rate of core	15, 20, 30	mL/min
Flow rate of shell	35, 40, 50	mL/min
Applied voltage	0, 1000	Volt
Frequency	400	Hz
Core diameter	450	µm
Shell diameter	700	µm

2.5 Determination of bakuchiol content in beads

The amount of bakuchiol encapsulated in the beads was determined using UV–Vis spectroscopy. The absorbance of the bead samples was measured at a wavelength of 262 nm on days 0, 14, 30, and 60. The bakuchiol content per bead (µg per bead) was quantified from a calibration curve prepared using standard bakuchiol solutions in methanol.

The percentage of bakuchiol retention was calculated according to the following equation:

$$\%\,Retention = (M_t / M_0) \times 100 \quad (1)$$

where M_t represents the bakuchiol content at each time point, and M_0 is the initial content at day 0.

2.6 Stability study

The stability of the beads during storage was evaluated under various conditions. The beads were immersed in calcium chloride solution, distilled water, and solutions with pH values of 1, 3, 5, 7, and 9. The samples were stored at room temperature. Sampling was conducted on days 0, 14, 30 and 60 to assess morphological changes and quantify the encapsulated compound.

2.7 Particle sizes of the beads

The particle sizes of the beads were characterized by capturing microscopic images and measuring the average bead diameter size using ImageJ software.

3 Results and Discussion

3.1 Formation of the beads

3.1.1 Effect of sodium alginate concentration and flow rates

The formation of beads was investigated by varying sodium alginate concentrations and core-to-shell flow rates. A bakuchiol concentration of 1.0% w/v was selected, along with a calcium chloride crosslinking bath at 2.0% w/v, an applied voltage of 1000 V, and a frequency of 400 Hz.

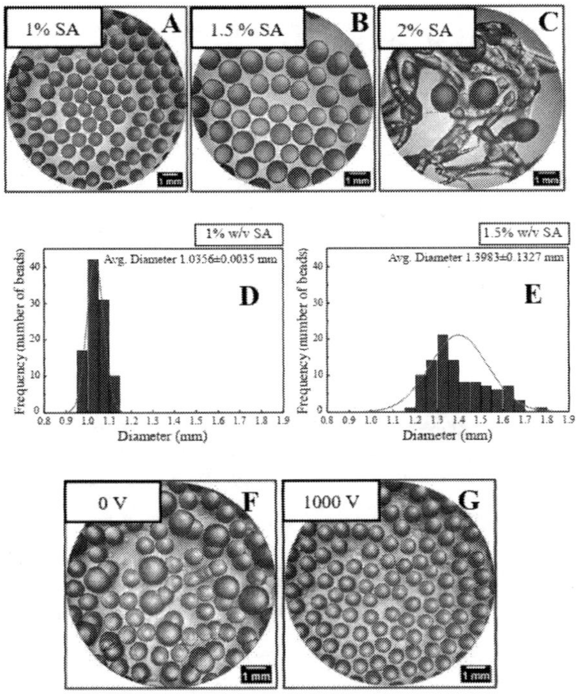

Fig. 2. Effect of sodium alginate concentration, flow rates, and applied voltage on bead formation. (A-C) Optical images of beads prepared with 1.0%, 1.5%, and 2.0% w/v sodium alginate; (D-E) size distribution of beads prepared with 1.0% and 1.5% w/v sodium alginate at optimal flow rates; (F-G) effect of applied voltage on bead morphology (F: 0 V, G: 1000 V).

The core-shell structures of the beads were clearly identified based on their morphological characteristics observed under optical microscopy. Optimal bead formation was observed at an alginate concentration of 1.0% w/v with a core-to-shell flow rate of 20:40 mL/min (Figure 2A), resulting in spherical beads with well-defined morphology and uniform size distribution. In contrast, lower flow rates (15:35 and 15:40 mL/min) produced beads with irregular shapes. At a higher flow rate of 30:50 mL/min, the shell layer appeared thick and uneven, and the core was inconsistently encapsulated, suggesting incomplete or unstable droplet formation. At an alginate concentration of 1.5% w/v (Figure 2B), the beads exhibited a broader size distribution, while at 2.0% w/v (Figure 2C), elongated and thread-like structures were observed, indicating that the higher solution viscosity hindered the formation of discrete droplets [25, 26].

3.1.2 Effect of applied voltage

The effect of applied voltage on the formation of alginate beads was investigated using sodium alginate concentrations of 1.0% w/v, with core-to-shell flow rate ratios of 20:40 mL/min. The crosslinking bath contained 2.0% w/v calcium chloride solution, and the electrospray frequency was fixed at 400 Hz.

At 0 V (Figure 2F), the electrospraying process failed to produce well-defined beads. Instead, irregular and aggregated structures were observed. This result is attributed to the absence of an electric field, which is critical for inducing the formation of a stable Taylor cone and promoting the breakup of the liquid into discrete droplets. In the absence of sufficient electrostatic repulsion, the droplets tended to coalesce upon contact, resulting in non-uniform bead morphology [32]. In contrast, applying a voltage of 1000 V (Figure 2G) yielded uniform, spherical beads. The applied electric field at this voltage promoted the formation of a stable Taylor cone at the nozzle tip, which led to the generation of a fine liquid jet that disintegrated into charged droplets. The mutual electrostatic repulsion between these charged droplets minimized aggregation and enabled uniform dispersion into the crosslinking bath. Additionally, the electric field accelerated the movement of the droplets toward the grounded collector, reducing the time available for droplet coalescence and allowing rapid gelation upon contact with the calcium chloride solution [33].

3.1.3 Effect of calcium chloride concentration

Beads were prepared using 1.0% w/v sodium alginate, a core-to-shell flow rate ratio of 20:40 mL/min, an applied voltage of 1000 V, and an electrospray frequency of 400 Hz. These parameters had previously produced well-defined core-shell structures.

Calcium chloride concentrations of 1.0%, 2.0%, and 3.0% w/v were tested. The mean bead diameter decreased from 1.081 mm at 1.0% calcium chloride to 0.945 mm at 3.0% (Figure 3). The decrease in bead size can be attributed to enhanced ionic crosslinking between calcium ions and the guluronic acid residues of sodium alginate, resulting in a dense gel network through the "egg-box" model. Stronger crosslinking produced smaller and more compact beads. These results confirm that calcium ion concentration is a key parameter for tuning particle morphology and size [34].

https://doi.org/10.1051/e3sconf/202567901016

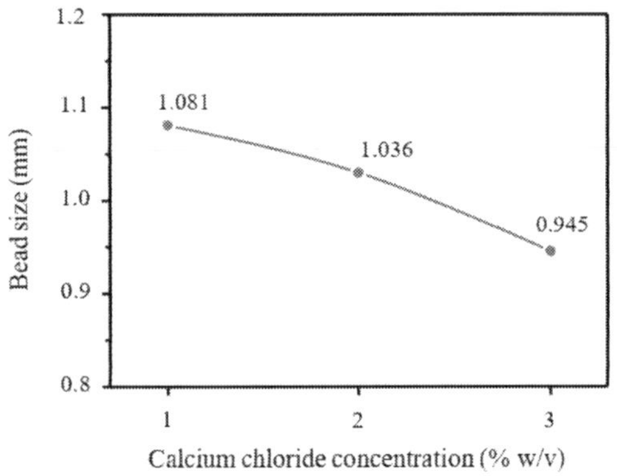

Fig. 3. Effect of calcium chloride concentration (1.0%, 2.0%, and 3.0% w/v) on the average bead diameter.

3.2 Fourier transform infrared spectroscopy

The FT-IR spectra of bakuchiol (a), sodium alginate (b), coconut oil (c), and the prepared beads (d) were displayed in Figure 4. The characteristic peaks of bakuchiol were observed at 3359.24 cm^{-1} (O–H stretching), 2966.08 cm^{-1} (C–H stretching), and 1632.48 cm^{-1} (C=C aromatic stretching). Sodium alginate showed characteristic peaks at 3445.95 cm^{-1} (O–H stretching), 2925.07 cm^{-1} (C–H stretching), 1614.89 cm^{-1} (asymmetric COO^- stretching), 1445.98 cm^{-1} (symmetric COO^- stretching), and 1031.78 cm^{-1} (C–O stretching). Coconut oil exhibited peaks at 3471.26 cm^{-1} (O–H stretching), 2854.04 cm^{-1} (C–H stretching), 1746.81 cm^{-1} (C=O stretching), 1465.80 cm^{-1} (C–H bending), and 1160.30 cm^{-1} (C–O stretching). When the prepared beads were characterized, the spectrum showed absorption bands at 3466.46 cm^{-1} (O–H stretching), 2854.26 cm^{-1} (C–H stretching), 1513.87 cm^{-1} (C–H bending), 1465.80 cm^{-1} (C–H bending), and 1160.45 cm^{-1} (C–O stretching), confirming the successful encapsulation of bakuchiol within the alginate beads.

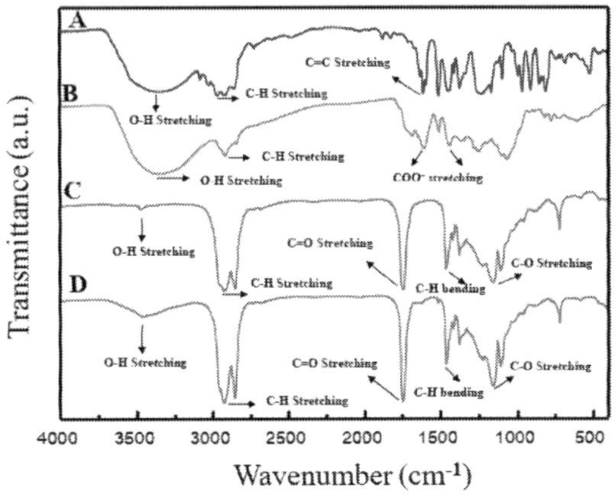

Fig. 4. FT-IR spectra of (A) bakuchiol, (B) sodium alginate, (C) coconut oil, and (D) prepared beads.

3.3 Stability under different conditions

3.3.1 Stability of beads in ultrapure water and calcium chloride solution

The stability of the prepared beads was evaluated over a 30-day storage period in both calcium chloride solution and ultrapure water (Figure 5). Beads stored in calcium chloride solution showed a gradual decrease in size over time. The bead diameter decreased from 1.024 mm at day 0 to 1.013 mm at day 30. This size reduction is attributed to the continued ionic crosslinking between calcium ions and the guluronic acid residues of sodium alginate in the shell layer. The formation of a more compact and ordered network, known as the "egg-box" structure, results in tighter packing of the polymer chains, thereby reducing the overall bead size. In contrast, swelling was observed in beads stored in ultrapure water, with bead size increasing from 1.027 mm at day 0 to 1.077 mm at day 30. The absence of calcium ions in the medium allows water to diffuse into the bead matrix, disrupting some of the ionic interactions and leading to minor expansion of the beads. The swelling is likely due to osmotic effects and water absorption within the alginate network [35, 36].

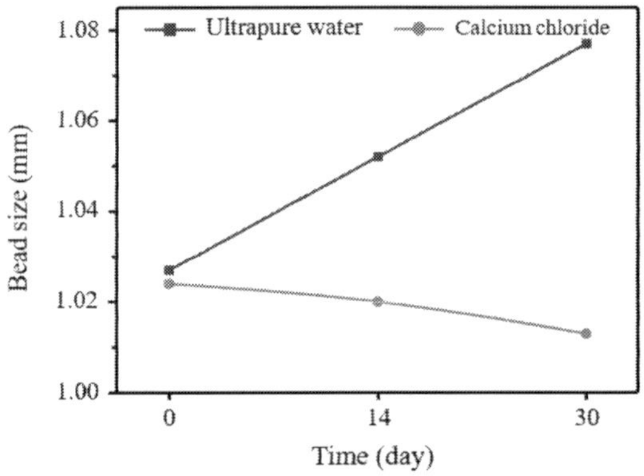

Fig. 5. Effect of storage solution (calcium chloride and ultrapure water) on the bead after 30 day storage.

3.3.2 Stability of beads in storage under light and dark conditions

The stability of BK-loaded beads was evaluated over a 60-day storage period under light and dark conditions at room temperature (Figure 6). The initial bakuchiol content was 6.53 µg per bead, corresponding to 100% remaining at day 0.

Under light exposure (Figure 6-A), the remaining bakuchiol content decreased to 99.68%, 95.65%, and 90.55% at days 14, 30, and 60, respectively. Similarly, under dark conditions (Figure 6-B), the remaining content was 99.85%, 95.66%, and 91.57% at days 14, 30, and 60. The similar degradation observed under both light and dark storage conditions suggests that light exposure had a minimal effect on the stability of bakuchiol within the alginate beads. The encapsulation provided sufficient protection against photo-degradation, likely due to the barrier properties of the alginate matrix. The gradual decrease in bakuchiol content over time can be attributed to chemical degradation and possible diffusion-related loss, rather than light-induced effects. These findings indicate that the prepared beads effectively maintain bakuchiol stability under typical storage conditions.

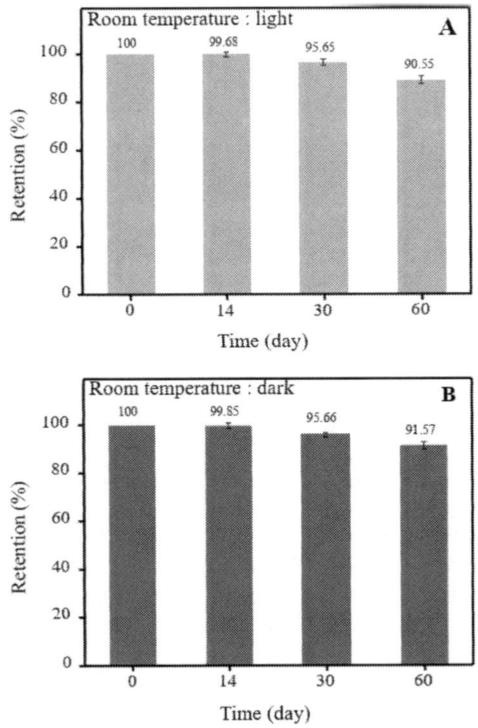

Fig. 6. Percentage of retention bakuchiol in beads during storage under (A) light and (B) dark conditions at room temperature after 60 day storage.

3.3.3 Stability of beads in different pH solutions

The stability of BK-loaded beads was evaluated in solutions of different pH values (pH 1, 3, 5, 7 and 9) over a 60-day storage period (Figure 7).

At neutral and acidic conditions (pH 3, pH 5, and pH 7), the beads maintained relatively high bakuchiol retention, with remaining content exceeding 80% after 60 days. In contrast, exposure to strongly basic conditions (pH 9) resulted in a more pronounced decrease in bakuchiol content, with values declining to below 60%. At alkaline pH, the alginate network may undergo swelling and partial decrosslinking due to ion exchange and matrix relaxation, which promotes the diffusion of the active compound out of the beads [37]. These findings suggest that the prepared beads effectively stabilize bakuchiol under neutral and moderately acidic conditions.

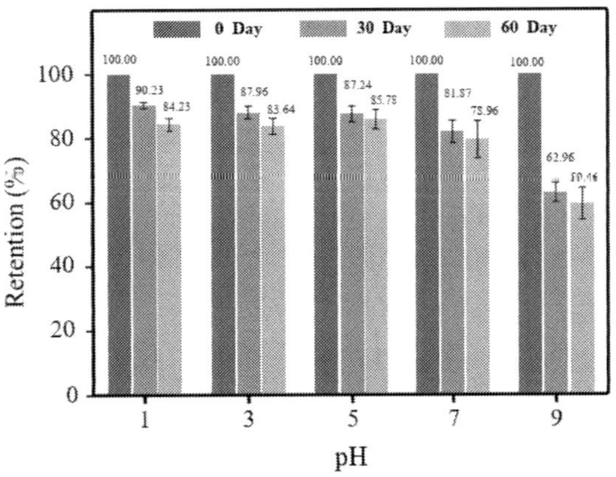

Fig. 7. Percentage of retention bakuchiol in beads after 0, 30, and 60 day storage in buffer solutions of different pH (pH 1, 3, 5, 7, and 9).

4 Conclusion

This study successfully demonstrated the synthesis of BK-loaded beads using coaxial electrospray, with systematic optimization of key processing parameters. Bead formation was highly dependent on sodium alginate concentration, core-to-shell flow rates, and applied voltage, with optimal conditions (1.0% w/v alginate; 20:40 mL/min flow rates; 1000 V) yielding spherical, well-defined beads with uniform size distribution. The Fourier transform infrared (FT-IR) spectroscopy confirmed the successful encapsulation of bakuchiol within the alginate gel matrix. Stability evaluations under various storage conditions revealed that the beads effectively maintained their structural integrity and bakuchiol content in both calcium chloride and ultrapure water over time. Furthermore, encapsulated bakuchiol exhibited high retention (greater than 80%) under neutral and moderately acidic conditions (pH 3, 5, and 7), and remained stable under both light and dark environments, highlighting the protective role of the alginate matrix. In contrast, exposure to alkaline pH led to increased degradation and potential diffusion-related loss. Overall, the findings indicate that coaxial electrospray-based alginate beads offer a promising delivery system for enhancing the stability of bakuchiol, supporting its future application in cosmetic formulations.

This research was supported by the Department of Industrial Chemistry, Faculty of Applied Science, King Mongkut's University of Technology North Bangkok. Special Thanks to Assoc. Prof. Dr. Sasithorn Kongruang for kindly providing the encapsulation machine to complete the research.

References

1. T. P. Adarsh Krishna, B. Edachery, S. Athalathil, Bakuchiol - a natural meroterpenoid, structure, isolation, synthesis and functionalization approaches. RSC Adv. **12**, 8815-8832 (2022). https://doi.org/10.1039/D1RA08771A
2. A. B. Lyons, I. Kohli, A. F. Nahhas, T. L. Braunberger, T. F. Mohammad, C. L. Nicholson, N. T. Nartker, K. Modi, M. S. Matsui, H.W. Lim, I. H. Hamzavi, Trichloroacetic acid model to accurately capture the efficacy of treatments for postinflammatory hyperpigmentation. Arch. Dermatol. Res. **312**, 437-446 (2020). https://doi.org/10.1007/s00403-020-02071-4
3. F. Mascarenhas-Melo, M.M. Ribeiro, K.H. Kahkesh, S. Parida, K.D. Pawar, K. Velsankar, A.C. Paiva-Santos, Comprehensive review of the skin use of bakuchiol, physicochemical properties, sources, bioactivities, nanotechnology delivery systems, regulatory and toxicological concerns. Phytochem. Rev. **23**, 1377-1413 (2024). https://doi.org/10.1007/s11101-024-09926-y
4. N. N. Nizam, S. Mahmud, S. M. A. Ark, M. Kamruzzaman, M. K. Hasan, Bakuchiol, a natural constituent and its pharmacological benefits. F1000Res. **12**, 29 (2023). https://doi.org/10.12688/f1000research.129072.2
5. R. K. Chaudhuri, K. Bojanowski, Bakuchiol, a retinol-like functional compound revealed by gene expression profiling and clinically proven to have anti-aging effects. Int. J. Cosmet. Sci. **36**, 221-230 (2014). https://doi.org/10.1111/ics.12117
6. J. Greenzaid, A. Friedman, P. Sodha, The use of bakuchiol in dermatology, a review of in vitro and in vivo evidence. J. Drugs Dermatol. 21, 624-629 (2022). https://doi.org/10.36849/JDD.6740
7. C. Puyana, N. Chandan, M. Tsoukas, Applications of bakuchiol in dermatology, systematic review of the literature. J. Cosmet. Dermatol. **21**, 6636-6643 (2022). https://doi.org/10.1111/jocd.15420
8. S. Dhaliwal, I. Rybak, S. R. Ellis, M Notay, M Trivedi, W Burney, A R Vaughn, M Nguyen, P Reiter, S Bosanac, H Yan, N Foolad, R K Sivamani, Prospective, randomized, double-blind assessment of topical bakuchiol and retinol for facial photoageing. Br. J. Dermatol. **180**, 289-296 (2019). https://doi.org/10.1111/bjd.16918
9. M. Kuśmierska, J. Kuśmierski, A. Martyka, P. Ujma, Redefining skin health, the potential of plant-based bakuchiol as a sustainable substitute for retinoids. Our Dermatol. Online **15**, 345-348 (2024). https://doi.org/10.7241/ourd.20244.3
10. A. Bluemke, A. P. Ring, J. Immeyer, A. Hoff, T. Eisenberg, W. Gerwat, F. Meyer, S. Breitkreutz, L.M. Klinger, J.M. Brandner, G. Sandig, M. Seifert, D. Segger, F. Rippke, Multidirectional activity of bakuchiol against cellular mechanisms of facial ageing - Experimental evidence for a holistic treatment approach. Int. J. Cosmet. Sci. **44**, 377-393 (2022). https://doi.org/10.1111/ics.12784
11. S. Adhikari, R. Joshi, B. S. Patro, T. K. Ghanty, G. J. Chintalwar, A. Sharma, S. Chattopadhyay, T. Mukherjee, Antioxidant activity of bakuchiol, experimental evidences and theoretical treatments on the possible involvement of the terpenoid chain. Chem. Res. Toxicol. **16**, 1062-1069 (2003). https://doi.org/10.1021/tx034082r
12. S. Y. Choi, S. Lee, W.-H. Choi, Y. Lee, Y.O. Jo, T.-Y. Ha, Isolation and anti-inflammatory activity of Bakuchiol from Ulmus davidiana var. japonica. J. Med. Food. **13**, 1019-1023 (2010). https://doi.org/10.1089/jmf.2009.1207
13. Y. Cui, X. Zeng, Y. Zeng, Q. Liu, H. Zeng, Constituents of Psoralea corylifolia Fruits and Their Effects on Methicillin-Resistant Staphylococcus aureus. Molecules. **20**, 12500-12511 (2015). https://doi.org/10.3390/molecules200712500
14. R. Chaudhuri, F. Marchio, Bakuchiol in the management of acne-affected skin. Cosmet. Toilet. **126**, 502-510 (2011).
15. Z.D. Draelos, H. Gunt, J. Zeichner, S. Levy, Clinical Evaluation of a Nature-Based Bakuchiol Anti-Aging Moisturizer for Sensitive Skin. J. Drugs Dermatol. **19**, 1181-1183 (2020). https://doi.org/10.36849/JDD.2020.5522
16. M. Hadiwidjaja, E. Romadhona, Y. Yulianto, N.A. Chauwito, M.G.E. Sidauruk, R. Kardiono, C. Avanti, Comparative efficacy of bakuchiol oil and encapsulated bakuchiol cream on facial skin quality: A 28-day pilot study. J. Pharm. Pharmacogn. Res. **12**, 477-486 (2024). https://doi.org/10.56499/jppres23.1812_12.3.477
17. N. Inmuangkham, P. Sukjarernchaikul, S. Thepwatee, Fatty acid profiles of olive oil and moringa oil and their influence on nanoemulsion formation via D-phase emulsification using bakuchiol as a model active compound. Ind. Crops Prod. **209**, 118052 (2024). https://doi.org/10.1016/j.indcrop.2024.118052
18. G. Wadhwa, S. Kumar, V. Mittal, R. Rao, Encapsulation of babchi essential oil into microsponges: Physicochemical properties, cytotoxic evaluation and anti-microbial activity. J. Food Drug Anal. **27**, 60-70 (2019). https://doi.org/10.1016/j.jfda.2018.07.006
19. K. Kurpet, G. Chwatko, Development of a new chromatographic method for the determination of bakuchiol in cosmetic products. Sci. Rep. **13**, 13893 (2023). https://doi.org/10.1038/s41598-023-41076-7
20. A. Rezagholizade-Shirvan, M. Soltani, S. Shokri, R. Radfar, M. Arab, E. Shamloo, Bioactive compound encapsulation: Characteristics, applications in food systems, and implications for human health. Food Chem.: X. **24**, 101953 (2024). https://doi.org/10.1016/j.fochx.2024.101953
21. M. Figueiredo, Z. Sárkány, F. Rocha, P. M. Martins, Challenges and Advances in the Encapsulation of Bioactive Ingredients Using Whey Proteins. Foods. **14**, 691 (2025). https://doi.org/10.3390/foods14040691

22. P. M. Junaid, S. Ali, K. Rasul, A. Abdullah, Polysaccharide-based hydrogels for microencapsulation of bioactive compounds: A review. J. Agric. Food Res. **15**, 101038 (2024). https://doi.org/10.1016/j.jafr.2024.101038
23. K. Y. Lee, D. J. Mooney, Alginate: properties and biomedical applications. Prog. Polym. Sci. **37**, 106-126 (2012). https://doi.org/10.1016/j.progpolymsci.2011.06.003
24. K. I. Draget, G. Skjåk-Braek, O. Smidsrød, Alginate based new materials. Int. J. Biol. Macromol. **21**, 47-55 (1997). https://doi.org/10.1016/s0141-8130(97)00040-8
25. G. T. Grant, E. R. Morris, D. A. Rees, P. J. C. Smith, D. Thom, Biological interactions between polysaccharides and divalent cations: The egg-box model. FEBS Lett. **32**, 195-198 (1973). https://doi.org/10.1016/0014-5793(73)80770-7
26. D. Zadeike, Z. Gaizauskaite, L. Basinskiene, R. Zvirdauskiene, D. Cizeikiene, Exploring Calcium Alginate-Based Gels for Encapsulation of Lacticaseibacillus paracasei to Enhance Stability in Functional Breadmaking. Gels. **10**, 641 (2024). https://doi.org/10.3390/gels10100641
27. A. Arevalo-Gallegos, S. P. Cuellar-Bermudez, E. M. Melchor-Martinez, H. M. N. Iqbal, R. Parra-Saldivar, Comparison of Alginate Mixtures as Wall Materials of Schizochytrium Oil Microcapsules Formed by Coaxial Electrospray. Polymers. **15**, 2756 (2023). https://doi.org/10.3390/polym15122756
28. A. Letocha, M. Miastkowska, E. Sikora, Preparation and Characteristics of Alginate Microparticles for Food, Pharmaceutical and Cosmetic Applications. Polymers. **14**, 3834 (2022). https://doi.org/10.3390/polym14183834
29. L. G. Gómez-Mascaraque, F. Tordera, M. J. Fabra, M. Martínez-Sanz, A. Lopez-Rubio, Coaxial electrospraying of biopolymers as a strategy to improve protection of bioactive food ingredients. Innov. Food Sci. Emerg. Technol. **51,** 2-11 (2019). https://doi.org/10.1016/j.ifset.2018.03.023
30. C. Chen, W. Liu, P. Jiang, T. Hong, Coaxial Electrohydrodynamic Atomization for the Production of Drug-Loaded Micro/Nanoparticles. Micromachines. **10**, 125 (2019). https://doi.org/10.3390/mi10020125
31. S. Tsai, Y. Ting, Synthesize of alginate/chitosan bilayer nanocarrier by CCD-RSM guided co-axial electrospray: A novel and versatile approach. Food Res. Int. **116**, 1163-1172 (2019). https://doi.org/10.1016/j.foodres.2018.11.047
32. A. M. Gañán-Calvo, J. M. Montanero, Revision of Capillary Cone-Jet Physics: Electrospray and Flow Focusing. Phys. Rev. E. **79**, 066305 (2009). https://doi.org/10.1103/PhysRevE.79.066305
33. M. R. Shaiqah, H. M. Salahuddin, A. Y. A. Huda, M. Izzuddin, N. I. M. N. Shafiq, M. A. N. Hakimah, S. R. Rahman, A. A. Budipratama, Screening of Electrospray-operating Parameters in the Production of Alginate-Royal Jelly Microbeads Using Factorial Design. J. Pharm. Bioallied Sci. **12**, S703-S706 (2020). https://doi.org/10.4103/jpbs.JPBS_249_19
34. C. Bennacef, A. Karim, S. El-Khaldi, M. Benyoussef, Influence of Alginate Properties and Calcium Chloride Concentration on Alginate Bead Reticulation and Size: A Phenomenological Approach. Polymers. **15**, 4163 (2023). https://doi.org/10.3390/polym15204163
35. S. K. Bajpai, R. Tankhiwale, Investigation of water uptake behavior and stability of calcium alginate/chitosan bi-polymeric beads: Part-1. React. Funct. Polym. **66**, 645-658 (2006). https://doi.org/10.1016/j.reactfunctpolym.2005.10.017
36. S.-L. Huang, Y.-S. Lin, The Size Stability of Alginate Beads by Different Ionic Crosslinkers. Adv. Mater. Sci. Eng. **2017**, 1-7 (2017). https://doi.org/10.1155/2017/9304592
37. N. Stachowiak, A. Kowalska, P. Zieliński, E. Romanowska, Stability Studies, Biodegradation Tests, and Mechanical Properties of Sodium Alginate and Gellan Gum Beads Containing Surfactant. Polymers. **15**, 2568 (2023). https://doi.org/10.3390/polym15112568

Effects of Metal Ions on the Stabilization of Anthocyanin Pigments Powder from Butterfly Pea Flowers

Piyachat Kranpukdee [1], *Voranuch* Somsongkul[1, 2*], and *Sarinya* Shawaphun[1†]

[1]Department of Industrial Chemistry, Faculty of Applied Science, King Mongkut's University of Technology North Bangkok, Wongsawang, Bang Sue, 10800 Bangkok, Thailand
[2]Integrated Chemistry Research Center for Sustainable Technology, King Mongkut's University of Technology North Bangkok, Wongsawang, Bang Sue, 10800 Bangkok, Thailand

Abstract. Butterfly pea (*Clitoria ternatea* L.) flowers have been recognized as a natural source of anthocyanins, particularly delphinidin, which is used as a natural colorant but is highly susceptible to degradation influenced by environmental factors such as pH and temperature. In this study, the co-pigmentation of butterfly pea anthocyanins with metal ions (Al^{3+}, Fe^{2+}, Zn^{2+}, Mg^{2+}, and Ca^{2+}) was evaluated under pH conditions of 4, 7, and 10, using a non-metal control for comparison. Total anthocyanin content (TAC), percentage of yield, and color measurement (L*, a*, b*, ΔE) were analyzed before and after accelerated heat and cooling cycle stability testing. The highest TAC (35.8 mg/L) and percentage of yield (98.95%) were obtained with Al^{3+} at pH 4. Minimal ΔE values (0.11–0.17) were observed in Al^{3+}treated samples across all pH levels, indicating excellent color stability, whereas significant color degradation (ΔE 4.64–8.29) was observed in the control group. These results indicate that anthocyanin stability can be significantly enhanced by Al^{3+}, followed by Fe^{2+} and Zn^{2+}, suggesting the potential of metal-assisted co-pigmentation in improving the stability and functionality of natural colorants for applications in food, cosmetics, and related industries.

1 Introduction

Butterfly pea (*Clitoria ternatea* L.) flowers are known to contain high concentrations of anthocyanins, which are utilized as natural pigments, particularly delphinidin. The hydroxyl (-OH) groups located at the 3′, 4′, and 5′ positions on the B-ring of delphinidin have been shown to promote co-pigmentation, thereby enhancing pigment stability [1, 2]. However, anthocyanins are susceptible to degradation, which is influenced by several environmental factors, including pH, light, temperature, oxygen, and enzymatic activity; these factors collectively reduce their stability and shelf life [3, 4]. Due to the ionic nature of anthocyanin molecules, their coloration is strongly affected by pH. Four main chemical forms of anthocyanins are known to exist, depending on the pH of the solution. Under strongly acidic conditions (pH = 1), the flavylium cation form is predominantly observed; this form is characterized by a positive charge, high water solubility, and red-to-purple coloration. As the pH increases to 2–4, quinonoidal blue species are formed. At pH 5–6, carbinol pseudo base or chalcone, at pH > 7, pyrocatechol forms are observed; both are colorless and may exhibit charge balance depending on the solution environment. At pH levels above 7, anionic forms become dominant, and anthocyanin degradation is promoted due to specific substituent groups (Figure 1.) [5]. Therefore, the development of anthocyanin pigment powder in a suitable form is considered essential for enhancing stability and extending shelf life. The stability of anthocyanins can be improved through the formation of co-pigmentation complexes with metal ions, a process in which interactions occur between the ligands of anthocyanin molecules and electron-accepting metal ions, which influence both the color characteristics and stability of the pigment. In this study, five metal ions—aluminum ion (Al^{3+}), iron ion (Fe^{2+}), zinc ion (Zn^{2+}), magnesium ion (Mg^{2+}), and calcium ion (Ca^{2+})—were selected as representatives of different metal categories based on variations in charge, ionic radius, and complex-forming abilities. Al^{3+} is classified as a post-transition metal from Group 13, while Fe^{2+} and Zn^{2+} are transition metals belonging to Groups 8 and 12, respectively. Mg^{2+} and Ca^{2+} are alkaline earth metals from Group 2 of the periodic table. These metal ions are capable of interacting with functional groups present in the anthocyanin structure, potentially altering the electronic structure of the molecules and affecting both color intensity and hue. This study aims to enhance the stability of natural pigments extracted from butterfly pea flowers by means of co-pigmentation with metal ions, without the need for

* Corresponding author: voranuch.s@sci.kmutnb.ac.th
† Corresponding author: sarinya.s@sci.kmutnb.ac.th

synthetic additives. Furthermore, the potential for application in food, cosmetics, and various bioproduct

Industries are demonstrated [6-8].

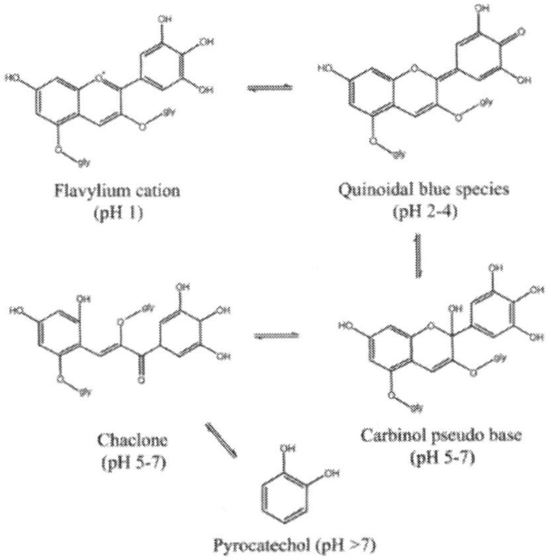

Fig. 1. Representative structural transformations of delphinidin under various pH conditions, including flavylium cation (pH = 1), quinonoidal base (pH 2–4), carbinol pseudo base or chalcone (pH 5–7), and pyrocatechol form (pH > 7).

2 Materials and Methods

2.1 Materials

Butterfly pea flower powder was obtained from Long Beach Co., Ltd. (Thailand) and subsequently stored in airtight containers under dry and dark conditions until use. Calcium chloride dihydrate ($CaCl_2 \cdot 2H_2O$), magnesium chloride hexahydrate ($MgCl_2 \cdot 6H_2O$), aluminum chloride hexahydrate ($AlCl_3 \cdot 6H_2O$), and anhydrous zinc chloride ($ZnCl_2$) were purchased from Kemaus (Australia), while iron (II) chloride tetrahydrate ($FeCl_2 \cdot 4H_2O$) was procured from QRe™. All chemical reagents used in this study were of analytical grade.

2.2 Extraction of Anthocyanins from Butterfly Pea Flowers

The extraction process was performed by weighing 1.000 g of butterfly pea flower powder, to which distilled water was added at a ratio of 1:10. The total volume was then adjusted to 10.00 mL using a volumetric flask, and the solution was thoroughly mixed. The initial pH of the extract was measured and subsequently adjusted to 1.0 using 10 wt% hydrochloric acid (HCl). Extraction was conducted at 40 °C for 60 minutes.

2.3 Preparation of Pigment Powder Using Co-pigmentation with Metal Ions

Metal salts, including $CaCl_2 \cdot 2H_2O$, $MgCl_2 \cdot 6H_2O$, $AlCl_3 \cdot 6H_2O$, $ZnCl_2$, and $FeCl_2 \cdot 4H_2O$, were each weighed at 0.01 mol based on their respective molecular weights and subsequently added to the butterfly pea flower extract. And co-pigmentation with metal ions was subsequently performed at 40°C for 60 minutes. The pH of each mixture was measured and adjusted to 4, 7, and 10 using 10 wt% ammonium hydroxide (NH_4OH) solution. The mixtures were then allowed to stand at room temperature for 30 minutes to promote co-pigmentation and precipitation between anthocyanin and metal ions. The resulting precipitates were separated by centrifugation at 6,000 rpm for 15 minutes. The pigment powder was dried at 50°C for 24 hours, after which the dried powders were analyzed for percentage of yield and color values using a colorimeter based on the CIE L*ab** system.

2.4 Determination of total anthocyanin content

The total anthocyanin content was determined by diluting the butterfly pea flower extract samples co-pigmented with Al^{3+}, Fe^{2+}, Zn^{2+}, Mg^{2+}, Ca^{2+}, and the control sample without metal ions at a ratio of 1:10 using two buffer systems: 0.025 M potassium chloride (KCl) at pH 1.0 and 0.4 M sodium acetate at pH 4.5. Absorbance measurements were performed using a UV–Visible spectrophotometer (SPECORD 210 PLUS, Analytic Jena, Germany) at wavelengths of 520 nm and 700 nm. The instrument was operated with a 1.0 nm slit width and medium scan speed, equipped with a silicon photodiode detector. Baseline correction was automatically applied using a solvent blank. The total anthocyanin content was determined using Equation (1):

$$Total\ Anthocyanins\ Content = \frac{A \times MW \times DF \times 10^3}{\varepsilon \times l} \quad (1)$$

where $A = (A_{520nm} - A_{700nm})_{pH1} - (A_{520nm} - A_{700nm})_{pH4.5}$; MW = molecular weight of cyanidin-3-glucoside ($g \cdot mol^{-1}$); DF = dilution factor; L = path length of the cuvette (cm); ε = molar absorptivity of cyanidin-3-glucoside ($L \cdot mol^{-1} \cdot cm^{-1}$).

2.5 Determination of the percentage of yield

The percentage yield was calculated based on the dried weight of the pigment powder obtained from the co-pigmentation of butterfly pea flower extract with Al^{3+}, Fe^{2+}, Zn^{2+}, Mg^{2+}, Ca^{2+}, and the control sample, relative to the initial weight of the butterfly pea flower powder used for extraction. The percentage yield was determined using Equation 2:

$$Percentage\ of\ Yield\ (\%) = \frac{Weight_d\ (g)}{Weight_i\ (g)} \times 100 \quad (2)$$

Where W_d = Dried weight of the pigment powder obtained from the co-pigmentation between the butterfly pea flower extract and metal ions (g), and W_i = Initial weight of butterfly pea flower powder used for extraction (g).

2.6 Heat and Cooling Cycle Stability Test

The stability of the pigment powders obtained from the co-pigmentation of butterfly pea flower extract with Al^{3+}, Fe^{2+}, Zn^{2+}, Mg^{2+}, Ca^{2+}, and the control sample was evaluated using an accelerated heat and cooling cycle stability test. The samples were initially stored at 4°C in a refrigerator for 48 hours, followed by incubation at 45°C in a hot air oven for an additional 48 hours. This procedure was defined as one thermal cycle and was repeated for a total of eight cycles [10].

2.7 Color measurement

Color measurements of the pigment powders obtained from the co-pigmentation of butterfly pea flower extract with Al^{3+}, Fe^{2+}, Zn^{2+}, Mg^{2+}, Ca^{2+}, and the control sample were conducted using a benchtop colorimeter (ColorFlex EZ 45-0 (LAV), HunterLab, USA). The instrument was operated under the CIE L*a*b* color system with the L*, a*, and b* scales, employing a D65 light source, a 10° observer angle, reflectance mode, and a 25 mm aperture size. Calibration was performed before each measurement using a physical white tile standard. Samples were placed in a glass cell at the measurement port, and L*, a*, and b* values were recorded in triplicate. The average values were subsequently used for analysis. The L* value indicates lightness, ranging from 0 (black) to 100 (white). The a* value corresponds to the red-green axis, with positive values indicating redness and negative values indicating greenness. The b* value corresponds to the yellow-blue axis, where positive values indicate yellowness and negative values indicate blueness [11]. The total color difference (ΔE) was determined using Equation 3.

$$\Delta E = \sqrt{(L_1^* - L_2^*)^2 + (a_1^* - a_2^*)^2 + (b_1^* - b_2^*)^2} \quad (3)$$

Where L1, a1, and b1 were recorded as the color measurements before the heat and cooling cycle stability test, and L2, a2, and b2 were recorded as the color measurements after the heat and cooling cycle stability test

ΔE is widely recognized in color science as a quantitative indicator of chromatic alteration and was interpreted according to standard perceptibility thresholds: $\Delta E < 1$ - imperceptible to the human eye; $1 \leq \Delta E < 2$ – detectable by trained observers; $2 \leq \Delta E < 3.5$ – perceptible by untrained observers; $3.5 \leq \Delta E < 5$ - perceptible; and $\Delta E > 5$ - distinctly different in appearance.

3 Results and Discussion

3.1 Determination of total anthocyanin content

The total anthocyanin content (TAC) of butterfly pea flower extract following co-pigmentation with various metal ions—Al^{3+}, Fe^{2+}, Zn^{2+}, Mg^{2+}, and Ca^{2+}—as well as a control sample, was evaluated at pH 4, 7, and 10. At pH 4 (Figure 2). The TAC values (mg/L) were observed in the following descending order: Al4 = 216.39, Fe4 = 212.24, Zn4 = 211.60, Mg4 = 210.14, Ca4= 208.88, and Control4 = 200.98.

The highest enhancement in TAC by Al^{3+} is attributed to its high positive charge (+3) and small ionic radius (~53 pm), resulting in a high charge density. Al^{3+} acts as a strong Lewis acid, forming stable co-pigmentation with electron-donating functional groups on anthocyanin molecules, such as hydroxyl and carbonyl groups. Furthermore, the empty orbitals of Al^{3+} facilitate co-pigmentation interactions that stabilize the anthocyanin in butterfly pea extract, thus effectively inhibiting anthocyanin degradation.

Fe^{2+}, a first-row transition metal, ranked second in stabilization efficiency. Although it carries a lower positive charge than Al^{3+}, its incomplete d-orbital configuration ($3d^6$) allows ligand-to-metal charge transfer (LMCT) and π–d interactions with anthocyanins, enhancing stability via co-pigmentation and resonance mechanisms. Its moderate ionic radius (~78 pm) also supports effective bonding with functional groups on anthocyanins.

Zn^{2+} displayed similar but slightly lower TAC enhancement compared to Fe^{2+}. As Zn^{2+} possesses a filled d-orbital shell ($3d^{10}$), it cannot participate in π-back bonding, though it can still undergo co-pigmentation with electron-donating ligands to a certain extent. Its lack of redox activity and resonance capabilities accounts for its lower efficiency.

Mg^{2+} and Ca^{2+}, classified as Group 2A metals, contributed less to TAC enhancement due to the absence of vacant d-orbitals, restricting interactions to electrostatic outer-sphere coordination. Although Mg^{2+} has a smaller ionic radius (~72 pm) than Ca^{2+} (~100 pm), resulting in a higher charge density and slightly better stabilization capacity, their co-pigmentation is inherently weaker compared to transition metals [12].

The control sample, which lacked metal ions, exhibited the lowest TAC, highlighting the critical role of metal ions and anthocyanin interactions in pigment stabilization under mildly acidic to basic conditions.

Experimental results further indicated that TAC significantly declined with increasing pH. At pH 4 (Figure 3), anthocyanins predominantly existed as quinonoidal blue species, which are relatively stable. Upon increasing the pH to 7, a structural transition to the carbinol pseudo base form—less stable—was observed, leading to reduced TAC values: Al7 = 212.04, Fe7 = 207.18, Zn7 = 200.93, Mg7 = 198.42, Ca7 = 195.74, and Control7 = 175.01 mg/L. At pH 10 (Figure 4), anthocyanins were largely present in the chalcone form, a degraded structure, resulting in a pronounced decrease in TAC: Al10 = 207.81, Fe10 = 193.78, Zn10 = 180.46, Mg10 = 170.09, Ca10 = 166.11, and Control10 = 143.95 mg/L. Nevertheless, the presence of metal ions consistently contributed to higher TAC values compared to the control across all pH conditions, confirming their role in mitigating anthocyanin degradation. This transformation abolishes the C6–C3–C6 flavonoid skeleton and the associated conjugated system, leading to a chemically unstable species that is prone to oxidation and degradation. Nonetheless, metal ions particularly Al^{3+} and Fe^{2+}—were still able to partially retard structural degradation, likely via electrostatic interactions or limited coordination, thus maintaining yields significantly above that of the control.

At pH 4, anthocyanins are predominantly found in the form of quinonoidal base species (Figure 5a), which are stabilized via resonance structures involving an extended conjugated double bond system across the aromatic rings. Through this structural arrangement, efficient electron delocalization over the π-system is facilitated, thereby reducing molecular susceptibility to nucleophilic attack and enhancing chemical stability. As a consequence, anthocyanins in this form can retain their coloration, and relatively high total anthocyanin content (TAC) is maintained. These quinonoidal species are less affected by pH-induced hydration or ring-opening reactions, rendering them comparatively more stable under mildly acidic conditions. At pH 7, structural transformation is triggered, disrupting the conjugated π-system and resulting in the formation of a carbinol pseudo base (Figure 5b), which is a colorless and chemically less stable intermediate. Simultaneously, tautomerization or molecular rearrangement may occur, yielding an open-chain chalcone structure (Figure 5c), which lacks aromatic stabilization and is prone to further degradation. Both the carbinol pseudobase and chalcone forms are considered thermodynamically unstable and more reactive than the quinonoidal base, thereby contributing to a significant decline in TAC. Under alkaline conditions (e.g., pH 10), extensive degradation of the anthocyanin structure is observed. The strongly basic environment promotes bond cleavage, particularly within the flavylium core, resulting in the irreversible breakdown of the chromophore. This degradation leads to the formation of smaller phenolic compounds, primarily pyrocatechol-type derivatives (Figure 5d), which no longer retain the original conjugated system essential for pigment functionality. Such irreversible transformations not only abolish the chromatic properties of anthocyanins but also substantially compromise their functional stability in food, cosmetic, and pharmaceutical applications [5, 13].

In summary, the results demonstrated a significant decrease in total anthocyanin content with increasing pH, attributable to the pH-dependent structural instability of anthocyanins in alkaline conditions. However, the co-pigmentation with metal ions was found to play a crucial role in enhancing the molecular stability of anthocyanins. The stabilization efficiency of metal ions followed the order: $Al^{3+} > Fe^{2+} > Zn^{2+} > Mg^{2+} > Ca^{2+} >$ Control, effectively delaying pigment degradation under basic conditions [14-18].

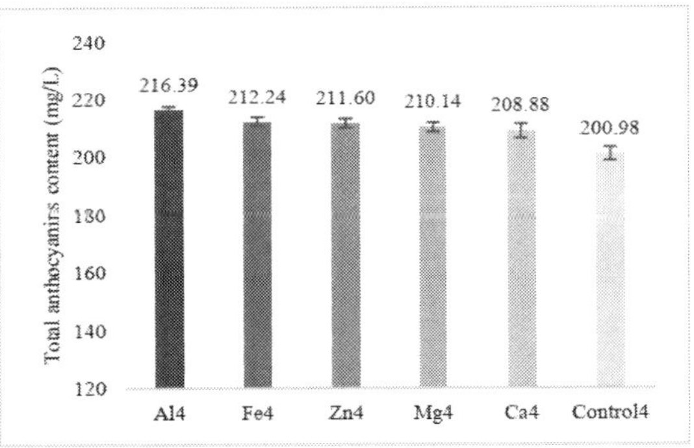

Fig. 2. Total anthocyanin content of butterfly pea flower extract after co-pigmentation with different metal ions at pH 4: Al^{3+} (Al4), Fe^{2+} (Fe4), Zn^{2+} (Zn4), Mg^{2+} (Mg4), Ca^{2+} (Ca4), and non-metal ions (Control4).

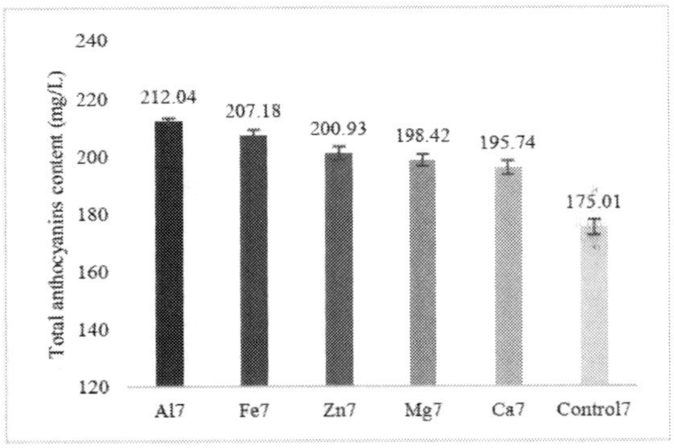

Fig. 3. Total anthocyanin content of butterfly pea flower extract after co-pigmentation with different metal ions at pH 7: Al^{3+} (Al7), Fe^{2+} (Fe7), Zn^{2+} (Zn7), Mg^{2+} (Mg7), Ca^{2+} (Ca7), and non-metal ions (Control7).

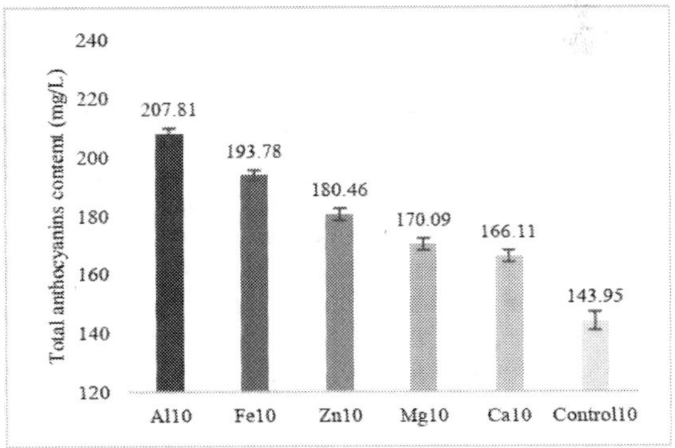

Fig. 4. Total anthocyanin content of butterfly pea flower extract after co-pigmentation with different metal ions at pH 10: Al^{3+} (Al10), Fe^{2+} (Fe10), Zn^{2+} (Zn10), Mg^{2+} (Mg10), Ca^{2+} (Ca10), and non-metal ions (Control10).

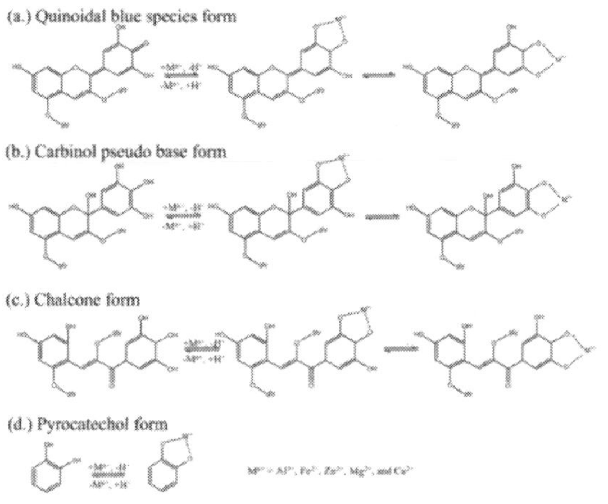

Fig. 5. Co-pigmentation between delphinidin and metal ions (M^{n+}) under different pH conditions: (a) quinonoidal blue species at pH 4, (b) carbinol pseudo base at pH 7, (c) chalcone form at pH 7, and (d) pyrocatechol form at pH 10.

3.2 Determination of the percentage of yield

The percentage yield of butterfly pea flower extract following co-pigmentation with various metal ions—Al^{3+}, Fe^{2+}, Zn^{2+}, Mg^{2+}, and Ca^{2+}—as well as a control sample, under pH conditions of 4, 7, and 10, was found to be consistent with the total anthocyanin content (TAC) previously described.

At pH 4 (Figure 6), the yields were as follows: Al4 = 98.95%, Fe4 = 88.80%, Zn4 = 75.32%, Mg4 = 67.72%, Ca4 = 52.50%, and Control4 = 35.91%. This pH level corresponds to the predominance of the quinonoidal blue species, whose structure is characterized by a conjugated system formed between the A and B rings through the flavylium backbone. The oxygen atom at the C4 position exists in the enol form, enabling interaction with hydroxyl groups on the B ring, which promotes extensive delocalization of π-electrons. This electronic delocalization contributes to the pronounced blue coloration and enhanced stability under mildly acidic conditions. The quinonoidal blue species possess a high capability for co-pigmentation with metal ions via hydroxyl and/or carbonyl groups located at the 3', 4', and 5' positions on the B-ring of delphinidin [15-17].

Al^{3+}, due to its trivalent charge and small ionic radius, exhibited the highest co-pigmentation ability, resulting in the maximum pigment yield. Fe^{2+}, as a transition metal with accessible d-electrons, facilitated stable co-pigmentation to a slightly lesser extent. Zn^{2+}, having an ionic radius similar to that of Mg^{2+} but a slightly greater coordination potential, led to a moderate pigment yield.

Mg^{2+}, although able to interact through hydroxyl groups, provided lower yields due to its lower coordination energy. Ca^{2+}, with its larger ionic radius and the weakest coordination ability among the tested ions, resulted in a relatively low yield. The control group, devoid of metal ions, produced the lowest pigment yield due to the absence of stabilizing interactions [12].

At pH 7 (Figure 7), the following yields were obtained: Al7 = 89.93%, Fe7 = 74.04%, Zn7 = 60.03%, Mg7 = 52.50%, Ca7 = 40.20%, and Control7 = 25.35%. Under this condition, anthocyanins are converted into the carbinol pseudo base form or chalcone. This conversion disrupts the conjugated π-system, resulting in diminished coloration (almost colorless) and reduced chemical stability. Although this form is unfavorable for efficient co-pigmentation, residual hydroxyl groups may still participate in weak interactions with metal ions, allowing the pigment yield to remain significantly higher than the control.

At pH 10 (Figure 8), the yields decreased further: Al10 = 72.29%, Fe10 = 62.26%, Zn10 = 45.19%, Mg10 = 37.22%, Ca10 = 19.76%, and Control10 = 10.79%. Under strongly alkaline conditions, anthocyanins are predominantly present in the pyrocatechol form, an open-ring structure resulting from cleavage of the C ring.

In conclusion, structural transformations of anthocyanins induced by pH shifts have been demonstrated to exert a direct influence on their co-pigmentation efficiency with metal ions. These pH-dependent conformational changes alter the chromophore stability and, consequently, affect pigment preservation and functionality. Based on the relative structural stabilities of the major anthocyanin forms observed under different pH conditions, the following order has been established: quinonoidal blue species (pH 4) > carbinol pseudo base or chalcone (pH 7) > pyrocatechol derivatives (pH 10). This trend correlates well with the measured percentage yields of total anthocyanin content (TAC), where greater molecular stability has been associated with higher pigment retention. Despite the inherent susceptibility of anthocyanins to degradation under neutral and alkaline conditions, co-pigmentation with metal ions has been found to play a critical role in enhancing the stability of anthocyanin structures, particularly those extracted from butterfly pea flowers. Through co-pigmentation, they have been stabilized to varying extents depending on the type of metal ion involved. The metal ions investigated in this study can be ranked according to their stabilizing efficacy as follows: Al^{3+} > Fe^{2+} > Zn^{2+} > Mg^{2+} > Ca^{2+} > Control. This ranking highlights the potential application of specific metal ions in mitigating pigment degradation across a range of environmental conditions, offering a practical strategy for improving the stability of anthocyanin-based colorants in food, pharmaceutical, and cosmetic formulations [14–18].

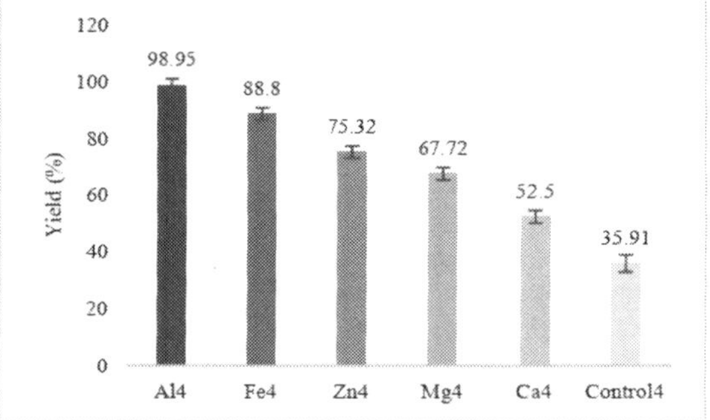

Fig. 6. The percentage yield of anthocyanin pigment powder from butterfly pea flowers after co-pigmentation with various

metal ions at pH 4: Al^{3+} (Al4), Fe^{2+} (Fe4), Zn^{2+} (Zn4), Mg^{2+} (Mg4), Ca^{2+} (Ca4), and non-metal ions (Control7).

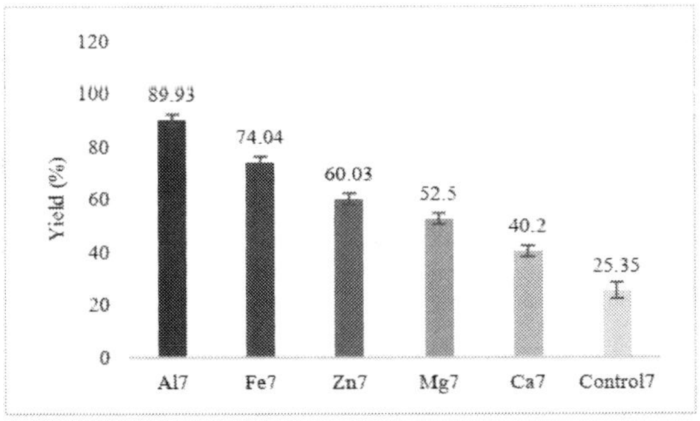

Fig. 7. The percentage yield of anthocyanin pigment powder from butterfly pea flowers after co-pigmentation with various metal ions at pH 7: Al^{3+} (Al7), Fe^{2+} (Fe7), Zn^{2+} (Zn7), Mg^{2+} (Mg7), Ca^{2+} (Ca7), and non-metal ions (Control7).

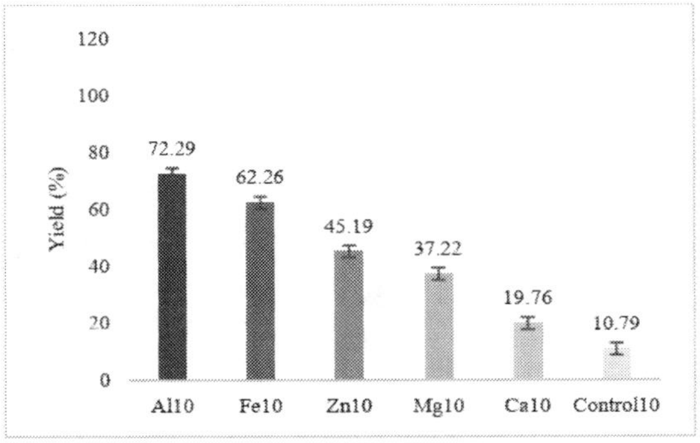

Fig. 8. The percentage yield of anthocyanin pigment powder from butterfly pea flowers after co-pigmentation with various metal ions at pH 10: Al^{3+} (Al10), Fe^{2+} (Fe10), Zn^{2+} (Zn10), Mg^{2+} (Mg10), Ca^{2+} (Ca10), and non-metal ions (Control10).

3.3 Color measurement before and after the Heat and Cooling Cycle Stability Test

The pigment powders obtained from the co-pigmentation of butterfly pea flower extract with Al^{3+}, Fe^{2+}, Zn^{2+}, Mg^{2+}, Ca^{2+} , and control samples under pH conditions of 4, 7, and 10 are presented in Table 1. Color parameters L*, a*, b* were analyzed both before and after stability testing under heat and cooling cycle conditions, which were designed to simulate thermal stress commonly encountered during product processing or storage when color is a critical attribute. These parameters provide essential information regarding hue and saturation. ΔE was calculated to evaluate the extent of color change, serving as an indicator of pigment powder stability [11].

The color measurement of anthocyanin pigment powders obtained through co-pigmentation with various metal ions and control samples was evaluated before Stability tests under accelerated heat and cooling cycles, revealing a wide range of hue variations under different pH conditions. At pH 4, the control sample (Control4) exhibited values of L* = 34.68, a* = 3.77, and b* = –5.28, indicating a deep reddish-purple hue characteristic of anthocyanins in the quinonoidal blue species form. In comparison, Ca4 (L* = 30.80, a* = 8.52, b* = –4.35) and Mg4 (L* = 32.48, a* = 8.19, b* = –4.60) displayed similarly deep reddish-purple tones. Fe4 (L* = 30.83, a* = 5.15, b* = 11.52) exhibited a reddish-yellow hue, while Zn4 (L* = 36.85, a* = 21.90, b* = 8.03) presented a vivid red coloration. Al4 (L* = 42.65, a* = 15.01, b* = 6.46) showed a distinctly purplish-red hue. At pH 7, the control sample (Control7) demonstrated a muted green tone (L* = 39.03, a* = –1.25, b* = –4.72), reflecting the persistence of quinoidal base and hemiketal forms. Ca7 (L* = 31.85, a* = –0.15, b* = –1.12) and Mg7 (L* = 34.83, a* = –0.45, b* = –1.27) appeared grayish-green in tone. Zn7 and Fe7 exhibited identical L* values of 36.81, with a* = 5.64 and b* = 1.26, resulting in light reddish-yellow hues. Al7 (L* = 46.78, a* = –3.92, b* = 11.76) was characterized by a bright bluish-green coloration. At pH 10, the control sample (Control10) presented a light green shade (L* = 42.77, a* = –2.72, b* = 1.02), attributed to the formation of the chalcone form. Ca10 (L* = 34.31, a* = –1.17, b* = 1.84) showed a yellowish-green tone, while Mg10 (L* = 48.84, a* = –5.72, b* = 15.23) exhibited a bright light green hue. Zn10 (L* = 40.80, a* = –2.72, b* = 1.15) appeared pale green. Fe10 (L* = 34.25, a* = 3.21, b* = 18.85) showed a reddish-yellow hue, and Al10 (L* = 54.83, a* = –4.76, b* = 17.03) demonstrated a light yellowish-green tone with a grayish tint.

After undergoing heat–cooling cycle stability testing, the control samples at all pH levels exhibited significant changes in color parameters. For Control4, the L* value increased to 39.16, while a* decreased to 2.54, and b* was recorded at –5.34, resulting in a ΔE of 4.64. Control7 presented L* = 43.77, a* = –3.86, and b* = –4.05, with a corresponding ΔE of 5.46. In the case of Control10, an L* value of 50.89, a* = –1.03, and b* = 1.15 was observed, with the ΔE reaching as high as 8.29—the highest among all tested conditions. These findings indicated substantial fading and structural degradation of the pigment molecules, particularly under alkaline conditions, where anthocyanin forms are inherently less stable and more thermally labile. In contrast, all samples co-pigmented with metal ions exhibited notable chromatic stability. At pH 4, minimal changes in ΔE were observed for Ca4 (ΔE = 0.15), Mg4 (ΔE = 0.15), Fe4 (ΔE = 0.12), Zn4 (ΔE = 0.12), and Al4 (ΔE = 0.11), with Al4 showing virtually unchanged L*, a*, and b* values, reflecting the superior color retention imparted by Al^{3+}. At pH 7, similarly low ΔE values were recorded for all metal-co-pigmented samples: Ca7 (ΔE = 0.23), Mg7 (ΔE = 0.21), Zn7 (ΔE = 0.17), Fe7 (ΔE = 0.16), and Al7 (ΔE = 0.12). In particular, Al7 showed an increase in the b* value to 11.87, suggesting an effective preservation of the bluish tone through the formation of a highly stable pigment complex. At pH 10, color stability was maintained across all metal ion treatments, with Ca10 (ΔE = 0.29), Mg10 (ΔE = 0.25), Zn10 (ΔE = 0.21), Fe10 (ΔE = 0.19), and Al10 (ΔE = 0.17) displaying only minor changes in color parameters. Remarkably, Al10 exhibited L* = 54.89, a* = –4.77, and b* = 17.19 after thermal cycling, underscoring the capability of Al^{3+} to form stable complexes with anthocyanin functional groups, effectively preventing pigment degradation under alkaline conditions.

In summary, the stability of pigment powders obtained from co-pigmentation of butterfly pea flower extracts with Al^{3+}, Fe^{2+}, Zn^{2+}, Mg^{2+}, Ca^{2+} and control samples under pH conditions of 4, 7, and 10 was investigated. It was found that Al^{3+} exhibited the highest efficacy in maintaining color stability due to its +3 charge and small ionic radius, which facilitated strong complex formation with the hydroxyl groups of anthocyanins. Fe^{2+} and Zn^{2+} also contributed effectively to color preservation under acidic and neutral conditions, whereas Mg^{2+} and Ca^{2+} demonstrated lower stability, particularly under alkaline conditions. Stability tests under accelerated heat and cooling cycles indicated that anthocyanins in the quinonoidal blue species form at pH 4 exhibited the greatest stability, while the pyrocatechol form observed at pH 10 showed the highest degree of color degradation in the control samples lacking metal ions. This degradation was attributed to the absence of stabilizing complexation by metal ions. Overall, metal ions—especially Al^{3+}—significantly enhanced the stability of anthocyanin pigments, rendering them suitable for applications in the pigment industry.

Table 1. Color Measurements of anthocyanin pigment powder from butterfly pea flowers after co-pigmentation with various metal ions at pH 4, 7, and 10

		pH 4	**L***	**a***	**b***	**pH 7**	**L***	**a***	**b***	**pH 10**	**L***	**a***	**b***
Control	Before		34.68	3.77	-5.28	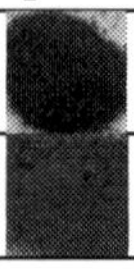	39.03	-1.25	-4.72		42.77	-2.72	1.02
	After		39.16	2.54	-5.34		43.77	-3.86	-4.05		50.89	-1.03	1.15
ΔE		4.64				5.46				8.29			
Ca	Before		30.80	8.52	-4.35		31.85	-0.15	-1.12		34.31	-1.17	1.84
	After		30.90	8.64	-4.35		31.96	-0.32	-1.01		34.60	-1.20	1.85
ΔE		0.15				0.23				0.29			
Mg	Before	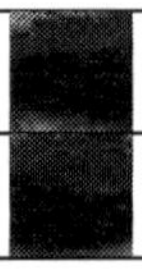	32.48	8.19	-4.60		34.83	-0.45	-1.27		48.84	-5.72	15.23
	After		32.63	8.19	-4.60		35.00	-0.44	-1.14		48.97	-5.64	15.42
ΔE		0.15				0.21				0.25			
Zn	Before		36.85	21.90	8.03	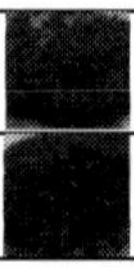	36.81	5.64	1.26		40.80	-2.72	1.15
	After		36.93	21.82	8.03		36.94	5.52	1.26		40.87	-2.89	1.24
ΔE		0.12				0.17				0.21			
Fe	Before	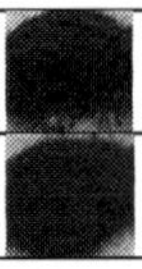	30.83	5.15	11.52		36.81	5.64	1.26		34.25	3.21	18.85
	After		30.84	5.20	11.63		36.94	5.52	1.26		34.29	3.25	19.03
ΔE		0.12				0.16				0.19			
Al	Before		42.65	15.01	6.46		46.78	-3.92	11.76		54.83	-4.76	17.03
	After		42.64	14.93	6.54		46.80	-3.97	11.87		54.89	-4.77	17.19
ΔE		0.11				0.12				0.17			

4 Conclusion

The effects of co-pigmentation between anthocyanin extracts from butterfly pea flower and various metal ions (Al^{3+}, Fe^{2+}, Zn^{2+}, Mg^{2+}, Ca^{2+}) under pH conditions of 4, 7, and 10 were investigated and compared with control samples lacking metal ions. The highest total anthocyanin content (TAC) was observed in samples co-pigmented with Al^{3+} at pH 4, followed by Fe^{2+} and Zn^{2+}, whereas markedly lower TAC values were detected in the presence of Mg^{2+} and Ca^{2+}. Control samples consistently showed the lowest TAC across all pH levels, suggesting the essential role of metal ions in delaying anthocyanin degradation. Pigment powder yield was found to correlate with TAC results, with the highest yields obtained in Al^{3+} and Fe^{2+} treated samples. Zn^{2+} yielded intermediate results, while Mg^{2+}, Ca^{2+}, and control samples showed reduced yields. Following thermal stability testing, color parameters L*, a*, b*, and ΔE were assessed. The smallest ΔE values, indicating enhanced color retention, were associated with Al^{3+} and Fe^{2+}. Conversely, the highest ΔE values were recorded for control samples, particularly at pH 10. These results confirm that Al^{3+} provided the most effective stabilization of anthocyanins.

This research was financially supported by the Department of Industrial Chemistry, Faculty of Applied Science, King Mongkut's University of Technology North Bangkok, with additional support in the form of research facilities and technical assistance.

References

1. R. Araki, A. Yada, H. Ueda, K. Tominaga, H. Isoda, Differences in the effects of anthocyanin supplementation on glucose and lipid metabolism according to the structure of the main anthocyanin: a meta-analysis of randomized controlled trials. Nutrients. **13**, 2003 (2021). https://doi.org/10.3390/nu13062003
2. H. E. Khoo, A. Azlan, S. T. Tang, S. M. Lim, Anthocyanidins and anthocyanins: colored pigments as food, pharmaceutical ingredients, and the potential health benefits. Food and Nutrition Research. **61**, 1361779 (2017). https://doi.org/-10.1080/16546628.2017.1361779
3. Y. Cheng, J. Liu, L. Li, J. Ren, J. Lu, F. Luo, Advances in embedding techniques of anthocyanins: Improving stability, bioactivity, and bioavailability. Food Chem. X **20**, 100983 (2023). https://doi.org/10.1016/j.fochx.2023.100983
4. C. Rodrigues, V. Souza, I. Coelhoso, A. Fernando, Bio-based sensors for smart food packaging—Current applications and future trends. Sensors. **21**, 2148 (2021). https://doi.org/10.3390/s2106-2148
5. B. Enaru, G. Dretcanu, T. D. Pop, A. Stanila, Z. Diaconeasa, Anthocyanins: Factors affecting their stability and degradation, Antioxidants. **10**, 1967 (2021). https://doi.org/10.3390/antiox1012-1967
6. M. Coulibaly, Applications of metal complexes dyes in analytical chemistry, IntechOpen. (2021).
7. A. R. Nedamani, Stability enhancement of natural food colorants – A review, Res. Innov. Food Sci. Technol. **10**, 369–388 (2022)
8. J. Sirirak, P. Suppharatthanya, K. Chantha, S. Girdthep, S. Chayabutra, Eco-friendly lake pigment from sappanwood: Adsorption study and its application as natural colorant for natural rubber toy balloon, J. Met. Mater. Miner. **31**, 27–37 (2021). https://doi.org/10.55713/jmmm.v31i2.1009
9. D. Aditiyarini, E.O. Iswuryani, Effect of various factors on anthocyanins extraction from butterfly pea flower (Clitoria ternatea L.), Nova Biotechnol. Chim. **20**(1), e817 (2021). https://doi.org/10.365-47/nbc.817
10. The European Cosmetic Toiletry and Perfumery Association (Colipa), Guidelines on stability testing of cosmetic products, (March 2004)
11. W. S. Mokrzycki, M. Tatol, Colour difference ΔE – A survey. *Mach. Graph. Vis.* **20**, (2011)
12. N. N. Greenwood, A. Earnshaw, Chemistry of the Elements, 2nd edn (Butterworth-Heinemann, Oxford, 1997). ISBN: 0 7506 3365 4.
13. V. S. Fedenko, S.A. Shemet, M. Landi, UV–vis spectroscopy and colorimetric models for detecting anthocyanin-metal complexes in plants: An overview of in vitro and in vivo techniques. *J. Plant Physiol.* **216**, 32–45 (2017). https://doi.org/10.10-16/j.jplph.2017.02.001
14. N. Jamil, M. N. M. Zairi, N. A. M. Nasim, F. Pa'ee, Influences of environmental conditions to phytoconstituents in *Clitoria ternatea* (butterfly pea flower) – A review. J. Sci. Technol. **10**, 208–228 (2018)
15. G. T. Sigurdson, R.J. Robbins, T.M. Collins, M.M. Giusti, Evaluating the role of metal ions in the bathochromic and hyperchromic responses of cyanidin derivatives in acidic and alkaline pH. Food Chem. **208**, 26–34 (2016). https://doi.org/10.1016/-j.foodchem.2016.03.109
16. D. F. Santosa, Beneficial health effects of butterfly pea (Clitoria ternatea): A literature review. Indonesia J. Biomed. Sci. **17**, 244–247 (2023). https://doi.org/10.15562/ijbs.v17i2.486
17. K. Kytidou, M. Artola, H.S. Overkleeft, J.M.F.G. Aerts, Plant glycosides and glycosidases: A treasure-trove for therapeutics. Front. Plant Sci. **11**, 356 (2020). https://doi.org/10.3389/fpls.2020.00-357
18. H. Xue, J. Zhao, Y. Wang, Z. Shi, K. Xie, X. Liao, J. Tan, Factors affecting the stability of anthocyanins and strategies for improving their stability: A review. Food Chem. X **24**, 101883 (2024). https://doi.org/10.1016/j.fochx.2024.101-883

Exploration of phytochemistry and their applications of *Sesamum indicum* L. and *Nyctanthes arbor-tristis* extracts

Pandey, Ram Darash[1, 2], and *Joshi*, Susan[1,*]

[1]Central Department of Chemistry, Kritipur, Nepal
[2]Amrit Campus, Thamel, Kathmandu, Nepal

Abstract. Nepal is one of the richest countries in plant biodiversity since a significantly large variety of medicinal plants are found at different altitudes. This research mainly focuses on searching for phyto-compounds in plant-leaf-derived methanolic extracts and their biological applications. Cultivated *S. indicum* and *N. arbor-tristis* plants were selected to prepare methanol extracts. Phenolics, flavonoids, saponins, alkaloids, etc., as secondary metabolites were identified from phytochemical screening tests, UV-vis, and FT-IR spectroscopic studies. Further, GC-MS analysis identified flavonoid, ester, ether, acid, alcohol, amide, and lactone. The total phenolic and the total flavonoid content were determined by the Folin-Ciocalteu and $AlCl_3$ colourimetric method, respectively, using a 96-well plate. The phenolic content of *S.indicum* and *N. arbor-tristis* extracts was 177.76 ± 3.40 mg/ g GAE and 131.32 ± 5.03 mg/ g GAE, respectively. Similarly, the flavonoid content of *S.indicum* and *N. arbor-tristis* extracts was 77.90 ± 0.78 mg/g QE and 173.75 ± 3.89 mg/ g QE, respectively. Both of these extracts exhibit eco-friendliness according to an oral acute toxicity test. The extracts possess remarkable antioxidant and anti-diabetic properties. However, they did not exhibit anti-fungal and anti-bacterial activity. These results may help in discovering pharmaceuticals and indicate that many plants in Nepalese forests are potent for medicine, and scientific study is essential for their use.

1. Introduction

Medicinal plants have been used in medicine and drug discovery for centuries. Many pioneering medications, such as antimalarials derived from Cinchona bark and opium from *Papaver somniferum*, have been obtained from plants [1]. Almost 80% of people worldwide rely on medicinal herbs for their primary healthcare [2]. Any part of the plant—including roots, stems, leaves, flowers, seeds, and bark—may hold therapeutic value since they are stores of secondary metabolites. This is one of the many benefits of phytomedicine [1]. The biochemical reactions and metabolic pathways within our body continually produce nitrogen and oxygen free radicals. These free radicals are harmful and contribute to ageing, neurological disorders, cancers, and cardiovascular diseases [3]. Treating these diseases has become difficult because synthetic antioxidants are either resistant or have numerous side effects. Plant-based antioxidants are highly effective, with minimal or no side effects, as they neutralise free radicals due to their abundance of phenolics and polyphenols [4]. In Nepal and other parts of the world, type-2 diabetes has become increasingly prevalent at an alarming rate, posing a serious issue. Plant-derived antidiabetics offer promising prospects because they are safer, less prone to resistance, and have fewer or no side effects. *Sesamum indicum* L. belongs to the Pedaliaceae family, which comprises 13 genera and 40 species, of which 36 are listed in the Kewensis index [5]. It is known by names such as tila (Sanskrit) and kalo tila (Nepali). This plant is cultivated in the Terai, Basi, and hill Tars of Nepal, as well as in various regions worldwide, including India, China, America, Africa, Brazil, the southern United States, Northwest and Southwest Ethiopia, North Gondar, Mexico, and Japan [6]. According to Hindu tradition, it appears to have originated in Indonesia. There are three varieties of sesame: black, white, and grey. In Nepal, black sesame is the most commonly cultivated variety. All parts of *S. indicum*—leaves, flowers, and seeds—possess medicinal properties. The decoction of *S. indicum* leaves is utilised to treat chronic dysentery, pain [7], catarrh, eye pain, erupted skin lesions, and bruises [8]. Root, seed, and leaf aqueous extracts showed ineffective inhibition against *Staphylococcus aureus*, *Bacillus cereus*, *Pseudomonas aeruginosa*, *Xanthomonas compestris*, and *E. coli*. However, methanol extracts from these sections demonstrated anti-*Pseudomonas aeruginosa* activity. Additionally, the methanol extract of seeds showed anti-*Staphylococcus aureus* and anti-*Xanthomonas compestris* activity. Antioxidant activity was present across all sections [9]. The leaf ethanol extract demonstrated excellent antibacterial activity against *Escherichia coli*, with no effect on *Staphylococcus aureus*, and low effectiveness against *Salmonella typhi* and *Klebsiella*

*Corresponding author: susanjoshi68@gmail.com

pneumoniae. Conversely, the aqueous extracts showed little activity against these bacteria [10]. The antimicrobial properties of white *S. indicum* leaf methanol extract from Nigeria were tested against several bacteria, revealing zones of inhibition; however, no zones were observed against *Corynebacterium ulcerans, Escherichia coli*, and *Candida stellatoidea* [11]. Another study investigated the antifungal properties of *S. indicum* extracts [12]. Two flavonoids, quercetin and kaempferol, were isolated from the leaves [13]. A pentacyclic triterpene, 3-epibartogenic acid, along with two flavonoids—epigallocatechin and kaempferol glycoside—was isolated from the methanol extract of *S. indicum* leaves and studied for their antidiabetic activity. The IC_{50} values for 3-epibartogenic acid and epigallocatechin were reported as 146.7 μM and 303.9 μM, respectively [14]. Three iridoids and seven polyphenols have been previously isolated from young *sesame* leaves [15]. Several phenolic compounds—including chlorogenic acid, quercetin, gallic acid, and catechin have been identified in the leaf extract through ultrasound-assisted and solvent extraction techniques [16]. Microwave-assisted extraction and mass spectrometry (LCMS-Q-TOF) of leaves identified fifty polyphenolic compounds [17]. The leaf extract demonstrated inhibitory effects on HT29 and another cell line, as well as in vitro antioxidant activity [18]. A recent molecular docking and simulation study of phytochemicals derived from this plant indicated inhibition of SARS-CoV-2's main protease [19].

Nyctanthes arbor-trisits, known as Parijata in Sanskrit. It has other names, such as Har-singer in Hindi, Night Jasmine in English, and Raatko Rani in Nepali. It belongs to the Oleaceae (Nyctaginaceae) family [20]. It is found in tropical and subtropical regions in Nepal, Australia, New Zealand, Japan, India, the USA, China, Mexico, and other countries. The leaves of *N.arbor-tristis* have many pharmacological significances and are used in burns, swelling, treatment of epilepsy, sciatica, rheumatism, chronic fever, internal worms, laxatives, diuretics, and diaphoretics [21]. The leaf extract is used as an antidote for reptile venoms, and combined with honey to cure fever, cough, and stomach problems [22]. The plant has a significant role as an analgesic, anti-inflammatory activity of stem bark [23], antimicrobial and antioxidant activity of essential oil [24], hepatoprotective activity of leaves [25], antibacterial activity of leaves, fruits, and seeds [26], antifungal activity of leaves, stem, bark, seeds, and flowers [27], antiviral [28], antioxidant and anti-inflammatory activity of leaves and flowers [29], the antispasmodic and anthelminthic activity of leaves, barks, flowers and seeds [30], tranquillising, antihistaminic, and purgative [31], anti-nociceptive and antipyretic [32]. The antimalarial activity of leaf extract against *Culex*, *Anopheles*, and *Aedes* mosquitoes has yielded encouraging results [34], and it has anticancer activity against breast cancer cell lines [33]. In addition to flavanol glycosides like astragaline (Kaempferol-3-glucoside) and nicotiflorinkaempferol-3-rhamnoglucoside, leaves have also yielded amorphous resin, mannitol, arborside-C, β-amyrin, β-sitosterol, hentriacontane, and benzoic acid [35].

Recognising the medicinal potential, the present authors have investigated the methanol extracts of *S. indicum* and *N. arbor-tristis* from Nepal to study their phytochemistry and to inform future directions for the pharmaceutical industry. The research is designed to prepare *S. indicum* and *N. arbor-tristis* extracts using a highly polar solvent, methanol, by a cold percolation method to study phytochemistry in qualitative and quantitative ways. Further, the biological applications of these extracts are studied with a target for medicinal applications. This research may be the door to the novel medicinal arena.

2. Materials and methods

2.1 Collection of plants

The *Sesamum indicum* and *Nyctanthes arbor-tristis* leaves were collected from Pigouna-2, Mahottari (*26.65, 85.82*), and Sifal Kathmandu (*27.71, 85.32*), respectively. The voucher codes for these plants, issued by the National Herbarium and Plant Laboratory Godavari, are RDP-03 and KATH-RDP0001, respectively.

Fig. 1. (a) *S. indicum* plant

Fig. 1. (b) *N. arbor-tristis* plant

2.2 Preparation of extract

The leaves were gathered, cleaned with purified water, allowed to dry in the shade, and then powdered using an electrical grinder. The powdered leaves were soaked in 99.8% methanol (solute: solvent = 1:5 w/v), left at ambient temperature for three days, and shaken occasionally. The filtration was performed first with cotton and then with Whatman paper 41. This process was repeated three times to ensure complete extraction. The solvent was concentrated at 40°C by rotatory evaporator to obtain the methanol extract, and preservation was done at 4°C until further use.

2.3 Qualitative phytochemical analysis

The chemical tests for secondary metabolites were performed on these plants' methanol extracts using the protocol described [36]for secondary metabolites. The UV-visible spectra of the plant extracts were recorded in the 200 to 800 nm range using a UV-visible (SPECCORD® 200, PLUS, Germany) double-beam spectrophotometer. The functional groups were inferred from spectral data. The crude methanol extracts were scanned for FTIR analysis in the 4000 to 500 cm^{-1} range using PerkinElmer Spectrum 2 IR Version 10.6.2. The functional groups were inferred from spectral data.

2.4 Quantitative phytochemical analysis

2.4.1 Total phenolic content analysis

The extract's total phenolic content was ascertained using the Folin-Ciocalteu reagent (FCR) [37]. 20 μL (1 mg/mL) of the extract and 100 μL (1:10 dilution in distilled water) of FCR reagent were placed in 96-well plates. For five minutes, the mixture was kept at room temperature in the dark. After that, 80 μL of sodium carbonate (7.5% in distilled water) was added to the mixture. The absorbance was measured at 765 nm using a microplate reader (BioTek, USA; Synergy/LX, multimedia reader) after the plates were incubated for 15 minutes in the dark. The results were reported as mg/g gallic acid equivalent, with gallic acid (1 mg/mL in ethanol) serving as a standard. Every experiment was carried out three times. The TPC is calculated using the formula,

TPC = C x V/m… (1), where V is the extract's volume in millilitres, m is its mass in grams, and C is the gallic acid concentration (mg/mL).

2.4.2 Total flavonoid content analysis

The $AlCl_3$ method was used to determine the extracts' total flavonoid content [38]. In short, a 96-well plate was filled with a 130 μL solution of aluminium chloride (20 μL extract + 110 μL distilled water) in triplicate. Initial absorbance was measured at 415 nm after standard quercetin 130 μL (0.1 mg/mL in methanol) was also taken in triplicate. Each plate was filled with 5 μL of $AlCl_3$, 5 μL of potassium acetate, and 60 μL of ethanol. The mixture was then allowed to stand at room temperature in the dark for half an hour. Using a microplate reader (Synergy/LX, multimedia reader BioTek, USA), the final absorbance was determined at 415 nm. The standard calibration curve was plotted for different quercetin concentrations in methanol. The TFC results were given in mg/g QE. Every experiment was carried out three times. TFC is calculated using the formula, TFC = C x V/m… (2),
Where C is the quercetin concentration in milligrams per millilitre, V is the extract volume in millilitres, and m is the extract mass in grams.

2.4.3 Identification of the chemical compositions

A Shimadzu GC-MS-QP2010 plus gas chromatograph with an AOC-20i autosampler was used to perform the GC-MS analysis. Helium was used as the carrier gas, and the separation was carried out on an Rtx-5MS capillary column (30 m × 0.25 mm × 0.25 μm) with primary pressures ranging from 500 to 900. The following temperatures were used: 60°C for the column oven, 200°C for the ion source, 280°C for the interface, 280°C for the injection, and splitless injection mode. The pressure was 80 kPa, the purge flow was 3.0 mL/min, the column flow was 2.89 mL/min, the total flow was 5.9 mL/min, and the linear velocity was 92.3 cm/sec. The mass (m/z) scan range was 40-500, the run time was 14.67 minutes, and the MS acquisition mode was set to normal scanning (scan speed 2500).

2.5 Applications of plant-based extracts

2.5.1 Acute oral toxicity

Albino mice were used in the acute oral toxicity test of plant leaf extract/powder following the OECD TG 425 Up and Down Procedure, 2001 [39]. Three female Albino mice of the same sex were given a single dose of leaf extract or powder based on their body weight using this technique. After that, they were watched for 14 days. During this observation period, special attention was given to the first four hours and then for the next twenty-four hours. The plant extract or powder is toxic if any of the three mice die within the allotted fourteen days; otherwise, it is non-toxic. To confirm the toxicity, additional observations with the lower dose are required if the initial result is toxic. The LD_{50} value serves as the quantitative basis for toxicity analysis. If there is no mortality at a single dose level of more than 2000 mg/kg body weight, the plant leaf extract or powder is considered non-toxic. If mortality is noted at a dose level greater than 2000 mg/kg body weight, the plant leaf extract or powder is toxic. This is ensured by repeated observations with a decreased dose twice and thrice

2.5.2 Antioxidant assay

Leaf extracts were subjected to an antioxidant assay using the 1, 1-diphenyl 1, 2-picrylhydrazyl (DPPH) assay [40]. A 96-well plate was filled with 100 μL of 0.1 mM DPPH solution (Sigma Aldrich, Germany) and 100 μL of plant extracts at different concentrations. After the plate was left in the dark for 30 minutes, its absorbance at 517 nm was measured using a microplate reader. Ascorbic acid was used as a reference to calculate the antioxidant capacity, and the result was expressed in µg/mL. The percentage scavenging was calculated using the following formula:

% scavenging = Ao-At /Ao ×100 %... (3), where Ao is the absorbance of the control solution (DPPH without sample) and At is the absorbance of the mixture solution or test sample and DPPH. The following formula is used to determine percentage inhibition: % inhibition $= A_{control} - A_{sample} / (A_{control}) \times 100$ %... (4).

2.5.3 Antidiabetic assay

The leaf extracts' in-vitro α-amylase inhibition activity was examined following the protocol [41]. The working sample was made by preparing 0.5 mg of α-amylase in 1 millilitre of phosphate buffer with a pH of 6 to 9. The concentrations of 100 µg/mL, 75 µg/mL, 50 µg/mL, and 25 µg/mL were obtained by further dissolving the plant extract (1 mg/mL) in methanol in phosphate buffer. 200 µL of each plant extract solution was combined with 200 µL of α-amylase, and the mixture was incubated for 10 minutes at 30°C. Each tube received 200 µL of a 1% w/v starch solution in water, which was then incubated for three minutes. Two millilitres of DNSA reagent (3, 5-dinitrosalicylic acid) were added to stop the reaction. The solution was added to the reaction mixture to create the positive control, which contained 1 mg/mL of metformin. The plant extract solution was not added when creating the 100% estimated enzyme activity tube. After that, each tube was incubated for ten minutes at 85°C. After 10 minutes, 5 mL of distilled water was added to each tube, and absorbance was taken at 540 nm. The following formula calculates the inhibition rate,

$$\frac{\text{Absorbance of 100\% enzyme activity} - \text{Absorbance of sample reaction}}{\text{Absorbance of 100\% enzyme activity}} \dots\dots (5)$$

2.5.4 Antibacterial assay

The Central Department of Microbiology, T.U., provided the gram-positive bacteria *Bacillus subtilis* (ATCC-6051) and *Staphylococcus aureus* (ATCC-25293), as well as the gram-negative bacteria *Escherichia coli* (ATCC-8739) and *Klebsiella pneumonia* (ATCC-13883). For the antibacterial assay, the well-diffusion method was employed [42]. Two different kinds of media were made: nutrient broth (NB) and nutrient agar (NA) plates. Following autoclaving, the media were allowed to cool to approximately 37°C. The 25 mL of media was poured into a 90 mm-diameter petri dish. Before being used, the prepared media plates were kept in the refrigerator. The sterile inoculating loop was used to aseptically cultivate the microorganisms in liquid nutrient media, and they were incubated for 24 hours at 37°C. After plating 100 µL of each strain's culture broth onto a nutrient agar plate, it was kept at 37°C for 15 minutes. The 10 µL sample of methanol extract was pipetted out and put into a 6 mm well-bored nutrient agar plate.

2.5.5 Antifungal assay

To evaluate the antifungal activity, the disk diffusion method was used to measure the zones of inhibition (ZOI) that methanol extracts produced on specific fungi [43]. At the Central Department of Microbiology, T.U. *Candida albicans* (ATCC-2091) fungi were gathered. The Nepal Agricultural Research Centre (NARC) provided *Alternaria* and *Fusarium* species. On nutrient agar, 100 µL of the strain's culture broth was plated, and it was incubated for 15 minutes at 37°C. After 15 minutes of incubation at 37°C, 10 µL of the methanol extract was pipetted out and poured onto a nutrient agar disk. All of this was done overnight at 37°C. The extract's antifungal properties against *Alternaria*, *Fusarium* and *Candida albicans* species were examined the following day. Cycloheximide 50 mg/mL as a positive control, DMSO as a negative control and the plant extract 50 mg/mL were employed in this investigation.

2.6 Statistical analysis

Every experiment was conducted three times. Standard deviation ± mean was used to express the data. The linear regression coefficient (R^2) values were calculated using the Origin Pro 2025 learning edition for Windows.

3. Results and discussion

3.1 Qualitative phytochemical analysis

The secondary metabolite profiling of crude methanolic extracts of *S. indicum* and *N. arbor-tristis* was performed following a standard protocol to explore them qualitatively. The results are listed in the following Table 1.

Table 1. Phytochemical Profiling of crude methanol leaf extracts.

S.N.	Secondary Metabolites	Test	*S.indicum* Extract	*N.arbor-tristis* extract
1.	Alkaloids	Dragendroff's	+	+
2.	Flavonoids	Shinoda's	+	+
3.	Glycosides	Keller-Killani's	+	+
4.	Polyphenols	Ferric chloride	+	+
5.	Fat/ Fixed oil	$CuSO_4$ test	-	-
6.	Tannins	Braemer's test	+	+
7.	Saponins	Foam	+	+
8.	Terpenoids	Salkowski test	+	+
9.	Quinones	NaOH test	+	+
10.	Coumarins	NaOH test	+	+

11.	Proteins	Biuret test	-	+
12.	Reducing sugars	Molisch's test	+	-

(Note: '+' refers to the presence of secondary metabolites, and '-' refers to the absence of secondary metabolites.)

Alkaloids, flavonoids, glycosides, polyphenols, tannins, saponins, terpenes, quinones and coumarins were reported in both extracts. Similarly, fat and volatile oils are absent in both extracts. Also, proteins were reported in *N. arbor-tristis* extract and reducing sugars were observed in *S. indicum* extract. Our results of *S. indicum* extracts' secondary metabolites align with previous reports [44-45]. Also, *N.arbor-tristis* extract results were compared and found to be similar to phytochemical results reported in [46].

The UV-Vis spectra of both extracts predict the presence of secondary metabolites, as observed in phytochemical testing. The metabolites, like alkaloids, flavonoids, phenolic and tannins, may be indicated by peaks in the UV-visible region [47]. The peaks observed in the UV range of 200-400 nm indicate the presence of unsaturated systems and heteroatoms such as oxygen, nitrogen, halogen, silicon and sulphur [48]. The peaks in the visible range of 400-600 nm indicate the presence of multiple bonds or heteroatoms in aromatic systems such as β-carotene or Lycopene systems [49].

Table 2. UV-Vis Spectra analysis for secondary metabolites in extracts

Wavelength	Secondary metabolites	
	S. indicum extract	*N. arbor-tristis* extract
415	-	Unsaturated chromophoric group
445	Chlorophyll group	
472	Highly conjugated aromatic systems	
533	Tannins	-
605	Anthocyanins	-
663	Chlorophyll	

Similarly, the idea of functional groups present in crude extracts was obtained by analysing absorption peaks in the FT-IR spectrum, as assigned in Table 3.

Table 3. FT-IR Spectra analysis for assignments of functional groups in extracts

Wavenumber (cm^{-1})		Assigned for Functional Groups
S.indicum extract	*N.arbor-tristis* extract	
3330	-	O-H stretch (Alcohols and Phenols)
-	3006	C-H symmetric Stretch (due to *Cis*-double bond vibration).
2920	2920	C-H symmetric stretch(Alkane)
2845	-	CH_2 andCH_3(vibrations of phospholipids, cholesterol and Creatine)
	2339	C≡N of nitrile
2083	-	C≡C of alkyne
-	1746	C=O ester of lipid and fatty acid
1695	-	C=O Stretch
-	1598	C=C stretch
-	1450	O-CH_2 bending vibration (due to in-plane deformation)
-	1370	O-H bending vibration (may be due to phenolic hydroxyl
1267	-	C-O stretch (may be due to lignin and Xylan)
1164	-	
-	1023	C-O-C bending vibration
806	-	C-H out-of-plane bending due to aromatic ring
-	710	C-H out of the plane bending

Therefore, qualitative chemical and spectroscopic analysis validated the presence of alkaloids, flavonoids, and phenolics as secondary metabolites, which justifies both extracts as suitable for biological applications and further studies.

3.2 Quantitative Phytochemical Analysis

As phenols and flavonoids were reported in both extracts, the total phenolic and total flavonoid content were quantified using the calibration curve of gallic acid and quercetin, respectively, as depicted in Figures. 2(a) and 2(b).

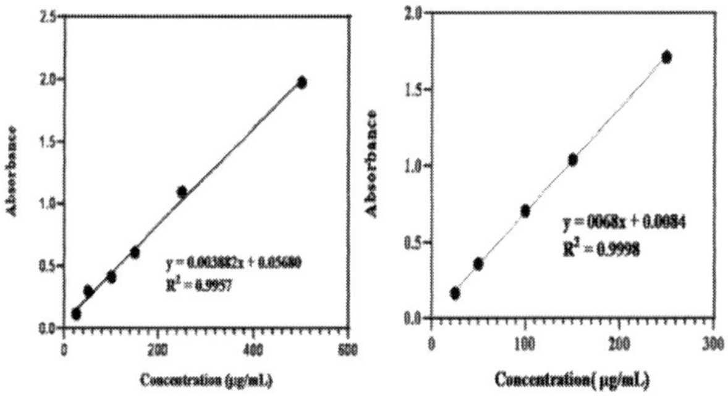

Fig. 2: Standard calibration curve for (a) gallic acid and (b) quercetin.

From the equations, $y = 0.00388x+0.05680$, and $y = 0.0068x+0.0084$, the value of C was determined from y as the average absorbance recorded from standard calibration curves. The phenolic content of *S. indicum* extract was 177.76 ± 3.40 mg/ g GAE, and *N. arbor-tristis* extract was 131.32 ± 5.03 mg/ g GAE. Therefore, a 26.12% higher TPC was determined in *S. indicum* extract than *in N. arbor-tristis* extract. This indicates that *S. indicum* extract should contain many phenolic compounds as secondary metabolites. Similarly, higher flavonoid content was responsible for the antioxidant properties of methanol extracts [50]. Between two experimental extracts, *N. arbor-tristis* extract was found to be richer in flavonoid content by 55.16% than *S. indicum* extract, since the flavonoid content in *N. arbor-tristis* extract is 173.75 ± 3.89 mg/ g QE and *S. indicum* extract is 77.90 ± 0.78 mg/g QE. In *S. indicum*, the total phenolic content is lower, and the flavonoid content is higher than our value, as reported in the other study [18]. Similarly, in *N.arbor-tristis,* a higher total phenolic content (260.3 ± 12.2 mg/g

GAE) than in our study has been reported elsewhere [51]. This is due to the differences in the extraction method, determination protocol, and climatic variation of the plant.

3.3 Chromatographic analysis

The biological applications of plant-based extracts are due to secondary metabolites. Hence, it is better to identify the compounds if possible. For this reason, GC-MS is an effective tool for determining compounds present in plant extract from retention time, area percentage, and mass [52]. The spectra of *S. indicum* reveal the presence of different secondary metabolites, as suggested by FT-IR and UV-Vis Spectroscopy. They are listed in Table 4 in tabular form.

Eighteen compounds were reported when the chromatogram obtained from GC-MS was analysed and compared with the NIST library database. The major compounds are 9, 12-Octadecadienoyl chloride, *(Z, Z)* -, (33.65 %), hexadecanoic acid, methyl ester (16 .16%), 9, 12-Octadecadienoic acid *(Z, Z)* - (12.94 %), 2-tetradecanone (9.77 %), D-erythro-Pentose, 2-deoxy- (6.18 %), Eicosanoic acid, methyl ester (5.03 %), Hexanoic acid, cyclohexyl ester (3.65 %), n-Tridecanoic acid, methyl(tetramethylene)silyl (2.88 %), and 2-hexadecen-1-ol, 3, 7, 11, 15-tetramethyl-, acetate (2.16 %). The compounds identified by GC-MS in our study are different from the previously reported compounds from leaves. Previously, twenty-six lignans from aerial organs and seeds [14], 50 phenolic compounds from leaves [15], and nineteen polyphenols from various organs were reported. Eight phenols were found in the seeds and aerial parts. Eight anthraquinones and three naphthoquinones were reported. Three iridoids lambalbid, Sesamoside and Shanzhiside methyl ester were also reported from the leaf [14]. The compounds identified from *N. arbor-tristis* methanolic extract are listed in Table 5.

Table 4. Compounds identified in the methanol extract of *S. indicum* from the GC-MS spectrum

Peak number	Retention Time (RT)	Area %	Base m/z	Name and Molecular formula	Mol wt.
1	3.060	0.64	44.00	Tetrahydro-4H-pyran-4-ol ($C_5H_{10}O_2$)	102.13
2	3.517	0.52	61.05	Diglycerol ($C_6H_{14}O_5$)	166.17
3	4.037	2.88	41.05	n-Tridecanoic acid, methyl(tetramethylene)silyl ($C_{18}H_{30}O_2Si$)	306.52
4	4.223	6.18	57.05	D-erythro-Pentose, 2-deoxy- ($C_5H_{10}O_4$)	134.13
5	4.323	0.90	75.05	4-(2-Fluorobenzoylamino)piperidine-1-carbo	
6					
7	4.410	2.16	43.05	2-Hexadecen-1-ol,3,7,11,15-tetramethyl-, acetate ($C_{22}H_{42}O_2$)	338.58
8	4.484	3.65	43.05	Hexanoic acid, cyclohexyl ester ($C_{12}H_{22}O_2$)	198.31
9	4.571	16.16	74.05	Hexadecanoic acid, methyl ester ($C_{17}H_{34}O_2$)	270.46
10	4.806	9.77	58.05	2-Tetradecanone ($C_{14}H_{28}O$)	212.38
11	4.924	33.65	55.05	9,12-Octadecadienoyl chloride, (Z, Z)- ($C_{18}H_{31}ClO$)	298.90
12	5.234	12.94	41.05	9,12-Octadecadienoic acid (Z,Z)- ($C_{18}H_{32}O_2$)	280.45
13	5.559	5.03	74.05	Eicosanoic acid, methyl ester ($C_{21}H_{42}O_2$)	326.57
14	5.878	0.63	129.10	Hexanedioic acid, dioctyl ester ($C_{22}H_{42}O_4$)	370.57
15	5.950	0.61	87.05	3-O-Methyl-d-glucose ($C_7H_{14}O_6$)	194.18
16	6.422	0.56	74.05	Docosanoic acid, methyl ester ($C_{23}H_{46}O_2$)	354.62
17	8.001	1.23	69.10	Squalene ($C_{30}H_{50}$)	410.73
18	8.490	0.16	43.05	2,4-bis(dimethylamino)-7,9-diethyl-10-imino-8-sulfanylidene-1,7,9-triazaspiro[4.5]deca-1,3-dien-6-one ($C_{15}H_{24}N_6OS$)	336.5

Table 5. Compounds identified in the methanol extract of *Arbor-tristis* from GC-MS spectrum.

Peak number	Retention Time (RT)	Area %	Base m/z	Name and Molecular formula	Mol wt.
4	3.372	1.71	105.05	Benzoic acid ($C_7H_6O_2$)	122.12
5	3.500	0.18	120.05	Bezofuran, 2,3-dihydro- (C_8H_8O)	120.15
7	3.756	0.42	164.10	*trans*-Isoeugenol ($C_{10}H_{12}O_2$)	164.20
8	3.896	1.55	60.00	d-Gluco-heptulosan($C_7H_{14}O_7$)	210.18
9	4.002	0.86	41.05	13,16-Octadecadienoic acid, methyl ester($C_{19}H_{34}O_2$)	294.48
10	4.094	1.85	194.05	n-Decanoic acid ($C_{10}H_{20}O_2$)	172.27
11	4.152	0.54	68.05	Neophytadiene ($C_{20}H_{38}$)	278.52
12	4.184	1.32	43.05	2-Undecanone, 6,10-dimethyl- ($C_{13}H_{26}O$)	198.35
13	4.267	0.58	41.05	Pentadecanoic acid ($C_{15}H_{30}O_2$)	242.40
14	4.309	4.67	74.00	Hexadecanoic acid, methyl ester ($C_{17}H_{34}O_2$)	270.46
15	4.391	2.33	216.10	Valerenic acid, methyl ester ($C_6H_{10}O_2$)	114.14
16	4.441	8.62	43.05	n-Hexadecanoic acid ($C_{16}H_{32}O_2$)	256.43
17	4.583	0.90	58.05	Tramadol ($C_{16}H_{25}NO_2$)	263.38
18	4.714	19.60	79.05	9,12,15-Octadecatrienoic acid, methyl ester, (*Z*) ($C_{19}H_{32}O_2$)	292.46
19	4.747	13.11	71.05	Phytol($C_{20}H_{40}O$)	296.54
20	4.894	21.81	79.05	9,12,15-Octadecatrienoic acid, (*Z,Z,Z*)- ($C_{18}H_{30}O_2$)	278.44
21	5.010	3.73	69.05	*trans*-Farnesol ($C_{15}H_{26}O$)	222.37
22	5.103	1.68	157.05	(*3R,6R*)-3-hydroperoxy-3-methyl-6-prop-1-en-2-ylcyclohexene ($C_{10}H_{16}O_2$)	168.24
23	5.166	1.52	79.05	Methyl (*Z*)-5,11,14,17-eicosatetraenoate ($C_{21}H_{34}O_2$)	318.50
24	5.307	1.48	74.00	Eicosanoic acid, methyl ester ($C_{21}H_{42}O_2$)	326.57
32	7.256	0.76	117.05	Doconexent ($C_{22}H_{32}O_2$)	328.50

Twenty one compounds were reported when the chromatogram obtained from GC-MS was analysed and compared with the NIST library database. The major compounds are 9, 12, 15-Octadecatrienoic acid, (Z, Z, Z) - (21.81%), 9, 12, 15-Octadecatrienoic acid, Methyl ester, (Z) (19.60%), Phytol (13.11 %), n-hexadecanoic acid (8.62 %), hexadecanoic acid, methyl ester (4.67 %), trans-farnesol (3.73 %), and valerenic acid, methyl ester (2.33 %). The compounds identified by the GC-MS in our study differ from the previously reported compounds from the leaf, flower, seed and stem [53-55]. Our methanol extract GC-MS data were also compared with ethanol extract data in another study [17].

3.4 Applications of plant-based extracts

Both extracts and their powdered form were subjected to acute oral toxicity tests with albino mice with a single dose. No mortality was observed in any of the cases tabulated in Table 6 up to 14 days of observation. According to OECD guidelines, all extracts and original leaf powder are safe for humans. Therefore, these extracts become crucial for the development of novel biological applications. This result is aligned with another study [56]

Table 6. LD_{50} values for the leaf powder and extract

Sample	LD_{50} value
Leaf powder of *S. indicum*	>2000 mg/kg BW
Leaf powder of *N. arbor-tristis*	>2000 mg/kg BW
S. indicum extract	>2000 mg/kg BW
N. arbor-tristis extract	>2000 mg/kg BW

Since both extracts are expected to be strong antioxidants, the DPPH method was used to analyse the antioxidant properties, using ascorbic acid as a reference. Antioxidant efficacy is correlated with IC_{50} values; a lower IC_{50} value indicates more antioxidant activity [57]. Ascorbic acid's standard calibration curve is used to evaluate IC_{50} values and is expressed as a percentage of inhibition versus concentration, as in Figure 3

https://doi.org/10.1051/e3sconf/202567901018

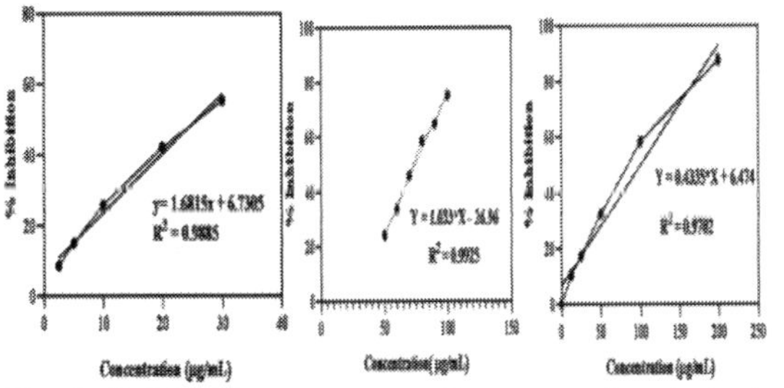

Fig. 3. % inhibition vs concentration curves for a) standard ascorbic acid, (b) *S. indicum* extract, and (c) *N. arbor-tristis* extract for antioxidant activity.

Thus, the IC_{50} values for ascorbic acid, methanolic crude extracts of *S. indicum*, and *N. arbor-tristis* calculated were 25.74 μg/mL (Figure 3a), 74.47 μg/mL (Figure 3b), and 100.40 μg/mL (Figure 3c), respectively. In our case, the IC_{50} value for *S. indicum* extract is nearly three times higher and for *N. arbor-tristis* extract, four times higher than standard ascorbic acid. The % inhibition for methanol extract of *S. indicum* ranges from 24.33% - 75.34%, which is higher than the values 31.60%- 49.42% reported by Sharma *et al.* [9]. The antioxidant efficacy of the plant extract has been divided into four levels, $IC_{50} <$ 50 μg/mL (very strong antioxidant), IC_{50} = 50-100 μg/mL (strong antioxidant), IC_{50} = 100-150 μg/mL (moderate antioxidant) and IC_{50} = 151-250 μg/mL (weak antioxidant) [58]. Hence, *S. indicum* and *N. arbor-tristis* have strong antioxidant potential, as described elsewhere [59].

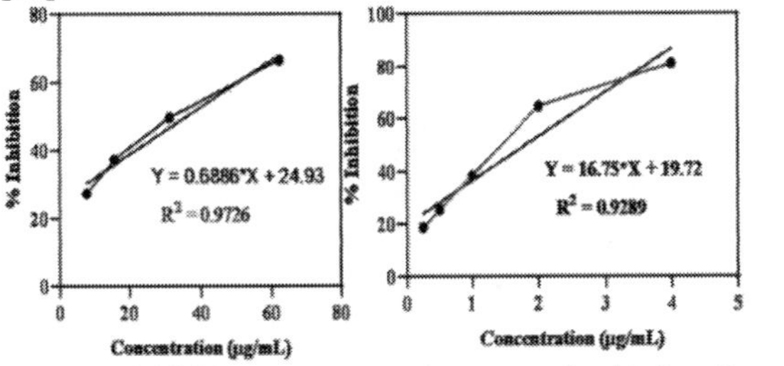

Fig. 4. % inhibition vs concentration curves for (a) *S. indicum* extract, (b) *N. arbor-tristis* extract

Since both extracts possess potent antidiabetic properties due to their high polyphenol content, the antidiabetic properties were analysed using the α-amylase inhibition method. Antidiabetic efficacy can be related to IC_{50} values; that is, lower IC_{50} values indicate greater antidiabetic efficacy. Therefore, the standard calibration curve of metformin is expressed as % inhibition vs concentration to estimate IC_{50} values, as in Figs. 4. Thus, IC_{50} values for methanolic crude extracts of *S. indicum*, *N. arbor-tristis* and metformin are 36.46 μg/mL (Figure 4a), 1.80 μg/mL (Figure 4b) and 19.4 ± 1.4 μM (Figure 4c), respectively. Low IC_{50} values indicate better antidiabetic efficacy of plant-based extracts compared to the standard metformin. Both extracts possess anti-diabetic properties, but the *N.arbor-tristis* extract possesses a lower IC_{50} value than standard metformin. Hence, it possesses better antidiabetic properties than the standard.

Correlation between TPC and TFC, determined as quantitative phytochemistry and applications as antioxidant and antidiabetic properties, was done with statistical approaches using Origin Pro, 2025 (Figure 5). The Karl Pearson correlation analysis was performed between the above parameters. A statistical analysis that shows how two variables relate to a change in one variable is called correlation analysis. There is a positive correlation between two variables if they change in the same direction. A negative correlation occurs when they are moving in the opposite direction. Studies indicate that the TPC and TFC are linearly correlated with antioxidant properties [18]. TPC is nearly orthogonal, i.e., -vely correlated to the antioxidant property with $R^2 = -0.933$(a high negative value, so there is a strong negative correlation) and p-value 0.020 (very significant).

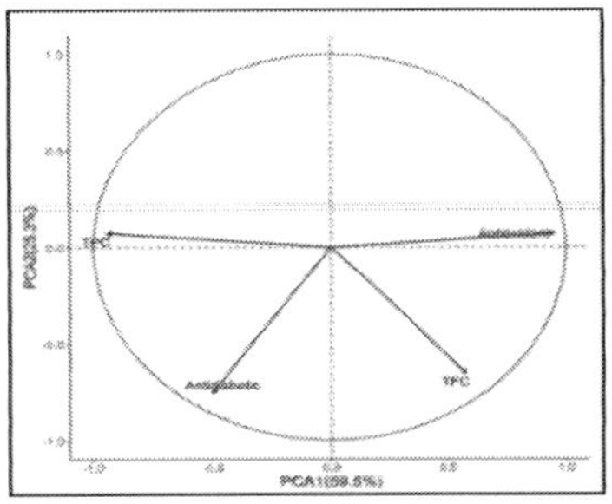

Fig. 5. Loading Plot between variables TPC, TFC, Antioxidant and Antidiabetic property

Similarly, the antibacterial and antifungal activities were assessed, but neither exhibited a zone of inhibition (ZOI). Therefore, they lack antibacterial and antifungal activity against the tested bacteria and fungi. These results are aligned with those of Sharma *et al.* [9]

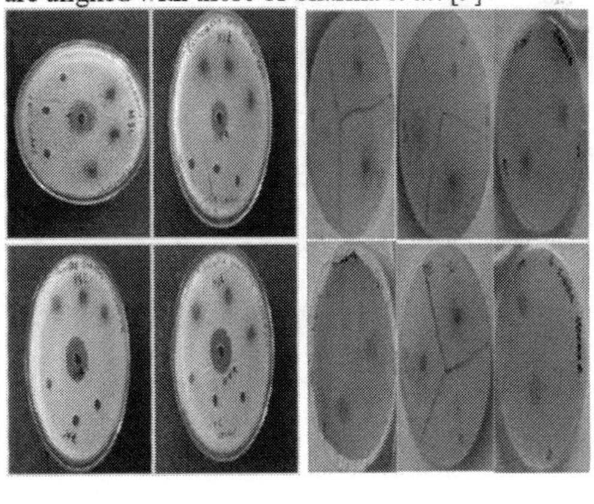

Fig. 6. Antimicrobial Test for (a) S. indicum and (b) N. arbor-tristis

4. Conclusions

Methanolic extracts of two Nepal-based plants, *S. indicum* and *N. arbor-tristis*, were examined for their phytochemistry. Both extracts confirmed the presence of secondary metabolites such as alkaloids, flavonoids, polyphenols, tannins, saponins, quinones, and others through phytochemical screening tests. UV and FT-IR spectroscopy supported these findings. Quantitatively, *N. arbor-tristis* extract was found to be richer in flavonoids by 55.16% compared to *S. indicum*, with flavonoid contents of 173.75 ± 3.89 mg/g QE and 77.90 ± 0.78 mg/g QE, respectively. Conversely, *S. indicum* extract contained a higher amount of phenolic compounds; a 26.12% higher total phenolic content (TPC) was measured in *S. indicum* than in *N. arbor-tristis*. Both extracts were non-toxic to albino mice in acute toxicity tests. Compounds such as 9, 12-Octadecadienoyl chloride, (Z, Z), 9, 12-Octadecadienoic acid (Z, Z), and hexadecanoic acid methyl ester were identified via GC-MS analysis. Both exhibited strong antioxidant activity, with IC_{50} values of 74.47 μg/mL and 100.40 μg/mL, respectively, for *S. indicum* and *N. arbor-tristis*. Anti-diabetic properties were also observed, with IC_{50} values of 36.46 μg/mL and 1.80 μg/mL, respectively. The extracts did not demonstrate anti-fungal or anti-bacterial activity against the tested fungi and bacteria. These findings could represent significant advancements for the pharmaceutical industry.

We deeply acknowledge UGC Nepal for funding this research with grant number PhD-76/77- S&T-25 under the category of faculty and type A. We also appreciate the National Herbarium and Plant Laboratory, Godavari, for providing plant identification and voucher codes, the Central Department of Microbiology for providing bacteria, and NARC for providing fungi.

References

1. G. M. Cragg, D. J. Newman, Natural Product Drug Discovery in the Next Millennium, Pharm. Biol. **39**, 8–17 (2001). https://doi.org/10.1076/phbi.39.s1.8.0009
2. C. W. J., Health-promoting properties of common herbs, Am. J. Clin. Nutr. **70**, 491–499 (1999).
3. S. G. Tumilaar, A. Hardianto, H. Dohi, D. Kurnia, A comprehensive review of free radicals, oxidative stress, and antioxidants: overview, clinical applications, global perspectives, future directions, and mechanisms of antioxidant activity of flavonoid compounds, Journal of Chemistry. **2024**, 1–21 (2024). https://onlinelibrary.wiley.com/doi/10.1155/2024/5594386
4. G. Pizzino et al., Oxidative stress: Harms and benefits for human health, Oxidative Medicine and Cellular Longevity. **2017**, (2017). https://doi.org/10.1155/2017/8416763
5. R. N. Syed, H. Laurentin, R. Splivallo, P. Karlovsky, Antifungal properties of extracts of sesame (*Sesamum indicum*), Int. J. Agric. Biol., vol. **17**, 575–581 (2015).
6. C. Wacal et al., Unravelling the potential benefits of *sesame* (*Sesamum indicum* L.) in cropping systems, nutritional, health, and industrial uses of its seeds – a review, Cogent Food & Agriculture. **10**, (2024). https://doi.org/10.1080/23311932.2024.2360766
7. S. Jarić et al., An ethnobotanical survey of traditionally used plants on Suva planina mountain (south-eastern Serbia), Journal of Ethnopharmacology. **175**, 93–108 (2015). https://doi.org/10.1016/j.jep.2015.09.002
8. A. J. Shittu Lukeman, K. Shittu Remilekun, O. Olufemi, O. Tayo Adetokunbo, A. A. Osunubi Abraham, Hypoglycaemia and improved testicular parameters in *Sesamum radiatum* treated normo-glycaemic adult male Sprague Dawley rats, African J. Biotechnol. **8**, 2878–2886 (2009).
9. S. Sandhya et al., In vitro evaluation of roots, seeds and leaves of *Sesamum indicum* L. for their potential antibacterial and antioxidant properties, African Journal of Biotechnology. **13**, 3692–3701 (2014).
10. O. Ogunsola, T. Fasola, The antibacterial activities of *Sesamum indicum* Linn. leaf extracts, Adv. Life Sci. Technol. **18**, 28–32 (2014).
11. C. Ogwuche, J. Amupitan, Antimicrobial activity of the leaf of the white species of *Sesamum indicum* from Benue State, Nigeria, International Journal of Biological and Chemical Sciences. **9**, 996 (2015).
12. R. N. Syed, H. Laurentin, R. Splivallo, P. Karlovsky, Antifungal Properties of Extracts of *Sesame* (*Sesamum indicum*), International Journal of Agriculture and Biology. **17**, 575–581 (2015).
13. P. Sharma, R. Sarin, Isolation and identification of flavonoids from *Sesamum indicum*, Indones. J. Pharm. **23**, 135–140 (2012).
14. N. T. Dat, N. H. Dang, L. N. Thanh, New flavonoid and pentacyclic triterpene from *Sesamum indicum* leaves, Natural Product Research. **30**, 311–315 (2015). https://doi.org/10.1080/14786419.2015.1057730
15. Y. Fuji, A. Uchida, K. Fukahori, M. Chino, T. Ohtsuki, H. Matsufuji, Chemical characterisation and biological activity in young *sesame* leaves (*Sesamum indicum* L.), and changes in iridoid and polyphenol content at different growth stages, PLoS ONE. **13**, 0194449 (2018). https://doi.org/10.1371/journal.pone.0194449
16. L. Sarma, S. Chakraborty, M. J. Das, R. K. Duary, Optimisation of ultrasound-assisted extraction of phenolic compounds from *Sesamum indicum*, Natural Product Research. **34**, 1931-1936 (2019). https://doi.org/10.1080/14786419.2018.1564294
17. S. A. Mousum, S. Ahmed, B. Gawali, M. Kwatra, A. Ahmed, M. Lahkar, *Nyctanthes arbor-tristis* leaf extract ameliorates hyperlipidemia- and hyperglycemia-associated nephrotoxicity by improving anti-oxidant and anti-inflammatory status in high-fat diet–streptozotocin-induced diabetic rats, Inflammopharmacology. **26**, 1415–1428 (2018). https://doi.org/10.1007/s10787-018-0497-6
18. S. Kim, H. Y. Yang, H. J. Lee, J. Ju, In Vitro Antioxidant and Anti-Colon Cancer Activities of *Sesamum indicum* L. Leaf Extract and Its Major Component, Pedaliin, Foods. **10**, 1216 (2021). https://doi.org/10.3390/foods10061216
19. A. Kumar, D. C. Mishra, U. B. Angadi, R. Yadav, A. Rai, D. Kumar, Inhibition Potencies of Phytochemicals Derived from *Sesame* Against

SARS-CoV-2 Main Protease: A Molecular Docking and Simulation Study, Frontiers in Chemistry. **9**, (2021).https://doi.org/10.3389/fchem.2021.744376
20. A. K. Daund, R. S. Jadhav, D. N. Vikhe, A Review on *Nyctanthes arbor-tristis* Leaves: a Potential Medicinal Herb, Certif. J. | Amol al. World J. Pharm. Med. Res. **8**, 128–132 (2022).
21. J. Agrawal, A. Pal, *Nyctanthes arbor-tristis* Linn - A critical ethno pharmacological review, J. Ethnopharmacol. **146**, 645–658 (2013). https://doi.org/10.1016/j.jep.2013.01.024
22. S. Chobhe, S. Kumar Sen, L.Mohan Behera, Ethno-Medicinal Uses of *Nyctanthes arbor-tristis* L. in Bargarh District, Odisha, Int. J. Herb. Med. **8**, 22–24 (2020).
23. B. B. Kakoti, P. Pradhan, S. Borah, K. Mahato, M. Kumar, Analgesic and Anti-Inflammatory activities of the methanolic stem bark extract of *Nyctanthes arbor-tristis*Linn., BioMed Research International. **2013**, 1–6 (2013). https://doi.org/10.1155/2013/826295
24. J. Kaur, S. Kaushal, Chemical Analysis, Antimicrobial and Antioxidant Activities of Harsingar (*Nyctanthes arbor-tristis*) essential oil, Journal of Essential Oil Bearing Plants. **23**, 230–245 (2020).
25. V. I. Hukkeri, K. S. Akki, R. R. Sureban, B. Gopalakrishna, V. V. Byahatti, S. V. Rajendra, Hepatoprotective activity of the leaves of *Nyctanthes arbor-tristis* Linn., Indian J. Pharm. Sci. **68**, 542–543 (2006). https://www.ijpsonline.com/articles/hepatoprotective-activity-of-the-leaves-of-nyctanthes-arbortristis-linn.html
26. M. Balasubramanian, Study on phytochemical screening and antibacterial activity of *Nyctanthes arbor-tristis*, J. Chem. Pharm. Res. **4**, 1686–1695 (2012).
27. H. N., K. A. Verma Laxmi, Tamrakar Vaibhav, Antifungal activity of different extracts from different parts of *Nyctanthes arbor-tristis* Linn. (Parijat) against clinical pathogens. 1–23 (2016).
28. P. Gupta, S. K. Bajpai, K. Chandra, K. L. Singh, J. S. Tandon, Antiviral profile of *Nyctanthes arbor-tristis* L. against encephalitis-causing viruses, Indian J. Exp. Biol. **43**, 1156–1160 (2005).
29. D. I. Dhinakaran, G. Sakthivel, Antioxidant and Anti-inflammatory Activities Of *Nyctanthes arbor-tristis* Extracts. **4**, 1–5 (2016).
30. S. Das, D. Sasmal, S. P. Basu, Antispasmodic and Anthelmintic Activity of *Nyctanthes arbor-tristis* Linn., Int. J. Pharm. Sci. Res. **1**, 51–55 (2010).
31. R. S. Saxena, B. Gupta, S. Lata, Tranquillising, antihistaminic and purgative activity of *Nyctanthes arbor-tristis* leaf extract, J. Ethnopharmacol. **81**, 321–325 (2002). https://doi.org/10.1016/S0378-8741(02)00088-0
32. C. Rani, S. Chawla, M. Mangal, A. K. Mangal, S. Kajla, A. K. Dhawan, *Nyctanthes arbor-tristis* Linn. (Night Jasmine): A sacred ornamental plant with immense medicinal potentials, Indian J. Tradit. Knowl. **11**, 427–435 (2012).
33. D. Benefit, Anticancer activity of *Nyctanthes arbor-tristis*, Int. J. Adv. Res. **5**, 84–87 (2019). [Online]. Available: www.IJARIIT.com
34. P. Kumari, D. Sahal, S. K. Jain, V. S. Chauhan, Bioactivity Guided Fractionation of Leaves Extract of *Nyctanthes arbor tristis* (Harshringar) against *P falciparum*, PLoS One. **7**, 1–7 (2012). https://doi.org/10.1371/journal.pone.0051714
35. J. Agrawal and A. Pal, *Nyctanthes arbor-tristis* Linn - A critical ethno pharmacological review," J. Ethnopharmacol. **146**, 645–658 (2013). https://doi.org/10.1016/j.jep.2013.01.024
36. J. B. Harborne, Phytochemical Methods : A Guide to Modern Techniques of Plant Analysis. (Second ed., Chapman and Hall, New York, USA. 1984).
37. X. Lu, C. F. Ross, J. R. Powers, D. E. Aston, B. A. Rasco, Determination of total phenolic content and antioxidant activity of garlic (*Allium sativum*) and elephant garlic (*Allium ampeloprasum*) by attenuated total reflectance-Fourier transformed infrared spectroscopy. J. Agric. Food Chem. **59**, 5215–5221 (2011). https://doi.org/10.1021/jf201254f
38. C. C. Chang, M. H. Yang, H. M. Wen, J. C. Chern, Estimation of total flavonoid content in propolis by two complementary colometric methods, J. Food Drug Anal. **10**, 178–182 (2002). https://doi.org/10.38212/2224-6614.2748
39. OECD, The Organisation of Economic Co-operation and Development Guidelines Test No. 423: Acute Oral toxicity - Acute Toxic Class Method, OECD Guidelines for the Testing of Chemicals, Section 4. OECD. 1–14 (2002).
40. J. Javanmardi, C. Stushnoff, E. Locke, J. M. Vivanco, Antioxidant activity and total phenolic content of Iranian *Ocimum* accessions, Food Chem. **83**, 547–550 (2003). https://doi.org/10.1016/S0308-8146(03)00151-1
41. Y. M. Kim, Y. K. Jeong, M. H. Wang, W. Y. Lee, H. I. Rhee, Inhibitory effect of pine extract on α-glucosidase activity and postprandial hyperglycemia, Nutrition. **21**, 756–761 (2005). https://doi.org/10.1016/j.nut.2004.10.014
42. E. A. Palombo, S. J. Semple, Antibacterial activity of traditional Australian medicinal plants, J. Ethnopharmacol. **77**, 151–157 (2001). https://doi.org/10.1016/S0378-8741(01)00290-2
43. D. Webster, P. Taschereau, R. J. Belland, C. Sand, R. P. Rennie, Antifungal activity of medicinal plant extracts; preliminary screening studies, J. Ethnopharmacol. **115**, 140–146 (2008). https://doi.org/10.1016/j.jep.2007.09.014
44. R. K. Mishra et al., Exploration of anti-Malarial potential of *Nyctanthes arbor-tristis* L. and their application to combat the infection caused by Mala s1, a novel allergen, BMC Complement. Altern. Med. **16**, 1–14 (2016). https://doi.org/10.1186/s12906-016-1092-2
45. M.P., Neeta, N., Mukta, K.Bilwa, Comparative Qualitative Phytochemical analysis of *Sesamum indicum* L, International Journal of Current

Microbiology and Applied Sciences. 172-181 (2015). ISSN: 2319-7706.

46. R. Ks, S. K. Naik, S. Satapathy, S. Mishra, Phytochemical analysis of the leaf extracts of *Nyctanthes arbor-tristis*, Plant Archives. **21**, (2021).
47. T. K. Patle, K. Shrivas, R. Kurrey, S. Upadhyay, R. Jangde, R. Chauhan, Phytochemical screening and determination of phenolics and flavonoids in *Dillenia pentagyna* using UV–vis and FTIR spectroscopy, Spectrochimica Acta Part a Molecular and Biomolecular Spectroscopy. **242**, 118717 (2020). https://doi.org/10.1016/j.saa.2020.118717
48. P. Jain, A. Soni, P. Jain, J. Bhawsar, Phytochemical analysis of Mentha spicata plant extract using UV-vis, FTIR and GC/MS technique, Journal of Chemical and Pharmaceutical Research, **8**, 1-6 (2016).
49. I. R. Bunghez, M. Raduly, S. Doncea, I. Aksahin, R. M. Ion, Lycopene determination in tomatoes by different spectral techniques (UV-vis, FTIR and HPLC), Digest Journal of Nanomaterials and Biostructures. **6**, 1349-1356 (2011).
50. S. H. Hassanpour, A. Doroudi, Review of the antioxidant potential of flavonoids as a subgroup of polyphenols and partial substitute for synthetic antioxidants, PubMed.**13**, 354–376 (2023). https://doi.org/10.22038/ajp.2023.21774
51. Peddinti, Ramya, Phytochemical, Antibacterial and in Vitro Antioxidant Analysis of *Nyctanthes arbor-tristis* Leaves, International Journal of Pharmaceutical Science Invention (IJPSI). **9,** 6-9 (2019).
52. N. Konappa, A. C. Udayashankar, S. Krishnamurthy, C. K. Pradeep, S. Chowdappa, S. Jogaiah, GC–MS analysis of phytoconstituents from *Amomum nilgiricum* and molecular docking interactions of bioactive serverogenin acetate with target proteins, Scientific Reports. **10**, (2020). https://doi.org/10.1038/s41598-020-73442-0
53. N. K. S. M. Dewi, N. Fakhrudin, S. Wahyuono, A comprehensive review on the phytoconstituents and biological activities of *Nyctanthes arbor-tristis* L., Journal of Applied Pharmaceutical Science. 9–17 (2022). https://doi.org/10.7324/japs.2022.120802
54. A. K. Mishra, K. N. Tiwari, R. Saini, J. K. Chaurasia, S. K. Mishra, Assessment of antioxidant potential in seed extracts of *Nyctanthes arbor-tristis* L. and phytochemical profiling by Gas Chromatography-Mass Spectrometry system, Brazilian Journal of Pharmaceutical Sciences. **58**, (2022). https://doi.org/10.1590/s2175-97902022e21180
55. S. N. Heendeniya et al., Therapeutic Efficacy of *Nyctanthes arbor-tristis* Flowers to Inhibit Proliferation of Acute and Chronic Primary Human Leukaemia Cells, with Adipocyte Differentiation and in Silico Analysis of Interactions between Survivin Protein and Selected Secondary Metabolites, Biomolecules. **10**, 165 (2020). https://doi.org/10.3390/biom10020165
56. S. Phongpaichit et al., Biological activities of extracts from endophytic fungi isolated from Garcinia plants, FEMS Immunology & Medical Microbiology. **51**, 517–525 (2007). https://doi.org/10.1111/j.1574-695x.2007.00331.x
57. J. Jumina, D. Siswanta, K. Zulkarnain, S. Triono, P. Priatmoko, E. Yuanita, N. Fatmasari, I. Nursalim, Development of C-Arylcalix [4] resorcinarenes and C-Arylcalix [4] pyrogallol as Antioxidant and UV-B Protector, Indonesian Journal of Chemistry. **19,** 273 (2019). https://doi.org/10.22146/ijc.26868
58. B. Setha, F. G. Febe, P. A. S. Idris, S. Rahman, M. N. Mailoa, Potential of Seaweed Padina Sp as a Source of Antioxidant, International journal of scientific & technology research. **2** (2013). ISSN 2277-8616.
59. M. A. Syabana, N. D. Yuliana, I. Batubara, D. Fardiaz, α-glucosidase inhibitors from *Syzygium polyanthum* (Wight) Walp leaves as revealed by metabolomics and in silico approaches," Journal of Ethnopharmacology. **282**, 114618 (2021). https://doi.org/10.1016/j.jep.2021.114618

Business Intelligence System for Management of Academic Organization's Carbon Dioxide Emission

Wachirapong Jirakitpuwapat[1], *Taweesak* Srithong[1], and *Chalida* Phanlert[1*]

[1]Faculty of Science, Energy and Environment, King Mongkut's University of Technology North Bangkok, Rayong Campus, 21120 Rayong, Thailand

Abstract. This paper investigated the assessment of carbon dioxide emissions in academic organizations affiliated with the Faculty of Science, Energy, and Environment at King Mongkut's University of Technology North Bangkok in Rayong campus, and presented business intelligence strategies to reduce carbon dioxide (CO_2) emissions. We calculate the tons of carbon dioxide equivalent (CO_2 eq) for 2 years (2023-2024) of data from surveys, sources, and various activities responsible for CO_2 emissions, presenting the results through charts on the dashboard in a visually compelling and understandable way. According to the study, total CO_2 emissions are 484.96 tons CO_2 eq, with the top four sources of CO_2 emissions being electricity, R410a, Diesel fuel, and garbage, respectively. Based on business intelligence methodologies, several strategies for reducing CO_2 emissions have been evaluated and identified, including immediate reduction measures, assigning responsibility and implementing monitoring, collaboration with specialists, raising awareness and promoting communication, and fostering innovation and incentives.

1 Introduction

Greenhouse gases (GHGs), such as sulfur dioxide (SO_2), nitrous oxide (N_2O), methane (CH_4), and carbon dioxide (CO_2), play a crucial role in our ecosystem, and it is vital to understand their impact on the environment [1]. Without these GHGs, the Earth's temperature would become unstable, leading to catastrophic consequences for our planet's atmosphere and environment. Despite their importance, human activities such as burning fossil fuels, deforestation, power generation, cement production, and industrial processes have led to a continuing increase in GHGs, especially CO_2. These activities are a primary factor in the rapid changes in Earth's climate and weather systems, resulting in the increasing average atmospheric temperature, commonly referred to as global warming. The primary factor contributing to global warming is CO_2, which has adverse effects on humans and other organisms [2]. Therefore, it is crucial to restrict CO_2 emissions to reduce the effects of climate change and its associated impacts.

The carbon footprint (CF) is the total amount of GHGs that an individual, organization, event, or product emits into the atmosphere, directly or indirectly. These emissions are expressed in equivalent tons of CO_2, taking into account the global warming potential (GWP) of each gas [3]. CF is a valuable metric for quantifying the impact of people, businesses, goods, and services on climate change. By measuring a company's CF, it can better understand its primary sources of emissions and find ways to minimize them. This can lead to more informed decisions, increased stakeholder participation, and a more substantial contribution to combating climate change [4].

The Sustainable Development Goals (SDGs) are comprehensive global development objectives consisting of 17 goals and 169 targets. On September 25, 2015, all 193 United Nations member countries unanimously adopted these goals [5-7]. These goals address global challenges, including poverty, inequality, climate change, environmental degradation, and the pursuit of peace and justice. This roadmap provides a framework for governments and organizations to work together towards a more sustainable and equitable future for everyone and the planet. In the context of academic organizations, the term "green campus" refers to the concept of sustainability on campus [8-11].

Over the past three decades, Business Intelligence (BI) has gained significant traction as organizations have realized the value of analyzing data for informed decision-making [12-14]. By leveraging BI tools, businesses can extract, interpret, and transform large volumes of data into meaningful insights, providing a competitive edge in today's fast-paced and data-driven business environment. This enables them to adopt energy-efficient practices, utilize sustainable materials, and promote low-carbon technologies [15]. As such, BI has become an essential component of any modern business strategy, enabling organizations to identify trends, patterns, and opportunities that would otherwise go unnoticed.

With the motivation above, we analyzed CO_2 emissions from the operations and activities of an academic organization for the period of 2023-2024. We primarily focused on the CO_2 emissions associated

* Corresponding author: chalida.p@sciee.kmutnb.ac.th

with the Faculty of Science, Energy, and Environment's operations at King Mongkut's University of Technology North Bangkok in Rayong Campus. We used BI techniques and developed a data dashboard to assess the factors responsible for CO_2 emissions. Based on our analysis, we have identified several strategies that could help reduce CO_2 emissions. Furthermore, our work aligns with SDG Goal 13, focusing on environmental sustainability, and we are actively implementing timely measures to mitigate the impacts of climate change and address its repercussions. In addition, the significant contributions and highlights of this paper are summarized in the following key points:

- We assess CO_2 emissions at academic organizations such as diesel fuel, R410a, electricity, A4 paper, and garbage.
- We apply a BI strategy to analyze problems and recommend solutions for reducing CO_2 emissions.
- We present our results using dashboards and diagrams.

2 Management

This section presents the process of taking action to achieve organizational goals [16].

2.1 Planning:

Planning entails establishing the scope of the business, setting goals and objectives, and determining the steps to achieve those goals. Based on the scope, the work's goals and procedures are evident. Having previously stated, the executives continued. The next task is to put together an organization.

2.2 Organization:

Management of organizations encompasses staffing, departmentalization, resource allocation, and management, enabling the company to implement its strategy and achieve its predetermined goals.

2.3 Commanding:

Giving commands is the act of issuing instructions in various contexts, particularly between superiors and subordinates.

2.4 Coordinating:

Coordinating involves reaching out to us with questions or requesting assistance to ensure the organization's operations are completed efficiently. The objective was achieved in relation to the group's goals.

2.5 Controlling:

Control refers to the organization's ability to maintain activities. Different organizational processes are guided by the norms, expectations, or strategies that have been established.

3 Business Intelligence

Business intelligence (BI) refers to the technologies, strategies, techniques, and practices that organizations employ to analyze information. The purpose of BI is to assist organizations in making more informed, data-driven decisions. BI tools help organizations understand complicated data through reports, dashboards, and data visualizations, uncovering trends and insights to drive strategic decisions [17].

3.1 Framework for business intelligence

3.1.1 Data warehouse:

The data warehouse is a centralized repository that accumulates data from both internal and external sources, holding large amounts of data in a format suitable for professional use. It plays a vital role in BI and analytics, providing firms with the necessary data to make decisions and gain a competitive advantage.

3.1.2 Business analytics:

Business analytics is the use of data, statistical analysis, and quantitative methods to gain insights and inform business decisions. It involves examining, analyzing, and interpreting data to identify trends and patterns that can be used to optimize business processes and improve outcomes. The purpose of business analytics is to enable organizations to make data-driven decisions that promote growth, enhance efficiency, and improve overall business performance.

3.1.3 Business process management:

Business process management is critical for every organization's governance and operational performance analysis. However, most firms have separate work processes, resulting in numerous applications, which makes it challenging to combine the systems efficiently. To address this challenge, the concept of gathering and improving procedures emerged. The idea is to arrange corporate processes so that they can be integrated and function together efficiently. This will help increase the efficiency and reuse of numerous systems, allowing enterprises to employ the services they require simultaneously. Each corporation uses business process management to govern and analyze operating results, linking and completing business tasks. Several efficient systems can be utilized and reused. The objective is to organize the company's operations so that services can be shared, enabling each organization to use the services it needs simultaneously.

3.1.4 User interface:

The user interface is a critical component within a system, serving as the primary means of interaction between the user and the system. It is responsible for facilitating communication, interpreting user input, and presenting output in a clear and concise manner. An effective user interface is crucial for ensuring an optimal user experience and satisfaction, and can directly impact the overall success of a system. Designing and implementing user interfaces that meet users' needs and provide a seamless and intuitive experience is crucial.

3.2 Business intelligence processes

Rick Sherman is considered an authority in BI and plays a significant role in advancing knowledge and practices within the industry. He has presented a definition of the BI process. This process, central to data analysis and decision-making, is crucial for organizations seeking to derive meaningful insights from their data. By providing a clear and concise definition of the BI process, he has contributed to advancing knowledge in this critical field. His insights will prove valuable to researchers, practitioners, and business leaders [18].

3.2.1 Data source:

The initial step in the BI process is identifying and defining the data sources. These sources are subsequently categorized into two types: internal and external, before being integrated into the data warehouse or data mart. This process lays the foundation for the subsequent stages of BI and is crucial for the accurate analysis of data and the generation of valuable insights.

3.2.2 Dimensional data model:

Data warehousing utilizes a specialized type of data model known as the dimensional data model. The dimensional model utilizes two primary types of tables to optimize the organization and structure of data for reporting and querying purposes.

- Dimension tables are essential to data analysis as they furnish crucial descriptive attributes about the items under scrutiny. The primary key in each dimension table is a unique identifier, while other columns provide supplementary information about the object.
- Fact tables comprise numerical data and foreign keys that establish a linkage to the dimension tables. The composite key that serves as the primary key is generally composed of foreign keys that interconnect to the dimension tables.

3.2.3 Data warehouse/Data marts:

To successfully import data into data warehouses or data markets, which are subsets of data warehouses, you must properly format the data according to the requirements of the data transformation process. The data formatting will ensure that the data is processed efficiently and that the insights generated are accurate and reliable.

- Extract is the process of choosing needed data from multiple sources and transforming it.
- Transform is selecting and filtering information. Raw data cannot be utilized to make well-informed decisions. Therefore, it must be modified to ensure it meets the required quality and standards before being used in subsequent data-filling and decision-making processes.
- Load is the process of storing transformed data in a data warehouse. This process is critical in ensuring efficient data management and seamless utilization when making informed business decisions.

3.2.4 Data creation in a cube pattern:

The data structure is multilayered, and dimensions facilitate data analysis. The various retrieval techniques are accessible, and the slice-and-dice approach yields significant savings in query time.

3.2.5 Report:

Dashboards and reports are essential to BI, providing executives with an overall picture of an organization. However, if they require more detailed information, they need supporting reports that can take the form of previously prepared reports. In situations where executives need immediate responses, ad-hoc reports come in handy. These reports provide management with the necessary information to make informed decisions.

4 Carbon Footprint

Compiling a comprehensive list of greenhouse gas emissions is necessary to determine an organization's CF. This process requires executing five crucial steps [19].

4.1 Organization boundary:

Establishing clear organizational boundaries is imperative to ensure effective management. Furthermore, keeping a record of greenhouse gas emissions and absorption within a designated timeframe is recommended. This practice not only helps monitor environmental impact but also enables informed decision-making.

4.2 Operational boundaries:

An organization's operational scope is quantified based on the volume of greenhouse gas emissions generated by every activity conducted within its premises, with activities categorized into three distinct classifications.

- Scope 1 is an organization's direct greenhouse gas emissions and absorption. These include emissions from internal operations, such as stationary and mobile combustion, as well as leaks.

- Scope 2 is indirect emissions and absorption of GHGs from energy consumption, such as the amount of GHGs produced during the generation of heat, steam, or electricity from sources outside the organization and then used internally.
- Scope 3 is indirect emissions from sources not owned or directly controlled by the entity, arising from activities other than those mentioned in categories 1 and 2, such as employee commuting, garbage amount, and A4 paper use.

4.3 Identifying sources of greenhouse gas emissions and evaluating the organization's CF:

In calculating an organization's CF, it is crucial to consider the resources available for gathering greenhouse gas emissions data and selecting the appropriate computational approach to determine the greenhouse gas emission factor, as in (1). It is essential to ensure that the following GHGs are included in the CF calculation: CO_2, hydrofluorocarbons gas group (HFCs), CH_4, SO_2, N_2O, and perfluorocarbon gas group (PFCs), as they have the potential to cause global warming. To determine the global warming potential of these GHGs over 100 years, refer to Table 1. [20].

$$GHG = \text{Activity data} \times EF, \qquad (1)$$

where *GHG* is the amount of greenhouse gases, activity data is information about activities that cause GHGs, and EF is the greenhouse gas emissions factor.

Table 1. The potential value of causing global warming.

greenhouse gases	Potential to cause global warming (times of carbon dioxide)
Carbon Dioxide (CO_2)	1
Methane (CH_4)	25
Nitrous Oxide (N_2O)	298
Hydrofluorocarbons (HFCs)	7462
Perfluorocarbons (PFCs)	9795
Sulfur Hexafluoride (SF_6)	22,800

4.4 Computation:

The process of preparing a greenhouse gas inventory involves collecting data from all three activity types to compute the quantity of GHGs produced accurately. Once the data has been gathered, the resulting figures are then summarized for further analysis and evaluation.

4.5 Identifying and tackling uncertainty:

This step is significant in ensuring the accuracy of the data collected on greenhouse gas emissions and absorption. It addresses the uncertainties that may arise from utilizing different greenhouse gas emission factors from various reference sources in the calculations. Thus, the organization responsible for the assessment must incorporate the findings of the uncertainty assessment into its review process. Tables 2 and 3 serve as an excellent illustration of this.

5 Business Intelligence for Management of Organization's CO_2 Emission

The Plan-Do-Check-Act (PDCA) management methodology is widely used in businesses to monitor and enhance their processes and products [21]. We have taken this approach one step further by incorporating BI into PDCA methodology, which we refer to as BI-PDCA, as illustrated in Figure 1.

5.1 Business intelligence planning:

A SWOT analysis is an essential strategic planning tool for identifying and evaluating an organization's Strengths, Weaknesses, Opportunities, and Threats. This tool can help organizations manage their CF more effectively by leveraging BI to create a comprehensive plan. Key performance indicators (KPIs) are established to measure success, and database models are developed for BI systems. These approaches can help organizations optimize their CF management efforts and achieve their goals more efficiently.

5.2 Business intelligence doing:

Proceed with the BI objectives as per the established plan.

Table 2. Reference score of data quality used in studies.

Value Type	Data Quality Level			
Activity Data	X = 6 points	Y = 3 points		Z = 1 points
	Automatic Continuous	Regular Measurement		Estimation
Emission Factor	C = 4 points	D = 3 points	E = 2 points	F = 1 point
	Quality Measurement	Manufacturer /National	Regional	International

Table 3. Level of uncertrainty and data quality.

Rating	Scoring	Description
1	1-6	High uncertainty & Poor quality
2	7-12	Little uncertainty & Moderate quality
3	13-18	Slightly uncertainty & Good quality
4	19-24	Low uncertainty & Excellent quality

Table 4. Level of uncertrainty and data quality.

Scope	Emission Sources	Data		Greenhouse gas emissions		
		Source	Amount	Factor	Tons CO_2eq	Factor Sources
1	Diesel fuel	Receipts	6672.809 L	2.7078	18.93	IPCC Vol.2 Table 3.3.1, DEDE
1	R140a	Receipts	27.27 kg	1923.5	52.45	IPCC: GWP (AR5)
2	Electricity	Receipts	795,386.6 KWh	0.4999	397.61	Thai National LCI Database, TIISMTEC-NSTDA, AR5 (with TGO electricity 2016-2018)
3	A4 Paper	Record	2696.1 Kg	0.6677	1.80	Thai National LCI Database, TIIS-MTEC-NSTDA
3	Garbage	Record	12,799.8 Kg	0.7933	10.15	Thai National LCI Database, TIISMTEC-NSTDA, AR5 (with TGO electricity 2016-2018)
3	Scrap paper	Record	1196.7 Kg	2.93	3.51	2006 IPCC Volume 5: Waste
3	Clear glass bottle	Record	209.7 Kg	0.8075	0.17	Thai National LCI Database, TIIS-MTEC-NSTDA
3	Aluminum can	Record	30.4 Kg	1.4682	0.05	Ecoinvent 2.2, IPCC 2007 GWP 100a
3	Plastic water bottle	Record	506.1 Kg	0.5751	0.29	Ecoinvent 2.2, IPCC 2007 GWP 100a

5.3 Business intelligence checking:

KPIs are employed to evaluate the success of a plan and assess whether it has met expectations. As the assessment process unfolds, it is essential to acknowledge that both successful and unsuccessful outcomes are possible. As an assessor, it is crucial to acknowledge this possibility. In the event of a successful plan, we must determine the contributing factors that led to its triumph rather than attributing it solely to chance. Conversely, if the plan did not unfold as intended, it is essential to ascertain the underlying reasons for its failure.

5.4 Business intelligence acting:

Upon completion of the examination, the team has identified areas for improvement that require incorporation into the relevant procedures. The team will conduct an in-depth analysis to identify the factors that impede the success of the original plan and devise appropriate mitigation strategies. Following the completion of the revised operational plan, the team will resume the cycle of continuously performing BI-PDCA to ensure sustained improvements.

Table 5. Assessing data uncertainty.

Emission Sources	Score		Evaluation Results	Quality Level
	Collect	EF		
Diesel fuel	3	2	9	2
R140a	3	2	9	2
Electricity	3	3	9	2
A4 Paper	3	3	9	2
Garbage	3	3	9	2
Scrap paper	3	3	9	2
Clear glass bottle	3	3	9	2
Aluminum can	3	3	9	2
Plastic water bottle	3	3	9	2

6 Case Study of Faculty of Science, Energy and Environment in King Mongkut's University of Technology North Bangkok in Rayong Campus

This research was conducted at the Faculty of Science, Energy, and Environment of King Mongkut's University of Technology North Bangkok in Rayong Campus. The CF will be calculated by considering all the activities of our academic organization that generate CO_2 emissions. We have all the necessary information, which was methodically collected from the academic organization's records and receipts.

6.1 Quantity of the organization's CF

The data emission source is obtained from receipts and documented in the office. The emission factor is obtained from regional and national sources, as shown in Tables 4 and 5.

The bar plot illustrates the CF from source emissions over 2 years (2023-2024), as shown in Figure 2. Electricity, R410a, diesel fuel, and garbage are the top 4 source emissions, as shown in Figure 3. Electricity has the highest emissions, at 397.61 tons CO_2 eq, accounting for 81.99% of the total. September shows the highest emissions, peaking at 40.02 tons CO_2 eq. Emissions appear relatively stable and consistent from April through December, ranging from 27.74 to 31.81 tons CO_2 eq, with minor fluctuations. R410a was only recorded in November, at 52.45 tons CO_2 eq, which is 10.82% of the total. Diesel fuel emissions are at 18.93 tons CO_2 eq, which is 3.90% of the total. May shows the highest emissions, peaking at 2.52 tons CO_2 eq. This peak is significantly higher than in other months. Garbage emissions are at 10.154 tons CO_2 eq, 2.09%. February shows the highest emissions, peaking at 1.04 tons CO_2 eq. The lowest value is observed in March, at a notably lower emission level of 0.43 tons CO_2 eq, which is an extreme outlier compared to the rest of the data. Garbage, scrap paper, clear glass bottles, aluminum cans, and plastic water bottles have a positive correlation, as shown in Figure 4.

6.2 Discussion

In 2023-2024, an assessment was conducted to determine the CF of the Faculty of Science, Energy, and Environment at King Mongkut's University of Technology North Bangkok in Rayong Campus. According to the assessment, the total amount of greenhouse gas emissions generated by the academic organization's operations was 484.96 tons CO_2 eq, equivalent to 1.28 tons CO_2 eq per person.

The assessment found that the academic organization's energy use was the second scope of its operating activity, contributing to greenhouse gas emissions. Specifically, the academic organization's electricity use for teaching and learning activities, including air conditioning, lighting, and lift usage, contributed significantly to these emissions. Additionally, almost all students and teachers require high electrical power to use experimental equipment.

Further, the assessment revealed that the academic organizations used diesel fuel for various activities, including meetings, training, cooperation, educational guidance, student affairs, and more. The educational guidance activities were frequent in May, while garbage production was low in March due to fewer people in the office and fewer purchases. The causes of greenhouse gas emissions are summarized in Figure 5.

https://doi.org/10.1051/e3sconf/202567901019

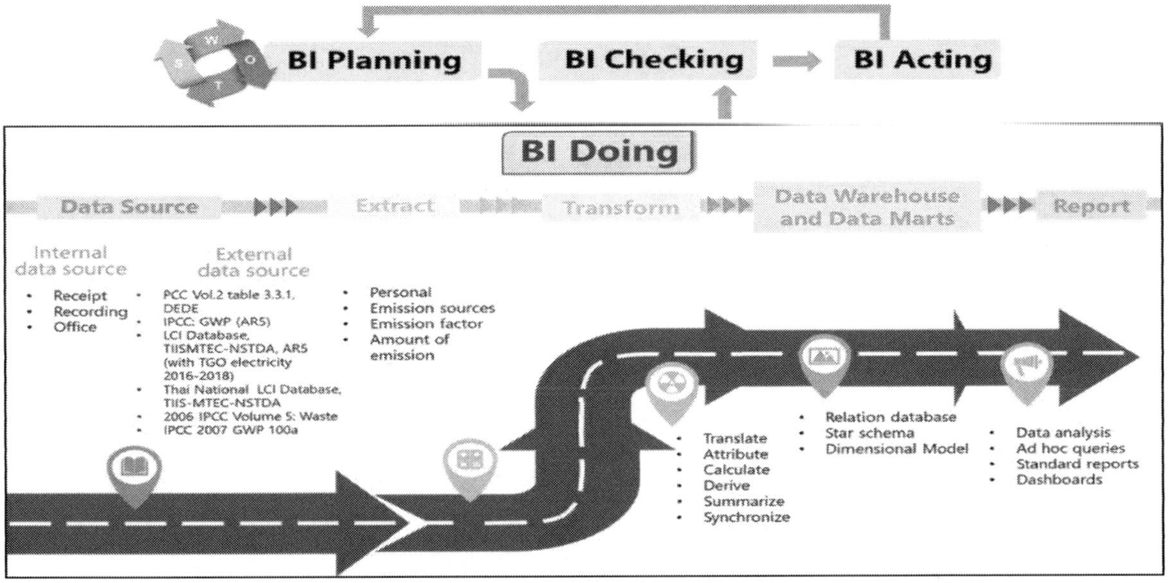

Fig. 1. Business intelligence system diagram.

6.3 Guidelines for reducing greenhouse gas emissions

The SWOT analysis provides the following recommendations for reducing greenhouse gas emissions:

6.3.1 Promptly implement measures to curtail greenhouse gas emissions in all aspects of operations, including cutting back on electricity consumption. It is of utmost importance to expeditiously implement measures aimed at curtailing greenhouse gas emissions

in all facets of operations, including reducing electricity consumption. These can be achieved by promoting energy conservation, substituting electric bulbs with LED bulbs, minimizing solar exposure in office buildings, and other similar measures.

6.3.2 Designating a person to evaluate the organization's CF is advisable as part of a complete management strategy to decrease greenhouse gas emissions. Establishing clear and precise metrics for reducing greenhouse gas emissions is essential, enabling continual monitoring and evaluation of operations.

6.3.3 Employees are recommended to establish a collaborative partnership with organizations that specialize in CF assessment. This will equip your employees with the necessary knowledge and skills to evaluate the company's CF.

6.3.4 Inform staff members and service recipients regularly about policies aimed at cutting greenhouse gas emissions. To encourage participation in and awareness of the need to reduce greenhouse gas emissions.

6.3.5 Employees should cultivate a culture of innovation and excellence by encouraging employees to develop energy-saving and management technologies.

One practical approach is to organize an inventiocompetitionon, which provides a platform for employees tshowcasese their talent and creativity. Rewarding outstanding performers can further incentivize them to strive for excellence and contribute to the organization'energy-saving endeavors.

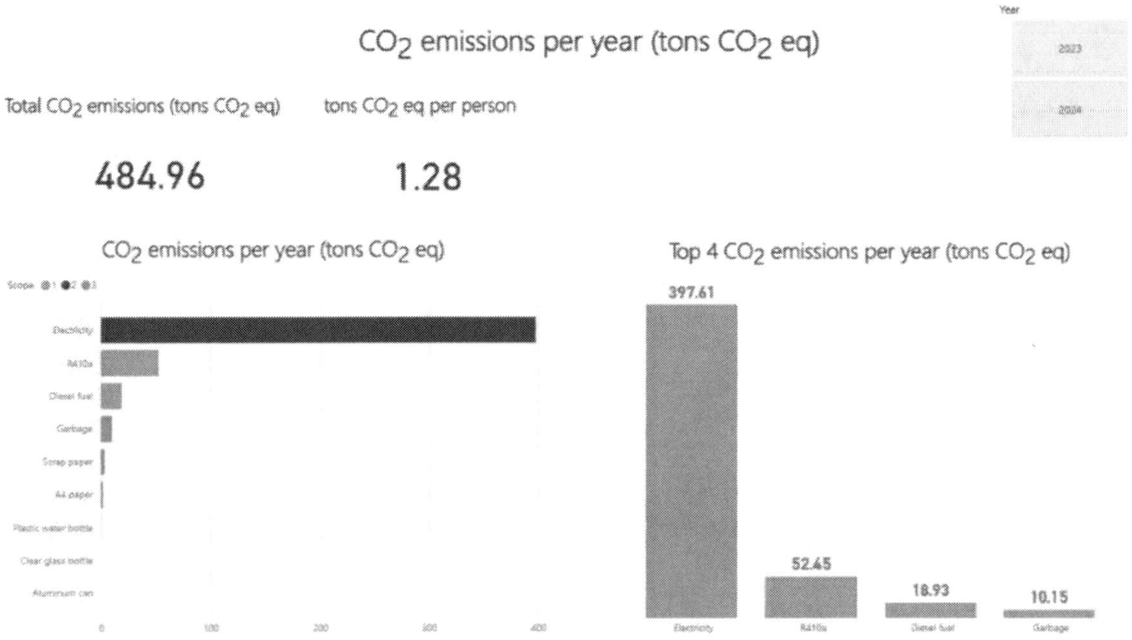

Fig. 2. CO_2 emissions per year (tons CO_2 eq).

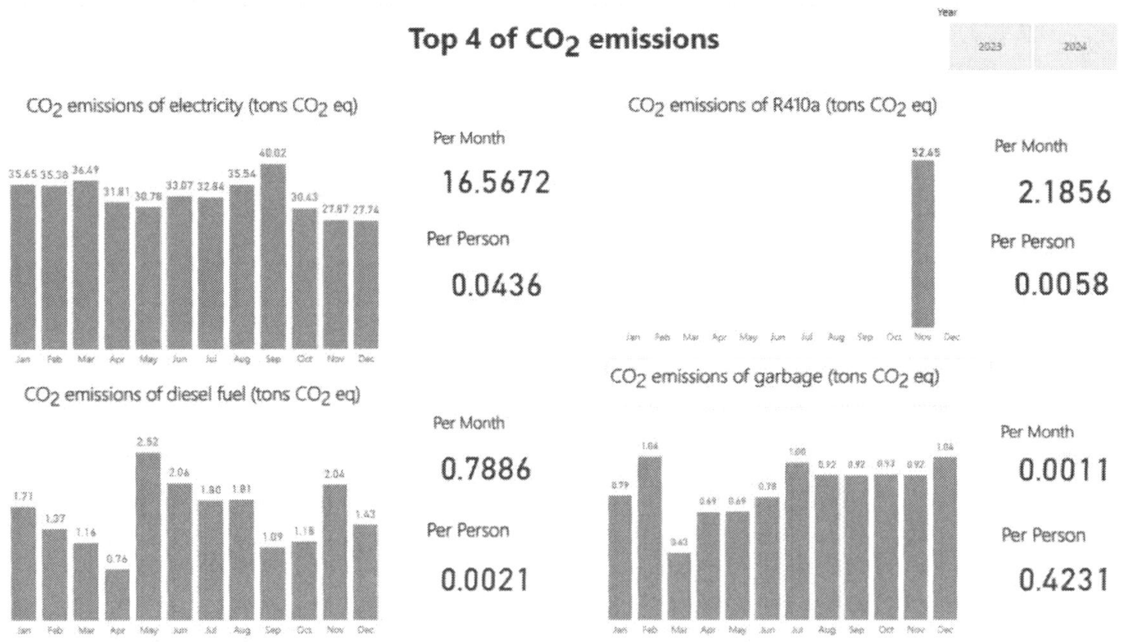

Fig. 3. Top 4 of CO_2 emissions.

7 Conclusion

Greenhouse gases, mainly carbon dioxide, are the principal causes of climate change. Climate change presents serious environmental risks. This study assessed the CF from an academic institution and offered methods for monitoring and decreasing CO_2 emissions by combining BI and management techniques. The Faculty of Science, Energy, and the Environment at King Mongkut's University of Technology North Bangkok (Rayong Campus) calculated a total carbon emissions value of 484.96 tons of CO_2 eq, or 1.28 tons CO_2 eq per person, for the 2023-2024 year. Carbon emissions were accounted in four major accounting categories, being electricity (81.99%), R410a refrigerant (10.82%), diesel (3.90%), and garbage (2.09%). Scope 2 emissions made up 397.62 tons of CO_2 eq. In this study, the main source is electricity. It was used for teaching in classrooms, air conditioning, lighting, and powering equipment in the laboratories. The greatest emissions occurred in months with high academic and laboratory activity. There is a primary necessity in the academic institution sector to control their CF in order to maintain compliance with regulations, meet stakeholder requirements, and remain socially responsible in the cataclysm of climate change. This study brought BI together with the PDCA cycle as a basis to monitor mitigation options to enhance informed decision-making and enable continuous improvement. The POCCC management framework was also utilized to demonstrate that BI-driven strategies can align with assessing management function to improve systems within the study organization. The use of this framework provides a concrete way to take action, communicate consistently, coordinate workflows and resources effectively, and provide oversight of the work plan, which will improve the reduction of emissions. By using BI tools and considering the PDCA and POCCC management function, academic institutions will be able to monitor emissions, target carbon hot spots, implement sustainable practices, and gain competitive and environmental benefits in the long run.

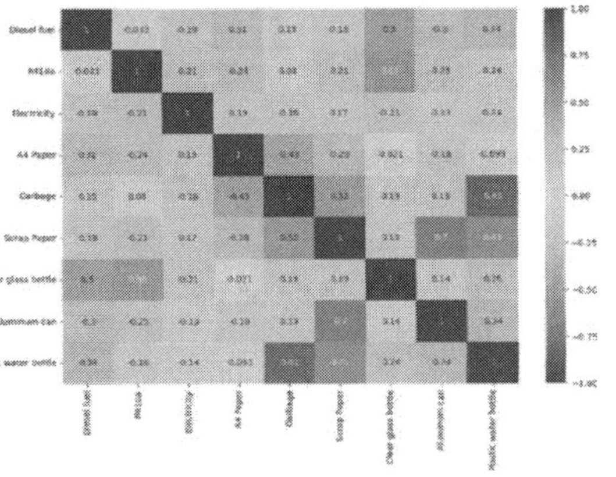

Fig. 4. Correlation matrix of emission sources.

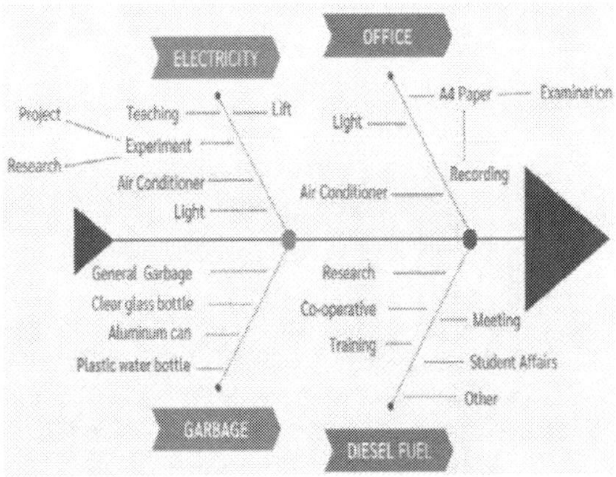

Fig. 5. The Causes of greenhouse gas emissions by fish bone diagram.

References

1. K. O . Yoro, M. O. Daramola, CO_2 emission sources, greenhouse gases, and the global warming effect. Adv. Carbon Capture. 3–28 (2020). https://doi.org/10.1016/B978-0-12-819657-1.00001-3
2. M. Audi, A. Ali, M. Kassem, Greenhouse gases: A review of losses and benefits. Int. J. Energy Econ. Policy. **10**, 403–418 (2019). https://doi.org/10.32479/ijeep.8416
3. Center for Sustainable Systems, Carbon footprint factsheet. University of Michigan (2018)
4. N. E. Selin, Carbon footprint. Encyclopedia Britannica (2024)
5. T. Bennich, N. Weitz, H. Carlsen, Deciphering the scientific literature on SDG interactions: A review and reading guide. Sci. Total Environ. **728**, 138405 (2020). https://doi.org/10.1016/j.scitotenv.2020.138405
6. P. Pradhan, L. Costa, D. Rybski, W. Lucht, J. P. Kropp, A systematic study of sustainable development goal (SDG) interactions. Earth's Future. **5**, 1169–1179 (2017). https://doi.org/10.1002/2017EF000632
7. F. Rosati, L. Faria, Addressing the SDGs in sustainability reports: The relationship with institutional factors. J. Cleaner Prod. **215**, 1312–1326 (2019). https://doi.org/10.1016/j.jclepro.2018.12.107
8. W. Zhao, Y. Zou, Green university initiatives in China: A case of Tsinghua University. Int. J. Sustain. Higher Educ. **16**, 491–506 (2015). https://doi.org/10.1108/IJSHE-02-2014-0021
9. M. M. Ulkhaq, P. Prayogo, M. Firmansyah, D. Agustina, Assessing campus sustainability: A report from Diponegoro University, Indonesia. Int. J. Inf. Educ. Technol. **6**, 616–621 (2016) https://doi.org/10.7763/IJIET.2016.V6.761

10. R. Castro, C. Jabbour, Evaluating sustainability of an Indian university. J. Cleaner Prod. **61**, 54–58 (2013). https://doi.org/10.1016/j.jclepro.2013.02.033
11. S. Syafrudin, B. Zaman, M.A. Budihardjo, S. Yumaroh, D.I. Gita, D.S. Lantip, Carbon footprint of academic activities: A case study in Diponegoro University. IOP Conf. Ser.: Earth Environ. Sci. **448**, 012008 (2020). https://doi.org/10.1088/1755-1315/448/1/012008
12. D. Larson, V. Chang, A review and future direction of agile, business intelligence, analytics and data science. Int. J. Inf. Manage. **36**, 700–710 (2016). https://doi.org/10.1016/j.ijinfomgt.2016.04.013
13. S. Adamala, L. Cidrin, Key success factors in business intelligence (2011)
14. Y. Niu, L. Ying, J. Yang, M. Bao, C. B. Sivaparthipan, Organizational business intelligence and decision making using big data analytics. Inf. Process. Manage. **58**, 102725 (2021). https://doi.org/10.1016/j.ipm.2021.102725
15. Ö. Işık, M.C. Jones, A. Sidorova, Business intelligence success: The roles of BI capabilities and decision environments. Inf. Manage. **50**, 13–23 (2013). https://doi.org/10.1016/j.im.2012.12.001
16. K. M. Bartol, D. C. Martin, Management (Irwin/McGraw-Hill, New York, 1999)
17. G. R. Gangadharan, S. N. Swami, Business intelligence systems: design and implementation strategies, in Proceedings of the 26th Int. Conf. Inf. Technol. Interfaces. June 7–10 (2004)
18. R. Sherman, Business intelligence guidebook (Morgan Kaufmann, Amsterdam, 2015)
19. M. Damert, J. Morris, E. Guenther, Carbon footprints of organizations and products. Responsible Consumption and Production, 59–72 (2020)
20. S. Erhart, K. Erhart, Environmental ranking of European industrial facilities by toxicity and global warming potentials. Sci. Rep. **13**, 1772 (2023)
21. P. J. Koiesar, What Deming told the Japanese in 1950. Qual. Manage. J. **2**, 9–24 (2018). https://doi.org/10.1080/10686967.1994.11918672

Exploration of plant-based leaf extracts as anti-corrosive concrete admixtures for extending the service life of reinforcement concrete infrastructures

Jivan Raj Dhungana[1], *Madhab* Gautam[1,2], *Dhruba Babu* Subedi[1], *Nootan Prasad* Bhattarai[1*], and *Jagadeesh* Bhattarai[1†]

[1]Central Department of Chemistry, Tribhuvan University, Kirtipur 44618, Kathmandu, Nepal.
[2]Department of Chemistry, Tribhuvan M. Campus, Tribhuvan University, Tansen 32500, Palpa, Nepal.

Abstract. This study intended to improve the service life of reinforcing mild steel (MS) within concrete beams (CBs) by incorporating leaf extracts from *Justicia adhatoda* L. (JAL) and *Persea americana* Mill. (PAL) as concrete admixtures in corrosive environmental conditions. The research involved monitoring the corrosion susceptibility levels of mild steel-reinforced concrete beams (MS-CBs) with varying concentrations of JAL and PAL extracts—specifically, 500, 1000, 2000, and 4000 ppm. Half-cell potential (HCP) and electrical resistivity (ER) data were collected for seven months or more, following ASTM standards, and were recorded at various time intervals to ensure accurate assessment. The outcomes indicated that the corrosion resistance of the MS in CBs significantly improved with 500-4000 ppm of these extracts as a concrete admixture, as compared with the corrosion level of the MS-CBs without extract (control). Phyto-screening analysis has identified key bioactive components, including alkaloids, flavonoids, and tannins. FTIR and UV-visible analysis results validate the conclusions drawn from the phyto-screening tests. Scanning electron microscopy (SEM) analysis provides pertinent surface information regarding the MS in CBs, yielding valuable insights into the chemical composition that may facilitate the development of novel anti-corrosive films for corroded MS, thereby mitigating early corrosion damage in MS-CBs and elucidating the corrosion inhibition mechanism. The study highlights the potential of plant-based inhibitors to enhance the durability of reinforced concrete, offering practical benefits for infrastructure longevity and guiding future research in sustainable construction materials.

1 Introduction

Concrete is one of the most widely used structural materials in modern engineering due to its excellent compressive strength; however, it exhibits relatively low tensile strength [1]. To address this limitation, reinforcement using steel rebar has become standard practice, leading to the development of reinforced concrete [2]. In its initial state, concrete has a high pH (above 12), which promotes the formation of a passive oxide layer on the reinforced metal surface, protecting it from corrosion [3]. However, the ingress of aggressive environmental pollutants through the concrete's pores can lower the pH below 10, dissolve or break down the passive layer, and hence initiate corrosion [4]. The results ultimately lost the structural integrity of the reinforcement concrete infrastructures [5].

Corrosion of reinforcement concrete is a progressive and unavoidable process. The interaction between environmental contaminants and MS surfaces, facilitated by the porous nature of concrete, is a key factor in MS-CBs corrosion [6]. It can mitigate but cannot be avoided completely. Many mitigation strategies include the use of coated rebars [7] and corrosion-inhibiting admixtures [8]. However, the coated reinforcement rebars did not provide total protection in reinforced concrete (RC). Their use does not effectively reduce the damage caused by chloride-induced corrosion when compared with uncoated bars embedded in concrete with similar characteristics [9].

Besides the use of coated rebars to control the early corrosion damage of MS in RC structures, synthetic organic and inorganic waterproofing chemicals effectively inhibit corrosion in reinforced concrete structures where safety is critical [10]. These waterproofing chemicals are commonly used in both commercial and residential projects to create impermeable concrete by reducing its porosity [11] and filling its pores and capillaries [12]. The ingress rate (Ri) of moisture or pollutants through concrete capillaries is proportional to the fourth power of the capillary radius (r), noted as $Ri \propto r^4$ [13]. It means even minor alterations in pore size can affect the rates at which corrosion-

* Corresponding author : neutan08@gmail.com
† Corresponding author : bhattarai_05@yahoo.com

https://doi.org/10.1051/e3sconf/202567901020

enhancing moisture penetrates and influence the permeability of pollutant gases.

The usage of cement-based WProf additives can help to reduce capillary diameter and slow down the degradation of concrete structures [14]. It is achieved through the formation of hydrated calcium silicate (C-S-H) gel when using waterproofing chemicals as concrete additives [15]. However, such waterproofing chemicals have exhibited toxic, carcinogenic, and environmentally harmful properties. Therefore, in recent decades, cost-effective and eco-friendly plant-based inhibitors have been crucial in mitigating the corrosion of metals and their alloys. Consequently, this work has prompted us to seek greener concrete admixtures.

There has been increasing interest in developing green corrosion inhibitors derived from components of natural plants found in Nepal to mitigate the corrosion of metals and their alloys including the mild steel. As a result, in response to the necessity for eco-friendly alternatives to synthetic waterproofing agents and the corrosion-prone inorganic and organic compounds affecting RC infrastructure, recent research has focused on the potential of green corrosion inhibitors derived from plant sources as concrete admixtures.

Nepal's flora offers significant opportunities to identify natural inhibitors that control concrete corrosion, integrating them into concrete formulations to enhance the durability of RC structures. In this context, a primary objective of this investigation is to develop an environmentally sustainable anti-corrosive concrete admixture derived from the leaves of two Nepali plants, *Justicia adhatoda* L. (JAL) and *Persea americana* Mill. (PAL), named as Asuroo (Malabar nut) and Avocado, respectively, in Nepali.

Both plant-based extracts are promising green alternatives for corrosion inhibition due to the formation of protective adsorption layers—either physically or chemically—on the surface of mild steel through interactions between their bioactive components and iron atoms. Avocado (*Persea americana* Mill.) has gained popularity because of its rich nutritional profile and potential health benefits [16]. Research has identified a wide range of secondary phytochemicals in avocado extracts, including carotenoids, flavonoids, alkaloids, terpenoids, and long-chain fatty alcohols [17]. Studies have also explored the use of avocado seed extract as an eco-friendly corrosion inhibitor for mild steel in 0.5 M sulfuric acid, employing both gravimetric and electrochemical methods [18]. Another study found that avocado leaf extract effectively acts as a green corrosion inhibitor in acidic solutions [19].

Similarly, *Justicia adhatoda* L., commonly known as Malabar nut in English, is a plant belonging to the Acanthaceae family. It contains various bioactive phytoconstituents, including alkaloids, phytosterols, polyphenols, and glycosides [20]. The effectiveness of the leaf extract from this plant as a corrosion inhibitor was evaluated on mild steel in aqueous neutral electrolyte using weight loss, corrosion potential, and potentiodynamic polarization methods [21].

To the best of the authors' knowledge, this study is the first to explore the use of *Justicia adhatoda* L. (JAL) and *Persea americana* Mill. (PAL) leaf extracts as corrosion-inhibiting concrete admixtures. The researchers investigate the anti-corrosive performance of these extracts under ambient conditions using the HCP and ER methods in compliance with ASTM standards [22]. Complementary surface analyses further support the findings. This work contributes to the development of eco-friendly, cost-effective, and sustainable corrosion inhibitors or concrete admixtures for use in reinforced concrete structures.

2 Materials and methods

Mature and healthy leaves of the *Persea americana* (Mill.) and *Justicia adhatoda* (L.) plants were collected from Tanglaphant in Kirtipur Municipality, Kathmandu, and Janaki Rural Municipality in the Durgauli area of Kailali district, respectively. The leaves were cleaned individually several times using distilled water and then air-dried, placing them in shaded areas for 25 days. An electric mill was used to grind the dried leaves of each plant into a fine powder for preparing individual plant extracts.

Roughly 400 g of pulverized leaf powder of each plant was weighed and mixed separately into seven 2000 mL conical flasks containing 800 mL of methanol. After being tightly sealed and thoroughly shaken, they were kept for 2 weeks or more with regular shaking. The mixtures were filtered using Whatman filter paper. Excess methanol in the filtrate was concentrated using a rotary evaporator (IKA RV 10 digital V, Germany) (as illustrated in Figure 1) to remove residual methanol from each extract, yielding semi-solid forms of the leaf extracts from *Persea americana* (PAL) and *Justicia adhatoda* (JAL), as described elsewhere [24].

Fig. 1. Steps for JAL and PAL preparation.

These extracts were subsequently transferred to a container to evaporate the remaining methanol, which acts as a concrete admixture or as an eco-friendly corrosion inhibitor. Both semi-solid extracts were stored separately in a freezer at 4°C or lower before being mixed with concrete aggregates.

A mold box measuring 36 cm × 9 cm × 9 cm was used for preparing the MS-CBs [Figure 2(d)]. Initially, sets of concrete mixtures were prepared using a ratio of 1:2:3 for cement, sand, and gravel [Figure 2(a)], with a water-to-cement ratio of 0.45 per ASTM C1582/C1582M-11 standard [22]. The required amounts of the plant extract dissolved in distilled water for preparing the concrete paste [Figure 2(c)]. The concrete paste, with or without the addition of plant extracts, was poured into the molds, embedding a 10 mm diameter mild steel rebar into each beam. The beams without any extracts served as the control MS-CB.

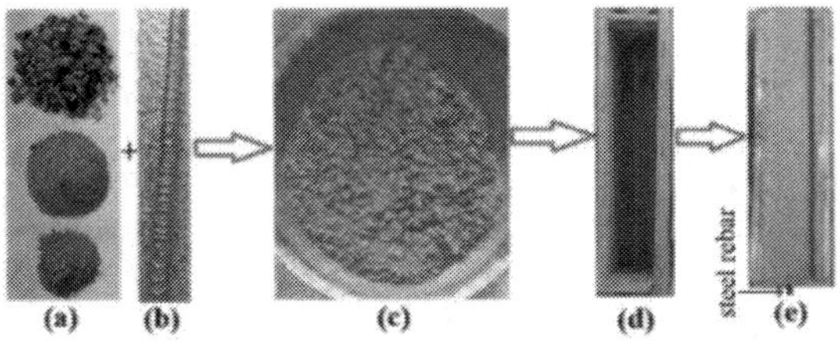

Fig. 2. Materials of MS-CB preparation [cement-sand-gravel (a), mechanically and chemically cleaned MS rod (b), concrete paste (c), MS rod fix in a casting box (d), and MS-CB (e)].

Before embedding, each mild steel rebar (MSR) was cleaned with silicon carbide sandpaper, treated in concentrated HCl and Na_2CO_3 solution, and then washed with distilled water. To record the half-cell potential (HCP), as demonstrated in previous research by Roka et al., 2 cm of the MS rebar was intentionally left exposed at one end of the MS-CB. The exposed end of the MS rebar (i.e., the 2 cm MS rebar left outside the reinforced concrete beam) functions as a working electrode to which the positive pole of the digital multimeter is connected, as demonstrated in Figure 2(e) as well as in Figure 3.

A total of eight sets of steel-reinforced concrete beams were produced using varying concentrations of JAL and PAL, ranging from 500 to 4000 parts per million (ppm) [Figures 3(a) and 3(b)]. Each MS-CB surface has marked four points just above the embedded MS to record the in-situ electrochemical properties of HCP and ER. The average of these four points of each MS-CB was calculated with standard error values (n=4).

After casting, all beams were cured at room temperature (25 ± 2°C) for one week. Following this period, the HCP and ER were recorded periodically over seven months. A digital multi-meter was employed for these measurements, utilizing a saturated calomel electrode (SCE) as the reference electrode (RE) and the exposed MS rebar as the working electrode (WE). For consistent measurement of HCP and ER, four equally spaced points labeled 1 through 4 were marked on the top of each MS-CB, as illustrated in Figures 3 (a) and 3(b).

The HCP and ER values were determined by connecting the negative terminal of the multi-meter to the reference SCE electrode and the positive terminal of the multi-meter to the exposed end of the MS rebar. To measure the HCP and ER, the SCE electrode was inserted in a moistened sponge and positioned directly above every four points of MS-CBs. The corrosion level can be inferred from the measured average values of HCP and ER, as outlined in Table 1 [24].

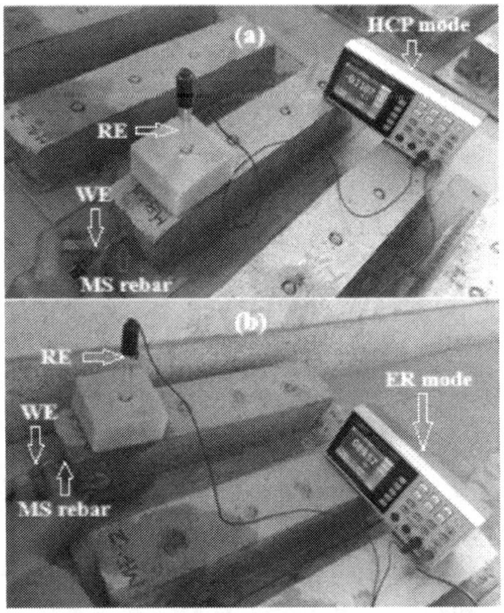

Fig. 3. Experimental set up for measurement of HCP (a) and ER (b).

Table 1. Correlation between HCP and ER values with corrosion risk level of MS-CBs [31].

HCP (mV vs SCE)	ER (kΩ.cm)	Corrosion risk level of MS-CBs
< -276	<10	High or more than 90 % corrosion risk (HiC)
−276 to −126	10 to 20	Mild or 10-90% of corrosion risk (MiC)
> −126	> 20	Low or less than 10 % of corrosion risk (LoC)

The JAL and PAL, utilized as concrete admixtures, were characterized using UV-Vis (SPECORD®200PLUS, Germany), FTIR (IR Affinity-1S, SCHIMADZU), GC-MS (Agilent 7890B Gas Chromatograph coupled with a 5977A Mass Selective Detector), and ultra-high-performance liquid chromatography (UHPLC) (XEVO G2-XS QTOF, Waters Corporation, USA) analysis to analyze the electronic properties of secondary metabolites (SeMBs), their functional groups, identify the number and confirm the presence of varieties of SeMBs in both plant extract. The surfaces of MS before and after reinforcement in CBs were analyzed using optical and scanning electron microscopic (Tabletop SEM-TM 4000, Hitachi).

The JAL and PAL, utilized as concrete admixtures, were characterized using UV-Vis (SPECORD®200PLUS, Germany), FTIR (IR Affinity-1S, SCHIMADZU), GC-MS (Agilent 7890B Gas Chromatograph coupled with a 5977A Mass Selective Detector), and ultra-high-performance liquid chromatography (UHPLC) (XEVO G2-XS QTOF, Waters Corporation, USA) analysis to analyze the electronic properties of secondary metabolites (SeMBs), their functional groups, identify the number and confirm the presence of varieties of SeMBs in both plant extract. The surfaces of MS rebar before and after reinforcement in CBs were analyzed using optical and scanning electron microscopic (Tabletop SEM-TM 4000, Hitachi).

3 Results and discussion

Based on the phytochemical screening test [21], the methanolic leaf extracts of *Justicia adhatoda* (JAL) and *Persea americana* (PAL) show positive tests for phenols, alkaloids, flavonoids, and terpenoids. In contrast, both plant extracts show negative tests for saponins and steroids (as shown in Table 2).

These phyto-compounds have shown prospective action, developing a corrosion-resistant passive film on the surface of MS rebar in CBs. The findings of the phyto-compound screening tests conducted in this study are consistent with previously reported data on the methanol extract prepared from the leaves of *Justicia adhatoda* [25] and *Persea americana* [26].

Table 2. Screening tests for constituents present in JAL and PAL.

Constituent	Test name/agent	JAL	PAL
Phenols	Lead acetate	+	+
Alkaloids	Dragendroff's test	+	+
Saponins	Foam	–	–
Flavonoids	Alkaline	+	+
Glycosides	Legal	–	+
Tannins	Ferric chloride	+	–
Terpenoids	Salkowski	+	+
Carbohydrates	Molisch Reagent	–	+

('+' refers to the presence and '-' refers to the absence)

The UV-Vis peaks of JAL and PAL were recorded between 200-800 nm wavelength due to the presence of secondary metabolites [27], as illustrated in Figures. 4(a) and 4(b), respectively. The JAL and PAL exhibited distinctive peaks at the range of 250-700 nm wavelength or ultraviolet/visible region and for the π-conjugation of single-double bonds in secondary metabolites or chlorophyll when subjected to UV-visible spectroscopy, which revealed the presence of alkaloids, flavonoids, terpenoids, and phenols, as reported in the literature [28]. Doublet peaks at 268 nm and 273 nm for JAL are due to the presence of -OH, $-OCH_3$, -CN, or -COOH groups attached to aromatic ring compounds [29], which are difficult to observe for PAL. Literature has noticed that the UV-Vis peak around 270-280 nm represents the presence of phenolic groups in guava leaf extract [30]. Furthermore, the UV-Vis bands at 288 nm and 332 nm demonstrated the existence of tannins and phenolic compounds, respectively, as in the literature [31].

Similarly, peaks observed around 330 nm and 380 nm are due to the presence of flavonoids in PAL and are difficult to observe for JAL. A peak at 405 nm is due to the presence of terpenoids, as reported elsewhere [29]. The peak around 663-665 nm is due to the presence of chlorophyll. The peak observed around 320-332 nm is due to the presence of flavonoids in the plant extracts. In the same way, any peaks that are not around 210-220 nm indicate the absence of saponins in both JAL and PAL extracts [32]. The depicted phyto-compounds contain σ-bonds, π-bonds, lone pairs of electrons, chromophores, and aromatic ring compounds, per existing literature [33].

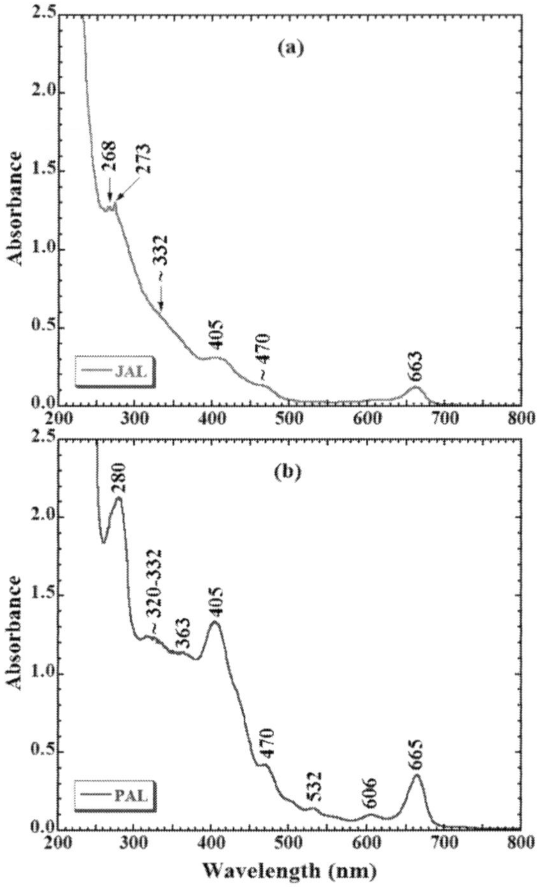

Fig. 4. UV-Vis Spectra analysis of JAL (a) and PAL (b).

FTIR analysis allows for the identification of functional groups present in plant extracts. Figures 5(a) and 5(b) display the FTIR spectra recorded for the JAL and PAL, respectively. The symmetric and broad absorption peak around 3340-3230 cm^{-1} corresponds to the O-H stretching of hydroxyl compounds [34]. These functional groups are characterized by specific peaks, at around 3200-3400 cm^{-1} for O–H stretching vibration in aromatic compounds [35], 1606-1617 cm^{-1} for aromatic C = C stretching [36], 1446 cm^{-1} for C–H stretching [37], 1201 cm^{-1} for –COOH group [38], 1038 cm^{-1} for O–H or C–H bending of aromatics [39], suggesting the presence of phenolic or alcoholic compounds [40]. Besides, Peaks around 2927 cm^{-1} represent asymmetric C-H stretching vibrations of both the JAL and PAL. These results are consistent with previous studies on the same plant extracts [41]. The presence of secondary or tertiary amino in the JAL is confirmed by two peaks around the 1100-1200 cm^{-1} range, indicating the C-N stretching vibration [42].

GC-MS analysis revealed the presence of 25 and 28 secondary metabolites (SecMs) in JAL and PAL extracts respectively, as demonstrated in Figure 6. It is meaningful to mention that the methanol leaf extract of this plant yielded only 13 phyto-compounds from GC-MS analysis [43]. GC-MS analysis data are imported into MZmine software in the form of mzML files to encourage the matching of m/z values and retention times with reference database libraries. This procedure is critical for the identification and quantification of compounds within complex samples.

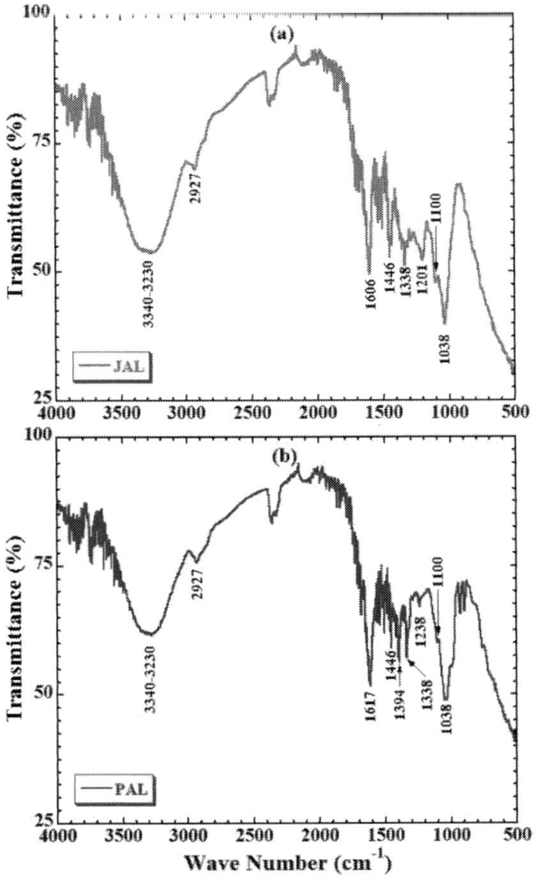

Fig. 5. FTIR Spectra analysis of JAL (a) and PAL (b).

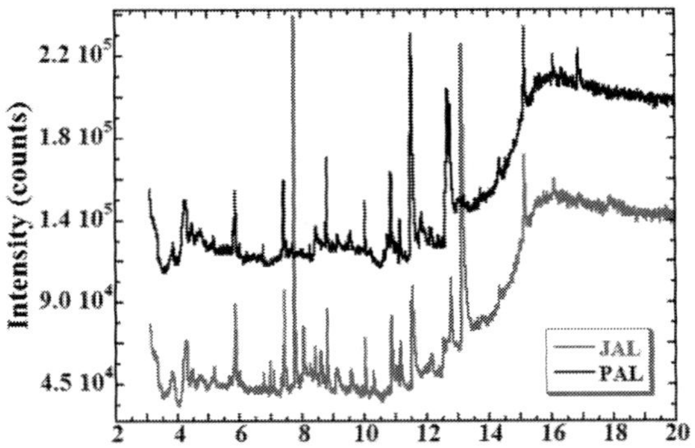

Fig. 6. GC spectra of JAL and PAL for qualitative phyto-compounds analysis.

It suggested that the presence of β-caryophyllene, 3-methylene-7, 11-dimethyl-1-dodecene, nonadecanoic acid methyl ester; 9, 12-octadecadienoic acid (Z, Z)-methyl ester, and 2-napthalene sulfonic acid are the main phyto-compounds in JAL extract, while DL-2-hydroxybutyric acid, penta-ethylene glycol dimethyl ether, 3-methylene-7, 11-dimethyl-1-dodecene, nonadecanoic acid methyl ester, 5-phenyl-3, 5, 7-triaza-tetracyclo, 2-napthalene sulfonic acid, *etc.* are in PAL extract. These qualitative consequences exhibited that both JAL and PAL have powerful anti-corrosive effects, contributing to the corrosion prevention of MS-CBs.

An ultra-high performance liquid chromatography (UHPLC) method, which is assumed to be more reliable than UV-Vis, FTIR, and GC-MS methods, was employed to detect the presence of various SeMBs in the methanolic extracts of JAL and PAL. Although the complete analysis and identification of all compounds by UHPLC analysis can be challenging when using crude extracts instead of isolated compounds [44], the most abundant compounds are expected in PAL and JAL, as summarized in Tables 3 and 4, respectively. Alkaloids, flavonoids, terpenoids, and phenolic compounds were in both extracts through the MassBank search page (https://massbank.eu/MassBank/Search), which provides access to a comprehensive database of mass spectral data.

Table 3. Major presumed phyto-compounds present in JAL.

Ret. Time (min.)	Molecular Formula and Molecular Weight (g/mol)	Phyto-compounds	Classification
4.94	$C_{15}H_{20}O_4$ (264)	Abiscisic acid	Terpenoid
6.77	$C_{40}H_{56}$ (537)	Beta-carotene	Terpenoid
14.26	$C_{21}H_{14}O_7$ (378)	Justicidin G	Lignan/Phenol
15.19	$C_{20}H_{24}N_2O_2$ (324)	Quinine	Alkaloid
15.36	$C_{25}H_{20}O_{10}$ (482.4)	Silychrystin	Flavonoid

Table 4. Major presumed phyto-compounds present in PAL.

Ret. Time (min.)	Molecular Formula & Molecular Weight (g/mol)	Phyto-compounds	Classification
5.26	$C_{15}H_{14}O_6$ (290.3)	Epicatechin	Flavonoid
7.70	$C_{21}H_{20}O_{11}$ (448.4)	Maritimein	Flavonoid
14.71	$C_{21}H_{24}O_6$ (372.4)	Arctigenin	Polyphenol
18.28	$C_{25}H_{22}O_{10}$ (482.4)	Silychristin	Flavonoid
18.83	$C_{33}H_{49}NO_8$ (587.7)	Pseudojervine	Alkaloid
20.03	$C_{25}H_{22}O_{10}$ (482.4)	Silybin B	Flavonoid

The presence of these alkaloids, flavonoids, terpenoids, and phenolic phyto-compounds, which are characterized by aromatic rings, heteroatoms, and conjugated systems, as indicated by UV-Vis, FTIR, and phytochemical profiling tests also. These secondary metabolites in JAL and PAL extracts are supposed to be the basis of the results of UHPLC analysis using mass bank matching. These metabolites included flavonoids, alkaloids, terpenoids, pyridine, and phenolic compounds, as illustrated by their molecular formula in Figures 7 and 8.

These aromatic rings, heteroatoms, and conjugated systems present in phyto-compounds improve both physical and chemical adsorption processes, as proposed in the literature [45]. This interaction helps to form a diffusion-barrier passive film between the corroded MS rebar and the concrete mix. These findings underline the perspective of JAL and PAL as anti-corrosive agents for preventing the corrosion of MS-CBs. Moreover, the secondary metabolites (SecMBs) found in both plant extracts offer insights into the adsorption mechanisms that create a protective passive film on the surfaces of corroded MS in CBs, as discussed in a succeeding section.

 https://doi.org/10.1051/e3sconf/202567901020

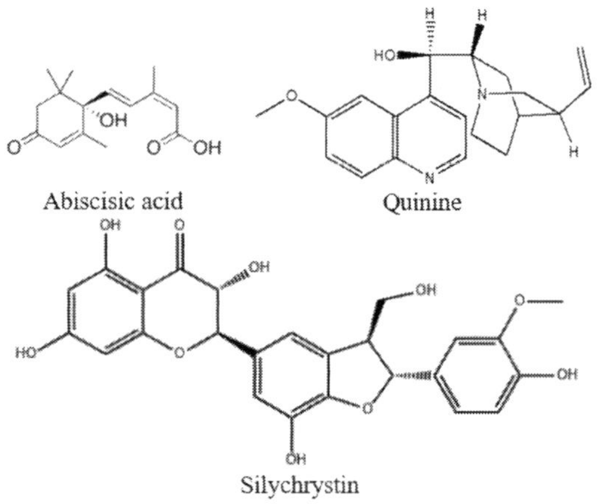

Fig. 7. Molecular structure of some phyto-compounds assumed to be present in JAL from UHPLC analysis.

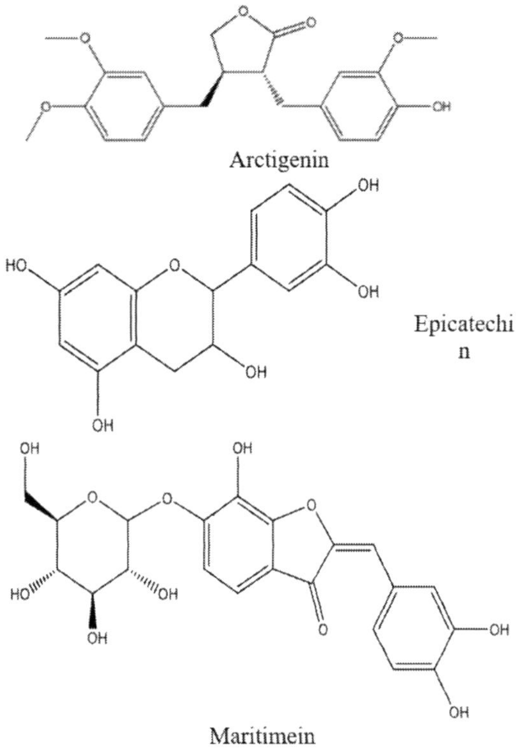

Fig. 8. Molecular structure of some phyto-compounds assumed to be present in PAL from UHPLC analysis.

The half-cell potential (HCP) values were measured at four different points on the surface of the MS-CB for 220 days to investigate the effect of 500-4000 ppm JAL and PAL. The trend of HCP changes of all four types of MS-CBs with 500 ppm, 1000 ppm, 2000 ppm, and 4000 ppm JAL and PAL are almost the same except in the case of control-MS in CB without extract, as illustrated in Figures 9(a) and 9(b), respectively. These findings suggest a positive impact of JAL and PAL on the corrosion-resistant properties of MS in CBs.

The results of the HCP measurements indicate that the potential value of the control-MSReC shifted to more negative values (i.e., at the MiC zone) with exposure times after 31 days, as illustrated in Figure 9. However, at the initial exposure time between 7 and 31 days, the CorP of the control-MS in CB shifted to less negative potential regions than -126 mV (SCE) with exposure times until about two months, suggesting the corrosion risk remains in LoC regions (with less than a 10% probability of corrosion risk) even the control-MS in CB according to the ASTM C876-22b standard [24].

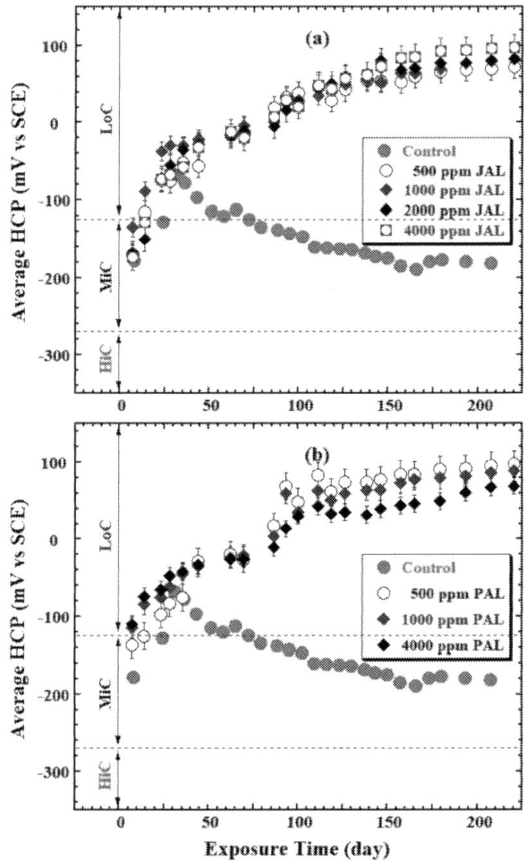

Fig. 9. Variation of average HCP of ReMS in ReC beams without and with 500-4000 ppm of (a) JAL and (b) PAL in ambient environment, as a function of exposure time.

In contrast, the concrete beams treated with 500-4000 ppm plant extracts showed HCP values in the MiC regions at the initial 3 to 4 weeks of exposure. These values likely indicate a preliminary stage of a protective thin film formation on the MS rebar in CBs with various concentrations of the plant extract. As a result, the probability of reinforced concrete corrosion located between 10% and 90% (MiC), with HCP values ranging from -276 mV to -126 mV (SCE). This phenomenon occurs during the early stages of the corrosion process, triggered by the penetration of moisture, oxygen, CO_2, and other harmful atmospheric agents into the MS-CBs.

Therefore, it is crucial to address this issue promptly to prevent further deterioration and ensure the long-term durability of the reinforced concrete structures. The HCP values shifted towards a more noble region or greater than -126 mV (SCE), indicating a low corrosion risk with less than 10% corrosion probability (LoC). This shift of HCP

 https://doi.org/10.1051/e3sconf/202567901020

from MiC to LoC region, attributing to the formation of a protective thin film over the MS rebar in concrete mix with different concentrations of JAL or PAL, as shown in Figures 9(a) and 9(b). The formation of such thin and diffusion barrier film protects the concrete beams efficiently from corrosion with the addition of JAL and PAL extract as concrete admixtures.

The determination of electrical resistivity (ER) values, based on the results obtained from HCP data, becomes a valuable supportive tool for assigning three corrosion levels of the MS-CBs corrosion, as per the ASTM C876-22b standard [21]. The recoded ER-values for the control MS-CB without plant extract over 220 days decreased during the measurement period due to the penetration of aggressive or corrosive ions of molecules like Cl^-, SO^{2-}_4, H_2O, and O_2 through the pollutant atmosphere, and thus are responsible for the higher conductivity in the embedded MS surface as there was no formation of thin film in the absence of plant extract. Therefore, in turn, this resulted in increased conductivity on the surface of the embedded MS, as illustrated in Figure 10.

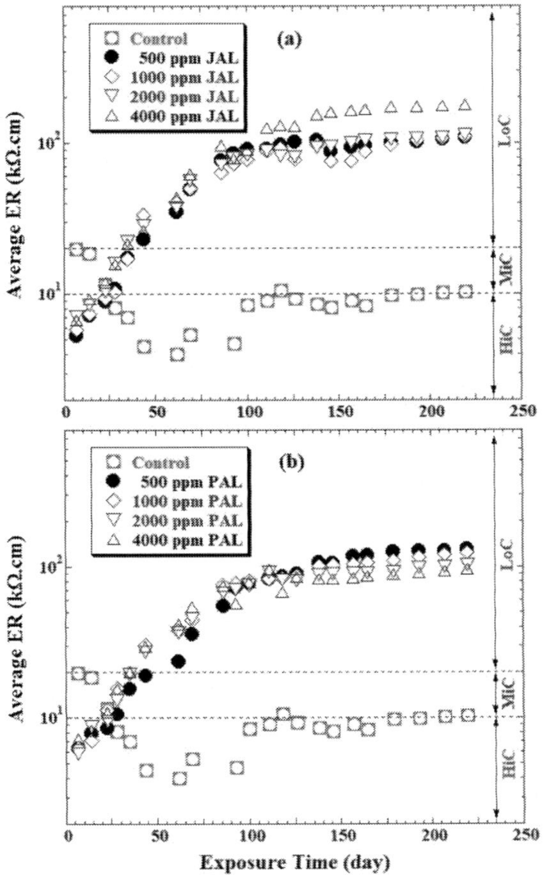

Fig. 10. Variation of average electrical resistivity (ER) of reinforcing MS in different CBs without and with 500-4000 ppm of (a) JALE & (b) PALE in ambient environment, as a function of exposure time.

The lack of a thin film formation on the surface of MS rebar in the absence of plant extract facilitated the ease with which the pollutant gases, molecules, or ions could penetrate the concrete surface. Conversely, the other eight CBs, each reinforced with different concentrations of individual plant extracts (500-4000 ppm of JAL or PAL), demonstrated a consistent increase in resistivity value up to 220 days, as shown in Figure 10, attributing to the reduced possibility of aggressive ions ingress to the embedded MS rebar surface. It is noteworthy that these findings have practical significance since they can enhance the durability and longevity of reinforced concrete structures.

Moreover, these results of the present work are compatible with the previous study, which reported the efficacy of the leaf extracts of *Ziziphus budhensis* and *Tagetes erecta* L. [22] and *Sesamum indicum* L. [46], as eco-friendly corrosion inhibitors in a saturated $Ca(OH)_2$ solution with a pH 12 ± 0.5, considered as SCPS (simulated concrete pore solution), and mango fruit extract in SCPS [54], which mimics the environment of CB. The weight loss and electrochemical polarization assessed the ability of these plant-based extracts to inhibit steel corrosion, and the highest corrosion-inhibition efficiency was reported to be 80%-95%. These extracts contain secondary phyto-molecules that adhere to the metal surface in SCPS.

An analysis of the MS-CBs containing varying amounts of JAL and PAL extracts indicates a low corrosion risk of MS rebar in CB. This outcome was attributed to the formation of a protective thin film over the surface of the embedded rebar. Consistent with this finding, HCP measurements also indicated a reduced likelihood of corrosion. These observations suggest that the use of plant extract in MS-CBs could be a promising approach to mitigating reinforcement corrosion in concrete structures.

Further investigation of the morphological changes on the MS rebar surface after being embedded for seven months in the concrete beams, without (control) and with 2000 ppm JAL or PAL, was explored using SEM analysis. The SEM images of the MS surface in the control MS-CB without plant extract show patches of rust and pits over large areas of the sample, as illustrated in Figure 11. This surface of MS rebar indicates the corrosion of the rebar embedded in the control beam.

However, surface flaws related to rust are not visible in the SEM images of the MS in CB when mixed with 2000 ppm of JAL or PAL inhibitors, as shown in Figures 12(a) and 12(b), respectively. Smooth and uninterrupted corrosion-protective layers form on the MS surface by eliminating active corrosion sites through the adsorption mechanisms of the phyto-molecules present in these plant extracts, as outlined in previous studies [45].

The SEM images indicate that corrosion-related surface imperfections have been removed or minimized on the inhibited surface, highlighting the increased effectiveness of the two plant extracts in providing corrosion protection. As a result, incorporating 2000 ppm of JAL and PAL extract into the concrete mix reduces the likelihood of SR corrosion damage from the microbiologically influenced corrosion (MiC) zone to a passive state (i.e., LoC). According to the literature [48], the phyto-molecules of the plant extract acts as efficacious adsorbents, promoting the reduction of active corrosion sites on the surface of MS rebar.

Fig. 11: SEM images of the MS rebar surface after embedded for 7 months in control CB without extract.

(a) 2000 ppm JAL

(b) 2000 ppm PAL

Fig. 12. SEM images of the MS rebar surface after embedded for seven months in CBs with 2000 ppm of (a) JAL, and (b) PAL.

The SEM images of the MS embedded in CB with phyto-compounds furnish compelling evidence that surface flaws associated with corrosion have been successfully eliminated on the inhibited surface, thereby demonstrating the improved inhibition effectiveness of the JAL and PAL in MS-CB corrosion. Consequently, the probability of MS corrosion damage has shifted from MiC to LoC region with the addition of 500-4000 ppm JAL/PAL into the MS-CBs.

The findings from the SEM analysis align with the results related to HCP and ER measurement methods, as discussed previously. A superior inhibition potential of these two plant-based extracts furnishes evidence to sustain the electrochemical (i.e., HCP and ER) results from the SEM analysis, indicating the inhibition of corrosion-induced surface flaws. Therefore, the probability of ReC corrosion damage transitioning from the MiC zone to a passive state LoC area with 500-4000 ppm JAL or PAL additions in the concrete mix.

A pictorial articulation ascribes the corrosion-inhibiting mechanism of MS in CB without (control) and with 2000 ppm PAL in an ambient environment, as illustrated in Figure 13. This graphic is leveled in findings derived from a wide array of experimental methodologies, including screening tests, UV-Vis, FTIR, GC-MS, UHPLC, HCP, ER, and SEM analyses.

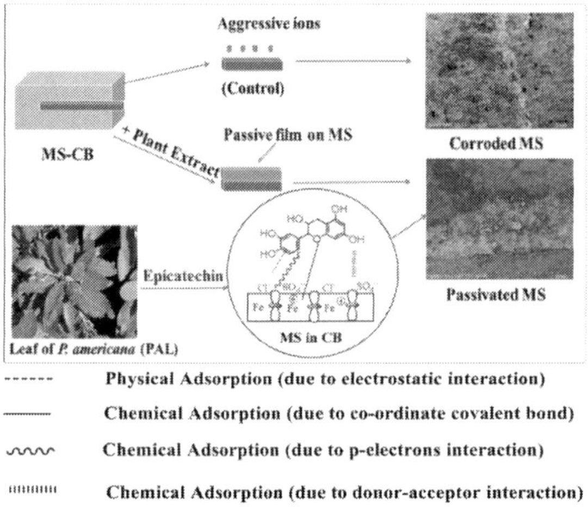

Fig. 13. Schematic graph showing corrosion inhibiting mechanism of MS-CBs.

The corrosion-inhibiting mechanism of the MS-CBs, along with associated adsorption phenomena, results from the displacement of aggressive ions and molecules from the surface of the MS rebar. Such interactions are possible by electron transfer between the electronegative elements—oxygen, nitrogen, and sulfur in the PAL extract and the iron substrate. Such interactions, which may involve either chemical or physical adsorption or a combination thereof, contribute significantly to the enhanced protection of the MS rebar from corrosion induced by the reinforced concrete beam (Fig. 13), as illustrated the following four processes.

* Phyto-molecule (PM) protonate in concrete to form positively charged ions, which adsorb to the MS by physical adsorption or electrostatic interactions with negatively charged ions (Cl^-, SO_4^{2-}) in the concrete matrix, until they thoroughly shield the reactive anions, enhancing the corrosion-inhibition [22].
* Chemical adsorption (CA) occurs through the formation of coordination bonds between the lone-

pair electrons of O or N in PM and the vacant d-orbitals of Fe on the rebar surface [49], helping to prevent corrosion by blocking aggressive ions.

* CA promoted by π-electron interactions between an aromatic ring of PM and the vacant d-orbitals of Fe on the rebar, to assemble a passive film with high resilience to enhance the corrosion-inhibition [45].
* CA due to retro-donation or vice versa between d-electrons of Fe and empty antibonding molecular orbitals of PM constituents [43].

4 Conclusions

An anti-corrosive effect of plant-based extracts as concrete admixtures was explored with *in situ* electrochemical analysis with periodic monitoring of HCP and ER values of reinforced rebar in concrete beam (CB). Based on the findings of this study, it was concluded that the leaf extracts of *Justicia adhatoda* (JAL) and *Persea americana* (PAL) exhibit significant potential as green, eco-friendly corrosion inhibitors for steel-reinforced concrete. Phytochemical screening along with UV-visible, FTIR, and UHPLC analyses, confirmed the presence of key bioactive compounds such as phenols, alkaloids, flavonoids, tannins, and glycosides in both extracts.

Shifting of HCP and ER values of reinforced-SR from the zone of MiC or HiC (about 90% or more probability of corrosion) to LoC (Less than 10% probability of corrosion) when plant extracts are admixed to ReC. When added to concrete in concentrations ranging from 500 to 4000 ppm, these extracts notably enhanced the corrosion resistance of reinforcing steel bars, with effectiveness observed even at the lowest concentration. Surface analysis of SR in different conditions is in agreement with the prediction made by qualitative *in situ* electrochemical analysis.

These results consistently indicate that JAL and PAL are promising candidates for the development of sustainable anti-corrosive concrete additives, with the potential to extend the service life of reinforced concrete infrastructure and reduce corrosion-related deterioration. Besides, these plant-derived phyto-constituted extracts, as we believe, have diverse applications, including reinforced concrete additives, functioning as anticorrosion agents. It should not be limited only to academic research but also to industrial applications.

The authors acknowledge Dr. M.A. Fickenscher and Mr. N.K. Pandey from the University of Cincinnati, USA, for their contributions to SEM/EDS and GC-MS analysis, respectively. Additionally, they thank the University of Lucknow, India, particularly Dr. Anant Ram Rathor and Mr. Gulab Singh, for providing essential analytical facilities for UHPLC-MS.

References

1. J-Q. Wu, Z. Lu, Y-T. Chen, B. Ghiassi, W. Shi, B. Li, Mechanical properties and cracking behavior of lightweight engineered geopolymer composites with fly ash cenospheres. *Constr. Build. Mater.* **400**, 132622 (2023). https://doi.org/10.1016/j.conbuildmat.2023.132622
2. S. Ashraf, M. Rucka, Comparative study on fracture evolution in steel fiber and bar reinforced concrete beams using acoustic emission and digital image correlation techniques. *Case Stud. Constr. Mater.* **20**, e03359 (2024). https://doi.org/10.1016/j.cscm.2024.e03359
3. R. R. Hussain, Passive layer development and corrosion of steel in concrete at the nano-scale. *J. Civ. Environ. Eng.* **04**, e116 (2014). https://doi.org/10.4172/2165-784X.1000e116
4. K. N. Hoque, F. Presuel-Moreno, Long-term corrosion behavior of reinforced concrete: impact of supplementary cementitious materials and reservoir size under accelerated chloride ingress. *Const. Mater.* **5**, 33 (2025). https://doi.org/10.3390/constrmater5020033
5. A. Hameed, M. F. Afzal, A. Javed, A. M. Rasool, M. Qureshi, A. Mehrabi, I. Ashraf, Behavior and performance of reinforced concrete columns subjected to accelerated corrosion. *Metals.* **13**, 930 (2023). http://dx.doi.org/10.3390/met13050930
6. S. Akduman, H. Öztürk, Effect of reinforcement corrosion on structural behavior in reinforced concrete structures according to initiation and propagation periods. *Buildings*, **14**(12), 4026 (2024). http://dx.doi.org/10.3390/buildings14124026
7. M. S. H. S. Mohammed, R. S. Raghavan, G. M. S. Knight, V. Murugesan, Macrocell corrosion studies of coated rebars. *Arab. J. Sci. Eng.*, **39**, 3535–3543 (2014). https://doi.org/10.1007/s13369-014-1006-x
8. S. A. Civjan, J. M. Lafave, J. Trybulski, D. Lovett, J. Lima, D. W. Pfeifer, Effectiveness of corrosion inhibiting admixture combinations in structural concrete. *Cem. Concr. Compos.* **27**, 688–703 (2005). https://doi.org/10.1016/j.cemconcomp.2004.07.00
9. H. Qian, J. Mao, S. Ye, Z. Xu, S. Chen, Y. Liu, D. Yan, Coated rebars for reinforced concrete structures: A review. *J. Build. Eng.* **109**, 113000 (2025). https://doi.org/10.1016/j.jobe.2025.113000
10. R. Drochytka, M. Ledl, J. Bydzovsky, N. Zizkova, J.J. Bester, Use of secondary crystallization and fly ash in waterproofing materials to increase concrete resistance to aggressive gases and liquids. *Adv. Civ. Eng.* **2019**, 7530325 (2019). https://doi.org/10.1155/2019/7530325
11. J. Li, S. Li, M. A. Haque, B. Chen, Water-resistance performance analysis of Portland composite concrete containing waterproofing liquid membrane. *J. Build. Eng.* **76**, 106889 (2023). https://doi.org/10.1016/j.jobe.2023.106889
12. F. Wang, T. Xie, J. Ou, M. Xue, W. Li, Cement based superhydrophobic coating with excellent robustness and solar reflective ability. *J. Alloys Compd.* **823**, 153702 (2020). https://doi.org/10.1016/j.jallcom.2020.153702
13. R. Kumar, B. Bhattacharjee, Porosity, pore size distribution, and in situ strength of concrete. *Cem.*

Con. Res. **33**, 155–164 (2003). https://doi.org/10.1016/S0008-8846(02)00942-0

14. V. G. Cappellesso, N. S. Petry, D. C. C. D. Molin, A. B. Masuero, Use of crystalline waterproofing to reduce capillary porosity in concrete. *J. Build. Pathol. Rehabil.* **1**, 9 (2016). https://doi.org/10.1007/s41024-016-0012-7
15. S. C. Gnanaraj, R. B. Chokkalingam, G. L. Thankam, Effects of admixtures on the self-compacting concrete state of the art report. *IOP Conf. Ser.: Mater. Sci. Eng.* **1006**, 012038 (2020). https://doi.org/10.1088/1757-899X/1006/1/012038
16. M. R. Louis, L. Rani, V. Pushpa, K. Balakrishna, P. Ganesan, Mosquito larvicidal activity of avocado (*Persea americana* Mill.) unripe fruit peel methanolic extract against *Aedes aegypti*, *Culex quinquefasciatus* and *Anopheles stephensi*. *South Afr. J. Bot.* **133**, 1–4 (2020). http://dx.doi.org/10.1016/j.sajb.2020.06.020
17. D. J. Bhuyan, M. A. Alsherbiny, S. Perera, M. Low, A. Basu, O. A. Devi, M. S. Barooah, C. G. Li, K. Papoutsis, The odyssey of bioactive compounds in avocado (*Persea americana*) and their health benefits. *Antioxidants (Basel, Switzerland).* **8**, 426 (2019). https://doi.org/10.3390/antiox8100426
18. A. C. Ehiemere, R. O. Anyanwu, P. Emele, U. G. Nwokeke, Anti-corrosion potentials of fresh extracts of old *Persea americana* var. *Americana* seed in 0.5 m H_2SO_4 on mild steel. *Chem. Mater. Res.* **13**, 60–71 (2021). http://dx.doi.org/10.7176/CMR/13-2-03
19. K. Muazu, M. M. Aliyu, A. T. Mohammed, S. Lasisi, R. Dahiru, I.Y. Suleiman, Ethanol extract of *Avocado* leaf as corrosion inhibitor for the protection of mild steel in acidic environment. *J. Mater. Environ. Sci.* **13**, 1343–1354 (2022). http://dx.doi.org/10.6084/m9.figshare.21699587
20. Isha, P. Kumar, A. N. Singh, An overview of *Justicia adhatoda*: A medicinal plant but native invader in India. *Conservation.* **5**, 2 (2025). https://doi.org/10.3390/conservation5010002
21. K. S. Beenakumari, *Justicia adhatoda* (Vasaka) leaf extracts as eco-friendly corrosion inhibitor for mild steel in potable water. *Orient. J. Chem.* **29**, 369–373 (2013). http://dx.doi.org/10.13005/ojc/290159
22. ASTM C1582/C1582M-11, *Standard Specification for Admixtures to Inhibit Chloride Induced Corrosion of Reinforcing Steel in Concrete.* In Annual book of ASTM standards, ASTM International, West Conshohocken, USA (2017) 10 https://doi.org/10.1520/C1582_C1582M-11R17E01
23. M. Gautam, N. P. Bhattarai, J. Bhattarai, Leaf-based extracts of Nepal origin plants as efficient inhibitors for controlling rebar corrosion in concrete pore solution. *Int. J. Corros. Scale Inhib.* **13**, 2087–2111 (2024). http://dx.doi.org/10.17675/2305-6894-2024-13-4-10
24. ASTM C876-22b, *Standard Test Method for Corrosion Potentials of Uncoated Reinforcing Steel in Concrete.* In: Annual book of ASTM standards, ASTM International, West Conshohocken, USA (2022). https://doi.org/10.1520/C0876-22B
25. A. Basit, T. Shutian, A. Khan, S. M. Khan, R. Shahzad, A. Khan, M. Khan, Anti-inflammatory and analgesic potential of leaf extract of *Justicia adhatoda* L. (Acanthaceae) in carrageenan and formalin-induced models by targeting oxidative stress. *Biomed. Pharmacother.* **153**, 113322 (2022). https://doi.org/10.1016/j.biopha.2022.113322
26. A. Thoume, I. N. Irahal, N. Benzbiria, D. B. Left, R. Achagar, A. Elmakssoudi, A. El foulani, M. Dakir, M. Azzi, N. Bourhim, M. Zertoubi, In vitro and in silico antibacterial and anti-corrosive properties of Persea americana leaves extract as an environmentally friendly corrosion inhibitor for carbon steel in a hydrochloric acid medium. *Colloids Surf. A: Physicochem. Eng. Aspects.* **674**, 131848 (2023). https://doi.org/10.1016/j.colsurfa.2023.131848
27. R. Paji, A. Samrot, B. R. Fernando, P. Kumar, R. Geetika, V. Sharma, K. Dhanabal, Extraction, characterization and *in vitro* bioactivity evaluation of alkaloids, flavonoids, saponins and tannins of *Cassia alata, Thespesia populnea, Euphorbia hirta* and *Wrightia tinctoria*. *Rasayan J. Chem.* **12**, 123–137 (2019). http://dx.doi.org/10.31788/RJC.2019.1214054
28. L. Akinpelu, O. Idowu, G. Ogundepo, A. Adegoke, G. Olayiwola, T. Idowu, Spectroscopic analysis and anti-inflammatory effects of *Milicia excelsa* (Moraceae) leaf and fractions. *GSC Biol. Pharm. Sci.* **6**, 51–60 (2019). http://dx.doi.org/10.30574/gscbps.2019.6.3.0035
29. A. Williams, D. Flemming, *Spectroscopic Methods in Organic Chemistry*, (Springer, 2019) 55–81. https://doi.org/10.1007/978-3-030-18252-6
30. P. Somchaidee, K. Tedsree, Green synthesis of high dispersion and narrow size distribution of zero-valent iron nanoparticles using guava leaf (*Psidium guajava* L) extract. *Adv. Nat. Sci.: Nanosci. Nanotechnol.* **9**, 035006 (2018). https://doi.org/10.1088/2043-6254/aad5d7
31. A. Barbasz, M. Oćwieja, J. Barbasz, Cytotoxic activity of highly purified silver nanoparticles sol against cells of human immune system. *Appl. Biochem. Biotechnol.* **176**, 817-834 (2015). https://doi.org/10.1007/s12010-015-1613-3
32. C. Yuan, Y. Li, Q. Li, R. Jin, L. Ren, Purification of tea saponins and evaluation of its effect on alcohol dehydrogenase activity. *Open Life Sci.* **13**, 56–63 (2018). https://doi.org/10.1515/biol-2018-0008
33. D. I. Njoku, M. A. Chidiebere, K. L. Oguzie, C. E. Ogukwe, E.E. Oguzie, Corrosion inhibition of mild steel in hydrochloric acid solution by the leaf extract of *Nicotiana tabacum*. *Adv. Mater. Corros.* **1**, 54–61 (2013). https://api.semanticscholar.org/CorpusID:92074940
34. J. Coates, Interpretation of infrared spectra, a practical approach, in R. A. Meyers (Ed.),

Encyclopedia of Analytical Chemistry (1st ed.), Wiley (2000).

35. A. Sulistiawan, W. Setyaningsih, A. Rohman, A new FTIR method combined with multivariate data analysis for determining aflatoxins in peanuts (*Arachis hypogaea*). *J. Appl. Pharm. Sci.* **12**, 199–206 (2022). https://doi.org/10.7324/JAPS.2022.120720
36. P. P. Yue, Y. J. Hu, G. Q. Fu, C. X. Sun, M. F. Li, F. Peng, R. C. Sun, Structural differences between the lignin-carbohydrate complexes (LCCs) from 2- and 24-months old bamboo (*Neosinocalamus affinis*). *Int. J. Mol. Sci.* **19**, 1 (2018). https://doi.org/10.3390/ijms19010001
37. J. M. Barcelo, A. M. Gatchallan, I. J. B. Aquino, D. R. E. Ollero, F. L. D. Cortez, T. M. Costales, L. A. Q. Marzo, FTIR spectrum and anti-mutagenicity of *Coffea arabica* pulp and *Arachis hypogaea* test in relation to their *in vitro* antioxidant properties. *Asia Pac. J. Multidiscip. Res.* **3**, 99–108 (2015)
38. M. Maczka, A. Ciupa, A. Gągor, A. Sieradzki, A. Pikul, B. Macalik, M. Drozd, Perovskite metal formate framework of [NH_2-CH^+-NH_2] Mn $(HCOO)_3$]: phase transition, magnetic, dielectric, and phonon properties. *Inorg. Chem.* **53**, 5260–5268 (2014). https://doi.org/10.1021/ic500479e
39. K. K. Veedu, T. P. Kalarikkal, N. Jayakumar, N. K. Gopalan, Anticorrosive performance of *Mangifera indica* L. leaf extract-based hybrid coating on steel. *ACS Omega*. **4**, 10176–10184 (2019)
40. V. M. Oliveira, R. C. A. Neri, F. T. D. Monte, N. A. Roberto, H. M. S. Costa, C. R. D. Assis, A. L. F. Porto, Crosslink-free collagen from *Cichla ocellaris*: structural characterization by FTIR spectroscopy and densitometric evaluation. *J. Mole. Struct.* **1176**, 751–758 (2019). https://doi.org/10.1016/j.molstruc.2018.09.023
41. B. Kumar, L. Cumbal, UV-Vis, FTIR and antioxidant study of *Persea americana* (avocado) leaf and fruit: a comparison. *Rev. Fac. Cien. Quím.* **14**, 13–20 (2016)
42. M. Bedair, L.W. Sumner, Current and emerging mass-spectrometry technologies for metabolomics. *Trends Anal. Chem.* **27**, 238–250 (2008). https://doi.org/10.1016/j.trac.2008.01.006
43. G. Jayapriya, F. Gricilda Shoba, GC-MS analysis of bioactive compounds in methanolic leaf extracts of Justicia adhatoda (Linn.). *J. Pharmacog. Phytochem.* **4**, 113–117 (2015)
44. I. M. Abu-Reidah, M. S. Ali-Shtayeh, R. M. Jamous, D. Arráez-Román, A. Segura-Carretero, Comprehensive metabolite profiling of *Arum palaestinum* (Araceae) leaves by using liquid chromatography–tandem mass spectrometry. *Food Res. Int.* **70**, 74–86 (2015). http://dx.doi.org/10.1016/j.foodres.2015.01.023
45. M. Gautam, D. B. Subedi, J. R. Dhungana, M. Dhakal, K. P. Bohara, N. P. Bhattarai, J. Bhattarai, A sustainable approach for mitigating rebar corrosion in adverse conditions using *Phyllanthus emblica* (L.) leaf extract as concrete scale inhibitor. *Int. J. Corros. Scale Inhib.* **14**, 1522–1554 (2025). https://doi.org/10.17675/2305-6894-2025-14-3-26
46. M. Gautam, N. P. Bhattarai, J. Bhattarai, *Sisamum indicum* leaf extract as environmentally benign inhibitor to mitigate mild steel corrosion in cement pore solution. *J. Inst. Sci. Technol.* **30**, 101–113 (2025). https://doi.org/10.3126/jist.v30i1.74723
47. M. H. Rahmani, A. Dehghani, M. Salamati, G. Bahlakeh, B. Ramezanzadeh, Mango extract behavior as a potent corrosion inhibitor against simulated chloride-contaminated concrete pore solution; coupled experimental and computer modeling studies. *J. Indus. Eng. Chem.* **130**, 368–381 (2024). https://doi.org/10.1016/j.jiec.2023.09.040
48. L. Casanova, F. Ceriani, E. Messinese, L. Paterlini, S. Beretta, F.M. Bolzoni, M. Pedeferri, Recent advances in the use of green corrosion inhibitors to prevent chloride-induced corrosion in reinforced concrete. *Materials* (Basel, Switzerland). **16**, 7462 (2023). https://doi.org/10.3390/ma16237462
49. C. Verma, A. R. Pathania, I. Barsoum, K. Y. Rhee, Y. Qiang, A. Alfantazi, Coordination chemistry in corrosion science and engineering: Role of coordination bonding and coordination materials. *Coord. Chem. Rev.* **549**, 217258 (2026). https://doi.org/10.1016/j.ccr.2025.217258

Carbon Footprint Evaluation of Polylactic Acid Production via Process Simulation

Pichan Tantichaipakorn[1], *Peerada* Yodkaew[1], *Kewalin* Preesong[1], *Aleena* Ketiam[1], and *Prakorn* Kittipoomwong[1,*]
[1]Chemical Engineering Department, King Mongkut's University of Technology North Bangkok, 10800 Bangkok, Thailand

Abstract. This study examines the design process for producing Polylactic Acid (PLA) by optimizing its production using Aspen Plus®. The objective is to enhance the quality and purity of lactide by adjusting various parameters, such as temperature. The research findings have been verified against reported data, revealing that the quantities of essential substances measured at each production stage closely match those reported in existing literatures. A sensitivity analysis reveals that lowering reactor temperatures can reduce energy consumption in both the condenser and reboiler while maintaining the quality of PLA, leading to improved cost efficiency. Additionally, the study evaluates the carbon dioxide emissions resulting from PLA synthesis, which total approximately 656 kg of CO_2 per ton of PLA. Most emissions occur during the oligomerization phase. Therefore, reducing the operational temperature during this phase to 170°C can significantly decrease the carbon footprint of PLA production. This approach helps identify an optimal operational point that maximizes energy savings.

1 Introduction

Plastic waste is one of the pressing world issues since it has become an indispensable material for human activities. In particular, the heavy use of plastic bags and plastic as packaging materials creates a tremendous volume of plastic waste. Unfortunately, only a small fraction of plastics is treated and properly managed, such as through incineration to generate electricity. The remaining plastic waste undergoes a simple landfill option with little regard to the grave consequences.

There is a pressing need for large-scale plastic waste management to eliminate as much plastic as possible from landfills, which leads to environmental pollution by contaminating water resources and exacerbating greenhouse gas emissions [1]. Although plastic wastes are mostly recyclable, the recycling efforts have fallen short of keeping pace with the growing volume of plastic waste generated. A more practical approach is necessary to resolve the problematic issues stemming from non-degradable and high carbon footprint of petroleum-based plastics. This environmental crisis has prompted the need for alternative solutions, such as employing sustainable materials like bioplastics, which are biodegradable.

Polylactic acid offers an attractive solution because of its biodegradability and sustainable material sources. The fermentation of corn or cassava starch is typically the starting step to produce lactic acid, which serves as a precursor for PLA through a polymerization reaction. The use of sustainable sources serves as a significant advantage over the option of petroleum-based raw material, which also contributes to the production of greenhouse gases, with carbon dioxide emissions around 3 kg CO_2 per kilogram of plastic [2]. On the contrary, the use of sustainable raw materials enables PLA to complete a closed carbon cycle. In other words, PLA offers a smaller overall carbon footprint by offsetting the CO_2 generated during PLA production and other phases, through the reduction of CO_2 derived from using plant-based raw materials. In addition, by carefully designing and adapting an energy-efficient production process, the greenhouse gas emissions of PLA can be further decreased compared to conventional plastics. This is even before considering the biodegradability which makes it even more attractive than conventional petroleum-based plastics from a practical perspective. Nevertheless, a challenge persists in achieving efficient degradation of PLA in industrial composting conditions.

Process simulation is an indispensable tool for understanding the impact of various process variables on achieving high yields while minimizing carbon footprints. In case of process simulation of the polylactide synthesis via lactic acid polymerization, the computational tool can emulate the complex and evolving relationships between operating parameters, including temperature, pressure, and catalyst loading, and their corresponding effects on product yield and desired specifications, including molecular weight [3].

In another case of batch production of PLA for biomedical products, a process simulation has demonstrated the ability to provide insights into the reaction kinetics and operating variables such as reactor temperature, pressure, and reactant concentration, and the product yield [4]. The authors elaborated the advantage of the computational approach in analyzing and optimizing operating conditions to achieve product specification in the article [5].

The Aspen process simulator is a valuable tool for process simulation. It was utilized in a thesis study focusing on the production of PLA [6]. The study sought

*Corresponding author : prakorn.k@eng.kmutnb.ac.th

to improve the PLA manufacturing process. Aspen Polymer Plus was utilized to model and simulate the generation of lactic acid and the polymerization process. A dynamic model was developed to assess the stability and controllability of the process. Additionally, the heat operations within the process could be optimized using the Aspen Energy Analyzer to improve the overall heat exchanger network.

The life cycle analysis of polylactic acid offers important insights into the environmental effects associated with every phase of its life cycle. [7]. The two most critical environmental concerns are: 1) the cultivation of agricultural feedstock, such as sugarcane, and 2) the production process that converts this feedstock into PLA. Process simulation can significantly enhance production efficiency and energy usage, which in turn helps reduce CO_2 emissions and energy consumption. A comprehensive approach to process design can mitigate the carbon footprint associated with each production step while ensuring high yield and product quality. The study indicates that, in combination with efficient cultivation techniques, the overall environmental impact of polylactic acid can be substantially lowered, potentially leading to a carbon-neutral production process [8].

Process simulation serves as an effective tool for conducting a thorough design of the production process for polylactic acid. It allows for the optimization of operating conditions while also focusing on minimizing the carbon footprint associated with polylactic acid production. This research goal is to create a platform for a process simulation to analyze the operating parameters affecting polylactic acid yield, as well as the corresponding carbon dioxide emissions.

2 Methodology

There are two principal methods for producing polylactic acid: direct condensation and ring-opening polymerization. The condensation method presents challenges due to being an equilibrium reaction, which makes the removal of water during the process difficult. As a result, this limitation restricts the maximum attainable molecular weight of PLA [9]. Consequently, ring-opening polymerization has emerged as the favored method due to its capacity to provide enhanced control over the reaction and yield PLA with a greater molecular weight [10].

In the ring-opening polymerization method for producing polylactic acid, the process begins with the generation of lactide monomers. These monomers are then transformed into the final PLA product using a catalyst. The entire process is divided into three distinct stages: oligomerization, depolymerization, and polymerization. This structured approach enhances the efficiency and control over the production, resulting in high-quality PLA.

$$5(C_3H_6O_3) \rightarrow 3(H_2O) + C_6H_{10}O_5 + C_9H_{14}O_7 \quad (1)$$

In the initial oligomerization reaction, five molecules of lactic acid combine through a condensation process. During this reaction, three water molecules are eliminated, resulting in the formation of oligomers. This results in the formation of dilactic (L2) and trilactic (L3) oligomers, while water is produced as a byproduct of the reaction.

$$2(C_6H_{10}O_5) + 2(C_9H_{14}O_7) \rightarrow 5(C_6H_8O_4) + 4(H_2O) \quad (2)$$

In this stage of the process, dilactic and trilactic acid experience depolymerization, which entails the breaking of the ester bonds. When heat or a suitable catalyst is applied, these oligomers react to produce lactide and water as a byproduct. This reaction is generally reversible, allowing larger oligomers to break down into smaller lactide molecules. These smaller molecules can then be polymerized again, resulting in the formation of higher molecular weight compounds.

$$C_6H_8O_4 \rightarrow 2\,(C_3H_4O_2) \quad (3)$$

The last step in the procedure involves polymerizing lactide to produce polylactic acid. This polymerization is categorized as addition polymerization. In this process, lactide molecules break their ester linkages when they come into contact with a catalyst. Lactide units combine to form polylactic acid (PLA) through a chain-growth process that occurs under heat, often facilitated by an initiator and catalyst to commence polymerization.

The synthesis process of polylactic acid was simulated using Aspen Plus. Initially, data were collected on key chemical species such as lactic acid, oligomers, lactide, and PLA, with a focus on ensuring accuracy through the property libraries available in Aspen Plus. The Poly-NRTL model was employed to address reaction kinetics and equilibrium.

The polylactic acid production process, illustrated in Fig. 1., begins with lactic acid being dissolved in water and subsequently introduced into the primary reactor. In this reactor, a condensation reaction takes place, joining lactic acid molecules to form dilactic and trilactic oligomers, with water generated as a by-product. A portion of the oligomer products is returned to the reactor to enhance efficiency.

The oligomers are subsequently moved to a second reactor, where depolymerization happens at elevated temperatures under vacuum conditions, yielding lactide, a crucial precursor for PLA. The unreacted substances are separated; some are recycled, and a small portion is eliminated to avoid contamination.

Following this, the lactide mixture is processed through two distillation columns to eliminate any remaining lactic acid and water, resulting in refined lactide. This purified lactide is then placed into a third reactor for ring-opening polymerization, employing a catalyst to generate high-quality PLA. The entire procedure includes recycling loops to optimize conversion rates and enhance overall efficiency.

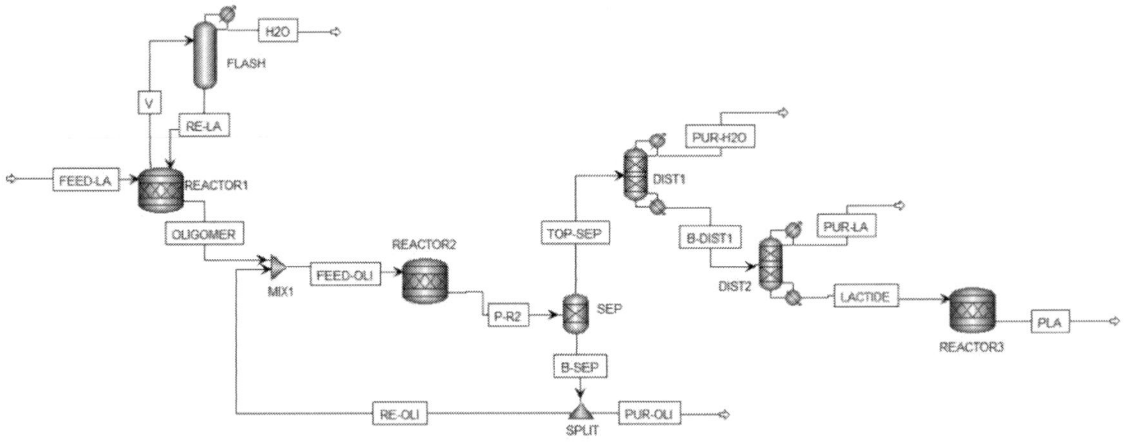

Fig. 1. Simulation flowsheet of the Polylactic acid synthesis process

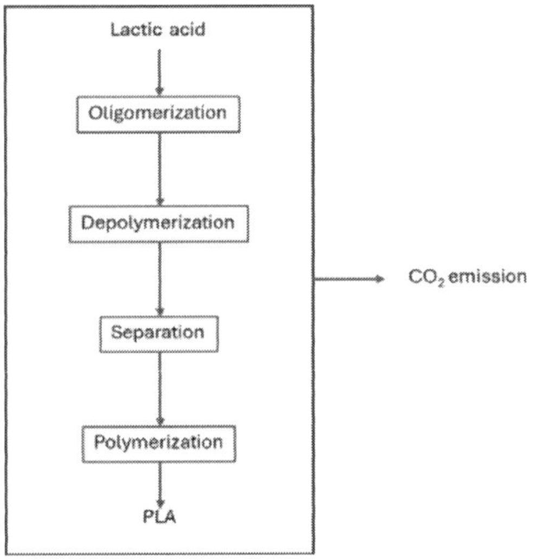

Fig. 2. System boundary

The research employs a Gate-to-Gate approach, focusing on the production process of Polylactic Acid (PLA) within the facility. It tracks the progression from the intake of Lactic Acid to the final PLA product, which is visually represented in Figure 2. To evaluate this process, a process simulator is utilized to analyze input and output balances while also measuring CO2 emissions. The study emphasizes the importance of accounting for carbon emissions related to energy consumption, particularly from grid electricity, as these contribute significantly to the facility's greenhouse gas footprint. Furthermore, it assesses emissions using natural gas as the primary energy source, highlighting the impact of heat and cooling (referred to as SCOPE 2 emissions) on the overall carbon footprint.

3 Result and Analysis

3.1 Process modelling of PLA production

First, the oligomerization undergoes in REACTOR1 where lactic acid is used as a feedstock to produce L2 and L3 oligomers at a rate of approximately 11,500 kg/h. Subsequently, the L2 and L3 are fed into REACTOR 2 for a depolymerization reaction, yielding lactide at a rate around 9,100 kg/h. Following this, two distillation units are employed to purify lactide, resulting in approximately 8,900 kg/h of refined product. Finally, refined lactide undergoes a ring-opening polymerization in REACTOR 3, generating polylactic acid at an output rate of about 8,900 kg/h. Overall, this synthesis process achieves a total yield of 77% in the production of PLA.

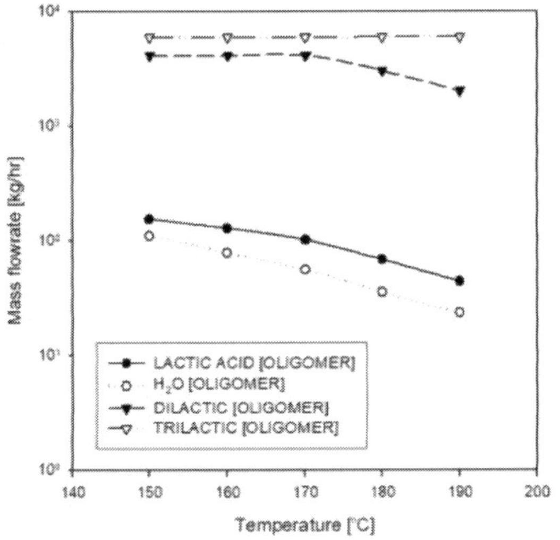

Fig. 3. Mass flow rate of various components in the OLIGOMER stream of REACTOR1 as a function of temperature.

The production rate of components from REACTOR1 exhibits a clear temperature-dependent behavior, as illustrated in Figure 3. As the temperature increases from 150°C to 190°C, there is a notable reduction in the levels of unreacted lactic acid and water, signaling improved conversion efficiency and effective water removal. The flow rate of dilactic acid initially rises, peaking at 4100 kg/h at 170°C, but subsequently declines sharply to around half that amount by 190°C. In contrast, the flow rate of trilactic acid continues to increase with temperature, rising from 5892 kg/h to 5942 kg/h. This suggests that while higher temperatures favor the production of longer-chain oligomers, excessively high temperatures can adversely affect the yield of shorter-chain products such as dilactic acid.

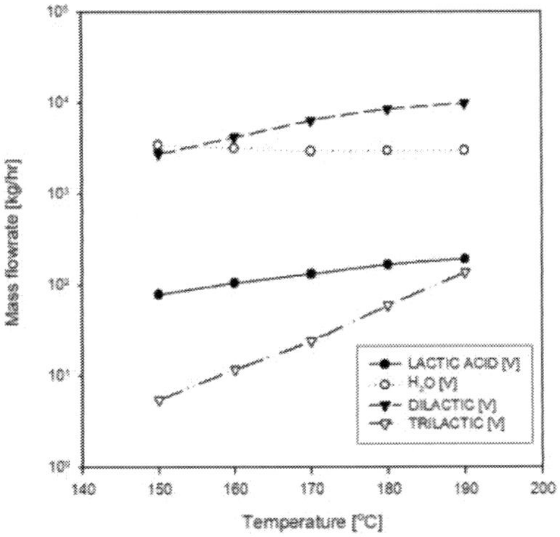

Fig. 4. Mass flow rate of various components in the V stream of REACTOR1 as a function of temperature.

Stream "V" primarily comprises L2 oligomers and water, with an increasing concentration of dilactic acid at elevated temperatures, indicating enhanced efficiency of the condensation reaction as illustrated in Figure 4. Meanwhile, the "OLIGOMER" stream is predominantly made up of dilactic and trilactic acids, with trilactic becoming more prevalent at temperatures exceeding 170°C. However, at these higher temperatures, the quantity of dilactic acid significantly decreases due to its evaporation into stream "V," resulting in a reduced mass in the "OLIGOMER" stream. This loss poses a challenge as it diminishes the availability of reactants for further reactions. Therefore, to minimize product loss and optimize process efficiency, it is recommended to maintain the reactor temperature at 170°C.

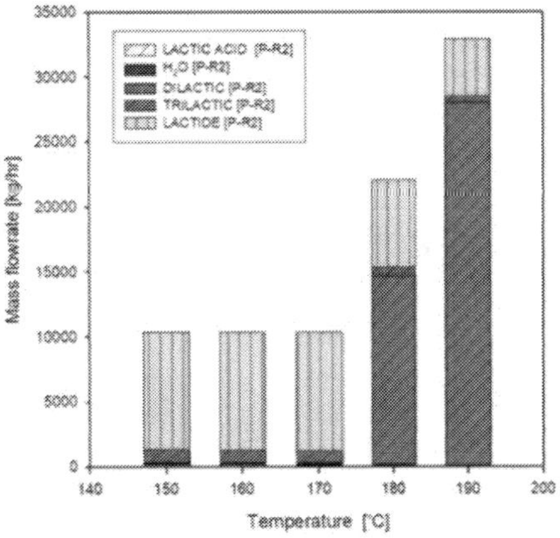

Fig. 5. Mass flow rate and component distribution in the P-R2 stream of REACTOR2 as a function of temperature.

The operating conditions of oligomerization in REACTOR1 significantly impact the compositions present in both REACTOR2 and REACTOR3, with temperature playing a crucial role in this process. It is essential to maintain an operational temperature between 150 and 170°C to stabilize oligomer concentrations. However, an increase in temperature to the range of 180 to 190°C leads to substantial changes, primarily due to an uptick in the recirculation of dilactic acid. Furthermore, at these elevated temperatures, the flow rate of the "RE-OLI" recycled stream, which returns unreacted L2 and L3 to REACTOR2, decreases, indicating an effective conversion process.

As illustrated in Figure 5, the increase in temperature correlates with a rise in the stream P-R2 from REACTOR2. This aligns with anticipated feed patterns and supports the overall mass balance continuity. Nonetheless, the higher temperature conditions result in an increased presence of trilactic acid, suggesting that some incomplete conversion may occur. This aspect necessitates careful monitoring during the downstream separation processes.

Recent validation against prior studies shows that substance quantities remain consistent throughout different production stages. Specifically, the mass flow rate of OLIGOMER from REACTOR1 corresponds well with earlier observations [5], confirming OLIGOMER as the primary component, alongside smaller amounts of lactic acid and water. Our model predicts a water mass flow rate of 55 kg/h, notably lower than the 72 kg/h reported in other studies, indicating improved efficiency in water removal. Furthermore, as depicted in Figure 6, our model achieves an oligomer production rate of approximately 10,000 kg/h, which exceeds the reported production figures of 8,469 kg/h and 8,531 kg/h from previous research [3, 6]. These findings underscore the advantages of optimized reaction conditions, resulting in increased oligomer yields and decreased levels of unreacted lactic acid in the system.

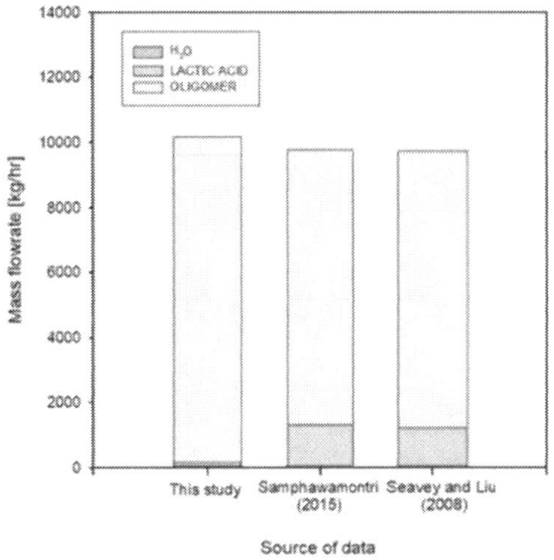

Fig. 6. Comparison of mass flow rates and component distributions in oligomerization across various studies.

In this study, the depolymerization step focused on optimizing lactide production while reducing the formation of undesirable byproducts. The outcomes achieved were found to be comparable to those reported in two other studies as shown in Figure 7. Notably, the absence of water and lactic acid during the process indicates a more efficient separation method. However, the detection of some oligomers suggests potential inefficiencies within the depolymerization process or the associated distillation units. Although the yield of lactide obtained in this study is lower than that found in other literature, the purity of the product is notably higher, underscoring an improvement in product quality.

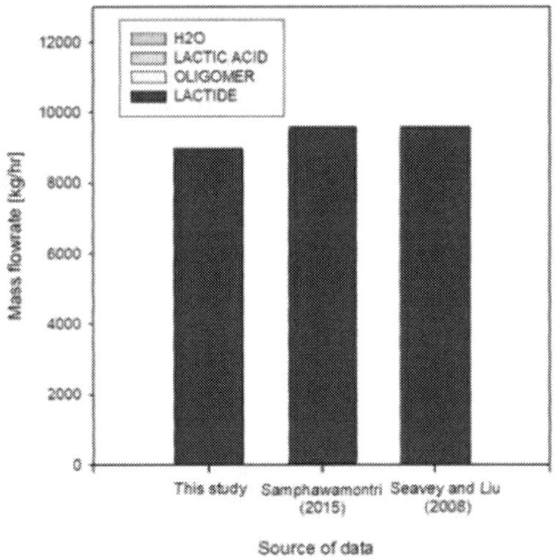

Fig. 7. Comparison of mass flow rates and component distributions in depolymerization across various studies.

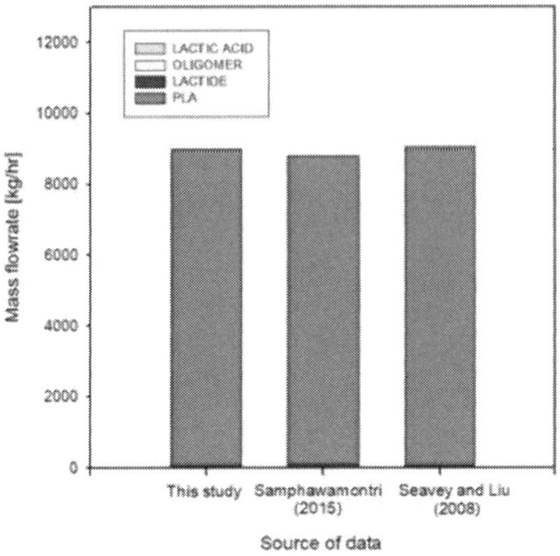

Fig. 8. Comparison of mass flow rates and component distributions in ring-opening polymerization across various studies.

The ring-opening polymerization phase effectively produces polylactic acid, yielding 90 kg/h of lactide and 8,896 kg/h of PLA. These outcomes are consistent with previous research, such as that conducted by Samphawamontri [6], which reported lactide residuals of 93 kg/h and a PLA yield of 8,693 kg/h. Additionally, Seaviy and Liu [3] documented a lactide production rate of 95 kg/h alongside a PLA yield of 8,963 kg/h. As shown in Figure 8, our process notably distinguishes itself by generating a clean product stream that eliminates lactic acid and oligomers, emphasizing the significance of optimized reaction conditions and separation processes. While our lactide content is slightly lower, our model demonstrates a promising approach for synthesizing high-purity PLA.

3.2 Carbon footprint evaluation of polylactic acid production

An analysis of CO_2 emissions associated with the various stages of polylactic acid production reveals that oligomerization is the largest contributor, emitting 274 kg of CO_2 per ton of PLA, as shown in Figure 9. This significant emission is primarily due to the high energy requirements for heating and maintaining the necessary reaction conditions. Following oligomerization, the depolymerization phase generates 169 kg of CO_2 per ton, driven by the energy needed to convert oligomers into lactide. The distillation process contributes the least, accounting for 72 kg of CO_2 per ton, while the polymerization phase emits 141 kg of CO_2 per ton, stemming from the energy-intensive thermal and catalytic processes involved. These findings suggest that improving energy efficiency—such as optimizing the operating temperature in Reactor 1—could significantly reduce the overall carbon footprint of PLA production.

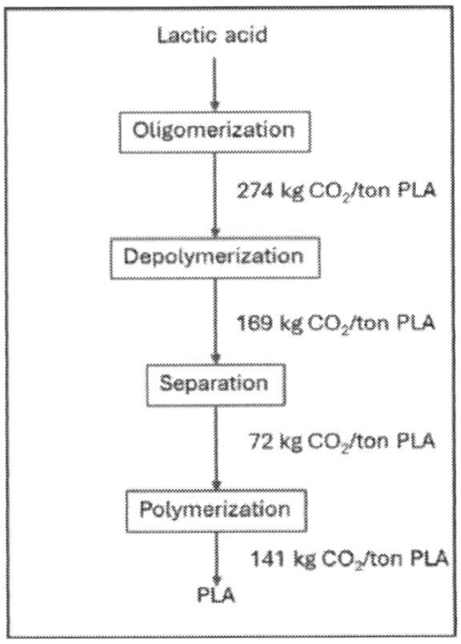

Fig. 9. CO_2 emissions across various stages of PLA production.

The simulation results indicate that oligomerization temperature significantly influences both CO_2 emissions and lactide production as illustrated in Figure 10. An optimal temperature of around 170°C or lower was identified, where both CO_2 emissions and lactide output consistently increase. However, temperatures above 170°C led to a notable increase in CO_2 emissions and a sharp decrease in lactide production. This decline is attributed to the reduced formation of shorter-chain products, like dilactic acid, during the oligomerization reaction at higher temperatures, negatively affecting the overall production of lactic acid and polylactic acid.

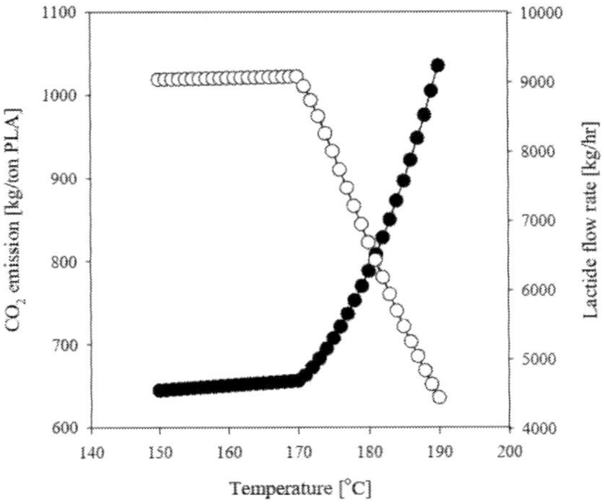

Fig. 10. The overall CO_2 emissions and mass flow rate of lactide in relation to oligomerization temperature.

At an oligomerization temperature of 170°C, the production of polylactic acid results in approximately 656 kg of CO_2 emissions per ton. This figure aligns closely with a previously reported estimate of 691 kg CO_2 per ton [7]. The slight difference in these estimates can be attributed to the current study's use of a natural gas-based energy source, which produces less CO_2 compared to the fossil fuel utilized in the earlier research. It is important to note that these findings originate from idealized conditions and may not fully capture the complexities encountered in real-world scenarios. Factors such as energy losses, equipment wear, and variability in operations could potentially increase emissions. Despite this, the consistent results from both studies enhance the credibility of the simulation methods and the analysis of CO_2 emissions conducted.

4 Summary

The study investigates the synthesis of polylactic acid (PLA) using Aspen Plus process simulation software, highlighting its potential for industrial applications. It outlines a three-step reaction process comprising oligomerization, depolymerization, and ring-opening polymerization, ultimately yielding a high-purity PLA output of 77%, which is consistent with current benchmarks. A significant aspect of the findings is the optimization of reactor temperatures, particularly during the oligomerization phase, which proves to be most effective at 170°C. This temperature not only enhances product yield but also minimizes energy losses and prevents the degradation of raw materials. From an environmental perspective, the oligomerization stage plays a pivotal role in reducing the carbon footprint. The analysis indicates CO_2 emissions of approximately 656 kg per ton of PLA, in line with existing literature. Overall, the study underscores the importance of integrating process simulation with CO_2 emission analysis, reinforcing the value of such models in the evaluation of industrial processes.

We are grateful for the support received from the Chemical Engineering Department at the Faculty of Engineering, King Mongkut's University of North Bangkok, which provided partial funding for this research.

References

1. R. Geyer, J. R. Jambeck, K. L. Law, Production, use, and fate of all plastics ever made. Sci Adv. **3**, e1700782 (2017). https://doi.org/10.1126/sciadv.1700782
2. E. T. H. Vink, K. R. Rabago, D. A. Glassner, P. R. Gruber, Application of life cycle assessment to Nature Works™ polylactide (PLA) production, Polymer Degradation and Stability. **80**, 403 (2003). https://doi.org/10.1016/S0141-3910(02)00372-5.
3. K. C. Seavey, Y. A. Liu, Polylactide and Nylon-6,6 Polymerization Process Modeling in Polymers Plus. In Step-Growth Polymerization: Process Modeling and Product Design, (John Wiley and Sons, New Jersey, 2008)

4. G. Martinez, A. Lasprilla, B. Lunelli, A. Jardini, R. Filho, A computer tool for the development of poly (lactic acid) synthesis process from renewable feedstock for biomanufacturing. Comp. Aid. Chem. Eng. **29**, 346 (2011).

   http://dx.doi.org/10.1016/B978-0-444-53711-9.50070-5

5. G. Martinez, A. Lasprilla, M. Barbosa, A. Jardini, R. Filho, Modeling and simulation of Poly-lactic acid synthesis in batch process for biomedical applications. Computer Aided Chemical Engineering. **30**, 997 (2012).

   http://dx.doi.org/10.1016/B978-0-444-59520-1.50054-3

6. Y. Samphawamontri, Process Modeling and Simulation of Polylactic Acid, Master thesis, Kasetsart University, Department of Chemical Engineering (2015)

7. A. Morão, F. Bie, Life Cycle Impact Assessment of Polylactic Acid (PLA) Produced from Sugarcane in Thailand, Journal of Polymers and the Environment, **27**, 2523 (2019).

   https://link.springer.com/article/10.1007/s10924-019-01525-9

8. U. Suwanmanee, T. Leejarkpai, Y. Rudeekit, T. Mungcharoen, Life cycle energy consumption and greenhouse gas emissions of polylactic acid (PLA) and polystyrene (PS) trays, Kasetsart Journal - Natural Science. **44**, 703 (2010)

9. L. Mou, J. Li, Y. Lu, G. Li, Juan Li, Polylactic acid: A future universal biobased polymer with multifunctional performance from monomer synthesis, and processing to applications: A review. J. of Hazardous Materials Advances. **18**, 100757 (2025).

   https://doi.org/10.1016/j.hazadv.2025.100757

10. M. C. D'Alterio, I. D'Auria, L. Gaeta, C. Tedesco, S. Brenna, and C. Pellecchia, Are Well Performing Catalysts for the Ring Opening Polymerization of l-Lactide under Mild Laboratory Conditions Suitable for the Industrial Process? The Case of New Highly Active Zn (II) Catalysts. Macromolecules. **55**, 5515 (2022).

    https://doi.org/10.1021/acs.macromol.2c00719

11. Rahmayetty, Y. Whulanza, Sukirno, S. F. Rahman, E. A. Suyono, M. Yohda, and M. Gozan, Use of Candida rugosa lipase as a biocatalyst for L-lactide ring-opening polymerization and polylactic acid production, Biocatalysis and Agricultural Biotechnology. **16**, 683 (2018).

    https://doi.org/10.1016/j.bcab.2018.09.015

The Study of the Antioxidant Activity and Skin Moisturizing Efficacy of Polysaccharides in Mung Bean Shell Extracts from Industrial By-Product

Panitpim Atthapatiphant [1], *Phusanisa* Burakorn[1], *Rattiyakorn* Waisan [1], *Aekkran* Thongwilai [1], *Worawikunya* Kiatponglarp[2], and *Kongaphisith* Tongpoolsomjit [1*]

[1]Department of Industrial Chemistry, Faculty of Applied Science, King Mongkut's University of Technology North Bangkok, Wongsawang, Bangsue, 10800 Bangkok, Thailand
[2]Thai Wah Public Company, Tungmahamek, Sathorn, 10120 Bangkok, Thailand

Abstract. Natural products are gaining popularity in the cosmetics industry, especially those containing plant-based extracts with properties such as anti-inflammatory effects, antioxidant activity, skin hydration, and pollution protection. Many plant extracts show potential for development into dietary supplements or healthcare products. This study investigated polysaccharides extracted from mung bean (*Vigna radiata*) shells using a reflux extraction method at different times. The total sugar content was determined by the phenol-sulfuric acid colorimetric assay, along with antioxidant activity. The highest sugar content (52.28 mg/g) was obtained after 1 hour. Longer extraction times led to sugar loss compared to the xylose standard. The antioxidant capacity of the extract, evaluated using the DPPH free radical scavenging assay, showed an IC_{50} of 0.47 mg/mL, while ascorbic acid had an IC_{50} of 0.03 mg/mL. Moisturizing tests showed that the moisture absorption rate (Ra) and retention rate (Rh) were comparable to standard humectants such as chitosan, sodium hyaluronate, and sodium alginate. These findings indicate that mung bean polysaccharides possess antioxidant and moisturizing properties and have potential for further development into effective cosmetic and healthcare products, adding value to mung bean shells, which are typically discarded as industrial by-products.

1 Introduction

Mung bean (*Vigna radiata* L.) is a leguminous crop primarily cultivated in Southeast and East Asia. [1]. It is widely used in many industries, especially in food production, due to its high nutritional value. The bean contains a good amount of protein, vitamin C, lysine, phosphorus, and vitamin A [2]. People often use it to make vermicelli, sweet dishes, and different kinds of food. Due to their high nutritional value and low cost compared to animal-based proteins, mung beans have become an noticeable plant-based protein source. Despite the growing use of mung beans, their processing result in significant by-products, especially mung bean shell, which are often discarded as waste. However, this shell possess potential for further utilization. They have been used as animal feed [3], compost material, and more recently, as a source of bioactive substances for uses with added value [4].

These bioactive substances include, polysaccharides extracted from mung bean shells have obtained increasing interesting for their useful properties. These complex carbohydrates exhibit strong antioxidant activity, effectively scavenging free radicals and protecting skin cells from oxidative stress, which is a major cause of skin aging and inflammation. Additionally, mung bean shell polysaccharides display anti-inflammatory effects, helping to smooth irritated skin and promote the restoration of the skin barrier. Their strong moisture retention helps hydrate skin and enhance its elasticity and texture. Compared to other widely used polysaccharides such as hyaluronic acid and alginate, those derived from mung bean shells are notable for their natural origin, biodegradability, and availability as an agricultural by-product, combining in ideally with the growing demand from consumers for environmentally friendly and sustainable cosmetic ingredients.

Although the promising biological activities of mung bean shell polysaccharides have been showed in initial research, detailed investigations into their extraction, characterization, and efficacy in topical applications remain limited. This study sets out to explore these issues by carefully examining both the antioxidant properties and the moisturizing ability of polysaccharides extracted from mung bean shells, thereby supporting their potential use in the health and beauty industries.

Several studies have reported that mung bean shell contains antioxidants and other phytochemicals that are beneficial for skin care. Natural extracts with antioxidants

* Corresponding author: kongaphisith.t@sci.kmutnb.ac.th

[5], anti-inflammatory [6], and moisturizing properties have gained popularity in cosmetic and health product development to meet consumer demand for natural and environmentally friendly products [7].

Mung bean-derived ingredients, particularly from its shell, have shown potential to be developed into scrubs, moisturizers, and functional skin-care formulations [8]. Given these prospects, The goal of this study is to explore the antioxidant activity and skin moisturizing efficacy of mung bean shell for its possible use in the cosmetics and health industries.

2 Materials and methods

2.1 Materials

Mung bean shell was a kind gift from Thai Wah Public Company (TWPC)., Thai Wah Tower 1, 21/59, 21/63-64 South Sathorn Road, Tungmahamek, Sathorn, Thailand. The fresh mung bean shells were stored at 4°C to maintain quality before processing. All substances used were acquired from Sigma-Aldrich (St. Louis, MO, USA) and were analytical grade.

2.2 Polysaccharide extraction from mung bean shell

Fresh mung bean shells were promptly collected and stored at 4°C to minimize microbial growth and enzymatic degradation, ensuring the preservation of polysaccharide content and quality prior to extraction. The extraction was modified according to a previously reported procedure [9]. Mung bean shell powder (10.000 g) was combined with 200.0 mL of deionized water. The mixture was extracted by refluxing for 1, 2, and 3 hours, respectively. Following extraction, Whatman No. 1 filter paper was used to filter the mixture under vacuum. The clear supernatant was then separated from the filtrate by centrifuging it for 10 minutes at 6000 rpm, which was collected as the polysaccharide extract from mung bean shell. An ethanol precipitation method was employed by adjusting the extract to 80% (v/v) ethanol using 95% ethanol, and the mixture was then incubated at 4°C for 16 hours.

For the collection of the precipitated polysaccharides, the solution was centrifuged for 12 minutes at 6,000 rpm following incubation. (Figure 1), which were then retained for further use.

2.3 Total sugar analysis

The phenol-sulfuric acid method was employed to quantify total sugar content, with D-xylose serving as the calibration standard. [11]. A test tube was filled with 1.60 mL of the polysaccharide extract. After that, 2.00 mL of 98% sulfuric acid and 0.40 mL of a 5% (w/v) phenol solution were added. After thoroughly mixing the mixture using a vortex mixer, it was allowed to stand for half an hour at room temperature. The absorbance was determined at a wavelength of 490 nm with a Spectronic 21 spectrophotometer.

2.4 Fourier transform infrared (FTIR) analysis

The chemical composition of the polysaccharide extract was analyzed using Fourier Transform Infrared (FTIR) spectroscopy. The sample was mixed with potassium bromide (KBr) and pressed into a pellet. FTIR spectra were recorded in the range of 400–4000 cm^{-1} using a Fourier Transform Infrared Spectroscope (PerkinElmer, Spectrum 100, USA).

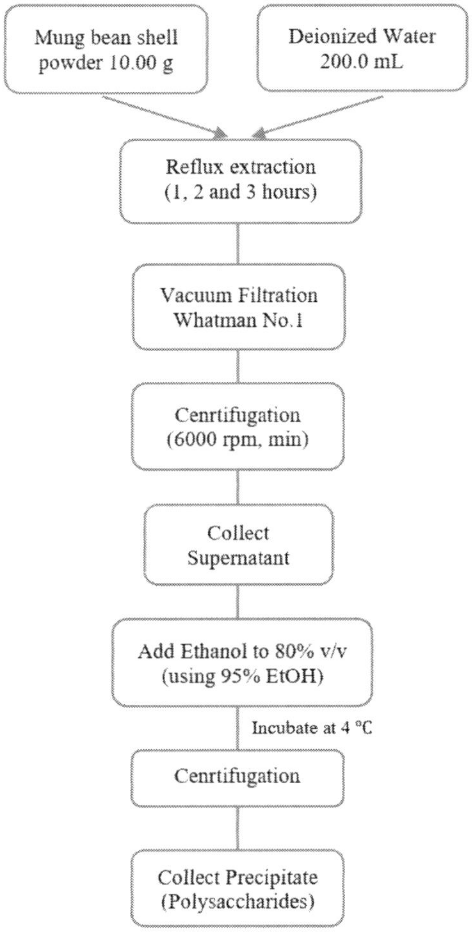

Fig. 1. Extraction procedure of polysaccharides from the shell of *Vigna radiata*.

2.5 Antioxidant assay

The DPPH radical scavenging assay was employed to assess antioxidant activity, with ascorbic acid (vitamin C) serving as the positive control. [9]. A 0.50 mL portion of the polysaccharide extract was added to a test tube, followed by 1.50 mL of deionized water. Subsequently, 2.00 mL of DPPH radical solution was introduced into the mixture. The solution was mixed thoroughly using a vortex mixer and incubated in darkness at ambient temperature for 30 minutes. Absorbance was recorded at

517 nm with a UV-visible spectrophotometer. The following formula was used to determine the capacity to scavenge the DPPH:

$$\text{DPPH scavenging effect (\%)} = [1 - (A_2 - A_1)/A_0] \times 100\% \quad (1)$$

where A_0 is the absorbance of DPPH solution without sample
A_1 is the absorbance of the control sample (without DPPH solution)
A_2 is the absorbance of the sample mixed with DPPH solution

2.6 Evaluation of moisturizing efficacy

Moisture absorption and retention were assessed by placing dried samples in desiccators containing saturated salt solutions of sodium carbonate (Na_2CO_3; 43% RH) and ammonium sulfate ($(NH_4)_2SO_4$; 81% RH). The samples were maintained at room temperature, and weight changes were recorded over time to evaluate their interaction with moisture under varying humidity conditions [12].

2.6.1 Moisture Absorption

Polysaccharide extracts and commonly used cosmetic humectants—chitosan, sodium hyaluronate, and sodium alginate—were each weighed at 100 mg per sample. After that, the samples were dried for 4 hours at 100°C in a hot-air oven. Following drying, the samples were placed in moisture absorption chambers with saturated solutions of sodium carbonate (Na_2CO_3) and ammonium sulfate ($(NH_4)_2SO_4$), which generate relative humidities of 43% and 81%, respectively, at 25°C. Moisture absorption was measured over a period of 0 to 48 hours. The relative absorption (Ra) was calculated as follows:

$$R_a\ (\%) = \frac{A_1 - A_0}{A_0} \times 100\% \quad (2)$$

where A_0 represents the weight of the sample before exposure to the moisture absorption chamber.
A_1 represents the weight of the sample after exposure to the moisture absorption chamber.

2.6.2 Moisture Retention

Polysaccharide extracts and commonly used cosmetic humectants—chitosan, sodium hyaluronate, and sodium alginate—were each weighed at 100 mg per sample. From this, the samples were dried for four hours at 100°C in a hot-air oven. Following drying, each sample obtained 20 mL of distilled water. The hydrated samples were then placed in moisture retention chambers containing silica gel and saturated salt solutions of sodium carbonate (Na_2CO_3) and ammonium sulfate ($(NH_4)_2SO_4$), which produced atmospheric relative humidities of 43% and 81%, respectively, at 25°C. The test duration ranged from 0 to 48 hours. The moisture retention capacity (Rh) was determined using the equation below:

$$R_h\ (\%) = \frac{B_1}{B_0} \times 100\% \quad (3)$$

where B_0 is the weight of the sample prior to placement in the moisture retention chamber.
B_1 is the weight of the sample after being placed in the moisture retention chamber.

3 Results and discussion

3.1 Extract yield from mung bean shells (%)

Table 1. Yield of dried polysaccharide extract based on fresh mung bean shell.

Time (hours)	Yield of polysaccharide extract per gram of fresh mung bean shell (mg/g)
1	55.5
2	70.4
3	83.7

Extraction of polysaccharides from mung bean shell using hot water for 1, 2, and 3 hours revealed that the highest yield of 83.73 mg/g was obtained after 3 hours. This is nearly double the yield reported in a previous study using water extraction on mung bean hulls [11]. The discrepancy could be due to differences in extraction conditions, such as extraction time, temperature, material to solvent ratio, or physical characteristics of the raw material shell. In addition, prolonged heating may have enhanced the breakdown of cell wall components, facilitating the release of bound polysaccharides into the solution. These results suggest that optimizing the extraction parameters can significantly influence the recovery and efficiency of beneficial polysaccharides extraction from agricultural by products.

3.2 Total sugar content

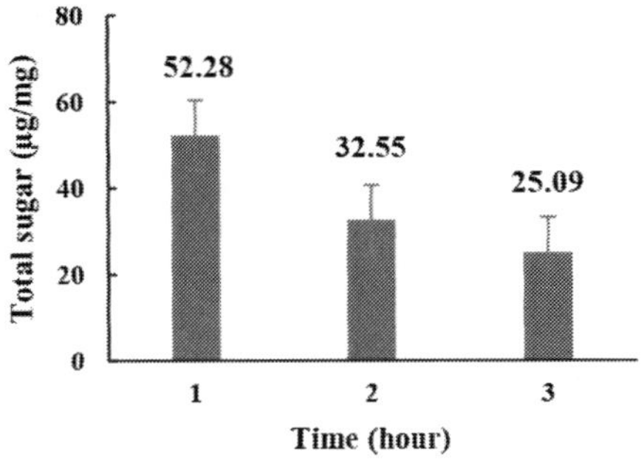

Fig. 2. Comparison of total sugar content extracted under varying reflux durations.

The total sugar content of polysaccharide extracts obtained by hot water extraction at different extraction times (1, 2, and 3 hours) was analyzed, as presented in (Figure 2). The highest total sugar content was observed at 1 hour, yielding 52.28 µg/mg. In contrast, a previous study reported a significantly higher total sugar content of 634.30 µg/mg after 3 hours of extraction [9]. The difference in yield may be due to variations in raw materials, extraction conditions, and difficulty in controlling temperature during extraction. This discrepancy may be caused by thermal degradation and structural changes in polysaccharides during prolonged extraction. Such changes can break down sugar chains into smaller fragments or form derivatives that are not detectable by the phenol–sulfuric acid method. Similar results were reported in a previous study [10], where increased polysaccharide yield but decreased reducing sugar content was observed after extended hot water extraction of *Agaricus bisporus*. These findings suggest that longer extraction times may increase overall polysaccharide yield but reduce measurable sugar content due to degradation. These findings support the hypothesis that prolonged heating may induce thermal degradation of heat-sensitive sugar structures, leading to lower detectable sugar content.

3.3 FT-IR spectroscopy

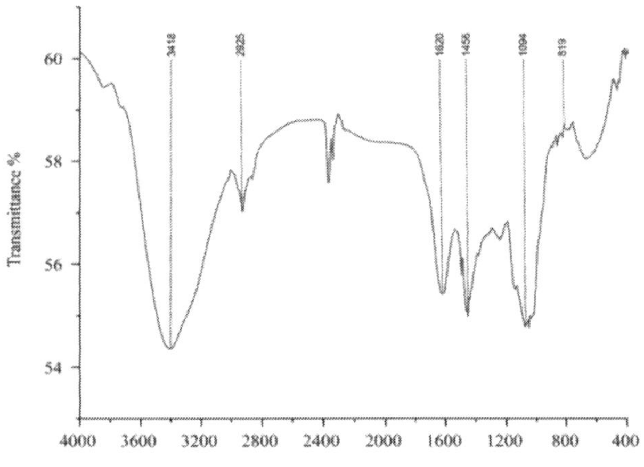

Fig. 3. FT-IR spectra of polysaccharides extracted from mung bean shells.

The FTIR analysis of the polysaccharide structure extracted from mung bean shell was (extracted for 3 hours) recorded in the range of 4000–400 cm^{-1}, as illustrated in (Figure 3). A broad stretching vibration peak was observed at approximately 3,418 cm^{-1}, corresponding to the O–H stretching vibration, suggesting that hydroxyl groups, which frequently appear in polysaccharide structures, are present. These groups are essential for water solubility and hydrogen atom donation, which may be related to the extracted material's antioxidant activity. Moreover, hydroxyl groups can form hydrogen bonds with water molecules, which contributes significantly to the water-holding capacity of polysaccharides [13]. A weaker stretching region appeared around 2,925 cm^{-1}, which is characteristic of C–H bond stretching and bending motions [14]. The FTIR spectrum shows an absorption band near 1,620 cm^{-1}, which is attributed to the asymmetric stretching vibration of carboxylate ions (COO^-), which corresponds with previous findings locating this vibration in the 1,630 to 1,600 cm^{-1} [15]. This suggests the presence of functional groups that may enhance the bioactivity of the extracted polysaccharides, including antioxidant and metal-chelating properties. A peak at 1456 cm^{-1} was observed, which corresponds to the asymmetric bending of CH_3 groups in lignin. Previous studies have reported this vibration in the range of 1456–1465 cm^{-1}, indicating the presence of lignin [16]. This is significant because lignin influences the composition and quality of the polysaccharide, which affects extraction optimization. The peaks around 1094 cm^{-1} are typical of C–O stretching in polysaccharides, which generally absorb at 1050–1150 cm^{-1} [17, 18]. The peak around 819 cm^{-1} is attributed to C–O–C stretching of pyranose rings and COH ring vibrations [14].

3.4 Antioxidant

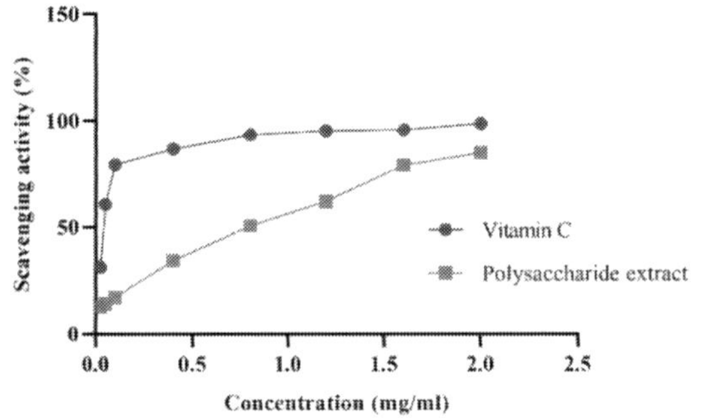

Fig. 4. Antioxidant activity of polysaccharide extract evaluated by DPPH radical scavenging assay.

Antioxidants are compounds that inhibit oxidative damage by neutralizing free radicals. The evaluation of free radical scavenging is a standard way to measure antioxidant activity in natural compounds [19]. The positive control for antioxidant activity assessment was vitamin C. The polysaccharides extracted after 3 hours were selected for further testing. As shown in (Figure 4), the ability of the polysaccharide extract to scavenge free radicals improved with increasing sample concentrations between 0.025 to 2 mg/mL At the highest tested concentration of the polysaccharide extract (2 mg/mL), the scavenging activity reached 85.24% (IC_{50} = 0.47 mg/mL). When compared at the same concentration, this value was lower than that of ascorbic acid, which showed 98.583% (IC_{50} = 0.03 mg/mL). Previous studies reported that polysaccharides extracted from mung bean shell using hot water exhibited antioxidant activity, as indicated by an IC_{50} of 0.73 mg/mL [9]. It is important to note that the reduced antioxidant activity observed in this study may result from variations in extraction conditions. Specifically,

a shorter extraction time might result in the incomplete release of bioactive polysaccharides. Additionally, variations in temperature during hot water extraction can affect both extraction efficiency and antioxidant stability. Bioactive polysaccharides are carbohydrate polymers that have positive effects on cells, like decreasing blood sugar levels, enhancing lipid levels, acting as antioxidants, reducing inflammation, improving immune response, and exhibit anticancer activity [20, 21]. These compounds are increasingly explored for their potential applications in functional foods, nutraceuticals, pharmaceuticals, and cosmetics.

3.5 Evaluation of moisturizing efficacy

3.5.1 Moisture Absorption

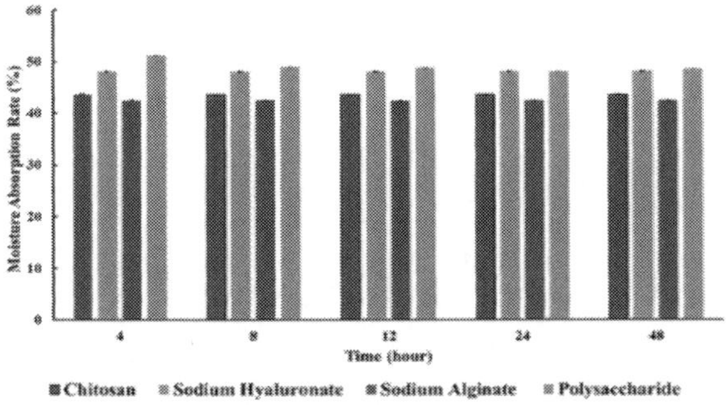

Fig. 5. Moisture absorption of chitosan, sodium hyaluronate, sodium alginate and polysaccharide extract at 43% relative humidity over the indicated time periods.

The moisture absorption capacity (Ra) of polysaccharides extracted from mung bean shell (extracted for 3 hours) was investigated under two different relative humidity (RH) conditions: 43% (Figure 5) and 81% (Figure 6). The results revealed a consistent ability to retain moisture over time, with comparatively better performance than commonly used standard moisturizers. At 43% RH, the polysaccharide sample showed its highest recorded moisture absorption at 51.25% ± 0.02% during the testing period. After 48 hours, the value slightly decreased to 48.57% ± 0.02%, reflecting a reduction of only 5.23%, which was significantly lower *($p < 0.001$)* than the reductions observed in standard moisturizers such as chitosan, sodium hyaluronate, and sodium alginate. This relatively small change indicates excellent moisture retention stability, especially when compared with standard moisturizers such as chitosan, sodium hyaluronate, and sodium alginate, which generally exhibited a more substantial decline in moisture absorption over time.

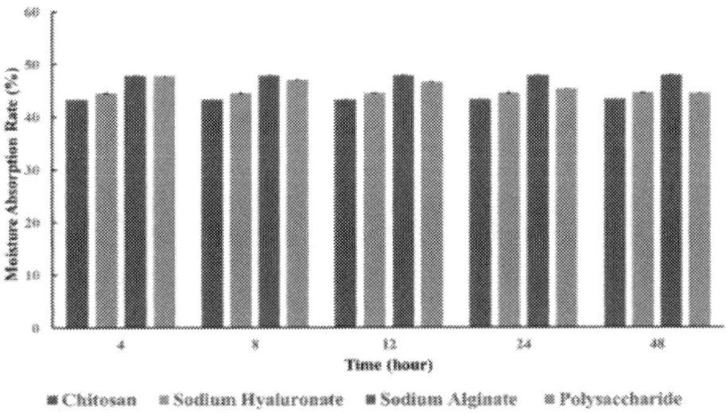

Fig. 6. Moisture absorption of chitosan, sodium hyaluronate, sodium alginate and polysaccharide extract at 81% relative humidity over the indicated time periods.

These results indicate that the mung bean shell polysaccharides possess a continuous moisture absorption capacity along with structural stability under varying levels of relative humidity. Notably, under 81% RH conditions, where typical moisturizers often experience saturation or moisture desorption, the polysaccharide samples were still able to maintain relatively stable Ra values throughout the testing period. This suggests a strong affinity for water and a robust matrix structure capable of sustaining moisture uptake over time.

The mechanism underlying this behavior may be attributed to the polysaccharide structure containing abundant hydroxyl (–OH) and carboxyl (–COOH) groups, which are particularly able to forming long-term hydrogen bonds with molecules of water. Moreover, the physical structure of the polysaccharides is reported to consist of a tightly packed, complex three-dimensional network formed by associated molecular chains capable of efficiently trapping water molecules within. [22, 23]. This network may act as a hydrogel-like matrix capable of swelling and retaining water over extended periods, resulting in a slow and gradual decrease in moisture absorption [13, 24].

3.5.2 Moisture Retention

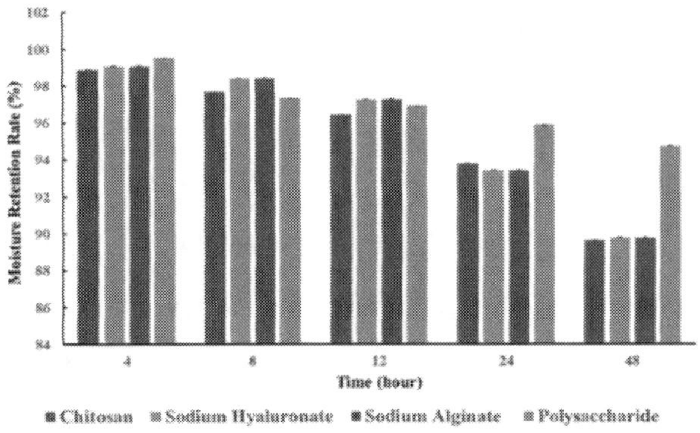

Fig. 7. Moisture retention of chitosan, sodium hyaluronate, sodium alginate and polysaccharide extract at 43% relative humidity over the indicated time periods.

The moisture retention capacity of polysaccharides extracted from mung bean shell (extracted for 3 hours) was evaluated under two relative humidity (RH) conditions: 43% and 81%. Under 43% RH (Figure 7), which represents a low humidity environment, the polysaccharide samples demonstrated a remarkably high initial moisture retention of 99.525 ± 0.035%. After 48 hours, the value slightly decreased to 94.735 ± 0.045%, indicating only a 4.81% reduction *($p < 0.001$)*, which was significantly lower than the declines observed in standard moisturizers such as chitosan, sodium hyaluronate, and sodium alginate.

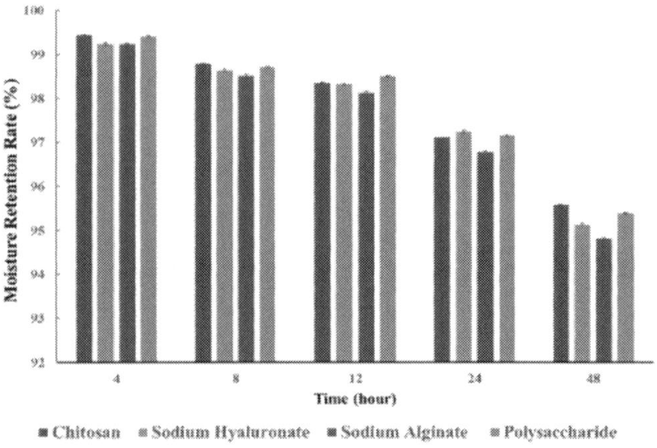

Fig. 8. Moisture retention of chitosan, sodium hyaluronate, sodium alginate and polysaccharide extract at 43% relative humidity over the indicated time periods.

Furthermore, under high humidity conditions 81% RH (Figure 8.), where conventional moisturizers often reach saturation or experience moisture desorption, the mung bean shell polysaccharides still retained excellent moisture retention properties. The highest recorded retention at the beginning of the test was 99.405 ± 0.025 %, which gradually decreased to 95.39 ± 0.03% after 48 hours, reflecting a minimal reduction of only 4.04% ($p < 0.001$), significantly lower than the moisture loss typically observed in standard moisturizers such as chitosan, sodium hyaluronate, and sodium alginate. These results indicate that the polysaccharides can maintain consistent hydration performance and structural integrity even under varying environmental humidity

Together, these findings confirm that mung bean shell polysaccharides possess high and stable moisture retention properties under both low and high RH conditions, making them highly suitable for applications in cosmetic, cosmeceutical, or biopolymer film products that require long term moisture control.

4 Conclusion

This study demonstrated that polysaccharides extracted from mung bean (*Vigna radiata*) shells, an underutilized industrial byproduct, possess notable antioxidant and skin moisturizing properties. The highest yield of polysaccharides was obtained after 3 hours of hot water extraction, while the greatest total sugar content was observed at the 1-hour extraction mark. The extracts showed antioxidant activity, with an IC_{50} value of 0.47 mg/mL, was concentration dependent, though slightly lower than that of ascorbic acid. Moisturization tests revealed that the extracted polysaccharides exhibited high moisture absorption and retention capacities under both low (43% RH) and high (81% RH) humidity conditions. Compared to standard moisturizers such as chitosan, sodium hyaluronate, and sodium alginate, the mung bean shell polysaccharides showed more stable hydration performance over time. The results show that polysaccharides extracted from mung bean shells have antioxidant and moisturizing properties, which means they could be useful as ingredients in cosmetics or biopolymer products. However, more biological tests are needed to confirm how well they work for health and beauty uses. This work also highlights a way to add value to agricultural waste in an eco-friendly way.

This research was funded by Faculty of Applied Science, King Mongkut's University of Technology North Bangkok, Thailand contract no. 671185. The authors would like to thank Department of Industrial Chemistry, Faculty of Applied Science, King Mongkut's University of Technology North Bangkok for their continual supports in providing efficient information and operations. The authors also thank Thai Wah Public Company (TWPC) for supplying the mung bean shells used in this study.

References

1. S. A. Esmaeilzadeh-Hosseini, M. Azadvar, M. G. Reddy, M. Salehi, G. P. Rao, Update on phytoplasma diseases associated with legumes in Asia. In: Phytoplasma Diseases. Elsevier. 243–261 (2023)
2. M. H. Shahrajabian, W. Sun, Q. Cheng, A short review of health benefits and nutritional values of mung bean in sustainable agriculture. J. Med. Plants Stud. **37**, 31–36 (2019)
3. P. L. Sherasia, M. R. Garg, B. M. Bhanderi, Pulses and their by-products as animal feed. Food and Agriculture Organization of the United Nations, Rome (2017)
4. D. Hou, L. Yang, Q. Shen, Y. Li, F. Ren, X. Tang, X. Zhang, Mung Bean (*Vigna radiata* L.): Bioactive Polyphenols, Polysaccharides, Peptides, and Health Benefits. Nutrients **11**, 1238 (2019)
5. Z. Karami, C. Changsiripun, K. Duangmal, N. Chotechuang, Health Benefits and Challenges of Mung Bean Bioactive Compounds: A Systematic Review of In Vivo Evidence for Functional Food Applications. Food Rev. Int. 1–28 (2023). https://doi.org/10.1080/87559129.2025.2452240
6. N. Buathong, K. Chandarajoti, S. Sae-tan, Anti-inflammatory potential of mung bean seed coat water extract in lipopolysaccharide-induced 3T3-L1 adipocytes. Agric. Nat. Resour. **55**, 777–786 (2021).

7. Inekwe G., Kiniyi B. U., Umunna M., Udensi N. K, Effect of Moisture Content on Physical Properties of Mung Bean (*Vigna radiata* L.). Int. J. Eng. Res. Technol. **8**, 56–61 (2019)
8. P. Husni, F. Dewi, Formulation of Peel-off Gel Mask containing Mung Bean (*Vigna radiata* (L.) Wilczek) Extract. Indones. J. Pharm. **1** (2019)
9. L. Jiang, W. Wang, J. Xie, W. Zhao, W. Han, Y. Wang, Two water-soluble polysaccharides from mung bean skin: Physicochemical characterization, antioxidant and antibacterial activities. Food Hydrocoll. **100**, 105412 (2020). https://doi.org/10.1016/j.foodhyd.2019.105412
10. R. Khalil, M. Lukasiewicz, The optimization of the hot water extraction of the polysaccharide-rich fraction from Agaricus bisporus. Molecules 29, 4783 (2023). https://doi.org/10.3390/molecules29194783
11. M. DuBois, K. A. Gilles, J. K. Hamilton, P. A. Rebers, F. Smith, Colorimetric Method for Determination of Sugars and Related Substances. Anal. Chem. **28**, 350–356 (1956)
12. Y. Liu, Q. Guo, S. Zhang, Y. Bao, M. Chen, L. Gao, Y. Zhang, H. Zhou, Polysaccharides from Discarded Stems of Trollius chinensis Bunge Elicit Promising Potential in Cosmetic Industry: Characterization, Moisture Retention and Antioxidant Activity. Molecules **28** (2023). https://doi.org/10.3390/molecules28073114
13. T. Zhang, Q. Guo, Y. Xin, Y. Liu, Comprehensive review in moisture retention mechanism of polysaccharides from algae, plants, bacteria and fungus. Arab. J. Chem. **15**, 104163 (2022). https://doi.org/10.1016/j.arabjc.2022.104163
14. Y. Wang, B. Zhang, J. Xiao, Q. Huang, C. Li, X. Fu, Enrichment, purification and in vitro antioxidant activities of polysaccharides from Umbilicaria esculenta macrolichen. Biochem. Eng. J. **130**, 10–20 (2018). https://doi.org/10.1016/j.bej.2017.11.004
15. M. Szymanska-Chargot, A. Zdunek, Use of FT-IR Spectra and PCA to the Bulk Characterization of Cell Wall Residues of Fruits and Vegetables Along a Fraction Process. Food Biophys. **8**, 29–42 (2013)
16. C. G. Boeriu, D. Bravo, R. J. A. Gosselink, J. E. G. van Dam, Characterisation of structure-dependent functional properties of lignin with infrared spectroscopy. Ind. Crops Prod. **20**, 205–218 (2004). https://doi.org/10.1016/j.indcrop.2004.04.022
17. S. Diblan, P. K. Kelebek, L. Y. Aydemir, FT-IR spectroscopy characterization and chemometric evaluation of legumes extracted with different solvents. Food Health **4**, 80–88 (2018)
18. B. Gieroba, G. Kalisz, M. Krysa, M. Khalavka, A. Przekora, Application of vibrational spectroscopic techniques in the study of the natural polysaccharides and their cross-linking process. **24**, 2630 (2023). https://doi.org/10.3390/ijms24032630
19. J. Alamed, W. Chaiyasit, D. J. McClements, E. A. Decker, Relationships between Free Radical Scavenging and Antioxidant Activity in Foods. J. Agric. Food Chem. **57**, 2969–2976 (2009)
20. R. Huang, J. Zhang, X. Xu, M. Sun, L. Xu, C. Xu, C. Xu & L. Guo, The multiple benefits of bioactive polysaccharides: From the gut to overall health. Trends Food Sci. Technol. **152**, 104677 (2024). https://doi.org/10.1016/j.tifs.2024.104677
21. Y. Xu, Y.-J. Wu, P.-L. Sun, F.-M. Zhang, R.J. Linhardt, Chemically modified polysaccharides: Synthesis, characterization, structure activity relationships of action. Int. J. Biol. Macromol. **132**, 970–977 (2019). https://doi.org/10.1016/j.ijbiomac.2019.03.213
22. Q. Wu, N. Cheng, D. Fang, H. Wang, F.-U. Rahman, H. Hao, Y. Zhang, Recent advances on application of polysaccharides in cosmetics. J. Dermatol. Sci. Cosmet. Technol. **1**, 100004 (2024). https://doi.org/10.1016/j.jdsct.2024.100004
23. Y. Chi, H. Ye, H. Li, Y. Li, H. Guan, H. Mou, P. Wang, Structure and molecular morphology of a novel moisturizing exopolysaccharide produced by Phyllobacterium sp. 921F. Int. J. Biol. Macromol. **135**, 998–1005 (2019). https://doi.org/10.1016/j.ijbiomac.2019.06.019
24. S. K. Patra, R. Poddar, M. Brestic, P. U. Acharjee, P. Bhattacharya, S. Sengupta, P. Pal, N. Bam, B. Biswas, V. Barek, P. Ondrisik, M. Skalicky, A. Hossain, Prospects of Hydrogels in Agriculture for Enhancing Crop and Water Productivity under Water Deficit Condition. Int. J. Polym. Sci. 2022, 1–16 (2022). https://doi.org/10.1155/2022/4914836

Encapsulation of Probiotic by Gellan Gum-Protein Peptide and Polysaccharides

Yanisa Sangkamjan[1], *Wiboon* Riansa-ngawong[1], *Sriwiang* Rittisak[2], *Kriangkrai* Phattayakorn[3], and *Wanticha* Savedboworn[1*]

[1] Department of Agro-Industry Technology and Management, Faculty of Digital Agro-Industry, King Mongkut's University of Technology North Bangkok, Noen Hom, 25230 Prachin Buri, Thailand
[2] Department of Innovation and Product Development Technology, Faculty of Digital Agro-Industry, King Mongkut's University of Technology North Bangkok, Noen Hom, 25230 Prachin Buri, Thailand
[3] Department of Food Technology and Nutrition, Faculty of Natural Resources and Agro-Industry, Kasetsart University, Chiang Khruea, Mueang Sakon Nakhon, 4700 Sakon Nakhon, Thailand

Abstract. Over the years, consumers have become more interested in healthy eating. As a result, the probiotic food market has grown. The development of these products ensures that probiotics remain intact throughout storage. This study examined the survival of the probiotic *Lactobacillus casei* TISTR 1463 through an encapsulation process using extrusion techniques. Encapsulation of probiotics using alginate, gellan gum, sea cucumber peptides and konjac glucomannan coated with chitosan and fucoidan (AGSK-CF) had the highest encapsulation efficiency (%EE) of 99.275%. The results of light microscopy and stereo microscopy showed that gel beads had spherical, elliptical shapes and smooth surface. Free water content values were found in the range of 0.972-0.974. Control exhibited more green than other encapsulants. Hue values of most samples tended to be yellow and chroma values were in the range of 6 – 14. Mechanical characterization analysis of samples showed that AGSK-CF exhibited higher values of Coating Hardness (N), Interior Hardness (N) and Work of cutting/Toughness (N/sec) than other samples.

1 Introduction

Over the past decade, consumer interested in healthy eating has grown steadily, leading to a rise in the availability of probiotic-fortified foods. A major challenge in developing these products have to ensure that probiotics remained viable throughout storage. According to Global Market Insights, the probiotic market was valued at US$5.56 billions in 2023 and is expected to grow at a compound annual growth rate (CAGR) of 6.9% from 2024 to 2032, reaching US$10.28 billions. [1]. One effective solution to improve probiotic stability is encapsulation which protects probiotics from harsh environmental conditions and helps them survive exposure to stomach acid during digestion. Probiotics have gained attention due to their ability to control and maintain microbial ecosystems in the human gastrointestinal tract (GI) [2]. However, the effectiveness and survival rate of probiotics are influenced by several factors including the presence of acids, and bile nutrient depletion, osmotic pressure and oxidative stress [3]. Encapsulation is a technique used to enhance the survival of probiotics by enclosing probiotics cells within a protective material. This barrier helps prevent the degradation of the probiotics, reduces their evaporation rate, and masks any unpleasant tastes, colors, or odors [4]. Encapsulation methods, such as extrusion and emulsification, have been effectively used to protect probiotic cells. These techniques improve cells stability and survival under harsh conditions, including the acidic environment of the stomach, digestive enzymes the presence of bile salts, oxygen, and other microorganisms in the upper gastrointestinal tract [5].

Encapsulants are materials used to protect probiotic strains and support their growth. One of the most commonly used encapsulants is alginate, an edible polymer made up of polysaccharides with strong gelling properties. When alginate interacts with divalent ions such as calcium (Ca^{2+}) or magnesium (Mg^{2+}), it forms a stable three-dimensional gel bead. However, alginate alone is not stable in highly acidic environments, especially at pH levels below 2. To improve its performance under these conditions, it is often combined with other hydrogels, such as proteins or prebiotics, which can enhance the stability and provide additional benefits [6, 7]. Another effective encapsulating material is gellan gum, an anionic polysaccharide that also forms gels in the presence of cations like sodium (Na^{2+}), potassium (K^{+}), and calcium (Ca^{2+}). Gellan gum is more stable than alginate at high temperatures and in acidic environments, and it resists rapid breakdown, making it a strong candidate for probiotic delivery systems [6, 7].

In addition, the incorporation of gellan gum with other polymers enhances gel pellet strength and improves the survival of probiotics in simulated gastric fluid (SGF) [8]. Based on the research of Thinkohkaew et al. [9], encapsulated *Lactobacillus. casei* with a combination of

*Corresponding author: wanticha.s@agro.kmutnb.ac.th

alginate and gellan gum with chitosan coating showed encapsulation efficiency (%EE) of 96.7%. Furthermore, after 6 hours of immersion in intestinal fluid, the gel tablets maintained probiotic levels above 8 log CFU/g even after 30 days of storage.

Numerous studies have demonstrated that incorporating proteins enhanced the efficiency of probiotic encapsulation. Sea cucumber peptides (SCPs), derived from the skin of sea cucumbers, are formed through the self-aggregation of small peptides into fibrous structures, which can bind solvents and form gels. Researches indicated that both temperature and acid concentration significantly influence the quality of sea cucumbers, as the rigid wall structure of sea cucumbers becomes more flexible under heat and acidic conditions, eventually forming a gel-like texture [10]. de Farias et al. [11], suggested that polysaccharides when combined with gelling agents like sea cucumbers, enhanced the protective matrix around probiotics and contributed to positively effect on gastrointestinal health.

In addition, the preservation of encapsulated probiotics to a high survival number can be improved by coating a layer of gel pellets, of which chitosan is one of the most widely used materials. This was probably because a positive electrostatic charge that can be encapsulated with negatively charged of probiotics. This technique has advantages to protect probiotics in the stomach system, severe pH and heat treatment [12]. Fucoidan is polysaccharides located in the cell walls of algae, soluted in water [13]. and known for its high stability under acidic and alkaline conditions. Fucoidan also has a strong ability to bind to compounds [14].

A major challenge in developing encapsulation techniques is ensuring that post-encapsulation probiotics remain survive throughout storage. This research explored the use of alginate and gellan gum as encapsulants, both of which have the ability to create strong gel and are resistant to acidic environments. The incorporation of sea cucumbers in food products presents an interesting option for the future. Sea cucumber peptides enhance the encapsulation efficiency and flexibility of gel beads, which in turn enhances the viability of probiotics under gastrointestinal conditions. In addition, the coating of survival rate more than one layer increases the survival rate of probiotics under inappropriate conditions [10, 13].

The objective of this research was to evaluate the survival of *L. casei* TISTR 1463 encapsulated with sea cucumber peptides and different polysaccharides including konjac glucomannan, yeast β-glucan and *Lycium barbarum* and coated with chitosan - fucoidan. The determination of physical properties including size, a_w, color values, and mechanical characteristics were also conducted.

2 Materials and methods

2.1 Preparation of probiotic *L. casei* TISTR 1463

A culture of *L. casei* TISTR 1463 was grown in MRS broth at 37°C for 30 hr. The culture was then centrifuged at 4000 rpm for 15 min, yielding approximately 5 mL of cell pellets. The drop plate method was used to determine the initial microbial load, which was approximately 10 log CFU/g. The pellet was then mixed with the encapsulating agent as described in section 2.2 [1].

2.2 Preparation of encapsulation probiotics

Solutions of 1.5% sodium alginate (w/v) (Aldrich, Iceland) and 0.5% gellan gum (w/v) (MySkinRecipes,Thailand) were prepared, along with a 1% sea cucumber peptide solution (w/v) (MySkinRecipes,Thailand). Encapsulant formulations were also prepared by combining each with 1% (w/v) of various polysaccharide, as shown in Table 2-1. The mixtures were thoroughly blended, and 5 mL obtained from section 2.1 were added. Mixtures were then transferred into a 20G syringe and dropped into 100 mL of 0.2 M $CaCl_2$ solution under constant stirring to form gel beads.

The resulting gel beads were soaked on and stirred gently for 30 minutes, then washed with 100 mL of 0.1% (w/v) sterile peptone solution under gentle agitation for 10 seconds. Encapsulated beads were coated using chitosan and fucoidan solutions. Coating solutions of 0.3% chitosan (w/v) (Aldrich, Iceland) and 0.3% fucoidan (w/v) (MySkinRecipes, Thailand) were dissolved in 100 mL of water. The beads were soaked in the chitosan solution and stirred gently for 30 minutes to form the first coating layer.

A second layer was then applied using fucoidan under the same condition. After coating, the gel beads were collected and the encapsulation efficiency (%EE) of each encapsulant formulation was calculated [1, 15].

Table 2-1. Encapsulated probiotic treatments.

Abbreviation	Materials	1% Sea cucumber peptide	1% Polysaccharides	Chitosan - Fucoidan coating
Control	1.5%Alginate + 0.5%Gellan gum	✖	✖	✖
AGS-CF		✓	✖	✓
AGSK-CF		✓	Konjac glucomannan	✓
AGSY-CF		✓	Yeast β – glucan	✓
AGSL-CF		✓	*Lycium barbarum*	✓

Note: Control: 1.5%Alginate + 0.5%Gellan gum; **AGS-CF:** 1.5%Alginate + 0.5%Gellan gum + 1%Sea cucumber peptide (Coating with Chitosan and Fucoidan); **AGSK-CF:** 1.5%Alginate + 0.5%Gellan gum + 1%Sea cucumber peptide + 1% Konjac glucomannan (Coating with Chitosan and Fucoidan); **AGSY-CF:** 1.5%Alginate + 0.5%Gellan gum + 1%Sea cucumber peptide + 1%Yeast β – glucan (Coating with Chitosan and Fucoidan); **AGSL-CF:** 1.5%Alginate + 0.5%Gellan gum + 1%Sea cucumber peptide + 1% *Lycium barbarum* (Coating with Chitosan and Fucoidan)

2.3 Probiotic cell encapsulation efficacy test

0.5 gram sample of gel beads were added to 4.5 mL of 2% sodium citrate solution and allowed to stand for 10 minutes to release the encapsulated cells. The suspension was then diluted with 0.1% (w/v) steriled peptone solution. The number of viable cells were determined using the drop plate method on MRS agar (Himedia, India) containing 0.5% calcium carbonate. The plates were incubated at 37°C for 30 hr. The results were reported as log CFU/g. Encapsulation efficiency was calculated using the following equation.

$$\text{Encapsulation efficiency (\%)} = \frac{xt}{x0} \times 100 \qquad (1)$$

Assign X_0 as the number of viable cells prior to encapsulation (log CFU/g)
X_t is the number of viable cells after encapsulation (log CFU/g)

2.4 Free water content measurement (a_w)

The water activity (a_w) value was measured using an AquaLab 3TE a_w meter. Two grams of gel beads were placed in a sample container for each measurement. Three measurements were taken to collect consistent analysis results.

2.5 Color measurement

Color analysis was performed using a ColorFlex colorimeter (HunterLab, USA). Two grams of gel beads were placed in a sample container, and the color was measured using the CIELAB color system (CIELAB). The results were displayed on a computer screen, and three measurements were taken to ensure consistency.

2.6 Measuring the size of gel beads

Ten gel beads were randomly selected, and their sizes were measured in millimetres (mm) using a digital vernier calliper. The average size was then calculated from the measured values.

2.7 Gel beads characteristics by a conventional optical microscope and a stereo microscope

Gel bead were placed on a glass slide and examined under a microscope (NIKON, Japan) using standard lighting. The microscope was set to 40X magnification by combining a 4X objective lens with a 10X ocular lens. The image was adjusted for clarity, and then saved. Gel beads were on the stereo microscope (Motic, China) saucer and placed a black pad under the gel saucer.

2.8 Mechanical characterization analysis

One gel tablet was placed in the Texture Analyser (T. A. XT. plus, Thailand) to determine its pressure resistance (MPa). A selected indenter was mounted on the device and applied vertical pressure from top to bottom. During compression, the force exerted on the indenter was recorded. The results were then averaged across the tested samples [16].

2.9 Statistical analysis

A factorial experiment was planned to test the differences in different encapsulants by analyzing the variance by ANOVA at a confidence level of 95%, and analyzing the differences in the means by means (Duncan's new Multiple Range Test, DMRT) using the statistical SPSS version 28.0 (IBM SPSS, USA).

3 Results and discussions

3.1 Encapsulation efficiency of probiotics with various encapsulants

Encapsulation efficiency (EE) indicates the quantity of probiotics contained with in a particle or structure [4]. According to Figure 3-1, it can be seen that AGSK-CF added with konjac glucomannan has the highest encapsulation efficiency of 99.275%, and control showed the lowest encapsulation efficiency of 97.502%. This was probably because control treatment did not contain polysaccharides as an adjunct supplemented in encapsulation and peptides from sea cucumbers to reinforce the encapsulant spaces or pores. The supplementation of konjac glucomannan with other polymers helps form elastic gels, promotes the growth of beneficial bacteria, and also serves as a prebiotic source [17-19]. This is consistent with the experimental results of Phumsombat et al. [20], that *L. rhamnosus* L34 and *L. acidophilus* LA5 encapsulated with konjac glucomannan exhibited a maximum survival rate of 97.92% and 88.94%, respectively. AGSY-CF, AGSL-CF and AGS-CF supplemented with polysaccharide, sea cucumber peptides, and yeast β-glucan had the encapsulation efficiency lower than konjac glucomannan with the encapsulation efficiency of 98.068%, 98.115% and 98.188%, respectively, with no statistically significant difference ($p \geq 0.05$). Polysaccharide and yeast β - glucan are substances influenced the growth of beneficial bacteria. Polysaccharide is a source of nutrients, allowing probiotics to be used in intestinal growth. Polysaccharide also has a surface suitable for probiotic adhesion and increases transmission live probiotics to the small intestine [21]. In addition, the structure of yeast β - Glucan is porous. This makes probiotics easily, attached to the mesh structure, increasing the survival rate of probiotics [22]. Several studies have confirmed that both temperature and acid concentration influence the quality of sea cucumber peptides. When exposed to heat and acid, these peptides gradually transform into a flexible gel structure [23]. This gel is effective in encapsulating probiotics and significantly enhances their survival rate after encapsulation. In this study, the control treatment was encapsulated using both alginate and gellan gum without the addition of polysaccharide and coating material. Employing alginate solely for cell encapsulation produced highly porous gel beads [10]. However, when encapsulated with other polymers, the gel was formed with calcium ions (Ca^{2+}) and other cations of sodium alginate. Therefore, the structure was similar to "egg box junction", making the structure stronger than alginate alone [22]. Encapsulating more than 0.1% alginate stabilized the gel beads and increased their strength [22]. In addition, the two-layer coating (layer by layer) also increased the efficiency of encapsulation. The first layer of the coating was chitosan, and fucoidan was used as the second layer. Kraithong et al. [24] proposed that fucoidan may occupy spaces between the bonds of encapsulated substances, there by enhancing encapsulation efficiency. Upon analyzing the statistical results, the comparison of the survival efficacy among the five probiotic samples revealed no statistically significant difference.

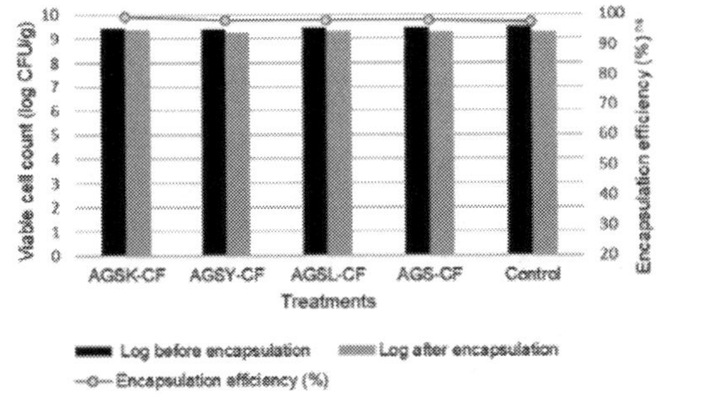

Fig. 3-1. Viable cell count and encapsulation efficiency of encapsulated probiotics with various encapsulants.
Note: ns Revealed no statistically significant difference. ($p \geq 0.05$).

3.2 Size of gel beads

Measurements of the gel granule size, following encapsulation via the extrusion technique, were conducted to assess their consistency. As shown in Table 3-2, the results revealed that sizes of AGSK-CF, AGSY-CF and AGSL-CF ranged from of 3.330 to 3.340 mm, which was not significantly difference ($p \geq 0.05$). In addition, gel tablets with polysaccharides showed a slightly larger size than controland AGS-CF. The larger gel pellet size and higher viscosity were observed in the samples containing polysaccharides due to the distinct properties of the polysaccharides used as encapsulants. These polysaccharides form a more robust gel matrix compared to control and AGS-CF samples. Without polysaccharides added, prepared gel solution with lower viscosity was observed [9]. This may come from the sample being very viscous with a slow flow rate through the needle tips, resulting in a large size of gel pellets. It has a positive effect on the survival of probiotic cells. This is because when the gel pellets are large, the surface area will be less exposed to various conditions, reducing the death of probiotics. While small gel pellets have a large surface area exposed to various conditions, increasing the death of probiotics [25].

Table 3-2. Size of microcapsule pellets.

Samples	Size of encapsulated beads ^{ns} (mm) ± SD
Control	3.300±0.240
AGS-CF	3.310±0.197
AGSK-CF	3.330±0.195
AGSY-CF	3.340±0.143
AGSL-CF	3.330±0.258

Note: ns Revealed no statistically significant difference.($p \geq 0.05$).

3.3 Physical analysis under light microscope and stereo microscope of gel beads

Structural characterization of gel pellets using conventional light microscopy and stereo microscopy revealed structural features. As shown in Figure 3-2, the gel beads were spherical, elliptical shapes, and smooth under a light microscope and a stereo microscope. Using alginate alone has a disadvantage, such as large porosity which affects cell encapsulation [9]. The addition of gellan gum effectively affects the strength of the gel and the survival of probiotic cells. This aligns with the findings of Koh et al. [26], which indicated that the combination of alginate and gellan gum enhances biological function and the flexible modulus of gel beads, thereby promoting structural cohesion.

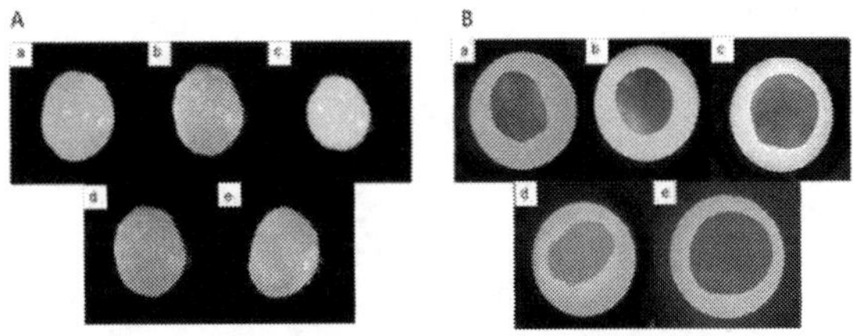

Fig. 3-2. Gel beads under a light microscopy (A) and a stereo microscopy (B)
Note: a: AGSK-CF; b: AGSY-CF; c: AGSL-CF; d: AGS-CF; e: Control

3.4 Free water content (a_w) of the gel beads

The a_w value is one of the most important variables indicating the shelf life of probiotics. The samples had free water contents ranged from of 0.972 to 0.974, which was not significant difference ($p \geq 0.05$) (Table 3-3). This is consistent with the reporting of Rather et al. [27], stated that the presence of prebiotics could protect the probiotics from moisture and had no effect on the a_w value. Moreover, alginate helps encapsulate probiotics to pass well into the intestines. It is estimated to have a pore size of less than 17 nm [28].

Table 3-3. Free water contents of various microcapsules

Samples	Free water content [ns] (a_w)± SD
Control	0.972±0.001
AGS-CF	0.973±0.002
AGSK-CF	0.973±0.002
AGSY-CF	0.972±0.002
AGSL-CF	0.974±0.001

Note: [ns] Revealed no statistically significant difference. ($p \geq 0.05$).

3.5 Colorimetric measurement

Color measurement of gel beads was shown in Table 3-4. Control sample showed a value of –a* greater than other samples. The mixture of alginate and gellan gum causes green color more than other encapsulated beads, and also exhibited the highest brightness. However, AGSK-CF has a lower brightness value than control sample, and the a* value tended to be more yellow than the control sample. The +b* value tended to be less green than the other treatments, resulting in a pale yellow-green color for the gel beads. In AGSY-CF and AGS-CF, a similar brightness and the -a* and +b* values were found, and tended to have same direction resulted in a yellow-green color of gel beads. AGSY-CF showed a slightly darker color. However, AGSL-CF has a lower brightness value than other samples because *Lycium barbarum* has a reddish-brown color with a tendency of +a* value indicating redness and +b* value indicating yellowness. Hue value indicated the color tone or the color of the sample (0° or 360° = red, 90° = yellow, 180° = green, and 270° = blue). Most samples tended to be yellow with hue values in the range of 95°- 106°. Chroma value is an indicator of the color intensity of or the color saturation. Chroma values of encapsulated beads were in the range of 6-14. Sample with a high chroma value exhibited more vivid or saturated [29]. All samples were green due to the color of fucoidan, which is consistent with the experimental results of Morsy et al. [30], that *Lactobacillus rhamnosus* GG was encapsulated with alginate and anthocyanin, which gave the structure of the gel granules a red color caused by the anthocyanin pigment.

3.6 Mechanical characterization analysis of gel beads

The use of different encapsulating agents may affect the properties of the gel beads. The mechanical strength of the gel beads indicated the encapsulation efficiency of the probiotic. From the experimental results in Table 3-5, it was found that AGSK-CF samples had the highest values of Coating Hardness (N), Interior Hardness (N), and Work of cutting/Toughness (N/sec) than other encapsulating agents, resulting in higher gel compressive force than the other samples. Konjac glucomannan was encapsulating agent which showed the highest pressure resistance. The addition of konjac glucomannan together with gellan gum can improve the flow characteristics and the formation of gels with better elasticity [17, 18]. This is consistent with the experimental results of Lia et al. [31], that alginate enhances the hardness of the gel granules, with an average hardness of 131.1 ± 9.7 N. However, adding pectin, gellan gum, and κ-carrageenan decreased the hardness while increasing the elasticity of the gel granules.
AGS-CF sample had higher Coating Hardness (N), Interior Hardness (N), and Work of cutting/Toughness (N/sec) values than control sample. This is because the sea cucumber peptides are formed by the self-assembly of small peptides into fibers, which can bind to the solvent and form a gel. By using sea cucumber peptides as an encapsulating agent, many reports have confirmed that heating and increasing the concentration of acid will help sea cucumber peptides form gels. The inflexible sea cucumber surface wall will gradually change to a flexible gel structure when exposed to heat and acid [11]. As a result, the samples with sea cucumber peptides were more flexible than the control sample, and required higher compression force.

Table 3-4. Color values of encapsulated gel with different encapsulants

Samples	Color values of encapsulated pellets				
	L*	a*	b*	Hue	Chroma
Control	64.290±0.360[a]	-1.907±0.067[a]	8.743±0.117[c]	102.323±0.331[b]	8.947±0.126[c]
AGS-CF	62.867±0.015[c]	-1.503±0.046[b]	9.633±0.031b[c]	98.893±0.237[c]	9.750±0.036b[c]
AGSK-CF	64.187±0.189[a]	-1.817±0.012[a]	6.180±0.053[d]	106.387±0.117[a]	6.443±0.057[d]
AGSY-CF	63.317±0.025[b]	-1.117±0.035[c]	10.730±0.075[b]	95.927±0.166[c]	10.783±0.076[b]
AGSL-CF	59.407±0.029[d]	0.203±0.061[d]	14.343±0.117[a]	89.187±0.244[d]	14.343±0.117[a]

Note: The superscripts (a-d) in each column mean statistical significant difference (p<0.05)

Table 3-5. Strength values of encapsulated pellets with different encapsulants

Samples	Strength values of encapsulated pellets		
	Coating Hardness (N)	Interior Hardness (N)	Work of cutting/Toughness (N.sec)
Control	0.521±0.018[d]	0.521±0.018[d]	0.142±0.003[d]
AGS-CF	0.523±0.014[c]	0.523±0.014[c]	0.147±0.002[c]
AGSK-CF	0.527±0.018[a]	0.527±0.018[a]	0.153±0.003[a]
AGSY-CF	0.526±0.024[ab]	0.526±0.024[ab]	0.150±0.002[ab]
AGSL-CF	0.526±0.025[ab]	0.526±0.025[ab]	0.150±0.006[ab]

Note: The superscripts (a-d) in each column mean statistical significant difference (p<0.05)

4 Conclusion

An encapsulation experiment of *Lactobacillus casei* TISTR 1463 was conducted using the extrusion technique. AGSK-CF showed the highest encapsulation efficiency of 99.275%, which positively affects the survival of probiotics. The gel bead sizes were in the range of 3.300-3.340 mm and the size of the gel beads with different compositions were not significantly different (p≥0.5). Gel beads were spherical, elliptical, and smooth under light microscopy and stereo microscopy. The free water content values were in the range of 0.972-0.974. Prebiotic supplementation could protect the probiotics from moisture. Therefore, it did not affect the change of a_w value. The color analysis of the samples showed that AGSK-CF were green and the brightest. AGSL-CF is less bright than the other samples. The hue values of most samples tended to be yellow with values in the range of 95°-106°. Chroma values of samples were in the range of 6-14. In addition, the mechanical analysis showed that AGSK-CF has higher Coating Hardness (N), Interior Hardness (N), and Work of cutting/Toughness (N/sec) values than the other coated samples. The addition of konjac glucomannan together with gellan gum (AGSK-CF) can help in the formation of gels with better elasticity, resulting in requiring more pressure to compress the gel beads than other samples. Based on all experimental results, AGSK-CF exhibited higher survival efficiency and also showed higher Coating Hardness (N), Interior Hardness (N), and Work of cutting/Toughness (N/sec) values than the other coated samples. However, the study of the number of probiotics that survive through the gastrointestinal tract and storage needs to be further studied.

References

1. K. Pulidindi, K. Ahuja, Probiotics Market Size - By Ingredients (Lactobacilli, Bifidobacterium, Streptococcus, Bacillus), By End-Use (Human, Animal), By Application (Food and Beverages, Dietary Supplements, Animal Feed) & Forecast. 2024 – 2032 (2023). https://www.gminsights.com/toc/details/probiotics-market.
2. P. Apiwattanasiri, S. Jantrasee, R. Charoen, W. Savedboworn, S. Rittisak, Co-encapsulation efficiency of silk sericin-alginate-prebiotics and the effectiveness of silk sericin coating layer on the survival of probiotic Lactobacillus casei, Food Bioscience. **46**, 101576 (2022). https://doi.org/10.1016/j.fbio.2022.101576
3. C. Sun, M. Zhang, D. Feng, S. Wang, M. Li, Effects of dietary D-mannose supplementation on growth performance, intestinal digestive capacity, gut microbiota, and ammonia tolerance of largemouth bass

micropterus salmoides, Aquaculture Reports **36**, 102054 (2024). https://doi.org/10.1016/j.aqrep.2024.102054

4. J. M. Bae, Prophylactic efficacy of probiotics on travelers' diarrhea: An adaptive meta-analysis of randomized controlled trials. Epidemiol, Health. **40**, (2018). https://doi.org10.4178/ epih.e2018043
5. F. J. Rodrigues, M. F. Cedran, J. L. Bicas, H. H. Sato, Encapsulated probiotic cells: relevant techniques, natural sources as encapsulating materials and food applications-a narrative review. Food Res Int. **137**, 1016 (2020). https://doi.org/10.1016/ j.foodres. 2020.109682
6. D. Gomes, J. P. Batista-Silva, A. Sousa, L. A. Passarinha, Progress and opportunities in gellan gum-based materials: A review of preparation, characterization and emerging applications, Carbohydrate Polymers, **311**, 120782 (2023). https://doi.org10.1016/ j.carbpol.2023.120782
7. S. Rittisak, R. Charoen, S. Seamsin, J. Buppha, T. Ruangthong, S. Muenkhling' W. Riansa ngawong, S. Eadmusik, K. Phattayakorn, S. Jantrasee, W. Savedboworn, Effects of incorporated collagen/prebiotics and different coating substances on the survival rate of encapsulated probiotics, Food Sci Biotechnol, **34**, 1383–1399 (2025). https://doi.org/ 10.1007/s10068-024-01794-8
8. A. Nag, K.S. Han, H. Singh, Microencapsulation of probiotic bacteria using pH-Induced gelation of sodium caseinate and gellan gum, Int. Dairy J. **21**, 247–253 (2011). https://doi.org/ 10.1016/j.idairyj.2010.11.002
9. K. Thinkohkaew, V. Jonjaroen, N. Niamsir,A. Panya, I. Suppavorasatit, P. Potiyaraj, Microencapsulation of probiotics in chitosan-coated alginate/gellan gum: Optimization for viability and stability enhancement, Food Hydrocolloids. **151**, 109788 (2024). https://doi.org/10.1016/j.foodhyd.2024.109788
10. W. J. Li, L. Li, W. Y. Zhen, L. F. Wang, M. Pan, J. Qian Lv, F. Wang, Y.F.Yao, S. P. Nie, M.Y. Xie, Ganoderma atrum polysaccharide ameliorates ROS generation and apoptosis in spleen and thymus of immunosuppressed mice, Food Chem Toxicol. **99**, 199–208 (2017). https://doi.org/10.1016/j.fct.2016.11.033
11. T. G. S. de Farias, H. F. L. Ladislau, T. C. M. Stamford, J. A. C. Medeiros, B. L. M. Soares, T. M. S. Arnaud, T. L. M. Stamford, Viabilities of Lactobacillus rhamnosus ASCC 290 and Lactobacillus casei ATCC 334 (in free form or encapsulated with calcium alginate-chitosan) in yellow mombin ice cream, LWT. **100**, 391-396 (2019). https://doi.org10.1016/ j.lwt.2018.10.084
12. Y. Zhu, Z. Wang, L. Bai, J. Deng, Q. Zhou, Biomaterial-based encapsulated probiotics for biomedical applications : current status and future perspectives, Materials and Design. **210**, 110018 (2021). https://doi.org/10.1016/ j.matdes.2021.110018
13. C. L. Okolie, B. Mason, A. Mohan, N. Pitts, C. C. Udenigwe, Extraction technology impacts on the structure-function relationship between sodium alginate extracts and their in vitro prebiotic activity, Food Bioscience. **37**, (2020). https://doi.org/10.1016/j.fbio.2020.100672
14. R. Sakthivel, K. P. Devi, Antioxidant, anti-inflammatory and anticancer potential of natural bioactive compounds from seaweeds, Studies in Natural Products Chemistry. **63**, 113–160 (2019). https://doi.org/10.1016/B978-0-12-817901-7.00005-8
15. H. Michida, S. Tamalampudi, S. S. Pandiella, C. Webb, H. Fukuda, A. Kondo, Effect of cereal extracts and cereal fiber on viability of Lactobacillus plantarum under gastrointestinal tract conditions, Biochem Eng J. **28**, 73-78 (2006). https://doi.org/10.1016/j.bej.2005. 09.004
16. A. Kistaubayeva, M. Abdulzhanova, S. Zhantlessova, I. Savitskaya, T. Karpenyuk, A. Goncharova, Y. Sinyavskiy, The Effect of encapsulating a prebiotic-based biopolymer delivery system for enhanced probiotic survival, Polymers. **15**, 1752 (2023). https://doi.org10.3390/polym15071752
17. Y. Yuan, L. Wang, R.J. Mu, J. Gong, Y. Wang, Y. Li, J. Ma, J. Pang, C. Wu, Effects of konjac glucomannan on the structure, properties, and drug release characteristics of agarose hydrogels, Carbohydrate Polymers. **190**, 196–203 (2018). https://doi.org/10.1016/ j.carbpol. 2018.02.049
18. D. Qiao, W. Shi, M. Luo, F. Jiang, B. Zhang, Poly vinyl alcohol inclusion can optimize the sol-gel, mechanical and hydrophobic features of agar/konjac glucomannan system, Carbohydrate Polymers. **277**, 118879 (2022). https://doi.org/10.1016/j.carbpol.2021.118879
19. R. A. Rastall, V.Maitin, Prebiotics and synbiotics: towards the next generation, Curr Opin Biotechnol, **13**, 490-496 (2002). https://doi.org/ 10.1016/ S0958-1669(02)00365-8
20. P. Phumsombat, S. Lekhavat, C. Borompichaichartkul, S. Devahastin, N. Chiewchan, Enhancing probiotic encapsulation with konjac glucomannan hydrolysate, IJFST. **59**, 7887–7896 (2024). https://doi.org/ 10.1111/ijfs.17084
21. H. Liu, M. Xie S. Nie, Recent trends and applications of polysaccharides for microencapsulation of probiotics, Food Frontiers. **1**, 45–59 (2020). https://doi.org/10.1002/fft2.11

22. A. Shah, A. Gani, M. Ahmad, B. A. Ashwar, F. A. Masoodi, β-Glucan as an encapsulating agent: Effect on probiotic survival in simulated gastrointestinal tract, Int. J. Biol. Macromol. **82**, 217-222 (2016). https://doi.org/10.1016/j.ijbiomac.2015.11.017
23. X. Song, L. Si, X. Sun, X. Zhu, Z. Li, Y. Li, Y. Wang, H. Hou, Rheological properties, thermal stability and conformational changes of collagen from sea cucumber (Apostichopus japonicas), Food Chemistry. **389**,133033 (2022). https://doi.org/10.1016/j.foodchem. 2022.133033
24. S. Kraithong, A. Theppawong, Y. Liu, P. Sangsawad, R. Huang, Fucoidan as an encapsulant material: applications and advantages in active agents and probiotic encapsulations, Food Chemistry. **477**, 143570 (2025). https://doi.org10.1016/ j.foodchem. 2025.143570
25. A. Kikuchi, M. Kawabuchi, M. Sugihara, Y. Sakurai, T. Okano, Pulsed dextran release from calcium-alginate gel beads, J. Contr. Release, 47, 1 (1997). https://doi.org10.1016/S0168-3659(96)01612-4.
26. W.Y. Koh, X. X. Lim, T.C. Tan, R. Kobun, B. Rasti, Encapsulated probiotics: potential techniques and coating materials for non-dairy food applications, Applied Sciences. **12**, 19 (2022). https://doi.org/10.3390/app121910005
27. S. A. Rather, R. Akhter, F. A. Masoodi, A. Gani, S. M. Wani, Effect of double alginate microencapsulation on in vitro digestibility and thermal tolerance of Lactobacillus plantarum NCDC201 and Lactobacillus casei NCDC297, LWT. **83**, 50–58 (2017). https://doi.org/10.1016/j.lwt.2017.04.036
28. P. Smrdel, M. Bogataj, A. Zega, O. Planinsek, A. Mrhar, Shape optimization and characterization of polysaccharide beads prepared by ionotropic gelation, J. Microencapsul. **25**, 90-105 (2008). https://doi.org/10.1080/02652040701776109
29. C. Saldanha do Carmo, C. Maia,ab Joana Poejo, I. Lychko,ab P. Gamito, I. Nogueira, M. R. Bronze, Ana Teresa Serra, Catarina M. M. Duarte, Microencapsulation of α-tocopherol with zein and β-cyclodextrin using spray drying for colour stability and shelf-life improvement of fruit beverages, Rsc Advances. **7**, 32065, (2017). https://doi.org/10.1039/C6RA25946D
30. M. K. Morsy, O.M. Morsy, M. A. Abdelmonem, R. Elsabagh, Anthocyanin Colored Microencapsulation Effects on Survival Rate of Lactobacillus rhamnosus GG, Color Stability, and Sensory Parameters in Strawberry Nectar Model. FBT. **15**, 352-367 (2022). https://doi.org/10.1007/s11947-022-02758-8
31. Q. Lia, H. Lina, J. Lia, L. Liua, J. Huanga, Y. Caoa, T. Zhaoa, D. J. McClementsb, J. Chenc, C. Liuc, J. Liud, P. Shenb, M. Zhoua, Improving probiotic (Lactobacillus casei) viability by encapsulation in alginate-based microgels: Impact of polymeric and colloidal fillers, Food Hydrocolloids. **138**, (2023). https https://doi.org/10.1016/j.foodhyd.2022.108028

Development of Triple-Polymer Beads for the Delivery of Probiotics under Simulated Gastrointestinal Digestion

Chonlatorn Buaroy[1*], *Nicharee* Wisuthiphaet[1], and *Sasithorn* Kongruang[1*]

[1]Department of Biotechnology, Faculty of Applied Science, King Mongkut's University of Technology North Bangkok, Wong Sawang, Bang Sue, 10800 Bangkok, Thailand

Abstract. This study developed triple polymer beads composed of alginate, inulin and chitosan for encapsulating *Bifidobacterium bifidum* TISTR 2129 and *Lactobacillus sporogenes* BC 208. Four formulations were prepared by the extrusion method, representing alginate (A), alginate with chitosan coating (AC), alginate with inulin (AI), and alginate with both inulin and chitosan coating (AIC). The beads were evaluated for encapsulation efficiency, swelling behavior, and probiotic release under simulated gastrointestinal digestion using the INFOGEST protocol. AI and AIC beads exhibited higher encapsulation efficiency (up to 92%) compared to A and AC, suggesting that inulin improved the interaction between the matrix and probiotic cells. All formulations showed contraction in acidic conditions (pH 3), with AI and AIC showing the lowest swelling, indicating a more compact network. In intestinal conditions (pH 7), swelling increased, particularly in A bead. Notably, AIC beads demonstrated the highest probiotic release (7.32 ± 0.03 log CFU/mL) at 10.25 h, despite exhibiting the lowest swelling, indicating a sustained and controlled release. These results confirm that the combination of inulin and chitosan enhances bead stability, encapsulation efficiency, and targeted delivery, supporting the application of triple polymer systems in functional food development.

1 Introduction

Recently, probiotic-enriched foods have grown to be an important market in the functional food industry due to their potential to enhance human health beyond primary nutrition. Probiotics are living bacteria that provide health benefits when ingested in adequate amounts (at least 6 log CFU/g) and are crucial for maintaining gastrointestinal microbiota and improving host immunity [1-3]. Among the various probiotics, *Bifidobacterium bifidum* TISTR 2129 and *Lactobacillus sporogenes* BC 208 are important for their beneficial effects on gut microbiomes. However, the effective delivery of probiotics to the intestine was an important challenge because these bacteria must endure the harsh conditions of the gastrointestinal tract, especially the acidic pH of the stomach and bile salts, which can significantly reduce their survival. [4].

Encapsulation is known as a technique for enhancing the stability and viability of probiotics during storage and gastrointestinal transit [5]. Sodium alginate is a naturally generated anionic polysaccharide consisting of β-D-mannuronic acid (M) and its epimer, α-L-guluronic acid (G), with the 1, 4-glycosidic linkages commonly used in probiotic encapsulation due to its ability to form hydrogels that interact with divalent cations such as calcium ion. [6]. Nevertheless, alginate beads could be at risk for disintegration in acidic environments, especially in the stomach (pH ~2), since the protonation of carboxyl groups diminishes electrostatic connections and weakens the gel network [7]. To enhance protective efficiency, researchers have incorporated inulin, a fructooligosaccharide that acts as a prebiotic and a non-digestible dietary fiber for beneficial gut microbiota, into encapsulation systems. This addition improves matrix strength and supports selective probiotic growth in the colon [8]. Moreover, the application of chitosan, a naturally sourced cationic polysaccharide produced through the deacetylation of chitin, has attracted considerable attention for its ability to strengthen the structural integrity of encapsulated beads. Chitosan consists of repeated units of β-(1→4)-linked D-glucosamine and N-acetyl-D-glucosamine, containing free amino groups ($-NH_3^+$) in the glucosamine units providing a positive charge under acidic environment. [9-11]. The positive charge causes chitosan to form strong ionic links with the negatively charged alginate matrix, leading to a stable and cohesive coating layer [12]. This coating enhances the strength of the beads and protects them against harmful gastric conditions, particularly low pH and digestive enzymes, thus preventing the leakage of internal bacteria and maintaining bead stability at varying pH levels [13]. Alginate constructs the hydrogel structure, inulin acts as a prebiotic and matrix enhancer, and chitosan offers a protective cationic coating that increases stability in acidic conditions, thereby utilising the unique properties of each polymer to establish a strong encapsulating matrix. This combination offers controlled release in the colon and has improved probiotic viability

* Corresponding author: sasithorn.k@sci.kmutnb.ac.th, s6604071810011@email.kmutnb.ac.th

during gastrointestinal transit. These encapsulating techniques have great potential to advance dietary supplements and functional foods where the preservation of bacterial viability is crucial. Moreover, studying the swelling behaviour of beads is essential since it influences their probiotic release and interaction with intestinal fluids.

Recent studies in probiotic delivery have investigated the integration of inulin into encapsulation systems with diverse materials. Guo et al. (2024) [14] examined the thermo-kinetic properties of co-encapsulated inulin and *Lactobacillus rhamnosus* GG within alginate/pectin composite beads during *in vitro* digestion and colonic fermentation. The results indicated that inulin improved thermal stability and controlled the release of encapsulated probiotics, although it also promoted colonic fermentation action, thereby maintaining probiotic viability and prebiotic efficacy throughout the gastrointestinal tract. Sakoui et al. (2022) [15] found that encapsulated *Enterococcus mundtii* SRBG1 within an inulin–maltodextrin–sodium alginate matrix increased probiotic viability and improved the rheological properties of fermented milk. Maleki et al. (2023) [16] developed synbiotic ice cream by microencapsulating *Lactobacillus rhamnosus* with a composite of whey protein, bacterial cellulose, and inulin. The research demonstrated that this encapsulation method successfully maintained probiotic viability during freezing and storage, while simultaneously improving the functional and sensory attributes of the ice cream.

This study aims to evaluate the production of triple-polymer beads based on alginate (A), alginate with chitosan coating (AC), alginate with inulin (AI), and alginate with both inulin and chitosan coating (AIC) for the encapsulation of two probiotic strains, *Bifidobacterium bifidum* TISTR 2129 and *Lactobacillus sporogenes* BC 208. The encapsulation efficiency, release under simulated gastrointestinal conditions, and swelling behaviour of the beads were assessed to evaluate their efficacy for protecting probiotics and promoting targeted delivery in the gastrointestinal tract.

2 Materials and methods

2.1 Chemicals, probiotics and pathogenic strains

Alginate, chitosan and inulin were purchased from CTi & Science Co., Ltd., Thailand. De -man, rogosa and sharpe (MRS broth and agar) were purchased from Sisco Research Laboratories Pvt. Ltd. (Mumbai, India). The probiotic strains used in this study were *Bifidobacterium bifidum* TISTR 2129 derived from Thailand Institute of Scientific and Technological Research (TISTR) (Pathum Thani, Thailand) and *Lactobacillus sporogenes* BC 208 purchased from New Bellus Enterprises Co., LTD. (Taiwan).

2.2 Probiotic culture preparation

The fermentation of *B. bifidum* TISTR 2129 and *L. sporogenes* BC 208 was carried out in a 5L stirred tank bioreactor (BioFlo 120, Eppendorf, USA) that contained MRS medium. *B. bifidum* TISTR 2129 was maintained at a pH of 6.0 with an agitation rate of 100 rpm, while *L. sporogenes* BC 208 was maintained at a pH of 6.5 with an agitation speed of 150 rpm. Both strains were inoculated with a 10% inoculum size, and the fermentation was maintained at a constant temperature of 37°C. After fermentation, the broth was centrifuged at 3000 rpm for 10 min at 4°C, followed by washing twice with 0.85% NaCl. The probiotic cells were prepared for the encapsulation process.

2.3 Encapsulation process

The beads were encapsulated using the extrusion method, as described by Thinkohkaew et al. (2024) [17], with slight modifications. Four bead formulations were developed to evaluate the individual and combined effects of inulin and chitosan. The formulations were designated as A, AC, AI, and AIC, indicating alginate only, alginate with chitosan coating, alginate with inulin, and alginate with both inulin and chitosan coating, respectively. To prepare the base solution, 2% (w/v) sodium alginate was solubilized in deionized water and heated to 80°C for 30 min. The solution was afterwards sterilized at 121 °C for 15 min. In formulations containing inulin (AI and AIC), 3% (w/v) inulin was added to the sterile alginate solution, and the mixture was then heated at 80°C for 30 min to achieve complete dissolution. After the alginate or alginate–inulin solution had cooled to room temperature, a probiotic mixture consisting of *L. sporogenes* BC 208 and *B. bifidum* TISTR 2129 was added at a final concentration of approximately 10 log CFU/mL. The mixture was then gently stirred for 2 h to ensure homogeneous distribution of the bacterial cells. Encapsulation was conducted using a Büchi B-390 encapsulator (Switzerland) equipped with a 450 µm nozzle. The operational settings were a vibration frequency of 1000 Hz, an electrode potential of 1000 V, and an air pressure of 600 bar. The extrusion procedure was carried out in a 0.1 M calcium chloride ($CaCl_2$) solution with stirring for 30 min. The formed beads were collected and rinsed with sterile distilled water. The produced beads were collected and washed with sterile distilled water. For formulations with chitosan coating (AC and AIC), the beads were immersed in a 0.4% (w/v) chitosan solution for 30 min to form a surface coating. The composition of the prepared bead formulations is summarized in Table 1.

Table 1. The composition of the prepared bead formulations.

Formulations	Alginate (% w/v)	Inulin (% w/v)	Chitosan coating (% w/v)
A	2	-	-
AC	2	-	0.4
AI	2	3	-
AIC	2	3	0.4

2.4 Encapsulation efficiency

Mahmoud et al. (2020) [18] explained the process of assessing the number of viable cells encapsulated in the beads. In brief, 1 g of beads was suspended in 9 mL of sterile 2% (w/v) trisodium citrate solution and vortexed until completely dissolved. Subsequently, 1 mL of the resulting solution was serially diluted using phosphatebuffered saline (PBS). The number of viable cells was determined by plating the diluted samples on MRS agar media, followed by incubation at 37°C for 48 h. Viable cell counts were expressed as colony-forming units per milliliter (CFU/mL). The encapsulation efficiency of beads was subsequently determined using Equation (1).

$$\%EE = Log_{10}N / Log_{10}N_0 \times 100 \qquad (1)$$

Where N_0 and N were the initial number of probiotic cells (CFU/mL) and the number of cells encapsulated in beads, respectively.

2.5 Release study of probiotics under *in vitro* gastrointestinal digestion

The *in vitro* gastrointestinal digestion was carried out following the standardized INFOGEST protocol established by Brodkorb et al. (2019) [19], with slight adaptations to suit the experimental conditions. The *in vitro* digestion phase involved three consecutive phases: the oral phase, the gastric phase, and the intestinal phase, using simulated salivary fluid (SSF), simulated gastric fluid (SGF), and simulated intestinal fluid (SIF), respectively. For the oral phase, the sample was mixed with SSF at a 1:1 weight ratio, supplemented with 0.3 M $CaCl_2$ and salivary amylase to achieve a final enzymatic activity of 75 U/mL. The pH of the fluid was adjusted to 7.0 by 1 M NaOH. The mixture was subsequently incubated at 37°C with continuous agitation at 100 rpm for 2 min to mimic the limited exposure duration to salivary amylase. The gastric phase started with a solution of SGF containing pepsin at an activity of 2000 U/mL and gastric lipase at an activity of 60 U/mL. The pH was adjusted to 3.0 with 1 M HCl, and the mixture was incubated at 37°C with shaking at 100 rpm for 2 h to simulate stomach conditions. The intestinal phase was carried out by providing SIF with bile extract at a final concentration of 10 mM and pancreatin at a final enzymatic activity of 100 U/mL. The pH was adjusted to 7.0 using 1 M NaOH, and the mixture was shaken continuously at 100 rpm at 37°C for 8 h to simulate intestinal digestion. Upon completion of each digestion phase, samples were taken for analysis. The total number of living cells released was counted and shown as colony-forming units per millilitre (CFU/mL).

2.6 Swelling studies

The swelling behaviour of beads under simulated gastrointestinal digestion was previously described by Gbassi et al. (2011) [20], with modifications. Initially, 1 g of beads was immersed in 50 mL of simulated gastric fluid (SGF) adjusted to a pH of 3.0 by 1M NaOH and incubated at 37°C with continuous shaking at 100 rpm for 2 h. After the gastric simulation, the beads were placed into simulated intestinal fluid (SIF) maintained at pH 7.0 and incubated for an additional 8 hours. At certain times, the swollen beads were extracted and carefully wiped with filter paper to remove excess surface moisture before weighing. The swelling index (SI) was determined by calculating the weight gain according to Equation (2). All experiments were conducted in triplicate.

$$S_i = [M_2 - M_1] / M_1 \qquad (2)$$

Where M_1 was the initial weight of the beads before immersion in the fluid. M_2 was the weight of the beads after immersion in the fluid.

2.7 Statistical analysis

All experiments were conducted in triplicate. Data were expressed as mean values ± standard deviation (SD). One-way analysis of variance (ANOVA) was employed to assess differences among treatments, followed by Tukey's test for multiple comparisons. Statistical significance was defined at $p < 0.05$. All analyses were performed using SPSS 21.0 software (Chicago, IL, USA).

3 Results and discussion

3.1 Encapsulation efficiency

As shown in Figure 1, encapsulation efficiency of A, AC, AI and AIC were 82.11 ± 0.07%, 83.41 ± 0.01%, 90.06 ± 0.10% and 92.56 ± 0.09%, respectively, with AI and AIC exhibiting higher encapsulation efficiency compared to A and AC. No significant difference was found between A and AC ($p = 0.544$), nor between AI and AIC ($p = 0.112$). The results indicated that the incorporation of inulin produced a greater impact on encapsulation efficiency than the chitosan coating under the studied conditions. Although chitosan was recognized for improving the barrier characteristics and mechanical strengths of alginate beads [21], the chitosan layer was more likely to improve long-term stability, protect against environmental stress, and help with controlled release in the digestive system rather than significantly increase encapsulation efficiency [22–24]. Importantly, previous studies have reported that the encapsulation efficiency of similar systems incorporating inulin ranged from 83% to 90% [17, 25, 26]. In comparison, the encapsulation efficiency achieved in our study was notably higher, indicating the superior performance of the developed encapsulation system. The enhanced efficiency might be attributed to the addition of inulin, which reinforces the alginate matrix and promotes stronger interactions between the encapsulating shell and probiotic cell surfaces, thereby improving cell retention. Figure 2 shows the freshly produced probiotic-encapsulated beads. All exhibited a consistently spherical form and a milky-white hue. These attributes are crucial for ensuring regularity in probiotic delivery and efficient protection. Pamela et al. (2024) [27] indicated that probiotic-encapsulated beads composed of 3% alginate and 10% inulin presented a spherical morphology, attaining an encapsulation efficiency of 99% and enhanced probiotic viability in low pH environments.

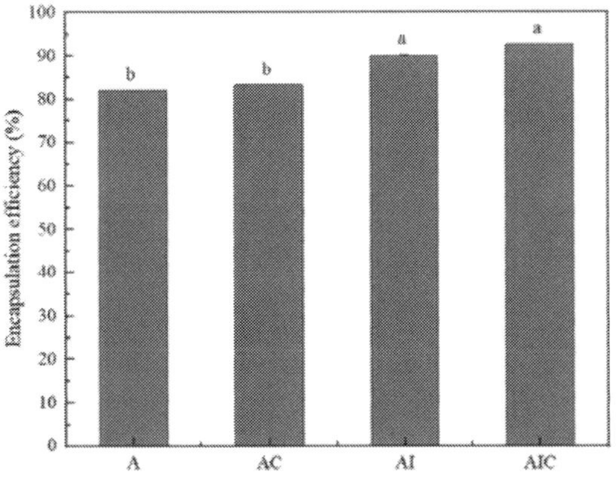

Fig. 1. Encapsulation efficiency for four formulations: alginate (A), alginate with chitosan coating (AC), alginate with inulin (AI), and alginate with both inulin and chitosan coating (AIC). Different letters represent statistically significant differences (p < 0.05).

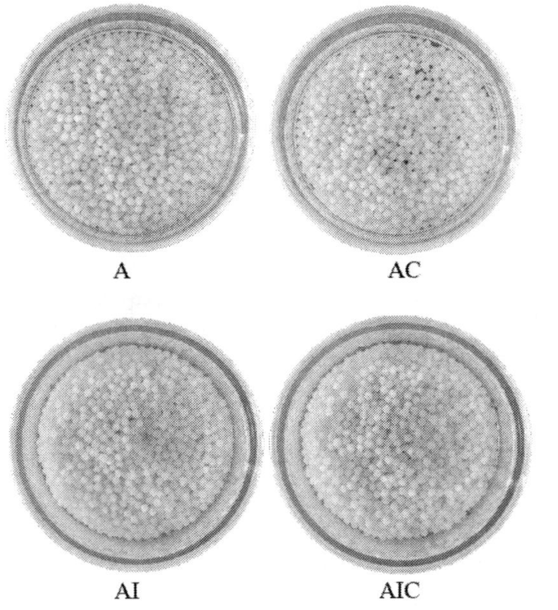

Fig. 2. Apparent images of freshly probiotic-encapsulated beads.

3.2 Swelling behavior

The swelling index of the beads was determined in simulated gastrointestinal digestion, initially with the stomach phase and then transitioning to the intestinal phase, as shown in Figure 3. For the gastric phase at pH 3, all beads demonstrated negative swelling behavior during a 2 h digestion period. A and AC beads presented slight differences in swelling, which were -0.10 ± 0.04 and -0.11 ± 0.04, respectively, with no significant difference (p = 0.97), indicating that the chitosan coating did not substantially alter their swelling behavior in an acidic environment. On the other hand, AI and AIC beads were -0.32 ± 0.06 and -0.27 ± 0.05, proving significantly more reduced than A and AC beads (p = 0.003, p = 0.011, p = 0.017 and p = 0.004), reflecting a more compact structure. However, there was no significant distinction between AI and AIC beads, indicating that the addition of a chitosan coating to the inulin-loaded beads did not significantly affect their swelling behavior under these conditions.

In the intestinal phase transition at pH 7, all beads indicated significantly enhanced swelling behavior. At 5.25 h, A beads exhibited the highest swelling index of 1.07 ± 0.05, followed by AC beads at 0.69 ± 0.09, AI beads at 0.64 ± 0.03, and AIC beads at 0.62 ± 0.02. Statistical analysis indicated substantial disparities between the alginate beads and all other beads (p < 0.0001). At the final time point of 9.25 h, the swelling indexes attained their greatest. A bead showed the highest swelling index of 1.58 ± 0.10, while AC, AI and AIC beads demonstrated similar swelling indices of 1.39 ± 0.03, 1.41 ± 0.04 and 1.38 ± 0.09, respectively.

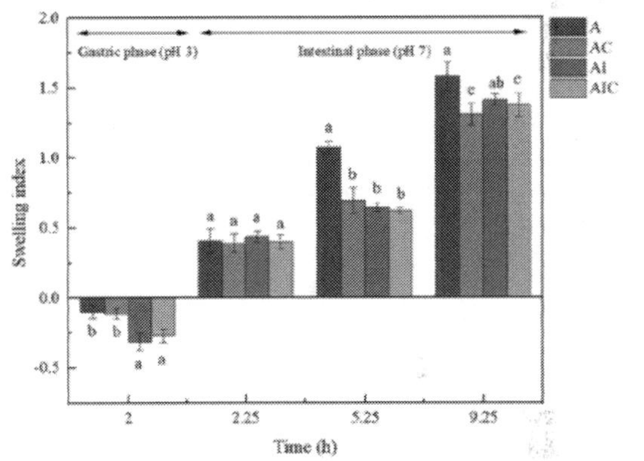

Fig. 3. Swelling behavior of beads under simulated gastrointestinal digestion. Different letters represent statistically significant differences (p < 0.05).

3.3 *In vitro* release under the gastrointestinal digestion

The *in vitro* release of probiotic-loaded beads was assessed according to the INFOGEST protocol to simulate gastrointestinal conditions, as shown in Figure 4. In the oral phase (pH 7, 2 min), free probiotic cells exhibited the maximum release of 9.62 ± 0.10 log CFU/mL. Conversely, all encapsulated beads exhibited no quantified release, signifying successful encapsulation and protection within the oral environment. In the gastric phase transition (pH 3, 2 h), a slight increase in release was observed in all beads, with A and AI exhibiting releases of 2.86 ± 0.03 log CFU/mL and 2.69 ± 0.04 log CFU/mL, respectively, while the other beads presented no probiotic release. In the intestinal phase (pH 7, 2.25–10.25 h), all beads exhibited a slow enhancement in probiotic release. At 10.25 h, AIC achieved the highest release among the encapsulated, at 7.32 ± 0.03 log CFU/mL. AC and AI showed moderate release at 6.98 ± 0.01 log CFU/mL and 6.79 ± 0.14 log CFU/mL, respectively. A showed the lowest release among the encapsulated beads, with release at 6.02 ± 0.03 log CFU/mL. The results indicate that the composition of the encapsulating matrix, specifically alginate and inulin coated with chitosan, significantly influences probiotic release during gastrointestinal digestion. The probiotic release observed in this study demonstrates that the encapsulation method effectively protected the probiotics, ensuring their viability throughout gastrointestinal delivery. The probiotics maintained a viability of a minimum of 6 log CFU/mL, which is the required concentration for providing health benefits [1]. The results of the present study corresponded with those of a previous study that confirmed the improved survival of *Lactobacillus casei* when encapsulated in alginate/inulin coated with chitosan by the extrusion method [17].

The swelling behavior of the beads, as observed under simulated gastrointestinal conditions, strongly correlates with their probiotic release profiles, as shown in Figure 3. All beads showed negative swelling induced in the stomach phase at pH 3, which indicated that the gel matrix contracted. This behavior was typical of alginate-based hydrogels, where network contraction and reduced electrostatic repulsion result from carboxyl groups becoming protonated in an acidic environment [28]. As a result, limited probiotic cell release was seen during this phase, especially in AC and AIC beads, where the presence of inulin or chitosan coating caused the matrix to become denser and further prevented diffusion. On the other hand, all beads indicated significant improvement during the intestinal phase at pH 7. According to Jin et al. (2009) [29], this was explained by the ion exchange mechanism between Na^+ in PBS and Ca^{2+} in the alginate matrix, particularly within the polymannuronate. Probiotic diffusions were assisted by chain relaxation and increased gel swelling caused by the consequent increase in ionized carboxyl groups and lower cross-linking hardness. Interestingly, AIC beads demonstrated the maximum overall release at 10.25 h even though they had the lowest swelling index of all beads. This suggests that additional inulin assisted continuous probiotic release along with controlling swelling, possibly because of its porous structure and prebiotic-enhancing properties. The importance of composite matrix design for reaching desired delivery performance was highlighted by the less controlled release of the pure alginate beads (A), which had the greatest swelling index.

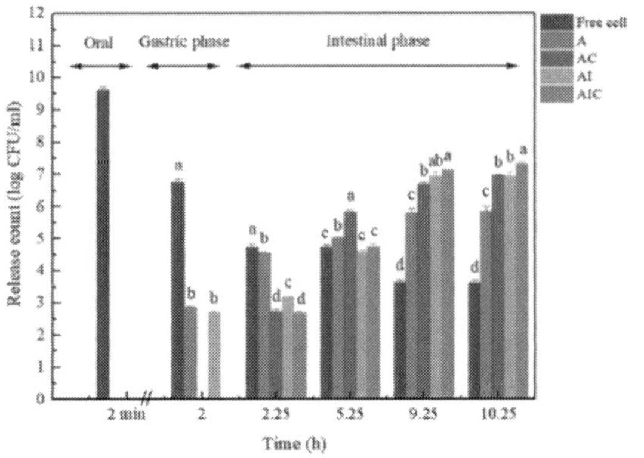

Fig. 4. *In vitro* release profile under simulated gastrointestinal digestion (INFOGEST protocol. Different letters represent statistically significant differences ($p < 0.05$).

4 Conclusion

The triple-polymer encapsulation system comprising alginate, inulin, and chitosan successfully enhanced the structural integrity and functionality of probiotic beads under simulated gastrointestinal digestion. The inclusion of inulin notably improved encapsulation efficiency and contributed to a more compact bead structure, while chitosan coating offered additional protection in acidic conditions. Swelling studies revealed that all beads contracted in gastric conditions and expanded in intestinal fluid, correlating closely with their probiotic release behavior. Among all formulations, AIC beads demonstrated the most desirable performance, with a controlled swelling profile and the highest probiotic release during intestinal digestion. These results emphasize the synergistic potential of combining biopolymers to optimize probiotic encapsulation and delivery, offering promising applications in the development of functional foods and synbiotic products.

This partly supported by Sweet D international company limited under Enserv Holding CO., LTD., and the Department of Biotechnology, Faculty of Applied Science, KMUTNB, for their facilities support.

References

1. FAO/WHO. Probiotics in food: health and nutritional properties and guidelines for evaluation. FAO Food Nutr. Pap. **85**, Rome (2001). http://www.fao.org/3/a-a0512e.pdf
2. C. Mazziotta, M. Tognon, F. Martini, E. Torreggiani, J. C. Rotondo, Probiotics mechanism of action on immune cells and beneficial effects on human health. Cells. **12**, 184 (2023). https://doi.org/10.3390/cells12010184
3. X. Wang, P. Zhang, X. Zhang, Probiotics regulate gut microbiota: an effective method to improve immunity. Molecules **26**, 6076 (2021).
4. S. Han, Y. Lu, J. Xie, Y. Fei, G. Zheng, Z. Wang, J. Liu, L. Lv, Z. Ling, B. Berglund, M. Yao, L. Li, Probiotic gastrointestinal transit and colonization

after oral administration: a long journey. Front. Cell. Infect. Microbiol. **11**, 609722 (2021). https://doi.org/10.3389/fcimb.2021.609722

5. S. Agriopoulou, M. Tarapoulouzi, T. Varzakas, S. M. Jafari, Application of encapsulation strategies for probiotics: from individual loading to co-encapsulation. Microorganisms. **11**, 2896 (2023). https://doi.org/10.3390/microorganisms11122896
6. R. Abka-Khajouei, L. Tounsi, N. Shahabi, A.K. Patel, S. Abdelkafi, P. Michaud, Structures, properties and applications of alginates. Mar. Drugs **20**, 364 (2022). https://doi.org/10.3390/md20060364
7. H. Malektaj, A. D. Drozdov, E. Fini, J. d. C. Christiansen, The effect of pH on the viscoelastic response of alginate–montmorillonite nanocomposite hydrogels. Molecules. **29**, 244 (2024). https://doi.org/10.3390/molecules29010244
8. A. Anand, S. N. Manjula, N. K. Fuloria, H. Sharma, K. Mruthunjaya, Inulin as a prebiotic and its effect on gut microbiota (Inulin for Pharmaceutical Applications: A Versatile Biopolymer, Springer Nature Singapore, Singapore, 2025)
9. F. Hong, P. Qiu, Y. Wang, P. Ren, J. Liu, J. Zhao, D. Gou, Chitosan-based hydrogels: From preparation to applications, a review. Food Chem. X. **21**, 101095 (2024). https://doi.org/10.1016/j.fochx.2023.101095
10. K. M. Rudall, Chitin and its association with other molecules. J. Polym. Sci. C Polym. Symp. **28**, 83–102 (1969). https://doi.org/10.1002/polc.5070280110
11. N. Desai, D. Rana, S. Salave, R. Gupta, P. Patel, B. Karunakaran, A. Sharma, J. Giri, D. Benival, N. Kommineni, Chitosan: A potential biopolymer in drug delivery and biomedical applications. Pharmaceutics **15**, 1313 (2023). https://doi.org/10.3390/pharmaceutics15041313
12. N. Wathoni, Y. Herdiana, C. Suhandi, A. F. A. Mohammed, A. El-Rayyes, A. C. Narsa, Chitosan/alginate-based nanoparticles for antibacterial agents delivery. Int. J. Nanomedicine 19, 5021–5044 (2024). https://doi.org/10.2147/IJN.S469572
13. W. Y. Koh, X. X. Lim, T.-C. Tan, R. Kobun, B. Rasti, Encapsulated probiotics: Potential techniques and coating materials for non-dairy food applications. Appl. Sci. **12**, 10005 (2022). https://doi.org/10.3390/app121910005
14. Y. Guo, Y. Liu, Q. Han, H. Yang, L. Cai, Y. Zhang, Thermo-kinetic studies of *in vitro* digestion and colonic fermentation of inulin/*Lactobacillus rhamnosus* GG co-encapsulated composite beads. Food Hydrocoll. **149**, 109541 (2024). https://doi.org/10.1016/j.foodhyd.2024.109541
15. S. Sakoui, R. Derdak, O. L. Pop, D. C. Vodnar, B. Addoum, B.E. Teleky, B. El Khalfi, Effect of encapsulated probiotic in inulin–maltodextrin–sodium alginate matrix on the viability of *Enterococcus mundtii* SRBG1 and the rheological parameters of fermented milk. Curr. Res. Food Sci. **5**, 1713–1719 (2022). https://doi.org/10.1016/j.crfs.2022.11.034
16. O. Maleki, A. Khosrowshahi Asl, M. Alizadeh Khaledabad, S. Amiri, Production and characterization of synbiotic ice cream using microencapsulation and cryopreservation of *Lactobacillus rhamnosus* in whey protein/bio-cellulose/inulin composite microcapsules. J. Food Meas. Char. **17**, 3909–3917 (2023). https://doi.org/10.1007/s11694-023-01922-8
17. Thinkohkaew, K., Aumphaiphensiri, N., Tangamornsiri, T., Niamsiri, N., Potiyaraj, P., Suppavorasatit, I, Inulin extracted from burdock root (*Arctium lappa* L.) incorporated alginate/chitosan hydrogel beads for probiotics encapsulation. J. Agric. Food Res. **18**, 101405 (2024). https://doi.org/10.1016/j.jafr.2024.101405
18. M. Mahmoud, N. A. Abdallah, K. El-Shafei, N. F. Tawfik, H. S. El-Sayed, Survivability of alginate-microencapsulated *Lactobacillus plantarum* during storage, simulated food processing and gastrointestinal conditions. Heliyon. **6**, (2020). https://doi.org/10.1016/j.heliyon.2020.e03541
19. Brodkorb, A., Egger, L., Alminger, M., Alvito, P., Assunção, R., Ballance, S., Bohn, T., Bourlieu-Lacanal, C., Boutrou, R., Carrière, F., Clemente, A., Corredig, M., Dupont, D., Dufour, C., Edwards, C., Golding, M., Karakaya, S., Kirkhus, B., Le Feunteun, S., Lesmes, U., INFOGEST static *in vitro* simulation of gastrointestinal food digestion. Nat. Protoc. **14**, 991–1014 (2019). https://doi.org/10.1038/s41596-018-0119-1
20. G. K. Gbassi, T. Vandamme, F. S. Yolou, E. Marchioni, *In vitro* effects of pH, bile salts and enzymes on the release and viability of encapsulated *Lactobacillus plantarum* strains in a gastrointestinal tract model. Int. Dairy J. **21**, 97–102 (2011)
21. L. Zhang, B. Shen, C. Zheng, Y. Huang, Y. Liang, P. Fei, W. Lai, Chitosan/oxidized sodium alginate/Ca^{2+} hydrogels: Synthesis, characterization and adsorption properties. Food Hydrocoll. **156**, 110368 (2024). https://doi.org/10.1016/j.foodhyd.2024.110368
22. S. Senthil Kumar, S. Sheik Mohideen, Encapsulation of L. fermentum with chitosan-alginate enhances its bioactivity against acrylamide toxicity in *D. melanogaster*. Sci. Rep. **15**, 11324 (2025). https://doi.org/10.1038/s41598-025-11324-0
23. S. Arora, R.D. Budhiraja, Chitosan-alginate microcapsules of amoxicillin for gastric stability and mucoadhesion. J. Adv. Pharm. Technol. Res. **3**, 68–74 (2012). https://doi.org/10.4103/2231-4040.93555
24. S. Masoomi Dezfooli, C. Bonnot, N. Gutierrez-Maddox, A.C. Alfaro, A. Seyfoddin, Chitosan coated alginate beads as probiotic delivery system for New Zealand black footed abalone (Haliotis iris). J. Appl. Polym. Sci. **139** (2022). https://doi.org/10.1002/app.52626

25. Y. Parsana, M. Yadav, S. Kumar, Microencapsulation in the chitosan-coated alginate-inulin matrix of *Limosilactobacillus reuteri* SW23 and *Lactobacillus salivarius* RBL50 and their characterization, Carbohydr. Polym. Technol. Appl. **5**, 100285 (2023). https://doi.org/10.1016/j.carpta.2023.100285
26. V. Serrano-Casas, M. L. Pérez-Chabela, E. Cortés-Barberena, A. Totosaus, Improvement of lactic acid bacteria viability in acid conditions employing agroindustrial co-products as prebiotic on alginate ionotropic gel matrix co-encapsulation, J. Funct. Foods **38**, 293–297 (2017). https://doi.org/10.1016/j.jff.2017.09.048
27. V. Y. Pamela, F. R. Eris, S. Kusumasari, B. Meindrawan, The development of microencapsulated lactic acid bacteria and its application on yoghurt powder products. Food Res. **8**, 421–429 (2024). https://doi.org/10.26656/fr.2017.8(5).107
28. H. Malektaj, A. D. Drozdov, J. deClaville Christiansen, Swelling of homogeneous alginate gels with multi-stimuli sensitivity, Int. J. Mol. Sci. **24**, 5064 (2023). https://doi.org/10.3390/ijms24065064
29. L. Jin, Y. Hong, J.-W. Pyo, H. Song, K. No, Monitoring of swelling and degrading behavior of alginate beads using optical tweezers. BioChip J. **3**, 213 (2009)

Preliminary Performance Assessment of polyculture vertical flow constructed wetland for campus greywater treatment

Mohan Marumudi[1], *Nida* Arshad[2], *Sai Priya* Botta[3], *Devi* Teppala[3], *Malinee* Sriariyanun[2], and *Keerthi* Katam[1*]

[1]Department of Civil Engineering, Mahindra University, Hyderabad, 500043 Telangana, India
[2] Biorefinery and Process Automation Engineering Centre, Department of Chemical and Process Engineering, The Sirindhorn Thai-German International Graduate School of Engineering, King Mongkut's University of Technology North Bangkok, 10800 Thailand
[3]Department of Civil Engineering, Baba Institute of Technology and Sciences, Visakhapatnam, 530041 Andhra Pradesh, India

Abstract. Constructed wetlands (CW) are recognized as one of the best nature-based, sustainable solutions for wastewater treatment. This study evaluates the effectiveness of polyculture wetlands in treating campus greywater (GW). A pilot-scale CW, measuring 6 x 3 x 0.7 m (L x B x D), was set up on campus, containing three layers of filter media with plant species *Chlorophytum Comosum, Codiaeum Variegatum, and Cyperus Laxus*. CW was operated at a flow rate of 120 m³/d over 35 days. This study observed removal efficiencies of 97.8% for turbidity, 52.7% for chemical oxygen demand, 41.1% for biological oxygen demand, 41.7% for total coliforms, 38.2% for phosphorus, 36.7% for oil and grease, and 19.4% for total suspended solids The significant reduction in turbidity reflects the filter bed's efficiency, while organic matter removal demonstrates the biological activity facilitated by the plant- microbe interactions. These results prove that polyculture-based constructed wetlands offer a sustainable, efficient, and scalable wastewater treatment option applicable for campus decentralized applications. It presents a viable method to minimize environmental pollution and encourage water reuse with an eco-friendly, low-maintenance system, in line with institutional sustainability goals.

1 Introduction

Globally, most of the developing countries will face water shortages in the near future. Climate change exacerbates water scarcity through altered precipitation patterns, increased frequency of extreme weather events, and rising temperatures, which collectively strain existing water resources. Urban areas, with their high population densities and significant water demands, are particularly susceptible to these changes [1]. The existing water sources are contaminated because untreated sewage and industrial wastewater are discharged into surface waters, resulting in an impairment of water quality [2]. Increasing pressure on water resources worldwide has raised interest in recycling and reusing wastewater, driving the need for sustainable treatment solutions, especially in urban areas. Studies revealed that nearly 50–75% of potable water is used for non-potable applications [2]. Rainwater harvesting is a seasonal process, but greywater (GW) is available throughout the year. Reuse of untreated GW can cause health risks; therefore, GW should be properly treated and it should meet the specified standards before it is reused for certain applications [2]. On-site reuse of treated greywater for non-potable purposes such as toilet flushing, garden irrigation, and car washing is one of the alternatives to meet the increasing water demand and to reduce the load on sewage treatment plants [3]. In recent years, significant developments have been recorded worldwide in GW reuse practices and policies. GW treatment is one of the viable options for implementing the reclamation of wastewater. GW includes a significant portion of domestic wastewater originating from sinks, showers, and laundry [4]. GW is commonly referred to as "light" and "mixed", the former consisting of bath, shower, and bathroom sink water, and the latter including laundry and kitchen sink water [5]. The treatment of GW for reuse should be sustainable and affordable. The low capital and maintenance requirements of constructed wetlands (CW) make it a suitable small-scale treatment option for GW [4].

CWs are technologies based on natural processes for pollutant removal and have gained increasing acceptance in the treatment of domestic and industrial wastewater [6]. These are manmade wetlands designed to operate and mimic natural wetlands. The whole process is mediated by complex interactions between water, plants, media, microorganisms, and the atmosphere by using the power of nature and energy from the sun [7]. Key aspects of CW include the selection of vegetation, substrate, and a proper system of construction at suitable locations. However, previous studies showed that CW was used with monoculture plantations like any one particular plant species [4, 6], [8-15]. Emergent macrophytes like *Typha spp. Cattails, Scirpus spp. Bulrushes, Phragmites Australis Common Reed, and Lemna spp. Duckweed* are known for their high growth rate and tolerance to a wide range of environmental conditions and are the most widely used plant type in CWs [16]. They were effective in removing nutrients like nitrogen and phosphorus and in degrading organic pollutants. The use

*Corresponding author: kkatam810@gmail.com

of multiple plant species in a single wetland system approach has gained a lot of interest recently due to its advantages over monoculture using a single plant species in improving the efficiency and resilience of wastewater treatment [17-18]. The polyculture in CW enhanced pollutant removal efficiency, increased biodiversity and system resilience, improved habitat for microbial communities, reduction of invasive species, risk-optimized oxygen transfer, water flow dynamics, aesthetic, and multifunctional benefits [19]. This study aims to evaluate the removal efficiency of a CW using polyculture with three different plant species in treating campus GW.

2 Materials

2.1 Collection of material

Three different substrates of filter media were used: 20 mm gravel, 30 mm pebbles, and a sand layer. These materials are locally sourced. The three different plant species *Chlorophytum Comosum, Codiaeum Variegatum,* and *Cyperus Laxus* used to treat the GW were purchased from a local nursery.

2.2 Source of GW

The GW used in this study was pumped from the outlet drain of the college campus. The drain receives the GW from both the boys' and girls' hostel blocks, mess, and administrative buildings, having a population of 1600 members.

3 Methodology

3.1 Construction of wetland

The Schematic diagram illustrating the CW is displayed in Fig. 1. The detailed step-by-step construction of the wetland is shown in Fig. 2. Marking of basin excavation as pilot scale wetland measurements were assumed to hold and treat, based on the generated GW quantity. Basin excavation with inlet and outlet was made in the ground to a size of 6 meters in length, 3 meters in width, and with a depth of 0.70 meters. The excavated basin was lined with a polysheet to prevent GW from infiltrating into the groundwater, and a 60 cm difference was maintained between the inlet and outlet of the CW to accommodate the GW to maintain the effective treatment. The wetland was then filled with locally sourced materials as three substrate layers of pebbles, gravel, and sand, with each layer having a thickness of 200 mm. The bottom layer consisted of pebbles, the middle layer was gravel, and the top layer was sand, integrated with poly mesh to separate and reduce the internal clogging of substrate filling. The arrangements to divert the water through gravity into the reservoir for treatment and maintaining the constant discharge of the water level in the inlet reservoir, and the selected locally sourced plants of *Chlorophytum Comosum, Codiaeum Variegatum, and Cyperus Laxus* were then introduced into the wetland. *Chlorophytum Comosum (Spider plant)* is a native of tropical and southern Africa, belongs to the Asparagaceae family, and has long, aching green leaves that can grow up to 15 inches with yellow and white stripes and produces small white flowers and baby offshoots called spiderettes. This is a fast-growing plant that thrives in bright or indirect sunlight, and rhizobium zone enhances the microbial activity in pollutant removal. *Codiaeum Variegatum (Garden croton plant)* originates in Southeast Asia and belongs to the Euphorbiaceae family, having thick, glossy, vibrant colour leaves that thrive in warm and humid environments. *Cyperus Laxus (Loose Flatsedge)* originates from tropical regions of the Western Hemisphere and Africa, having narrow, grass-like leaves that form a dense clump thrives in wet environments and spreads through underground rhizomes, which may help in microbial growth and pollutant removal can tolerate seasonal flooding and enhances filtration.

3.2 Operation of CW

A tank was built to provide a consistent flow of GW to the wetland. The flow rate was approximately 120 cubic meters per day, and the entire experiment lasted for 35 days. This consistent flow helped to reduce the continuous

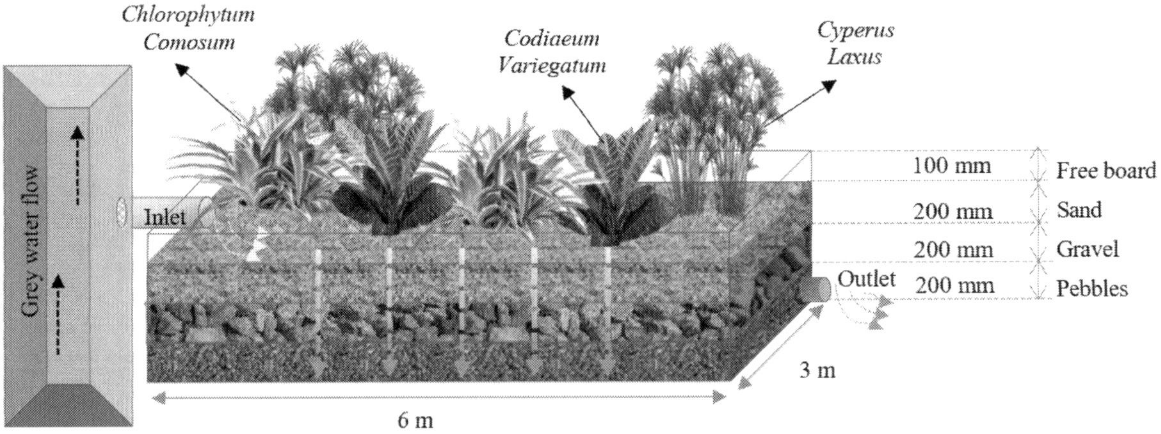

Fig. 1. Schematic illustration of the CW

overloading that led to a loss of treatment capacity due to excessive suspended solids, sludge, or other pollutants. The inlet and outlet flow were regularly monitored to prevent clogging in the substrate.

Fig. 2. Construction stages of the constructed wetland (CW): (1) Basin marking; (2) Excavation with inlet and outlet; (3) Laying the pipelines; (4) Polysheet lining with layering of pebbles (each 200 mm); (5) Sand layer; (6 & 7) Gravity-fed water inlet tank; (8) *Chlorophytum comosum*, *Codiaeum variegatum*, and *Cyperus laxus* plants.

3.3 Water quality analysis

The influent GW that enters the CW and the effluent treated water that flows out of the bottom of the CW samples were characterized for total suspended solids (TSS), turbidity, biological oxygen demand (BOD), chemical oxygen demand (COD), oil & grease, total coliforms (TC), and phosphorus (P). Samples were collected before and after 35 days of treatment in the constructed wetland, with each sample collected in triplicate and subsequently analysed. The turbidity was measured using a Nephelometer (Make: Elico). The dissolved oxygen (DO) was measured using a DO meter (Make: Elico). COD and P were measured following the protocols given in the Standard Methods for the Examination of Water and Wastewater [20]. The removal efficiency of the CW was calculated by subtracting the effluent concentration from the influent concentration and dividing the obtained value by the influent concentration. The obtained decimal value was multiplied by 100 to convert it to a percentage.

4 Results and discussion

The data from different previous studies were compared with the water quality parameters abounding in this study, and the results are shown in Table 1. The parameters include TSS, turbidity, phosphorus, BOD, COD, oil and grease, and total coliforms. Each parameter provides important information about ecosystem health and water pollution. The TSS level in the current study was 72 mg/L, which is within the range of 204 ± 41 mg/L that has been reported by Aygun 2014 [21] and 29–505 mg/L in Domestic and campus GW reported by Arden 2020 [5]. In this study, turbidity was measured at 58 NTU. This figure is greater than the majority of the values found across other studies, including 19.2–119 NTU reported by Liu 2016 [22] and 8.4 NTU reported by Kuo 2018 [25]. However, a slightly higher turbidity of 65 NTU was observed by Laaffat 2019 [24].

The phosphorus concentration of 11 mg/L, compared with other reported results, such as 2.4 ± 0.9 mg/L reported by Tuttolomondo 2020 [17] and 0.8 mg/L reported by Laaffat 2019 [24], is significantly higher. In aquatic systems, too much phosphorus can cause eutrophication, which results in algal blooms and oxygen depletion. Here, the BOD level was 190 mg/L, which is a clear symptom of serious organic pollution. It is in line with the range of 111–290 mg/L observed by Liu 2016 [22], although it is significantly higher than values found in other studies by Tuttolomondo 2020 [17] and Laaffat 2019 [24]. Increased organic matter decomposition is indicated by elevated BOD, which can damage aquatic life and reduce dissolved oxygen. COD values of 440 mg/L was found in this study, indicating significant amounts of chemical and organic pollutants. This is comparable to the 383 ± 57 mg/L reported by Aygun 2014 [21], but higher than the values of 189.4 ± 38.6 mg/L reported by Tuttolomondo 2020 [17] and 77.2 mg/L reported by Laaffat 2019 [24]. The high amounts of BOD and COD indicate a large amount of untreated wastewater. In this study, oil and grease levels were measured at 3 mg/L; however, no comparable results from other studies were presented. Despite the seemingly tiny concentration of 3 mg/L, even minute amounts can produce surface coatings that restrict oxygen exchange and damage aquatic life. In this study, the total coliform counts were 3.6×10^5 MPN/100 ml, falling between the $1–7.4 \times 10^5$ MPN/100 ml range observed by Arden 2020 [5]. Fecal contamination is strongly indicated by elevated coliform levels. These results underscore potential public health risks and the need for improved sanitation practices.

The variability and heterogeneity in the wastewater characteristic concentrations across the studies are influenced by multiple factors, like college population density, water usage patterns, cafeteria waste discharge,

Table 1. Initial characterization of GW

TSS mg/L	Turbidity NTU	Phosphorous mg/L	BOD mg/L	COD mg/L	Oil and grease mg/L	Total Coliforms MPN/100 ml	Wastewater Type	Reference s
72	58	11	190	440	3	3.6×10^5	Campus greywater	[This Study]
29-505	12.5-240	0.1-48.8	20-240	100-633	n.d.	$1\text{-}7.4 \times 10^5$	Domestic wastewater	[5]
17.6 ± 4.6	n.d.	2.4 ± 0.9	86.9 ± 29.3	189.4 ± 38.6	n.d.	n.d.	Campus greywater	[17]
n.d.	n.d.	n.d.	n.d.	374	n.d.	n.d.	Domestic wastewater	[18]
204 ± 41	n.d.	8.85 ± 2.7	280 ± 32	383 ± 57	n.d.	n.d.	Campus greywater	[21]
n.d.	19.2 -119	n.d.	111 -290	n.d.	n.d.	n.d.	Campus greywater	[22]
n.d.	n.d.	24.7-39.3	n.d.	164 -256	n.d.	n.d.	Campus greywater	[23]
0.8	65	0.8	44.2	77.2	n.d.	n.d.	Campus greywater	[24]
10.1	8.4	3.7	n.d.	35.1	n.d.	n.d.	Campus greywater	[25]

Table 2. Performance (removal efficiency %) of polyculture in CW in treating greywater

Plant species	Bed Substrate	Root zone microbial activity	TSS mg/L	Turbidity NTU	Phosphorous mg/L	Nitrogen mg/L	BOD mg/L	COD mg/L	Oil and Grease mg/L	Total Coliforms MPN/ 100 ml	References
Chlorophytum Comosum, Codiaeum Variegatum, Cyperus Laxus	Sand, gravel, and pebbles	High [a], n.d., High [b]	9.4	93.3	38.2	n.d.	41	52.7	36.7	41.7	[This Study]
Phragmites Australis	Clay and gravel	High [c]	88.9	98.2	n.d.	n.d.	84	58.6	n.d.	2.1	[4]
Phragmites Australis	Coarse gravel	High [c]	63	n.d.	n.d.	2	51	36	n.d.	n.d.	[9]
Eichhornia Crassipes	n.d.	High [d]	96.6	100	n.d.	n.d.	93.7	88.5	n.d.	n.d.	[10]
Phragmites Australis, Arundo Donax L	Silica quartz river gravel	High [c], High [e]	50.8	n.d.	21	59	75.2	62.5	n.d.	n.d.	[17]
Cannax Generalis, Equisetum Giganteum	Gravel, blast furnace slag, soil with geotextile blanket	Moderate [f], Moderate [g]	n.d.	n.d.	n.d.	n.d.	n.d.	66	n.d.	n.d.	[18]
Typha Latifolia	Coarse gravel	High [h]	90	88	50	42	87	89	n.d.	n.d.	[24]
Pittosporum Tobir	Coarse gravel, fine gravel, sand	n.d.	95.3	n.d.	21.7	n.d.	92.7	97.2	n.d.	41	[34]

[a] [26], [b] [27] , [c] [28] , [d] [29] , [e] [30], [f] [31], [g] [32] , [h] [33]. n.d.- no data

sanitation infrastructure, and mostly seasonal fluctuations and existing wastewater management practices. These collective practices contribute to the pollutant profiles of the campus wastewater. The findings of this study highlight significant variations across key water quality parameters compared to other studies. Elevated levels of BOD, COD, phosphorus, and coliforms suggest notable pollution stress. The comparison highlights that campus GW has considerable contamination, making it unsuitable for direct use without treatment.

The CW displayed varying levels of efficiency in removing different pollutants from GW, as indicated by the results given in Table 2. Various plant species used in GW treatment systems, along with their associated bed substrates. The study's findings suggest that different plants excel in different aspects of wastewater treatment, making species selection crucial depending on the target pollutant and the root zone microbial activity, which were evaluated based on the root zone structure, density, and surface area, as high, medium, and low, which helps the microbial mechanism in pollutant degradation. The choice of bed substrate significantly influences pollutant removal efficiency. Clay and gravel systems with *Phragmites australis* demonstrate strong TSS and phosphorus removal, while coarse gravel systems with *Typha latifolia and Phragmites australis* also perform well in these aspects, which was observed by. Lava rock- based membrane filters excel in reducing BOD with 97% and COD with 84% [35], indicating that high surface area media enhance microbial activity. Conversely, with silica quartz river gravel, *Phragmites Australis* and *Arundo donax L* achieved only 21% phosphorus reduction [17], showing that substrate alone is insufficient for effective phosphorus removal. The presence of gravel, blast furnace slag, and geotextile blankets, with *Carex generalis* and *Equisetum giganteum,* contributes to COD reduction of 66% [18], demonstrating the importance of integrated systems for optimal treatment. Among the listed species, *Phragmites Australis* with clay and gravel achieved 98.2% in turbidity reduction, along with *Pittosporum Tobira* with gravel and clay also showed strong turbidity and TSS removal efficiencies of 88.9% and 94.8% respectively [34]. In terms of BOD reduction, *Phragmites Australis* with clay and gravel achieved an 84% reduction, followed by *Eichhornia Crassipes* 93.7% has been reported by Tandekar 2022 [10]. The significant BOD reduction by *Eichhornia Crassipes* suggests its suitability for nutrient-heavy wastewater, indicating its strong biological treatment capacity. For COD removal, *Pittosporum tobira*, *Eichhornia crassipes*, and membrane filters achieved reductions of 97.2%, 88.5%, and 84%, respectively, demonstrating significant treatment efficiency. COD measures the organic matter in water, and high reduction rates indicate the system's ability to break down pollutants effectively. Regarding oil and grease and total coliform (TC) removal, *Chlorophytum comosum*, *Codiaeum variegatum*, and *Cyperus laxus* achieved moderate performance, with removal efficiencies of 36.7% and 41.7%, respectively. Oil and grease removal is crucial for wastewater treatment in industrial and urban areas. All these highlight variabilities in treatment efficiencies due to different experimental conditions. The current study's system, *Chlorophytum Comosum, Codiaeum Variegatum, and Cyperus Laxus* with sand, gravel, and pebbles as substrate media, shows moderate removal across all parameters, performing best in removing turbidity (97.8%) and COD (52.7%). On the other hand, the efficiency of *Chlorophytum Comosum and Codiaeum Variegatum* in removing pollutants like TSS, BOD, total coliforms, and nutrients was found to be moderate in comparison to more commonly used species like *Phragmites Australis*, indicating the potential for improvement through system optimization. These species with dynamic growth are adapted to the local climate, and their removal efficiency for total coliforms, COD, and oil and grease are optimal compared to other studies. Notably, terrestrial species like *Codiaeum Variegatum* have been less explored in the literature for GW treatment, which adds a novel aspect to this study compared with traditional aquatic macrophytes, potentially expanding the range of effective plant species used in CW. Integrating these plant species, particularly *Cyperus Laxus*, could enhance treatment efficiency for specific pollutants, especially in systems requiring significant microbial load reduction. The primary limitations of this study is its relatively short operational period of 35 days. While the observed removal efficiencies are encouraging, this duration may be insufficient to fully evaluate the long-term performance and stability of the constructed wetland system, particularly with regard to issues such as substrate clogging. Moreover, the study does not encompass the effects of varying climatic conditions or seasonal fluctuations, which are critical for assessing the robustness and optimizing the performance of the system under real-world conditions.

5 Conclusion

This study demonstrates the effectiveness of CWs employing polyculture plant species in removing pollutants from GW produced in educational institutions. It was observed that major pollutants such as COD, Phosphorus, and microbial indicators are removed in considerable quantities. The removal efficiencies obtained in the present study reveal that the CW technique may be applied to mitigate the environmental impacts of GW. The use of polyculture, plant species was particularly positive in CWs, where it seems to enhance general treatment performance through the uptake of more nutrients and an increase in microbial activity. More importantly, the adaptability of CWs to different kinds of environmental conditions makes their utility suitable even for areas with problems of water shortage. From the findings of this study, it can be concluded that CWs integrated with polyculture plant species are practical for GW treatment. Future studies should, therefore, focus on the long-term performance and maintenance requirements addressing potential clogging and seasonal variance of such systems, as well as their applicability in other urban areas, in further establishing their role in environmental sustainability and resource conservation.

References

1. G. Borah, Urban Water Stress: Climate Change Implications for Water Supply in Cities. *Water Conservation Science and Engineering*. **10**, 20 (2025). https://doi.org/10.1007/s41101-025-00344-5
2. D. Narayan Paithankar, Shashi Ranjan Kumar, Greywater Reuse and Treatment Methods for Quality Improvement: A Review. *Advances in Manufacturing Technology and Management*. 328–338 (2022). https://doi.org/10.1007/978-981-16-9523-0_37
3. M. Daniel, M. M. Ahammed, I. N. Shaikh, Selection of Greywater Reuse Options Using Multi-Criteria Decision-making Techniques. *Water Conservation Science and Engineering*. **8**, 2 (2023). https://doi.org/10.1007/s41101-023-00181-4
4. L. M. Avery *et al.*, Constructed wetlands for grey water treatment. *Ecohydrology and Hydrobiology*, **7**, no. 3–4, pp. 191–200 (2007). https://doi.org/10.1016/S1642-3593(07)70101-5
5. S. Arden, X. Ma, Constructed wetlands for greywater recycle and reuse: A review. *Science of The Total Environment,* **630**, pp. 587-599 (2018) https://doi.org/10.1016/j.scitotenv.2018.02.218
6. S. X. De Campos, M. Soto, The Use of Constructed Wetlands to Treat Effluents for Water Reuse. *Environments – MDPI*. **11**, 1–26 (2024). https://doi.org/10.3390/environments11020035
7. Constructed Building Ideas. Online. Available :(2024). https://theconstructor.org/environmental-engg/constructed-wetlands-components-mechanism
8. M. Mohan, C. G. Evangelin, V. N. S. Sindhuja, A. U. Kumar, Phytoremediation (Plants as reactors). *International Journal of Engineering, Science and Mathematics* **6**, 283–291 (2017). https://www.ijesm.co.in/uploads/68/4249.pdf
9. C. Hernández-Crespo, N. Oliver, M. Peña, M. Añó, M. Martín, Valorisation of drinking water treatment sludge as substrate in subsurface flow constructed wetlands for upgrading treated wastewater. *Process Safety and Environmental Protection*. **158**, 486–494 (2022). https://doi.org/10.1016/j.psep.2021.12.035
10. R. Tandekar, P. Kochrekar, R. Jadhav, S. Ubale, M. Janbandhu, Treatment of Greywater Using Constructed Wetland. *International Research Journal of Engineering and Technology*. **09**, 2109–2112 (2022). https://www.irjet.net/archives/V9/i7/IRJET-V9I7385.pdf
11. D. M. Ghaitidak, K. D. Yadav, Characteristics and treatment of greywater—a review. *Environmental Science and Pollution Research*. **20**, 2795–2809 (2013). https://doi.org/10.1007/s11356-013-1533-0
12. A. Dixon, D. Butler, A. Fewkes, Water saving potential of domestic water reuse systems using greywater and rainwater in combination. *Water Science and Technology*. **39**, 25–32 (1999). https://doi.org/10.1016/S0273-1223(99)00083-9.
13. B. K. Biswal, R. Balasubramanian, Constructed Wetlands for Reclamation and Reuse of Wastewater and Urban Stormwater: A Review. *Frontiers in Environmental Science* **10,** (2022). https://doi.org/10.3389/fenvs.2022.836289
14. R. Shukla, D. Gupta, G. Singh, V. K. Mishra, Performance of horizontal flow constructed wetland for secondary treatment of domestic wastewater in a remote tribal area of Central India. *Sustainable Environment Research*. **31**, (2021). https://doi.org/10.1186/s42834-021-00087-7
15. S. C. Reed, D. Brown, Subsurface flow wetlands—A performance evaluation. *Water Environment Research*. **67**, 244–248 (1995). https://doi.org/10.2175/106143095X131420
16. J. Vymazal, Plants used in constructed wetlands with horizontal subsurface flow: a review. *Hydrobiologia*. **674**, 133-156 (2011). https://doi.org/10.1007/s10750-011-0738-9
17. T. Tuttolomondo, G. Virga, M. Licata, C. Leto, S. La Bella, Constructed wetlands as sustainable technology for the treatment and reuse of the first-flush stormwater in agriculture-A case study in Sicily (Italy). *Water (Switzerland)*. **12**, (2020). https://doi.org/10.3390/w12092542
18. R. Mascoli Junior, C. M. Passoni, F. M. Santos, F. S. Bernardes, F. J. C. Magalhães Filho, P. L. Paulo, Assessment of Surfactant Removal Capacity and Microbial Community Diversity in a Greywater-Treating Constructed Wetland. *Resources*. **12**, (2023). https://doi.org/10.3390/resources12030038
19. D. Q. Zhang et al, Application of constructed wetlands for wastewater treatment in developing countries–A review of recent developments (2000–2013). *Journal of Environmental Management*. **141**, 116-131 (2014). https://doi.org/10.1016/j.jenvman.2014.03.015
20. APHA/AWWA/WEF, 2012, Online. Available: https://www.standardmethods.org/doi/book/10.2105/SMWW.2882
21. A. Aygun, B. Nas, A. Berktay, H. Ates, Application of sequencing batch biofilm reactor for treatment of sewage wastewater treatment: effect of power failure, *Desalination and Water Treatment*. **52**, 6956–6965 (2014). https://doi.org/10.1080/19443994.2013.823354
22. X. Liu, N. Dong, Q. Chen, Y. Luo, J. Guo, S. Tang, Study on treatment of campus domestic wastewater for landscape water treatment by

hydrolytic acidification - biological contact oxidation process. *Chemical Engineering Transactions*. **55**, 157– 162 (2016). https://doi.org/10.3303/CET1655027

23. K. Katam, Y. Tiwari, T. Shimizu, S. Soda, D. Bhattacharyya, Start-up of a trickling photobioreactor for the treatment of domestic wastewater. *Water Environment Research*, **93**, 1690–1699 (2021). https://doi.org/10.1002/wer.1554

24. J. Laaffat, F. Aziz, N. Ouazzani, L. Mandi, Biotechnological approach of greywater treatment and reuse for landscape irrigation in small communities. *Saudi Journal of Biological Sciences*. **26**, 83–90 (2019). https://doi.org/10.1016/j.sjbs.2017.01.006

25. W. C. Kuo, C. W. Pan, L. F. Lin, Wastewater Treatment and Reuse on Campus: A Case Study in Kun Shan University. *4th International Conference on Green Technology and Sustainable Development (GTSD)*, Ho Chi Minh City, Vietnam. 583-586 (2018). https://doi: 10.1109/GTSD.2018.8595652

26. G Langergraber, The role of plant uptake on the removal of organic matter and nutrients in subsurface flow constructed wetlands: a simulation study – PubMed. *Water Science and Technology*. **51**, 213–23 (2005). https://doi.org/10.2166/wst.2005.0322

27. T. Pincam, H. Brix, A. Jampeetong, Growth performance of tropical wetland species (Cyperus involucratus Rottb. and Thalia geniculata L.) in anaerobic digester effluent and their water treatment efficiency. *Ecological Engineering*. **143**, 105667 (2020). https://doi.org/10.1016/j.ecoleng.2019.105667

28. Q. Wang, Y. Hu, H. Xie, Z. Yang, Constructed Wetlands: A Review on the Role of Radial Oxygen Loss in the Rhizosphere by Macrophytes. *Water*. **10**, 678 (2018). https://doi.org/10.3390/w10060678

29. A. G. Patel *et al.*, Intensifying Nutrient Removal in Hybrid-Constructed Wetlands Treating Urban Streamwater. *ACS Omega*. **10**, 13943–13953 (2025). https://doi:10.1021/acsomega.4c10124

30. Z. A. Mumtaj, S. Khan, N. Ahmad, A. R. Khan, M. Q. Alkahtani, R. El Morabet, Evaluating Arundo donax efficiency for pharmaceutical compounds removal from synthetic wastewater in horizontal flow constructed wetland. *Scientific Reports*. **15**, 13781 (2025). https://doi.org/10.1038/s41598-025-94808-2

31. H. D. Tran, H. M. T. Vi, H. T. T. Dang, R. M. Narbaitz, Pollutant removal by Canna Generalis in tropical constructed wetlands for domestic wastewater treatment. *Global Journal of Environmental Science and Management*. **5**, 331–344 (2019). https:// doi:10.22034/gjesm.2019.03.06

32. H. D. Di Giorgi, A. Mariñelarena, J. Cochero, Sustained nutrient removal in constructed wetlands using Equisetum giganteum. *Science of the Total Environment*. **994**, (2025). https://doi.org/10.1016/j.scitotenv.2025.180046

33. J. G. Martinez-Martínez *et al.*, Bacterial Communities Associated with the Roots of *Typha* spp. and Its Relationship in Phytoremediation Processes. *Microorganisms*, **11**, 1587 (2023). https://doi.org/10.3390/microorganisms11061587

34. D. Kotsia, A. Deligianni, N. M. Fyllas, A. S. Stasinakis, M. S. Fountoulakis, Converting treatment wetlands into 'treatment gardens': Use of ornamental plants for greywater treatment. *Science of the Total Environment*. **744**, 140889 (2020). https://doi.org/10.1016/j.scitotenv.2020.140889

35. F. H. Lakho *et al.*, Decentralized grey and black water reuse by combining a vertical flow constructed wetland and membrane based potable water system: Full scale demonstration. *Journal of Environmental Chemical Engineering*. **9**, (2021). https://doi.org/10.1016/j.jece.2020.104688

Mathematical Modeling of Citric Acid Production and Microbial Growth Kinetics Using *Aspergillus niger* in Batch Fermentation

Kanjana Detchomphoo[1*], *Nicharee* Wisuthiphaet[1], *Rittipun* Rungruang[2], and *Sasithorn* Kongruang[1*]

[1]Department of Biotechnology, Faculty of Applied Science, King Mongkut's University of Technology North Bangkok, Wong Sawang, Bang Sue, 10800 Bangkok, Thailand
[2]Department of Cosmetic Science, Faculty of Science and Technology, Suan Dusit University, 10300 Bangkok, Thailand

Abstract. This study investigates the microbial growth kinetics and citric acid production by *Aspergillus niger* in batch fermentation, employing Monod, Logistic, and Gompertz models to analyze the dynamic relationships between biomass growth, substrate consumption, and citric acid formation. A series of experiments were conducted in a 5 L stirred tank batch bioreactor with 3 L working volume, using glucose (97 g/L) as the carbon source. Model predictions were validated using experimental data from batch fermentation runs. The results showed that *A. niger* exhibited typical microbial growth behavior, with biomass concentration increasing from 2.65 g cell/L at 0 hours to a peak of 14.58 g cell/L at 192 hours, before declining to 12.39 g cell/L by the end of the fermentation. Citric acid production followed a similar trend, reaching a maximum of 24.75 g/L at 240 hours and subsequently declining. Model fitting results revealed that the Gompertz model provided the best fit and yield, maximum specific growth rate μ_{max} 15 h^{-1} exhibiting the highest goodness-of-fit ($R^2 = 0.989$) compared to the Monod ($R^2 = 0.974$) and Logistic models ($R^2 = 0.988$). The Gompertz model effectively captured the S-shaped growth and product formation patterns, including the deceleration phase associated with nutrient depletion and product inhibition. This study highlights the effectiveness of the Gompertz model in describing the fermentation process and emphasizes the importance of model selection in evaluating fermentation performance and improving the understanding of citric acid production kinetics.

1 Introduction

Citric acid, also known as 2-hydroxy-1, 2, 3-propane-tricarboxylic acid, derives its name from the Latin word citrus, referring to plants within the Citrus genus, including lemon trees [1]. It is a colorless, weak organic acid that is highly soluble in water in its pure form. This acid can be produced from both natural and synthetic sources, and its global production has significantly increased in recent years. In 2020, global citric acid production reached 2.39 million tons, with projections indicating an increase to 2.91 million tons by 2026 [2]. This weak acid is widely used in various industries, such as food and beverage, medicines, cosmetics, and animal feed, due to its versatile nature. In the food industry, citric acid is commonly used as an acidulant due to its high solubility and low toxicity. It is also utilized for cleaning specialized steam boilers. Within the beverage, food, and confectionery industries, citric acid serves as an antioxidant, emulsifier, buffer, chelating agent, flavor enhancer, and acidulant [3].

Citric acid can be extracted from natural sources such as lemons, guavas, and oranges, or produced through microbial fermentation. However, due to the insufficient yields from plant sources to meet global demand, microbial fermentation has become the primary method for citric acid production. A wide variety of microorganisms, including bacterial and fungal species, are employed in large-scale citric acid production. These include *Bacillus licheniformis*, *Arthrobacter paraffinens*, *Penicillium janthinellum*, *Candida species*, *Yarrowia lipolytica*, *Hansenula anamola*, and various strains of the *Aspergillus* genus [4]. Among these, *Aspergillus niger* has become the preferred microorganism for large-scale citric acid production due to its ability to utilize a diverse range of substrates and its high citric acid production capacity [5]. Research has shown that *A. niger* can produce up to 90 g/L of citric acid through submerged fermentation when using sucrose as the carbon source [6].

Citric acid is particularly important in the food sector, where it accounts for a significant portion of global consumption. In 2016, it comprised 62.53% of global citric acid consumption within the food and beverage industry, shown in Figure 1., with an anticipated growth rate of 6.03% from 2016 to 2021 [5]. In the pharmaceutical industry, this acid is essential in regulating mineral formation and stimulating nerve cells [9]. It is also used in the treatment of kidney stones [10] and is a key ingredient in drug formulations and healthcare products [11]. In the cosmetics industry, this compound functions as an antioxidant and exfoliant, improving product stability and absorption [12].

* Corresponding author : sasithorn.k@sci.kmutnb.ac.th, s660407181004@email.kmutnb.ac.th

Additionally, in agriculture, it enhances nutrient absorption and stimulates plant growth. Furthermore, citric acid is utilized in the textile and detergent industries for cleaning and descaling equipment. A 2022 evaluation of the global citric acid market projected that its market value would grow at an annual rate of 3.82% through 2032 [13].

Despite its widespread application, the kinetic understanding of citric acid production remains a significant challenge due to the complexities of the fermentation process. This complexity arises from the wide variety of substrates that can be utilized, the dynamic interactions between *A. niger* and these substrates, and the inhibitory effects exerted by both substrates and products. Such factors complicate the development of a universal kinetic model capable of accurately describing citric acid fermentation. Nevertheless, mathematical modeling has proven valuable for predicting system behavior, identifying optimal bioprocess designs, and defining key operating parameters, ultimately enhancing process efficiency [14]. To support this, Woinaroschy et al. studied and improved kinetic models for citric acid fermentation using molasses and whey, comparing different models with experimental results. Their findings underscored the critical influence of substrate concentration and inhibition effects on fermentation performance[15, 16]. Building upon this foundation, Sharifzadeh Baei et al. applied the logistic model to describe microbial growth and incorporated the Luedeking-Piret equation to model citric acid production from apple pomace by *A. niger*, revealing that citric acid synthesis in this system is closely associated with microbial growth [17]. Complementing these efforts, Baei et al. and other researchers have reported essential kinetic parameters, including the maximum specific growth rate (μ_{max}), yield coefficients, and substrate affinity constants across different microbial strains and fermentation conditions. These insights have provided a more detailed understanding for the calibration and refinement of fermentation models [17, 18]. By utilizing these mathematical modeling methods, researchers can significantly reduce the need for extensive empirical experimentation under varying conditions, resulting in notable savings in both time and research costs while accelerating process development.

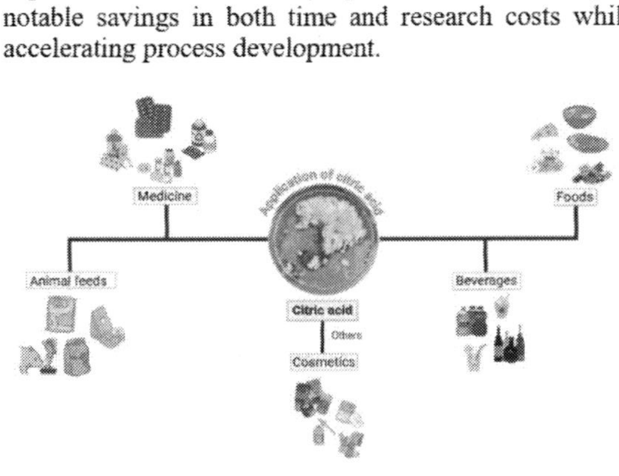

Fig. 1. Applications of citric acid in various industries

In recent years, scientific investigations into *A. niger* fermentation have focused on enhancing citric acid production due to its substantial industrial importance and the organism's favorable metabolic characteristics, such as high citrate synthase activity and the ability to metabolize a wide spectrum of carbon sources [13]. These studies have systematically examined both fermentation parameters and genetic improvements to elevate citric acid yields [13]. To quantitatively characterize and evaluate *A. niger* growth and metabolite formation, several mathematical models have been applied.

The Monod model is widely used to describe microbial growth as a function of substrate concentration and has been applied to *A. niger* fermentations for estimating essential kinetic parameters such as maximum specific growth rate and substrate affinity [18, 19]. In addition, the Logistic model has been effectively utilized to capture the typical sigmoidal growth patterns observed in *A. niger*, particularly under nutrient-limited conditions. This model has proven useful for fitting empirical data and estimating maximum biomass concentrations in both submerged and solid-state systems [20]. The Gompertz model, which has gained increasing attention in the field of fungal kinetics, offers a comprehensive description of the lag, exponential, and deceleration phases of growth. It has demonstrated a strong ability to fit data related to biomass accumulation and citric acid production, especially under conditions exhibiting S-shaped growth curves [21]. Comparative assessments indicate that while each model possesses specific advantages depending on the fermentation context, the Gompertz and Logistic models are particularly well-suited to capture the complex kinetics of filamentous fungi like *A. niger* [20, 21]. Furthermore, some studies have introduced alternative or hybrid modeling approaches to improve predictive accuracy in specialized fermentation scenarios [13]. Overall, the use of these mathematical models plays a pivotal role in refining process control, improving yield prediction, and reducing experimental effort in industrial-scale citric acid fermentation processes [13, 19, 20].

Within this context, the present study proposes and evaluates the Monod, Logistic, and Gompertz kinetic models to describe citric acid production and biomass formation by *A. niger* in batch fermentation systems. The investigation involves monitoring changes in biomass, glucose concentration, and citric acid levels to assess the models' ability to capture experimental trends. These models aim not only to describe microbial behavior but also to facilitate improved control strategies and efficiency in scale up fermentation operations.

2 Material and methods

2.1 Chemicals

The Potato Dextrose Broth (PDB) and Potato Dextrose Agar (PDA) were obtained from Himedia Laboratories Pvt. Ltd., Mumbai, India. D-glucose ($C_6H_{12}O_6$), monopotassium phosphate (KH_2PO_4), dipotassium phosphate (K_2HPO_4), magnesium sulfate heptahydrate ($MgSO_4 \cdot 7H_2O$), calcium chloride ($CaCl_2$), and calcium carbonate ($CaCO_3$) were purchased from Sisco Research

Laboratories Pvt. Ltd., Taloja, India. Urea was obtained from Honeywell International Inc., New Jersey, USA. Tween 80 was purchased from Scharlab S.L., Sentmenat, Spain. 3, 5-Dinitrosalicylic acid was procured from Sisco Research Laboratories Pvt. Ltd., Taloja, India. Hydrochloric acid (HCl) and sodium hydroxide (NaOH) were purchased from QReC™, USA.

2.2 Microorganism and inoculum

A. niger TISTR 2365 were obtained from Thailand Institute of Scientific and Technological Research (Pathumthani, Thailand). Fungal strain was inoculated into Erlenmeyer flask containing 100 mL Potato Dextrose Broth (PDB) and maintained at 4°C for stock cultures.

2.2.1 Inoculum preparation

A. niger TISTR 2365 from stock cultures were transferred to sterile plate containing Potato dextrose agar (PDA). The cultures were incubated at 30°C in control incubater (Shaker Incubator, INC 125 FS digital, IKA-Werke GmbH & Co. KG., Staufen, Germany). After 168 hours the cultures were used as inoculum for batch cultivations in shake flask.

2.2.2 Starter preparation of A. niger

The PDA culture of *A. niger* was prepared by directly suspending the spores from the mycelium growth in the modified media. The spore suspension of *A. niger* was prepared in sterile Tween 80 to a final concentration of 3 x 10^8 spores/mL using a Thomas hemocytometer.

2.3 Kinetics of growth and citric acid production

2.3.1 Media Composition

The medium consisted of glucose ($C_6H_{12}O_6$) at concentrations of 97 g/L of D-glucose, 1 g of urea, 0.3 g/L of KH_2PO_4, 0.3 g/L of K_2HPO_4, 0.3 g/L of $MgSO_4 \cdot 7H_2O$, 0.1 g/L of $CaCl_2$. The pH of the medium was adjusted to 4 using hydrochloric acid. The medium was prepared and transferred into a batch bioreactor with a working volume of 3 L. The medium was sterilized by autoclaving at 121 °C for 15 minutes at 15 lb/in² to ensure aseptic conditions before inoculation.

2.3.2 Citric Acid Production and Kinetic Analysis of A. niger TISTR 2365 in the Stirred Tank Bioreactor

The bioreactor system was assembled in accordance with the manufacturer's guidelines and connected to all necessary operational equipment. The fungal inoculum was prepared following the procedure outlined in Section 2.2.1, using the optimized culture conditions. To ensure reproducibility and reliability of the results, the fermentation process was carried out in triplicate. A volume of 300 mL of fungal pre-culture was inoculated into the 5 L batch bioreactor containing 3 L of sterilized liquid medium in the bioreactor (MDFT-N-5L, B.E. MARUBISHI CO., LTD., Bangkok Thailand) accordingly to the setup. The cultivation was initiated under the specified conditions: agitation speed of 300 rpm with 1L/min aeration rate at 30°C, and sampling was performed every 48 hours. Each sample, with a volume of 50 mL, was collected over a total cultivation period of 384 hours to monitor fungal growth kinetics and citric acid production.

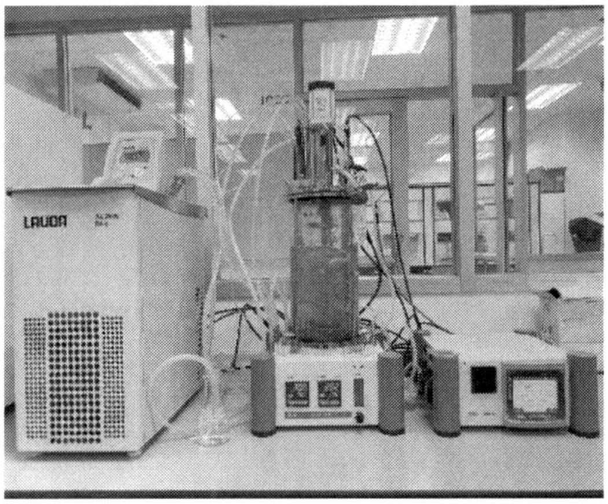

Fig. 2. Citric acid production in 5 L bioreactor using *A.niger* grown in modified media.

2.4 Analytical measurement

2.4.1 Analytical Techniques

Fermentations were performed in triplicate. Samples were withdrawn at the end of the fermentation period. The broth culture was centrifuged at 15,000 rpm to separate the mycelia. The collected filtrate was used to estimate residual sugar and citric acid production. The dry weight of mycelium was obtained by filtering broth samples through pre-weighed filter discs. Biomass concentration was determined by dry weight measurement. The harvested biomass was washed with 0.85% saline solution, followed by deionized water, then dried overnight at 80°C, cooled in a desiccator, and weighed [22]. Sugar concentration was measured using the dinitrosalicylic acid (DNS) method [23], while citric acid was quantified by titration with 0.1 N sodium hydroxide using phenolphthalein as an indicator [24]. The volume change of the sample solution from colorless to pink to red was recorded, calculated, and reported as the citric acid concentration.

2.4.2 Investigation of Growth Kinetics of A. niger

The study focused on analyzing the growth kinetics of *A. niger* during fermentation, with particular attention to biomass production, citric acid formation, and glucose consumption. All measurements in this study were conducted in triplicate to ensure accuracy and reproducibility of the results. Key experimental rates were calculated based on data collected over a 384-hour fermentation period. These include rate of biomass production r_x, where (r_x = d[X]/dt) and [X] represents biomass concentration, the rate of citric acid formation r_p, where (r_p = d[P]/dt) and [P] is citric acid concentration, and glucose consumption rate r_s, where (r_s = d[S]/dt) and [S] denotes glucose concentration.

2.5 Comparison of model kinetics

Predicted data with the consideration of the mathematical modeling using OriginPro V.2021 (OriginLab corporation, MA, USA) for evaluating parameter values in the context of nonlinear regression.

3 Mathematical modelling

Mathematical models are essential for explaining the citric acid production process through fermentation by the microorganism *A. niger*. The application of these mathematical models aids in the calculation and analysis of cell growth, sugar consumption, and product formation. This approach enables researchers to determine effective kinetic parameters that enhance fermentation yield. In this study, three mathematical models, namely the Monod Model, Logistic Model, and Gompertz Model, were applied to fit the experimental data of the fermentation process. Kinetic parameters were determined through the examination of experimental profiles and their corresponding production. The validity of the models was confirmed using three independent sets of experimental data, encompassing biomass production and product formation. The equations for biomass production models are defined in Eq. 1-3.

Monod kinetics is a model that describes the growth of microorganisms based on the concentration of the substrate available in the system. It employs an equation that expresses the growth rate as a function of the substrate concentration and a saturation value, which represents the maximum growth rate. When the substrate concentration reaches a certain level, the microorganisms reach their maximum growth capacity, and the growth rate no longer increases. The equations for monod kinetics are given in Equation 1:

$$\mu = \frac{\mu_{max} \cdot S}{K_S + S} \qquad (1)$$

where: μ is the specific growth rate (h^{-1})
μ_{max} is the maximum growth rate (h^{-1})
S is the substrate concentration (g/L)
K_S is the Monod constant, which indicates the substrate concentration at which the microorganism grows at half of its maximum rate.

The Logistic Model is another mathematical model used to describe S-curve growth, which is similar to the Gompertz model but simpler in terms of calculations and explaining the growth with a limiting factor. In this model, the population or product grows rapidly in the initial stages and then gradually slows down as it approaches the maximum growth limit, also known as the carrying capacity. The equations for logistic kinetics are shown in Equation 2:

$$\ln\left(\frac{X}{X_0}\right) = \frac{a}{1-exp(b-cx)} \qquad (2)$$

where: X is the population size or cell concentration at time (g/L)
X_0 is the initial population size (initial cell concentration) (g/L)
a is a constant that reflects the difference between the maximum population size and the initial population size.
b is a constant that relates to the initial growth rate (h^{-1})
c is a constant that defines the rate of growth slowdown (h^{-1})
t is the time (h)

The Gompertz Model is a widely used mathematical model to describe growth processes exhibiting an S-curve. It begins with slow growth, accelerates, and then decelerates as the system approaches its maximum limit. In biological production processes or the growth of living organisms (such as microorganisms) or population dynamics, growth is often limited by resource constraints, preventing continuous expansion without bounds. The Gompertz equation is expressed are:

$$\ln\left(\frac{X}{X_0}\right) = a\ exp\{-\ exp(b - ct)\} \qquad (3)$$

where: X represents the population size or cell concentration at time (g/L)
X_0 is the initial population size (initial cell concentration) (g/L)
a is a constant associated with the maximum growth rate
b is a constant that defines the starting point of growth (h^{-1})
c is a constant related to the rate of growth slowdown (h^{-1})
t is the time (h)
To assess the biological behavior of the fermentation process, the modified Gompertz model was employed to estimate key kinetic parameters related to citric acid and biomass formation. This model was selected based on its superior statistical performance compared to alternative models. The primary biological parameters evaluated include the maximum production potential (A), the specific formation rate (μ), and the duration of the lag phase (λ). These were calculated using multi-parametric nonlinear regression based on the modified Gompertz equation as proposed by Zwietering et al. (1990), which is expressed as follows Equation 4:

$$y = A \exp\left\{-\exp\left[\frac{\mu e}{A}(\lambda - t) + 1\right]\right\} \qquad (4)$$

In this equation: y represents the citric acid or biomass concentration (g/L) at a given time t (days)
A (g/L) denotes the asymptotic maximum concentration
μ (g/L/day) is the specific citric acid (or biomass) formation rate
λ (days) represents the lag phase duration
The use of mathematical models helps in analyzing the microbial growth behavior and product formation in batch fermentation processes. The parameters obtained from these models can help predict and control the fermentation process, thus improving the efficiency of biomass production and metabolite formation.

3.1 Complete Model for Parameter Estimation

In this study, a system of three Ordinary Differential Equations (ODEs) is used to represent the changes in biomass concentration [X], substrate concentration [S], and product concentration [P] based on batch experimental data. These equations describe the dynamic relationships of these components during the fermentation process. The system of equations is as follows:

- The rate of change of biomass concentration:

$$\frac{dX}{dt} = \mu \cdot X - k_d \cdot X$$

- The rate of change of substrate concentration:

$$\frac{dS}{dt} = \frac{1}{Y_{X/S}} \cdot \mu \cdot X - m_s \cdot X$$

- The rate of change of citric acid concentration:

$$\frac{dP}{dt} = Y_{P/X} \cdot \mu \cdot X - \mu_P \cdot X$$

In these equations, the following parameters are used:

- $Y_{X/S}$: The yield coefficient of biomass per substrate (g/g)
- $Y_{P/X}$: The yield coefficient of product (citric acid) per biomass (g/g)
- m_S: The maintenance coefficient for substrate utilization (-)
- k_d: The death rate coefficient of microorganisms (h^{-1})

These equations and parameters are crucial for modeling the fermentation process and estimating key parameters that determine the efficiency of citric acid production under the given experimental conditions.

4 Result and discussion

4.1 Model validation and parameter estimation

The batch fermentation model was validated using experimental data obtained throughout the course of this study. This validation was accomplished by estimating the parameters of the various kinetic models under experimented runs over fermentation time. Table 1. displays the estimated parameters along with the optimal values for the kinetic models considered. The estimation of the maximum specific growth rate (μ_{max}) using both the Logistic and Gompertz models yielded similar results. However, the Monod model provided the highest μ_{max} value of 19.08 h^{-1}. For the substrate affinity constant (K_s), the Monod model yielded a result of 93.98 g/L. Figure 3. showed the mathematical model graphs for three models: Monod, Logistic, and Gompertz, using data for substrate concentration (sugar), biomass (dry *A. niger* cells), and product (citric acid).

The main objective of the fermentation process is to maximize substrate utilization, thereby achieving the highest possible yield. To ensure that fermentation proceeds under optimal conditions, it is crucial to develop an accurate mathematical model and precisely determine the associated parameters. This model should include equations that describe cell growth, substrate consumption, and product formation, while also accounting for the interrelationships between these factors. Both the Gompertz and logistic curves exhibit an S-shaped pattern, making them well-suited for modeling processes that involve an initial adaptation phase, followed by rapid growth, and eventually a slower phase as the system reaches saturation. Despite their visual and numerical similarities, these two models are fundamentally distinct.

In this study, the Gompertz model was found to be the most effective in explaining citric acid production and biomass formation, providing the highest goodness-of-fit (R^2) with μ_{max} 15 h^{-1}, P_{max} 24.97 g/L and R^2 0.995 as shown Table 4. when compared to other models such as the logistic and Monod models under all experimental conditions. This aligns with recent studies, such as that of Chaichol et al. (2023), who applied the Andrews model to describe substrate inhibition effects in Aspergillus species during citric acid fermentation. Their findings showed that the Andrews model offered a better fit than classical Monod kinetics, particularly at high glucose concentrations [17]. Similarly, Chaleewong et al. (2022) used a combined Contois-Gompertz hybrid model to more accurately capture biomass growth and product formation during batch fermentation of filamentous fungi, highlighting the significance of accounting for biomass-dependent substrate uptake [26]. These studies underline the evolving nature of kinetic modeling in fermentation research, demonstrating how hybrid or modified models often outperform traditional ones. By incorporating complex biological phenomena such as inhibition, biomass aggregation, and morphological changes, these advanced models provide a more comprehensive and accurate representation of fermentation dynamics.

Table 1. Results of *A. niger* cultivation experiments in batch bioreactor.

Fermentation time (h)	Biomass (g cell/L)	Glucose Concentration (g glucose/L)	Citric acid concentration (g citric acid/L)
0	2.65	98.58	2.13
48	6.51	83.60	2.56
96	7.39	69.81	16.64
144	8.06	54.29	18.35
192	14.58	29.77	21.76
240	12.27	28.51	24.75
288	14.41	26.70	24.32
336	12.63	24.66	23.47
384	12.39	22.73	22.61

 https://doi.org/10.1051/e3sconf/202567901026

4.2 Substrate Consumption

For the consumption of sugar by *A. niger*, Table 1. shows a gradual decrease in the amount of residual sugar from an initial value of 98.58 g/L, which decreased to 22.73 g/L by the end of the fermentation, after 384 hours. The observed decrease was due to the sugar consumption by the microorganisms during fermentation. Our findings align with those reported by Amenaghawon & Aisien (2012) [26], who observed a similar reduction in the residual sugar content due to the formation of citric acid from the sugar consumption of corn starch hydrolysate *A. niger*.

The parameters for sugar consumption, $Y_{x/s}$ and K_s, obtained from the Monod model were 0.0743 g cell / g glucose and 1.622 g/L, appeared in Tables 2 and 4 respectively.

4.3 Microbial Growth

The growth of the fermented *A. niger* is shown in Table 1. It was observed that the concentration of *A. niger* cells increased from 2.65 g cell/L at the initial stage to 14.58 g cell/L after approximately 192 hours. After this point, the microbial concentration slightly decreased towards the end, with the final concentration being 12.39 g cell/L. The observed trend indicates that microbial growth occurred between 0 and 192 hours of fermentation, while growth slowed between 192 and 384 hours. The observed decrease is often due to the complete utilization of the substrate and may be caused by the high levels of citric acid are toxic to cells, when excessive citric acid accumulates [13], which could inhibit the activity of the fermenting microorganisms. The parameters for the growth of *A. niger*, μ_{max} and $Y_{x/s}$, as shown in Table 2., were 0.14 h^{-1} and 0.13 (g cell/g glucose), respectively. The experimental results are consistent with the findings of Amenaghawon & Aisien (2012) [26], who observed that the concentration of *A. niger* cells increased during the initial stages of fermentation, reaching a maximum value, after which the concentration decreased. The observed trend of decline is commonly attributed to the exhaustion of the substrate, which is consistent with Table 3 showing the kinetic parameters related to the microbial growth and citric acid production in the batch fermentation process. The microbial growth rate (r_x) started from 0.08 g cell/L h and gradually decreased, the sugar consumption rate (r_s) and citric acid production rate (r_p) also changed with the fermentation time, and the cell production rate (q_x), sugar consumption per cell (q_s), and citric acid production per cell (q_p) were also changed. These data can be used to improve and control the fermentation process to effectively increase the yield and reduce the cost of citric acid production from *A. niger*.

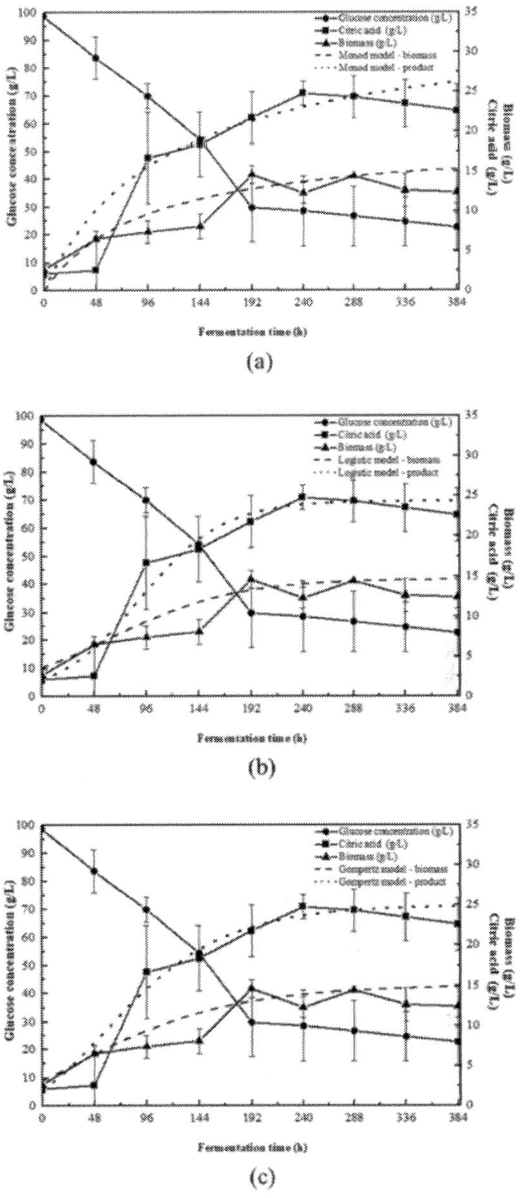

Fig. 3. Fitting of the (a) Monod model, (b) Logistic model and (c) Gompertz model to substrate, biomass and product concentrations by *A. niger* TISTR 2365 in 5 L bioreactor.

Table 2. Summary of *A. niger* TISTR 2365 growth kinetics data for batch cultivation in bioreactors.

μ_{max} (h^{-1})	$Y_{x/s}$ (g cell / g glucose)	$Y_{p/s}$ (g citric acid / g glucose)	$Y_{p/x}$ (g citric acid / g cell)	t_d (h)	Productivity (g/g/h)
0.14	0.13	0.27	2.10	398.26	0.15

4.4 Product Formation

Figure 3. shows the time profile of citric acid concentration during fermentation. It was observed that citric acid production exhibited a nearly linear relationship with cell growth from the onset of fermentation up to approximately 192 hours, indicating that citric acid production is closely linked to microbial cell growth. The citric acid concentration increased steadily from 2.13 g/L to around 24.75 g/L, after which it plateaued and subsequently declined after 240 hours. These observations are consistent with those of Nadeem et al. (2010), who reported a similar decline in citric acid production after reaching a peak. According to Al-Sheri & Mostafa (2006) [28], Alvarez-Vasquez et al. (2000) [29], Arzumanov et al. (2000) [30], and Kristiansen & Sinclair (1978) [31], the decline in citric acid yield was attributed to reduced microbial growth in the fermentation after 96 hours, as citric acid formation is closely linked to microbial growth. Additionally, this decline may be due to inhibitory effects from high citric acid concentrations, reduced nitrogen levels in the fermentation medium, and the depletion of sugar sources. The parameters for citric acid production, specifically $Y_{p/x}$, were calculated and presented in Table 2, showing a value of 2.10 g of citric acid per gram of cells. High variability observed in Figure 3 can be attributed to several factors, including biological variability inherent to the microorganism, limitations in analytical techniques, and heterogeneity within the bioreactor environment. Biological variability, such as differences in spore germination, hyphal morphology, and pellet formation, can influence microbial growth and metabolite production across replicates. Furthermore, measurement techniques like dry weight determination and colorimetric assays may introduce significant experimental error, especially when sample preparation lacks consistency. In the earlier phase of this study, citric acid concentrations were analyzed using High-Performance Liquid Chromatography (HPLC). The results obtained from HPLC were found to be consistent with those obtained using the titration method, showing no significant differences in measurement accuracy. Therefore, to simplify the modeling and evaluation of the kinetic equations, the titration method was selected for subsequent analyses. This approach allows for efficient model validation while maintaining reliable accuracy in the assessment of citric acid production. Additionally, spatial gradients of nutrients and oxygen within the bioreactor could contribute to these discrepancies. To address these issues and enhance data reliability, high-performance liquid chromatography (HPLC) is recommended due to its superior sensitivity and specificity. HPLC provides more accurate quantification, reduces analytical errors, and improves reproducibility, thereby significantly enhancing the reliability of fermentation data. [26, 32]

Table 4. Values of estimated parameters using different models

Model	μ_{max} h^{-1}	P_{max} g/L	K_S g/L	R^2_b	R^2_p
Monod	19.08±0.98	33.83±14.54	93.98	0.97	0.92
Logistic	14.66±0.46	24.36±0.71	-	0.99	1.00
Gompertz	15.01±0.66	24.97±1.15	-	0.99	0.99

R^2_b: regression coefficient for fitted biomass concentration.

R^2_p: regression coefficient for fitted product concentration

Table 3. Kinetic parameters associated with biomass growth and citric acid production

r_x (g cell/L·h)	r_s (g glucose/L·h)	r_p (g product/L·h)	q_x (g cell/g glucose)	q_s (g glucose/g cell)	q_p (g product/g cell)
-	-	-	0.03	37.20	0.80
0.08	-0.31	0.01	0.08	12.84	0.39
0.02	-0.29	0.29	0.11	9.45	2.25
0.01	-0.32	0.04	0.15	6.74	2.28
0.14	-0.51	0.07	0.49	2.04	1.49
-0.05	-0.03	0.06	0.43	2.32	2.02
0.04	-0.04	-0.01	0.54	1.85	1.69
-0.04	-0.04	-0.02	0.51	1.95	1.86
-0.01	-0.04	-0.02	0.55	1.83	1.82

Note: q_x = biomass productivity (g/L h), q_s = sugar consumption rate (g/L h) and q_p = citric acid productivity (g/L h)

5 Conclusions

This study successfully demonstrated the use of Monod, Logistic, and Gompertz models to analyze microbial growth and citric acid production by *A. niger* in a batch fermentation system. The application of these models provided a deeper understanding of the kinetics involved in citric acid production, highlighting the importance of mathematical models in optimizing fermentation processes. Among the models tested, the Gompertz model showed the best fit to the experimental data, providing the highest goodness-of-fit (R^2) values. This model effectively captured the sigmoidal growth patterns and product formation kinetics, making it the most suitable for describing the dynamics of citric acid production under the given experimental conditions. The Logistic model, while also suitable, exhibited asymmetry compared to the more symmetric Gompertz model.

The findings confirm that microbial growth and citric acid production are closely linked, with the fermentation process following an initial exponential growth phase, followed by a deceleration period. The concentration of citric acid peaked at approximately 24.75 g/L, after which it declined due to the exhaustion of nutrients and accumulation of inhibitory products. These results are consistent with prior studies, which indicate that high citric acid concentrations and nutrient limitations can inhibit further microbial growth and acid production. Overall, the study emphasizes the importance of precise parameter estimation and model selection for optimizing industrial-scale fermentation processes. The insights gained from this research can aid in the efficient production of citric acid and similar metabolites, contributing to the advancement of biotechnological applications.

This research was partly supported by Sweet D international company limited under Enserv Holding CO., LTD., and the Department of Biotechnology, Faculty of Applied Science, KMUTNB, for their facilities support.

References

1. B. Max, J. M. Salgado, N. Rodríguez, S. Cortés, A. Converti, J. M. Domínguez, Biotechnological production of citric acid. *Brazilian Journal of Microbiology*. **41**, 862–875 (2010). https://doi.org/10.1590/s1517-83822010000400005
2. M. Lambros, T. Tran, Q. Fei, M. Nicolaou, Citric acid: a multifunctional pharmaceutical excipient. *Pharmaceutics*. **14**, 972 (2022). https://doi.org/10.3390/pharmaceutics14050972
3. B. C. Behera, Citric acid from *Aspergillus niger*: a comprehensive overview. *Critical Reviews in Microbiology*. **46**, 727–749 (2020). https://doi.org/10.1080/1040841x.2020.1828815
4. S. Mores *et al.*, Citric acid bioproduction and downstream processing: Status, opportunities, and challenges. *Bioresource Technology*. **320**, 124426 (2020). https://doi.org/10.1016/j.biortech.2020.124426
5. C. R. Soccol, L. P. S. Vandenberghe, C. Rodrigues, A. Pandey, New perspectives for citric acid production and applications. *Food Technol. Biotechnol.* **44**, 141-149 (2006). [Online]. Available: https://www.scirp.org/reference/referencespapers?referenceid=2149898
6. Kinetic studies on citric acid production by *Aspergillus niger*. II. The two-stage process. *PubMed*. (1975). [Online]. Available: https://pubmed.ncbi.nlm.nih.gov/5858/.
7. A. Pandey, C. R. Soccol, J. A. Rodriguez-Leon, P. Nigam, *Solid-State Fermentation in Biotechnology-Fundamentals and Applications*. New Delhi: Asiatech Publishers Inc., (2001). [Online]. Available:https://www.scirp.org/reference/referencespapers?referenceid=1934530.
8. C. R. Soccol, L. P. S. Vandenberghe, Overview of applied solid-state fermentation in Brazil. *Biochemical Engineering Journal*. **13**, 205–218 (2003). https://doi.org/10.1016/S1369-703X(02)00121-3
9. L. P. S. Vandenberghe, C. R. Soccol, A. Pandey, J.-M. Lebeault, Microbial production of citric acid. *Brazilian Archives of Biology and Technology*. **42**, 263–276 (1999). https://doi.org/10.1590/s1516-89131999000300001
10. R. Salihu *et al.*, Citric acid: A green cross-linker of biomaterials for biomedical applications. *European Polymer Journal*. **146**, 110271 (2021).https://doi.org/10.1016/j.eurpolymj.2021.110271
11. R. Ciriminna, F. Meneguzzo, R. Delisi, M. Pagliaro, Citric acid: emerging applications of key biotechnology industrial product. *Chemistry Central Journal*. **11**, (2017). https://doi.org/10.1186/s13065-017-0251-y
12. A. Latif *et al.*, An overview of key industrial product citric acid production by *Aspergillus niger* and its application. *Journal of Industrial Microbiology & Biotechnology*. (2025). https://doi.org/10.1093/jimb/kuaf007
13. H. Andres, Z.-R. Hu, S. Snowling, O. Schraa, Model-Based Optimum Design of Sequencing Batch Reactors for COD and Nitrogen Removal from a Slaughterhouse Wastewater. *Proceedings of the Water Environment Federation*. **2006**, 5100–5107 (2006).
14. E. Książek, Citric acid: Properties, microbial production, and applications in industries. *Molecules*. **29**, 22 (2023). https://doi.org/10.3390/molecules29010022
15. A. Woinaroschy, A. Nica, I. D. Ofițeru, V. Lavric, Kinetic Models for Citric Acid Production. *Rev. Chim. (Bucharest)*. **61**, 979-982 (2010).
16. M. S. Baei, M. Mahmoudi, H. Yunesi, A kinetic model for citric acid production from apple pomace by *Aspergillus niger*. *Afr. J. Biotechnol.* **7**, 3487-3489 (2008). [Online]. Available: http://www.academicjournals.org/AJB. [Accessed: Jul. 4, 2025].
17. N. Amenaghawon, O. Osazuwa, C. Okieimen, Dynamic Modelling and Simulation of Citric Acid Production from Dilute Acid Hydrolysed Corn Starch Using Aspergillus Niger. *Nigerian Journal of Technology*. **33**, 222 (2014). https://doi.org/10.4314/njt.v33i2.12

18. H. Pagarra, A simplified model of Aspergillus niger growth using Nephrolepis biserrata leaves for exo-polygalacturonase production. *Proceeding International Conference on Mathematic, Science, Technology, Education and Their Applications*. **1**, (2016). [Online].Available:https://ojs.unm.ac.id/icmstea/article/download/2702/1441
19. S. Saithi, M. Nopharatana, Mathematical Modeling of Biomass and Enzyme Production Kinetics by Aspergillus niger in Solid-State Fermentation at Various Temperatures and Moisture Contents. Journal of Microbial & Biochemical Technology. **08**, (2016).
20. F. Chen, M. Gullo, 4th International Conference on Acetic Acid Bacteria - Vinegar and other products (AAB 2015). *Acetic Acid Bacteria*. **4**, (2015). https://doi.org/10.1080/19476337.2024.2393758
21. S. Sirisansaneeyakul, S. Singhasuwan, W. Choorit, N. Phoopat, J. L. Garcia, Y. Chisti, Photoautotrophic production of lipids by some *Chlorella* strains. *Mar. Biotechnol.* **13**, 928-941 (2011).
22. G. L. Miller, Use of dinitrosalicylic acid reagent for determination of reducing sugar) Analytical Chemistry. **31**, 426–428 (1959). https://doi.org/10.1021/ac60147a030
23. D. V. Guebel, N. V. T. Darias, Optimization of the citric acid production by *Aspergillus niger* through a metabolic flux balance model. Electronic Journal of Biotechnology. **4**, 7–8 (2001). DOI:10.4067/S0717-34582001000100001
24. P. Chaichol, et al., Modeling substrate inhibition kinetics of *Aspergillus* spp. in citric acid fermentation, *J. Ind. Microbiol. Biotechnol.* **50**, 45-58 (2023)
25. S. Chaleewong, et al., Hybrid Contois-Gompertz kinetic modeling of filamentous fungal growth in batch fermentation. *Biochem. Eng. J.* **180**, 108345 (2022)
26. N. A. Amenaghawon, F. A. Aisien, Modelling and Simulation of Citric Acid Production from Corn Starch Hydrolysate Using *Aspergillus Niger*. *Environment and Natural Resources Research*. **2**, (2012). https://doi.org/10.5539/enrr.v2n1p73
27. M. Al-Sheh, Yasser S. Mostafa, Citric Acid Production from Date Syrup using Immobilized Cells of *Aspergillus niger*, *Biotechnology(Faisalabad)*. **5**, 461–465 (2006). https://doi.org/10.3923/biotech.2006.461.465
28. Metabolism of citric acid production by *Aspergillus niger*: model definition, steady-state analysis and constrained optimization of citric acid production rate. *PubMed*. (2000). https://doi.org/10.1002/1097-0290(20001005)70:1<82::aid-bit10>3.0.co;2-v
29. T. E. Arzumanov, N. V. Shishkanova, T. V. Finogenova, Biosynthesis of citric acid by *Yarrowia lipolytica* repeat-batch culture on ethanol. *Applied Microbiology and Biotechnology*. **53**, 525–529 (2000). https://doi.org/10.1007/s002530051651
30. B. Kristiansen, C. G. Sinclair, Production of citric acid in batch culture. *Biotechnology and Bioengineering*. **20**, 1711–1722 (1978). https://doi.org/10.1002/bit.260201103
31. D. Ibrahim, Effect of agitation speed on the morphology ofAspergillus nigerHFD5A-1 hyphae and its pectinase production in submerged fermentation. *World Journal of Biological Chemistry*. **6**, 265 (2015).
32. R. T. Hagemann, *Causes and consequences of Aspergillus niger pelleting behavior in industrial cultivation*, Technical University of Denmark. (2018).
33. O. Erkmen, E. Alben, Mathematical modeling of citric acid production and biomass formation by *Aspergillus niger* in undersized semolina. *Journal of Food Engineering*. **52**, 161–166 (2002). https://doi.org/10.1016/s0260-8774(01)00099-1

E3S Web of Conferences **679**, 01027 (2025) https://doi.org/10.1051/e3sconf/202567901027
RI²C 2025

Starch Citrate Synthesis from Diverse Thai Rice Cultivars: A Study on Resistant Starch Enhancement and Physicochemical Changes.

Napassakorn Pasriwong [1*], *Nicharee* Wisuthiphaet[1], *Thitinun* Ungtrakul [2], and *Sasithorn* Kongruang [1*]

[1] Department of Biotechnology, Faculty of Applied Science, King Mongkut's University of Technology North Bangkok, 10800 Bangkok, Thailand
[2] Department of Materials and Production Engineering (MPE), The Sirindhorn International Thai German Graduate School of Engineering (TGGS), King Mongkut's University of Technology North Bangkok, 10800 Bangkok, Thailand

Abstract. This study investigates the synthesis and characterization of starch citrate derived from five Thai rice cultivars: Rice, Riceberry, Homnil, Red Jasmine, and Thubtim Chumphae using citric acid esterification. The objective was to enhance resistant starch (RS) content and assess changes in structural and functional properties. Native rice starches were chemically modified and evaluated through resistant starch assays, Fourier-transform infrared spectroscopy (FTIR), Rapid Visco Analyzer (RVA), scanning electron microscopy (SEM) and water absorption index. Results showed a significant increase in RS content in citrate-modified flours, with white rice exhibiting the highest RS value (55.04%). FTIR confirmed ester bond formation through the appearance of C=O stretching bands at 1734–1740 cm⁻¹, SEM images revealed pronounced granule surface disruption post-modification. The physicochemical changes confirm successful citric acid crosslinking, which improves starch resistance to enzymatic digestion. These findings highlight the potential of citric acid esterification in developing functional starches with health-promoting properties and enhanced thermal and morphological characteristics.

1 Introduction

Rice (*Oryza sativa L.*) is a vital staple crop worldwide and a major source of starch used extensively across food, pharmaceutical, and industrial sectors. Thailand is home to a wide array of rice cultivars, each exhibiting distinct physicochemical properties that influence their functional applications.

A key focus of this research is resistant starch (RS), a form of starch that escapes digestion in the small intestine and undergoes fermentation in the large intestine, where it contributes to gut health, glycemic regulation, and the production of beneficial short-chain fatty acids. RS is classified into five types based on its origin and structural resistance to enzymatic breakdown: RS1, physically protected starch found in whole grains and seeds; RS2, native granular starch with crystalline structure such as in raw potatoes and unripe bananas; RS3, retrograded starch formed upon cooling of gelatinized starch; RS4, chemically modified starch produced through reactions like esterification or etherification; and RS5, complexes of amylose and lipids that resist digestion. Among these, RS4, particularly through citric acid modification, offers promising potential for developing functional starches with enhanced health benefits. Various processes exist to produce RS; each suited to different applications. Conventional hot air oven treatment (120–160°C) induces starch reorganization to form RS [1] Autoclaving uses high temperature and pressure to promote retrogradation, enhancing resistance [2]. Stirred reactors allow controlled modification of starch digestibility through precise regulation of temperature and pressure. Extrusion is widely employed in large-scale RS production due to its efficiency and precise process control [4, 5]. Compared to methods such as autoclaving, extrusion, stirred-tank bioreactors, or microwave treatment, the conventional hot air oven method offers a convenient, easy, and promising approach for producing starch citrate.

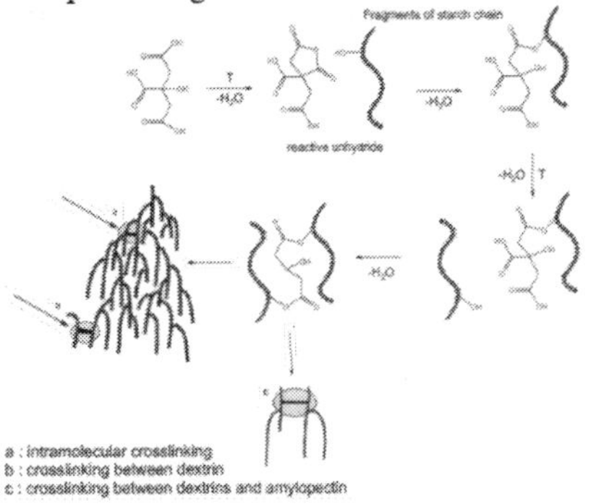

Fig. 1. Mechanism and molecular structure of starch esterification by citric acid

* Corresponding author : sasithorn.k@sci.kmutnb.ac.th, s6604071810029@email.kmutnb.ac.th

Native starch granules consist of crystalline and amorphous regions: crystalline areas mainly formed by amylopectin double helices, while amylose and amylopectin intertwine in amorphous zones. Differences in crystalline structure, polymerization degree, and amylose-to-amylopectin ratio among starch sources affect their physicochemical properties. During esterification, citric acid crosslinks starch molecules by forming anhydride bonds upon heating, which react with hydroxyl groups to produce mono- and diesters. This crosslinking creates intramolecular (Type A) and intermolecular (Types B and C) linkages, increasing structural rigidity and reducing solubility in starch citrate (Figure 1). Among chemical modifications, esterification of native starch with citric acid is well-documented [6-9]. Industrially, citrate is primarily produced by fermentation and utilized as a food additive (E330) for its acidity-modifying and antioxidant properties. Citrate-modified starches exhibit enhanced resistant starch content and potential functional benefits such as hypoglycaemic effects, making them attractive ingredients in functional foods, as well as in non-food applications like textile dressings and drilling fluids [6].

Given the rising interest in RS as a functional ingredient for health-promoting foods, this study evaluates the modification of starch from selected Thai rice cultivars via citric acid esterification and investigates the resultant structural and functional properties, with an emphasis on resistant starch content and gelatinization behaviour. These cultivars were modified by esterification with citric acid to produce starch citrate, followed by characterization of resistant starch content and structural properties via FTIR, RVA, water absorption index and SEM.

2 Materials and methods

2.1 Chemicals

Five Thai rice cultivars were used to study the gelatinization. Rice flour (*Oryza sativa L.*), Riceberry rice (*Oryza sativa L.*), Homnil rice (*Oryza sativa var. indica*), Red jasmine rice (*Oryza sativa var. indica*), and Thapthim Chumphae rice (*Oryza sativa var. indica*) were obtained from Nana Rice, (Bangkok, Thailand). Citric acid and sodium bicarbonate were purchased from the Chemipan Cooperation Co., Ltd (Bangkok, Thailand). Resistant starch assay kit was brought from Megazyme International Ireland Ltd., (Wicklow, Ireland). All other chemicals and solvents were of analytical grade.

2.2 Starch preparation

A starch was prepared by milling five Thai rice varieties using a SUS304 grinder (Vientian Tool, China). The resulting rice flour was then subjected to particle size separation by sieving, using a 125-mesh sieve, to obtain flour with uniform particle size suitable for further processing.

2.3 Characterization of starch: pasting viscosity

The pasting properties of five Thai rice starch varieties: Rice flour, Riceberry, Homnil rice, Red Jasmine rice and Thapthim Chumphae rice were determined using a Rapid Visco Analyser (RVA-3D; Newport Scientific, NSW, Australia). Starch samples (2.24 g, dry basis) were weighed directly into RVA canisters, followed by the addition of distilled water to bring the total sample weight to 28 g. The starch suspensions were equilibrated at 50°C for 2 minutes, after which the temperature was increased to 95°C at a rate of 12°C/min and held at 95°C for 2 minutes. The temperature was then decreased back to 50°C at the same rate (12°C/min) and held for an additional 2 minutes. Throughout the analysis, the paddle rotated at a constant speed of 160 rpm. Pasting parameters such as peak viscosity, breakdown, setback, and final viscosity were recorded and used to characterize the starch pasting behaviour.

2.4 Preparation of starch citrate using a convection drying

Citrate starch was synthesized by esterification with citric acid. A 20% (w/v) citric acid solution was prepared by dissolving citric acid in distilled water, adjusting the pH to 3.5 using 10 M NaOH, and diluting to a final volume of 1000 mL. Then, 1000 mL of this solution was thoroughly mixed with 1000 g of native rice starch. The mixture was incubated in a hot-air oven at 50°C for 16 hours to allow for initial absorption and equilibration. After incubation, the sample was finely ground, and its moisture content was adjusted to approximately 10% (w/w). The starch was then subjected to a thermal reaction by heating at 160°C for 5 hours to promote ester bond formation. Following thermal treatment, the product was ground again and passed through a 125-mesh sieve. To remove unreacted citric acid, the modified starch was washed four times with absolute ethanol, followed by a final wash with 1 M sodium bicarbonate until the pH of the wash solution reached approximately 7. The resulting starch was then air-dried at 45°C and passed through a 125-mesh sieve to obtain citrate-modified starch in powder form.

2.5 Characterization of starch citrate

2.5.1 Resistant starch contents

The resistant starch (RS) content of starch citrate was determined using a commercial Resistant Starch Assay Kit (K-RSTAR; Megazyme Ltd., Australia), following the manufacturer's protocol. Finely ground starch citrate samples (100 ± 5 mg) were weighed into capped test tubes. To each tube, 4.0 mL of a freshly prepared enzyme mixture containing pancreatic α-amylase and amyloglucosidase (AMG) was added. The mixture was vortexed and incubated at 37°C in a shaking water bath at 200 rpm for 16 hours to allow enzymatic hydrolysis of digestible starch. Following incubation, 4.0 mL of 99% ethanol was added to each tube to precipitate the resistant starch, and samples were centrifuged at 1,500× g for 10 minutes. The resulting pellet was washed twice with 50% (v/v) ethanol, followed by centrifugation under the same conditions. The pellet was then resuspended in 2.0 mL of 2 M KOH and stirred in an ice bath for 20 minutes to solubilize the resistant starch. Afterward, 8.0 mL of 1.2 M sodium acetate buffer (pH 3.8) and 0.1 mL of AMG were added, and the mixture was incubated at 50°C for 30 minutes to hydrolyze the solubilized starch into glucose. The sample was centrifuged again at 1,500 × g for 10 minutes, and the supernatant was collected for glucose determination. Glucose content was quantified calorimetrically using the glucose oxidase-peroxidase (GOPOD) reagent, with absorbance measured at 510 nm using a spectrophotometer (Molecular Devices, USA). Resistant starch content was calculated based on the amount of glucose released.

2.5.2 Fourier transform infrared spectroscopy (FTIR)

Pulverized and dried samples (10 mg) were analyzed using Fourier Transform Infrared (FTIR) spectroscopy in attenuated total reflectance (ATR) mode with an INVENIO S spectrometer (BRUKER, Germany). Spectra were recorded in the range of 4000–400 cm^{-1} with a spectral resolution of 2 cm^{-1}, averaging 25 scans per sample to enhance signal quality. The degree of crystallinity was assessed by calculating the crystallinity index using Equation (1), based on the absorbance ratio of characteristic peaks at 1047 cm^{-1} (crystalline region) and 1022 cm^{-1} (amorphous region):
Crystallinity of peaks was calculated using Eq. (1)

$$\text{Crystallinity} = \frac{A_{1047}}{A_{1022}} \quad (1)$$

This method of crystallinity estimation is based on the approach described by Liu, Mingyue, et al. [10]

2.5.3 Scanning electron microscopy (SEM)

The surface morphology of starch citrate was examined using a scanning electron microscope (JEOL JSM-IT500HR, Japan). Samples were mounted onto aluminum stubs using double-sided conductive carbon tape. Imaging was conducted at an accelerating voltage ranging from 3.0 to 5.0 kV. SEM micrographs were captured at a magnification of 5,000× to observe surface features and particle morphology.

2.5.4 Determination of Water Absorption Index (WAI)

The WAI were determined based on the method described by [11]. 0.1 g of rice flour was mixed with 10 mL of distilled water and vortexed for 1 minute. The mixture was then gently stirred and incubated in a water bath at 30°C for 30 minutes. After incubation, the samples were centrifuged at 3000 rpm for 10 minutes. The WAI were calculated using the following equations:

$$\text{WAI (g/g)} = \frac{\text{Weight of wet sediment (g)}}{\text{Dry weight of flour (g)}} \quad (2)$$

Each analysis was performed in triplicate, and the results are expressed as mean values with standard deviations.

2.5.5 Determination of Moisture Content

The moisture content of flour was determined using a moisture analyzer (Shimadzu MOC-63u, Japan) based on the thermogravimetric method. Approximately 2 g of sample was evenly spread on the aluminum sample pan and analyzed at 105°C using automatic mode. The result was recorded as percentage moisture content (%MC) when the weight loss stabilized. Each sample was measured in triplicate.

2.5.6 Determination of Moisture Content

The total phenolic content was determined using a modified Folin–Ciocalteu method [12]. Briefly, 200 µL of rice extract was mixed with 1.0 mL of freshly prepared and diluted (1 : 10, v/v) Folin–Ciocalteu reagent. The mixture was vortexed for 1 minute, followed by the addition of 800 µL of 10% (w/v) sodium carbonate (Na_2CO_3) solution. After mixing thoroughly, the reaction mixture was incubated at room temperature for 2 hours. The volume was adjusted to 5.0 mL with distilled water. Absorbance was measured at 760 nm using a UV–Visible spectrophotometer. The total phenolic content was calculated from a gallic acid standard curve and expressed as milligrams of gallic acid equivalents per 100 g of dry weight (mg GAE/100 g DW).

2.6 Statistical analysis

The analytical experiments were conducted in triplicate. The SPSS 22.0 software (Chicago, IL, USA). was employed to conduct an ANOVA analysis of the results. The Tukey's test was adopted to conduct multiple comparisons of the means at a significance level of 0.05.

3 Results and discussion

3.1 Pasting viscosity

In this study, a distinct difference in color was observed between native rice flour and citrate-modified rice flour, as shown in Figure 2. The native flours, derived from five Thai rice cultivars—Riceberry, Homnil, Red Jasmine, Thapthim Chumphae, and standard white rice—exhibited a range of natural hues that closely resembled the pigmentation of their corresponding rice grains. However, after modification with citric acid under thermal treatment, all samples showed significantly darker coloration. This was particularly evident in flours from pigmented rice varieties such as Riceberry and Red Jasmine, which changed from light greyish or purplish tones to deep brown or golden shades. The notable color transformation is primarily attributed to the Maillard reaction, a non-enzymatic browning process that occurs when reducing sugars react with free amino acids or proteins under high-temperature conditions. This reaction results in the formation of melanoidins, which are irreversible brown polymers responsible for the dark coloration [13, 14]. In this case, the citric acid modification was carried out at 160°C, a temperature conducive to efficient Maillard reaction activity [15]. Pigmented rice varieties, particularly those rich in phenolic compounds such as anthocyanins, flavonoids, and tannins—as well as higher levels of proteins and free amino acids compared to white rice—serve as ideal precursors for accelerating browning reactions [16, 17].

The pasting properties of starches derived from five Thai rice cultivars: Rice flour, Riceberry, Homnil, Red Jasmine, and Thapthim Chumphae were evaluated using a rapid visco analyzer to understand their gelatinization behavior and functional characteristics. Among the samples as shown in Figure1 and results in Table 1, native rice starch exhibited the highest peak viscosity (189.17 cP), indicating strong swelling and water absorption capacity during heating. Red Jasmine rice followed with a peak viscosity of 160.58 cP, while Homnil (94.83 cP), Thapthim Chumphae (88.92 cP), and Riceberry (50.00 cP) showed progressively lower values. The breakdown viscosity, which reflects the stability of the starch granules under heat and shear, was greatest in Red Jasmine rice (43.00 cP), suggesting moderate structural integrity, whereas Thapthim Chumphae displayed the lowest breakdown (5.58 cP), indicating higher stability. Final viscosity, representing the viscosity after cooling, was highest in Rice flour (325.17 cP), indicating significant retrogradation tendency, while Riceberry had the lowest (38.58 cP), reflecting limited ability to reassociate. Setback viscosity, the difference between final and trough viscosity, was also highest in Rice (169.50 cP), signifying greater retrogradation, and lowest in Riceberry (11.42 cP). Peak times ranged from 5.87 to 6.47 minutes across all samples, with Thapthim Chumphae starch requiring the longest time to reach peak viscosity. The pasting temperature varied between cultivars, from 73.5°C in Riceberry to 83.0 °C in Thapthim Chumphae, reflecting differences in granular resistance to swelling and gelatinization. The peak time and pasting temperature parameters reflect the kinetic and thermal properties of starch gelatinization. Thubtim Chumphae rice required the longest time to reach peak viscosity (6.47 min) and had the highest pasting temperature (83°C), indicating slower gelatinization kinetics and higher thermal stability, possibly due to variations in starch granule size or protein matrix effects [18]. These findings reveal distinct pasting profiles among the rice starches, emphasizing the influence of cultivar-specific properties on starch functionality and modification potential. Collectively, these RVA profiles highlight significant varietal differences in starch pasting behaviour, with implications for processing and product development in the rice industry. The understanding of these physicochemical properties is crucial for tailoring rice-based products with desired textural and functional attributes [19].

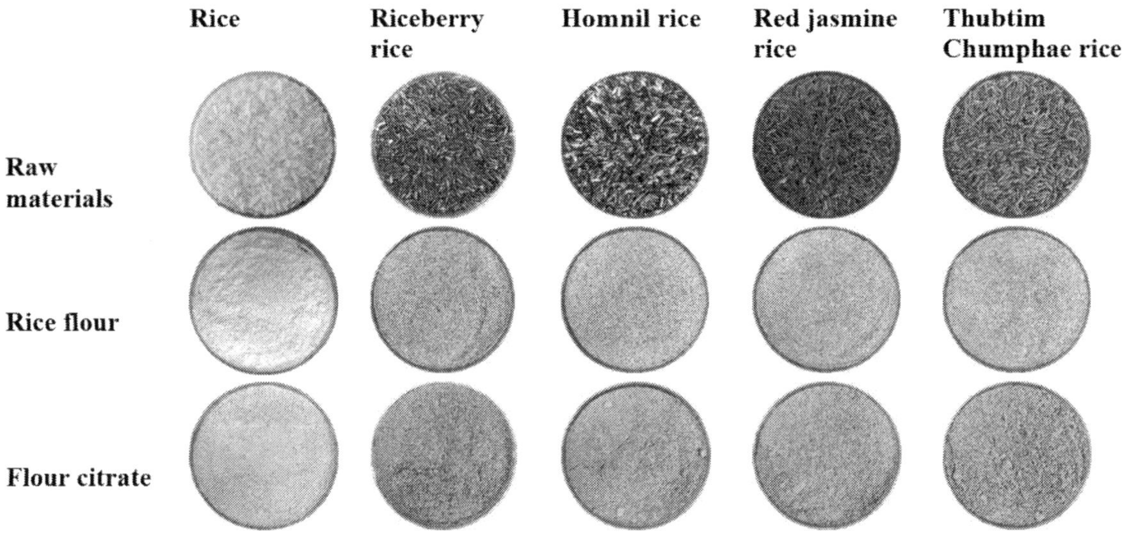

Fig. 2. Comparison five Thai rice of native and flour citrate.

Table 1. Pasting viscosity parameters of Thai rice.

Sample	Pasting viscosity parameters						
	Peak viscosity (cP)	**Trough viscosity (cP)**	**Breakdown viscosity (cP)**	**Final viscosity (cP)**	**Setback viscosity (cP)**	**Peak time (min)**	**Pasting temperature (° C)**
Rice flour	189.17	155.67	33.5	325.17	169.5	6.33	79.1
Riceberry Rice	50	27.17	22.83	38.58	11.42	3.73	73.5
Homnil rice	94.83	80.08	14.75	158.92	78.83	6	76.7
Red jasmine rice	160.58	117.58	43	260.17	142.58	5.87	82.3
Thubtim Chumphae rice	88.92	83.33	5.58	151.42	68.08	6.47	83

Different letters indicate statistically significant differences ($p < 0.05$)

3.2 Resistant starch contents

The resistant starch content of modified starch citrate derived from five Thai rice cultivars varied significantly, reflecting the impact of botanical source and modification efficiency. As shown in Table 2, rice starch citrate showed the highest resistant starch (RS) content at 55.04%, followed by Thapthim Chumphae (46.49%), Riceberry (46.34%), Red Jasmine (45.82%), and Homnil rice (45.47%). These values were markedly higher compared to the native starch control, which exhibited only 9.22%, confirming the effectiveness of citric acid esterification in enhancing starch resistance to enzymatic digestion The resistant starch (RS) content of native flours derived from different rice varieties exhibited significant variation, with white rice (*Oryza sativa*) demonstrating the highest RS content at 55.04%. This finding aligns with previous studies reporting elevated RS levels in native starches extracted from specific rice cultivars due to their unique amylose to amylopectin ratios and granular structures [20, 21]. In contrast, the RS content in pigmented rice varieties such as Riceberry, Homnil, Red Jasmine, and Thubtim Chumphae ranged from 45.47% to 46.49%, consistent with findings by [22], who noted lower RS in pigmented rice attributed to differences in starch granule morphology and the presence of phenolic compounds.

Table 2. Resistant starch content (%) of native and starch citrate.

Sample	Native		modified	
	Resistance starch content (%)	**Moisture content (%)**	**Resistance starch content (%)**	**Moisture content (%)**
Rice flour	1.11±0.19ᵃ	12.47±0.35ᵃ	55.04 ± 0.61ᵇ	12.50 ± 1.04ᵃ
Riceberry rice	0.96±0.11ᵃ	1.54±0.71ᵃ	46.34 ± 0.35ᵇ	1.88 ± 0.69ᵃ
Homnil rice	0.27±0.03ᵃ	1.59±1.37ᵃ	45.47 ± 0.35ᵇ	2.15 ± 0.34ᵇ
Red jasmine rice	0.13±0.01ᵃ	2.28±0.27ᵃ	45.82 ± 0.67ᵇ	2.35 ± 0.31ᵃ
Thubtim Chumphae rice	0.14±0.10ᵃ	4.78±1.07ᵃ	46.49 ± 0.37ᵇ	4.78 ± 0.27ᵃ

3.3 FTIR spectra of native and flour citrate

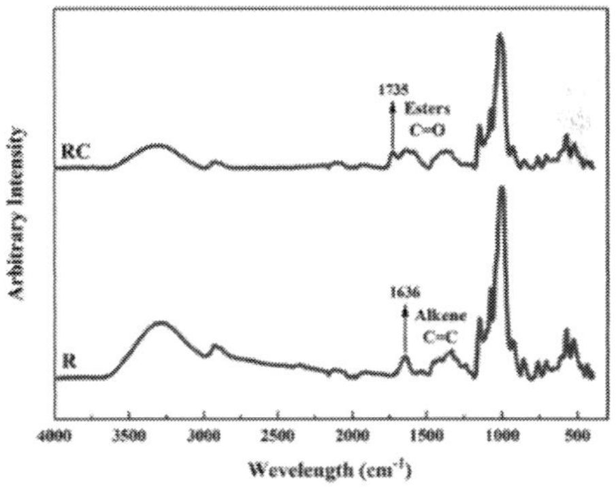

(a)

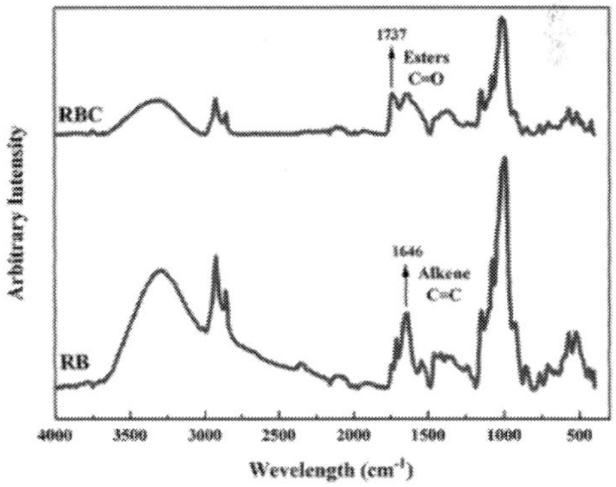

(b)

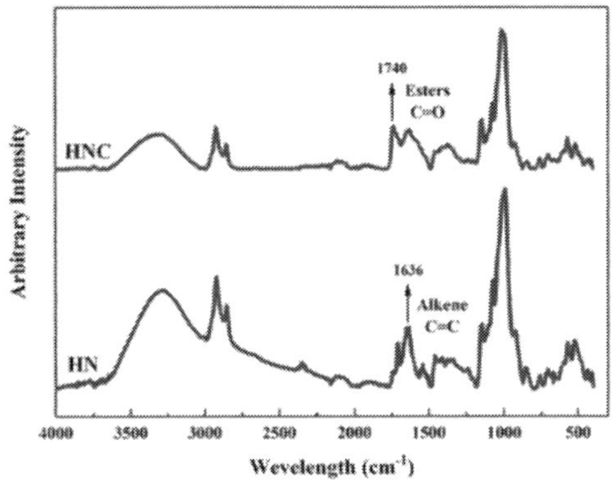

(c)

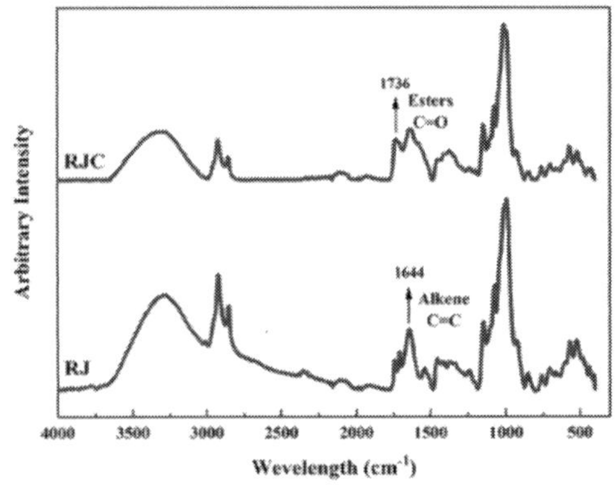

(d)

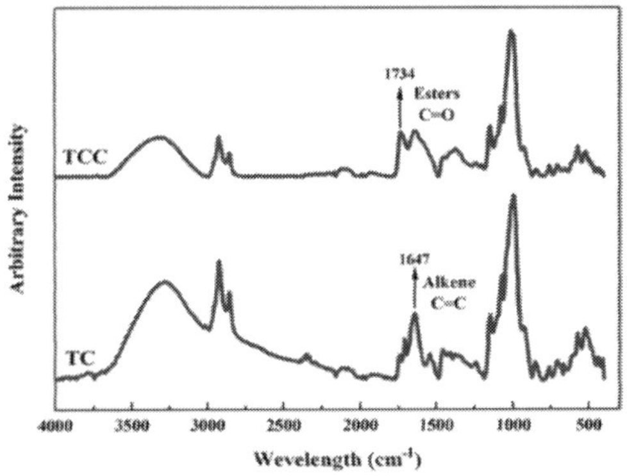

(e)

Fig. 3. FTIR spectra of native and flour citrate: (a) Native flour Rice (R) and Rice citrate (RC), (b) Riceberry rice (RB) and Riceberry rice citrate (RBC), (c) Homnil rice (HN) and Homnil rice citrate (HNC), (d) Red jasmine rice (RJ) and Red jasmine rice citrate (RJC), and (e)Thubtim Chumphae rice (TB) and Thubtim Chumphae rice citrate (TBC)

Table 3. Crystallinity Index from fourier transform infrared spectroscopy (FTIR)

Sample	Crystallinity Index	
	Native	Modified
Rice flour	0.62	0.58
Riceberry rice	0.74	0.65
Homnil rice	0.72	0.62
Red jasmine rice	0.71	0.62
Thubtim Chumphae rice	0.73	0.64

Fourier Transform Infrared (FTIR) analysis of native and citric acid-modified rice flours revealed significant changes in the chemical composition and structure of the starch molecules after modification. All modified rice flours exhibited an absorption band at 1734ó1740 cm^{-1}, which was absent from native flours (with some exceptions). This band corresponds to the carbonyl bond (C=O) vibration of the ester group, suggesting the formation of an ester bond between the hydroxyl group of starch and the carboxyl group of citric acid. This confirms the success of the chemical modification via esterification [1 ,5 ,6 ,27], which affects functional properties of the starch, such as its resistance to digestion (resistant starch type 4 : RS4).

Furthermore, the absorption band at 1636-1647cm^{-1}, associated with the C=C bond vibration or water bending (H–O–H bending), was reduced in the modified starches compared to the native flours. This reflects a change in molecular structure or a decrease in unsaturated substances in the starch that may decompose under acidic conditions [17, 18].

Meanwhile, the Crystallinity Index (CI) of all rice flours decreased significantly after modification, indicating a partial loss of crystal structure and an increase in amorphous regions, which may promote starch swelling, water solubility, and resistance to digestion. In particular, Hom Nil rice flour exhibited the highest CI reduction (0.10), followed by Riceberry, Hom Mali Daeng, and Tubtim Chumphae rice (0.09 reduction). White rice flour exhibited only a 0.04 reduction [1, 3, 6]. Also, a weak absorption band was observed at approximately 1735 cm^{-1} in the flours of native rice, Riceberry, Hom Mali Daeng, and Tubtim Chumphae, even without modification. This is different from white rice flour, which lacks this signal at all. This is due to the presence of fatty or phenolic compounds with natural ester groups in unmilled rice varieties, which can provide a signal in this range. As white rice undergoes intensive milling, these compounds are removed [16, 17].

Furthermore, the O–H stretching bands in the 3100-3600 cm^{-1} region, associated with hydroxyl groups, decreased in intensity in the modified starch, reflecting the partial replacement of hydroxyl groups with ester groups by chemical reactions. Meanwhile, the fingerprint region (900ó1200 cm^{-1}), particularly at 1040 and 1020 cm^{-1}, exhibited changes in the intensity of the absorption bands, indicating changes in the structure of glycosidic bonds and the polysaccharide backbone, which are associated with intramolecular crosslinking of the starch molecules [6, 21, 27].

Overall, the FTIR analysis results indicated significant structural changes at the chemical bond level due to the citric acid modification process.

3.4 Scanning electron microscopy

The morphological characteristics of native and citrate-modified rice flours were examined using scanning electron microscopy (SEM), as shown in Figure 4. Native flours from all rice varieties: Rice (R), Riceberry (RB), Homnil (HN), Red Jasmine (RJ), and Thubtim Chumphae (TC) exhibited irregular, angular granules with well-defined edges and compact, smooth surfaces, indicative of intact starch granule structures. In contrast, their citrate-modified counterparts (RC, RBC, HNC, RJC, and TCC) showed significant structural disruption. The modified granules appeared more fragmented, with rougher surfaces, reduced size, and a more porous and eroded morphology. These changes suggest that citric acid treatment disrupted the semi-crystalline granular architecture through esterification and crosslinking, leading to granule disintegration and surface modification. The loss of structural integrity was especially evident in the modified samples, supporting the findings from FTIR that confirmed chemical modification and amorphization of the starch. [3, 25-27]. Overall, the SEM images illustrate that citric acid significantly alters starch granule morphology, which may impact the functional and physicochemical properties of the modified flours. Comparative analysis clearly indicates that citrate modification induces
extensive physical and structural changes to native starch granules, which can be correlated with altered physicochemical behaviors and potentially improved techno-functional attributes.

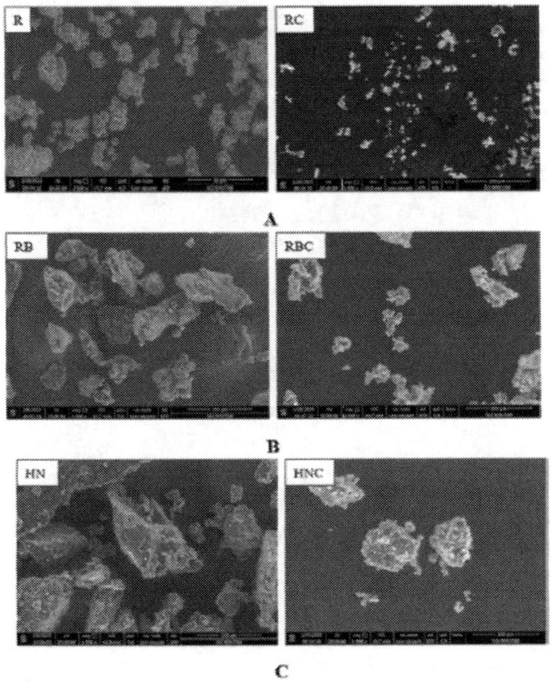

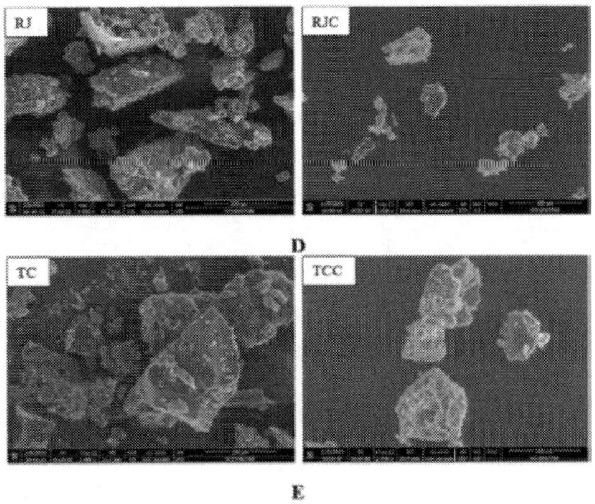

Fig. 4. SEM images of native and flour citrate: (a) Native flour Rice (R) and Rice citrate (RC), (b) Riceberry rice (RB) and Riceberry rice citrate (RBC), (c) Homnil rice (HN) and Homnil rice citrate (HNC), (d) Red jasmine rice (RJ) and Red jasmine rice citrate (RJC), and (e)Thubtim Chumphae rice (TB) and Thubtim Chumphae rice citrate (TBC)

3.5 Determination of Water Absorption Index (WAI)

In raw starch, the Water Absorption Index (WAI) tends to increase continuously with temperature due to the destruction of the starch crystal structure, allowing the starch to absorb more water [28, 30]. For example, red jasmine rice flour's WAI increased from 3.50 ± 0.10 at 30°C to 8.87 ± 0.16 at 70°C due to the breakdown of hydrogen bonds within the amylopectin molecule and partial dissolution of amylose, which increased the surface area for water absorption [28–30].

In contrast, when starch was crosslinked with citric acid, the WAI decreased significantly, especially at high temperatures. For example, modified riceberry flour's WAI decreased from 7.83 ± 0.06 to 3.27 ± 0.12 at 70°C [31–34]. This is due to citric acid's ability to form ester bonds with hydroxyl groups in the starch. This results in a stronger starch structure and limits swelling and water absorption [31, 32]. Especially at 70°C, the difference between raw and modified starches is clear. For example, raw red jasmine flour has a WAI of 8.87 ± 0.16 g/g, but after modification, it decreases to only 3.00 ± 0.19 g/g ($p<0.05$) [29, 32]. This is consistent with research indicating that crosslinked starches exhibit reduced heat resistance and water absorption due to their reinforced structure [29, 32–34].

These results indicate that at higher temperatures, native starch granules undergo extensive swelling due to the breakdown of crystalline structures and the disruption of hydrogen bonds, enabling greater water absorption. Meanwhile, citric acid-modified starches, which have undergone crosslinking, retain a more stable granular structure, thereby limiting swelling and water uptake even under heat. The chemical mechanism underlying this behavior is attributed to esterification or hydrogen bonding between the citric acid's carboxyl groups and the starch's hydroxyl groups. This results in a crosslinked network that reinforces the granule structure, enhancing thermal stability and reducing its ability to swell and absorb water [32]. This finding aligns with the report by Singh et al. [29], which demonstrated that chemically crosslinked starches tend to exhibit lower WAI values due to their reinforced, compact structure that resists water penetration. In summary, citric acid modification effectively reduces excessive water absorption at elevated temperatures by enhancing the structural integrity of starch granules.

Table 4. Water Absorption Index (WAI) of flour and flour citrate

Sample	WAI (g/g) 30°C		WAI (g/g) 50°C		WAI (g/g) 70°C	
	Native	Modified	Native	Modified	Native	Modified
Rice flour	3.30±0.00[a]	3.27±0.33[a]	3.30±0.33[a]	3.27±0.33[a]	5.80±0.17[b]	3.27±0.07[a]
Riceberry rice	3.53±0.89[a]	3.27±0.03[a]	3.53±0.15[a]	3.47±0.15[a]	7.83±0.06[b]	3.27±0.12[a]
Homnil rice	3.53±0.09[a]	3.47±0.15[a]	3.87±0.33[ab]	3.50±0.33[a]	7.83±0.23[c]	3.00±0.03[a]
Red jasmine rice	3.50±0.10[a]	3.47±0.15[a]	4.1±0.20[ab]	3.97±0.24[ab]	8.87±0.16[c]	3.00±0.19[a]
Thubtim Chumphae rice	3.87±0.03[a]	3.50±0.03[a]	4.03±0.07[a]	3.67±0.67[a]	8.87±0.06[b]	3.77±0.07[a]

Different letters indicate statistically significant differences ($p < 0.05$)

3.6 Total Phenolic Content

Table 5. Total Phenolic Content of flour and flour citrate

Sample	Total phenol (mg/g)	
	Native	Modified
Rice flour	0.03±0.002[a]	0.02±0.008[a]
Riceberry rice	0.06±0.005[a]	0.05±0.007[a]
Homnil rice	0.05±0.001[a]	0.04±0.001[a]
Red jasmine rice	0.07±0.026[a]	0.05±0.004[a]
Thubtim Chumphae rice	0.06±0.011[a]	0.05±0.005[a]

Different letters indicate statistically significant differences (p < 0.05).

Total Phenolic Content (TPC) of native and citric acid-modified rice flours showed a decrease in phenolic content after modification, although the decrease was not statistically significant (p > 0.05) for all sample groups. For Riceberry, Hom Nil, Red Jasmine, and Tubtim Chumphae rice, the phenolic content of the modified flours decreased by approximately 0.01ó0.02 mg GAE/g compared to the native flours. White rice flour showed the lowest values for both the native (0.03 ≤ 0.002 mg/g) and post-modification (0.02 ≤ 0.008 mg/g) forms. The trend of phenolic content decrease may be due to the citric acid modification process, which requires high temperatures, resulting in the degradation or loss of some phenolic compounds. Furthermore, washing and drying processes may also leach some phenolic compounds from the flour. However, the measured TPC values still reflect the characteristics of each rice variety. In particular, colored rice such as Riceberry and Red Jasmine rice retained higher phenolic values compared to white rice even after modification, reflecting the potential of colored indigenous rice as a source of natural antioxidants.

4 Conclusion

This study demonstrates that citric acid modification significantly enhances the resistant starch (RS) content and alters the physicochemical properties of starches derived from various Thai rice cultivars. The increase in RS content is closely linked to the structural transformation of starch granules, particularly the interplay between amylose and amylopectin fractions. A higher amylose content typically promotes RS formation due to its linear structure that facilitates retrogradation and crystallization, while high amylopectin content favors a more branched and amorphous configuration. FTIR analysis confirmed the formation of ester bonds via C=O stretching bands and revealed a decrease in the crystallinity index across all modified starches. This suggests a disruption of the native crystalline regions—primarily formed by amylopectin double helices—and an increase in amorphous domains, which enhances the resistance of starch to enzymatic digestion. SEM images further supported this by showing granule surface erosion and increased porosity after modification, indicating granule disintegration and structural reorganization.

Additionally, the decreased water absorption capacity in citrate-modified starches highlights their reinforced structure due to crosslinking between citric acid and hydroxyl groups of starch. These structural changes result in improved mechanical integrity and thermal stability. In conclusion, the citric acid esterification process effectively modifies starch by modulating the amylose/amylopectin ratio's influence on crystalline versus amorphous regions, thereby enhancing RS content. This makes citrate-modified starches suitable for applications in functional foods, where resistance to digestion and controlled water interaction are desired.

This research was partly supported by Sweet D international company limited under Enserv Holding CO., LTD., and the Department of Biotechnology, Faculty of Applied Science, KMUTNB, for their facilities support.

References

1. J. Y. Kim, Y.-K. Lee, Y. H. Chang, Structure and digestibility properties of resistant rice starch cross-linked with citric acid. International Journal of Food Properties. **20**, 1–12 (2017). https://doi.org/10.1080/10942912.2017.1368551
2. Lilia-Baby, K. T. Suman, S. Krishnan, V. Indira, Effect of autoclaving and cooling on resistant starch formation in rice starch. Asian Journal of Dairy and Food Research. **35**, 2 (2016). https://doi.org/10.18805/ajdfr.v35i2.10722
3. J. S. Hong, H.-J. Chung, B.-H. Lee, H.-S. Kim, Impact of static and dynamic modes of semi-dry heat reaction on the characteristics of starch citrates. Carbohydrate Polymers. **233**, 115853 (2020). https://doi.org/10.1016/j.carbpol.2020.115853
4. E. Rudnik, E. Zukowska, Studies on preparation of starch succinate by reactive extrusion. Polimery. **49**, 132–134 (2004). https://doi.org/10.14314/polimery.2004.132
5. J. Ye, S. Luo, A. Huang, C. Liu, D. J. McClements, Synthesis and characterization of citric acid esterified rice starch by reactive extrusion: A new method of producing resistant starch. Food Hydrocolloids, **92**, 135–142 (2019). https://doi.org/10.1016/j.foodhyd.2019.01.064
6. M. Kapelko-Żeberska, K. Buksa, A. Szumny, T. Zięba, A. Gryszkin, Analysis of molecular structure of starch citrate obtained by a well-stablished method. LWT - Food Science and Technology. **69**, 334–341 (2016). https://doi.org/10.1016/j.lwt.2016.01.066
7. M. Kapelko-Żeberska et al., Effect of Long-Term Potato Starch Retention with Citric Acid on Its Properties. Molecules. **27**, 2454 (2022). https://doi.org/10.3390/molecules27082454
8. E. Olsson, M. S. Hedenqvist, C. Johansson, L. Järnström, Influence of citric acid and curing on moisture sorption, diffusion and permeability of starch films. Carbohydrate Polymers. **94**, 765–772 (2013). https://doi.org/10.1016/j.carbpol.2013.02.006
9. X. Xie, Q. Liu, Development and Physicochemical Characterization of New Resistant Citrate Starch from Different Corn Starches, Starch - Stärke, **56**, 364–370 (2004). https://doi.org/10.1002/star.200300261
10. M. Liu et al., *Effect of amylose content and crystal type on the structure and digestibility of starch-fatty acid complex nanoparticle*. Food Structure. **37**, 100336 (2023). https://doi.org/10.1016/j.foostr.2023.100336
11. S. Kraithong, S. Lee, S. Rawdkuen, Physicochemical and functional properties of Thai organic rice flour. Journal of Cereal Science. **79**, 259–266 (2018)
12. Cicco, N., Lanorte, M. T., Paraggio, M., Viggiano, M., Lattanzio, A Reproducible, Rapid and Inexpensive Folin-Ciocalteu Micro-Method in Determining Phenolics of Plant Methanol Extracts. Microchemical Journal. **91**, 107-110. - References - Scientific Research Publishing. Scirp.org, 2019. https://www.scirp.org/reference/referencespapers?referenceid=2601095 (accessed Jul. 29, 2025)
13. S. I. F. S. Martins, W. M. F. Jongen, M. A. J. S. van Boekel, A review of Maillard reaction in food and implications to kinetic modelling. Trends Food Sci. Technol. **11**, 364–373 (2001). https://doi.org/10.1016/S0924-2244(01)00022-X
14. J. O'Brien, P. A. Morrissey, J. M. Ames, Nutritional and toxicological aspects of the Maillard browning reaction in foods. Crit. Rev. Food Sci. Nutr. **28**, 211–248 (1989). https://doi.org/10.1080/10408398909527499
15. J. A. Rufián-Henares, F. J. Morales, Functional properties of melanoidins:In vitro antioxidant. antimicrobial and antihypertensive activities. Food Res. Int. **40**, 995–1002 (2007). https://doi.org/10.1016/j.foodres.2007.05.002
16. P. Goufo, H. Trindade, Rice antioxidants: phenolic acids, flavonoids, anthocyanins, proanthocyanidins, tocopherols, tocotrienols, γ-oryzanol, and phytic acid. Food Sci. Nutr. **2**, 75–104 (2014). https://doi.org/10.1002/fsn3.86
17. F. Finocchiaro, B. Ferrari, A. Gianinetti, A study of biodiversity of flavonoid content in the rice caryopsis evidencing simultaneous accumulation of anthocyanins and proanthocyanidins in a black-grained genotype. J. Cereal Sci. **51**, 28–34 (2010). https://doi.org/10.1016/j.jcs.2009.09.001
18. Z. Zhou, X. Wang, X. Si, C. Blanchard, P. Strappe, The ageing mechanism of stored rice: A concept model from the past to the present. Journal of Stored Products Research. **64**, 80–87 (2015). https://doi.org/10.1016/j.jspr.2015.09.004
19. K. N. Nakorn, T. Tongdang, P. Sirivongpaisal, Crystallinity and Rheological Properties of Pregelatinized Rice Starches Differing in Amylose Content, Starch – Stärke. **61**, 101–108 (2009). https://doi.org/10.1002/star.200800008
20. N. Poomsa-ad, L. Wiset, S. Suwannarong, N. Pakdeenarong, Increasing resistant starch of processed Thai rice using citric acid, extra virgin coconut oil and herbs. Food Science and Technology Research. **30**, 37–46 (2024). https://doi.org/10.3136/fstr.fstr-d-23-00104
21. A. Golachowski, W. Drożdż, M. Golachowska, M. Kapelko-Żeberska, B. Raszewski, Production and Properties of Starch Citrates—Current Research Foods. **9**, 1311 (2020). https://doi.org/10.3390/foods9091311
22. A. Gani et al., Resistant starch from five Himalayan rice cultivars and Horse chestnut: Extraction method optimization and characterization. Scientific Reports. **10**, (2020). https://doi.org/10.1038/s41598-020-60770-4
23. C. Zhong et al., Preparation and characterization of rice starch citrates by superheated steam: A new strategy of producing resistant starch. LWT. **154**,

112890 (2021). https://doi.org/10.1016/j.lwt.2021.112890

24. K. O. Falade and O. E. Ayetigbo, Influence of physical and chemical modifications on granule size frequency distribution, fourier transform infrared (FTIR) spectra and adsorption isotherms of starch from four yam (Dioscorea spp.) cultivars. Journal of Food Science and Technology. **59**, 1865–1877 (2021). https://doi.org/10.1007/s13197-021-05200-7
25. T. Taguchi et al., Evaluation of starch retrogradation by X-ray diffraction using a water-addition method, LWT. **173**, 114341 (2023). https://doi.org/10.1016/j.lwt.2022.114341
26. R. Kaliyappan, P. Ramanathan, The Impact of Citric Acid Hydrolysis on Starch Functionality in Mangifera Indica of Sindoor Variety: A Comprehensive Analysis. Oriental Journal Of Chemistry. **40**, 247–257 (2024). https://doi.org/10.13005/ojc/400130
27. M. He, J. Chen, W. Liu, J. Lin, Solvent-free synthesis of starch citrate via dry heat reaction: An in-depth analysis on structural and physicochemical properties. LWT. **208**, 116634 (2024). https://doi.org/10.1016/j.lwt.2024.116634
28. R. F. Tester, W. R. Morrison, Swelling and Gelatinization of Cereal Starches. VI. Starches from Waxy Hector and Hector Barleys at Four Stages of Grain Development. Journal of Cereal Science. **17**, 11–18 (1993). https://doi.org/10.1006/jcrs.1993.1002
29. N. Singh, L. Kaur, N. S. Sodhi, K. S. Sekhon, Physicochemical, cooking and textural properties of milled rice from different Indian rice cultivars. Food Chemistry. **89**, 253–259 (2005). https://doi.org/10.1016/j.foodchem.2004.02.040
30. R. Hoover, Composition, molecular structure, and physicochemical properties of tuber and root starches: a review, Carbohydrate Polymers. **45**, 253–267 (2001). https://doi.org/10.1016/S0144-8617(00)00260-5
31. H. F. Zobel, Starch crystal transformations and their industrial importance. Starch – Stärke. **40**, 1–7 (1988). https://doi.org/10.1002/star.19880400102
32. H. Wu, Y. Lei, J. Lu, R. Zhu, D. Xiao, C. Jiao, R. Xia, Z. Zhang, G. Shen, Y. Liu, S. Li, M. Li, Effect of citric acid induced crosslinking on the structure and properties of potato starch/chitosan composite films. Food Hydrocolloids. **97**, 105208 (2019). https://doi.org/10.1016/j.foodhyd.2019.105208
33. U. Shah, F. Naqash, A. Gani, F. A. Masoodi, Art and science behind modified starch edible films and coatings: A review. Comprehensive Reviews in Food Science and Food Safety. **15**, 568–580 (2016). https://doi.org/10.1111/1541-4337.12197
34. A. Gunaratne, R. Hoover, Effect of heat–moisture treatment on the structure and physicochemical properties of tuber and root starches, Carbohydrate Polymers. **49**, 425–437 (2002). https://doi.org/10.1016/S0144-8617(01)00352-0

Optimizing the conditions of deep eutectic solvents pretreatment for the production of bioethanol from Water hyacinth using Response Surface Methodology (RSM)

Sukunya Areeya [1], *Frauke* Weber [2], *Malinee* Sriariyanun [1], *Atthasit* Tawai [1] and *Suksun* Amornraksa [1*]

[1]Biorefinery and Process Automation Engineering Center, Department of Chemical Engineering and Management, The Sirindhorn International Thai-German Graduate School of Engineering, King Mongkut's University of Technology North Bangkok, Bangkok, Thailand

[2]Faculty of Chemistry, Aalen University, Aalen, Germany

*corresponding author: suksun.a@tggs.kmutnb.ac.th

Abstract. Water hyacinth reproduces rapidly, causing numerous issues across various sectors, including irrigation, agriculture, and invasion to native plant species and ecosystems. As a lignocellulosic biomass, water hyacinth holds potential as a raw material in chemical and biotechnological applications. However, its resistance to enzymatic breakdown during hydrolysis necessitates pretreatment to enable the efficient production of bioproducts from its components. This study aimed to determine the optimal Deep Eutectic Solvent (DES) pretreatment conditions for water hyacinth using the Box-Behnken design under the Response Surface Methodology (RSM) in order to maximize the sugar recovery rate. The DES pretreatment conditions, using a mixture of choline chloride and monoethanolamine (ChCl:MEA) in a 1:4 molar ratio, were optimized by varying the solid-to-liquid ratio (1:5 to 1:15, w/w), temperature (90–130 °C), and reaction time (60–240 min). The RSM model estimated the optimal pretreatment conditions to be a solid-to-liquid ratio of 1:9.58 (w/w) at 90 °C for 60 min, resulting in a maximum sugar recovery rate of 44.22%. The impact of pretreatment on chemical structure, as revealed by Fourier Transform Infrared (FTIR) spectroscopy and X-ray diffraction (XRD) analyses, confirmed the efficiency of the DES pretreatment (ChCl:MEA). Therefore, this study highlights the potential of water hyacinth as a source for producing value-added compounds..

1 Introduction

In times of the search for alternative energy options approaches that tackle more than one problem seem favorable. The use of water hyacinth as biomass for generating bioethanol fits this concept. Water hyacinth (*Eichhornia crassipes*) is an invasive aquatic plant that spread all over the world on five continents [1]. It originated from Brazil, the Amazon basin and the Ecuador region [2] before invading over 50 countries [1]. With a grow rate of up to 140 tons of dry matter per hectare per year water hyacinth is counted to be one of the most productive plants [3]. Imported originally as ornamental plants for gardens, it is necessary to face the severe ecological and socio-economic effects caused by the excessive spreading of the plant [1]. As an alien plant without natural enemies and competition in most places, the massive growth endangers waterbodies and their affected ecosystem [2]. The invasion has an influence on the physic-chemical characteristics of the water by changing the temperature, pH and nutrient levels [3]. Even in times of drought, the seeds are able to survive for months or years [2]. This makes it hard to get control of the excessive growth and invasion. Nevertheless, water hyacinth has been applied for various beneficial purposes, such as removal of heavy metals and inorganic and organic components from water [2,4]. Additionally, the rapid growth of water hyacinth with limited needs for nutrient supplies and lands make it become potential raw materials for lignocellulose biomass for production of biofuels and biochemicals with low cost [5].

Lignocellulose biorefining process is a multiple-step process including pretreatment, hydrolysis, fermentation and product recovery. Hydrolysis step has a main function to break the lignocellulose into monomeric sugars that are subsequently fermented to produce biofuels and biochemicals. The goal of pretreatment is to reduce the size of the biomass and promote vulnerability of lignocellulose for enzymatic saccharification by removing lignin and hemicellulose. [6]. The process to generate bioethanol from biomass involves chemical pretreatment which allows lignin to be solubilized and dissolves hemicellulose. One sustainable pretreatment method involves deep eutectic solvents (DES) [7]. Their properties are similar to ionic liquids at the advantage of lower cost and less toxicity [6]. One of the key elements of successful pretreatment is the removal of lignin or modification of its structure [8]. DES helps to remove the lignin while the cellulose stays unaffected [7].

Water hyacinth is a promising biomass as it was shown to be high in cellulose and hemicellulose while being low on lignin [9]. So far, various pretreatment methods like acid, alkali, biological and physical were tested for water hyacinth, [10] however the DES application is kept nearly untouched. Umai et al worked with a DES synthesized out of choline chloride and urea to optimize the delignification of water hyacinth, achieving a lignin removal of 64.32% (w/w) [11]. Previous work from Sun et al. (2023) studied the pretreatment of Pennisetum giganteum (PG) using different types of DES [13]. The results showed that among these DESs, ChCl/MEA exhibited the highest potential for PG biomass pretreatment, achieving the highest lignin removal of 79.8 % while retaining 89.5 % of cellulose. Furthermore, this DES pretreatment reached a 95.6 % glucose yield and 88.0 % xylose yield [12]. To optimize the efficiency of DES pretreatment, response surface methodology (RSM) was used. It is a statistical tool for the optimization of parameters in processes. Based on quadratic polynomial equations an experiment plan is developed with minimal runs of experiments. It allows us to observe interactions between the pretreatment parameters and to give the accurate predictions of optimal condition comparing to other statistical methods [13].

This study aimed to determine the optimal pretreatment conditions using RSM with a Box-Behnken design to assess the effectiveness of DES pretreatment on water hyacinth using choline chloride and monoethanolamine (ChCl/MEA). The efficiency of DES pretreatment was evaluated through chemical characterization by using Fourier Transform Infrared (FTIR) spectroscopy and X-ray diffraction (XRD) to understand the effect of ChCl/MEA on water hyacinth biomass.

2 Materials and Method

2.1 Materials

Chlorine chloride (ChCl) was purchased from Sigma Aldrich, St. Louis, USA. Monoethanolamine (MEA) was acquired from TCI (Tokyo Chemical Industry Co., Ltd., Tokyo, Japan), with a purity of at least 99%. All reagents used in this research were of analytical grade. The commercial cellulase enzyme, Ctec2, was procured from Sigma Aldrich, St. Louis, USA. Distilled water was sourced from the chemical department's processing laboratory.

2.2 Preparation of Water hyacinth

Water hyacinth biomass utilized for feedstock in this study was collected from the local freshwater river in Nonthaburi province, Thailand. The biomass was chopped and dried at 60 °C overnight to reduce moisture content, then ground using a food grinder to decrease particle size. The material was subsequently sieved through a 20-mesh (0.841 mm) aluminium screen to achieve uniformity. The resulting powder was sealed in an airtight container and stored at room temperature until further use.

2.3 Preparation of deep eutectic solvents

A DES, ChCl/MEA, was prepared by combining two components: choline chloride (ChCl) as the hydrogen bond acceptor (HBA) and monoethanolamine (MEA) as the hydrogen bond donor (HBD), in a molar ratio of 1:4. The synthesis process was carried out using a magnetic stirrer set at 100 rpm and maintained at 80 °C for 20 min, following the method by Sun et al. (2023) [12]. After synthesis, the DES was stored in a sealed reagent bottle and kept in a vacuum desiccator containing silica gel to prevent moisture absorption [14].

2.4 RSM experiment design

RSM is a statistical tool commonly used to efficiently design experiments with a minimal number of trials, thereby reducing time and costs [13]. It involves mathematical and statistical techniques to develop empirical models based on experimental data aligned with a specific design strategy [15]. RSM helps assess the influence of different variables on the response and optimizes the independent parameters. Among its approaches, the Box–Behnken Design (BBD) is frequently employed to analyze the effects of experimental factors in various studies [13,16-17]. The designed experimental conditions based on the Box–Behnken design (BBD) with three independent variables were conducted using 8 factorial points, 6 axial (star) points, and 3 duplicate center points.

The experimental results were analyzed using a second-order polynomial equation (quadratic model), as shown in Equation (1) [15], to assess the influence of individual variables on the response and identify the optimal processing conditions [13]. Variables with a statistically significant effect on the response were identified based on a confidence level exceeding 95%, corresponding to a p-value below 0.05. [18].

$$Y=\beta_0+\beta_1 A+\beta_2 B+\beta_3 C+\beta_{11} A^2+\beta_{22} B^2+\beta_{33} C^2+\beta_{12}AB+\beta_{13} AC+\beta_{23} BC \quad (1)$$

In this equation, y represents the response, while A, B, and C denote the independent variables. β_0 is the constant term, β_1, β_2, and β_3 are the linear coefficients, β_{11}, β_{22}, and β_{33} are the quadratic coefficients, and β_{12}, β_{13}, and β_{23} represent the interaction coefficients. [13].

The coefficients and interaction effects of the parameters in Eq. (1) were determined, and Analysis of Variance (ANOVA) was applied to assess the significance of the three independent variables [13]. These variables included pretreatment temperature (A, °C), reaction time (B, min), and the solid-to-liquid ratio (C, w/w), with value ranges set at 90–130 °C, 60–240 min, and 1/5–1/15 w/w, respectively. A total of 17 experimental runs were recommended by the design, varying the process variables at different levels (Table 1). To identify the optimal conditions for maximizing biomass recovery from water hyacinth pretreatment, this study utilized Design-Expert 7.0.0 software (Stat-Ease Inc., Minneapolis, MN, USA) to analyze the influence of each variable across the 17 experiments and predict the corresponding recovery rates.

2.5 Deep eutectic solvents pretreatment

The ground and dried water hyacinth underwent ChCl/MEA pretreatment using a stirring mantle under the conditions specified in Table 1. Following the DES treatment, the samples were left to cool at room temperature to stop the reaction process [19]. The solid portion was rinsed with 50 mL of distilled water per gram of biomass to eliminate any remaining DES. The washed solution was then adjusted to a neutral pH prior to enzymatic saccharification and then filtered through 125 mm filter paper (chm Cat No. F1001 125). Solid fraction was dried overnight at 60 °C in a hot air oven and subsequently stored in an airtight container for further saccharification and analysis (Figure 1) [20].

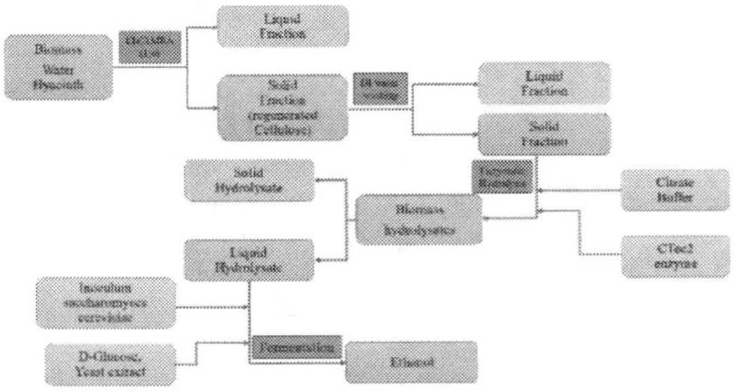

Fig. 1. Process flow of pretreatment, enzymatic saccharification, and fermentation process of water hyacinth biomass.

Table 1. Experimental design of response surface methodology for pretreated water hyacinth biomass.

Run	S/L ratio (w/w)	Temperature (°C)	Time (min)	Sugar yield (%)
1	5	120	150	22.494
2	20	120	150	26.628
3	12.5	95	150	26.265
4	5	70	150	23.769
5	20	95	240	28.778
6	12.5	70	240	25.055
7	12.5	70	60	17.352
8	12.5	95	150	29.165
9	12.5	120	60	20.488
10	5	95	240	18.371
11	12.5	95	150	24.350
12	20	95	60	21.771
13	20	70	150	32.126
14	5	95	60	26.191
15	12.5	120	240	25.722
16	12.5	95	150	25.970
17	12.5	95	150	21.794

2.6 Chemical characterization of raw and pretreated sugarcane leaves

2.6.1 Fourier-transform infrared spectroscopic analysis (FTIR)

FTIR spectroscopy was employed to precisely determine the chemical composition of biomass and to identify functional groups. In this study, an FTIR spectrometer (Spectrum 2000, Perkin-Elmer, USA) was used to examine structural changes in untreated and pretreated water hyacinths. Each sample was analyzed in triplicate, with spectra recorded in transmission mode across a wavenumber range of 400 to 4000 cm^{-1}, using 16 scans per minute at a resolution of 4 cm^{-1} to observe shifts in wavenumber [21].

2.6.2 X-ray diffraction analysis

The structure of lignocellulose, especially of the amorphous and crystalline structure can be evaluated using X-ray diffraction (XRD) analysis [15]. The XRD analysis provides information on the crystalline regions of cellulose within the biomass. In this study, the crystallinity of both untreated and pretreated water hyacinth was examined using a powder XRD instrument (Model: SmartLab Studio II, Rigaku, Japan), operating within a 2θ range of 5° to 80°, at a scan speed of 5°/min, and utilizing Cu-Kα radiation (λ = 0.154 nm) as the monochromatic source [14]. The crystallinity index (CrI) was determined via the peak intensity method, calculated as the ratio between the maximum peak intensity at 2θ = 22.0 (I_{002}) and the minimum intensity at 2θ = 18.0 (I_{am}), which lies between the 001 and 002 diffraction peaks. [22].

$$\text{Crystalinity Index, CrI (\%)} = \frac{I_{002}-I_{am}}{I_{002}} \times 100 \quad (2)$$

2.7 Enzymatic saccharification

The process of enzymatic saccharification is well known for breaking the bonds of the cellulose and hemicellulose components in lignocellulosic biomass [23]. A 2.5% (w/v) of solid loading was used to hydrolyze the untreated and pretreated water hyacinth with 50 mM citrate buffer (pH 4.8 ± 0.2) and the cellulase enzyme Ctec2 (30 FPU/g biomass) at 50 °C and 150 rpm for 72 h [16].

2.8 Reducing sugar analysis by using DNS assay

The reducing sugar concentration was measured using the 3,5-dinitrosalicylic acid (DNS) method as described by Miller [24]. In this assay, 50 μL of the hydrolysate supernatant was mixed with 150 μL of DNS reagent. The mixture was vortexed, heated at 95 °C for 5 min in a water bath, and then cooled on ice for another 5 min. Afterward, 1 mL of deionized water was added, and the absorbance was recorded at 540 nm using a UV-Vis spectrophotometer (T80+ UV/Vis Spectrometer, PG Instrument Ltd., USA).

3 Results and Discussions

3.1 Results and Discussions

In this study, RSM was utilized to optimize the process parameters of DES pretreatment for maximizing total sugar yield (g/g) and enhancing the recovery rate of water hyacinth. Multiple regression analyses were applied to evaluate the experimental data. BBD [25], a common RSM approach, was used with three input variables: pretreatment temperature (A), reaction time (B), and solid-to-liquid ratio (C). A total of 17 experimental runs were performed, and the recovery rate was measured as the response. Analysis of variance (ANOVA) was employed to assess the significance of the quadratic model. A high F-value and a low p-value ($p<0.0001$) indicated strong model significance across all variables, whereas a low F-value would suggest the presence of random variation or noise in the results. [22]. The ANOVA results confirmed the model's significance (Table 2), presenting an F-value of 27.28 with the model's regression coefficient (R^2) at 0.9550. Based on p-values ($p<0.05$), the linear terms (A, B, and C), the interaction term AC, and all quadratic terms (A^2, B^2, and C^2) were statistically significant at a 95% confidence level. The interaction parameters AB and BC were eliminated because they were not significant according to the significance criterion ($p < 0.05$), in order to reduce model complexity and improve model accuracy [25]. The optimal conditions for DES pretreatment of water hyacinth, as suggested by the model, were a temperature of 90 °C for 60 min at a solid-to-liquid ratio of 1:9.58 (w/w), resulting in a maximum recovery rate of 44.22%. Experimental results under these optimal conditions yielded a reducing sugar concentration of 0.31 g/g and a recovery rate of 45.46%. The reducing sugar obtained in this study (0.31 g/g) was 22.53% higher than that reported in previous research (0.253 g/g) [24], which used 3% KOH pretreatment of water hyacinth. The predicted recovery rate (44.22%) was compared with the validated experimental value (45.46%), with an error percentage of 2.80%. Therefore, this model demonstrates good accuracy and potential to predict the optimized conditions and recovery rate of the pretreatment process of water hyacinth using ChCl/MEA.

Table 2. ANOVA results for the response surface quadratic model (response: recovery rate (%)).

Source	Sum of squares	df	Mean square	F-value	p-value	
Model	65.43	7	9.35	27.28	<0.0001	**
A - Temperature	30.23	1	30.23	88.22	<0.0001	
B - Time	5.50	1	5.50	16.05	0.0031	
C – S/L ratio	7.62	1	7.62	22.24	0.0011	
AC	2.94	1	2.94	8.57	0.0168	
A^2	14.12	1	14.12	41.22	0.0001	
B^2	2.98	1	2.98	8.70	0.0162	
C^2	2.09	1	2.09	6.10	0.0356	
Residual	3.08	9	0.34			
Lack of fit	3.08	5	0.62			
Pure error	0.000	4	0.000			
Cor Total	68.51	16				

**Significant, NS not significant

Figure 2 illustrates a 3D surface plot showing how the three independent variables, such as S/L ratio, temperature, and reaction time, influence the recovery rate during enzymatic saccharification of pretreated water hyacinth. A notable interaction was observed between the S/L ratio and temperature, which had a significant effect on the recovery rate (Fig. 2a). In contrast, the interaction between temperature and time did not show a meaningful impact on the response (Fig. 2b). The regression equation that models the predicted recovery rate (Y) as a function of temperature (A), reaction time (B), and S/L ratio (C) is presented below.

$$Y=38.77-1.94A-0.83B-0.98C-0.86A\times C+1.83A^2+0.84B^2-0.7C^2 \quad (3)$$

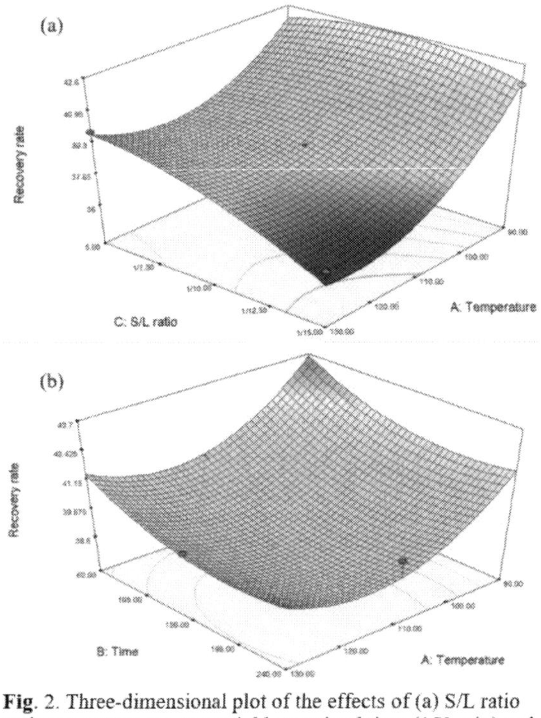

Fig. 2. Three-dimensional plot of the effects of (a) S/L ratio and temperature on sugar yield at optimal time (150 min) and (b) temperature and time on sugar yield at optimal S/L ratio (1/5)

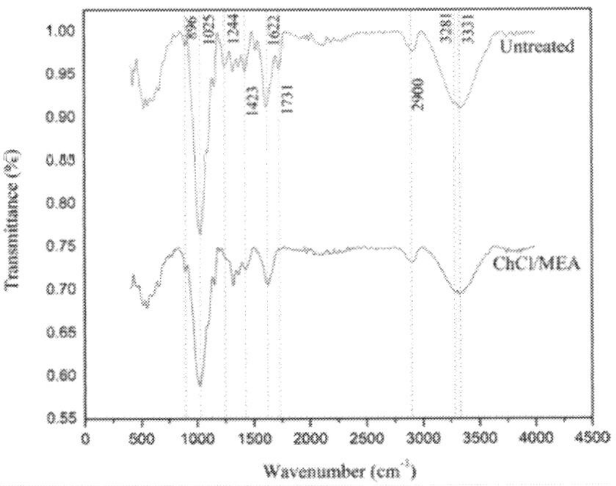

Fig. 3. Fourier-transform infrared spectroscopy (FTIR) spectra of untreated and pretreated water hyacinth biomass.

3.2 Effect of Structural changes in biomass after DES pretreatment using FT-IR Spectroscopy

FTIR analysis is commonly used to reveal bond breakage and stretching vibrations, offering insights into the structural integrity of lignocellulosic biomass [27]. This type of biomass is mainly composed of cellulose, hemicellulose, and lignin, where cellulose exhibits a crystalline structure, while lignin is largely amorphous [22]. In this study, FTIR spectroscopy was employed to investigate the structural alterations in untreated and DES-pretreated water hyacinth at optimized condition (temperature of 90 °C, a reaction time of 60 min, and a solid-to-liquid ratio of 1:9.58 (w/w)) through the spectral range of 400–4000 cm^{-1} (Figure 3). The absorption band near 896 cm^{-1} corresponds to β-glucosidic linkages, indicating CH deformation specific to cellulose [28,29]. A sharp peak at 1025 cm^{-1} is linked to C-O-C stretching vibrations in the pyranose rings found in cellulose and hemicellulose [30]. Additionally, a band at 1244 cm^{-1} appeared exclusively in the DES-pretreated sample, suggesting that remnants of chemical modifications in lignin persisted post-treatment [31,32]. A spectral band near 1423 cm^{-1} is associated with asymmetric C=O stretching vibrations, indicating the presence of carbonate compounds in biomass ash [33]. The peak at 1622 cm^{-1} corresponds to H–O–H bending vibrations, which become more pronounced and shift slightly due to component interactions [34]. The band at 1731 cm^{-1} reflects complex ester linkages between hemicellulose and lignin, such as acetyl, feruloyl, and p-coumaroyl groups [35]. After pretreatment, this 1731 cm^{-1} peak diminished, suggesting cleavage of those ester bonds. Absorption in the 3500–2800 cm^{-1} range typically indicates the presence of cellulose (strong signal), hemicellulose (strong), or lignin (weak) in lignocellulosic biomass [36]. Following ChCl/MEA treatment, a slight increase in intensity around 2900 cm^{-1} was observed, attributed to enhanced C–H stretching in cellulose [30]. Additionally, the bands at 3281 and 3331 cm^{-1} were linked to hydrogen-bonded O–H stretching on the cellulose surface [23].

3.3 Effect of DES pretreatments on cellulose crystallinity structure using XRD method

Cellulose crystallinity plays a crucial role in determining the efficiency of pretreatment processes. To assess this, XRD analysis was performed to examine the crystalline structure of cellulose, offering valuable insight into the effectiveness of the pretreatment. Figure 4 presents the XRD patterns for both untreated and DES pretreatment at optimized condition (temperature of 90 °C, a reaction time of 60 min, and a solid-to-liquid ratio of 1:9.58 (w/w)) of water hyacinth biomasses. The diffraction profiles revealed two prominent peaks at 22° and 18°. Notably, the pretreated biomass showed a more pronounced reduction in the peak intensity at 18°, indicating a higher degree of hemicellulose removal and structural disruption in the amorphous regions compared to the untreated sample [15]. The CrI values indicate that the pretreated water hyacinth biomass (49.31%) exhibits greater crystallinity compared to the untreated sample (35.28%). This increase in CrI after DES pretreatment is likely because of structural alterations in the biomass, specifically the removal of amorphous components like the lignin–hemicellulose matrix. This matrix typically surrounds the cellulose, and its removal during pretreatment exposes more of the crystalline cellulose regions, resulting in a higher CrI. [15].

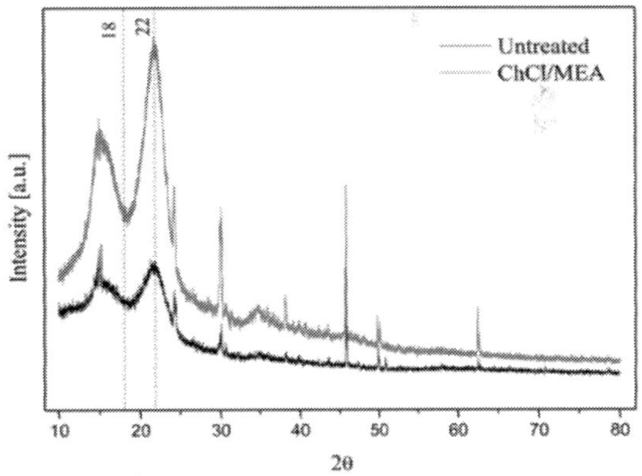

Fig. 4. Fourier-transform infrared spectroscopy (FTIR) spectra of untreated and pretreated water hyacinth biomass.

4 Conclusion

The mathematical model predicted the optimal pretreatment conditions with a regression coefficient (R^2) of 0.9550, identifying a solid-to-liquid ratio of 1:9.58 (w/w) at 90 °C for 60 minutes, which yielded a maximum recovery rate of 44.22%. Under these optimal conditions, the pretreatment significantly enhanced the amount of reducing sugars in enzymatic hydrolysis. The results of Fourier Transform Infrared (FTIR) spectroscopy and X-ray diffraction (XRD) confirmed the effectiveness of DES pretreatment on the water hyacinth biomass. Therefore, this study indicates that DES pretreatment under the identified optimal conditions can facilitate the valorization of water hyacinth waste for the production of value-added products within the biorefinery sector.

The authors would like to thank King Mongkut's University of Technology North Bangkok (Research Grant Contract No. KMUTNB-68-BASIC-27.

References

1. A. M. Villamagna, B. R. Murphy, Ecological and socio-economic impacts of invasive water hyacinth (*Eichhornia crassipes*): a review. Freshwater Biology, **55**, 282-298 (2010)
2. S. Rezania, M. Ponraj, A. Talaiekhozani, Shaza E. Mohamad, M. F. M. Din, S. Md Taib, F. Sabbagh, F. Md Sairan, Perspectives of phytoremediation using water hyacinth for removal of heavy metals, organic and inorganic pollutants in wastewater. Journal of Environmental Management, **163**, 125-133 (2015)
3. P. P. D. Omo; V. Spena; S. L. Froscia, Assessment of a Mechanical Pretreatment to Enhance Biogas Production from the Noxious Weed Eichhornia Crassipes on Industrial Scale. in Proceedings of 5th International Symposium on Environment-Friendly Energies and Applications (EFEA), September September 24-26 (2018)
4. S. Pandey, N. Singh, A. K. Nirala, A. Gir, Dynamics of Water Weed Eichhornia Crassipes: A Review. IJRASET. **3** (2015)
5. G. K. Gaurav, T. Mehmood, L. Cheng, J. J. Klemeš, D. K. Shrivastava, Water hyacinth as a biomass: A review. Journal of Cleaner Production, **277**, 122214 (2020)
6. D. Jose, K. Rattanaporn, N. Kittiborwornkul, A. A. Adediran, and M. Sriariyanun, Biorefining Processes for Valorization of Lignocellulosic Biomass for Sustainable Production of Value-Added Products (CRC Press, Boca Raton, London, New York, 2023)
7. H. El-gendi, E. M. El-Fakharany, M. H El-Sayed, D.A. Alenazi, R. Jame, N. Alkhathami, A. S. Khera, M. Abdelaziz, A comprehensive overview of lignocellulosic biomass exploiting for sustainable bioethanol production: recent advances and emerging challenges towards commercial implementation. Egypt. J. Chem. **67**, 2053-2072 (2024)
8. O. M. Perrone, M. M. de S. Moretti, S. E. Bordignon, J. de C. Pereira, R. da Silva, E. Gomes, M. Boscolo, Improving cellulosic ethanol production using ozonolysis and acid as a sugarcane biomass pretreatment in mild conditions. BioResources. **13**, 100628 (2021)
9. T. Ruan, R. Zeng, X. Y. Yin, S. Zhang, Z.-H. Yang, Water Hyacinth (Eichhornia crassipes) Biomass as a Biofuel Feedstock by Enzymatic Hydrolysis. BioResources. **11**, 2372-2380 (2016)
10. B. K. Show, G. Shivakumaran, A. Koley, A. Ghosh, S. Chaudhury, A. K. Hazra, S. Balachandran, Effect of thermal and NaOH pretreatment on water hyacinth to enhance the biogas production. Environmental Science and Pollution Research, **30**, 120984–120993 (2023)
11. R. D. Umai, S. Jacob, V. Kumar, Deep Eutectic Solvent Pretreatment of Water Hyacinth for Improved Holocellulosic Saccharification and Fermentative Co-Production of Xylitol and Lipids Using *Rhodosporidium toruloides* NCIM 3547. Fermentation, **8**, 591 (2022)
12. Y.-Q. Sun, Y. Yuan, K.-X. Dai, Z.-L. Xiu, The pretreatment of the sustainable biomass feedstock of Pennisetum giganteum for biorefinery using deep eutectic solvents. Bioresource Technology, **384**, 129289 (2023)
13. M. Sulaiman, H. Mahmood, H. M. Khan, T. Iqbal, N. U. Khan, M. M. Abbas, M. N.-E.-Alam, M. E. M. Soudagar, Cellulosic rich biomass production with optimized process parameters by using glycerol pretreatment for biofuels applications. Energy Nexus, **14**, 100298 (2024)
14. K. Narayanan, P. Venkatachalam, E. J. Panakkal, P. Tantayotai, A. Tandhanskul, R. Selvasembian, S. Chuetor, M. Sriariyanun, Exploring Ternary Deep Eutectic Solvent Pretreatment in a One-Pot Process with Napier Grass for Bioethanol Production. BioEnergy Research, **17**, 2213–2225 (2024)
15. S. L. Sunar, R. K. Oruganti, D. Bhattacharyya, D. Shee and T. K. Panda, Pretreatment of sugarcane bagasse using ionic liquid for enhanced enzymatic saccharification and lignin recovery: process optimization by response surface methodology. Cellulose, **31**, 2151–2173 (2024)
16. S. Areeya, M. P. Gundupalli, B. Dharmalingam, B. Paramasivam, P. Tantayotai, P. Yasurin, E. J. Panakkal, Process Optimization of Deep Eutectic Solvent Pretreatment of Coffee Husk Biomass. E3S Web of Conferences, **428**, 01010 (2023)
17. D. Pradhan, S. Jaiswal, B. K. Tiwari, A. K. Jaiswal, Nanocellulose separation from barley straw via ultrasound-assisted choline chloride – Formic acid deep eutectic solvent pretreatment and high-intensity ultrasonication. Ultrasonics Sonochemistry, **110**, 107048 (2024)
18. B. Timoteo-Cruz, R. M. Gómez-Espinosa, R. Sánchez-Orozco, J. J. García-Sánchez, F. Ureña-Núñez and G. Roa-Morales, Pretreatment of Typha latifolia biomass with imidazolium ionic liquid as a strategy for sugar production. Biomass Conversion and Biorefinery, **14**, 4591–4604 (2024)
19. M. Pawłowska, M. Zdeb and M. Nieścioruk, Efficiency of Chemical Pretreatment of Sugar Beet Pulp Biomass Intended to Energy Production via Biological Processes, Energies, **16**, 574 (2023)
20. R. P. Martins, A. A.Schmatz, L. A. de Freita, M J. R. Mutton, M. Brienzo, Solubilization of

hemicellulose and fermentable sugars from bagasse, stalks, and leaves of sweet sorghum. Industrial Crops and Products, **170**, 113813 (2021)

21. M. Ivanović, D. Grujić, J. Cerar, M. I. Razboršek ,L. Topalić-Trivunović, A. Savić, D. Kočar, Mitja Kolar, Extraction of Bioactive Metabolites from Achillea millefolium L. with Choline Chloride Based Natural Deep Eutectic Solvents: A Study of the Antioxidant and Antimicrobial Activity. Antioxidants, **11**, 724 (2022)
22. O. Govindaraj, G. N. Olaganathan, R. ASM, S. Uthandi, An eco-friendly EnZolv pretreatment optimization in banana fiber biomass using response surface methodology (RSM) and its structural characterization. Biomass Conversion and Biorefinery, **14**, 1329–1342 (2023)
23. P. Kahar, Synergistic Effects of Pretreatment Process on Enzymatic Digestion of Rice Straw for Efficient Ethanol Fermentation. Environmental Biotechnology - New Approaches and Prospective Applications, 65-87 (2013)
24. G.L. Miller, Anal. Chem. **14**, 426-428 (1959)
25. E.K. Tetteh, S. Rathilal, Response Surface Optimization of Biophotocatalytic Degradation of Industrial Wastewater for Bioenergy Recovery, **9**, 3 (2022)
26. R.H. Jadhav and A. Dey, Pre-Treatment and Characterization of Water Hyacinth Biomass (WHB) for Enhanced Xylose Production Using Dilute Alkali Treatment Method, Water, **17**, 301 (2025)
27. J.L. Morales-Martinez, M.G. Aguilar-Uscanga, E. Bolaños-Reynoso, L. López-Zamora, Optimization of chemical pretreatments using response surface methodology for second-generation ethanol production from coffee husk waste. BioEnergy Research, **14**, 815–827 (2021)
28. Z. Yao, G. Chong, H. Guo, Deep Eutectic Solvent Pretreatment and Green Separation of Lignocellulose. Appl. Sci. **14**, 7662 (2024)
29. K. C. Patil, R. H. Patil, Qualitative characterization of pretreated fruit waste to produce an effective fertilizer by using FTIR. 2022 IJCRT. **10**, 12 (2022)
30. J. E. H. Rodríguez, D. E. Rincón, D. F. H. Rojas, I. G. C. Orjuela, L. M. Socolovsky, D. G. E. Rondón, C. L. L. Calderón, Effects of Hydrolysis and Bleaching Conditions on the Efficiency of Cellulose Microribbons Extraction from Coffee Parchment Through a Design of Experiments, Cellulose (2022)
31. W. Wang, C. Wang, Zahoor, X.Chen, Q. Yu, Z. Wang, X. Zhuang, Z. Yuan, Effect of a Nonionic Surfactant on Enzymatic Hydrolysis of Lignocellulose Based on Lignocellulosic Features and Enzyme Adsorption, ACS Omega. **5** 15812–15820 (2020)
32. R. Vârban, I. Crişan, D. Vârban, A. Ona, L. Olar, A. Stoie, R. Ştefan, Comparative FT-IR Prospecting for Cellulose in Stems of Some Fiber Plants: Flax, Velvet Leaf, Hemp and Jute. Appl. Sci. **11**, 8570 (2021)
33. J. Kalembkiewicz, D. Galas, E. Sitarz-Palczak, The Physicochemical Properties and Composition of Biomass Ash and Evaluating Directions of its Applications, Pol. J. Environ. Stud. **27**, 6 (2018)
34. A. Mudzakir, A. B. D. Nandiyanto, E. Heraldy, J. Efendi, K. M. Rizky, M. Widyaningsih, L.S. Anggiat, Dissolution Study of Lignin from Coconut Fiber as Lignocellulosic Biomass Using Eutectic Based Ionic Liquids, in Proceedings of the 9th Mathematics, Science, and Computer Science Education International Seminar (MSCEIS 2023)
35. Z. Zhu, R. Simister, S. Bird, S. J. McQueen-Mason, L. D. Gomez, D. J. Macquarrie, Microwave assisted acid and alkali pretreatment of Miscanthus biomass for biorefineries, AIMS Bioengineering **2**, 449-468 (2015)
36. S. Machmudah, Wahyudiono, P. N. Trisanti, H. Setyawan, S. Madhania, K. Sambodho, S. Winardi, T. Adschiri, M. Goto, Hydrothermal alkaline treatment of lignocellulosic biomass for microcrystalline cellulose generation at subcritical water, South African Journal of Chemical Engineering. **51**, 45-56 (2025)

Optical evaluation of antioxidant activity: a comparison between a spectrophotometer and a homebuilt photometer.

Pitcha Luengviriya[1], *Kornkamon* Kiatsommart[1], *Chanida* Leelakanok[1], *Supanun* Patumorathai[1], *Kwanruthai* Sibsiri[2], and *Thidarat* Wangkham[3*]

[1]Mahidol University International Demonstration School, Salaya, Phuttamonthon, 73170 Nakhon Pathom, Thailand
[2]Department of Physics, Kasetsart University, Jatujak, 10900 Bangkok, Thailand
[3]Biomedical Engineering program, Department of Industrial Physics and Medical Instrumentation, Lasers and Optics Research Center, King Mongkut's University of Technology North Bangkok, Wongsawang, Bangsue, 10800 Bangkok, Thailand

Abstract. The antioxidant activity of an orange peel extract is determined using a DPPH (2,2-diphenyl-1-picrylhydrazyl) solution. Sample absorption is measured with both a commercial spectrophotometer and a homebuilt photometer equipped with a 525-nm LED. Small, dried pieces of orange peel are extracted using 95% ethanol. Seven DPPH solutions with concentrations ranging from 0.1 to 0.4 mM are measured to establish calibration equations. For the spectrophotometer, absorbance exhibits a linear increase with DPPH concentration at both 517 nm (absorbance peak) and 525 nm (matching the LED in the photometer). In the homebuilt photometer, three piecewise linear fittings for concentration 0.1– 0.4 mM provide a better representation of absorption data compared to a single overall fitting across 0.1–0.4 mM. Different volumes of orange peel extract are added into the DPPH solution (0.4 mM DPPH after mixing) and stored in darkness for 30 minutes before the measurement. In both spectrophotometer and photometer analyses, antioxidant activity increases with the extract volume. Using spectrophotometer measurements as reference, the photometer with piecewise fittings produces significantly lower errors compared to those obtained with overall fitting.

1 Introduction

Free radicals are highly reactive molecules that can lead to oxidative damage to biological systems, leading to cell aging and various diseases, such as inflammation, neurodegenerative disorders, cardiovascular diseases, and cancer [1, 2]. These reactive species are generated by endogenous metabolic processes and environmental factors like pollution, radiation, and unhealthy diets [3, 4]. Over time, excessive oxidative stress can overwhelm the body's natural defense mechanisms, resulting in cellular dysfunction and disease progression [5]. Recent studies indicate that oxidative stress is not only a consequence of external environmental factors but is also closely linked to metabolic disorders such as diabetes and obesity, emphasizing the need for effective antioxidant strategies to mitigate these effects [6].

Antioxidants are key agents in neutralizing free radicals and reducing oxidative harm, thereby protecting cells from premature aging and disease development [7, 8]. These protective compounds are found in a variety of food sources, including fruits, vegetables, and medicinal plants, and have been extensively studied in food science, medicine, and nutrition research [9, 10]. Researchers are exploring bioactive compounds from natural sources, including marine algae, fungi, and novel plant extracts, as potential therapeutic antioxidants for combating oxidative stress-related disorders [11-13].

The ability to assess antioxidant activity accurately is essential for understanding their potential benefits and applications in health and disease prevention [14, 15]. One widely used method for evaluating antioxidant activity is the DPPH (2, 2-diphenyl-1-picrylhydrazyl) assay. This technique relies on the scavenging ability of antioxidants to reduce the DPPH radical, causing a measurable color change [16, 17]. The reaction is quantified using spectrophotometry, a reliable and well-established technique for determining antioxidant potency [18].

Although commercial spectrophotometers provide precise results, they can be expensive and require laboratory infrastructure, which may limit accessibility for some researchers and institutions [19-21]. Recent advancements have led to the development of cost-effective, homebuilt optical devices, such as photometers utilizing LED technology. These alternative devices offer an affordable solution for antioxidant measurement, making this research more accessible to broader scientific communities [22, 23]. Studies have demonstrated that such homemade optical tools can effectively quantify antioxidant activity with reasonable accuracy, presenting a viable alternative to traditional spectrophotometry.

* Corresponding author: thidarat.w@sci.kmutnb.ac.th

Innovations in smartphone-integrated optical sensors are emerging as promising tools for real-time antioxidant analysis, further expanding accessibility [24, 25]. Current developments include wearable sensors capable of detecting oxidative stress biomarkers, which could facilitate early disease diagnosis and personalized health monitoring [26].

Natural products, including citrus fruits, are sources of antioxidants. Orange peels contain bioactive compounds, which are flavonoids, carotenoids, and phenolic acids, exhibit strong radical-scavenging properties [27, 28]. Investigating the antioxidant activity of orange peel extracts can provide insights into their potential health benefits and applications in food science and nutraceuticals [29]. Beyond dietary applications, orange peel antioxidants are also being explored for their use in skincare, cosmetics, and biodegradable packaging materials due to their antimicrobial and preservative properties, highlighting their multifunctional potential [30-32].

In this article, we present a comparative study evaluating a commercial spectrophotometer and a homebuilt LED-based photometer for measuring the antioxidant activity of orange peel extract. By testing various concentrations and wavelengths, we assess whether a low-cost optical device can serve as an effective alternative to traditional spectrophotometric methods.

2 Methods

2.1 Preparation of DPPH Stock Solution

A stock solution of 100 mL DPPH (2, 2-diphenyl-1-picrylhydrazyl) with a concentration of 1 mM in 95% ethanol is prepared as follows. The required amount of DPPH powder is calculated based on its molecular weight (394.32 g/mol), yielding approximately 39.43 mg of DPPH for the solution. Using a high-precision balance, this amount is carefully weighed to ensure accuracy. The weighed DPPH is then transferred into a clean 100-mL volumetric flask, followed by gradual addition of 95% ethanol with continuous gentle stirring to facilitate complete dissolution.

Once fully dissolved, the solution volume is adjusted to 100 mL using the same solvent. To prevent degradation due to light exposure, the container is wrapped in aluminum foil and stored at 4°C in a refrigerator. The solution is allowed to reach room temperature before use to ensure consistency in measurements.

2.2 Preparation of Diluted DPPH Solutions

To study the relationship between absorbance and concentration, a set of seven diluted DPPH solutions is prepared with concentrations of 0.10, 0.15, 0.20, 0.25, 0.30, 0.35, and 0.40 mM in 95% ethanol. These solutions are obtained by precisely diluting the stock solution in clean volumetric flasks, ensuring uniform mixing. Each dilution step is carried out using calibrated micropipettes for accuracy.

2.3 Preparation of Orange Peel Extract

The extraction of orange peel antioxidants begins with thoroughly washing fresh orange peels under running tap water to remove any dirt or contaminants. The cleaned peels are then cut into small uniform pieces and dried in a well-ventilated dry area for approximately one week, ensuring complete moisture removal.

Following the drying step, 5 grams of completely dried orange peel pieces are accurately weighed using an analytical balance. These pieces are then placed in a 50-mL extraction bottle and extracted using 25 mL of 95% ethanol. The extraction process is carried out over 24 hours at room temperature, ensuring efficient diffusion of bioactive compounds into the solvent. After extraction, the liquid phase is separated from solid residues through filtration using Whatman filter paper and is then stored at 4°C for subsequent analysis.

2.4 Spectrophotometric Analysis

The absorbance measurements of the DPPH solutions and orange peel extract are conducted using LAMBDA 365 UV/Vis spectrophotometer (Perkin Elmer). Each sample solution is placed into 1-cm spectrophotometric quartz cells to minimize optical interference.

The absorbance spectra of the DPPH solutions are investigated across a wavelength range of 400–700 nm. The primary absorbance peak occurs at 517 nm, which is commonly used for antioxidant evaluation. Additionally, measurements at 525 nm are performed to match the LED source in the homebuilt photometer.

Using the absorbance values obtained, linear calibration equations are constructed to establish the relationship between absorbance (x) and concentration (y), expressed as:

$$y = a\,x + b \qquad (1)$$

where a and b are coefficients determined from experimental data.

2.5 Homebuilt Photometer Operation

Our homebuilt photometer is designed to provide a cost-effective and accessible method for measuring antioxidant activity. It consists of an Arduino Uno microcontroller board, a 525-nm LED light source, a light-dependent resistor (LDR) detector, and an LCD monitor for displaying the results.

The 525-nm LED is the primary illumination source for the photometric measurements. To ensure stable and adjustable light intensity, the LED is controlled using pulse-width modulation (PWM), which allows precise regulation of brightness. The LED is connected in series with a resistor and capacitor to stabilize the voltage and prevent fluctuations during operation. The PWM signal, generated from the Arduino Uno, modulates the duty cycle of the LED, controlling the brightness dynamically depending on the required intensity.

The transmitted light passing through the 1-cm spectrophotometric cuvette containing the sample solution is detected by the LDR sensor. The LDR is incorporated into a voltage-divider circuit, where it is connected in series with a fixed resistor and powered by a 5V DC supply. The voltage across the LDR changes proportionally to the light intensity it receives—higher illumination results in lower resistance, leading to higher voltage readings.

The Arduino Uno board reads the voltage signal from the LDR sensor and performs an analog-to-digital (A/D) conversion with a 10-bit resolution (1024 levels) over a 0–5V range. The resulting digitized voltage (v) represents the detected light intensity and is displayed on an LCD screen for real-time monitoring. To ensure accurate measurements, background noise and fluctuations are minimized by shielding external light interference.

To eliminate errors caused by variations in initial light intensity, a blank measurement is conducted using 95% ethanol solution before each DPPH test. The corresponding blank voltage (v_0) is recorded, and the absorption (Δv) is determined by calculating the difference between blank and sample voltage: $\Delta v = v_0 - v$. This difference represents the absorption and is used for constructing a calibration equation describing the linear relationship between absorption and concentration (y):

$$y = a\,\Delta v + b \tag{2}$$

where a and b are calibration coefficients determined experimentally.

2.6 Antioxidant Activity Measurement

The antioxidant activity of orange peel extract is evaluated at varying concentrations using a DPPH assay. A total of four test tubes are prepared, each containing 2 mL of 0.60 mM DPPH solution. The orange peel extract is then added in precise volumes of 0, 0.2, 0.4, and 0.6 mL, respectively. To ensure that the final volume remains consistent at 3 mL and that the initial DPPH concentration is uniformly adjusted to 0.40 mM, 95% ethanol is used to make up the remaining volume in each tube.

To prevent degradation due to light exposure, the prepared test tubes are covered with aluminum foil and kept in darkness for 30 minutes to allow the reaction between DPPH and antioxidant compounds to stabilize before absorption measurements.

After incubation, the DPPH-extract mixtures are carefully transferred into 1-cm spectrophotometric quartz cells to minimize external optical interference. The absorption of each sample is measured using both the UV/Vis spectrophotometer and the homebuilt photometer, providing comparative results.

For measurements using a LAMBDA 365 UV/Vis spectrophotometer, the antioxidant activity (AA%) is calculated based on the absorbance values of solutions without and with the orange peel extract using the equation:

$$AA(\%) = \frac{x_{ref} - x_{ext}}{x_{ref}} \times 100\% \tag{3}$$

where x_{ref} and x_{ext} are the absorbance of the solutions without and with the orange peel extract.

For measurements using our homebuilt photometer, the antioxidant activity is determined based on the voltage difference (Δv) recorded from the light-dependent resistor (LDR) sensor:

$$AA(\%) = \frac{\Delta v_{ref} - \Delta v_{ext}}{\Delta v_{ref}} \times 100\% \tag{4}$$

where Δv_{ref} and Δv_{ext} are the voltage difference, corresponding to the absorption of the solutions without and with the orange peel extract.

3 Results and discussion

3.1 Visual Observation of DPPH Solutions

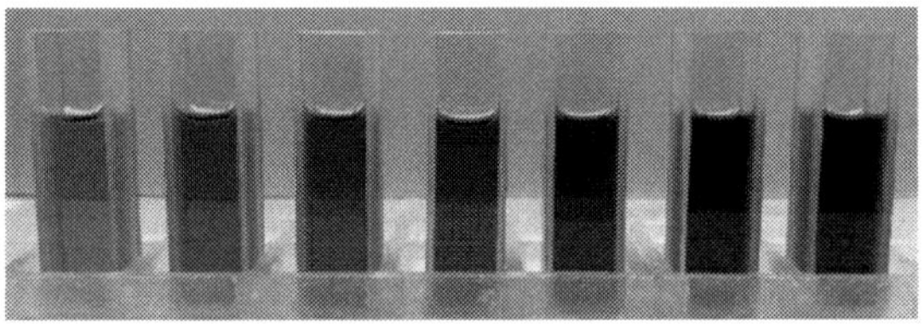

Fig. 1. Images of the diluted DPPH solutions with seven concentrations arranged sequentially from left to right: 0.10, 0.15, 0.20, 0.25, 0.30, 0.35, and 0.40 mM..

Figure 1 presents seven diluted DPPH solutions, each exhibiting a characteristic violet color. The intensity of the violet hue darkens as the concentration of DPPH increases, visually confirming that higher concentrations result in greater absorption of visible light. This observation aligns with the expected behavior of radical scavenging reactions, where higher molecular densities absorb more light, reducing transmission

3.2 Absorption Spectra of DPPH

Figure 2 illustrates the absorption spectra of the prepared DPPH solutions over the wavelength range of 400–700 nm, revealing a distinct absorption peak at 517 nm, characteristic of DPPH radical activity. Notably, all recorded spectral curves remain separate and well-defined, demonstrating that absorbance values increase consistently with higher DPPH concentrations. This confirms the expected relationship between concentration and optical absorption, where a greater number of radical molecules enhance light absorption, resulting in a darker solution appearance, as visually observed in figure 1.

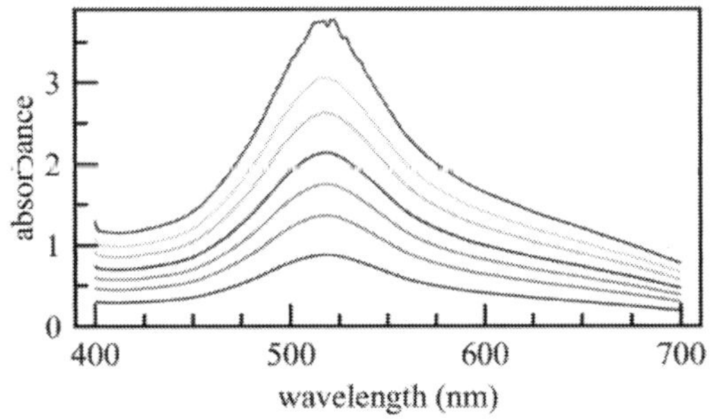

Fig. 2. Absorbance spectra of diluted DPPH solutions, with curves ordered from bottom to top, corresponding to concentrations of 0.10, 0.15, 0.20, 0.25, 0.30, 0.35, and 0.40 mM.

3.3 Calibration from Spectrophotometer

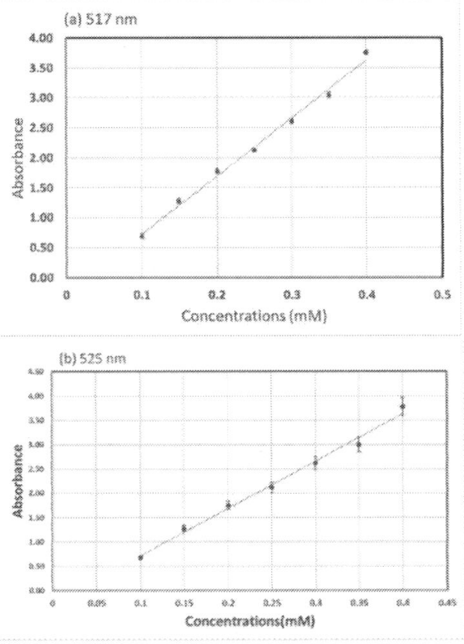

Fig. 3. Calibration curves of DPPH solutions at (a) 517 nm and (b) 525 nm, derived from spectrophotometric measurements. Circles represent the seven concentrations of the diluted DPPH solutions, plotted against the absorbance measured by the spectrophotometer. The lines denote the linear fits of the data.

The correlation between DPPH concentration and absorbance was analyzed using a linear regression model, formulated as Equation (1). Two distinct calibration equations were derived for measurements taken at 517 nm and 525 nm, expressed as:

$$y = 9.728\ x - 0.0255 \quad \text{(at 517 nm)} \qquad (5)$$

$$y = 9.731\ x - 0.258 \quad \text{(at 525 nm)} \qquad (6)$$

In both cases, the coefficient of determination (R^2) is exceptionally close to unity (0.9916 and 0.9921, respectively), indicating a strong fit to the linear regression, as illustrated in figure 3. These values suggest that both wavelengths are effective for DPPH analysis, though slight variations in slope (a) imply minor differences in light absorption efficiency.

3.4 Absorption of DPPH from Photometer

Table 1 shows the detailed measurements of the diluted DPPH solutions obtained from the homebuilt photometer. To minimize the electronic noise, each value of these digital voltages derived from an average of a thousand of raw data measured within a few seconds. The final values are rounded to two decimal places.

The blank voltages (v_0) of all seven measurements, in which a cuvette of 95% ethanal is placed in the photometer, are very similar. They are within a range of 951.46 – 951.93. The difference of the minimal and maximal values is only 0.47 which results in very small corresponding percentage difference of 0.049% [|951.46 – 951.93| / (951.46 + 951.93) ×2×100%]. This indicates that the homebuilt photometer works very reliable.

For the diluted DPPH solutions, the sample voltages (v) are lower than the blank voltage as the light is additionally absorbed by DPPH. When the DPPH concentration increases, the sample voltage (v) decreases. These results in the difference of the two voltages which taken as the sample absorption ($\Delta v = v_0 - v$) increases with the DPPH concentration.

Table 1. Absorption of diluted DPPH solutions measured by using the homebuilt photometer: the blank voltage (v_0), the sample voltage (v), and the absorption ($\Delta v = v_0 - v$).

DPPH (mM)	v_0	v	Δv
0.10	951.62	802.13	149.49
0.15	951.46	647.62	303.84
0.20	951.51	524.10	427.41
0.25	951.48	360.58	590.90
0.30	951.93	214.11	737.82
0.35	951.51	133.61	817.90
0.40	951.49	73.06	878.43

3.5 Calibration from Photometer

The digital voltage difference (Δv), obtained from the homebuilt photometer, exhibits a clear linear relationship with the DPPH concentration, similar to the absorbance behavior observed with the UV/Vis spectrophotometer. This reinforces the effectiveness of the LED-based detection system in quantifying DPPH concentration.

3.5.1 Overall Fitting

Figure 4(a) presents the calibration fitting results using equation (2). An overall fitting is performed using all collected data points, yielding the equation:

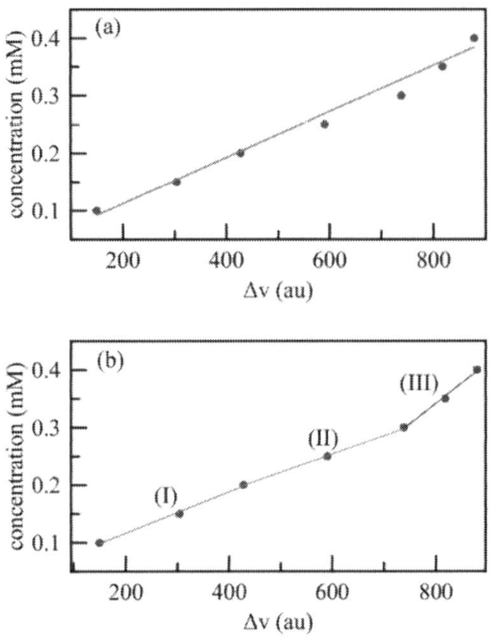

Fig. 4. Calibration curve of DPPH solutions obtained from measurements using the homebuilt photometer: (a) an overall fitting and (b) three piecewise fittings. Circles represent the seven concentrations of the diluted DPPH solutions, plotted against the digital voltage difference (Δv) measured by the photometer. The lines denote the linear fits of the data.

$$y = 3.90\times10^{-4}\,\Delta v + 0.0325 \qquad (7)$$

with the R^2 value of 0.9816. While this fitting confirms a strong correlation between DPPH concentration and voltage difference, the slightly lower R^2 value compared to those obtained from the spectrophotometric calibration (figure 3) suggests variations in measurement precision with the homebuilt photometer.

3.5.2 Piecewise Fitting

To enhance model accuracy and reduce residual errors, three piecewise fittings are performed for different concentration ranges of DPPH, as shown in figure 4(b):

range I: 0.1 mM $\leq y \leq$ 0.2 mM

$$y = 3.58\times10^{-4}\,\Delta v + 0.0448 \qquad (8)$$

with the R^2 value of 0.99959,

range II: 0.2 mM $\leq y \leq$ 0.3 mM

$$y = 3.22\times10^{-4}\,\Delta v + 0.0616 \qquad (9)$$

with the R^2 value of 0.9991, and

range III: 0.3 mM $\leq y \leq$ 0.4 mM

$$y = 7.07\times10^{-4}\,\Delta v - 0.2234 \qquad (10)$$

with the R^2 value of 0.9936.

The R^2 values for all three piecewise fittings are very close to unity, confirming that segmented calibration models better fit the experimental data compared to the overall fitting approach. This refinement improves measurement precision by accounting for subtle variations in photometric response at different concentration levels.

3.6 Visual Observation of Mixtures

Figure 5 illustrates the visual transformation of DPPH solution color upon reaction with orange peel extract after being kept in darkness for 30 minutes. While the initial DPPH concentration remains at 0.4 mM, the volume of added extract varies, influencing the degree of radical scavenging activity. The progressive shift from violet to pale yellow is an observable indication of antioxidant action, where bioactive compounds in the extract neutralize DPPH radicals. The gradual color transition corresponds to the interaction between phenolic compounds and flavonoids from the orange peel extract with DPPH radicals, resulting in the observed reduction in light absorption.

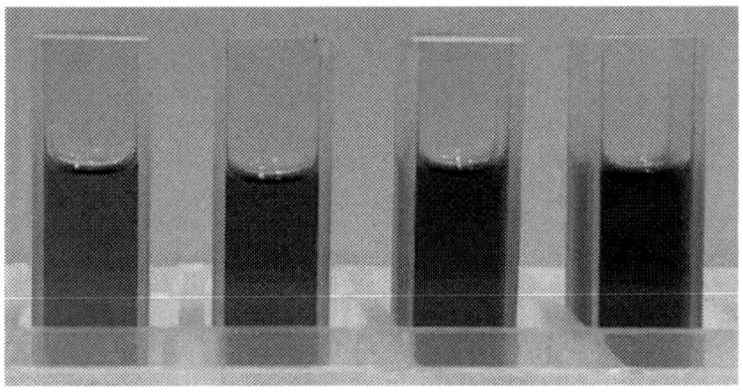

Fig. 5. Images of the mixtures containing DPPH and orange peel extract solutions, arranged sequentially from left to right with extract volumes of 0.6, 0.4, 0.2, and 0.0 ml.

3.7 Antioxidant Activity

Table 2. Antioxidant activity (AA) calculated from measurements by the spectrophotometer.

extract	AA (%)		
(ml)	517 nm	525 nm	average
0.0	0.0	0.0	0.0
0.2	24.8	26.5	25.7
0.4	48.5	50.1	49.3
0.6	64.3	66.0	65.2

The antioxidant activity (AA) calculated from absorption measurements in the spectrophotometer are summarized in table 2. AA increases with the added volume of the orange peel extract. Using equation 3, the measurements by the spectrophotometer with the wavelengths of 517 and 525 nm results very similar AA values with the difference about 1.6% - 1.7%. The average AA is also calculated and shown in table 2.

Table 3 shows AA values obtained from the measurements by the homebuilt photometer with the overall fitting and using equation 4. Similar to AA in table 2, it increases with the added volume of the extract. However, for each added volume, the AA value is quite different from those obtained from the spectrophotometer.

For quantitative comparison, we calculate the error by taking the AA value obtained from the spectrometer as reference. Even though for a given added volume of the extract the error depends on the reference (517nm, 525 nm, or average), the error increases with the added volume of the extract. from 0.2 to 0.6 ml, the error increases from 1.8% - 3.5% to 10.5% - 12.2%. We expect that the error comes from the fact that the single linear regression [figure4 (left)] does not fit well to the whole set data of the diluted DPPH solutions.

Table 3. Antioxidant activity (AA) calculated from measurements by the homebuilt photometer with overall fitting and the error in comparison to the results from the spectrometer.

extract (ml)	AA (%)	error (%) with ref.		
		517 nm	525 nm	average
0.0	0.0	0.0	0.0	0.0
0.2	23.0	1.8	3.5	2.7
0.4	55.9	7.4	5.8	6.6
0.6	76.5	12.2	10.5	11.3

Such error of AA obtained from the homebuilt photometer with overall fitting can be reduced when AA values are calculated based on the three piecewise fittings [figure4 (right)]. In this case, AA is not calculated from equation 4 but the equivalent DPPH concentration is calculated from Δv and the piecewise fitting before AA is calculated using equation (11) in which AA is defined as

$$AA(\%) = \frac{C_{ref} - C_{ext}}{C_{ref}} \times 100\% \quad (11)$$

where C_{ref} and C_{ext} are the equivalent DPPH concentration without and with the orange peel extract.

Table 4. Antioxidant activity (AA) calculated from measurements by the homebuilt photometer with piecewise fittings and the error in comparison to the results from the spectrometer.

extract (ml)	AA (%)	error (%) with ref.		
		517 nm	525 nm	average
0.0	0.0	0.0	0.0	0.0
0.2	27.5	2.7	1.0	1.8
0.4	52.3	3.8	2.2	3.0
0.6	68.9	4.6	2.9	3.7

Table 4 shows AA values calculated from the piecewise fitting method. They are different from those calculated from the overall fitting method in table 3. When the added volume of the extract is increased from 0.2 - 0.6 ml, the error also increases from 1.0% - 2.7% to 2.9% - 4.6% but much less than the error from the overall fitting method in table 3.

4 Conclusion

Absorption-based measurements of antioxidant activity obtained from both the homebuilt photometer and the commercial spectrophotometer showed consistent results. In the case of the homebuilt photometer, the use of three piecewise linear fittings provided a more accurate representation of the absorption data than overall fitting. Moreover, the findings of this study further substantiate the applicability of LED-based detection systems for antioxidant analysis and highlight the advantages of refined calibration procedures in enhancing measurement accuracy. Future work may focus on further optimizing homebuilt photometers to improve precision, sensitivity, limits of detection, and other parameters that contribute to reducing variability in concentration estimation.

We thank the Department of Industrial Physics and Medical Instrumentation, King Mongkut's University of Technology North Bangkok and the Department of Physics, Kasetsart University for financial support.

References

1. V. Lobo, A. Patil, A. Phatak, N. Chandra, Free radicals, antioxidants, and functional foods: Impact on human health. Pharmacognosy Reviews **4**, 118-126 (2010).
2. N. Chandimali, S. G. Bak, E. H. Park, H. J. Lim, Y. S. Won, E. K. Kim, S. I. Park, S. J. Lee, Free radicals and their impact on health and antioxidant defenses: a review. Cell Death Discov. **11**, 19 (2025)
3. H. Sies, Oxidative stress: A concept in redox biology and medicine. Redox Biology **4**, 180-183 (2015).
4. G. Liguori, R. Ingrassia, A. C. Maio, Reactive oxygen species, toxicity, oxidative stress, and antioxidants. Arch. Toxicol. 97, 2737–2763 (2023).
5. M. Valko, C.J. Rhodes, J. Moncol, M. Izakovic, Free radicals, metals and antioxidants in oxidative stress-induced cancer. Chem. Biol. Interact. **160**, 1-40 (2006).
6. L. Di Meo, C. Natalucci, S. Percario, et al., Oxidative stress and metabolic disorders: relevance and therapeutic perspectives. Front. Nutr. **9**, 994309 (2022)
7. G. Alamdari, M. Mohseni, S. Sadeghi, et al., Free radicals, antioxidants and functional foods: impact on human health. J. Med. Food **14**, 795–802 (2011).
8. S. Smith, J. Jones, and R. Taylor, Free radicals and their impact on health and antioxidant defenses. Cell Death Discov. **10**, 1234 (2024)
9. M. P. Kahkonen, A. T. Hopia, H. J. Vuorela, Antioxidant activity of plant extracts containing phenolic compounds. J. Agric. Food Chem. **47**, 3954-3962 (1999)
10. M. M. Rahaman, R. Hossain, J. Herrera-Bravo, et al., Natural antioxidants from some fruits, seeds,

foods, natural products, and associated health benefits: An update. Food Sci. Nutr. **11**, 1657–1670 (2023).

11. I. N. Monroy-García, S. Torres-Romero, L. D. Castro-Ochoa, A. Mendoza-Acosta, E. Viveros-Valdez, F. Ayala-Zavala, Bioactive compounds from marine macroalgae: A natural defense against oxidative stress-related diseases. Stresses **5**, 22 (2025)
12. F. Menaa, U. Wijesinghe, G. Thiripuranathar, et al., Marine algae-derived bioactive compounds: a new wave of nanodrugs? Mar. Drugs **19**, 484 (2021)
13. S. Ghosh, T. Sarkar, S. Pati, et al., Novel bioactive compounds from marine sources as a tool for functional food development. Front. Mar. Sci. **9**, 1–28 (2022)
14. R. L. Prior, X. Wu, K. Schaich, Standardized methods for the determination of antioxidant capacity in food and dietary supplements. J. Agric. Food Chem. **53**, 4290-4302 (2005)
15. C. A. Rice-Evans, N. J. Miller, G. Paganga, Structure-antioxidant activity relationships of flavonoids and phenolic acids. Free Radic. Biol. Med. **20**, 933-956 (1996)
16. W. Brand-Williams, M. E. Cuvelier, C. Berset, Use of a free radical method to evaluate antioxidant activity. LWT - Food Science and Technology **28**, 25-30 (1995)
17. K. Benzie, J. Strain, Ferric reducing/antioxidant power assay: Direct measure of total antioxidant capacity. Methods in Enzymology. **299**, 15-27 (1999)
18. A. Bocco, M. E. Cuvelier, H. Richard, C. Berset, Antioxidant activity and phenolic composition of citrus peel and seed extracts. J. Agric. Food Chem. **46**, 2123-2129 (1998).
19. P. Kolesnichenko, A. Eriksson, L. Lindh, D. Zigmantas, J. Uhlig, Viking spectrophotometer: a home-built, simple, and cost-efficient absorption and fluorescence spectrophotometer for education in chemistry. J. Chem. Educ. **100**, 1561–1567 (2023)
20. V. R. Pereira, B. S. Hosker, Low-cost (<€5), open-source, potential alternative to commercial spectrophotometers. PLoS Biol. **17**, e3000321 (2019)
21. A. B. D. Nandiyanto, R. Zaen, R. Oktiani, et al., Techno-economic feasibility study of low-cost and portable home-made spectrophotometer for analyzing solution concentration. J. Eng. Sci. Technol. **14**, 599–609 (2019)
22. H.-Y. Chen, H.-M. Nieh, M.-F. Yang, et al., Implementation of a low-cost automated LED photometer for enzymatic reaction detection to teach basic bioelectronics technologies in vocational high schools. IEEE Trans. Educ. **59**, 194–201 (2016)
23. E. M. Paiva, J. Rohwedder, C. Pasquini, C. Pereira, Method for building a portable near infrared photometer based on LEDs and interference filters chosen by a spectral variable selection algorithm. Microchem. J. **146**, 842–849 (2019)
24. R. Shi, C. Wang, M. Zhu, C. Xie, W. Cui, Q. Zhou, A smartphone-assisted colorimetric paper sensor based on MnO_2 nanozymes for rapid evaluation of total antioxidant capacity in foods. Microchim. Acta **192**, 414 (2025)
25. D. Calabria, M. Guardigli, P. Severi, I. Trozzi, A. Pace, S. Cinti, M. Zangheri, M. Mirasoli, A smartphone-based chemosensor to evaluate antioxidants in agri-food matrices by in situ AuNP formation. Sensors **21**, 5432 (2021)
26. Z. Ying, L. Qiao, B. Liu, L. Gao, P. Zhang, Development of a microfluidic wearable electrochemical sensor for the non-invasive monitoring of oxidative stress biomarkers in human sweat. Biosens. Bioelectron. **261**, 116502 (2024)
27. R. K. Saini, A. Ranjit, K. Sharma, P. Parchuri, X. Shang, K. Gowda, Y.-S. Keum, Bioactive compounds of citrus fruits: A review of composition and health benefits of carotenoids, flavonoids, limonoids, and terpenes. Antioxidants **11**, 239 (2022)
28. B. Singh, J. P. Singh, A. Kaur, N. Singh, Phenolic composition, antioxidant potential and health benefits of citrus peel. *Food Res. Int.* **132**, 109114 (2020)
29. J. H. Park, M. Lee, E. Park, Antioxidant activity of orange flesh and peel extracted with various solvents. Prev. Nutr. Food Sci. **19**, 291-298 (2014)
30. S. Jaiswal, S. S. Gaur, Orange peel and skin health: An exploratory study on potential benefits. J. Food Chem. Nanotechnol. **9**, S91-S99 (2023)
31. A. El-Sayed, M. Shehata, N. Abdel-Haleem, et al., Bioactive preservative nano-packaging films based on orange peel waste extracts: antioxidant and antimicrobial efficacy. Bioresour. Bioprocess. **12**, 1–18 (2025)
32. D. Gabrić, M. Kurek, M. Ščetar, M. Brnčić, K. Galić, Characterization of synthetic polymer coated with biopolymer layer with natural orange peel extract aimed for food packaging. Polymers **15**, 2569 (2023)

Effect of surfactant concentration on the synthesis of hydrogel microbeads using the emulsion polymerization process for acrylamide/acrylic acid copolymers

Nutthakritta Philaiwan [1], *Siriporn* Pranee[2], and *Samitthichai* Seeyangnok[1*]

[1]Department of Industrial Chemistry, Faculty of Applied Science, King Mongkut's University of Technology North Bangkok, Wong Sawang, Bang Sue, 10800 Bangkok, Thailand
[2]Department of Veterinary Technology, Faculty of Veterinary Technology, Kasetsart University, Lat Yao, Chatuchak, 10900 Bangkok, Thailand

Abstract. Personal care and cosmetic goods frequently contain microplastic particles, specifically microbeads with an average diameter of 250 mm, which make up about 5% of the product weight. Pollution may result from these microbeads' persistence in the environment. The goal of this study is to use emulsion polymerization to synthesize hydrogel microbeads from copolymers based on acrylamide. The study focuses into the surfactant concentrations affects swelling behavior and particle size. Scanning electron microscopy (SEM) is used to assess particle size and determine the swelling ratio, and Fourier transform infrared spectroscopy (FTIR) is used for chemical analysis. The results show that while swelling capacity decreases with increasing surfactant concentration, smaller and more homogeneous particles are produced. The result provides a systematic method to creating microbeads with adjustable characteristics. Additionally, the chosen synthesis materials have the potential to sustainably minimize water contamination and lessen the accumulation of hazardous residues.

1 Introduction

Microbeads are frequently found in a variety of personal care and cosmetic products (PCCPs), including toothpaste, soap, face cleansers, and sunscreen. Synthetic polymers, such as high-density polyethylene (HDPE), polyester (PES), polyvinyl chloride (PVC), and polyethylene (PE), are frequently used to create the main ingredients [1]. It has been reported that synthetic polymers can accumulate in living organisms, potentially causing long-term adverse effects, and negatively impacting overall environmental quality. The synthesis of microbeads with a three-dimensional covalently crosslinked network allows for excellent water absorption, effective encapsulation of active substances, and contributes to exfoliation, stain removal, and improved cleansing efficiency. These typically particles have an average size ranging from 10 to 250 μm, and variations in particle size influence their suitability for different types of applications. The appropriate selection of polymeric materials is a key factor in enhancing the performance of microbeads. Therefore, the development of alternative materials such as acrylamide-based polymers, which possess biocompatible properties, can be applied in the development of medical materials, including hydrogels for wound dressings, drug delivery systems, or tissue scaffolds. These materials can be designed with structures that allow for controlled release of active substances and efficient fluid absorption, while also not causing irritation to cells or tissues in the body [2]. Additionally, acrylamide-based polymers tend to be more environmentally friendly compared to other synthetic polymers.

However, there are still certain limitations that need to be addressed, including mechanical weakness that can lead to structural degradation prior to use, and irregular control over the encapsulation and release rates of active substances. These factors could affect the stability of formulations and the overall efficacy of the products. Emulsion polymerization provides benefits in regulating particle size, maintaining system stability, and adapting to different types of materials. It also enables adjustment of system composition to fine-tune polymer characteristics like water uptake, mechanical durability, and controlled release of active agents [3]. According to a study by Sarva Mangala Praveena, Siti Norashikin, and Akizuki (2018) [4], the population group of students to working adults aged between 21 and 29 years uses PCCPs on average three times per day. The two most used products are toothpaste and facial foam/scrubs, which often contain synthetic microbeads. Each use can release between 4,000 and 94, 500 microbead particles into wastewater [5]. Although some microbeads are removed in wastewater treatment plants, many still escape directly into the environment. This has made PCCPs a significant source of microplastic pollution in natural water bodies,

* Corresponding author: samitthichai.s@sci.kmutnb.ac.th

particularly in marine ecosystems. Currently, there are no effective and sustainable methods for the long-term removal of microplastics. For the reasons mentioned above, this research aims to develop hydrogel microbeads from synthetic acrylamide polymers using the emulsion polymerization technique. The goal is enhancing the properties of the microbeads to make them suitable for use in PCCPs, focusing especially on particle size and swelling behavior by examining the influence of varying surfactant concentrations. Ultimately, this research aims to provide guidelines for designing microbeads that balance both effective performance and reduced environmental impact by utilizing materials with potential biodegradability or long-term ecological compatibility.

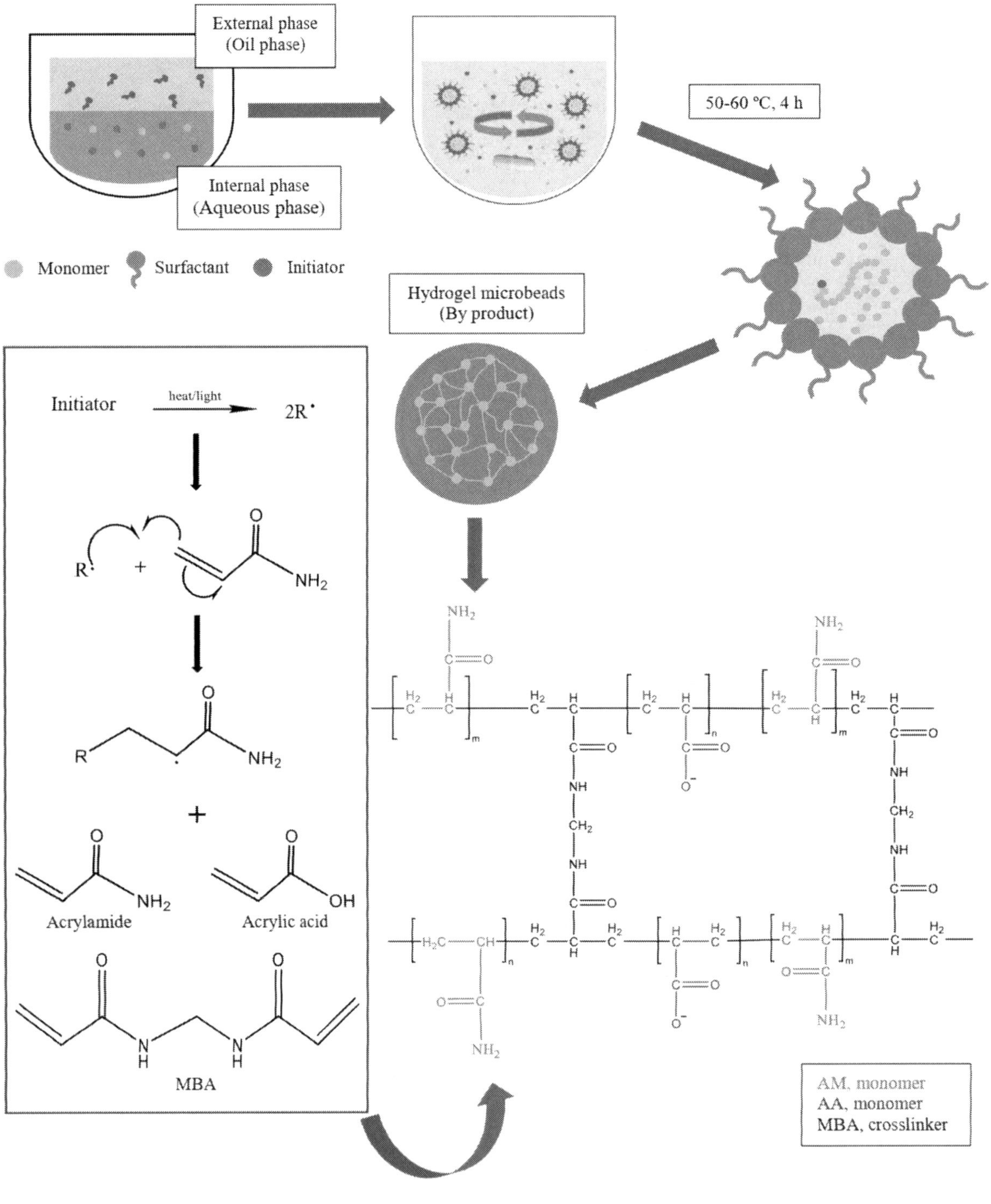

Fig. 1. Overview of the synthetic route employed in the preparation of hydrogel microbeads.

2 Materials and Methods

2.1 Materials

Acrylamide (AM) and acrylic acid (AA) (Acros Organics, 99 %) were used as monomers. N, N-methylenebisacrylamide (MBA) served as the crosslinker. Ammonium persulfate (APS) was used as the initiator. Cyclohexane was employed as the continuous oil phase in the emulsion system, while sorbitan monooleate (Span 80) acted as the surfactant. All chemicals were used as received without further purification.

2.2 Preparation of hydrogel microbeads

The hydrogel microbeads were prepared via an emulsion polymerization. Briefly, 30 mL of cyclohexane was mixed with Span 80 as the surfactant in a 250 mL reaction flask and stirred at room temperature for 15 min to form the external (oil) phase. For the internal (aqueous) phase, AM, AA monomers, and MBA were dissolved in 30 mL of deionized water in a 50 mL beaker and stirred at room temperature for 15 min. Afterwards, the aqueous phase was gradually added into the oil phase under continuous stirring to form the emulsion. The reaction flask was then purged with nitrogen gas for 10 min to remove oxygen. Next, APS (initiator) was added to initiate the polymerization. The reaction was carried out at 50–60 °C for 4 h under nitrogen atmosphere, allowing free radical polymerization to proceed (Figure 1). After completion, the reaction mixture was cooled to room temperature. The product was separated by centrifugation to remove cyclohexane, and the resulting white solid microbeads were washed twice with cyclohexane to remove residual surfactant. Finally, the microbeads were dried in a vacuum oven and stored in a desiccator [6]. The yield was approximately 95% (Figure 2). The formulation ratios are presented in Table 1.

Table 1. Mole ratio of prepare hydrogel microbeads for synthesis.

%Surfactant (%v/v)	AM (mmol)	AA (mmol)	MBA (mmol)	Particle size
2.0	35.20	34.70	0.65	25.29±6.07
4.0	35.20	34.70	0.65	11.07±2.78
6.0	35.20	34.70	0.65	9.67±2.61
8.0	35.20	34.70	0.65	7.73±2.77
10.0	35.20	34.70	0.65	6.66±1.66

A free radical polymerization is a polymerizing approach by which successive addition of free radicals takes place to form a polymer unit. It is a type of chain-growth polymerization, with a cationic, anionic and coordination polymerization. It is an essential technique for obtaining different polymers and material composites. Free radical polymerization via the emulsion technique was effectively employed to synthesize polymer microbeads. In this process, monomer droplets were dispersed in an aqueous phase stabilized by surfactants, forming a stable emulsion system. polymerization was initiated by free radicals generated from an initiator dissolved in the continuous aqueous phase. During polymerization, free radicals diffused from the aqueous phase into the monomer droplets, triggering chain reactions that resulted in polymer growth within the droplets. The surfactants played a critical role in stabilizing the monomer droplets, preventing coalescence and ensuring uniform polymerization. Consequently, polymer particles with controlled size and morphology were obtained.

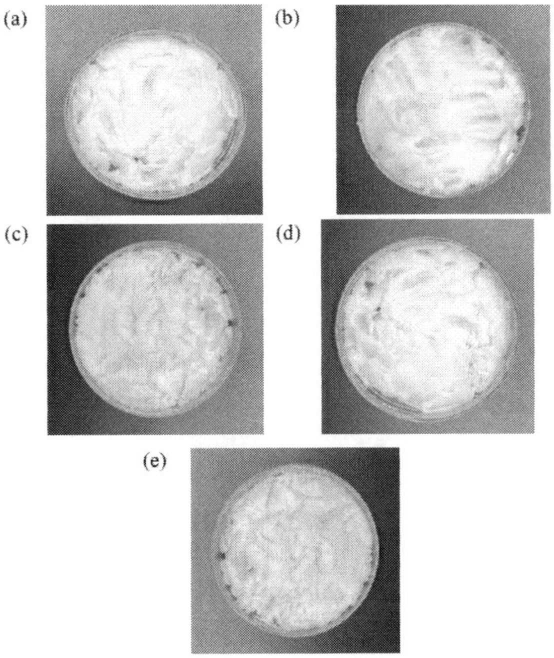

Fig. 2. Hydrogel microbead products synthesized via polymerization at varying concentrations of surfactant. (a-e). 2%, 4%, 6%, 8%, and 10%, respectively.

2.3 Fourier Transforms Infrared (FTIR) Spectroscopy

The prepared samples were finely ground and mixed with anhydrous potassium bromide (KBr) in a 1:100 (w/w) ratio. The mixture was then pressed into pellets (approximately 1 cm in diameter) using a hydraulic press at 1 ton of pressure for 30 sec. Fourier Transform Infrared Spectroscopy (FTIR) analysis was carried out over the wavenumber range of 4000–400 cm^{-1}.

2.4 Scanning Electron Microscopy

The morphology and particle size distribution of the microbeads were analyzed by preparing dried samples, which were ground using a mortar. Approximately 0.05 g of the sample was spread onto carbon tape mounted on a stub. The surface morphology was imaged, and preliminary particle sizes were determined using a Scanning Electron Microscope (SEM; Thermo Fisher Quanta 450) operated in low-vacuum mode. Particle sizes were measured from SEM images using ImageJ software.

 https://doi.org/10.1051/e3sconf/202567901030

2.5 Swelling test

The swelling test of the microbeads was conducted by weighing approximately 1.00 g of the dried sample and placing it in a nylon fiber bag. The sample was then immersed in deionized water at room temperature for specific time intervals. At each time point, the sample was removed, weighed, and the weight was recorded. The swelling ratio (%SR) was calculated using the following formula.

$$\textit{Swelling Ratio (\%SR)} = \frac{W_S - W_0}{W_0} \times 100 \qquad (1)$$

Where W_s is the weight of the microbeads in the swollen state and W_0 is the initial dry weight of the microbeads before swelling.

3 Results and Discussion

3.1 FTIR characterization

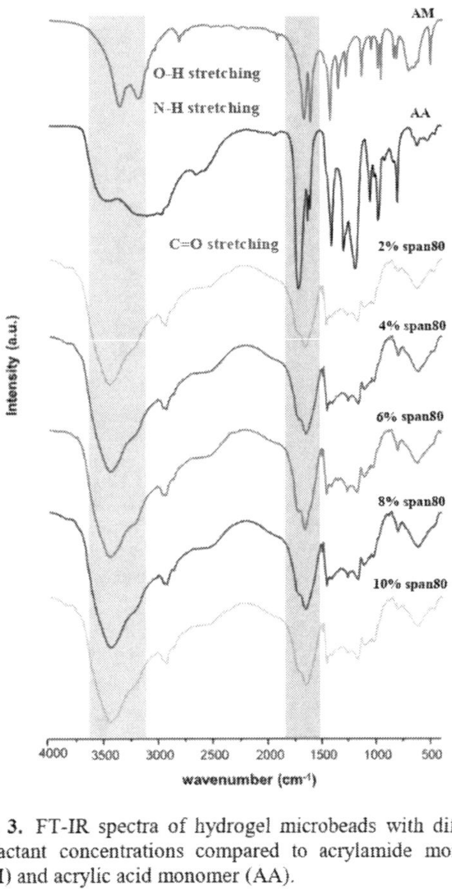

Fig. 3. FT-IR spectra of hydrogel microbeads with different surfactant concentrations compared to acrylamide monomer (AM) and acrylic acid monomer (AA).

The chemical structure of these 5 hydrogel microbeads with difference surfactant concentration is compared to AA and AM monomer were investigated by FTIR spectroscopy shows in the Figure 3 AM and AA monomer, characteristic absorption bands were observed at 3600-3400 cm^{-1} broad peaks attributed to -OH or -NH stretching vibrations, indicating the presence of hydroxy and amide groups. The peaks around 2950-2900 cm^{-1} are assigned to $-CH_2$ stretching vibrations from the polymer backbone. The absorption band at 1750-1700 cm^{-1} is attributed to the C=O stretching of the carboxylic groups (-COOH, from AA), while a second carbonyl peaks observed around 1650-1600 cm^{-1} corresponding to the amide group (C=O, from AM). These two peaks confirm the successful incorporation of both monomers into the hydrogel matrix. In the copolymer, key peaks from both AM and AA are observed, confirming successful polymerization.

The broad band at ~3400 cm^{-1} is due to overlapping –OH and –NH stretching vibrations, indicating the coexistence of hydroxyl and amide groups in the network. The C=O stretching vibrations from both the carboxylic acid and amide groups are seen at ~1715 cm^{-1} (AA) and ~1650 cm^{-1} (AM) respectively. Importantly, the disappearance of the vinyl groups C=C stretching peak (normally observed in the monomer form around 800–900 cm^{-1} in the copolymer spectrum indicates the completion of polymerization. FTIR analysis verifies that both AM and AA monomers have been efficiently polymerized into the copolymer chain using free radical polymerization. The detection of signature chemical groups and the absence of vinyl group peaks validate the formation of the poly (AM-*co*-AA) hydrogel network.

3.2 Morphology and particle size

The morphology of hydrogel microbeads is examined using SEM as shown in Figure 4., the diameters of particles were measured from the ImageJ program to calculate the average particle size. The physical appearance of particles in all conditions is spherical in shape with smooth surfaces. The average value of particle size distribution of microbeads with different surfactant concentrations at magnification 2000x, 2%, 4%, 6%, 8% and 10% were 25.29 ± 6.07, 11.07 ± 2.78, 9.67 ± 2.61, 7.73 ± 2.77 and 6.66 ± 1.66 respectively (Figure 4 (a, d, g, j, m)), the particle size was found to decrease inversely with increasing surfactant concentration. These results are consistent with the study by ISHAK, W.M.W. and M.H. ZULFAKAR [7], The low concentrations, Span 80 does not fully adsorb onto the surface of newly formed droplets, allowing them to coalesce and resulting in larger droplet sizes. This observation aligns with previous reports on the importance of optimal emulsifier concentrations for droplet stabilization. Increasing the concentration of Span 80 provides more surfactant molecules to effectively reduce interfacial tension and cover the droplet surfaces, thereby minimizing coalescence and leading to a reduction in overall droplet size. The distribution graphs (Figure 4 (c, f, i, l, o)) an increase in surfactant concentration resulted. in a relatively uniform reduction in particle size. At the same time, a narrower particle size distribution and a leftward shift were observed, which also increased with higher surfactant concentration.

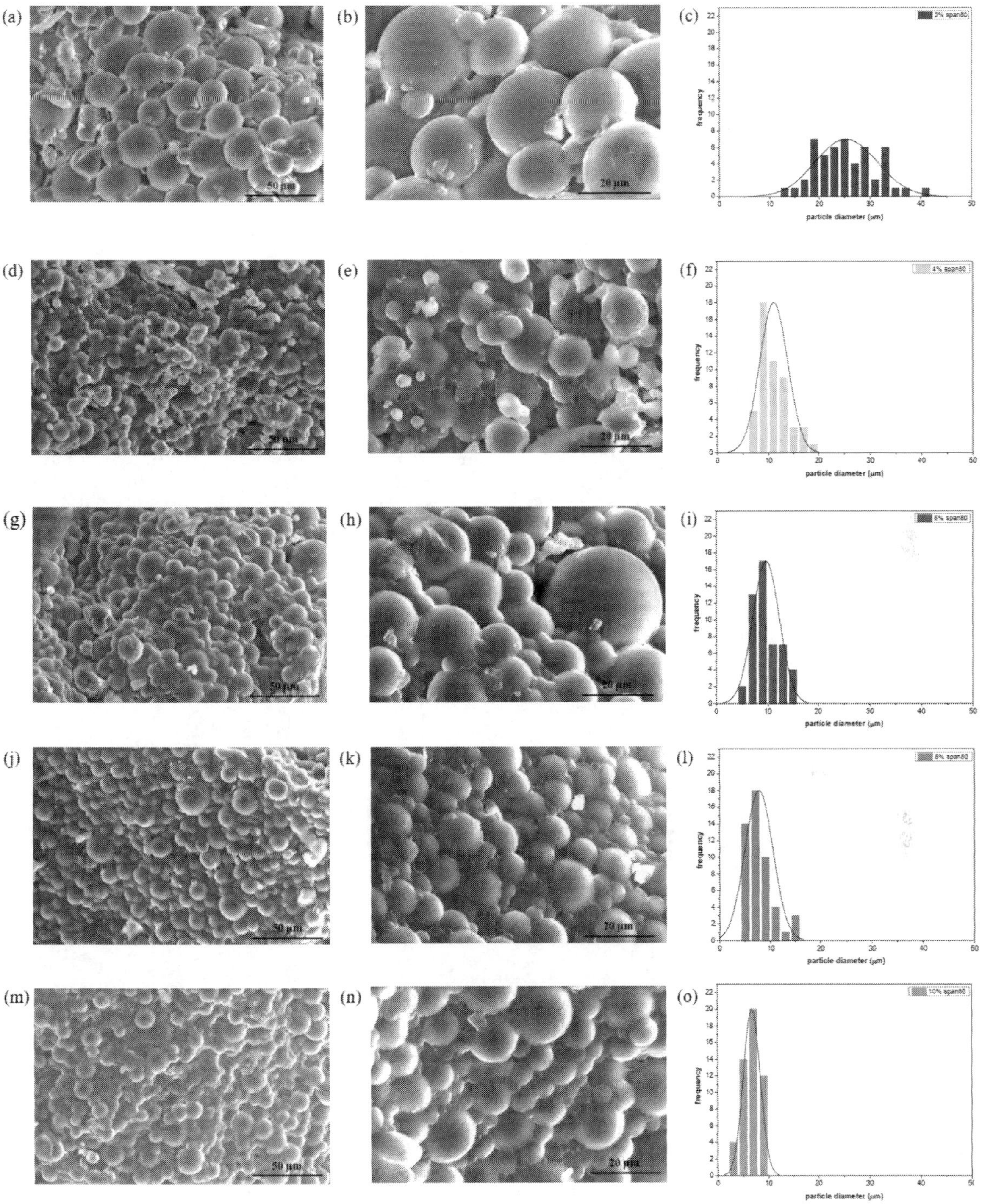

Fig. 4. SEM micrographs of hydrogel microbeads with different surfactant concentrations prepared by emulsion polymerization. (a-c). 2% span80 at magnifications 2000x, 5000x and average value of particle size distribution respectively, (d-f). 4% span80 at magnifications 2000x, 5000x and average value of particle size distribution respectively, (g-i). 6% span80 at magnifications 2000x, 5000x and average value of particle size distribution respectively, (j-l). 8% span80 at magnifications 2000x, 5000x and average value of particle size distribution respectively, (m-o). 10% span80 at magnifications 2000x, 5000x and average value of particle size distribution respectively.

3.3 Swelling behavior

Ability of hydrogel microbeads to absorb and retain an aqueous medium inside the network (Figure 5.), and it is evaluated by immersing the preweighted dried sample in the media. At the beginning solvent molecules attack the surface of the hydrogel and start penetrating the network, causing the expansion of gel meshes that allows other solvent particles to enter the network. Basically, the more hydrophilic the polymer structure, the stronger the polymer-water interaction becomes. Hydrogels with hydrophilic functional groups swell in water exclusively as result of polymer-water interaction forces.

Chemical gels are considered permanent when their polymer networks are stabilized by covalent cross-links, resulting in durable and irreversible structures. Reactive functional groups along the polymer chains enable the formation of these strong and stable covalent bonds, creating a robust gel network. Hydrogel microbeads swell until they reach equilibrium, a state influenced by the strength of polymer–water interactions and the degree of cross-linking. This swelling behavior also depends on the type of polymer and the number of reactive functional groups present along the polymer chain [8].

The swelling ratio of vary surfactant concentrations of hydrogel microbeads were determined based on weight changes in fiber bags as illustrated in Figure 6(a), the study found that the hydrogel microbeads began to reach swelling equilibrium after being immersed in deionized water for 150 min. At surfactant concentrations of 2% and 4%, the resulting emulsions were unstable, indicating that low surfactant levels were insufficient to effectively reduce the interfacial tension between the oil and water phases.

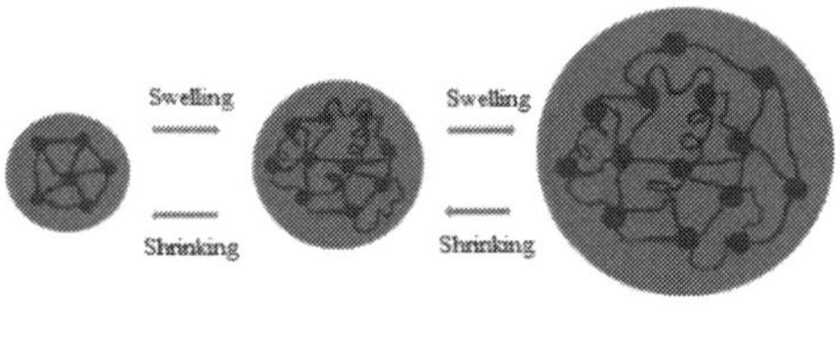

Fig. 5. Swelling property of the polymer matrix, which can uptake and hold significant quantities of water.

Under these conditions, polymerization process was incomplete, resulting in a polymer structure with low mechanical strength due to insufficient crosslinking. Consequently, the swelling ratios at 672.34 ± 7.76% and 673.21 ± 17.56%, respectively. Increasing the surfactant concentration to 6% significantly enhanced the emulsion stability, indicating that a higher amount of surfactant could adsorb at the interface between the oil phase and the internal aqueous phase. This resulted in a stronger adsorption layer and improved emulsion stability, as evidenced by the swelling ratio of 1111.06 ± 12.28%.

However, when the surfactant concentration was increased to 8% and 10%, the emulsion began to exhibit greater stability. The particle size of the emulsion increased and became more uniform. This result is consistent with the particle size distribution illustrated in Figure 4. (c, f, i, l, o), Which shows that increasing surfactant concentration results in smaller and more uniformly distributed particles. It is presumed that polymerization is more complete under these conditions, resulting in increased crosslinking within the polymer network.

This structural improvement contributed to a reduction and stabilization in the swelling ratio, at 916.33 ± 8.99% and 820.45 ± 12.24%, respectively. Similarly, the study conducted by Jusoh and Othman (2016) [9], reported an increase in particle formation at higher surfactant concentrations.

The swelling behavior observed in this system can be explained by Figure 6(b), During the initial immersion period, within the first 60 minutes, water penetrated the outer layer of the microbeads but could not evenly distribute into the internal structure. This led to the release or backflow of some of the absorbed water, causing a temporary decrease in the swelling ratio at the early stage. As time progressed, from 80 to 150 minutes, water gradually diffused into the inner polymer network, resulting in an increase in the swelling ratio again. The system eventually reached equilibrium after approximately 160 minutes. Moreover, the incomplete polymerization and the heterogeneity of the polymer network, which arose from the unstable emulsion, are likely key factors contributing to this two-phase swelling behavior. Similar swelling characteristics have been reported in other studies involving hydrogel materials with irregular porous structures [10, 11].

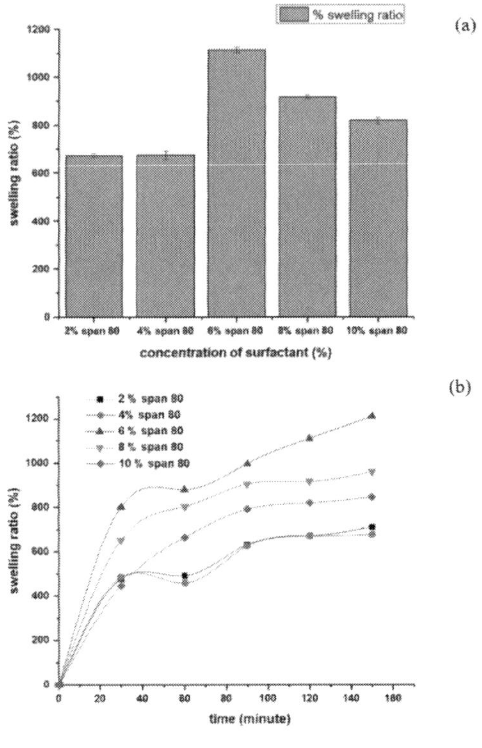

Fig. 6. The effect of different surfactant concentrations on the swelling behavior of hydrogel microbeads. (a). Relationship between surfactant concentration and the swelling ratio (%), (b). Relationship between time and the swelling ratio (%).

4 Conclusions

The results of this study demonstrated that the concentration of surfactant had a significant effect on the stability of the emulsion, which is a key factor influencing the completeness of the polymerization process within the hydrogel microbeads. The experiment revealed that the most stable emulsions were obtained using Span 80 at concentrations of 8% and 10%, which resulted in average particle sizes of 7.73 ± 2.77 μm and 6.66 ± 1.66 μm, respectively.

The swelling ratios of the hydrogel microbeads under these conditions were 916.33% and 820.45%, respectively, indicating a polymer structure with a higher crosslinking density. However, this experiment may have been subject to certain limitations and deviations caused by various factors, such as the accuracy of the equipment or temperature control during the emulsion formation process. Therefore, further studies are recommended to optimize the formulation and synthesis conditions for maximum efficiency. The findings from this study can serve as a guideline for developing high-performance hydrogel microbeads for use in PCCPs, supporting the development of sustainable products that reduce microplastic contamination and encourage ecological responsibility.

The authors would like to extend their appreciations to Department of Industrial Chemistry, Faculty of Applied Science, Graduate College, King Mongkut's University of Technology North Bangkok for their continual supports in providing efficient information and operations.

References

1. J. Li, X. Qu, L. Su, W. Zhang, D. yang, K. Prabhu, D. li, H. Shi, Microplastics in mussels along the coastal waters of China. Environ. Pollut. **214**, 177–184(2016). https://doi.org/10.1016/j.envpol.2016.04.012
2. E. Caló, V. V. Khutoryanskiy, Biomedical applications of hydrogels: A review of patents and commercial products. Eur. Polym. J. **65**,
3. Eliseeva, V. I., et al., Emulsion polymerization and its applications in industry. Springer Science & Business Media. (2012)
4. Sarva Mangala Praveena, S. M. P., M. Siti Norashikin, S. Akizuki, Exploration of microplastics from personal care and cosmetic products and its estimated emissions to marine environment: an evidence from Malaysia. Mar. Pollut. Bull. **136**, 135-140 (2018). https://www.sciencedirect.com/science/article/pii/S0025326X18306519
5. I. E. Napper, A. Bakir, S. J. Rowland, R. C. Thompson, Characterisation, quantity and sorptive properties of microplastics extracted from cosmetics. Mar. Pollut. Bull. **99**, 178–185 (2015). https://doi.org/10.1016/j.marpolbul.2015.07.029
6. Puanglamjeak, M., S. Pranee, S. Seeyangnok, Preparation of Crude Turmeric Extract Loaded Poly (Acrylamide-co-Acrylic Acid) Microspheres for Drug Release System. in Materials Science Forum. Trans Tech Publ. (2020).
7. ISHAK, WAN MAZNAH WAN ZULFAKAR, MOHD HANIF, Optimization, Development, And safety evaluation of olive oil nanoemulsion for topical application : A response surface methodology.**15**, (2022)
8. Redaelli, F., M. Sorbona, F. Rossi, Synthesis and processing of hydrogels for medical applications, in Bioresorbable polymers for biomedical applications. Elsevier. 205-228 (2017)
9. Li, J., D. J. Mooney, Designing hydrogels for controlled drug delivery. Nature Reviews Materials. **1**, 1-17 (2016)
10. Moustafa, A., A. Abd-El-Hakim, Ferric oxide-catalyzed polymerization of methyl methacrylate. Journal of Polymer Science: Polymer Chemistry Edition. **14**, 433-440 (1976)

Development of Cream Serum from Mung Bean Hull Extract Derived from Industrial By-Product: Phenolic Content, Antioxidant Activity, and Formulation

Kongaphisith Tongpoolsomjit[1] *, *Jiratchaya* Kiatkhuntod[1], *Supanida* Jettanavilai[1], *Viroj* Kaewmoon[1], *Vorrameth* Netsawang[1], and *Worawikunya* Kiatponglarp[2]

[1]Department of Industrial Chemistry, Faculty of Applied Science, King Mongkut's University of Technology North Bangkok, Wong Sawang, Bang Sue, 10800 Bangkok, Thailand
[2]Thai Wah Public Company, Tungmahamek, Sathorn, 10120 Bangkok, Thailand

Abstract. Mung beans hull is by-product from food industry containing polyphenol compounds with antioxidant properties. It is often used in animal feed industry, as inexpensive raw material, but the use in cosmetic products is not yet widespread. This work aims to develop a skin cream serum from polyphenols by extracting the substance from mung bean hull by refluxing and determining the phenolic content by Folin-Ciocalteu method. Antioxidant properties were exhibited by using DPPH method. Subsequently, the formulation and stability test of cream serum were performed. The experimental results showed that the phenolic content was as high as 17.9 mg/g GAE and the IC_{50} free radical inhibition value was 381.9 ug/mL. Three formulas of cream serum were formulated and tested their stability. The comparison of pH, viscosity and CIE color values between the first day and the 30th day showed that those parameters of the three cream serum formulas in each condition did not change significantly. At the same time, no change of the cream serum texture was also observed. These findings could be value addition to mung beans hull by converting for health and beauty industry.

1 Introduction

The global agricultural processing industry generates substantial quantities of by-products that have traditionally been discarded as waste [1]. Recent study has recognized these materials as possible sources of bioactive chemicals with considerable commercial worth [2]. This paradigm shift toward sustainable valorization aligns with circular economy principles and addresses growing concerns regarding resource conservation [3]. Among these underutilized resources, mung bean (*Vigna radiata*) hulls, the outer coverings removed during seed processing which reported as one of the most by-product from legumes industry [4], have emerged as promising candidates for upcycling into high-value products [5].

Mung bean hulls contain a diverse array of phenolic constituents, including protocatechuic acid, isovitexin, vitexin, and various other flavonoids [6]. The average percentage composition of polyphenols in mung bean hull extracts was reported as 55.27 ± 1.14 mg gallic acid equivalent (GAE)/g of mung bean hull [7]. These compounds have demonstrated considerable antioxidant capacity through multiple mechanistic pathways, including free radical scavenging, metal chelation, and enhancement of endogenous antioxidant defence systems [8]. Recent investigations have further elucidated that specific phenolics extracted from mung bean hulls can effectively modulate cellular oxidative stress responses and autophagy pathways in dermal fibroblasts and keratinocytes, suggesting potential applications in combating photoaging and environmental skin damage [9].

Phenolic compounds in mung bean hulls can be extracted using both traditional and modern techniques. Conventional methods include maceration and Soxhlet extraction [10, 11]. For solvent selection, ethanol is commonly employed, though acetone also proves effective. More advanced extraction approaches include ultrasound-assisted extraction [9], pressurized liquid extraction [7], and microwave heating [12].

The cosmeceutical industry represents an ideal for such bioactive compounds, as it increasingly demands naturally-derived ingredients with demonstrable efficacy [13-15]. Several beans have emerged as a significant botanical ingredient in the cosmetic industry, particularly within the realm of skincare products. This legume, traditionally valued in Asian cuisines and folk medicine, has transitioned into contemporary cosmetic formulations due to its remarkable dermatological benefits [16-18]. However, specific commercial cosmetics solely made from mung bean hulls are quite limited and not widely available as standalone products in mainstream markets. Some products that incorporate mung bean hulls or extracts include exfoliating scrubs, face masks, and toners.

* Corresponding author: kongaphisitht@kmutnb.ac.th

Cream serums—hybrid formulations combining the penetrative capabilities of serums with the hydrating properties of creams—offer an optimal delivery vehicle for phenolic compounds due to their balanced lipophilic-hydrophilic character [19]. The development of such formulations requires consideration of extract stability, ingredient compatibility, rheological properties, and sensory attributes to ensure both efficacy and consumer acceptance [20].

Herein, we investigate the systematic development of a cream serum incorporating phenolic-rich mung bean hull extract derived from industrial by-products. Our methodology encompasses extraction optimization, phenolic content quantification, antioxidant activity assessment, and formulation development with stability evaluation. The work aims to demonstrate not only the functional benefits of this cosmeceutical for skin protection but also its contribution to sustainable product innovation and waste valorization strategies. The findings presented provide a comprehensive framework for transforming agricultural processing residues into efficacious skincare ingredients.

2 Materials and methods

Mung bean hull powder was provided by Thai Wah Public Company, Bangkok, Thailand. Ethanol, Folin-Ciocalteu solution, sodium carbonate, DPPH solution, ascorbic acid, and EDTA were analytical grade from Sigma-Aldrich, Missouri, USA. All formulation ingredients, including glycerin 99.9 % USP, Silsense DW-18, Schercemol 318 Ester, 1,3 – butylene glycol, carbopol ultrez 30 polymer, and phenoxyethanol, were cosmetic grade and purchased from Namsiang Co., Ltd., Bangkok, Thailand.

2.1 Extraction of polyphenol from mung bean hull

The extraction was modified according to a previous report [7]. To a suspension of 10 g of mung bean hull powder in a 250 mL round-bottom flask using 100 mL of ethanol-water solution (40:60) as the solvent for reflux at 80°C for 1, 2, and 3 hours, respectively. Then each suspension was filtered with Whatman filter paper no. 1 and centrifuged at 4000 rpm for 20 minutes, after which it was evaporated using a rotary evaporator to remove ethanol, leaving polyphenol in water.

2.2 Determination of total phenolic content by Folin-Ciocalteu colorimetric assay

Determination of total phenolic content (TPC) by Folin-Ciocalteu colorimetric assay was modified according to a previously reported procedure [9]. Pipette 0.5 mL of diluted extract solution into a 10-mL test tube. Then add 4.5 mL of distilled water followed by 0.2 mL of Folin-Ciocalteu solution. Then add 0.5 mL saturated sodium carbonate and then add 4.3 mL distilled water. Mix well with a vortex mixer and leave the solution in the dark at room temperature (RT: 32 ± 3°C) for 30 minutes. Measure an absorption at 765 nm with a UV-Vis spectrophotometer.

2.3 Antioxidant activity test using DPPH radical scavenging assay

The antioxidant activity test using the DPPH radical scavenging assay was modified according to a previously reported procedure [21]. Pipette 0.5 mL of diluted extract solution into a 10-mL test tube. Then add 1.5 mL of distilled water and 2 mL of DPPH solution. Mix well with a vortex mixer and leave the mixed solution in the dark at RT (32 ± 3 °C) for 30 minutes. Measure an absorption at 517 nm with a UV-Vis spectrophotometer. Ascorbic acid was used as a standard for testing.

2.4 Formulation of cream serum

The formulation of cream serum was performed by varying concentration of glycerin (Table 1). The method for preparing the cream serum products was mixing the substances in Part A; DI water, 2Na EDTA, glycerin 99.9 % USP, 1,3–butylene glycol, and carbopol ultrez 30 polymer using T 25 Ultra-Turrax® homogenizer (IKA Works (Thailand) Co., Ltd., Bangkok, Thailand) at 10,000 rpm for 5 min. at RT (32 ± 3°C), followed by the substances in Part B, C and D. Then the substances in Part E; phenoxyethanol and polyphenol extract from mung bean hull were added. The mixture was then stirred until homogeneous and packaged.

Table 1. The formulation of cream serum.

Part	Ingredients	Formulation (%w/w)		
	INCI name	F_1	F_2	F_3
A	DI water	86.40	87.40	86.90
	Carbopol Ultrez 30 Polymer	0.15	0.15	0.15
	2 Na EDTA	0.1	0.1	0.10
	Glycerin 99.9% USP	3.00	2.00	2.50
	1,3-Butylene Glycol	5.00	5.00	5.00
B	Silsense 318 Ester	1.50	1.50	1.50
C	Schercemol 318 Ester	1.50	1.50	1.50
D	NaOH (18% Solution)	0.15	0.15	0.15
E	Phenoxyethanol	2.00	2.00	2.00
	Polyphenol extract from mung bean hull	0.20	0.20	0.20

2.5 Stability tests of formulated cream serum

Three cream serum formulations (F1, F2, F3) were prepared and divided into two parts for testing under two storage conditions: RT (32 ± 3°C) and 4 °C refrigeration. The assessments at the first day (D0) include phase separation, pH measurement, viscosity determination using Brookfield DV2T, and color analysis in the CIE system using Hunter Lab Colorflex: EZ 45-0 (LAV). For colorimetry, in CIE L*a*b* color space:

$$\Delta E = \sqrt{(L_1 - L_2)^2 + (a_1 - a_2)^2 + (b_1 - b_2)^2}$$

Where, L = Lightness (0=black, 100=white)
a = Red (+) to Green (-)
b = Yellow (+) to Blue (-)

After 30 days of storage (D30), the same parameters were reassessed to compare with D0. Comparative analysis between D0 and D30 measurements involves calculating delta values (Δ) for pH and viscosity, while color changes were quantified using the ΔE value.

3 Results and discussion

3.1 Determination of polyphenol extract yield

Sample extractions were performed under reflux conditions which utilizes controlled heating under condensation to maintain constant solvent volume [22]. The 40-50 % ethanol-water blend provides the right balance of polarity, solubility, and synergistic action to efficiently extract a broad spectrum of phenolic compounds from mung bean hulls while being a practical and safe choice of solvent [7].

Analysis of polyphenol extracts yield using reflux method at different times; 1, 2, and 3 hours in 40 % or 50 % ethanol as the solvent was exhibited in Tables 2. The experimental result demonstrated a relationship between ethanol concentration, extraction duration, and polyphenol yield. When comparing the extraction conditions, it was found 50% ethanol mostly produced higher yields than 40% ethanol, with one notable exception. The highest overall yield (170.9 mg/g dried-based mung bean hull) was achieved using 50% ethanol with a 1-hour extraction time, contradicting the general expectation that longer extraction times produce higher yields.

Table 2. Yield of polyphenol extracts using reflux method.

Conditions		mg/g of dried-based seed coat
%EtOH	Time (h)	
40	1	87.1 ± 0.5
	2	97.6 ± 0.3
	3	108.9 ± 0.4
50	1	170.9 ± 0.5
	2	92.5 ± 0.4
	3	103.9 ± 0.2

The results indicated that solvent polarity plays a crucial role in the extraction efficiency of polyphenols [23]. The 50% ethanol solution provided an optimal balance of polar and non-polar characteristics that effectively solubilizes a broader spectrum of polyphenolic compounds from the mung bean hull matrix. This intermediate polarity appeared effective for the initial extraction phase (1 hour), suggesting that shorter extraction times are preferred to minimize the degradation of polyphenols [9].

3.2 Determination of total phenolic content by Folin-Ciocalteu colorimetric assay

The Folin-Ciocalteu colorimetric assay, widely recognized for quantifying total phenolic content (TPC) in various matrices [9, 24], was employed to identify optimal parameters for maximizing phenolic yield using gallic acid as a standard. The result revealed a clear trend regarding ethanol concentration and extraction duration (Figure 1.). First, 50% ethanol consistently outperformed 40% ethanol across all time points, yielding significantly higher phenolic content values. This suggests that the increased polarity of the 50% ethanol solution provided a more favorable environment for extracting the target phenolic compounds from the sample matrix [25]. Second, a notable inverse relationship was observed between extraction duration and phenolic yield, with the 1-hour extraction consistently producing superior results compared to longer extraction periods (2 and 3 hours).

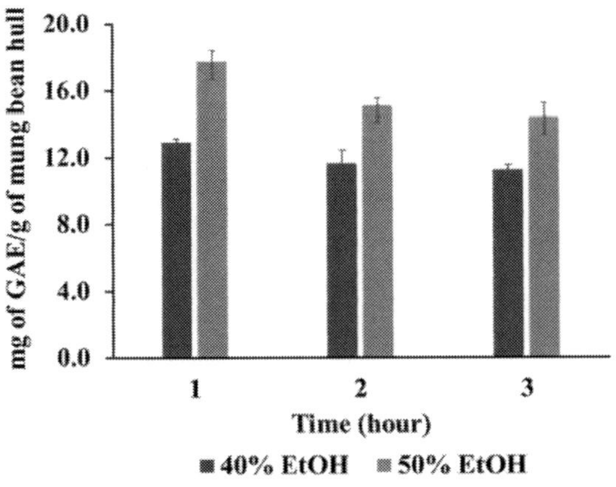

Figure 1. Total phenolic content of mung bean hull extracts.

The highest TPC of 17.9 mg GAE/g of mung bean hull was achieved using 50% ethanol with a 1-hour reflux duration, however, it was lower than the previous report [7]. This signified a 37% increase over the best-performing 40% ethanol condition. The progressive decrease in phenolic content with extended extraction times observed in both ethanol concentrations suggested potential degradation of phenolic compounds during prolonged thermal exposure which would be a critical consideration for optimizing extraction protocols [26].

3.3 Antioxidant activity using DPPH assay

According to the optimal duration and solvent concentration for the extraction procedure, a 1-hour period and 50% ethanol were then selected to assess antioxidant activity utilizing the DPPH assay.

The 2, 2-diphenyl-1-picrylhydrazyl (DPPH) assay represents one of the most widely utilized methodologies in natural product research for quantifying free radical scavenging capacity. This spectrophotometric assay offers several advantages including operational simplicity, rapid results, and high reproducibility, making it an essential tool for preliminary screening of potential antioxidant compounds from plant extracts [27].

In our investigation, the relationship between inhibition percentage and extract concentration was analyzed by plotting inhibition percentage against the logarithm of concentration (Figure 2.). Our result demonstrated that extraction yielded the antioxidant activity with an IC_{50} value of 381.9 µg/mL, which was higher than the previous report [28]. While this value was approximately 12.5 times higher than that of ascorbic acid or vitamin C (30.6 µg/mL), it represents antioxidant potential for a crude plant extract. This IC_{50} value represents a moderate antioxidant activity when compared to values reported in existing literature [29, 30].

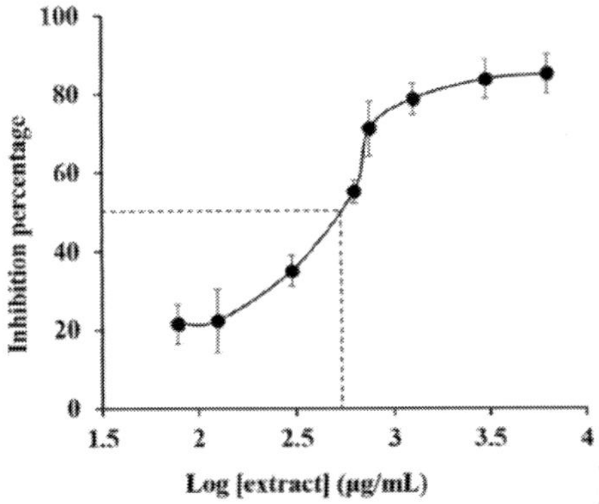

Figure 2. Plot of inhibition percentage against log concentration of mung bean hull extract.

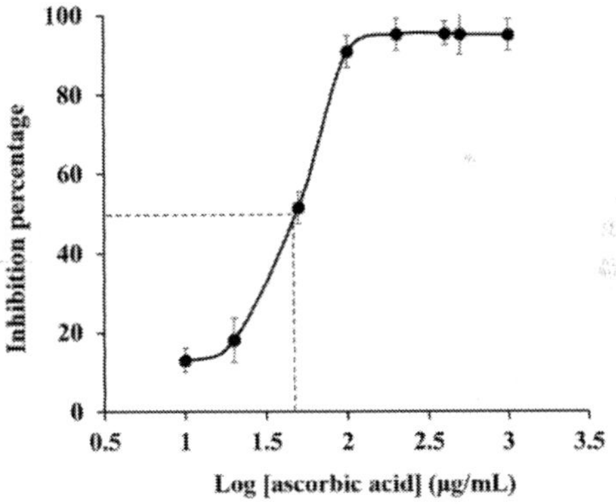

Figure 3. Plot of inhibition percentage against log concentration of ascorbic acid.

 https://doi.org/10.1051/e3sconf/202567901031

3.4 Stability tests of formulated cream serum

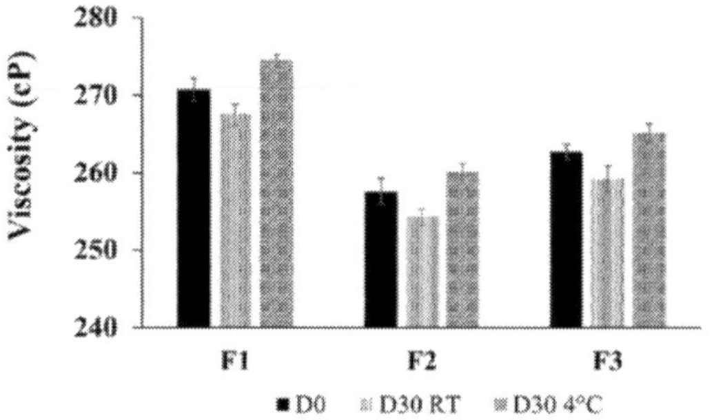

Figure 4. Viscosity of cream serum formulations over the 30-day storage period at RT (32 ± 3°C) and 4°C.

The physical stability of three cream serum formulations was rigorously evaluated through multiple parameters under two storage conditions: RT (32 ± 3°C) and refrigeration (4°C). This comprehensive analysis provides critical insights into the formulations' behavior under typical storage conditions over a 30-day period.

Visual inspection of the cream serum formulations from D0 to D30 revealed stability in terms of consistency. All three formulations maintained homogeneous textures without any noticeable changes in appearance when stored at RT (32 ± 3°C) (Table 3.). The serums preserved their white color and maintained an appealing texture throughout the testing period. At 4°C, while a slight increase in opacity was observed, the formulations remained homogeneous with no significant changes in their application characteristics.

Phase separation analysis demonstrated excellent stability across all formulations. No evidence of layer separation or sedimentation was observed in any of the samples at either storage condition. This stability aligns with the reported quality standards, which emphasize that cream and serum formulations should maintain phase integrity regardless of storage conditions or temperature variations [31, 32].

Table 3. Visual inspection and phase separation of cream serum formulations.

Formulation	D0	D30	
		RT	4°C
F1	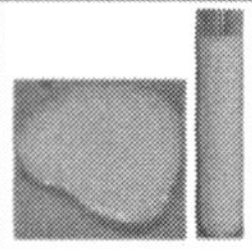	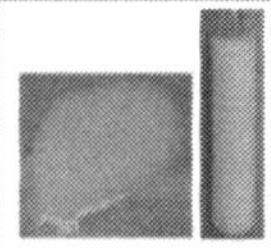	
F2	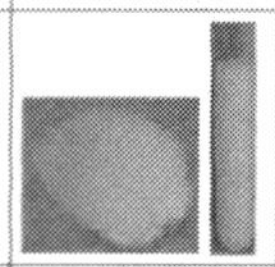		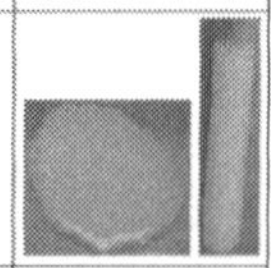
F3			

Viscosity analysis of the cream serum formulations revealed minimal changes over the 30-day storage period (Figure 4.). At RT (32 ± 3°C), the viscosity changes were 3.2 cP, 3.3 cP, and 3.5 cP for formulations F1, F2, and F3, respectively. Under refrigeration at 4°C, the formulations exhibited slightly higher viscosity values compared to RT (32 ± 3°C) samples due to reduced molecular kinetic energy at lower temperatures, which increases flow resistance. However, the changes from initial values remained minimal at 3.8 cP, 2.6 cP, and 2.5 cP for F1, F2, and F3, respectively.

The viscosity range of 200-270 cP observed across all formulations was optimal for serums, providing the lightweight, non-sticky texture that characterizes high-quality serum products [33]. This highlighted the lightweight texture and quick absorption as distinctive properties of effective serums.

The pH stability analysis discovered exceptional consistency across all formulations during the 30-day storage period (Figure 5.). At RT (32 ± 3°C), the pH changes were minimal at 0.01, 0.03, and 0.05 units for formulations F1, F2, and F3, respectively. Under refrigeration at 4°C, the formulations exhibited slightly higher pH values compared to RT samples, which can be attributed to decreased hydrogen molecule solubility at lower temperatures, leading to slightly increased alkalinity. However, the changes from initial values remained negligible at 0.01, 0.01, and 0.04 pH units for F1, F2, and F3, respectively.

Importantly, all formulations maintain pH values within the optimal range of 4-6, which is ideal for skin application. This is an importance of maintaining appropriate pH levels to protect the skin's natural hydrolipid film barrier [34]. Excessive alkalinity can disrupt this protective barrier, leading to moisture loss and skin dryness.

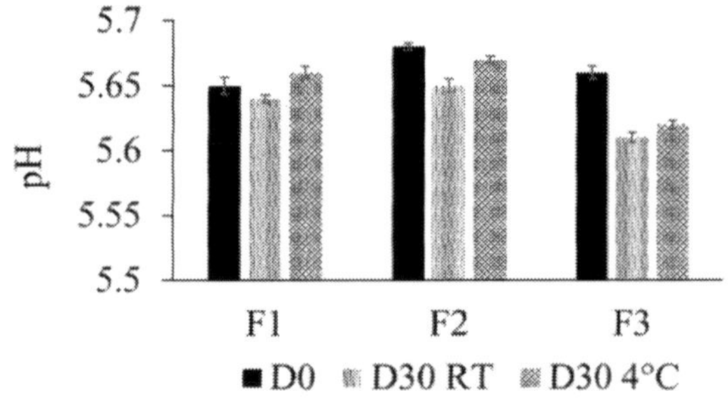

Fig. 5. pH of cream serum formulations over the 30-day storage period at RT (32 ± 3°C) and 4°C.

Color stability analysis using the CIE color system demonstrated excellent stability, particularly at RT (32 ± 3°C) (Table 4.). The color difference values (ΔE) for RT samples were 0.92, 0.90, and 0.97 for formulations F1, F2, and F3, respectively. Since these values are less than 1.0, the color changes are invisible to the human eye, indicating good color stability.

Table 4. Color in the CIE system of cream serum formulations over the 30-day storage period at RT (32 ± 3°C) and 4°C.

Color (L*, A*, B*)			
Formulation	Day/state		
	D0	D30	
		ΔE (RT)	ΔE (4°C)
F1	(92.88, -1.11, 1.02)	0.92	1.29
F2	(91.71, -1.37, -0.58)	0.90	1.17
F3	(91.57, -1.33, 0.52)	0.97	1.32

Under refrigeration at 4°C, slightly higher color difference values were observed: 1.29, 1.17, and 1.32 for F1, F2, and F3, respectively. These values exceed 1.0, suggesting that the color changes might be just perceptible to the human eye. This was visually confirmed as a slight increase in opacity in the refrigerated samples. The increased opacity is a visual indicator of changes at the molecular or microscopic level within the cream serum, primarily driven by the reduced temperature affecting ingredient solubility, viscosity, and emulsion stability. Nevertheless, these changes were minimal and did not significantly affect the overall appearance or quality of the formulations.

4 Conclusion

This research successfully demonstrates the potential of mung bean hull, an industrial by-product, as a valuable source of bioactive compounds for cosmetic applications. The study systematically developed a cream serum formulation incorporating phenolic-rich extracts from mung bean hulls, addressing both sustainability concerns and consumer demand for naturally-derived skincare ingredients. The extraction optimization revealed that 50% ethanol with a 1-hour reflux duration yielded the highest total phenolic content (17.9 mg GAE/g) and demonstrated significant antioxidant activity with an IC_{50} value of 381.9 µg/mL in the DPPH assay. Three cream serum formulations were developed and subjected to comprehensive stability testing over a 30-day period under both RT (32 ± 3°C) and refrigerated conditions. All formulations exhibited excellent stability in terms of physical appearance, phase separation, viscosity, pH, and color. This provides a comprehensive framework for transforming agricultural processing residues into efficacious skincare ingredients, contributing to sustainable product innovation and waste valorization strategies.

This research was funded by King Mongkut's University of Technology North Bangkok, Thailand Contract no. KMUTNB-67-NEW-08. The authors express gratitude to the Department of Industrial Chemistry, Faculty of Applied Science, King Mongkut's University of Technology North Bangkok for their ongoing help in delivering effective information and operations. The authors express gratitude to Thai Wah Public Company (TWPC) for providing the mung bean shells utilized in this study.

References

1. L. M. Reguengo, M. K. Salgaço, K. Sivieri, M. R. Maróstica Júnior, Agro-industrial by-products: Valuable sources of bioactive compounds. Food Research International. **152**, 110871 (2022)
2. P. V. Devi, J. Islam, P. Narzary, D. Sharma, F. Sultana, Bioactive compounds, nutraceutical values and its application in food product development of oyster mushroom. Journal of Future Foods. **4**, 335-342 (2024)
3. H. Yang, Q. Feng, J. Zhu, G. Liu, Y. Dai, Q. Zhou, S. Xia, Z. Wu, Y. Zhang, Towards sustainable futures: A review of sediment remediation and resource valorization techniques. Journal of Cleaner Production. **435**, 140529 (2024)
4. J. C. Yu, Y. J. Wu, From waste to value: Integrating legume byproducts into sustainable industrialization. **24**, e70174 (2025)
5. J.-C. Yu, Y.-J.-Z. Wu, W.-S. Shin, From waste to value: Integrating legume byproducts into sustainable industrialization. Comprehensive Reviews in Food Science and Food Safety. **24**, e70174 (2025)
6. Q.-Q. Yang, Y.-Y. Ge, A. Gunaratne, K.-W. Kong, H.-B. Li, K. Gul, K. Kumara, L. V. Arachchi, F. Zhu, H. Corke, R.-Y. Gan, Phenolic profiles, antioxidant activities, and antiproliferative activities of different mung bean (Vigna radiata) varieties from Sri Lanka. Food Bioscience. **37**, 100705 (2020)
7. B. Supasatyankul, M. Saisriyoot, U. Klinkesorn, K. Rattanaporn, S. Sae-Tan *Extraction of Phenolic and Flavonoid Compounds from Mung Bean (Vigna radiata L.) Seed Coat by Pressurized Liquid Extraction*. Molecules. **27**, (2022). DOI: 10.3390/molecules27072085
8. P. Chaudhary, P. Janmeda, A. O. Docea, B. Yeskaliyeva, A. F. Abdull Razis, B. Modu, D. Calina, J. Sharifi-Rad, Oxidative stress, free radicals and antioxidants: potential crosstalk in the pathophysiology of human diseases. Frontiers in Chemistry. **11,** (2023)
9. R. Hao, M. Li, F. Li, D. Sun-Waterhouse, D. Li, Protective effects of the phenolic compounds from mung bean hull against H2O2-induced skin aging through alleviating oxidative injury and autophagy in HaCaT cells and HSF cells. Science of The Total Environment. **841**, 156669. (2022)
10. A. Oreopoulou, D. Tsimogiannis, V. Oreopoulou, *Chapter 15 - Extraction of Polyphenols From Aromatic and Medicinal Plants: An Overview of the Methods and the Effect of Extraction Parameters*, in *Polyphenols in Plants (Second Edition)*. R.R. Watson. Editor. Academic Press. 243-259 (2019)

11. Y. Eriyanto, S. Sutrisno, K. Afandi, Total Phenolic Content and Antioxidant Activity of Mung Bean Seed Cultivars From Optimized Extraction Treatment. Buletin Palawija. **17**, 1-9 (2019)
12. J. Azmir, I. S. M. Zaidul, M. M. Rahman, K. M. Sharif, A. Mohamed, F. Sahena, M. H. A. Jahurul, K. Ghafoor, N. A. N. Norulaini, A. K. M. Omar, Techniques for extraction of bioactive compounds from plant materials: A review. Journal of Food Engineering. **117**, 426-436 (2013)
13. J. I. Alvarez-Leite, The Role of Bioactive Compounds in Human Health and Disease. Nutrients. **17**, 1170 (2025)
14. C. Putthong, P. Temkitthawon, P. Phimnuan, J. Viyoch, K. Tongpoolsomjit, Formulation of chewable nutraceuticals prepared from banana fruit pulp and hemp seed oil. ScienceAsia. **50**, 1-8 (2024)
15. C. Putthong, T. Panmanee, P. Charoensit, S. Ross, K. Tongpoolsomjit, J. Viyoch, Efficacy of Natural β-Carotene Chewable Tablets Derived from Banana (Musa AA) Pulp in Reducing UV-Induced Skin Erythema. Nutrients. **17,** (2025)
16. D. Fonseca-Hernández, E. D. C. Lugo-Cervantes, A. Escobedo-Reyes, L. Mojica, Black Bean (Phaseolus vulgaris L.) Polyphenolic Extract Exerts Antioxidant and Antiaging Potential. Molecules. **26**, 6716 (2021)
17. J. Shin, Y. Kang, W. Kim, A Study on the Whitening and Anti-Wrinkle Effects of Red Sword Bean Extract in Functional Cosmetics for Skin Care. European Journal of Engineering and Technology Research. **7**, 44-50 (2022)
18. K. Wojciechowska, E. Rostkowska, G. Ginalska, Ł. Zimmer, E. Poleszak, New Insights into Common Bean (Phaseolus vulgaris L.) Sprouts: Pilot Studies on the Formulation of a Cosmeceutical Based on Micellar Extracts Bean Sprouts. Applied Sciences. **15**, 1831 (2025)
19. N. Wangpradit, S. Macha, N. Phooteh, N. Yusohyo, A. Waedoloh, S. Manee, Determination of required hydrophilic-lipophilic balance of Amesiodendron chinense (Merr.) Hu oil and development of stable cream formulation. OCL. **29**, 29 (2022)
20. A. Z. M. Badruddoza, D. E. Moseson, H.-G. Lee, A. Esteghamatian, P. Thipsay, Role of rheology in formulation and process design of hot melt extruded amorphous solid dispersions. International Journal of Pharmaceutics. **664**, 124651 (2024)
21. S. R. Kanatt, A. K, and A. Sharma, Antioxidant and antimicrobial activity of legume hulls. Food Research International. **44**, 3182-3187. (2011)
22. M. Zhang, J. Zhao, X. Dai, X. Li, Extraction and Analysis of Chemical Compositions of Natural Products and Plants. Separations. **10**, 598 (2023)
23. D. Palaiogiannis, T. Chatzimitakos, V. Athanasiadis, E. Bozinou, D. P. Makris, S. I. Lalas, Successive Solvent Extraction of Polyphenols and Flavonoids from Cistus creticus L. Leaves. Oxygen. **3**, 274-286 (2023)
24. P. Torres, S. Osaki, E. Silveira, D. Y. A. C. dos Santos, F. Chow, Comprehensive evaluation of Folin-Ciocalteu assay for total phenolic quantification in algae (Chlorophyta, Phaeophyceae, and Rhodophyta). Algal Research. **80**, 103503 (2024)
25. O. R. Alara, N. H. Abdurahman, C. I. Ukaegbu, Extraction of phenolic compounds: A review. Current Research in Food Science. **4**, 200-214 (2021)
26. R. ElGamal, C. Song, A. M. Rayan, C. Liu, S. Al-Rejaie, G. ElMasry, Thermal Degradation of Bioactive Compounds during Drying Process of Horticultural and Agronomic Products: A Comprehensive Overview. Agronomy. **13**, 1580 (2023)
27. S. Baliyan, R. Mukherjee, A. Priyadarshini, A. Vibhuti, A. Gupta, R. P. Pandey, C. M. Chang, Determination of Antioxidants by DPPH Radical Scavenging Activity and Quantitative Phytochemical Analysis of Ficus religiosa. Molecules. **2,** (2022)
28. N. Buathong, K. Chandarajoti, S. Sae-tan, Anti-inflammatory potential of mung bean seed coat water extract in lipopolysaccharide-induced 3T3-L1 adipocytes. Agriculture and Natural Resources. **55**, 777–786 (2021)
29. M. Tao, R. Li, T. Xu, Z. Zhang, T. Wu, S. Pan, X. Xu, Flavonoids from the mung bean coat promote longevity and fitness in Caenorhabditis elegans. Food & Function. **12**, 8196-8207. (2021)
30. S. A. Basha, U. J. S. P. Rao, Bioactivities of fractions obtained from green gram (Vigna radiata) milled by-products. Food Bioscience. **19**, 134-141 (2017)
31. A. Marjani, Effect of Storage Time and Temperature on Serum Analytes. American Journal of Applied Sciences. **5,** (2008)
32. S. Vaidya, Review on Face Serum. Asian Journal of Pharmaceutics. **18,** (2024)
33. S. Sasidharan, P. Joseph, Junise, Formulation and evaluation of fairness serum using polyherbal extracts. (2014)
34. M. Lukic, I. Pantelic, S. Savic, Towards Optimal pH of the Skin and Topical Formulations: From the Current State of the Art to Tailored Products. Cosmetics. **8**, 69 (2021)

Optimization of blend formulation of agar/κ-carrageenan hydrogels for transdermal delivery of vitamin B12

Paul Jake Nalzaro[1*], *China Nicole* Alterado[1], *Tina Marie* Ong[1], *Camille Ann* Venturina[1], and *Terence* Tumolva[1]

[1]Department of Chemical Engineering, University of the Philippines, Quezon City, Philippines

Abstract. Cancer patients require a new method of vitamin B delivery due to the ineffective and invasive methods currently practiced. A biopolymer hydrogel of agar/κ-carrageenan was proposed to transdermally deliver vitamin B12 to cancer patients. Varying mass ratios were considered for the agar/κ-carrageenan: 25/75, 50/50, 75/25, and 100/0. A reference of 1 mg vitamin B12 was used for the loading coefficients of 1x, 1.5x, and 2x. The percent release of vitamin B12 and time required to reach equilibrium release concentration were the response variables used to determine the optimal hydrogel blend. The vitamins were loaded into the biopolymer solution over a double boiler and the resulting gel was dried and sent for release analysis via colorimetry. The hydrogel blend of 50/50 at a loading coefficient of 1x was found to have the highest vitamin release of 314%, and shortest time to reach equilibrium release concentration at 337 minutes. Increasing loading coefficient increases the time to reach equilibrium response concentration. To further improve the study, other essential B-group vitamins may be added and other mass ratios and loading coefficients may be incorporated in the optimization.

1 Introduction

The B group vitamins, specifically B12 or cobalamin, are nutrients essential to many metabolic and physiological processes such as energy metabolism, cell reproduction, and protein synthesis. Despite their integral role in several biosynthesis processes in the body, humans are unable to synthesize these and are reliant on B-rich food to provide the necessary B-group vitamin intake [1, 2]. Deficiencies in the B-group vitamins lead to adverse health effects such as impaired physiological functions like megaloblastic anemia and neurologic symptoms, as well as impaired antioxidant defense and immune response that leave DNA and proteins vulnerable to tissue damage [2, 3].

Cancer patients have been found to be especially susceptible to vitamin B12 deficiency driven primarily by malnutrition, weight loss, and use of medication that interfere with vitamin B12 absorption [1-2]. Cancer-related surgical procedures have also been found to cause metabolic disturbances related to poor macronutrient absorption [4]. Vitamin B12 depletion has also been found to contribute to increased tumor cell proliferation and energy demands [1, 2].

With cancer being the third leading cause of death in the Philippines, providing affordable yet effective means to deliver vitamin B12 in B-deficient patients has become a necessity [5]. The most common delivery of the vitamin B complex for B-deficient patients is through oral supplements or intramuscular injection. Oral administration may not be effective for cancer patients due to the metabolic disturbances [4]. Meanwhile, intramuscular injection tends to cause significant pain. Injections may also pose risks to individuals who have autoimmune disorders or are taking anticoagulant medication [6]. A trending approach is the transdermal delivery of vitamin B12 such as using diffusion cells and via iontophoresis [7]. However, such technologies are too expensive to be accessible.

A viable alternative is the transdermal delivery of vitamin B12 via hydrogel dressings which are painless and non-invasive. Hydrogels are superabsorbent water-swollen materials that maintain a three-dimensional matrix [8]. Hydrogels used in biomedical applications can be produced from natural polymers as they are cheap, biocompatible, and biodegradable [9]. Notable biopolymers include alginate, agar, and κ-carrageenan which are seaweed-based.

To improve material performance, different polymers may be blended to form a hydrogel that exhibits all the advantageous properties of each component; however, several factors such as miscibility and crosslinking behavior must be considered when establishing the blend formulation. κ-carrageenan and agar exhibit desirable properties for this particular biomedical application. κ-carrageenan is mainly used as a gelling and thickening agent in the food industry [10]. It is capable of absorbing water 20 times its own weight as well as forming thermoreversible gels making it resistant to heat degradation [11]. Similarly, agar is also used as a gelling agent in the food industry. Powdered agar, the more commercially available form of agar, sets to a firm gel even at low concentrations [10]. Agar gels are not

*Corresponding author: pbnalzaro@up.edu.ph

susceptible to heat degradation and can also hold a water content 20 times its own weight [12, 13]. Figure 1 shows the thermal crosslinking of κ-carrageenan and agar.

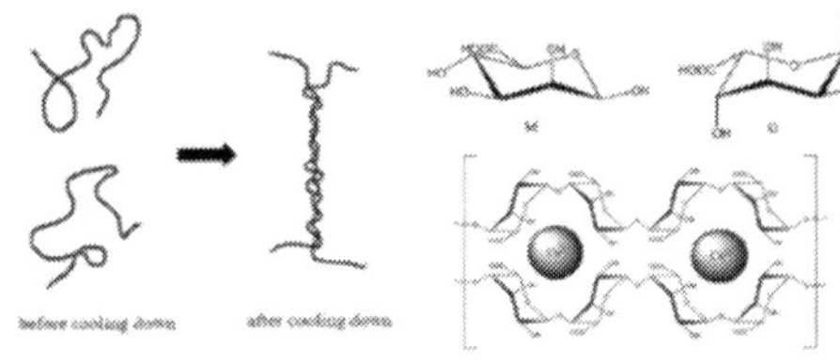

Fig. 1. Crosslinking of agar and κ-carrageenan (left) and alginate (right).

Currently, there is a need to explore the use of inexpensive and locally available materials in hydrogel technology for a non-invasive delivery of vitamin B12. This research aims to develop and contribute a simple and affordable method for vitamin delivery to make medical solutions more accessible. Specifically, this aims to determine the optimum hydrogel blend using seaweed-based biopolymers for the transdermal delivery of at least 1 mg of vitamin B12. The evaluation of this study involved identifying the effect that the agar/κ-carrageenan mass ratio and the vitamin loading coefficient have on the percentage of vitamin released and the time it took for the hydrogel to achieve its equilibrium release concentration. The optimum blend for this study was selected based on the highest percentage of release and quickest diffusion time.

2 Materials and methods

2.1 Chemicals

The bio-based polymers used were agar (Don Frank agar agar powder), alginate (Makintal high precision alginate), and κ-carrageenan (food grade). Vitamin B12 loaded into the hydrogel samples were sourced from Mason Natural.

2.2 Blend formulation and synthesis

Hydrogels of different biopolymers were synthesized. The individual gelling abilities of these biopolymers were investigated. As for the blended hydrogels, the formulation was derived from the study of Zhao et al. (2020) and Gupta et al. (2020) where they studied the physicochemical properties of agar/κ-carrageenan hydrogels along with their gelling properties [14, 15]. To determine the optimum blend, various mass ratios of agar and κ-carrageenan in the total biopolymer content were utilized. The ratios used for the agar/κ-carrageenan mixture were 100/0, 75/25, 50/50, 25/75, 0/100. Moreover, various loading coefficients of vitamin B12 were used to further determine the optimum blend formulation. For a target reference of 1 mg of vitamin B12, the loading coefficients used are 1x, 1.5x, and 2x.

The hydrogel formulation was made by mixing the total biopolymer components at 1.5wt% into 100 mL distilled water that was previously directly loaded with vitamin B12. The biopolymer-water-vitamin mixture was then heated to 90°C for thermal crosslinking while maintaining a constant stir. Once completely dissolved, the hot solutions were left to set at room temperature for 16 hours with a thickness of 1 mm in a 10-cm cylindrical silicone mold. Then, the firmed hydrogel samples were dried to a film for 3 hours in a turbo oven at 70°C. The same procedure was done for all mass ratios and loading coefficients in triplicate.

2.3 Vitamin B12 release

The dried vitamin-loaded hydrogels were subjected to release analysis by submerging in 0.9% brine solution. Through time, the solution changes its color as the pink-colored vitamin B12 diffuses from the hydrogels to the surrounding solution. To determine the amount of vitamin B12 released into the supernatant solution, samples of colored solutions were subjected to smartphone colorimetry via the Colorimeter® application. The generated absorbance results were then related to the mass of vitamin B12 released.

The response parameters were: (1) the percentage of vitamin B12 released, and (2) the time it took for the hydrogel to reach its equilibrium release concentration. The time was determined directly from the smartphone colorimetry procedure while percentage release was calculated from the ratio of vitamin B12 detected in solution and vitamin B12 loaded into the hydrogel. OFAT (one factor at a time) analysis was performed for each variable pair listed below to identify the effect each control parameter has on its corresponding response parameter.

- % vitamin B12 released vs mass ratio
- time it took to reach equilibrium concentrations vs mass ratio
- % vitamin B12 released vs loading coefficient
- time it took to reach equilibrium concentrations vs loading coefficient

For the blend optimization of the hydrogel blend, two independent variables (agar mass ratio, vitamin B12 loading coefficient) and two response variables (% vitamin B12 release, time to reach equilibrium release) were identified. Equation 1 was utilized to calculate the percent release for each trial.

$$\%\ vit.B12\ released = \frac{mass\ vit.released\ in\ supernatant}{mass\ vit.loaded\ into\ hydrogel} \times 100 \qquad (1)$$

Meanwhile, the optimum blend was determined through a central composite response surface generated using Design-Expert®.

3 Results and discussion

3.1 Biopolymer selection

All biopolymers underwent the same method as stated in the methodology for the unloaded hydrogels. The 100% κ-carrageenan mixture did not form a gel after it was set to rest. This is due to the lack of ability of the κ-carrageenan to form gels without chemical crosslinkers [10]. The same was observed for the 100% alginate mixture. The mixture remained liquid because of the lack of a chemical crosslinker. The 100% agar mixture was the only mixture that formed a gel since agar can form hydrogels at low concentrations even without any chemical crosslinkers.

To investigate the optimal biopolymer blend, the three biopolymers were blended at equal ratios. Table 1 shows the summary of gelling results of the three biopolymers [14]. For two-component mixtures, a ratio of 50:50 was used for each biopolymer component while three-component mixtures used a 33:33:33 ratio. All blends utilized thermal crosslinking and did not have any chemical crosslinkers.

Table 1. Synthesis of different hydrogel blends.

Blend	Result
alginate/κ-carrageenan	no gel formed
agar/κ-carrageenan	gel formed
agar/alginate/κ-carrageenan	gel formed

As shown in Figure 2, the alginate and κ-carrageenan blend remained liquid after setting time which is not ideal for a gel formulation. Both commonly require a chemical crosslinker to form rigid gels. κ-carrageenan is a polysaccharide composed of alternating copolymers of β-D-galactose and α-D-galactose bound by glycosidic linkages. It contains several OH groups and one sulfate group causing strong anionic behavior [16]. The most commonly used crosslinkers for κ-carrageenan are potassium and calcium salts [6, 14]. Since the scope of the experiment does not include the use of a chemical crosslinker, the alginate/κ-carrageenan blend was not optimal for the desired gelling conditions.

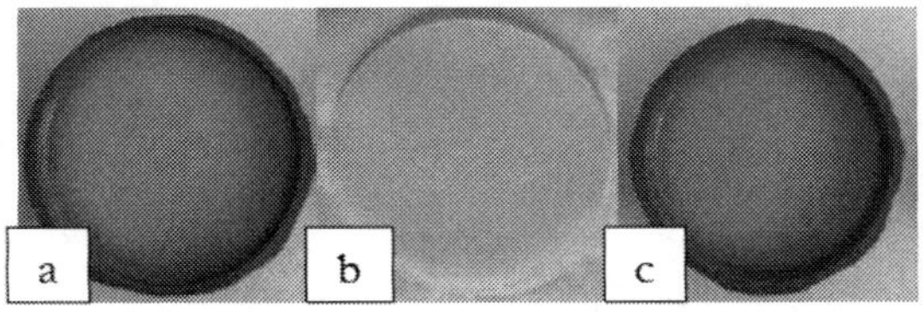

Fig. 2. Synthesized hydrogels of (a) alginate/κ-carrageenan, (b) agar/κ-carrageenan, and (c) agar/alginate/κ-carrageenan.

Using agar and κ-carrageenan as the components of the blend achieved a rigid gel. Agar is disaccharide composed of D-galactose and 3, 6-anhydro-L-galactopyranose with several OH functional groups [17]. Agar readily dissolves in hot water and forms a gel after cooling. It also does not require high concentrations of the polymer to form the gel. Ratios of 0.5% of agar with water are able to form rigid gels. The structure of agar contributes to the gel formation of the agar/κ-carrageenan blend. Agar gels are also thermoreversible making its property resistant to heat [13]. This achieved translucent gels which are ideal for the colorimetry method.

Typically, vitamin release from blended polymer matrices is dependent on several interactions such as polymer-polymer and vitamin-polymer [17]. Sol-gel experiments illustrated no associative interactions between the two biopolymers. This was likely due to their thermodynamic incompatibility which caused segregative phase separation within the mixture. Due to thermal crosslinking, the polymer matrix was likely formed by a continuous phase of agar. However, without the presence of a chemical crosslinker, the process yielded a discontinuous phase for κ-carrageenan. Since there were minimal polymer-polymer interactions within the matrix, the drug release mechanism can be attributed primarily to vitamin-polymer interactions instead.

The third blend analyzed in the experiment used the three biopolymers: agar, alginate, and κ-carrageenan. Similar to the agar/κ-carrageenan blend, using the three biopolymers formed a rigid gel. Although the components formed a gel, it was not visually fit for the method of determining the vitamin release. The gel formed using the three biopolymers formed a semi-green opaque hydrogel since the alginate component of the blend is green. This can disrupt the colorimetry method which is a limitation to this study.

With the firm and rigid gel that agar formed along with its blending with κ-carrageenan, the vitamin B12-loaded hydrogels did not experience any degradation and instability. Thus, among the three biopolymer blend variations, the agar/κ-carrageenan biopolymer blend showed the most desirable gelling conditions for this study.

3.2 Vitamin B12 release

To identify the effect that the mass ratio and loading coefficient have on the percentage of vitamin B12 released as well as the time it takes to reach equilibrium concentration, OFAT (one factor at a time) analysis was performed for each response-to-control variable pair.

3.2.1 Varying mass ratio

The experiment monitored the behavior of the response parameters following the variation of the agar/κ-carrageenan blend concentrations of each sample.

From visual inspection of hydrogel samples shown in Figure 3., it is evident that increasing the κ-carrageenan concentration also increases the opacity of the hydrogel sample. Meanwhile, physical handling of the samples illustrated that increasing agar concentrations result in firmer hydrogels.

Once dried, the hydrogels become thin yet pliable making them suitable for skin applications. No noticeable differences in thickness or texture were observed in any of the samples shown in Figure 4.

The percentage release data of the hydrogels with different mass ratios were plotted accordingly. It can be gathered from Figure 5 that the smartphone colorimetry experiment resulted in release values of over 100%. This was attributed to the development of turbidity in the solution. Potential sources of error can also be attributed to the use of the Colorimeter® application. Nevertheless, it was assumed that the driving force for the vitamin release was uniform across all samples and can thus be analyzed relative to each other rather than as individual magnitudes.

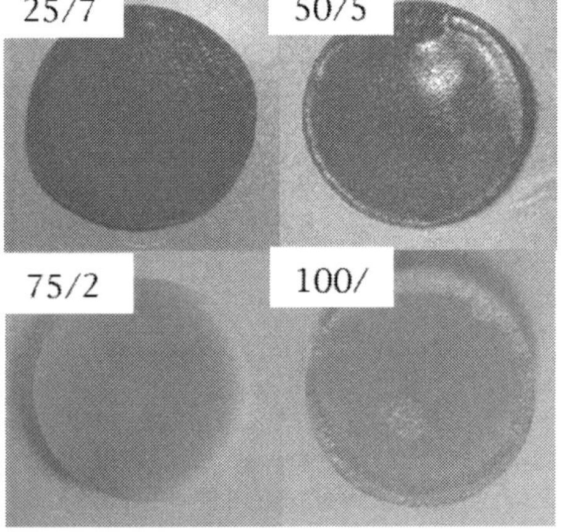

Fig. 3. Agar/κ-carrageenan samples before drying.

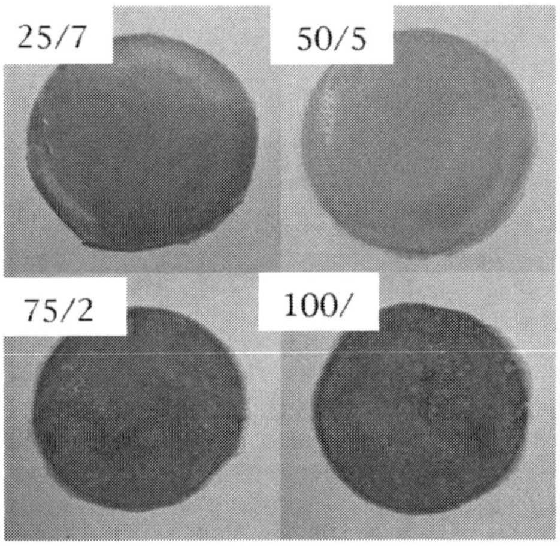

Fig. 4. Agar/κ-carrageenan samples after drying.

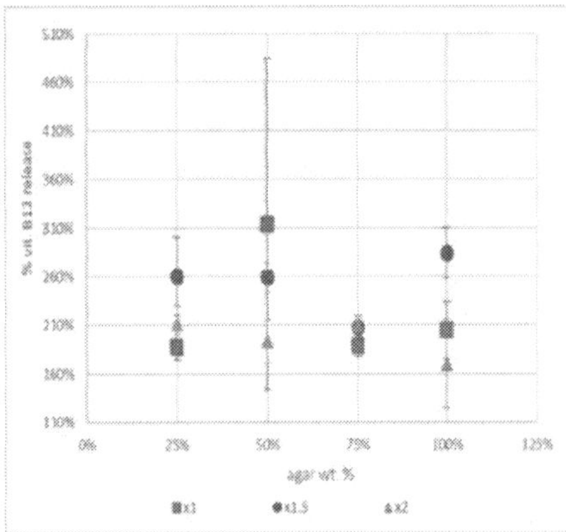

Fig. 5. % release of vitamin B12 against agar wt% at various vitamin loading coefficients.

From Figure 5, the hydrogel blend yielding the highest relative release was found to be the mass ratio 50/50 at the loading coefficient of 1. For most mass ratios, the highest release occurred at the loading coefficient of 1.5 however, this is not true for 50/50. Experimental data showed that one trial yielded an unusually high % release value of 498% compared to the other trials that reached only 281% and 163% released amounts. However, results of the Grubb's test validated the trial as not an outlier making 50/50 the mass ratio of highest average release. Meanwhile, the lowest vitamin B12 release occurred at the pure agar blend with a loading coefficient of 2. Fundamentally, no clear trend was observed between the biopolymer mass ratios to its % vitamin B12 released.

A shorter diffusion period to reach equilibrium concentration was considered a more desirable feature of the hydrogel. It was observed from Figure 6 that reaching this equilibrium concentration took longer as mass ratios exceeded 50% agar at loading coefficients of 1 and 2. Meanwhile, the opposite was true at a loading coefficient of 1.5 wherein diffusion time decreased with increasing agar concentration. Among all the mass ratios, the fastest diffusion occurred at 50/50 with a loading coefficient of 1.

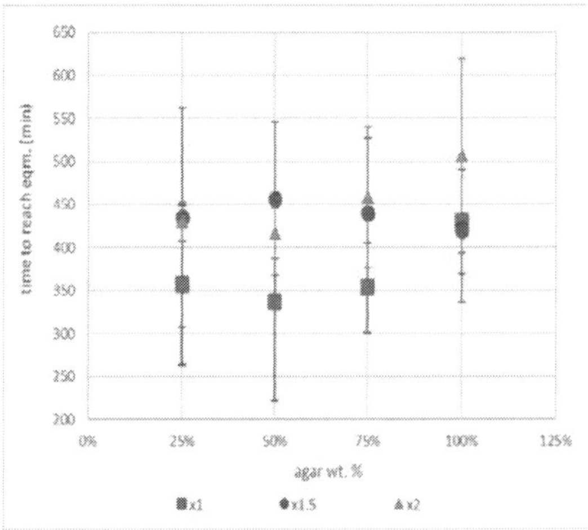

Fig. 6. Time to reach equilibrium release concentration against agar wt% at various vitamin loading coefficients.

3.2.2 Varying loading coefficient

The amount of vitamin B12 added to the hydrogel blend was manipulated to observe its effect on the response variables. As mentioned previously, the reference amount was 1 mg of vitamin B12.

As loading coefficient was manipulated, the most notable change in the physical properties of the hydrogel was the change in intensity of the color of the hydrogel brought by the increase in amount of vitamin B12. The procured vitamin B12 was a bright shade of pink which provides the distinctive color of the hydrogel formed, as shown in Figure 7. The color intensity was observable with the dried hydrogel compared to the pre-dried hydrogel. The change in shades of pink of the hydrogel can be seen in Figure 8, taken from the hydrogels with an agar wt% of 50/50 at varying loading coefficients.

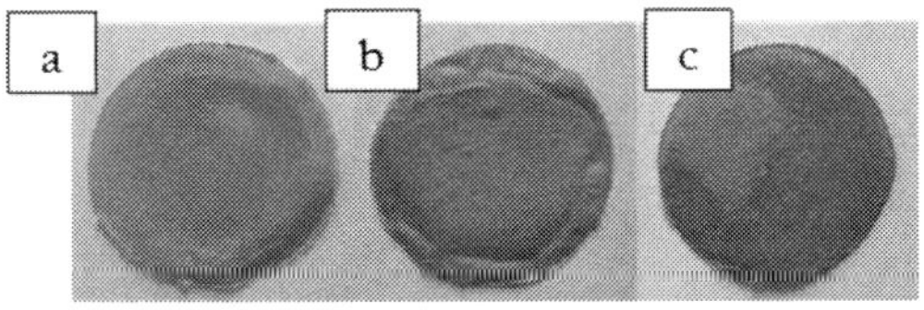

Fig. 7. Hydrogel color variation.

Fig. 8. Observable color change of (a) 1x, (b) 1.5x, and (c) 2x loading coefficients at a fixed 50/50 agar wt%.

As seen in Figure 9, the 1.5x loading coefficient had the highest average release, specifically, an average of 253% vitamin B12 released. The 1x loading and 2x loading coefficients had averages of 224% and 196% respectively. There were no significant trends on vitamin B12 release observed.

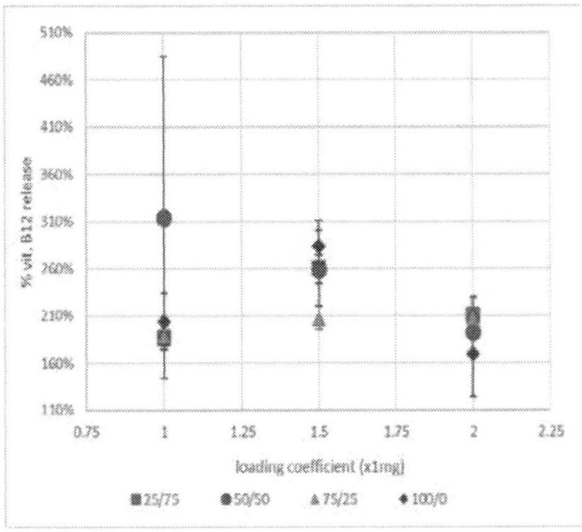

Fig. 9. % release of vitamin B12 against loading coefficient at various agar wt%.

In Figure 9, the highest relative release was found to be 314% which occurred at a vitamin loading coefficient of 1x with a biopolymer concentration of 50/50. This was 30 % higher than the % release of the hydrogel at a loading coefficient of 1.5% and a biopolymer concentration of 100/0, which was the second highest with a release of 284%.

As mentioned previously, a shorter time frame for the hydrogel to reach equilibrium release was preferred to reduce the probability of a bacterial infection in the wound. Based on Figure 10, the trend was evident that the time to reach its equilibrium release concentration increased as the loading coefficient increased. This trend was reasonable as more vitamin was loaded whenever the loading coefficient increased.

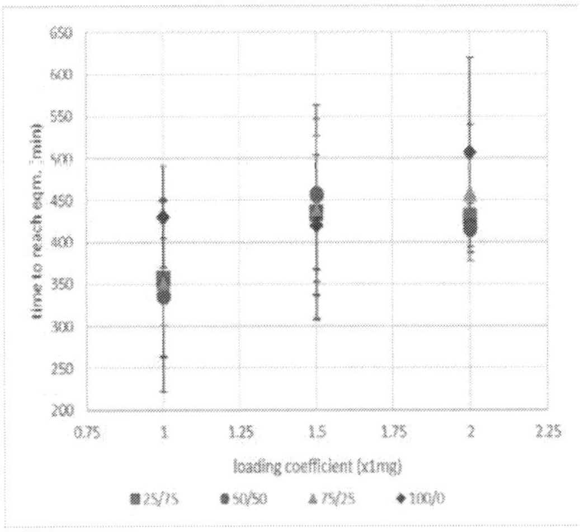

Fig. 10. Time to reach equilibrium release concentration against loading coefficient at various agar wt%.

The hydrogel at a loading coefficient of 2x and an agar wt% of 100/0 took the longest, which made it the least desirable hydrogel blend among all the blends. For the hydrogel at a loading coefficient of 1x and 50/50 agar wt.%, the equilibrium release was achieved after 337 minutes, making it the most desired hydrogel blend in terms of equilibrium release time as a function of loading coefficient.

3.3 Optimized blend selection

To select for the optimal blend, it is ideal that the hydrogel has a high vitamin release to maximize the amount of vitamins loaded. The desirable diffusion time of release needed to reach equilibrium optimal for the transdermal release of vitamins should have the shortest time.

3.3.1 Optimal release of vitamin B12

The effect of the amount of vitamin B12 loaded to a hydrogel and its mass ratio in terms of agar wt% was plotted against the % release of vitamin B12 through a central composite response surface. Through these plots, the optimal blend was determined. Figure 11 shows a contour and 3D plot of the response of the vitamin B12 in relation to the set parameters.

It is ideal that the hydrogel has a high release of the vitamin. This means that the amount of vitamins loaded was released at the maximum amount ensuring that less of the vitamins loaded were wasted.

The highest point of release can be seen at the red region of the plot in Figure 11 at the 50/50 mass ratio with a loading coefficient of 1. It can also be clearly seen in the 3D graph that the highest point is located at the 314% release. The hydrogel was able to release an average of 314% across three trials with the same loading coefficient and mass ratio.

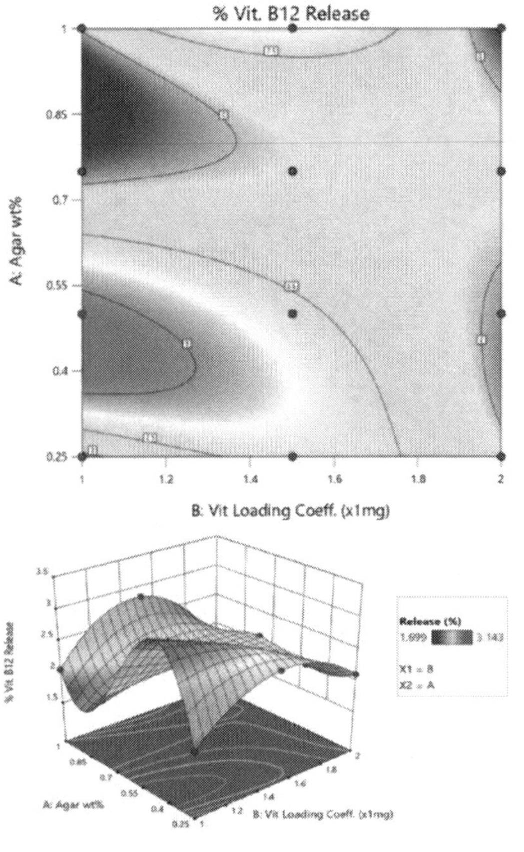

Fig. 11. Contour plot (top) and 3D plot (bottom) of the effect of loading coefficient and agar wt% to the % release of vitamin B12.

An earlier study on carrageenan-based drug delivery systems showed that agar and κ-carrageenan hydrogel blends used as metformin hydrochloride (MET) carriers displayed release profiles that are being dominated by electrostatic interactions between the pharmaceutical and polysaccharide [18]. It can be inferred that a similar release mechanism was present in the system evaluated in this study since the optimum agar/κ-carrageenan blend obtained was 50/50. Typically, for an agar and κ-carrageenan system, the loading efficiency for vitamin B12 is increased as κ-carrageenan concentrations increase as well. The anionic sulfate functional groups introduced by κ-carrageenan into the polymer matrix easily attracts the positively charged cobalamin molecules dispersed in solution. However, since no chemical crosslinker was used, once κ-carrageenan concentrations exceeded that of agar, the gel's structural integrity was compromised resulting in a poorer transport channel. Thus, it was gathered that insufficient agar concentrations resulted in ineffective transport media while insufficient κ-carrageenan concentrations exhibited inadequate release quantities. The blend formulation 50/50 struck a balance between structural integrity of the matrix and favorable electrostatic conditions for vitamin B12 delivery.

Using Design Expert®, the equation for optimization in terms of % release of vitamin B12 as a function of the wt% of agar and the loading coefficient was shown in Equation 2 where:

x – agar wt% of the hydrogel blend
y – loading coefficient of vitamin B12
z – total % release of vitamin B12

$$z = -27.07 + 137.17x - 103.14xy - 185.36x^2 - 5.94y^2 + 103.57x^2y + 15.00xy^2 + 69.92x^3 - 1.26x^2y^2 - 16.33x^3y - 11.66x^3y^2 \quad (2)$$

3.3.2 Optimal time to reach equilibrium release

The effect of the amount of vitamin B loaded to a hydrogel as well as its mass ratio in terms of agar wt% was plotted against the time it takes for the release to reach equilibrium through a central composite response surface. The plots were used to determine the optimal blend in terms of the time needed to reach equilibrium release. Figure 12 shows a contour and 3D plot of the equilibrium release time in relation to the set parameters.

It is ideal that the time needed to reach equilibrium release is faster. Open wounds are exposed to more bacterial infection and other foreign materials that may cause wound complications. Faster release time reduces the hazards that the patients may experience given that the loaded hydrogel application is for open wounds.

Figure 12 shows the fastest and slowest release at equilibrium. It was observed that the time of equilibrium release at the loading coefficient of 1.5 has a similar range. The slowest release was observed at the 100/0 mass ratio and with a loading coefficient of 2. The fastest release time was at the 50/50 mass ratio and the loading coefficient of 1 at 337 minutes making it the optimal blend in terms of time of release to reach equilibrium.

Similar to the % release correlation in Equation 2, the time needed to reach equilibrium release for the hydrogel as a function of the agar wt% and the loading coefficient was obtained using Design Expert® where:

x – agar wt% of the hydrogel blend
y – loading coefficient of vitamin B12
z – time needed to reach equilibrium release

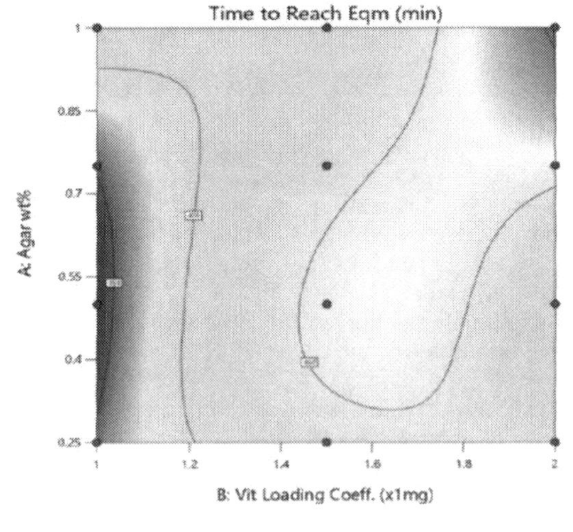

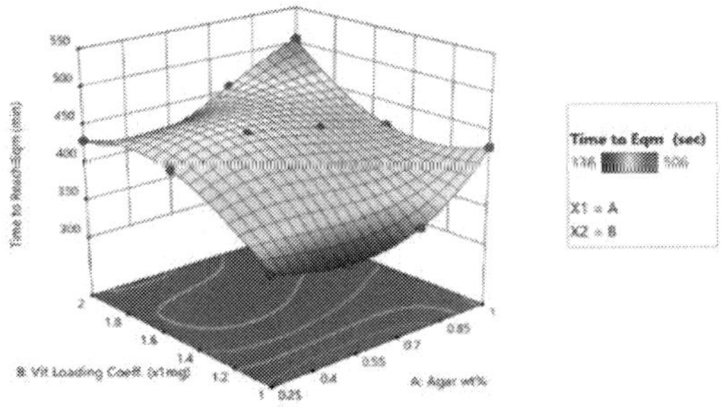

Fig. 12. Contour plot (top) and 3D plot (bottom) of the effect of loading coefficient and agar wt% to the time needed to reach equilibrium release.

$$z = 1238 - 7460x - 1352y + 11302.67xy + 9904x^2 + 504y^2 - 15624x^2y - 3976xy^2 - 2944x^3 + 5648x^2y^2 + 5173.33x^3y - 1948x^3y^2 \quad (3)$$

4 Conclusion

In synthesizing a seaweed-based biopolymer hydrogel, the agar/κ-carrageenan hydrogel blend showed the most desirable characteristics of a vitamin B loaded hydrogel to be used for open wounds of cancer patients. Agar forms rigid gels at low concentrations even without a chemical crosslinker. On the other hand, κ-carrageenan was proven to have anti-cancer activity and increases the strength of the synthesized hydrogel.

Five mass ratios were performed at three different loading coefficients for each mass ratio. The mass ratio where the hydrogel contained 100% κ-carrageenan (0/100) did not form into a gel since it did not have any chemical crosslinker. The four other mass ratios (27/75, 50/50, 75/25, 100/0) all formed gels ranging from soft to rigid. The loading coefficients did not influence the rigidness of the hydrogels although as the loading increased, the color intensity also increased.

For the intended application, the optimal hydrogel blend should have a high % release, and a short amount of time needed for the release to reach equilibrium. The data shows limited trends between the parameters. The only observable trend based on the data shows that as the loading coefficient increased, the time of equilibrium release also increased. The highest % release of 314 % was observed at the 50/50 mass ratio with a loading coefficient of 1. The shortest amount of time needed for the release to reach equilibrium was found to be at 337 minutes and was also found at the same mass ratio and loading coefficient. Given these data, it was concluded that the optimal blend uses the agar and κ-carrageenan biopolymers, has a mass ratio of 50/50 agar/κ-carrageenan, and has a loading coefficient of 1.

For further studies, it is recommended to include other essential B-group vitamins such as B1 and B6 in future formulations. Other loading methods such as the post-loading method for vitamin loaded may also be studied for further experimentations. Smaller increments for mass ratios and other loading coefficients for the samples may also be investigated to add further insight on the hydrogel behavior. Additionally, a validation test may be included to further prove the validity of the optimal blend investigated.

This research work was funded by the University of the Philippines System Enhanced Creative Work and Research Grant (ECWRG-2020-2-19R). The dissemination of this research work was supported by the University of the Philippines Diliman through the Office of the Vice Chancellor for Research and Development.

References

1. C. T. Peterson, D. A. Rodionov, A. L. Osterman, S. N. Peterson, B vitamins and their role in immune regulation and cancer. Nutrients **12**, 3380 (2020). https://doi.org/10.3390/nu12113380
2. C. Lin, M. Yin, B vitamins deficiency and decreased anti-oxidative state in patients with liver cancer. Eur J Nutr. **46**, 293–299 (2007). https://doi.org/10.1007/s00394-007-0665-8
3. E. C. R. de M. Viana *et al.*, Malnutrition and nutrition impact symptoms (NIS) in surgical patients with cancer. PLoS One **15**, e0241305 (2020). https://doi.org/10.1371/journal.pone.0241305
4. I.-H. Kim *et al.*, Korean practice guidelines for gastric cancer 2024: An evidence-based, multidisciplinary approach (Update of 2022 guideline). J Gastric Cancer. **25**, 5–114 (2025). https://doi.org/10.5230/jgc.2025.25.e11
5. 2024 Causes of Death in the Philippines. Accessed: Jul. **13**, (2025). [Online]. Available: https://psa.gov.ph/content/2024-causes-death-philippines-provisional-30-april-2025
6. H. Wang, L. Li, L. L. Qin, Y. Song, J. Vidal-Alaball, T. H. Liu, Oral vitamin B_{12} versus intramuscular vitamin B_{12} for vitamin B_{12} deficiency. Cochrane Database of Systematic Reviews **2018** (2018). https://doi.org/10.1002/14651858.CD004655.pub3
7. A. V. Sabiev, M. A. Korsten, W. A. Bauman, A comparison among three skin preparations for the transdermal delivery of vitamin B12 by iontophoresis: A novel approach to determine systemic absorption. (2021).
8. M. Rizwan, S. Naseem, S. R. Gilani, A. I. Durrani, Optimization of swelling and mechanical behavior of Acer platanoides cellulose combo hydrogel. Kuwait Journal of Science. **51**, 100177 (2024). https://doi.org/10.1016/j.kjs.2024.100177
9. Y. Ren *et al.*, Alginate-based hydrogels mediated biomedical applications: A review. International Journal of Biological Macromolecules. **279**, 135019 (2024). https://doi.org/10.1016/j.ijbiomac.2024.135019
10. D. J. McHugh, *A guide to the seaweed industry*. in FAO fisheries technical paper, no. 441. Rome: Food and Agriculture Organization of the United Nations (2003).
11. N. Jabeen *et al.*, Silymarin nanocrystals-laden chondroitin sulphate-based thermoreversible hydrogels; A promising approach for bioavailability

enhancement. International Journal of Biological Macromolecules. **218**, 456–472 (2022). https://doi.org/10.1016/j.ijbiomac.2022.07.114

12. R. C. Nissa *et al.*, The processability and properties of agar/gelatin film in a melt-mixing process. Green Materials. 1–9 (2024). https://doi.org/10.1680/jgrma.24.00002
13. Carrageenans, in *Carbohydrate Chemistry for Food Scientists*. Elsevier. 279–291 (2019) https://doi.org/10.1016/b978-0-12-812069-9.00013-3
14. J. Zhao, C. Sun, H. Li, X. Dong, X. Zhang, Studies on the physicochemical properties, gelling behavior and drug release performance of agar/κ-carrageenan mixed hydrogels. International Journal of Biological Macromolecules. **154**, 878–887 (2020). https://doi.org/10.1016/j.ijbiomac.2020.03.087
15. A. Gupta, J. Bhasarkar, M. R. Chandan, A. H. Shaik, B. Kiran, D. K. Bal, Diffusion kinetics of vitamin B_{12} from alginate and poly(vinyl acetate) based gel scaffolds for targeted drug delivery. Journal of Macromolecular Science, Part B. **59**, 713–730 (2020). https://doi.org/10.1080/00222348.2020.1800246
16. V. E. Santo *et al.*, Carrageenan-based hydrogels for the controlled delivery of PDGF-BB in bone tissue engineering applications. Biomacromolecules. **10**, 1392–1401 (2009). https://doi.org/10.1021/bm8014973
17. A. Saxena, A. Tahir, M. Kaloti, J. Ali, H. B. Bohidar, Effect of agar-gelatin compositions on the release of salbutamol tablets. Int J Pharm Investig. **1**, 93–98 (2011). https://doi.org/10.4103/2230-973X.82407
18. E.-M. Pacheco-Quito, R. Ruiz-Caro, M.-D. Veiga, Carrageenan: Drug Delivery Systems and Other Biomedical Applications. Marine Drugs. **18**, 583 (2020). https://doi.org/10.3390/md18110583

The combined pretreatment using ultrasonication with different chemical pretreatments to enhance lignin production and enzymatic hydrolysis efficiency

Kitilux Viwatmetawut [1*], *Santi* Chuetor [1], *Suchata* Kirdponpattara [1], and *Wanwitoo* Wanmolee [1]

[1] Department of Chemical Engineering, Faculty of Engineering, King Mongkut's University of Technology North Bangkok, 10800 Bangkok, Thailand

Abstract. Sugarcane bagasse is a lignocellulosic biomass and an abundant agricultural residue in Thailand. Therefore, it has been studied to maximize and convert it into high value bioproducts. However, due to its complex structure, pretreatment processes are important for enhancing the efficiency of component recovery. This study presents the combined ultrasonication and chemical pretreatment methods, specifically alkaline pretreatment and deep eutectic solvent (DES), to investigate their effects on lignin yield and enzymatic hydrolysis efficiency. The study examined the use of ultrasonication with 1M sodium hydroxide (Power rate 60%, 30 min) and the process sequence between ultrasonication before alkaline pretreatment (UBA) and ultrasonication after alkaline pretreatment (UAA) under the same conditions. Results showed that UBA obtained the highest lignin yield of 94%. The enzyme hydrolysis efficiency has higher reduced sugar yields from 44 to 189-190 mg/g biomass. In terms of DES pretreatment using a mixture of choline chloride-ethylene glycol-lactic acid (ChCl-EG-LA), different solid-liquid ratios 1:20 (20DES) and 1:40 (40DES). Lignin yields are 30% and 12%, respectively, which were less than those of ultrasonic combined with alkaline. The enzyme hydrolysis efficiency of 20DES has reducing sugar yields 186.79 mg/g biomass ,while 40DES has highest reducing sugars yields 186.79 mg/g biomass.

1 Introduction

The globe is currently dealing with the issue of rising greenhouse gases, which are causing global temperature increases and climate change, primarily because of human activities that consume fossil fuels. As a result, alternative energy sources have become an important role in replacing fossil fuels because it is clean energy that is never exhausted and does not pollute the environment. Agricultural waste materials are one of the interesting alternative energy sources represents a sustained renewable, widespread and low-cost source [3].

Sugarcane bagasse (SCB), a lignocellulosic biomass and agricultural residue from the sugar industry, is abundantly available in Thailand. It is commonly used as fuel in power generation, animal feed, or for composting. Lignocellulosic biomass mainly consists of three natural polymers: cellulose, hemicellulose, and lignin. These components can convert it into high-value products through a biorefinery process [5]. This process resembles petroleum refining, except it uses biomass as the feedstock. It allows for the fractionation of biomass into its key components to produce high-value products such as bioethanol from cellulose and hemicellulose, or natural adhesives and biochemicals from lignin.

Due to the complex molecular structure of lignocellulosic biomass, some factors make biomass recalcitrant like degree of lignification, heterogeneous structure, and complex nature of the cell wall. Hence, the pretreatment process becomes a crucial role in enhancing the accessibility of each component and improving the overall yield that direct conversion to bioethanol is often inefficient. Pretreatment methods are generally categorized into four types: physical, chemical, physicochemical, and biological [1].

Among these, alkaline pretreatment is widely employed due to its simplicity and efficiency in removing lignin, hemicellulose, and reducing cellulose crystallinity. That makes the biomass more amenable to downstream processing. However, it often requires large amounts of chemicals, raising environmental concerns [2].

To solve this problem, Deep Eutectic Solvents (DES) have emerged as an eco-friendly alternative. Its green solvents, biodegradability, low toxicity, easy to synthesize, and low cost of production [18]. DES are mixtures comprising hydrogen bond donors (HBD) and hydrogen bond acceptors (HBA) that form a eutectic mixture with lower melting points than their constituents [14]. The types of DES depend on different types of HBDs, including polyalcohol, acids, alkaline, and ternary DESs. Ternary DESs constructed with HBA, acid, and different contents of diols as HBD inhibited the formation of lignin and the quality of the lignocellulosic components

* Corresponding author: s6601031810041@email.kmutnb.ac.th

[16]. Though their high viscosity can affect the efficiency of biomass decomposition.

To further enhance chemical pretreatment effectiveness, integration with physical methods such as ultrasonication has gained interest. Ultrasonication generates cavitation bubbles and shear forces in the liquid medium, which promote better penetration of solvent molecules into the biomass structure, thereby improving pretreatment efficiency [1].

M. M. Kininge and P. R. Gogate investigated the enhancement of sugarcane bagasse delignification by comparing the performance of an ultrasonic horn and an ultrasonic bath. It was found that the efficacy of the ultrasonic horn is superior compared to the ultrasonic bath. The optimized condition was 1 M sodium hydroxide at biomass loading ratio 1:20 (1 h, 70°C, power 100 W and 70% duty cycle) yielding 67.30% as the delignification extent, which resulted of delignification 67.30% [12] but ultrasonic horn only suitable for small quantity ultrasonic probes are therefore attractive because they have high power and can be further upscaled in the future [9].

This research focuses on the combined pretreatment using ultrasonication with two different chemical pretreatments, specifically alkaline 1 M sodium hydroxide, with the process sequence between ultrasonication before alkaline pretreatment (UBA) and ultrasonication after alkaline pretreatment (UAA) under the same conditions and DES (ChCl-EG-LA), different solid-liquid ratios 1:20 (20DES) and 1:40 (40DES). The objective is to investigate their effects on lignin yield and enzymatic hydrolysis efficiency.

2 Materials and methods

2.1 Materials

Sugarcane bagasse (SCB) was supplied by sugar industry, Thailand. After drying overnight in an oven at 60°C, SCB was milled and sieved to mesh size of ≤ 0.5 mm. and stored in a desiccator. The chemicals used in this study consist of sodium hydroxide (NaOH, purity 99%), sulfuric acid (H_2SO_4, purity 98%), Choline chloride (ChCl), Ethylene glycol (EG), lactic acid (LA), Ethanol, the commercial enzyme solution CTech 2 (cellulase), sodium acetate.

2.2 Combined pretreatment of SCB

2.2.1 Combined pretreatment of SCB using ultrasonication-alkaline pretreatment

The SCB was combined with 1 M sodium hydroxide (NaOH) at a solid-liquid loading of 5% (w/v). In which the first sample (ultrasonication after alkaline pretreatment, UAA) was heated on a hot plate at 80°C and stirred for 30 minutes at 250 rpm before being conducted with an ultrasonic probe (JY98-IIIDN, USA) on-time of 2 s and an off-time of 4 s at a power rate 60% for 30 min. The second sample (ultrasonication before alkaline pretreatment, UBA) was under the same conditions but performed with ultrasonication before being heated on a hot plate.

After the pretreatment liquid and solid fractions were separated by using a Vacuum pump. The solid residue was washed with distilled water and dried overnight at 60°C. The liquid fractions or black liquor were precipitated with 6 M H_2SO_4 dropwise while stirring until pH 4. The solution was left stirring for 1 hour until final pH 4. The lignin precipitate was collected by centrifugation at 5000 rpm for 20 minutes. Lignin was subsequently washed with DI water and dried overnight at 50°C.

2.2.2 Combined pretreatment of SCB using ultrasonication-DES

The ternary deep eutectic solvent (TDES) was synthesized from ChCl: EG: LA at a molar ratio is 1:1:2. The NATDES was stirred at 500 rpm at 80°C until it turned homogeneous.

The SCB was combined with NATDES at different solid-liquid loadings of 1:20 and 1:40 (w/w) and exposed to an ultrasonic probe with an on-time of 10 s and off-time of 5 s at a power rate of 50% for 20 min. Soxhlet extraction at 120°C and stirred for 3 h at 500 rpm. The solid residue was washed with a mixture of water and ethanol until a neutral pH was achieved and dried overnight at 60°C. DI water was added to the filtrate afterward to precipitate lignin. The precipitated lignin was collected after centrifugation at 5000 r/min for 20 min. Lignin was subsequently washed with DI water and dried overnight at 50°C.

2.3 Enzyme hydrolysis

Enzymatic hydrolysis of untreated and pretreated SCB was conducted using commercial enzymes CTech 2 (Cellulase). The enzyme activity was estimated to be 161.03 FPU/ml. The enzyme loading of 20 FPU/g substrate in sodium acetate buffer (50 mM, pH = 5) in assey tube 50 ml. All tubes were mixture in shaking incubator (JSSI-100C) with 200 rpm at 50°C for 72 h. Stop the enzyme reaction by boiling in water at 100 for 5-10 min. Withdraw 2 ml of supernatant into the eppendorfs centrifuge at 1300 rpm for 5 min and collect the supernatant into HPLC vial to determine the sugar concentration.

2.4 Characterization of SCB

2.4.1 Quantification of total lignin and carbohydrates

The components of SCB, i.e., cellulose, lignin, hemicellulose, extractives, and ash, were determined through compositional analysis by the standard protocol of the National Renewable Energy Laboratory (NREL) [4]. The lignin removal % was determined with the following equation:

$$\text{Lignin removal (\%)} = \left[1 - \frac{\%\text{Lignin}_{\text{pretreated SCB}} \times W_{\text{solid recovery}}}{\%\text{Lignin}_{\text{untreated SCB}} \times W_{\text{untreated SCB}}}\right] \times 100 \quad (1)$$

The acid soluble lignin was determined through the UV-Visible spectrophotometer (Genesys 10S, Thermo Scientific) absorbance measurement at 280 nm.

The carbohydrate composition of SCB was determined by high performance liquid chromatography (HPLC) using a BioRad Aminex HPX-87H column and 0.005 mol/L sulphuric acid as mobile phase.

2.4.2 Fourier transform infrared spectroscopy (FTIR)

The untreated, pretreated SCB and lignin samples were characterized by FTIR (Nicolet iS50, Thermo Scientific) scans within the wavenumber range of 4000 to 400 cm^{-1}, employing a spectral resolution of 4 cm^{-1}. This was conducted utilizing the attenuated total reflection mode (ATR).

2.4.3 X-Ray (XRD)

The untreated and pretreated SCB were characterized by XRD to determine the crystallinity between angles 2θ range of 5 to 51° at 0.04 step. The crystallinity index (CrI) was calculated by equation:

$$\text{CrI (\%)} = \left[\frac{I_{002} - I_{am}}{I_{002}}\right] \times 100 \quad (2)$$

I_{002} : The crystalline region $2\theta = 22°$ and I_{am} : The amorphous region $2\theta = 18°$.

3 Results and discussion

3.1 Composition analysis of SCB

Untreated SCB consists of cellulose 35.95%, hemicellulose 21.07% and lignin 26.89% as shown in Table 1. Generally, SCB is composed of approximately 35-45% cellulose, 26-35% hemicellulose, and 11-25% lignin [5]. In comparison, cellulose was within the general range, while hemicellulose and lignin were lower and higher than the range. This is because the composition of SCB varies from diverse sources and strains. Pretreated SCB can be seen that the composition of cellulose increased from the untreated SCB, while the hemicellulose and lignin decreased, which is in accordance with the main objective of pretreatment to decrease hemicellulose and lignin and increase the cellulose content [7].

Ultrasonication-alkaline pretreated SCB in this study produced a relatively high lignin yield, with UBA achieving 94.37%, which was higher than UAA at 72.38%. The calculation of lignin removal, based on equation (1), predicted a value of approximately 71%, which was lower than the lignin yield, indicating that the lignin product still contains other extractive substances. In previous studies, I. F. Mota et al. pretreated SCB with 6 % w/w NaOH for 1 h at 90°C, achieving 72.8% lignin removal [8]. The lignin removal reported in that study was comparable to the present work employing combined pretreatment, despite the lower concentration of the chemical used. Because the intense shear forces resulting from ultrasonication can modify SCB surface structure, which is expected to enhance the adsorption of solvent and allow better access of solvent to SCB. But of course, if the ultrasonic pretreatment sequence is combined after the alkaline pretreatment (UAA), the amount of lignin yield will be lower as seen in Table 1, since NaOH plays a crucial role in the solubilization of lignin, as the basicity of the solvent [15], and ultrasonication may not be able to assist in breaking down the structure.

Ultrasonication-DES pretreated with difference solid-liquid ratios of 1:20 (20DES) can obtain more lignin yield than 1:40 (40DES), which were 30.63% and 11.9%, respectively, though were lower than those obtained from ultrasonication-alkaline pretreated. The lignin removal was higher than the corresponding lignin yield, which were 63.33% and 76.98%, respectively. The relatively low lignin yield can be attributed to the dissolution of lignin into the solution, as the presence of diols acting as HBD inhibited lignin reformation [16].

From the lignin removal, 40DES achieved the highest lignin removal but exhibited the lowest lignin yield, while ultrasonication-alkaline pretreatment had less lignin removal; however, UBA gave the highest lignin yield.

Table 1. Effect of pretreatment on composition of untreated and pretreated SCB.

Pretreatment conditions	Biomass composition			Solid recovery (%)	Lignin removal (%)	Lignin yield (%)
	Cellulose (%w/w)	Hemicellulose (%w/w)	Lignin (%w/w)			
Untreated SCB	35.95	21.07	26.89	-	-	-
UAA SCB	68.10	18.27	15.06	60	71.44	72.38
UBA SCB	70.33	16.17	14.59	52.35	71.6	94.37
20DES SCB	63.73	9.77	15.40	63.33	63.74	30.63
40DES SCB	70.95	10.99	14.20	43.6	76.98	11.9

3.2 FTIR

FTIR was performed on untreated and pretreatment SCB to analyze the functional groups, as shown in Figure 1. The band at 3200-3500 cm^{-1} represents O–H stretching of intramolecular hydrogen bond and the peak at 2890 cm^{-1} indicates the stretching vibration of the C–H functional groups in cellulose [14-15]. The peak at 1730 cm^{-1} represented the C=O stretching vibrations of the acetyl group of hemicellulose or carbonyl ester of p-coumaric lignin [11]. The peak at 1160 cm^{-1} represented the C–O–C bonds of carbohydrate [6]. The peak at 1030 cm^{-1} represented the C-O bonds of cellulose, and the intensification of this peak after combined pretreatment translated to a higher composition of cellulose [10]. The peak at 893 cm^{-1} represented polysaccharide content, particularly cellulose, due to the removal of lignin and hemicellulose [6]. Pretreated SCB showed higher concentrations than the untreated SCB, especially the ultrasonic-DES pretreatment showed higher peak intensities of 3334, 1730, 1160, and 893 cm^{-1} because it was a mild pretreatment process that still retained the functional groups of lignin and hemicellulose in structure.

In terms of lignin samples obtained from the combined pretreatment from Figure 2. the peak of lignin from combined pretreatments looked like the standard of lignin. The band 1508-1600 cm^{-1} represented the aromatic skeletal C—C linkages from the lignin aromatic ring [15]. The peak at 1458 cm^{-1} represents the C-H deformation and aromatic vibration of lignin [6]. The peak at 1420 cm^{-1} is C=C stretching with C-H in plane deformation aromatic skeleton. The peak at 1138 cm^{-1} is C-H in plane aromatic deformation G-ring, which was observed in the ultrasonic–alkaline. The lignin obtained from ultrasonic-alkaline and ultrasonic-DES pretreatment are different types of lignin due to different peak characteristics. Lignin from ultrasonic-DES has peak intensity of 1597 cm^{-1} which is lignin aromatic ring and 832 cm^{-1} representing polysaccharide content, particularly cellulose.

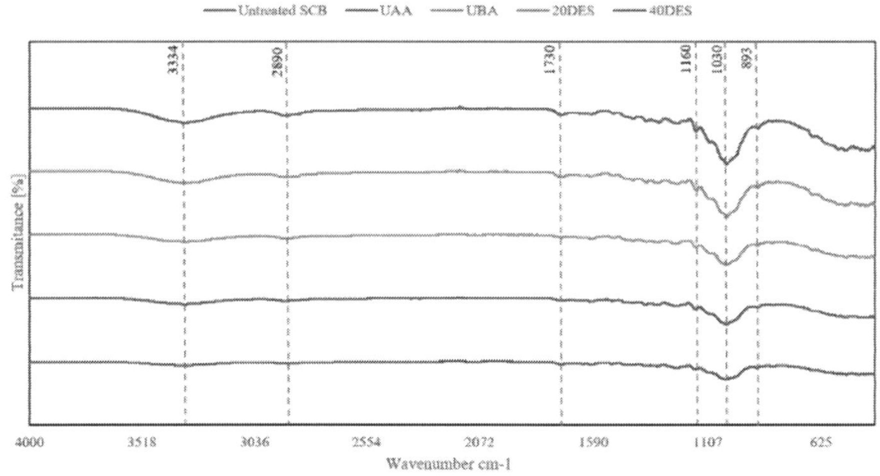

Fig. 1. FTIR spectra of raw and SCB pretreatment.

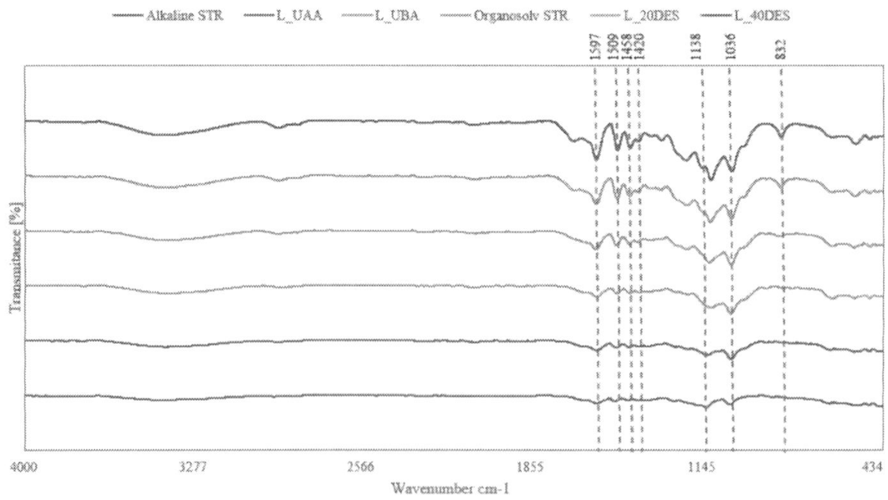

Fig. 2. FTIR spectra of standard lignin and lignin from combined pretreatment

3.3 XRD

The XRD analysis results of untreated and pretreated SCB are shown in Figure 3(a). According to equation (2). observed the CrI shown in Figure 3(b) of untreated was 24%, while the CrI of UBA, UBB, 20DES and 40DES were 44%, 51%, 49% and 56%. After pretreatment, the CrI value increased because the pretreatment removed the amorphous lignin, resulting in higher crystallinity, which affects the enzymatic hydrolysis [12].

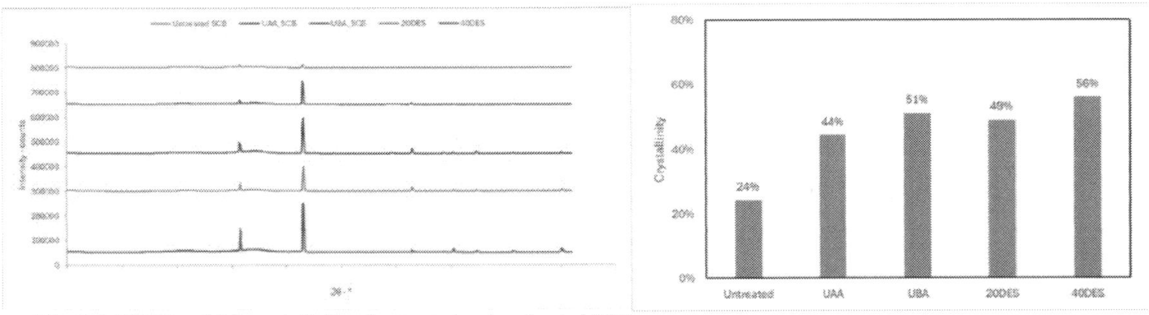

Fig. 3. (a) XRD and (b) crystallinity of untreated and pretreated SCB.

3.4 Enzymatic hydrolysis

Following enzymatic hydrolysis, the comparison among untreated, UAA, UBA, 20DES, and 40DES, as shown in Figure 4, revealed reducing sugars yield of 44.01, 189.44, 190.48, 186.79, and 194.46 mg/g biomass, respectively. The results clearly demonstrate that reducing sugars yield increased after pretreatment, consistent with the CrI obtained from XRD analysis. Moreover, the type of pretreatment influenced the composition of sugars released. Ultrasonic–alkaline pretreatment produced three sugars—glucose, xylose, and arabinose—with glucose at approximately 143–150 mg/g biomass. In contrast, ultrasonic–DES pretreatment produced two sugars, glucose and xylose, with 40DES achieving the highest glucose yield at 162 mg/g biomass.

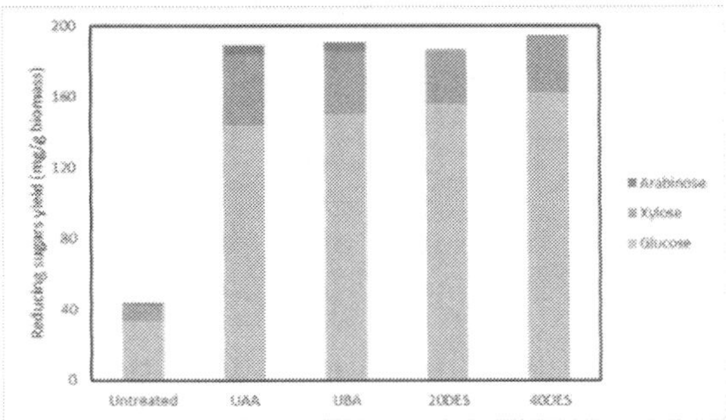

Fig. 4. Reducing sugars yield of untreated and pretreatment SCB.

4 Conclusions

The combined pretreatment using ultrasonication with different chemical pretreatments affected the lignin yield and enzyme hydrolysis efficiency. In terms of lignin yield, UBA achieved the highest yield at 94%. That means the sequence between ultrasonication before and after alkaline pretreatment had a significant effect on lignin yield. Nevertheless, lignin removal calculations suggested that the extracted lignin required further purification to eliminate impurities before utilization. In the part of ultrasonication-DES, lignin yields were less than 50%, attributable to the selected type of DES inhibiting lignin formation and causing most of the lignin to remain dissolved in solution. However, the solid-liquid ratio also affects lignin yield and using different chemicals that impact the type of lignin yield. Regarding enzymatic hydrolysis, pretreatment enhanced reducing sugar yields, with 40DES producing the highest yield at 194.46 mg/g biomass. Future studies should focus on analyzing the structural properties, identifying the most suitable agent for ultrasonic–DES to maximize lignin yield, evaluating the techno-economic analysis, and environmental impacts.

References

1. A. Kulshreshtha, Sustainable energy generation from municipal solid waste. (2022). https://doi.org/10.1016/B978-0-323-85387-3.00005-7
2. A. L. Woiciechowski, C. J. Dalmas Neto, L. P. de S. Vandenberghe, D. P. de Carvalho Neto, A. C. N. Sydney, L. A. J. Letti, S. G. Karp, L. A. Zevallos Torres, C. R. Soccol, Lignocellulosic biomass: Acid and alkaline pretreatments and their effects on biomass recalcitrance – Conventional processing and recent advances. (2020). https://doi.org/10.1016/j.biortech.2020.122848
3. A. R. Mankar, A. Pandey, A. Modak, K. K. Pant, Pretreatment of lignocellulosic biomass: A review on recent advances. (2021). https://doi.org/10.1016/j.biortech.2021.125235

4. A. Sluiter, B. Hames, R. Ruiz, C. Scarlata, J. Sluiter, D. Templeton, D. Crocker, Determination of Structural Carbohydrates and Lignin in Biomass, (LAP, 2012)
5. G. Guerriero, J. F. Hausman, J. Strauss, H. Ertan, K. S. Siddiqui, Lignocellulosic biomass: Biosynthesis, degradation, and industrial utilization. (Engineering in Life Sciences. **16**, 1-16 2016)
6. G. Xu, L. Wang, J. Liu, J. Wu, FTIR and XPS analysis of the changes in bamboo chemical structure decayed by white-rot and brown-rot fungi. (2013). https://doi.org/10.1016/j.apsusc.2013.05.065
7. H. Wu, X. Dai, S.-Li Zhou, Z.-Yao Xiong, Y.-Hang Qin, J. Ma, L. Yang, Z.-Kun Wu, T.-Lin Wang, C.-Wen Wang, Ultrasound-assisted alkaline pretreatment for enhancing the enzymatic hydrolysis of rice straw by using the heat energy dissipated from ultrasonication. (2017). https://doi.org/10.1016/j.biortech.2017.05.090
8. I. F. Mota, J. da Silva Burgal, F. Antunes, M. E. Pintado, P. S. Costa, High value-added lignin extracts from sugarcane by-products. (2023). https://doi.org/10.1016/j.ijbiomac.2023.123144
9. J. Luo, Z. Fang, R. L. Smith Jr., Ultrasound-enhanced conversion of biomass to biofuels. (2013). http://doi.org/10.1016/j.pecs.2013.11.001
10. J. Zhang, X. Ma, J. Yu, X. Zhang, T. Tan, The effects of four different pretreatments on enzymatic hydrolysis of sweet sorghum bagasse. (2011). http://doi.org/10.1016/j.biortech.2010.12.093
11. K. M. Lee, J. D. Quek, W. Y. Tey, St. Lim, H.Siang Kang, L. K. Quen, W. A. W. Mahmood, S. I. S. Jamaludin, K. H. Teng, K. S. Khoo, Biomass valorization by integrating ultrasonication and deep eutectic solvents: Delignification, cellulose digestibility and solvent reuse. (2022). https://doi.org/10.1016/j.bej.2022.108587
12. M. M. Kininge, P. R. Gogate, Intensification of alkaline delignification of sugarcane bagasse using ultrasound assisted approach. (2022). https://doi.org/10.1016/j.ultsonch.2021.105870
13. M. Kim, D. F Day, Composition of sugar cane, energy cane, and sweet sorghum suitable for ethanol production at Louisiana sugar mills. (2011). https://doi.org/10.1007/s10295-010-0812-8
14. V. R. Chourasia, A. Pandey, K. K. Pant, R. J. Henry, Improving enzymatic digestibility of sugarcane bagasse from different varieties of sugarcane using deep eutectic solvent pretreatment. (2021). https://doi.org/10.1016/j.biortech.2021.125480
15. V. Z. Ong, K. P. Y. Shak, T. Y. Wu, K. K. L. Chu, W. Y. Sun, A combined pretreatment with ultrasound-assisted alkaline solution and aqueous deep eutectic solvent for enhancing delignification and enzymatic hydrolysis from oil palm fronds. (2021). https://doi.org/10.1016/j.indcrop.2020.112974
16. Y. Bao, Y. Wang, C. Yan, Z. Xue, Deep eutectic solvents for fractionation and valorization of lignocellulose. (2025). https://doi.org/10.1016/j.gce.2024.04.001
17. Y. Xia, J. Zhuang, Enhancing enzymatic saccharification and valuable lignin recovery from wheat straw using a novel ternary deep eutectic solvent pretreatment. (2025). https://doi.org/10.1016/j.indcrop.2025.121245
18. Z. Chen, A. Ragauskas, C. Wan, Lignin extraction and upgrading using deep eutectic solvents. (2020). https://doi.org/10.1016/j.indcrop.2020.112241

AUTHOR INDEX

EDP Sciences – Web of Conferences
17, Avenue du Hoggar
Parc d'Activité de Courtabouf
BP 112
F-91944 Les Ulis Cedex A
France

ISBN 979-8-3313-3147-4
9 798331 331474